EFLECTIONS ON
OMMERCIAL LIFE

ANTHOLOGY OF CLASSIC TEXTS
OM PLATO TO THE PRESENT

lited by

ATRICK MURRAY

REFLECTIONS ON COMMERCIAL LIFE:

An Anthology of Classic Texts
from Plato to the Present

Routledge
New York and London

REFLECTIONS ON COMMERCIAL LIFE:

An Anthology of Classic Texts
from Plato to the Present

Edited by

Patrick Murray

Published in 1997 by
Routledge
29 West 35th Street
New York, NY 10001

Published in
Great Britain by
Routledge
11 New Fetter Lane
London EC4P 4EE

Copyright © 1997 by
Routledge
Printed in the United
States of America on acid–
free paper.

Library of Congress Cataloging–in–Publication Data

Reflections of commercial life : an anthology of classic texts from
    Plato to the present / edited with introductions by Patrick Murray.
        p.   cm.
    Includes bibliographical references and index.
    ISBN 0-415-91098-6. — ISBN 0-415-91099-4
    1. Capitalism—Philosophy.   2. Commerce—Philosophy.   I. Murray,
Patrick, 1948–   .
HB501.R356   1996
330.12'2—dc20   96-9481
                                                                    CIP

For my father, Jack Murray (1917–1962),
my mother, Muriel Stehney,
and my stepfather, George Stehney

CONTENTS

GENERAL INTRODUCTION: 1
    "On Studying Commercial Life" (with bibliographies)

chapter 1 PLATO   39
    From the *Republic* (Books I, II, and III)

chapter 2 ARISTOTLE   69
    From the *Politics* (Books I and II)

chapter 3 ST. THOMAS AQUINAS   87
    From the *Summa Contra Gentiles* ("That
    Man's Happiness does not Consist in Wealth"
    and "How Poverty is Good") and the *Summa
    Theologiae* (Question 66, "Of Theft and Robbery";
    Question 77, "Of Cheating, Which is Committed
    in Buying and Selling"; Question 78, "Of the Sin
    of Usury"; and Question 100, "On Simony")

chapter 4 ST. THOMAS MORE   117
    From *Utopia*

chapter 5 JOHN LOCKE   133
    From the *Second Treatise of Government*
    ("Of Property")

chapter 6   BERNARD MANDEVILLE   147
From *The Fable of the Bees* (Remark L.: Whilst
Luxury Employ'd a Million of the Poor, &c. and
Remark Q.: For frugally They now lived on
Their Salaray)

chapter 7   DAVID HUME   155
From *Essays, Moral, Political, and Literary* ("Of
Commerce" and "Of Refinement in the Arts")

chapter 8   ADAM SMITH   173
From *The Wealth of Nations* ("Of the Division of
Labour," "Of the Principle which Gives Occasion to
the Division of Labour," "Of the Accumulation of
Capital, or of Productive and Unproductive Labour."
"Of the Natural Progress of Opulence," "How the
Commerce of the Towns Contributed to the
Improvement of the Country," and "Of the
Expences of the Sovereign or Commonwealth")

chapter 9   JAMES MADISON   205
From *The Federalist Papers* (Number X)

chapter 10   FRIEDRICH SCHILLER   215
From *On the Aesthetic Education of Man:
In a Series of Letters* (Sixth Letter)

chapter 11   G.W.F. HEGEL   223
From the *Elements of the Philosophy of Right*
("Civil Society")

chapter 12   KARL MARX   253
From *Capital*, vol. I ("Commodities," "The
General Formula for Capital," and "The Buying
and Selling of Labour-Power")

chapter 13   JOHN STUART MILL   297
From the *Principles of Political Economy*
("Of the Grounds and Limits of the Laisser-Faire
or Non-Interference Principle")

chapter 14   THORSTEIN VEBLEN   317
From *The Theory of the Leisure Class* ("Pecuniary
Emulation" and "Conspicuous Consumption")

chapter 15   GEORG SIMMEL   333
"The Metropolis and Mental Life"

chapter 16 MAX WEBER 349
From *The Protestant Ethic and the Spirit of Capitalism* ("The Spirit of Capitalism")

chapter 17 MARCEL MAUSS 365
From *The Gift* ("Conclusions for Economic Sociology and Political Economy")

chapter 18 GEORGES BATAILLE 373
From *The Accursed Share* ("Theory of 'Potlatch'")

chapter 19 SIMONE WEIL 383
From *Oppression and Liberty* ("Sketch of Contemporary Social Life")

chapter 20 FRIEDRICH A. HAYEK 397
From *Law, Legislation and Liberty* ("The Discipline of Abstract Rules and the Emotions of the Tribal Society")

chapter 21 HANNAH ARENDT 417
From *The Human Condition* ("The Rise of the Social")

chapter 22 DANIEL BELL 429
From "The Cultural Contradictions of Capitalism"

chapter 23 JEAN BAUDRILLARD 447
From *Selected Writings* ("Consumer Society")

ix

COPYRIGHT PERMISSIONS

ACKNOWLEDGMENTS

MY FATHER was a traveling salesman, so I came by an interest in commerce early. As a college sophomore amid the upheavals of the late sixties, I told my high school physics teacher, Brother Joe Crane, that I was dropping out of physics to major in sociology. He stopped me cold with the observation that scientists create new wealth, whereas social workers and activists at best redistribute existing resources. I finished in physics and mathematics, but the social movements kept spilling over, and my questions about modern commercial life would not go away. Perhaps I sensed that the *social form of wealth* was as important as the how much question. I jumped the track and went to graduate school in philosophy. There, the pull of questions having to do with modern commercial life—Is capitalism the path to peace, prosperity, freedom, justice, and democracy or does it place obstacles in the way of achieving those ends?—bent my studies toward classical German philosophy, and especially Hegel and Marx. My question became: How are modern commerce, society, and philosophy involved with one another?

In Hegel, Marx, and Critical Theorists including Theodor Adorno, Herbert Marcuse, and Jürgen Habermas, I discovered thinkers who engaged that question profoundly. Thanks to the German Academic Exchange Program (DAAD), I deepened my knowledge of these writers while studying in Frankfurt, Germany. Over time, I felt the need to take up this joint study of modern philosophy and commerce on my native soil, Anglo-American philosophy. So I opened a continuing line of research into the commercial imagination of the British Empiricists, with emphasis on John Locke, George Berkeley, and David Hume. With the broader vision that this afforded, I got the idea for a course that would be a historical and topical reflection on commercial life. With the support of a grant from the Dean of the Creighton College of Arts and Sciences, Rev. Michael Proterra, S.J., I soon began teaching "Philosophy and Commercial Societies." Offering that course for the first time was a vivid teaching experience. My gratitude, then, extends to my students, whose spirited responses made the need for this volume apparent to me.

Many conversations over many years stand behind this book. For them I would like to thank James Collins (deceased), Albert William Levi (deceased), Paul Piccone, Mark Neilsen, Mary Beth Gallagher, Michael Bartz, Michael Goeke, James Marsh, Thomas Jeannot, Julie Kerksick, John Gardner, John Duggan, Daniel Dahlstrom, Thomas Nitsch, the Rev. Eugene Donahue, Michael Miller, Michael Gillespie, and my colleagues in the Department of Philosophy at Creighton University. To Rusty Reno I am especially grateful for comments on the "General Introduction."

Without benefit of the friendship and intelligence of the Rev. John F. Kavanaugh, Peter Fuss, Moishe Postone, and my companions in research Fred Moseley, Chris Arthur, Martha Campbell, Mino Carchedi, Paul Mattick, Geert Reuten, and Tony Smith, this book would not have been possible.

At Routledge, Maureen MacGrogan believed in this book when it mattered; she, Alison Shonkwiler, Laska Jimsen, Charles Hames, and the readers of the proposal for this book have my thanks for helping it through to publication. Thanks to Mark Rooks of the Intelex Corporation for providing several selections on diskette. In preparing the book I received support from Deans Michael Lawler and Barbara Braden of the Creighton Graduate School and was assisted by Craig Welch and also by Matthew Westerbeck. Margaret Troy's careful typing, editing, and proofreading greatly improved the finish of this book—my special thanks to her.

In my children, John Patrick, David, and Savita, I found the encouragement to complete this book. To my wife, Jeanne Schuler, who urged me to stick with this project and contributed her time, judgment, and words, I am most grateful.

xiv

GENERAL INTRODUCTION:

On Studying Commercial Life

NOT ALL societies have engaged in commerce, and of those that have, many have kept it at the margins; a society commercial to the bone can scarcely be imagined. When we speak of commercial societies, we think of places where commercial forms predominate. David Hume's observation that "the views most familiar to us are apt, for that very reason, to escape us" applies to those living in predominantly commercial societies: there, commercial forms have grown so familiar that they blend into the woodwork, like Coke into cola. We live in and through them, inhabiting them whether or not they awaken our thoughts. Ordinarily, our knowledge of these forms is practical: we get around in a commercial world without having to articulate the forms that open that world up—the commodity, money, wage labor, or capital. Like speakers who follow the rules of grammar without being able to name the differences between adjectives and adverbs, tense and mood, our awareness of commercial forms is tacit or subliminal. If a reflective knowledge of language came along with the ability to speak, we could take the grammar out of grammar school. Living in a commercial society does not endow us with a reflective knowledge of its structuring forms; we need to apply ourselves in order to grasp them. A good way to attain an articulate, reflective insight into commercial life is to begin with the writings of great grammarians of commerce, going back to Plato.

The seepage of commercial forms into disparate realms alters our discourse and aspirations. Ordinary language percolates with new words and usages that manifest or call attention to commercial forms. To "work" commonly means to engage in some activity that yields a wage. This usage carries the suggestion that the homemaker or volunteer does not work. Domestic or civic activities, while time consuming and socially purposive, lack standing as "real work." A "successful" person is admired for her hefty bank account. "Products" are goods and, increasingly, services that are bought and sold. An insurance or savings plan is a "product." If I clean my own apartment, only the commodities used will figure into the Gross Domestic Product, whereas if I hire cleaning professionals, their total bill will be counted. Just as ordinary usage equivocates on work, so do we slur over differences between needs, needs for commodities, and commodities themselves. Consider the scene from the Orson Welles film *The Stranger*, where a character browsing through a drugstore is told by the clerk: "You'll find all your needs up on the shelf." An odd location! Words like "interest," "riches," "value," "business," and "industry" have been so long subordinated to a commercial idiom that we have to switch gears to recall any other.

Consider the difference between a customer and a consumer. A customer looks to meet certain needs through the purchase of a commodity, say a pair of shoes. Still, the initiative belongs to the buyer. A consumer is that customer whose desires have been tilled and seeded by profitmaking enterprises. With the intensification of commerce, customers give way to consumers. The *Saturday Night Live* alien family the Coneheads parodies the consumer, not the customer, with the cry: "Consume mass quantities!" The adult suffering a Big Mac attack or the child squirming for a McDonald's Happy Meal are likewise consumers. In effect, the prefix "Mc" comes to serve as the consumer's logo. Thus, journalism redesigned under commercial imperatives wins *USA Today* the title of "Mcpaper."[1]

FORMAL AND REAL SUBSUMPTION UNDER COMMERCIAL FORMS

How different commercial forms (commodity, money, wages, capital, interest) insinuate themselves into human affairs can be clarified with a few distinctions.[2] *Formal* subsumption simply involves bringing something under a commercial form: what fell outside is drawn into the commercial nexus. Tomatoes growing in my backyard garden are not commodities, but they come to be formally subsumed under the commodity form if I take them to market and sell them. Take a different case: suppose my farm fails and my more prosperous neighbor buys my land and hires me to farm it. My capacity to farm has been formally subsumed under the wage form; I now farm as a wage laborer.

We can further distinguish between the broad and the narrow meanings of formal subsumption. The narrow sense means formally subsuming something without further meddling with it. Supposing that my new employer has hired me as part of a profitmaking agricultural business, my labor is subsumed under the form of capital. I now participate in a capitalist production process, still farming the land as before, yet under the more watchful eye of my neighbor, who owns the fruits of my labor. That is formal subsumption in the narrow sense. Suppose, by contrast, that my farm had been bought up by a large food processing corporation. Spurred by the goal of increasing profits, the corporation restructures farming operations. Now I not only work for a wage, I no longer work the way I used to; in this case, my labor is not simply formally subsumed (in the narrow sense) under capital. In being practically transformed it has undergone *real* subsumption. So formal subsumption in the narrow sense means that neither the product nor the labor have been reconfigured by commercial purposes; real subsumption means that they have, as with a Happy Meal or a store-bought tomato. Commercial forms encroach variously and by degrees. To return to a previous distinction, the consumption of the *customer is formally* subsumed (in the narrow sense), that of the *consumer is really* subsumed.

HOW COMMERCE AND CAPITALISM ARE RELATED

Since the word "consumer" conjures up images of capitalism, why speak of commercial society rather than capitalism? How do they differ? Spotlighting commercial practices keeps the present inquiry broader than a focus on capitalism and respects the ancient origins of many commercial forms. Not merely money and commodity exchange, but also *capital*, existed in traditional societies, chiefly in the forms of interest-bearing capital and merchant capital. However, capitalism in the modern sense—of the predominance of production and exchange on a capitalist basis—is the still unfolding reality of recent centuries. We may speak in a broad manner of commercial life, observing it wherever we find commodities exchanged, money coined, wages paid, interest demanded, and profits made. But commercial life more narrowly construed concerns the form of life characteristic of *commercial societies*, defined as societies where, as a rule, products pass through markets. Because of its peculiar features, capitalism provides the dynamism to turn noncommercial and marginally commercial societies into commercial ones. As we will see, capitalism and commercial society are intimately related, but not all societies in which commercial forms play a role are commercial societies in this restricted sense.

A commercial society (and, unless otherwise indicated, this phrase refers to the restricted sense defined above) is one where wealth generally takes the commodity form.[3] In such a society it is commonplace to slur the difference between wealth itself and wealth that passes through the market; that is, the commodity form blends into what it is a particular form of—wealth. This is just what happens under the rubric of the Gross Domestic Product: whatever is not bought or sold does not count as wealth. But how does the commodity form of wealth, once unknown or marginalized in human societies, come to be the norm? Why does an ever greater share of the wealth of a nation take the form of commodities? For an answer, consider how the generalization of the commodity form relates to the presuppositions and outcomes of capitalist investment.[4] Capitalism presupposes, reproduces, and extends commodity exchange, for capitalism is all about using money to make more money, and the ordinary way to do that is to sell commodities for more than it cost to buy them.[5] But to buy the inputs and sell the outputs, everything (including labor power) must be in the commodity form. Since capitalism cannot come into its own unless inputs and outputs are in the commodity form, capitalism requires a certain level of the development of commerce for it to succeed. Conversely, competition and the endlessness of capital accumulation push the generalization of the commodity form of wealth.[6] And in order for more of a society's productive activities to be organized on a capitalist basis, more people must be working for wages. For that to take place, those people must, as Marx put it, be free in a double sense: legally free and in possession of their capacity to labor so they can take it to market as their commodity to bargain with, and free of any alternative means of support.

The relationship between a commercial society and a capitalist one may be summarized as follows: "developed commodity production is itself capitalist commodity production."[7] In other words, a commercial society is a capitalist society, and a capitalist society is a commercial society. That goods and services are, as a rule, produced and delivered as commodities results from production's being undertaken on a capitalist basis, which continually extends the reach of the commodity form. To see the significance of this, take a closer look at the phrase "capitalist commodity production." What Marx unearths with that phrase is that commodities in a commercial society (which we now see is a capitalist one) must be characterized not simply as commodities (that is, goods and services up for purchase) but as *commodity capital* (that is, commodities produced by capitalist enterprises in order to bear a profit). Look at the commodities around you. How many are simply commodities and not produced for profit? A commodity in a commercial society, then, has a test to pass not required of a simple commodity: Will its sale return a suitable profit to its producer? Commodities that flunk this test vanish from the marketplace, like Edsels. Thus the commodity, the basic unit of a commercial society, is itself altered; as commodity capital, it possesses new characteristics. The plain notion of the commodity as any good or service up for sale oversimplifies the reality of capitalist commerce. In fact, as modern capitalism embraces the global economy, all commercial categories are transformed by becoming part of an expanding whole. "We see here how even economic categories appropriate to earlier modes of production acquire a new and specific historical character under the impact of capitalist production," writes Marx.[8] This important observation implies that we must be very wary of equivocations in the study of commercial forms.

IS THE MODERN COMMERCIAL ECONOMY "DISEMBEDDED"?

An influential scholar who called attention to the "great transformation" brought about by the emergence of commercial society was the economic historian Karl Polanyi. In his noted essay "Aristotle Discovers the Economy," Polanyi draws on the work of Hegel and Marx, and, more especially, Henry Sumner Maine and Ferdinand Tönnies, all of whom recognized the epochal differences between modern, commercial society and its predecessors. For Maine, contract relations dominate in commercial societies, while status predominates in pre-commercial societies. In language that has entered into common discourse, Tönnies distinguished between the impersonality of *gesellschaft* (commercial society) and the conviviality of *gemeinschaft* (noncommercial society). Polanyi coordinates these with his own distinction between "embedded" and "disembedded" economies: "It is now possible to say that status or *gemeinschaft* dominate where the economy is embedded in noneconomic institutions; *contractus* or *gesellschaft* is characteristic of the existence of a motivationally distinct economy in society."[9] It is not difficult to hear these oppositions clashing in current controversies between liberals and communitarians.[10]

Polanyi's talk of the economy being embedded in noneconomic institutions involving religious, cultural, or philosophical conceptions of the good can be misleading. The temptation to be misled into thinking (1) that the modern commercial economy is somehow "the economy" and (2) that it is not embedded in any particular constellation of "noneconomic" values and social relations comes naturally to participants in a commercial society. Here we come upon the scene of some of the most deep-seated and recurrent misconceptions about commercial societies. The root trouble lies with a vacillating use of the term "the economy." One meaning captures the prosaic idea that some sort of interchange of humans with nature, some sort of provisioning process, is required to sustain life. Polanyi expresses that meaning here: "until very recent times no name to sum up the organization of the material conditions of life existed in the languages even of civilized peoples."[11] This common notion of the economy can be called a general abstraction.[12] While we can speak of an economy in a general way, no economy in general exists. A second meaning refers to a particular type of provisioning process, namely, the (disembedded) modern commercial economy, which, unlike the economy in general, is something actual and has a specific social form.

Polanyi rightly insists that even embedded economies are examples of economic life in the general sense. Yet the language of embedded and disembedded may suggest on the one hand that the disembedded, commercial economy was somehow secretly operative under all the encumbrances of noneconomic institutions in embedded economies. Conversely, speaking of the modern commercial economy as "disembedded" suggests that it is the economy finally released into its pure state, as if the disembedded economy were the economy in general, finally standing on its own. Calling the modern commercial economy "disembedded" makes it sound as if it exists without any particular social form. The modern commercial economy does seem to be the economy pure and simple, but this seeming is a consequence of the peculiar opacity of its actual social form.

Thinking that "the economy" pure and simple can stand alone is like thinking that "the fruit" can actually exist alongside a cherry, pear, or peach. In reality, the modern commercial economy is, in the terms of this analogy, just as much a particular type of fruit as are the "embedded" economies: its nature is determined by definite social forms no less than theirs. True, modern commercial society differs remarkably from pre-commercial societies— Hegel, Marx, Maine, Tönnies, and Polanyi were right to be impressed by its distinctiveness—but the difference is one between different social forms of the provisioning process, not between those processes that have a social form (traditional, "embedded" economies) and one that does not ("disembedded," modern commerce). Noncommercial and commercial societies may differ as apples to oranges, but not as apples to fruit.

Here are two passages that point up Polanyi's vacillation in speaking of the economy. Polanyi holds that forming the general concept of the economy is a rather recent development precisely because of "the difficulty of identifying the economic process under conditions where it is embedded in noneconomic institutions."[13] But he does not mean that the economy, here in the general sense, is absent from any human society: "Only the concept of the economy, not the economy itself, is in abeyance, of course. Nature and society abound in locational and appropriational movements that form the body of man's livelihood."[14] But in the following passage Polanyi switches to the second meaning of "the economy": "as long as dependent labor predominates as an element in wealth, the economy has only a shadowy existence."[15] By "the economy" here, Polanyi must mean the modern commercial economy based on "free" labor, for there cannot be anything shadowy about the existence of "the economy" in the general sense—some provisioning process exists wherever we find human life. There is something shifty, then, about Polanyi's use of the term "the economy."

The trouble is not simply the ordinary logical problem of ambiguity, Polanyi's tendency to bait and switch. Even using "the economy" to refer to a particular type of economy, namely the modern commercial one, is itself objectionable: (1) This usage makes it appear as though the modern commercial economy were simply the instantiation of "the economy" in general, whereas the economy in general, like "the fruit," is not the sort of thing that can stand on its own. (2) Relatedly, it makes it seem as though the "disembedded" modern commercial economy lacks any specific social form at all, leading to a naturalistic or technical conception of the market economy. (3) That diverts attention from the actual social form of the modern commercial economy and from its peculiar content and consequences. (4) This way of looking at the modern commercial economy can privilege it for the wrong reasons, construing modern commerce as "the economy" in its natural form, rather than recognizing it as a particular form of the provisioning process and bothering to make the case that it is most appropriate.[16] That commercial forms are particular historical outcomes—not the natural forms of "the economy"—means that they are subject to judgment, intervention, revision, even overturning.

The notion that commercial forms are socially determinate was already apparent to Aristotle, who observed: "There are a number of different modes of subsistence; and the result is a number of different ways of life, both in the animal world and in the human."[17] While Aristotle recognized this general need to acquire goods as necessary and natural, he, like his teacher Plato, feared the specific powers of the commercial mode of acquisition: moneymaking tends to turn tyrant, transforming everything it touches to a means to an end that does not of itself make sense. Over two thousand years later Karl Marx praised Aristotle as "that great investigator who was the first to analyze the value form, like so many other forms of thought, society and nature," and, even more pointedly than Aristotle, called attention to the inescapable reality of social form.[18] He wrote: "All production is appropriation of nature on the part of an individual within and through a specific form of society."[19] In *Capital*, he renewed Aristotle's critical investigation of commerce as a particular social form of the art of acquisition.[20] The lessons here are: (1) acquiring what is needed to sustain and reproduce human life involves a social process that will always have a definite form and (2) the form of that process matters greatly.

What, then, is the social form of modern commerce? And what about it inclined Polanyi to speak of the "disembedded economy"? These questions can be given a provisional response. The characteristic features of modern commerce are: (1) a thin, formal sense of the sacred—namely, an abstract though high minded theory of human liberty; (2) a set of liberal juridical and political values and practices consonant with that thin theory of the sanctity of the person; (3) an undeclared but overarching goal or good, the endless pursuit of moneymaking, that anchors what Max Weber calls "the spirit of capitalism"; and (4) a set of property and class relations that make it possible for the capitalist form of production to take hold, predominate, and engender itself.[21]

7

COMPLEXITIES IN THE STUDY OF COMMERCIAL LIFE:
HISTORY AND THE SIDE EFFECTS OF COMMERCE

Though eager to call attention to the distinctiveness of modern commerce as the disembedded economy, Polanyi also cautioned: "In the nature of things the development from embedded to disembedded economies is a matter of degree."[22] The noneconomic institutions, customs, values, sensibilities, desires, tastes, and modes of thought in which pre-market economies were embedded do not necessarily vanish with the generalization of commercial life. So, what becomes of traditional ways as the market society becomes ascendant?[23] Any number of things, in any number of ways—this is the safest answer. Even if we grant in general that commercial forms of life pressure the old ways to contribute, conform, or collapse, how the myriad tensions, juxtapositions, intrusions, and synergies work themselves out in any actual society is a matter for detailed historical study.

The interplay between commercial and traditional forms poses many puzzles. How do various types of symbolic and gift exchange persist even in highly commercial societies? (Imagine reaching for your credit card as a dinner party at the home of good friends winds down, or exchanging checks along with rings with your marriage partner.) Why have forms of "unfree" labor, even chattel slavery, been so enduring under modern commercial conditions? How do racial, ethnic, and national prejudices that transgress the formal features of commodity exchange not only survive into the commercial era but break out with genocidal zeal? What possesses a merchant to say: "Your money is no good here?" And what of patriarchy, the systematic subjugation of women; why has that whiskered system of oppression been so lasting in the commercial era?

If lingering traditions contribute to the complexity of commercial life—we still hear that restaurants have "patrons," hotels have "guests," doctors have "patients," and universities have "students," though all might be more reductively termed "customers"—the spin-offs or side effects of commercial development introduce further complications. To cite only a handful of the more striking and influential such developments, consider the following. Religious changes: the separation of church and state, religious toleration, and mass secularization (the "disenchantment" of the world). Political developments: liberalization, the extension of the franchise, the bureaucratic welfare state. Modern science and technology: new methods of timekeeping, agricultural and medical technologies, technologies of communication and transportation (telegraph, telephone, radio, television, rail travel, automobiles, air and space travel), military innovations. Demographic changes: population growth, urbanization, colonization, contacts between peoples across the globe. New intellectual and moral sensibilities: the spread of doubt ("ours is the millennium of doubt" says Bertolt Brecht's Galileo), rationalization, the "matter-of-fact" mentality, a quantitative orientation, utilitarianism, an emphasis on "instrumental" virtues, irrationalism and emotivism in ethics. New aesthetic sensibilities: modernism and postmodernism. At the same time that we recognize that the modern, commercial world is a different place thanks to secularization, the extension of the franchise, effective public health measures, nuclear weapons, radio and television, and pop culture, we also need to remember the fundamental importance that the encompassing social form of the provisioning process retains.

These spin-offs that vastly complicate modern life may go with or against the grain of commercial forms. Thorstein Veblen observes that modern commerce unleashes a no-nonsense attitude of technical efficiency, "the instinct of workmanship." But that instinct runs counter to the ethos of conspicuous consumption, which is so handy for pumping up sales. Georg Simmel, on the other hand, detects affinities between certain effects of urban life and the coldness of money. Reversing once again, Daniel Bell finds in modernist and postmodernist cultural sensibilities a dangerous erosion of the "Protestant work ethic" expected of workers under capitalism.

Life in commercial society is further thickened by how its members envision their future. To take two important cases, the visions and efforts of working class and women's organizations over the past century and a half have made their mark on modern commercial life. Some people welcome commercial tendencies for extending ordinary liberal rights to all (for example, campaigners for human rights). Others champion a "new" capitalism with a lean, flexible, and consumer-friendly face. Libertarians relish the thought of a rollback of the welfare state. Yet others anticipate some reformed version of modern commerce through a bigger or better "New Deal," a return to some former place of grace,[24] an updated post-commercial Utopia, or an encouraging seismology of where pressures may be building along capitalism's cracks and fissures.[25]

If life in modern commercial societies is complicated by weathered bonds to the past and shiny hopes for the future, if what we are is not to be extricated from what we have been and what we hope for, then what do we make of the tendencies discerned by some contemporary commentators that in the planet's most commercial environments there is an atrophy of both memory and hope, consigning us to what one writer calls "this grinding present tense"?[26] David Gross observes that, though complaints that traditional ways are not being respected are not new, "one has to wait until relatively recent times to hear another, very different charge: that tradition itself is disappearing."[27] Frederic Jameson makes that charge, writing of "the disappearance of a sense of history, the way in which our entire contemporary social system has little by little begun to lose its capacity to retain its own past, has begun to live in a perpetual present and in a perpetual change that obliterates traditions of the kind which all earlier social formations have had in one way or another to preserve."[28] This suggests that the character of our experience of temporality is itself a variable sensitive to the power of social forms. More specifically, the present atmosphere of historical oblivion may be an effect of the capital form on memory and hope.

HOW COMMERCIALISM DIFFERS FROM COMMERCE

When studying commercial life we need to keep in mind the complexities just mentioned: the persistence of pre-commercial ways, the many side effects of the development of modern commerce, and the visions of the future that inhabit commercial life. Still, the center of attention for this volume remains the study of the commercial forms and the effects of formal and real subsumption under them. The common usages that distinguish between *commerce* and *commercialism* provide a global commentary on the merits of some of those effects. We speak of commercialism in situations where we sense that something is amiss or out of joint with commercial life. What sorts of situations are these and what is perceived to be going wrong in them? Reflecting on the distinction between commerce and commercialism leads us to the more fundamental question: What is the proper measure of wealth?

What is commercialism, and how does it differ from commerce? One staple of American popular culture, Frank Capra's film *It's a Wonderful Life*, can be viewed as a commentary on just this question. Capra pits (healthy) commerce against (corrupt) commercialism by contrasting two towns: Bedford Falls and Pottersville, the snakepit of commercialism that Bedford Falls would have sunk to but for the wonderful life of fair minded and self sacrificing George Bailey.[29] The modest Bailey family runs a building and loan operation that serves the community and checks the aggrandizing schemes of the crusty bachelor banker Mr. Potter. Traditional family values are intact in Bedford Falls, while Pottersville is depicted as a place of distrust and fear, with broken families, drunkenness, prostitution, and tacky rental properties. Bedford Falls has undergone formal subsumption under commercial forms, leaving traditional values in place, while Pottersville represents the soullessness of real subsumption. Though religion enters only fancifully into the story, the film has become an important ritual of the Christmas season: a sort of commercial antidote to Christmas commercialism. At the end of the film, George's friends file into his house with small handfuls of cash to save him and his building and loan service from ruin. In Capra's vision, this potluck of money and friendship triumphs over the rootless capital lurking down the block.[30] If we are vigilant and well-meaning, Capra implies, commerce and community values can go hand in hand; formal subsumption need not give way to real subsumption.

The following is a provisional categorization of four types of phenomena that could be classified as commercialism. (1) *Moneymaking as the end in itself:* When making money, as opposed to the specific activity that provides goods or services, is the controlling purpose of commercial activity, we can speak of commercialism. James Roderick, then Chairman of U.S. Steel, succinctly expressed this sort of commercialism, saying: "The duty of management is to make money, not steel."[31] U.S. Steel's new name, "USX," captures his point perfectly: USX is in the business of "X," where "X" is anything that turns the right profit. Here, what Aristotle called the proper end of a commodity, its use value (as opposed to its exchange value), has become a cipher, nothing but a means to make money. In fact, Aristotle identified this phenomenon of instrumentalization: "The proper function of courage, for example, is not to produce money but to give confidence. The same is true of military and medical ability: neither has the function of producing money; the one has the function of producing victory, and the other that of producing health. But those of whom we are speaking turn all such capacities into forms of the art of acquisition, as though to make money were the one aim and everything else must contribute to that aim."[32]

(2) *Corrupting the craft:* When the drive to make money leads to a corruption of the activity by which the money is being made, we can speak of commercialism, as when producers engage in planned obsolescence, popular music turns into corporate rock, or making films becomes subservient to the entertainment industry. In speaking here of the "corruption of the craft" I am setting aside what would commonly be regarded as unethical business practices, for example, charging a customer for an engine rebuild when the motor was simply tuned, or knowingly selling defective airplane engine parts.[33] The literature in business ethics attests to the fact that making this distinction presents no end of thorny problems. Is it a minimally fair commercial practice to engage in fashion-based planned obsolescence, styling products so they quickly are out-of-date and need to be replaced by new purchases? Probably so. But what of quality based planned obsolescence—that is, designing products so that they quickly break down or wear out? Again, probably so—you expect to "get what you pay for"—but here we might want to look at the details of particular cases.

(3) *Hype:* When commodities are presented in ways that blow their value out of proportion in order to increase sales, we speak of commercialism. Think of the marketing of children's toys, popular movies (with all their tie-ins and accessories), or athletic shoes. The use of image advertising has become so deeply entrenched in contemporary commercial culture that theorists like Guy Debord and Jean Baudrillard call ours the "society of the spectacle" and employ terms such as "hyperreality" and "simulation," claiming it is pointless any longer even to distinguish between "image" and "reality."[34] What is it, after all, that makes Marlboros a rugged man's smoke and Virginia Slims a cigarette for the liberated woman?

(4) *Simony:* When commerce transgresses certain boundaries by (a) turning a sacred object, activity, or role into a commodity or (b) invading sacred social (or geographical) spaces or sacred times, we speak of commercialism. If "si-

11

mony" seems too old fashioned a term for this phenomenon,[35] keep in mind that though the term ordinarily brings to mind cases involving religiously sacred events, offices, places, or times (such as the selling of Masses, indulgences, and church offices, or conducting commercial transactions on holy ground or holy days), even medieval discussions of simony include nonreligious topics. For example, St. Thomas Aquinas, in a selection on simony included in this volume, argues that scientific knowledge should not be handled as a commodity, a matter that vexes today's research universities. Even in highly commercialized societies, then, the concept of simony continues to be relevant. There is widespread agreement today that public offices and votes, spouses, sports championships, and academic degrees and honors are not to be bought and sold; nor should parents present children with a bill covering all the expenses of their upbringing once they reach maturity. Whether sexual acts, human body parts and fluids, or the use of wombs ought be made matters of commerce continues to stir debate.

A few more examples help show some of the different ways in which the simony issue is still with us. Consider two fictional cases. First, in a *Saturday Night Live* skit a rich man hires someone from a commercial service to inform women that he is terminating a romantic relationship with them. Second, as the film *Cadillac Man* opens, the lead character happens upon the scene of a stalled funeral motorcade and tries to sell new Cadillacs not only to the funeral director but—after a hapless attempt at soul-searching—to the outraged widow. In the first case it is the sort of activity involved, an intimate matter, that makes it a case of simony, whereas in the second what is objectionable is not what is being sold but the social circumstances of the sales pitch.

Struggles over commercial access to time and space arise from both religious and secular grounds. The cultural reasons why many Germans oppose longer store hours may have little to do with the Sabbath. In the United States, the introduction of for-profit, Channel One television (with commercials) into public and private school classrooms might be criticized on several points—for example, do students need more television? We may wonder too if instructional time in a schoolroom ought not be a time and place kept off limits to profitmaking commercial ventures. Neil Postman's observation that when a U.S. Presidential State of the Union address is broadcast on television, there are no commercials, no TV timeouts, illustrates the simony issue from another angle. The fact that networks treat these speeches as inviolable sends its own message about the rest of what is broadcast on commercial television. Of course, public sentiments and opinions change as to what counts as simony. Not so long ago the proposal for an investor-owned, for-profit chain of hospitals would have provoked the sort of moral incredulity that might yet greet a press conference at which a group of investors announced the opening of a chain of for-profit churches.

Though the generalized commodification of land and labor are among the recent and most decisive historical transformations easing the way for modern commercial life, simony issues still crop up here as well. New ecological and aesthetic awarenesses as well as a belated attitude of respect for aboriginal peoples are keeping the notion of simony alive with respect to land. With regard to the capacity for labor, by contrast, the simony issue is unavoidable. For modern, commercial society excludes both the nonvoluntary employment of another's labor power (as with slavery) and the sale of one's labor power to such an extent as to amount to the sale of one's person. I can sell what is mine but not what is me. The question arises: how much of what is mine can I sell off before I have effectively sold myself?[36] The sanctity of the person is what remains of the sacred in the economy of modern commercial life. As Immanuel Kant put it: "In the realm of ends everything has either a *price* or a *dignity*. Whatever has a price can be replaced by something else as its equivalent; on the other hand, whatever is above all price, and therefore admits of no equivalent, has a dignity."[37] Persons have dignity; everything else is disposable. So the border conflicts that erupt over what is involuntary or demeaning must be expected to be a regular feature of a commercial society.[38] What it means to be a person is a question always put into play by commercial societies.

Because they concern the *bounds* of commerce, there is no way to resolve simony issues *internally* to commerce. Their persistence discloses the presence of an "outside" to the commercial world capable of contesting its practices. A society commercial to the bone would lack an outside; there, charges of simony would not come up. Can we even imagine such a society?

13

WHAT IS THE PROPER MEASURE OF WEALTH?

This sketch of different types of commercialism poses the most fundamental question under discussion in this anthology: What is the measure, the limit, the end of wealth?[39] The different types of commercialism just described involve either taking the wrong measure or violating some proper one: money-making alone is the wrong measure of wealth; corrupting the craft means that the internal standards for an activity have been violated; hype misrepresents the true value of a thing; and simony involves transgressing the boundary markers for commercial forms. Commercialism involves some objectionable formal or real subsumption under a commercial form, be it the commodity, wage, or capital form. But what entitles us to make these judgments? What is the fitting measure of wealth and what are the proper limits to wealth-producing on which such judgments rely? Common language may distinguish between commerce and commercialism, but do we have a public, noncommercial measure by which to defend the distinction?[40]

Inquiring into the proper measure or limits of wealth reopens the issue of the embeddedness of the economy, for whatever embeds economic activity does so precisely by supplying some standard and limits. Furthermore, with the question of the proper measure and limits comes the question: what is the proper social form of the provisioning process? After all, is not form precisely the principle of measure or limit? And is not the social form of the provisioning process what allows us to speak of an economy's being "embedded"? So, the problematics of (1) measure or limit, (2) "embeddedness," and (3) social form converge. The authors included in this volume imply, propose, and criticize various answers to questions about the proper measure and limits of wealth and wealth-creating activities. What follows is an attempt to distinguish and assess several leading approaches; the actual views of these authors often revise, mix, or overlap possibilities sorted here for analytical purposes.

Traditionalism

Here traditional values give wealth its measure, and custom limits the activities of acquiring wealth. For the traditionalist, to know how to acquire wealth properly, just look to the past. The validity of customs, and of myths or religious representations of society and nature, is not a matter of the "rational reflection" identified with the secular philosophical or scientific standpoints. The customary can be parochial or local but not the rational. Allan Bloom remarks: "The ancestral is by its nature silent about its own foundations; it is an imposing presence that awes those who might be tempted to look too closely."[41] Max Weber identifies traditionalism as the mortal enemy of the spirit of modern commerce: "The most important opponent with which the spirit of capitalism, in the sense of a definite standard of life claiming ethical sanction, has had to struggle, was that type of attitude and reaction to new situations which we may designate as traditionalism."[42] For their part, traditional societies are seldom on friendly terms with either commerce or philosophy.

Assessment. As Kant observed two hundred years ago, "our age is, in especial degree, the age of criticism," and he foresaw and welcomed the persistence of the critical attitude. Custom cannot bear up as the standard for wealth: "Religion through its sanctity, and law-giving through its majesty, may seek to exempt themselves from it [criticism, P.M.]. But they then awaken just suspicion, and cannot claim the sincere respect which reason accords only to that which has been able to sustain the test of free and open examination."[43] Though customary practices may pass the test of reason, the way we were cannot dictate the way we will be.[44] To assert this is not, however, to deny that the customary remains an ineliminable ingredient of human needs and the provisioning process.

Divine Command Theory

John Locke was fond of quoting the Biblical injunction "be fruitful and multiply," and the reasoning by which he arrives at his seminal "labor theory of property" begins with the proposition that God has given the goods of the Earth to humankind in common. With hindsight, Locke may look like a prophet of the "disembedded economy," but he was at pains to locate the source of his advocacy of personal and property rights, industriousness, and the "improvement" of the land in the will of God.[45] For a divine command approach, God's law is the proper measure for wealth: I should act in a certain way for no further reason than that God wills I do so. God's law sets the ground rules for the provisioning process, as in the two principles that Locke cites: do not waste and do not take anything from the Common unless you leave as good and as much for others. A simpler example is the injunction to keep holy the Sabbath.

Assessment. This powerful and influential approach to the problem of the measure and limits of wealth faces at least these three challenging questions: (1) Are there any such divine commands? An answer to this question obviously turns on whether we can speak of God at all. (2) How could we recognize any imperative as truly a command of God? If we use our natural reason to screen out imposters, will that still allow us to recognize any commands that would add to or differ from principles we could arrive at through reason alone? (3) Is the divine command that I adopt a certain measure of wealth morally binding, or does it violate human autonomy?[46]

Modern Commerce

Modern commerce (modern capitalism) is indeed disembedded from traditional, thick conceptions of the good, whether poetic, religious, political, or philosophical, but that is a consequence of what it is embedded in—its peculiar social form, namely, the distinctive property division that makes capital and wage labor possible; a politically and juridically upheld, thin, though potent and high minded, doctrine of human liberty; and an uncanny historical project, namely, the ceaseless accumulation of money as an end in itself. Money is modern commerce's measure and goal: more is better, with no upper bound. Its limits are set by the formal conditions of its existence, those which insure freedom of action in the marketplace (*laissez faire* principles) and assure individuals the liberty, equality, and security of person and property needed for proper functioning in their roles as buyers and sellers. If we wonder whether it is good that potatoes are priced so high or that corporate executives are paid hundreds of times more than those they supervise, we need only ask: do these outcomes respect the rules of the marketplace? It is important to keep in mind that modern commerce is not simply a matter of the pursuit of money; as Max Weber observes, the "accursed love of gold" is an ancient phenomenon. No, capitalism involves a specific social form of the acquisition of money with a definite moral and political shape.[47]

15

Assessment. The pursuit of money for its own sake is a perversity pure and simple; the miser has been an object of scorn since the story of Midas. Max Weber harped on the irrationality of this *summum bonum*; and Marx did not intend a compliment when he called the capitalist the "rational miser." Who wants to be a clever Scrooge? While there is something sublime about the liberty involved in securing modern commerce's sphere of action, at the same time there is something skeletal about the "unencumbered self" that inhabits the "disembedded economy."[48] That a thicker human good than libertarian liberty should rule the provisioning process appears to be a conclusion long since reached by the commercial peoples of the world. And Karl Marx's complex argument— the liberty of the freely contracting agents in the marketplace is but the cheery exterior of the capitalist mode of production, which presupposes that wage laborers are "unencumbered" by having any means of maintaining themselves other than the sale of their labor power and which entails alienation and domination—brings to light several deep problems with modern commerce's measure of wealth and conception of liberty.[49]

Wealthism

We may wonder if modern commerce is ruled not by the craving for abstract wealth (money) but by the abstract mission of building up wealth per se (goods and services). Is it not the accumulation of wealth, rather than money, that spurs modern commerce? After all, Adam Smith did not entitle his classic book *The Moneymaking of Nations* but *The Wealth of Nations.* Is not wealth the goal and measure of modern commerce, and do not the demands of wealth creation establish its bounds?

16

Assessment. There are several difficulties with what may be termed "wealthism." (1) The deep problem parallels that discovered earlier with Polanyi's notion of "the economy." The notion of wealth in general covers all wealth in the particular, but it abstracts from the specific social form that any particular wealth possesses. There is nothing wrong with an abstract concept of wealth such as this, but there is something wrong with the thought that wealth can exist without a particular social form, just as it is a mistake to think that the economy can exist independently of a particular social form.

(2) Though there is no such thing as wealth in the abstract any more than there is an economy devoid of social form, the peculiar (asocial) social form of modern capitalism, with its impersonal market, where the social form of products bizarrely gets cornered in a thing (money),[50] naturally gives rise to such mirages as "wealth," "production (in general)," and "the economy." The deceptive picture of itself that capitalism puts out is that of a production process without any social form, accompanied by the circulation of commodities in the market.[51]

(3) As an account of capitalism, wealthism is false. Even if the creation of wealth is the ordinary means to make money, and even if capitalism is responsible for a tremendous outpouring of wealth, that does not make the creation of wealth capitalism's goal or measure. This disjuncture between the pursuits of wealth and money is played for laughs in the Alec Guinness film *The Man in the White Suit*. A young chemist discovers an artificial fabric that never gets dirty, never tears or wears out, and never needs pressing. Instead of receiving a hero's welcome, however, he ends up being hounded by both the owners and the workers of the textile factory, who see his discovery as a threat to their profits or wages.

(4) It is not clear how much of an improvement the unending accumulation of wealth per se is over the irrationality of the accumulation of abstract wealth. Long before those T-shirts that depict a heap of costly consumer goods above the words "whoever dies with the most toys wins." St. Thomas Aquinas argued that "riches" (money) and "wealth" (external goods) "are good to the extent that they contribute to virtue, but not in themselves."[52] Thinking along similar lines, Marx wrote in the *Grundrisse*: "Do we never find in antiquity an inquiry into which form of landed property, etc. is the most productive, creates the greatest wealth? Wealth does not appear as the aim of production. . . . The question is always which mode of property creates the best citizens. Wealth appears as an end in itself only among the few commercial peoples—monopolists of the carrying trade—who live in the pores of the ancient world, like the Jews in medieval society. . . . Thus the old view, in which the human being appears as the aim of production, regardless of his limited national, religious, political character, seems to be very lofty when contrasted to the modern world, where production appears as the aim of mankind and wealth as the aim of production."[53]

"POSITIVE" HUMAN RIGHTS

Sensing the shortfalls of free-market liberties, advocates of this approach thicken the libertarian conception of rights, without altogether dismantling the market. They declare that one or more of the following provisions must be secured for all: education, food, housing, medical care, employment, even co-ownership of the firm where one works—unfolding these requirements out of the concept of human liberty. Those who would thicken the conception of human liberty to include much that libertarians call "welfare" start from a phenomenology of the human being as free. The root of the limitations placed on commerce by this "positive" human rights approach remains the moral integrity of the individual person.[54] But here the judgments regarding what is requisite for securing that integrity result in a denser set of limits on the acquisition of wealth, in what remains in so many other respects a modern commercial setting.

Assessment. Whether a reasonable and convincing case can be made for such a thick set of human rights remains up for debate. Will we, a century from now, feel about the right to health care or employment the way we now feel about the right to vote or to a choose an occupation? Might we even feel about wage labor the way we now feel about slavery and serfdom? It is difficult to say. How a modern commercial society should be structured so as to insure the liberty of "thicker" selves raises a host of difficult ethical, economic, and policy questions, many of which have been under discussion for some time. And even if these more substantive needs could be addressed in some manner, others, such as the need for human solidarity or friendship, will still go unmet.[55] Finally, this approach does not cancel the fact that money still functions as the measure of wealth; it leaves many of the dynamics of capitalism in place. If it proves true that alienation, exploitation, and domination inhere in capitalism, the "thick" human rights approach would still be too thin.

Natural Function

The human body supplies the measure of wealth, says Epictetus: "The measure of possessions for each person is the body, as the foot is of the shoe. So if you hold to this principle you will preserve the measure; but if you step beyond it, you will in the end be carried as if over a cliff; just as in the case of the shoe, if you go beyond the foot, you get a gilded shoe, and then a purple embroidered one. For there is no limit to a thing once it is beyond its measure."[56] The human body's natural functions set the proper limits for acquiring wealth; cross those limits and you are on the slippery slope to an Imelda Marcos-sized collection of shoes. The necessities and (for those naturalists not ready to follow Diogenes all the way to the bare necessities) the conveniences of life can be read off from the natural features of the human frame and the functional challenges posed by nature. On this view, unnatural wealth, luxuries, and the endless accoutrements of cultured living spring up in the hothouse of human vanity. Uproot them!

This naturalism is a strain of rationalism, for its mighty acts of reflection want to cut through encrusted cultural norms, cleaving nature from nurture.[57] In addition to Cynicism, Stoicism, and Epicureanism, this sort of thinking comes up in various state-of-nature theorists and in the North American Diogenes, Henry David Thoreau. The Utopians invented by St. Thomas More adopted the measure of natural function and did so as a protest against the commercial measure: "For, in a society where we make money the standard of everything, it is necessary to practice many crafts which are quite vain and superfluous, ministering only to luxury and licentiousness. Suppose the host of those who now toil were distributed over only as few crafts as the few needs and conveniences demanded by nature."[58] It is a revealing thought experiment to draw up (and date) a list of those "few needs and conveniences."

Assessment. This view rests on a deep misunderstanding of the nature of needs, for human needs are not natural or fixed by function. Rather, they are ineradicably cultural and historical. Bernard Mandeville made this point by way of criticizing the possibility of actually distinguishing the necessary (natural) from the superfluous (luxurious): "If everything is to be luxury (as in strictness it ought) that is not immediately necessary to make man subsist as he is a living creature, there is nothing else to be found in the world, no not even among the naked savages; of which it is not probable that there are any but what by this time have made some improvements upon their former manner of living; and either in the preparation of their eatables, the ordering of their huts, or otherwise added something to what once sufficed them. This definition everybody will say is too rigorous; I am of the same opinion, but if we are to abate one inch of this severity, I am afraid we won't know where to stop."[59] In his evolutionary retelling of the first book of the Bible, *Genesis,* Kant identifies the radical turning of human desire away from the dictates of nature (instinct) with the fall (Adam and Eve's eating of the forbidden fruit) as the first step of our ancestors out of the animal kingdom and into the human realm of freedom and moral responsibility: "He [man, P.M.] stood as if at the edge of an abyss; for besides the particular objects of desire on which instinct had until now made him dependent, there opened up to him an infinitude of them, among which he could not choose, for he had no knowledge whatsoever to base choice on; and it was now equally impossible for him to turn back from his once tasted state of freedom to his former servitude (to the rule of instincts)."[60] That was and remains a scary step. Epictetus appears to be in flight from this terrifying prospect. The natural function view fails to come to grips with the actual character of human needing—as Rousseau recognized, once out of the state of nature, there is no turning back.[61]

Utility Theory

Some conceptual clarifications are in order prior to discussing utility theory. To avoid confusion, three concepts need to be discriminated: (1) the *general concept of the useful,* which covers anything that satisfies needs of whatever sort; (2) the *normative concept of the useful,* which opposes it to the wasteful, vain, or frivolous; and (3) the *concept of utility itself.* The scope of the first concept is wider than that of the second: if someone gets a kick out of driving around with a fake car phone, the phone counts as useful in the first sense, though presumably not in the second. John Stuart Mill sharply disavowed any association between the concept of utility and the puritanically normative concept of the useful: utility is just pleasure and avoidance of pain.[62] If the fake phone gives pleasure, it provides utility. The normative notion of the useful belongs to the natural function perspective just discussed. Grasping the distinction between the general concept of the useful and the concept of utility is perhaps the trickiest point, for here there is no difference in the scope of the concepts; both apply to anything that satisfies needs of whatever sort.[63] The difference is that the concept of utility posits that all useful things are commensurable, having in common something actual and homogeneous called utility. The general notion of the useful makes no such claim.

Optimizing utility (achieving the greatest happiness for the greatest number) presents another measure of wealth and principle for setting limits to the acquisition of wealth. At the beginning of his book *Utilitarianism*, John Stuart Mill sensibly invokes Epicurus as a forebear of utilitarianism. For utilitarianism is a variety of rationalistic naturalism, though different from the natural function kind. Once again it is assumed that human needs, satisfactions, and dissatisfactions can be sized up in abstraction from any constitutive social form that would itself set standards for wealth and its acquisition. Stripped of any defining social form, what could utility be but something natural? Utility theory rises from the putative ruins of all substantive moral theories.[64] Only the discrediting of such theories will reduce us to the threadbare considerations of pleasure and pain. If we already knew that murder or lying were wrong, whether either act brings pleasure or retards pain would be beside the point. The rationalism of utilitarianism comes forth not only in this leveling of substantial theories of the good or right but in its extracting from all particulars (we are asked to believe) the nectar of the goods: utility.

Assessment. Martha Nussbaum writes this splendid evocation of what utility theory would have us believe: "It is a startling and powerful vision. Just try to think it seriously: this body of this wonderful beloved person is exactly the same in quality as that person's mind and inner life. Both, in turn, the same in quality as the value of Athenian democracy; of Pythagorean geometry; of Eudoxan astronomy. What would it be like to look at a body and to see in it exactly the same shade and tone of goodness and beauty as in a mathematical proof—*exactly* the same, differing only in amount and in location, so that the choice between making love with that person and contemplating that proof presented itself as a choice between conversing with Socrates and administering those laws was, in the same way, a matter of qualitative indifference?"[65] The upshot of Nussbaum's phenomenological exercise is this: what utility theory is supposed to be a theory of, utility, is missing. While the concept of utility purports to carve away all formal determinations of pleasure and pain and still have something actual left over (pleasure or pain that is of no particular sort), it comes up empty handed. In a similar vein Alasdair MacIntyre writes that utility is a "pseudo-concept." It is but a shadow of modern commercial forms.[66] Utility theory is a creature of the peculiar social imagination of modern commercial life, where so many elements of wealth, all those in the commodity form, are in practice commensurated one with another.[67] They all have their price. Such commensurability is not part of the naturalism based on the functional needs of the body; neither, of course, is any restless suggestion of maximizing utility. In those particulars, utility theory mimics modern commercial life.

Nevertheless, utility theory has been and can be the inspiration for attacks on (as well as defenses of) the prevailing commercial societies.[68] In fact, utility theory has the stuff to become a bull in the proverbial china shop, inasmuch as it shadows only one element of commercial life (the commodity) and does not grant that other pillar of the marketplace (the commodity owner, the free person) a place as a primitive, nonnegotiable element of the theory. Compounding this problem is that the ordinary justification of property rights in a commercial society runs through the person, beginning with the proposition that as a free person my labor is mine, to conclude that what entitles me to property in a thing is my "mixing my labor" with it. The liberty and security of persons and private property can, at least in principle, be compromised if we accept utility theory, whereas they are constitutive features of commercial life. It is perhaps not surprising, then, that the history of utility theory is marked by developments that would either neutralize its capacity for radical critique (for example, one can deny the possibility of calculating interpersonal utilities, which could provide a rationale for massive redistributions of wealth) or attempt to squeeze liberalism out of Epicureanism by developing "rule utilitarian" versions of utility theory to secure the liberty of persons along with their property rights. Is it any wonder that in modern, commercial societies utility theory seems neither to triumph nor ever to be finally vanquished?[69]

21

Human Teleology

A teleological conception of human nature that offers a more or less thick and sociopolitical conception of the good, grounded in a more or less thick, sociopolitical conception of human nature, can propose a measure to wealth and set limits to the provisioning process. Its setting limits to wealth need not involve drawing up some determinate set of goods and services that, if provided for, would once and for all quench our needing. Rather, the teleological conception of the human good might be open-ended, not directing us to some preordained destination, but guiding as does a never completely attained aspiration or ideal.[70]

What the teleological theory has in common with all the others, except traditionalism (assuming a monotheistic divine command theory), is its aspiration to universality, its cosmopolitanism. In this it bears the marks of those encounters with commerce and money that so dislocate traditional societies as to activate decontextualized rational reflection on customary ways—a course Hegel calls spirit's "highway of despair." It too is a sort of naturalism and relies for its universality on that naturalism: human teleology is no parochial matter. Where it differs—and here it is not the creature of commercial forms that wealthism, natural function, and utilitarianism are—is that it takes the social and political character of human life to be not a supplement or accretion but one of our "original properties," to use David Hume's term. Thus Aristotle's "man is a political animal" is a statement about what we are, our essence; it is a phenomenological, not an ordinary empirical, claim. To treat human beings in abstraction from the forms of their social and political life, then, means to lose contact with the actuality of human existence.

Since the sociopolitical ingredient is incorporated into this theory of human nature, its theories of the measure and limits of wealth should attend to the fact that human needs and labor always have a specific social form, so that getting the proper measure and limits of wealth will involve getting the right social form of wealth creation. This means that the human teleology approach is not captive to popular representations of capitalism as the realm of "the economy" finally freed of all social form and roamed by *homo economicus*; rather it provides the conceptual wherewithal to challenge commercial forms on a more profound basis than the other theories just examined.

Assessment. Though the human teleology approach provides the most promising basis on which to generate an account of the proper measure and limits of wealth, it faces very challenging questions of its own. (1) Can a reasonable and convincing case be made that there is a human essence which establishes a common *telos*? (2) Is there, as Sartre insisted, something morally deranged in the very idea of a human essence? (3) If there is nothing morally objectionable about living in accordance with one's nature, is there any morally compelling reason to do so? Is it the case that what I ought to do cannot follow from what I am? Or is the urge to step back from our actual nature an existential dry heave? (4) If there is a morally compelling human *telos,* is it thick enough to provide a measure of wealth capable of being articulated in sufficient detail as to make a practical difference? (5) Could a provisioning process that had a social form designed to serve a reasonably thick human *telos* deserve the name "a free society"?[71]

Notes

1. Neil Postman quotes John Quinn, former editor of *USA Today*, as commenting in regard to the paper's chances of winning awards for its journalism: "They don't give awards for the best investigative paragraph" (*Amusing Ourselves to Death*, 112).

2. Here I am broadening the employment of distinctions set forth by Karl Marx in his manuscript *Results of the Immediate Production Process (Results)*, which is published in an English translation in the Penguin edition of the first volume of *Capital*. For reasons of space, I omit discussion of Marx's additional categories of *ideal* and *transitional* or *hybrid* subsumption.

3. William Leiss emphasizes the dramatic cultural consequences of this generalization of the commodity form: "Not market exchange as such, but the universalized version of exchange (the market economy) undermines the earlier practice of operat-

ing within discontinuous realms of objects (subsistence goods and prestige goods, for example) and constitutes the decisive alteration in the cultural context of economic activity" (*The Limits to Satisfaction,* 75).

4. What follows is indebted to Martha Campbell's essay "The Commodity as Necessary Form of Product."

5. Thus Karl Marx writes: "the capitalist production process is conditioned by circulation, trade. The circuit of money-capital is not just commodity production; it only comes into being by way of circulation, and presupposes this" (*Capital* II, 140).

6. Marx observes that the tendency of the capitalist mode of production "is to transform all possible production into commodity production" (*Capital* II, 190).

7. Marx, *Capital* II, 190.

8. Marx, *Results*, 950.

9. "Aristotle Discovers," 84. This suggests that the motivations of participants in a "disembedded economy" are "purely economic." In the following pages I will argue that the supposition underlying talk like this, namely, that there is actual economic life devoid of any specific social form, is mistaken. I will try to sort out the conceptual confusions that result in that misconception.

10. See Alasdair MacIntyre's *After Virtue*; Will Kymlicka's *Liberalism, Community, and Culture*; Michael Sandel's *Liberalism and the Limits of Justice* and the collection he edited, *Liberalism and Its Critics*; the book *Rights and the Common Good: the Communitarian Perspective*, compiled by Amitai Etzioni; Elizabeth Frazer and Nicola Lacey's *The Politics of Community: a Feminist Critique of the Liberal-Communitarian Debate*; and *Communitarianism and Individualism*, edited by Shlomo Avineri and Avner de-Shalit.

11. "Aristotle Discovers," 85–86.

12. On general and determinate abstractions, see Patrick Murray's *Marx's Theory of Scientific Knowledge*, Chapter 10.

13. "Aristotle Discovers," 86.

14. "Aristotle Discovers," 86.

15. "Aristotle Discovers," 93.

16. In *The Just Economy* Richard Winfield criticizes natural and "monological" conceptions of the market economy and then argues that modern market institutions, properly regulated and supplemented, do compose the just social form of the economy.

17. Aristotle, *Politics,* 1256a.

18. *Capital* I, 151. Marx improves on Aristotle in several ways. (1) When Marx says "there is no production in general" (*Grundrisse*, 86), he means that production is always specific in both the technical and the social senses. Production is always production of this or that (say, shoes or cigars) using this or that technique. And it always has a specific social form. Aristotle tends to slur this distinction, speaking sometimes as if distinguishing between hunting, herding, and fixed agriculture captured both the technical and the social specificities in one fell swoop. Marx makes a clear distinction between the two, which allows for the fact that hunting, herding, and agriculture can take a variety of social forms, including the capitalist one. (2) Aristotle is also prone to make the mistake of contrasting production to exchange as natural to social. Marx counters that both production and exchange have natural and social aspects, so both always have a specific social form. (3) Aristotle writes as if the distinction between instruments and possessions could be made on the basis of their technical properties

rather than their functional form in a particular social setting. But the beds at a hotel not only are means to make money for the hotel, they may be used by the "guests" for business or pleasure.

19. *Grundrisse*, 87. Simon Clarke contends that with this fundamental insight, Marx initiated a "scientific revolution" in the study of society that has been largely over-looked: "It was inaugurated by Marx's critique of the ideological foundations of classical political economy, which he located in the political economists' neglect of the social form of capitalist production, which was the basis of their naturalization of capitalist social relations" (*Marx, Marginalism and Modern Sociology*, 240).

20. See George McCarthy's *Dialectics and Decadence: Echoes of Antiquity in Marx and Nietzsche*.

21. Though a particular set of property and class relations are both presupposed and reproduced by capitalism, it would violate the rules governing persons and property if anything of this sort were legally stipulated. It is precisely the formal egalitarianism of capitalism that justifies speaking of "classes" rather than "estates," or some other term that entails explicit public sanctioning of the classification. In *The Just Economy* Richard Winfield maintains that these property arrangements can, in principle, be quite diverse. Perhaps more importantly, he rejects the suggestion that capital is in any sense predominant in a commercial economy. For a critique of Winfield on these and a number of other points, see Tony Smith's books *The Logic of Marx's "Capital": Replies to Hegelian Criticisms* and *Dialectical Social Theory and Its Critics: from Hegel to Analytical Marxism and Postmodernism*.

22. "Aristotle Discovers," 82.

23. A valuable recent inquiry into this question is made in David Gross's *The Past in Ruins: Tradition and the Critique of Modernity*.

24. See T.J. Jackson Lears' study, *No Place of Grace*.

25. See Moishe Postone's *Time, Labor, and Social Domination: A Reinterpretation of Marx's Critical Theory*.

26. Jeanne Schuler, "Back to Union Station," 65.

27. *The Past in Ruins*, 3.

28. "Postmodernism and Consumer Society," 125. Compare Jean Baudrillard's *The Illusion of the End*.

29. The popular 1980s romantic comedy *Pretty Woman* can be viewed as an update of the struggle between commerce and commercialism (as well as a retelling of the *Pygmalion* story). In this case the younger man is the cutthroat moneymaker—he buys, hacks apart, and sells off companies to make a hefty buck—while the older man (himself a major military contractor) embodies sturdy and benign commercial values.

30. See the conflicting assessments of *It's a Wonderful Life* by Tim Luke ("Xmas Ideology: Unwrapping the New Deal and the Cold War Under the Christmas Tree") and Paul Piccone ("Sometimes a Cigar is Just a Good Smoke: Xmas Ideology or Reaganism?") in *Telos* No. 82 (Winter 1989-90), 157–73 and 174–84, respectively.

31. As quoted in David Harvey's *The Condition of Postmodernity*, 158.

32. *Politics*, Book 1, chapter 9.

33. On the ground rules for fair trade, see the selections from St. Thomas Aquinas.

34. See Guy Debord's *The Society of the Spectacle* and Jean Baudrillard's "The Order of Simulacra" in his *Symbolic Exchange and Death*.

35. The term "prostitution" also comes to mind in this connection. Though it is frequently used beyond the narrow context of the sale of "sexual services," these wider uses, on the one hand, tend to focus on activities and, on the other, often express not simony but what was just categorized as "corrupting the craft," for example, the "prostituted" Hollywood screenwriter whose scripts pander to the corporate "bean counters" and audience testers.

36. Though the complete "alienation" of one's labor power violates a constitutive norm of modern commerce, it may be argued, as Carol Gould does quite powerfully in *Rethinking Democracy,* that one's capacities to work are so intimately related to one's personhood as to make wage labor per se morally illegitimate.

37. *Foundations of the Metaphysics of Morals,* 53.

38. The literature in business ethics corroborates this judgment.

39. Daniel Bell concluded his 1978 Foreword to *The Cultural Contradictions of Capitalism* on just this note: "We are groping for a new vocabulary whose keyword seems to be limits: a limit to growth, a limit to the spoilation of the environment, a limit to arms, a limit to the tampering with biological nature. . . . Can we set a limit to hubris?" (xxix). Three other books of that time that put the spotlight on limits are, William Leiss's *The Limits to Satisfaction* (1976), Fred Hirsch's *The Social Limits to Growth* (1978), and the Club of Rome report, *The Limits to Growth* (1972, 1974).

40. In *The Needs of Strangers,* Michael Ignatieff writes: "a decent and humane society requires a shared language of the good" (14) and worries that this shared language is slipping away from us.

41. "Interpretive Essay" to *The Republic,* 312–13.

42. *The Protestant Ethic,* 58–59.

43. *Critique of Pure Reason,* 9.

44. Joan Robinson observes: "One reason why modern life is so uncomfortable is that we have grown self-conscious about things that used to be taken for granted" (*Economic Philosophy,* 1).

45. See the treatment of Locke in C.B. McPherson's *The Political Theory of Possessive Individualism* and the contrasting assessments in John Dunn's *The Political Thought of John Locke* and his essay "From Applied Theology to Social Analysis: The Break Between John Locke and the Scottish Enlightenment" in *Virtue and Wealth* (edited by Michael Ignatieff and Istvan Hont), and in James Tully's *A Discourse on Property.*

46. Two classic treatments of this issue are Plato's brief dialogue *Euthyphro* and Leibniz's critique of Spinoza in his *Discourse on Metaphysics.*

47. This means rejecting any technical or natural conception of the market system. See Richard Winfield's *The Just Economy* and Robert Heilbroner's characterization of capitalism as a "regime" in *Behind the Veil of Economics.*

48. Michael Sandel employs the phrase the "unencumbered self" in his critical assessment of the limits of liberalism. See his *Liberalism and the Limits to Justice.* In the nineteenth century Hegel and Kierkegaard developed powerful criticisms, which were at the same time appropriations, of the notion of the pure or "infinite" self. See Hegel's *Philosophy of Spirit* and Kierkegaard's *Sickness Unto Death.* John Stuart Mill's critique of Kant's categorical imperative lodges its own objection to the unencumbered self: "when he begins to deduce from this precept any of the actual duties of morality, he fails, almost grotesquely, to show that there would be any contradiction,

any logical (not to say physical) impossibility, in the adoption by all rational beings of the most outrageously immoral rules of conduct. All he shows is that the *consequences* of their universal adoption would be such as no one would choose to incur" (*Utilitarianism*, 254). See also Alasdair MacIntyre's genealogy of the "emotivist self" in his *After Virtue* and Bernard Williams' critique of the purity of "morality" in his *Ethics and the Limits of Philosophy*.

49. On the abstract nature of social domination under capitalism see Moishe Postone's *Time, Labor, and Social Domination*.

50. Marx takes this up in his seminal analysis of the "value form," where he explores the question why is it that the value of one commodity appears in the body of another (and ultimately in money). Since what Marx means by "value" pertains to the specific social form of labor under capitalism, the question amounts to this: why does this social form appear as a thing? See his treatment of the value form and the "fetishism of commodities" included in this volume.

51. In his review of the three circuits of capital, one beginning with money (M . . . M′), the second with the production process (P . . . P′), and the third with the capitalistically produced commodity (C′ . . . C′′), Marx observes how a focus on the second circuit helps support the misperception that capitalist production is all about heaping up not money but wealth: "The general form of the movement P . . . P′ is the form of reproduction, and does not indicate, as does M . . . M′, that valorization [making money, P.M.] is the purpose of the process. For this reason, classical economics found it all the more easy to ignore the specifically capitalist form of the production process, and to present production as such as the purpose of the process—to produce as much and as cheaply as possible, and to exchange the product for as many other products as possible" (*Capital* II, 172).

52. *Summa Contra Gentiles*, 179.

53. *Grundrisse*, 487–88. Nevertheless, in the remainder of the paragraph Marx prizes the open-endedness of the modern world against the ancient.

54. An articulate, systematic development of this approach may be found in Carol Gould's *Rethinking Democracy*.

55. Michael Ignatieff makes this point in *The Needs of Strangers*; moreover, he finds in this a reason to supersede all strictly liberty-based approaches to needs in favor of a more Aristotelian one: "In the end, a theory of human needs has to be premissed on some set of choices about what humans need in order to be human: not what they need to be happy or free, since these are subsidiary goals, but what they need in order to realize the full extent of their potential" (15). At the same time that he holds out for a more robust theory of human needs, his critique of political utopianism leads him to the tragic conclusion that we cannot expect society to meet all our needs.

56. *The Enchiridion*, 39.

57. Though he is of the opinion that "It would be hazardous to assert that a useful purpose is ever absent from the utility of any article or of any service, however obviously its prime purpose and chief element is conspicuous waste; and it would be only less hazardous to assert of any primarily useful product that the element of waste is in no way concerned in its value, immediately or remotely" (*The Theory of the Leisure Class*, 101), Thorstein Veblen gives expression to the natural function view when he writes: "The popular reprobation of waste goes to say that in order to be at peace with

himself the common man must be able to see in any and all human effort and human enjoyment an enhancement of life and well-being on the whole. In order to meet with unqualified approval, any economic fact must approve itself under the test of impersonal usefulness—usefulness as seen from the point of view of the generically human" (*Theory of the Leisure Class*, 98). We are left to wonder when the first "generically human" person will turn up.

58. *Utopia*, 72.

59. *The Fable of the Bees,* 136–37.

60. "Speculative Beginning of Human History," in *Perpetual Peace*, 51.

61. See the telling conclusion to note i of the *Discourse on the Origins of Inequality*, which begins: "What! must we destroy societies, annihilate thine and mine, and go back to live in forests with bears? A conclusion in the manner of my adversaries, which I prefer to anticipate rather than leave them the shame of drawing it" (*Discourse on the Origins of Inequality*, 201).

62. Mill wrote: "A passing remark is all that needs be given to the ignorant blunder of supposing that those who stand up for utility as the test of right and wrong, use the term in that restricted and merely colloquial sense in which utility is opposed to pleasure. . . . Those who know anything about the matter are aware that every writer, from Epicurus to Bentham, who maintained the theory of utility, meant by it, not something to be contradistinguished from pleasure, but pleasure itself, together with the exemption from pain; and instead of opposing the useful to the agreeable or the ornamental, have always declared that the useful means these, among other things" (*Utilitarianism*, 256).

63. When, at the beginning of his entry "utility" in *The New Palgrave: A Dictionary of Economics*, R.D. Collison Black offers this definition of utility: "the capacity of a good or service to satisfy a want, of whatever kind" (776), he confuses the general concept of the useful—which is what his statement identifies—with the concept of utility.

64. In his dissertation, Karl Marx made the point that Epicurus's philosophy itself sprang from the demise of "substantial ethical life" and in so doing was a precursor of modern philosophy.

65. *Love's Knowledge*, 116.

66. One branch of utility theory, neoclassical economics, prides itself on its "purely subjective" value theory, but it cannot make sense of this notion. Thus, in his entry on "utility" in *The New Palgrave: A Dictionary of Economics*, R.D. Collison Black writes: "Utility in the sense of desiredness is a purely subjective concept, clearly distinct from usefulness or fitness for a purpose" (776). He calls attention to confusions among utility theorists over this distinction. But evidently the distinction is not so well fixed in Black's own mind as to keep him from writing in the sentence before the one quoted that "desiredness" is "the capacity of a good or service to satisfy a want, of whatever kind." Are such capacities of goods to serve the purpose of our satisfaction "purely subjective"? This points up another difference between the general concept of the useful and the concept of utility. Of usefulness Marx writes: "The usefulness of a thing makes it a use-value. But this usefulness does not dangle in midair. It is conditioned by the physical properties of the commodity, and has no existence apart from the latter" (*Capital* I, 126). Utility theories let usefulness "dangle in midair" and call it utility.

27

67. Thorstein Veblen observes that "hedonistic economics may be taken as an interpretation of human nature in terms of the marketplace" ("Preconceptions of Economic Science II," 141).

68. Simon Clarke writes of marginal utility theory: "Marginalism could embrace the reformist socialism of the Fabians and the revisionist wing of German Social Democracy, the liberal reformism of Wicksell, Cassel, Walras, Wieser, Marshall, Pigou, Keynes and Beveridge, and the conservative liberalism of Jevons, Hayek, von Mises and Milton Friedman" (*Marx, Marginalism and Modern Sociology*, 24).

69. In his article "utilitarianism" in *The New Palgrave: A Dictionary of Economics*, C. Welch comments: "Utilitarianism has achieved a paradoxical status; it dominates the landscape of contemporary thought in the social sciences not because of its own commanding presence, but because it has been necessary to create and recreate it in order to map out the relevant terrain. Its critics claim to look forward to the day when 'we hear no more of it' (Williams, 1973, 150), yet it continues to figure as the alter-ego of much modern moral and social inquiry" ("Utilitarianism," 775). (The reference is to Bernard Williams' "A Critique of Utilitarianism" in *Utilitarianism for and Against* by J.J.C. Smart and Bernard Williams.)

70. See Marx's criticism of Aristotle on just this point (*Grundrisse*, 488).

71. Of the most noteworthy thinker to entertain this prospect William James Booth writes: "We can now state with certainty that Marx, this most forceful and coherent of the critics of capitalism, was unable to provide the materials on which to found a feasible and superior alternative to the society he rejected. Or it may be . . . that it was not Marx's failure at all; perhaps it is the case that whatever the limitations of the economic institutions he so criticized, there is no feasible alternative that satisfies the desiderata he set out" (*Households*, 277). "It may be" does not close off our wondering if it may be otherwise.

28

General Bibliography (including works cited)

Adams, John. "Economy as Instituted Process." In *Journal of Economic Issues* XXIV, no. 2 (June 1994).

Ahrens, John, Fred D. Miller, Jr., Ellen Frankel Paul, and Jeffrey Paul, eds. *Capitalism* (Oxford: Basil Blackwell, 1989).

Appleby, Joyce O. *Economic Thought and Ideology in Seventeenth-Century England* (Princeton: Princeton Univ. Press, 1978).

Arnold, N. Scott. *The Philosophy and Economics of Market Socialism: A Critical Study* (New York: Oxford Univ. Press, 1994).

Avineri, Shlomo, and Avner de-Shalit, eds. *Communitarianism and Individualism* (Oxford: Oxford Univ. Press, 1992).

Bardhan, Pranab K., and John E. Roemer, eds. *Market Socialism: The Current Debate* (New York: Oxford Univ. Press, 1993).

Baudrillard, Jean. *The Illusion of the End* (Stanford: Stanford Univ. Press, 1994). Translated by Chris Turner.

_____. "The Order of Simulacra." In *Symbolic Exchange and Death* (London: SAGE Publications, 1993). Translated by Iain Hamilton Grant.

Becker, Gary. *The Economic Approach to Human Behavior* (Chicago: Univ. of Chicago Press, 1976).

Bell, Daniel. *The Cultural Contradictions of Capitalism* (New York: Basic Books, 1976).

Berger, Peter L. *The Capitalist Revolution* (New York: Basic Books, 1986).

Black, R.D. Collison. "Utility." In *The New Palgrave: A Dictionary of Economics,* Edited by John Eatwell et al. (London: Macmillan, 1987).

Bloom, Allan. "Interpretive Essay." *The Republic of Plato* (New York: Basic Books, 1968).

Bogart, Leo. *Commercial Culture: The Mass Media System and the Public Interest* (New York: Oxford Univ. Press, 1994).

Bonar, James. *Philosophy and Political Economy* (New Brunswick, N.J.: Transaction Books, 1991 [1893]).

Booth, William James. *Households: On the Moral Architecture of the Economy* (Ithaca, N.Y.: Cornell Univ. Press, 1994).

Campbell, Martha. "The Commodity as Necessary Form of Product." In *Economics as Worldly Philosophy: Essays in Political and Historical Economics in Honor of Robert L. Heilbroner.* Edited by Ron Blackwell et al. (New York: St. Martin's, 1993).

Chapman, John W., and J. Roland Pennock, eds. *Nomos 31: Markets and Justice* (New York: New York Univ. Press, 1989).

Clarke, Simon. *Marx, Marginalism and Modern Sociology* (Basingstoke, England: Macmillan, 1982).

Debord, Guy. *The Society of the Spectacle.* Translated by Donald Nicholson-Smith (New York: Zone Books, 1994).

de Tocqueville, Alexis. *Democracy in America.* Translated by George Lawrence and edited by J.P. Mayer. (Garden City, N.Y.: Anchor Books, 1969).

Durkheim, Émile. *The Division of Labor in Society* (Glencoe, Ill.: Free Press, 1960).

Dumont, Louis. *From Mandeville to Marx: The Genesis and Triumph of Economic Ideology* (Chicago: Univ. of Chicago Press, 1977).

Dunn, John. "From Applied Theology to Social Analysis: The Break Between John Locke and the Scottish Enlightenment." In Hont and Ignatieff, eds. *Wealth and Virtue: The Shaping of Political Economy in the Scottish Enlightenment* (Cambridge: Cambridge Univ. Press, 1983).

———. *The Political Thought of John Locke* (Cambridge: Cambridge Univ. Press, 1969).

Dworkin, Gerald, et al., eds. *Markets and Morals* (New York: John Wiley, 1977).

Epictetus. *The Enchiridion.* Translated by Thomas W. Higginson (New York: Macmillan, 1985).

Etzioni, Amitai. *Rights and the Common Good* (New York: St. Martin's, 1995).

Fine, Ben, and Ellen Leopold. *The World of Consumption* (London: Routledge, 1993).

Fischer, Norman. *Economy and Self: Philosophy and Economics from the Mercantilists to Marx* (Westport, Conn.: Greenwood Press, 1979).

Foucault, Michel. *The Order of Things: An Archaeology of the Human Sciences* (New York: Vintage Books, 1973).

Frazer, Elizabeth, and Nicola Lacey. *The Politics of Community: A Feminist Critique of the Liberal-Communitarian Debate* (Toronto: Univ. of Toronto Press, 1993).

Friedman, Milton. *Capitalism and Freedom* (Chicago: Univ. of Chicago Press, 1962).

Gould, Carol. *Rethinking Democracy: Freedom and Social Cooperation in Politics, Economy, and Society* (Cambridge: Cambridge Univ. Press, 1988).

Gross, David. *The Past in Ruins: Tradition and the Critique of Modernity* (Amherst: Univ. of Massachusetts Press, 1992).

29

Gross, Richard. "Speculation and History: Political Economy from Hobbes to Hegel." *Cultural Hermeneutics* 4 (Nov. 1976).

Harvey, David. *The Condition of Postmodernity* (Oxford: Basil Blackwell, 1989).

Hausman, Daniel M. *Essays in Philosophy and Economic Methodology* (New York: Cambridge Univ. Press, 1992).

Heilbroner, Robert L. *Behind the Veil of Economics* (New York: W.W. Norton, 1988).

Hirsch, Fred. *Social Limits to Growth* (Cambridge, Mass.: Harvard Univ. Press, 1978).

Hirschman, Albert O. *The Passions and the Interests: Political Arguments for Capitalism Before its Triumph* (Princeton: Princeton Univ. Press, 1977).

Hont, Istvan, and Michael Ignatieff, eds. *Wealth and Virtue: The Shaping of Political Economy in the Scottish Enlightenment* (Cambridge: Cambridge Univ. Press, 1983).

Ignatieff, Michael. *The Needs of Strangers* (Harmondsworth, England: Penguin, 1984).

Illich, Ivan. *Towards a History of Needs* (New York: Pantheon, 1978).

Jameson, Frederic. "Postmodernism and Consumer Society." In *The Anti-Aesthetic* by Hal Foster (Port Townsend, Wash.: Bay Press, 1983).

Kant, Immanuel. *The Critique of Pure Reason*. Translated by Norman Kemp Smith (London: Macmillan, 1929).

_____. *Foundations of the Metaphysics of Morals*. Translated with an introduction by Lewis White Beck (Indianapolis: Bobbs-Merrill, 1959).

Kierkegaard, Søren. *The Sickness Unto Death*. Edited and translated by Howard and Edna Hong (Princeton: Princeton Univ. Press, 1980).

Kymlicka, Will. *Liberalism, Community, and Culture* (Oxford: Clarendon Press, 1989).

Lears, T. Jackson. *No Place of Grace* (New York: Pantheon Books, 1981).

Leibniz, Gottfried. *Philosophical Essays*. Edited and translated by Roger Ariew and Daniel Garber (Indianapolis: Hackett, 1989).

Leiss, William. *The Limits to Satisfaction: An Essay on the Problem of Needs and Commodities* (Toronto: Univ. of Toronto Press, 1976).

Levine, David P. *Needs, Rights, and the Market* (Boulder, Colo. and London: Lynne Rienner, 1988).

Levy, David M. *The Economic Ideas of Ordinary People* (New York: Routledge, 1991).

Luke, Tim. "Xmas Ideology: Unwrapping the New Deal and the Cold War Under the Christmas Tree." *Telos 82* (Winter 1989–1990): 157–73.

Machan, Tibor R., ed. *The Libertarian Reader* (Totowa, N. J.: Rowman and Littlefield, 1982).

_____. ed. *The Main Debate: Communism versus Capitalism* (New York: Random House, 1987).

MacIntyre, Alasdair. *After Virtue* (South Bend, Ind.: Univ. of Notre Dame Press, 1984).

Macpherson. C.B. *The Political Theory of Possessive Individualism* (Oxford: Oxford Univ. Press, 1962).

_____. *The Rise and Fall of Economic Justice and Other Essays* (New York: Oxford Univ. Press, 1985).

Maine, Sir Henry. *Ancient Law* (New York: Henry Holt, 1864).

Mandeville, Bernard. *The Fable of the Bees* (Harmondsworth, England: Penguin, 1970). Edited by Phillip Harth.

Mansbridge, Jane J., ed. *Beyond Self-Interest* (Chicago: Univ. of Chicago Press, 1990).

Marx, Karl. *Results of the Immediate Production Process.* In *Capital,* vol. 1. Translated by Ben Fowkes (Harmondsworth, England: Penguin, 1976)..

Marx, Karl. *Capital,* vol. 2.. Translated by David Fernbach (Harmondsworth, England: Penguin, 1992).

Mattick, Paul, Jr. *Social Knowledge* (Armonk, N.Y.: M.E. Sharpe, 1986).

McCarthy, George. *Dialectics and Decadence: Echoes of Antiquity in Marx and Nietzsche* (Savage, Md.: Rowman and Littlefield, 1994).

McNally, David. *Political Economy and the Rise of Capitalism* (Berkeley: Univ. of California Press, 1988).

Meadows, Dennis L., et al. *The Limits to Growth: A Report for the Club of Rome's Project on the Predicament of Mankind* (New York: Universe Books, 1974).

Mill, John Stuart. *Utilitarianism, On Liberty, Essay on Bentham.* Edited by Mary Warnock (New York: Meridian Books, 1962).

More, St. Thomas. *Utopia* (New Haven: Yale Univ. Press, 1964). Edited by Edward Surtz, S.J.

Mosley, Fred, ed. *Marx's Method in Capital: A Reexamination* (Atlantic Highlands, N.J.: Humanities Press, 1993).

Murray, Patrick. *Marx's Theory of Scientific Knowledge* (Atlantic Highlands, N.J.: Humanities Press, 1988).

Needleman, Jacob. *Money and the Meaning of Life* (Garden City, N.Y.: Doubleday Currency Books, 1991).

Nussbaum, Martha. *Love's Knowledge: Essays on Philosophy and Literature* (Oxford: Oxford Univ. Press, 1990).

Nussbaum, Martha, and Amartya Sen, eds. *The Quality of Life* (New York: Oxford Univ. Press, 1993).

Olson, Mancur, Jr. *The Logic of Collective Action: Public Goods and the Theory of Groups* (Cambridge: Harvard Univ. Press, 1965).

Piccone, Paul. "Sometimes a Cigar is Just a Good Smoke: Xmas Ideology or Reaganism?" *Telos* 82 (Winter 1989–90): 174–84.

Piorie, Michael, and Charles Sable. *The Second Industrial Divide* (New York: Basic Books, 1984).

Plato. *Euthyphro.* In *Five Dialogues* (Indianapolis: Hackett, 1981). Translated by G.M.A. Grube.

Pocock, J.G.A. *The Machiavellian Moment: Florentine Political Thought and the Atlantic Republican Tradition* (Princeton: Princeton Univ. Press, 1975).

_____. *Virtue, Commerce, and History* (Cambridge: Cambridge Univ. Press, 1985).

Polanyi, Karl. "Aristotle Discovers the Economy." In *Primitive, Archaic, and Modern Economies: Essays of Karl Polanyi.* Edited by George Dalton. (Garden City, N.Y.: Doubleday, 1968).

Postman, Neil. *Amusing Ourselves to Death* (New York: Penguin, 1985).

Postone, Moishe. *Time, Labor, and Social Domination* (Cambridge: Cambridge Univ. Press, 1993).

Rainwater, Lee. *What Money Buys* (New York: Basic Books, 1976).

Reich, Robert. *The Work of Nations* (New York: Alfred A. Knopf, 1991).

Robinson, Joan. *Economic Philosophy* (Chicago: Aldine, 1962).

31

Rousseau, Jean-Jacques. *The First and Second Discourses* (New York: St. Martin's, 1964).

Roy, Subroto. *Philosophy of Economics: On the Scope of Reason in Economic Inquiry* (New York: Routledge, 1991).

Sandel, Michael, ed. *Liberalism and Its Critics* (New York: New York Univ. Press, 1984).

_____. *Liberalism and the Limits of Justice* (Cambridge: Cambridge Univ. Press, 1982).

Sayer, Derek. *Capitalism and Modernity: An Excursus on Marx and Weber* (London: Routledge, 1991).

Schuler, Jeanne. "Back to Union Station." *Telos* (Winter 1988–89): 55–69.

Schumpeter, Joseph. *Capitalism, Socialism and Democracy* (New York: Harper Torchbooks, 1942).

Sekora, John. *Luxury, The Concept in Western Thought, Eden to Smollett* (Baltimore, Md.: Johns Hopkins Univ. Press, 1977).

Sen, Amartya. *On Ethics and Economics* (Oxford: Basil Blackwell, 1987).

_____. *On Economic Inequality* (New York: Oxford Univ. Press, 1994).

Shell, Marc. *Money, Language, and Thought: Literary and Philosophical Economies from the Medieval to the Modern Era* (Berkeley: Univ. of California Press, 1982).

_____. *The Economy of Literature* (Baltimore: Johns Hopkins Univ. Press, 1978).

Smith, Tony. *Dialectical Social Theory and Its Critics: From Hegel to Analytical Marxism and Postmodernism* (Albany: State Univ. of New York Press, 1993).

_____. *The Logic of Marx's "Capital": Replies to Hegelian Criticisms* (Albany: State Univ. of New York Press, 1990).

Sombart, Werner. *The Quintessence of Capitalism: A Study of the History and Psychology of the Modern Business Man.* Translated and edited by M. Epstein (New York: Howard Fertig, Inc., 1967).

Springborg, Patricia. *The Problem of Human Needs and the Critique of Civilisation* (London: George Allen Unwin, 1981).

Tawney, R.H. *Religion and the Rise of Capitalism* (London: Penguin, 1966).

Teichgraeber, Richard, III. *Free Trade and Moral Philosophy* (Durham, N.C.: Duke Univ. Press, 1986).

Tribe, Keith. *Land, Labor, and Economic Discourse* (London: Routledge and Kegan Paul, 1978).

Tully, James. *A Discourse on Property: John Locke and His Adversaries* (Cambridge: Cambridge Univ. Press, 1980).

Veblen, Thorstein. "Preconceptions of Economic Science II." In *The Place of Science in Modern Civilisation, and other Essays* (New Brunswick, N.J.: Transaction Books, 1990).

Weber, Max. *The Protestant Ethic and the Spirit of Capitalism.* Translated by Talcott Parsons (New York: Scribner's, 1958).

Welch, C. "Utilitarianism." *The New Palgrave: A Dictionary of Economics,* vol. 4. Edited by John Eatwell et al. (London: Macmillan, 1987).

Williams, Bernard. "A Critique of Utilitarianism." In *Utilitarianism for and against.* Edited by J.J.C. Smart and Bernard Williams. (Cambridge: Cambridge Univ. Press, 1973).

_____. *Ethics and the Limits of Philosophy* (Cambridge: Harvard Univ. Press, 1985).

Winfield, Richard. *The Just Economy* (London: Routledge, 1990).

Xenos, Nicholas. *Scarcity and Modernity* (New York: Routledge, 1989).

Economics

Carchedi, Guglielmo. *Frontiers of Political Economy* (London:Verso, 1991).

Eatwell, John, Murray Milgate, and Peter Newman, eds. *The New Palgrave: A Dictionary of Economics* (London: Macmillan; New York: Stockton Press, c1987, 1988 printing).

Ekins, Paul, and Manfred Max-Neef. *Real-Life Economics: Understanding Wealth Creation* (New York: Routledge, 1992).

Ferber, Marianne A., and Julie Nelson. *Beyond Economic Man: Feminist Theory and Economics* (Chicago: Univ. of Chicago Press, 1993).

Heilbroner, Robert L. *Behind the Veil of Economics* (New York: W.W. Norton, 1988).

Hodgson, Geoffrey M. *Economics and Evolution: Bringing Life Back into Economics* (Ann Arbor: Univ. of Michigan Press, 1993).

Hutchison, T. W. *The Politics and Philosophy of Economics: Marxians, Keynesians, and Austrians* (New York: New York Univ. Press, 1981).

Levine, David P. *Economic Studies: Contributions to the Critique of Economic Theory* (London: Routledge, 1977).

Lowe, Adolph. *On Economic Knowledge* (New York: Harper and Row, 1965).

Menger, Carl. *Problems of Economics and Sociology* (Urbana: Univ. of Illinois Press, 1963).

Mosley, Fred, ed. *Heterodox Economic Theories: True or False?* (Brookfield, Vt.: Edward Elgar, 1995).

Prebrazhensky, I.A. *The New Economics.* Translated by Brian Pearce (Oxford: Clarendon Press, 1965).

Robinson, Joan. *Economic Philosophy* (Chicago: Aldine, 1962).

Economic History

de Vries, Jan. *The Economy of Europe in an Age of Crisis* (New York: Cambridge Univ. Press, 1976).

Dobb, Maurice. *Studies in the Development of Capitalism* (New York: International, 1964).

Finley, M.I. *The Ancient Economy* (Berkeley: Univ. of California Press, 1973).

Garnsey, Peter, et al., eds. *Trade in the Ancient Economy* (Berkeley: Univ. of California Press, 1983).

Goldsmith, R.W. *Premodern Financial Systems* (Cambridge: Cambridge Univ. Press, 1987).

Hasebroek, Johannes. *Trade and Politics in Ancient Greece* (New York: Biblo and Tannen, 1965).

Heilbroner, Robert L. *The Making of Economic Society.* 9th ed. (Englewood Cliffs, N.J.: Prentice-Hall, 1993).

Hilton, R.H. *The Transition from Feudalism to Capitalism* (London: New Left Books, 1976).

North, Douglass C. "Markets and Other Allocation Systems in History: The Challenge of Karl Polanyi." *Journal of European Economic History* 6 (1977).

_____. *Structure and Change in Economic History* (New York: W.W. Norton, 1981).

Polanyi, Karl. *The Great Transformation* (Boston: Beacon Press, 1957).

_____. *Primitive, Archaic, and Modern Economies: Essays of Karl Polanyi.* Edited by George Dalton. (Garden City, N.Y.: Doubleday, 1968).

33

Rosenberg, Nathan, and L.E. Birdzell. *How the West Grew Rich: The Economic Transformation of the Industrial World* (New York: Basic Books, 1986).

Sweezy, Paul. *The Theory of Capitalist Development* (New York: Monthly Review Press, 1968).

Vilar, Pierre. *A History of Gold and Money: 1450–1920* (London: Verso, 1991).

History

Austin, M.M., and Pierre Vidal-Naquet. *Economic and Social History of Ancient Greece.* Translated and revised by M.M Austin (Berkeley: Univ. of California Press, 1977).

Davies, J.K. *Democracy and Classical Greece* (Atlantic Highlands, N.J.: Humanities Press, 1978).

Dawson, Doyne. *Cities of the Gods: Communist Utopias in Greek Thought* (N.Y.: Oxford Univ. Press, 1992).

De Ste. Croix, G.E.M. *The Class Struggle in the Ancient Greek World* (Ithaca, N.Y.: Cornell Univ. Press, 1981).

Finley, M.I. *Economy and Society in Ancient Greece* (New York: Viking, 1982).

_____. *Studies in Ancient Society* (London: Routledge, 1974).

Landes, David S. *Revolution in Time: Clocks and the Making of the Modern World* (Cambridge: Harvard Univ. Press, 1983).

_____, ed. *The Rise of Capitalism* (New York: Macmillan, 1966).

Meijer, Fik, and Onno van Nijf. *Trade, Transport and Society in the Ancient World: A Sourcebook* (London and New York: Routledge, 1992).

History of Economic Theory

Blaug, Mark. *Economic Theory in Retrospect* (Homewood, Ill.: Richard D. Irwin, 1968).

Bowley, Marian. *Studies in the History of Economic Theory Before 1870* (London: Macmillan, 1973).

Deane, Phyllis. *The Evolution of Economic Ideas* (Cambridge: Cambridge Univ. Press, 1978).

Gordon, Barry. *Economic Analysis Before Adam Smith: Hesiod to Lessius* (London: Macmillan, 1975).

_____. *The Economic Problem in Biblical and Patristic Thought* (Leiden, N.Y.: E.J. Brill, 1989.

Heilbroner, Robert L. *The Worldly Philosophers,* 6th ed. (New York: Simon and Schuster, 1992).

Letwin, William. *The Origins of Scientific Economics: English Economic Thought 1660–1776* (London: Methuen, 1963).

Meek, Ronald. *Economics and Ideology* (London: Chapman and Hall, 1967).

_____. *Smith, Marx, and After* (London: Chapman and Hall, 1977).

Myrdal, Gunnar. *The Political Element in the Development of Economic Theory* (London: Routledge, 1953).

Napoleoni, Claudio. *Smith Ricardo Marx.* Translated by J.M.A. Gee (New York: John Wiley: Halsted Press, 1975).

Roll, Eric. *A History of Economic Thought,* 3rd ed. (Englewood Cliffs, N.J.: Prentice Hall, 1964).

34

Rubin, Isaac Ilych. *A History of Economic Thought*. Translated and edited by Donald Filtzer (London: Ink Links, 1979).

Schumpeter, Joseph. *History of Economic Analysis*. Edited by Elizabeth Brady Schumpeter (Oxford: Oxford Univ. Press, 1954).

Vickers, Douglas. *Studies in Theory of Money, 1690–1776* (Philadelphia: Chilton, 1959).

Viner, Jacob. *The Long View and the Short* (Glencoe, Ill.: Free Press, 1958).

_____. *Religious Thought and Economic Society: Four chapters of an unfinished work by Jacob Viner*. Edited by Jacques Melitz and Donald Winch. (Durham, N.C.: Duke Univ. Press, 1978).

Marxism and Critical Theory

Adorno, Theodor W. *Prisms* (Cambridge, MA.: MIT Press, 1981).

_____, and Max Horkheimer. *Dialectic of Enlightenment* (New York: Seabury Press, 1944).

Benhabib, Seyla. *Critique, Norm and Utopia: A Study of the Foundations of Critical Theory* (New York: Columbia Univ. Press, 1986).

Braverman, Harry. *Labor and Monopoly Capital: The Degradation of Work in the Twentieth Century* (New York: Monthly Review Press, 1974).

Castoriadis, Cornelius. *Crossroads in the Labyrinth* (Brighton: Harvester Press, 1983).

Colletti, Lucio. *From Rousseau to Lenin* (London: New Left Books, 1972).

della Volpe, G. *Rousseau and Marx* (London: Lawrence and Wishart, 1978).

Godelier, Maurice. *Rationality and Irrationality in Economics*. Translated by Brian Pearce (New York: Monthly Review Press, 1972).

Gorz, Andre. *Critique of Economic Reason* (New York: Verso, 1989).

Hartsock, Nancy. *Money, Sex, and Power: Toward a Feminist Historical Materialism* (New York: Longman, 1983).

Harvey, David. *The Urban Experience* (Baltimore: Johns Hopkins Univ. Press, 1989).

Lash, Scott and John Urry. *The End of Organized Capitalism* (Cambridge: Polity, 1987).

Lefebvre, Henri. *Critique of Everyday Life*. Translated by John Moore (London: Verso, 1991).

Lipietz, Alain. *Towards a New Economic Order: Postfordism, Ecology and Democracy* (New York: Oxford Univ. Press, 1992).

Lukács, Georg. *History and Class Consciousness*. Translated by Rodney Livingstone (Cambridge, Mass: MIT Press, 1971).

Marcuse, Herbert. *One-Dimensional Man: Studies in the Ideology of Advanced Industrial Society* (Boston: Beacon Press, 1964).

_____. *Eros and Civilization: A Philosophical Inquiry Into Freud* (New York: Random House, 1955).

_____. *Negations: Essays in Critical Theory* (Boston: Beacon Press, 1969).

O'Connor, James. *Accumulation Crisis* (New York: Basil Blackwell, 1984).

Offe, Claus. *Disorganized Capitalism* (Cambridge, Mass.: MIT Press, 1985).

Postone, Moishe, *Time, Labor, and Social Domination* (Cambridge: Cambridge Univ. Press, 1993).

Reuten, Geert, and Michael Williams. *Value-Form and the State* (London: Routledge, 1991).

Sohn-Rethel, A. *Intellectual and Manual Labor* (London: Macmillan, 1978).

35

Soper, Kate. *On Human Needs: Open and Closed Theories in a Marxist Perspective* (Brighton: Harvester Press, 1981).

Thompson, E.P. "Time, Work-Discipline, and Industrial Capitalism." *Past & Present* 38 (1967).

Political Theory

Barry, Norman P. *On Classical Liberalism and Libertarianism* (New York: St. Martin's, 1987).

Brittan, Samuel. *A Restatement of Economic Liberalism* (Atlantic Highlands, N.J.: Humanities Press, 1988).

Buckle, Stephen. *Natural Law Theory and the Theory of Property* (New York: Oxford Univ. Press, 1991).

Cropsey, Joseph. *Polity and Economy* (The Hague: Martinus Nijhoff, 1957).

_____. *Political Philosophy and the Issues of Politics* (Chicago: Univ. of Chicago Press, 1977).

Dworkin, Ronald. "Liberalism." In *Public and Private Morality.* Edited by Stuart Hampshire (Cambridge: Cambridge Univ. Press, 1978).

Ferguson, Thomas. *The Golden Rule: The Investment Theory of Party Competition and the Logic of Money-Driven Political Systems* (Chicago: Univ. of Chicago Press, 1995).

Gauthier, David. *Morals by Agreement* (Oxford: Clarendon Press, 1986).

Gough, Ian. *The Political Economy of the Welfare State* (London: Macmillan, 1979).

Gould, Carol. *Rethinking Democracy: Freedom and Social Cooperation in Politics, Economy, and Society* (Cambridge: Cambridge Univ. Press, 1988).

Guttman, Amy. *Liberal Equality* (New York: Cambridge Univ. Press, 1980).

Lindblom, Charles E. *Politics and Markets: The World's Political Economic Systems* (New York: Basic Books, 1977).

Macpherson, C.B. *Democratic Theory: Essays in Retrieval* (New York: Oxford Univ. Press, 1973).

_____. *The Real World of Democracy* (Oxford: Oxford Univ. Press, 1972).

Miller, David. *Market, State, and Community* (Oxford: Clarendon Press, 1989).

_____. *Social Justice* (Oxford: Clarendon Press, 1976).

Myers, Milton L. *The Soul of Modern Man: Ideas of Self-Interest—Thomas Hobbes to Adam Smith* (Chicago: Univ. of Chicago Press, 1983).

Oakeshott, Michael. *Rationalism in Politics and Other Essays* (Indianapolis: Liberty Press, 1991).

Okin, Susan Moller. *Women in Western Political Thought* (Princeton: Princeton Univ. Press, 1979).

Pateman, Carol. *The Problem of Political Obligation: A Critique of Liberal Theory* (Berkeley: Univ. of California Press, 1985).

Plant, Raymond, Harry Lesser, and Peter Laylor-Gooby, eds. *Political Philosophy and Social Welfare: Essays on the Normative Basis of Welfare Provision* (London: Routledge and Kegan Paul, 1980).

Rawls, John. *A Theory of Justice* (Cambridge, Mass.: Harvard Univ. Press, 1971).

Reiss, Hans, ed. *Kant: Political Writings* (Cambridge: Cambridge Univ. Press, 1991).

Rothbard, Murray. *Man, Economy and State* (Princeton: Princeton Univ. Press, 1962).

Ryan, Alan. *Property* (Minneapolis: Univ. of Minnesota Press, 1987).

_____. *Property and Political Theory* (Oxford: Basil Blackwell, 1984).

Sandel, Michael. *Liberalism and the Limits of Justice* (Cambridge: Cambridge Univ. Press, 1982).

Shklar, J.N. *Men and Citizens: A Study of Rousseau's Social Theory* (Cambridge: Cambridge Univ. Press, 1969).

Skinner, Quentin. *The Foundations of Modern Political Thought* (Cambridge: Cambridge Univ. Press, 1978).

Strauss, Leo. *Natural Right and History* (Chicago: Univ. of Chicago Press, 1950).

_____. *What is Political Philosophy?* (New York: Free Press, 1959).

Tuck, Richard. *Natural Rights Theories: Their Origin and Development* (Cambridge: Cambridge Univ. Press, 1979).

Walzer, Michael. *Spheres of Justice* (New York: Basic Books, 1983).

37

PLATO (c. 427–c.347 B.C)

"I WENT down to the Piraeus the other day," begins Plato's *Republic*. What sort of place was it and what sort of family did Socrates visit there? The Piraeus was the port of Athens, a center of trade and the mixing of peoples, and the family Socrates is roped into conversing with is headed by Cephalus. Cephalus, like many Athenian merchants, was not a citizen; he was a "resident alien" who came from Syracuse to make money dealing in armaments. So we begin in a commercial zone, on the margin of the city, with a merchant family at the margins of Athenian civic life. Is it accidental that the book to which Western philosophy owes such a debt opens this way? Or does it suggest that commerce, money, and moneymakers prove too intrusive to be isolated to the margins of traditional Athenian life and that they thrust themselves to the center of Plato's tandem theories of the just person and society? And what of that most dramatic figure of Book I, the Sophist Thrasymachus, whose pedagogy comes at a price? Is there an inner connection between his being a fee-taker and the "wisdom" he peddles: that perfect justice is really perfect injustice or tyranny? Is the *Republic* an anxious and profound set of reflections on commercial life?

In Book I, three characters pose definitions of justice, and all three are linked to moneymaking: Cephalus is identified as a rich, older man; Polemarchus, his son, is rebuked by Socrates for defining justice in the manner of a rich man, even a traitorous one. Thrasymachus, of course, belongs to that group of well paid fee-takers, the Sophists, who weigh so heavily on Plato's mind. Attention to money carries over into Book II with the story of the "ring of Gyges." In the story, a shepherd who pulls a gold ring (an early type of coin) off a corpse turns into a tyrant. The shepherd is described as an ancestor of Gyges, who was the Lydian king widely identified with instituting coined money and with tyranny. At the close of Book III, we learn that the just city provides for the needs of its rulers, the guardians, who are not permitted contact with silver or gold. Supposedly, the noble lie or "myth of the metals," which teaches that different classes of people have either base metal, silver, or golden souls, would help the guardians swallow this restriction.

Three tables of values clash in the *Republic* and throughout Plato's work: the ancestral Athenian values handed down by custom and in poetry; the commercial scale of values, which weighs out everything in silver and gold; and philosophy, which appeals to the nature or form of things—and above all to the ultimate form of the Good—as its measure of worth. Commerce and its standard of value, money, posed a peculiar threat to traditional values. For silver and gold were standards recognized as widely as commerce could fling itself. Commerce represented not one local custom vying with others, but a cosmopolitan outlook which acknowledged only one god, money. Plato judged that this challenge to traditional values could not be met by the traditional means of reaction and repression—that much he granted the Sophists. If traditional values were not to be swept away by commercial ones, they would need to be defended selectively and reflectively, on the basis of some newly conceived, non-parochial measure of worth. Philosophy was called upon to supply this new measure, thus doing battle on two fronts: against traditionalists, whose cause was lost, and against those with money in their mouths, whose rise would reduce human life to the meanest proportions.

Three moneymakers' notions of justice are presented in Book I, one more disturbing than the previous one. We are left wondering whether Thrasymachus's tyrant shares features with the seemingly benign merchant Cephalus, whose business depended upon servicing contracts honestly and repaying debts. The basic trouble facing moneymakers is how to figure out the meaning of justice without recourse to any substantive ideas about what is good for persons and for cities. Against this Plato insists: if justice is the art of rightly ordering one's soul and city, to what end are they to be ordered?

He wants to shock us with how empty-headed and dangerous the money-makers' answers to this question are.

We need to think through Plato's critique of the Sophists and the relation between their moneymaking and their moral skepticism and hedonism. What stands behind Protagoras's dictum "man is the measure" turns out to be "money is the measure." It could also be said of Aristotle's ethics that "man is the measure." But in the *Nicomachean Ethics,* the common intellectual, moral, political, and aesthetic nature of man gives the measure. For money to function as the measure for individuals and cities, traditional standards and substantial, philosophical measures of the good must be put out of play. For what about "man" is the Sophists' measure, after all? Doesn't it end up being pleasure and pain? Hedonism becomes the social norm precisely when we have the "disembedded" economy, for in an "embedded" economy, where custom or philosophy provide limits, hedonism is out of place. But what makes for a "disembedded" economy? An economy where money is the measure. So, "man is the measure" in the subjective Protagorean sense, precisely when money becomes the measure. Sophistical moral culture results when the acidic power of commerce is not contained. For Plato, money, not its Sophist mouthpieces, is the fundamental corrosive loosed into his world.

FROM THE *REPUBLIC,* BOOK I

I went down yesterday to the Piraeus with Glaucon, the son of Ariston, to pay my devotions to the goddess, and also because I wished to see how they would conduct the festival, since this was its inauguration.

I thought the procession of the citizens very fine, but it was no better than the show made by the marching of the Thracian contingent.

After we had said our prayers and seen the spectacle we were starting for town when Polemarchus, the son of Cephalus, caught sight of us from a distance as we were hastening homeward and ordered his boy run and bid us to wait for him, and the boy caught hold of my himation from behind and said, Polemarchus wants you to wait.

And I turned around and asked where his master was.

There he is, he said, behind you, coming this way. Wait for him.

So we will, said Glaucon. And shortly after Polemarchus came up and Adimantus, the brother of Glaucon, and Niceratus, the son of Nicias, and a few others apparently from the procession.

Whereupon Polemarchus said, Socrates, you appear to have turned your faces townward and to be going to leave us.

Not a bad guess, said I.

But you see how many we are? he said.

Surely.

You must either then prove yourselves the better men or stay here.

Why, is there not left, said I, the alternative of our persuading you that you ought to let us go?

But *could* you persuade us, said he, if we refused to listen?

Nohow, said Glaucon.

Well, we won't listen, and you might as well make up your minds to it.

Do you mean to say, interposed Adimantus, that you haven't heard that there is to be a torchlight race this evening on horseback in honor of the goddess?

On horseback? said I. That is a new idea. Will they carry torches and pass them along to one another as they race with the horses, or how do you mean?

That's the way of it, said Polemarchus, and, besides, there is to be a night festival which will be worth seeing. For after dinner we will get up and go out and see the sights and meet a lot of the lads there and have good talk. So stay and do as we ask.

It looks as if we should have to stay, said Glaucon.

Well, said I, if it so be, so be it.

So we went with them to Polemarchus' house, and there we found Lysias and Euthydemus, the brothers of Polemarchus, yes, and Thrasymachus, too, of Chalcedon, and Charmantides of the deme of Paeania, and Clitophon, the son of Aristonymus. And the father of Polemarchus, Cephalus, was also at home.

And I thought him much aged, for it was a long time since I had seen him. He was sitting on a sort of chair with cushions and he had a chaplet on his head, for he had just finished sacrificing in the court. So we went and sat down beside him, for there were seats there disposed in a circle.

As soon as he saw me Cephalus greeted me and said, You are not a very frequent visitor, Socrates. You don't often come down to the Piraeus to see us. That is not right. For if I were still able to make the journey up to town easily there would be no need of your resorting hither, but we would go to visit you. But as it is you should not space too widely your visits here. For I would have you know that, for my part, as the satisfactions of the body decay, in the same measure my desire for the pleasures of good talk and my delight in them increase. Don't refuse then, but be yourself a companion to these lads and make our house your resort and regard us as your very good friends and intimates.

Why, yes, Cephalus, said I, and I enjoy talking with the very aged. For to my thinking we have to learn of them as it were from wayfarers who have preceded us on a road on which we too, it may be, must sometime fare— what it is like. Is it rough and hard-going or easy and pleasant to travel? And so now I would fain learn of you what you think of this thing, now that your time has come to it, the thing that the poets call 'the threshold of old age.' Is it a hard part of life to bear or what report have you to make of it?

Yes, indeed, Socrates, he said, I will tell you my own feeling about it. For it often happens that some of us elders of about the same age come together and verify the old saw of like to like. At these reunions most of us make lament, longing for the lost joys of youth and recalling to mind the pleasures of wine, women, and feasts, and other things thereto appertaining, and they repine in the belief that the greatest things have been taken from them and that then they lived well and now it is no life at all. And some of them complain of the indignities that friends and kinsmen put upon old age and thereto recite a doleful litany of all the miseries for which they blame old age. But in my opinion, Socrates, they do not put the blame on the real cause. For if it were the cause I too should have had the same experience so far as old age is concerned, and so would all others who have come to this time of life. But in fact I have ere now met with others who do not feel in this way, and in particular I remember hearing Sophocles the poet greeted by a fellow who asked, How about your service of Aphrodite, Sophocles—is your natural force still unabated? And he replied, Hush, man, most gladly have I escaped this thing you talk of, as if I had run away from a raging and savage beast of a master. I thought it a good answer then and now I think so still more. For in very truth there comes to old age a great tranquillity in such matters and a blessed release. When the fierce tensions of the passions and desires relax, then is the word of Sophocles approved, and we are rid of many and mad masters. But indeed, in respect of these complaints and in the matter of our relations with kinsmen and friends there is just one cause, Socrates—not old age, but the character of the man. For if men are temperate and cheerful even old age is only moderately burdensome. But if the reverse, old age, Socrates, and youth are hard for such dispositions.

43

And I was filled with admiration for the man by these words, and desirous of hearing more I tried to draw him out and said, I fancy, Cephalus, that most people, when they hear you talk in this way, are not convinced but think that you bear old age lightly not because of your character but because of your wealth, for the rich, they say, have many consolations.

You are right, he said. They don't accept my view and there is something in their objection, though not so much as they suppose. But the retort of Themistocles comes in pat here, who, when a man from the little island of Seriphus grew abusive and told him that he owed his fame not to himself but to the city from which he came, replied that neither would he himself ever have made a name if he had been born in Seriphus nor the other if he had been an Athenian. And the same principle applies excellently to those who not being rich take old age hard, for neither would the reasonable man find it altogether easy to endure old age conjoined with poverty, nor would the unreasonable man by the attainment of riches ever attain to self-contentment and a cheerful temper.

May I ask, Cephalus, said I, whether you inherited most of your possessions or acquired them yourself?

Acquired, quotha? he said. As a money-maker, I hold a place somewhere halfway between my grandfather and my father. For my grandfather and namesake inherited about as much property as I now possess and multiplied it many times, my father Lysanias reduced it below the present amount, and I am content if I shall leave the estate to these boys not less but by some slight measure more than my inheritance.

The reason I asked, I said, is that you appear to me not to be overfond of money. And that is generally the case with those who have not earned it themselves. But those who have themselves acquired it have a double reason in comparison with other men for loving it. For just as poets feel complacency about their own poems and fathers about their own sons, so men who have made money take this money seriously as their own creation and they also value it for its uses as other people do. So they are hard to talk to since they are unwilling to commend anything except wealth.

You are right, he replied.

I assuredly am, said I. But tell me further this. What do you regard as the greatest benefit you have enjoyed from the possession of property?

Something, he said, which I might not easily bring many to believe if I told them. For let me tell you, Socrates, he said, that when a man begins to realize that he is going to die, he is filled with apprehensions and concern about matters that before did not occur to him. The tales that are told of the world below and how the men who have done wrong here must pay the penalty there, though he may have laughed them down hitherto, then begin to torture his soul with the doubt that there may be some truth in them. And apart from that the man himself either from the weakness of old age or possibly as being now nearer to the things beyond has a somewhat clearer view of them. Be that as it may, he is filled with doubt, surmises, and alarms and begins to reckon up and consider whether he has ever wronged anyone. Now he to whom the ledger of his life shows an account of many evil deeds starts up even from his dreams like a child again and again in affright and his days are haunted by anticipations of worse to come. But on him who is conscious of no wrong that he has done a sweet hope ever attends and a goodly, to be nurse of his old age, as Pindar too says. For a beautiful saying it is, Socrates, of the poet that when a man lives out his days in justice and piety, 'sweet companion with him, to cheer his heart and nurse his old age, accompanieth hope, who chiefly ruleth the changeful mind of mortals.' That is a fine saying and an admirable. It is for this, then, that I affirm that the possession of wealth is of most value, not it may be to every man but to the good man. Not to cheat any man even unintentionally or play him false, not remaining in debt to a god for some sacrifice or to a man for money, so to depart in fear to that other world—to this result the possession of property contributes not a little. It has also many other uses. But, setting one thing against another, I would lay it down, Socrates, that for a man of sense this is the chief service of wealth.

An admirable sentiment, Cephalus, said I. But speaking of this very thing, justice, are we to affirm thus without qualification that it is truthtelling and paying back what one has received from anyone, or may these very actions sometimes be just and sometimes unjust? I mean, for example, as everyone I presume would admit, if one took over weapons from a friend who was in his right mind and then the lender should go mad and demand them back, that we ought not to return them in that case and that he who did so return them would not be acting justly—nor yet would he who chose to speak nothing but the truth to one who was in that state.

You are right, he replied.

Then this is not the definition of justice—to tell the truth and return what one has received.

Nay, but it is, Socrates, said Polemarchus breaking in, if indeed we are to put any faith in Simonides.

Very well, said Cephalus, indeed I make over the whole argument to you. For it is time for me to attend the sacrifices.

Well, said I, is not Polemarchus the heir of everything that is yours?

Certainly, said he with a laugh, and at the same time went out to the sacred rites.

Tell me, then, you the inheritor of the argument, what it is that you affirm that Simonides says and rightly says about justice.

That it is just, he replied, to render to each his due. In saying this I think he speaks well.

I must admit, said I, that it is not easy to disbelieve Simonides. For he is a wise and inspired man. But just what he may mean by this you, Polemarchus, doubtless know, but I do not. Obviously he does not mean what we were just speaking of, this return of a deposit to anyone whatsoever even if he asks it back when not in his right mind. And yet what the man deposited is due to him in a sense, is it not?

Yes.

But rendered to him it ought not to be by any manner of means when he demands it not being in his right mind.

True, said he.

It is then something other than this that Simonides must, as it seems, mean by the saying that it is just to render back what is due.

Something else in very deed, he replied, for he believes that friends owe it to friends to do them some good and no evil.

I see, said I. You mean that he does not render what is due or owing who returns a deposit of gold if this return and the acceptance prove harmful and the returner and the recipient are friends. Isn't that what you say Simonides means?

Quite so.

But how about this—should one not render to enemies what is their due?

By all means, he said, what is due and owing to them, and there is due and owing from an enemy to an enemy what also is proper for him, some evil.

It was a riddling definition of justice, then, that Simonides gave after the manner of poets, for while his meaning, it seems, was that justice is rendering to each what befits him, the name that he gave to this was 'the due.'

What else do you suppose? said he.

In heaven's name! said I. Suppose someone had questioned him thus. Tell me, Simonides, the art that renders what that is due and befitting to what is called the art of medicine? What do you take it would have been his answer?

Obviously, he said, the art that renders to bodies drugs, foods, and drinks.

And the art that renders to what things what that is due and befitting is called the culinary art?

Seasoning to meats.

Good. In the same way tell me the art that renders what to whom would be denominated justice.

If we are to follow the previous examples, Socrates, it is that which renders benefits and harms to friends and enemies.

To do good to friends and evil to enemies, then, is justice in his meaning?
I think so.

Who then is the most able when they are ill to benefit friends and harm enemies in respect to disease and health?

The physician.

And who navigators in respect of the perils of the sea?

The pilot.

Well then, the just man, in what action and for what work is he the most competent to benefit friends and harm enemies?

In making war and as an ally, I should say.

Very well. But now if they are not sick, friend Polemarchus, the physician is useless to them.

True.

And so to those who are not at sea the pilot.

Yes.

Shall we also say this, that for those who are not at war the just man is useless?

By no means.

There is a use then even in peace for justice?

Yes, it is useful.

But so is agriculture, isn't it?—[Yes.]—Namely, for the getting of a harvest?
Yes.

But likewise the cobbler's art?—[Yes.]—Namely, I presume you would say, for the getting of shoes.

Certainly.

Then tell me, for the service and getting of what would you say that justice is useful in time of peace?

In engagements and dealings, Socrates.

And by dealings do you mean associations, partnerships, or something else?

Associations, of course.

Is it the just man, then, who is a good and useful associate and partner in the placing of draughts or the draughts player?

The player.

And in the placing of bricks and stones is the just man a more useful and better associate than the builder?

By no means.

Then what is the association in which the just man is a better partner than the harpist as a harpist is better than the just man for striking the chords?

For money dealings, I think.

Except, I presume, Polemarchus, for the use of money when there is occasion to buy in common or sell a horse. Then, I take it, the man who knows horses, isn't it so?

Apparently.

And again, if it is a vessel, the shipwright or the pilot.

It would seem so.

What then is the use of money in common for which a just man is the better partner?

When it is to be deposited and kept safe, Socrates.

You mean when it is to be put to no use but is to lie idle?

Quite so.

Then it is when money is useless that justice is useful in relation to it?

It looks that way.

And similarly when a scythe is to be kept safe, then justice is useful both in public and private. But when it is to be used, the vinedresser's art is useful?

Apparently.

And so you will have to say that when a shield and a lyre are to be kept and put to no use, justice is useful, but when they are to be made use of, the military art and music.

Necessarily.

And so in all other cases, in the use of each thing, justice is useless but in its uselessness useful?

It looks that way.

Then, my friend, justice cannot be a thing of much worth if it is useful only for things out of use and useless. But let us consider this point. Is not the man who is most skillful to strike or inflict a blow in a fight, whether as a boxer or elsewhere, also the most wary to guard against a blow?

Assuredly.

47

Is it not also true that he who best knows how to guard against disease is also most cunning to communicate it and escape detection?

I think so.

But again, the very same man is a good guardian of an army who is good at stealing a march upon the enemy in respect of their designs and proceedings generally.

Certainly.

Of whatsoever, then, anyone is a skillful guardian, of that he is also a skillful thief?

It seems so.

If then the just man is an expert in guarding money he is an expert in stealing it.

The argument certainly points that way.

A kind of thief then the just man it seems has turned out to be, and it is likely that you acquired this idea from Homer. For he regards with complacency Autolycus, the maternal uncle of Odysseus, and says, 'he was gifted beyond all men in thievery and perjury.' So justice, according to you and Homer and Simonides, seems to be a kind of stealing, with the qualification that it is for the benefit of friends and the harm of enemies. Isn't that what you meant?

No, by Zeus, he replied. I no longer know what I did mean. Yet this I still believe, that justice benefits friends and harms enemies.

May I ask whether by friends you mean those who seem to a man to be worthy or those who really are so, even if they do not seem, and similarly of enemies?

It is likely, he said, that men will love those whom they suppose to be good and dislike those whom they deem bad.

Do not men make mistakes in this matter so that many seem good to them who are not and the reverse?

They do.

For those, then, who thus err the good are their enemies and the bad their friends?

Certainly.

But all the same it is then just for them to benefit the bad and injure the good?

It would seem so.

But again, the good are just and incapable of injustice.

True.

On your reasoning then it is just to wrong those who do no injustice.

Nay, nay, Socrates, he said, the reasoning can't be right.

Then, said I, it is just to harm the unjust and benefit the just.

That seems a better conclusion than the other.

It will work out, then, for many, Polemarchus, who have misjudged men that it is just to harm their friends, for they have got bad ones, and to benefit their enemies, for they are good. And so we shall find ourselves saying the very opposite of what we affirmed Simonides to mean.

Most certainly, he said, it does work out so. But let us change our ground, for it looks as if we were wrong in the notion we took up about the friend and the enemy.

What notion, Polemarchus?

That the man who seems to us good is the friend.

And to what shall we change it now? said I.

That the man who both seems and is good is the friend, but that he who seems but is not really so seems but is not really the friend. And there will be the same assumption about the enemy.

Then on this view it appears the friend will be the good man and the bad the enemy.

Yes.

So you would have us qualify our former notion of the just man by an addition. We then said it was just to do good to a friend and evil to an enemy, but now we are to add that it is just to benefit the friend if he is good and harm the enemy if he is bad?

By all means, he said, that, I think, would be the right way to put it.

Is it then, said I, the part of a good man to harm anybody whatsoever?

Certainly it is, he replied. A man ought to harm those who are both bad and his enemies.

When horses are harmed does it make them better or worse?

Worse.

In respect of the excellence or virtue of dogs or that of horses?

Of horses.

And do not also dogs when harmed become worse in respect of canine and not of equine virtue?

Necessarily.

And men, my dear fellow, must we not say that when they are harmed it is in respect of the distinctive excellence or virtue of man that they become worse?

Assuredly.

And is not justice the specific virtue of man?

That too must be granted.

Then it must also be admitted, my friend, that men who are harmed become more unjust.

It seems so.

Do musicians then make men unmusical by the art of music?

Impossible.

Well, do horsemen by horsemanship unfit men for dealing with horses?

No.

49

By justice then do the just make men unjust, or in sum do the good by virtue make men bad?

Nay, it is impossible.

It is not, I take it, the function of heat to chill but of its opposite.—[Yes.]—Nor of dryness to moisten but of its opposite.

Assuredly.

Nor yet of the good to harm but of its opposite.

So it appears.

But the just man is good?

Certainly.

It is not then the function of the just man, Polemarchus, to harm either friend or anyone else, but of his opposite, the unjust.

I think you are altogether right, Socrates.

If, then, anyone affirms that it is just to render to each his due and he means by this that injury and harm is what is due to his enemies from the just man and benefits to his friends, he was no truly wise man who said it. For what he meant was not true. For it has been made clear to us that in no case is it just to harm anyone.

I concede it, he said.

We will take up arms against him, then, said I, you and I together, if anyone affirms that either Simonides or Bias or Pittacus or any other of the wise and blessed said such a thing.

I, for my part, he said, am ready to join in the battle with you.

Do you know, said I, to whom I think the saying belongs—this statement that it is just to benefit friends and harm enemies?

To whom? he said.

I think it was the saying of Periander or Perdiccas or Xerxes or Ismenias the Theban or some other rich man who had great power in his own conceit.

That is most true, he replied.

Very well, said I, since it has been made clear that this too is not justice and the just, what else is there that we might say justice to be?

Now Thrasymachus, even while we were conversing, had been trying several times to break in and lay hold of the discussion but he was restrained by those who sat by him who wished to hear the argument out. But when we came to a pause after I had said this, he couldn't any longer hold his peace. But gathering himself up like a wild beast he hurled himself upon us as if he would tear us to pieces. And Polemarchus and I were frightened and fluttered apart.

He bawled out into our midst, What balderdash is this that you have been talking, and why do you Simple Simons truckle and give way to one another? But if you really wish, Socrates, to know what the just is, don't merely ask questions or plume yourself upon controverting any answer that anyone gives—since your acumen has perceived that it is easier to ask questions than to answer them—but do you yourself answer and tell what you say the just is. And don't you be telling me that it is that which ought to be, or the beneficial or the profitable or the gainful or the advantageous, but express clearly and precisely whatever you say. For I won't take from you any such drivel as that!

And I, when I heard him, was dismayed, and looking upon him was filled with fear, and I believe that if I had not looked at him before he did at me I should have lost my voice. But as it is, at the very moment when he began to be exasperated by the course of the argument I glanced at him first, so that I became capable of answering him;

And said with a slight tremor, Thrasymachus, don't be harsh with us. If I, and my friend, have made mistakes in the consideration of the question, rest assured that it is unwillingly that we err. For you surely must not suppose that while, if our quest were for gold, we would never willingly truckle to one another and make concessions in the search and so spoil our chances of finding it, yet that when we are searching for justice, a thing more precious than much fine gold, we should then be so foolish as to give way to one another and not rather do our serious best to have it discovered. You surely must not suppose that, my friend. But you see it is our lack of ability that is at fault. It is pity then that we should far more reasonably receive from clever fellows like you than severity.

And he, on hearing this, gave a great guffaw and laughed sardonically and said, Ye gods! Here we have the well-known irony of Socrates, and I knew it and predicted that when it came to replying you would refuse and dissemble and do anything rather than answer any question that anyone asked you.

That's because you are wise, Thrasymachus, and so you knew very well that if you asked a man how many are twelve, and in putting the question warned him, Don't you be telling me, fellow, that twelve is twice six or three times four or six times two or four times three, for I won't accept any such drivel as that from you as an answer—it was obvious, I fancy, to you that no one could give an answer to a question framed in that fashion. Suppose he had said to you, Thrasymachus, what do you mean? Am I not to give any of the prohibited answers, not even, do you mean to say, if the thing really is one of these, but must I say something different from the truth, or what do you mean?— What would have been your answer to him?

Humph! said he. How very like the two cases are!

There is nothing to prevent it, said I. Yet even granted that they are not alike, yet if it appears to the person asked the question that they are alike, do you suppose that he will any the less answer what appears to him, whether we forbid him or whether we don't?

Is that, then, said he, what you are going to do? Are you going to give one of the forbidden answers?

I shouldn't be surprised, I said, if on reflection that would be my view.

What then, he said, if I show you another answer about justice differing from all these, a better one—what penalty do you think you deserve?

Why, what else, said I, than that which it befits anyone who is ignorant to suffer? It befits him, I presume, to learn from the one who does know. That then is what I propose that I should suffer.

I like your simplicity, said he. But in addition to 'learning' you must pay a fine of money.

Well, I will when I have got it, I said.

It is there, said Glaucon. If money is all that stands in the way, Thrasymachus, go on with your speech. We will all contribute for Socrates.

Oh yes, of course, said he, so that Socrates may contrive, as he always does, to evade answering himself but may cross-examine the other man and refute his replies.

Why, how, I said, my dear fellow, could anybody answer if in the first place he did not know and did not even profess to know, and secondly, even if he had some notion of the matter, he had been told by a man of weight that he mustn't give any of his suppositions as an answer? Nay, it is more reasonable that you should be the speaker. For you do affirm that you know and are able to tell. Don't be obstinate, but do me the favor to reply and don't be chary of your wisdom, and instruct Glaucon here and the rest of us.

When I had spoken thus Glaucon and the others urged him not to be obstinate. It was quite plain that Thrasymachus was eager to speak in order that he might do himself credit, since he believed that he had a most excellent answer to our question. But he demurred and pretended to make a point of my being the respondent. Finally he gave way and then said, Here you have the wisdom of Socrates, to refuse himself to teach, but go about and learn from others and not even pay thanks therefor.

That I learn from others, I said, you said truly, Thrasymachus. But in saying that I do not pay thanks you are mistaken. I pay as much as I am able. And I am able only to bestow praise. For money I lack. But that I praise right willingly those who appear to speak well you will well know forthwith as soon as you have given your answer. For I think that you will speak well.

Hearken and hear then, said he. I affirm that the just is nothing else than the advantage of the stronger. Well, why don't you applaud? Nay, you'll do anything but that.

Provided only I first understand your meaning, said I, for I don't yet apprehend it. The advantage of the stronger is what you affirm the just to be. But what in the world do you mean by this? I presume you don't intend to affirm this, that if Polydamas, the pancratiast, is stronger than we are and the flesh of beef is advantageous for him, for his body, this viand is also for us who are weaker than he both advantageous and just.

You are a buffoon, Socrates, and take my statement in the most detrimental sense.

Not at all, my dear fellow, said I. I only want you to make your meaning plainer.

Don't you know then, said he, that some cities are governed by tyrants, in others democracy rules, in others aristocracy?

Assuredly.

And is not this the thing that is strong and has the mastery in each—the ruling party?

Certainly.

And each form of government enacts the laws with a view to its own advantage, a democracy democratic laws and tyranny autocratic and the others likewise, and by so legislating they proclaim that the just for their subjects is that which is for their—the rulers'—advantage and the man who deviates from this law they chastise as a lawbreaker and a wrongdoer. This, then, my good sir, is what I understand as the identical principle of justice that obtains in all states—the advantage of the established government. This I presume you will admit holds power and is strong, so that, if one reasons rightly, it works out that the just is the same thing everywhere, the advantage of the stronger.

Now, said I, I have learned your meaning, but whether it is true or not I have to try to learn. The advantageous, then, is also your reply, Thrasymachus, to the question, what is the just—though you forbade me to give that answer. But you add thereto that of the stronger.

A trifling addition perhaps you think it, he said.

It is not yet clear whether it is a big one either, but that we must inquire whether what you say is true is clear. For since I too admit that the just is something that is of advantage—but you are for making an addition and affirm it to be the advantage of the stronger, while I don't profess to know—we must pursue the inquiry.

Inquire away, he said.

I will do so, said I. Tell me, then, you affirm also, do you not, that obedience to rulers is just?

I do.

May I ask whether the rulers in the various states are infallible or capable sometimes of error?

Surely, he said, they are liable to err.

Then in their attempts at legislation they enact some laws rightly and some not rightly, do they not?

So I suppose.

And by rightly we are to understand for their advantage, and by wrongly to their disadvantage? Do you mean that or not?

That.

But whatever they enact must be performed by their subjects and is justice?

Of course.

Then on your theory it is just not only to do what is the advantage of the stronger but also the opposite, what is not to his advantage.

What's that you're saying? he replied.

What you yourself are saying, I think. Let us consider it more closely. Have we not agreed that the rulers in giving orders to the ruled sometimes mistake their own advantage, and that whatever the rulers enjoin it is just for the subjects to perform? Was not that admitted?

I think it was, he replied.

Then you will have to think, I said, that to do what is disadvantageous to the rulers and the stronger has been admitted by you to be just in the case when the rulers unwittingly enjoin what is bad for themselves, while you affirm that it is just for the others to do what they enjoined. In that way does not this conclusion inevitably follow, my most sapient Thrasymachus, that it is just to do the very opposite of what you say? For it is in that case surely the disadvantage of the stronger or superior that the inferior are commanded to perform.

Yes, by Zeus, Socrates, said Polemarchus, nothing could be more conclusive.

Of course, said Clitophon, breaking in, if you are his witness.

What need is there of a witness? Polemarchus said. Thrasymachus himself admits that the rulers sometimes enjoin what is evil for themselves and yet says that it is just for the subjects to do this.

That, Polemarchus, is because Thrasymachus laid it down that it is just to obey the orders of the rulers.

Yes, Clitophon, but he also took the position that the advantage of the stronger is just. And after these two assumptions he again admitted that the stronger sometimes bid the inferior and their subjects do what is to the disadvantage of the rulers. And from these admissions the just would no more be the advantage of the stronger than the contrary.

Oh well, said Clitophon, by the advantage of the superior he meant what the superior supposed to be for his advantage. This was what the inferior had to do, and that this is the just was his position.

That isn't what he said, replied Polemarchus.

Never mind, Polemarchus, said I. But if that is Thrasymachus' present meaning, let us take it from him in that sense. So tell me, Thrasymachus, was this what you intended to say, that the just is the advantage of the superior as it appears to the superior whether it really is or not? Are we to say this was your meaning?

Not in the least, he said. Do you suppose that I call one who is in error a superior when he errs?

I certainly did suppose that you meant that, I replied, when you agreed that rulers are not infallible but sometimes make mistakes.

That is because you argue like a pettifogger, Socrates. Why, to take the nearest example, do you call one who is mistaken about the sick a physician in respect of his mistake or one who goes wrong in a calculation a calculator when he goes wrong and in respect of this error? Yet that is what we say literally—we say that the physician erred, and the calculator and the schoolmaster. But the truth, I take it, is, that each of these in so far as he is that which we entitle him never errs, so that, speaking precisely, since you are such a stickler for precision, no craftsman errs. For it is when his knowledge abandons him that he who goes wrong goes wrong—when he is not a craftsman. So that no craftsman, wise man, or ruler makes a mistake then when he is a ruler, though everybody would use the expression that the physician made a mistake and the ruler erred. It is in this loose way of speaking, then, that you must take the answer I gave you a little while ago. But the most precise statement is that other, that the ruler in so far forth as ruler does not err, and not erring he enacts what is best for himself, and this the subject must do, so that, even as I meant from the start, I say the just is to do what is for the advantage of the stronger.

So then, Thrasymachus, said I, my manner of argument seems to you pettifogging?

It does, he said.

You think, do you, that it was with malice aforethought and trying to get the better of you unfairly that I asked that question?

I don't think it, I know it, he said, and you won't make anything by it, for you won't get the better of me by stealth and, failing stealth, you are not of the force to beat me in debate.

Bless your soul, said I, I wouldn't even attempt such a thing. But that nothing of the sort may spring up between us again, define in which sense you take the ruler and stronger. Do you mean the so-called ruler or that ruler in the precise sense of whom you were just now telling us, and for whose advantage as being the superior it will be just for the inferior to act?

I mean the ruler in the very most precise sense of the word, he said. Now bring on against this your cavils and your shyster's tricks if you are able. I ask no quarter. But you'll find yourself unable.

Why, do you suppose, I said, that I am so mad as to try to beard a lion and try the pettifogger on Thrasymachus?

You did try it just now, he said, paltry fellow though you be.

Something too much of this sort of thing, said I. But tell me, your physician in the precise sense, of whom you were just now speaking, is he a money-maker, an earner of fees, or a healer of the sick? And remember to speak of the physician who is really such.

A healer of the sick, he replied.

And what of the pilot—the pilot rightly so called—is he a ruler of sailors or a sailor?

A ruler of sailors.

We don't, I fancy, have to take into account the fact that he actually sails in the ship, nor is he to be denominated a sailor. For it is not in respect of his sailing that he is called a pilot but in respect of his art and his ruling of the sailors.

True, he said.

Then for each of them is there not a something that is for his advantage?

Quite so.

And is it not also true, said I, that the art naturally exists for this, to discover and provide for each his advantage?

Yes, for this.

Is there, then, for each of the arts any other advantage than to be as perfect as possible?

What do you mean by that question?

Just as if, I said, you should ask me whether it is enough for the body to be the body or whether it stands in need of something else, I would reply, By all means it stands in need. That is the reason why the art of medicine has now been invented, because the body is defective and such defect is unsatisfactory. To provide for this, then, what is advantageous, that is the end for which the art was devised. Do you think that would be a correct answer, or not?

Correct, he said.

But how about this? Is the medical art itself defective or faulty, or has any other art any need of some virtue, quality, or excellence—as the eyes of vision, the ears of hearing—and for this reason is there need of some art over them that will consider and provide what is advantageous for these very ends? Does there exist in the art itself some defect and does each art require another art to consider its advantage and is there need of still another for the considering art and so on ad infinitum, or will the art look out for its own advantage? Or is it a fact that it needs neither itself nor another art to consider its advantage and provide against its deficiency? For there is no defect or error at all that dwells in any art. Nor does it befit an art to seek the advantage of anything else than that of its object. But the art itself is free from all harm and admixture of evil, and is right so long as each art is precisely and entirely that which it is. And consider the matter in that 'precise' way of speaking. Is it so or not?

It appears to be so, he said.

Then medicine, said I, does not consider the advantage of medicine but of the body?

Yes.

Nor horsemanship of horsemanship but of horses, nor does any other art look out for itself—for it has no need—but for that of which it is the art.

So it seems, he replied.

But surely, Thrasymachus, the arts do hold rule and are stronger than that of which they are the arts.

He conceded this but it went very hard.

Then no art considers or enjoins the advantage of the stronger but every art that of the weaker which is ruled by it.

This too he was finally brought to admit though he tried to contest it.

Can we deny, then, said I, that neither does any physician in so far as he is a physician seek or enjoin the advantage of the physician but that of the patient? For we have agreed that the physician, 'precisely' speaking, is a ruler and governor of bodies and not a moneymaker. Did we agree on that?

He assented.

And so the 'precise' pilot is a ruler of sailors, not a sailor?

That was admitted.

Then that sort of a pilot and ruler will not consider and enjoin the advantage of the pilot but that of the sailor whose ruler he is.

He assented reluctantly.

Then, said I, Thrasymachus, neither does anyone in any office of rule in so far as he is a ruler consider and enjoin his own advantage but that of the one whom he rules and for whom he exercises his craft, and he keeps his eyes fixed on that and on what is advantageous and suitable to that in all that he says and does.

When we had come to this point in the discussion and it was apparent to everybody that his formula of justice had suffered a reversal of form, Thrasymachus, instead of replying, said, Tell me, Socrates, have you got a nurse?

What do you mean? said I. Why didn't you answer me instead of asking such a question?

Because, he said, she lets her little snotty run about driveling and doesn't wipe your face clean, though you need it badly, if she can't get you to know the difference between the shepherd and the sheep.

And what, pray, makes you think that? said I.

Because you think that the shepherds and the neatherds are considering the good of the sheep and the cattle and fatten and tend them with anything else in view than the good of their masters and themselves. And by the same token you seem to suppose that the rulers in our cities, I mean the real rulers, differ at all in their thoughts of the governed from a man's attitude toward his sheep or that they think of anything else night and day than the sources of their own profit. And you are so far out concerning the just and justice and the unjust and injustice that you don't know that justice and the just are literally the other fellow's good—the advantage of the stronger and the ruler, but a detriment that is all his own of the subject who obeys and serves—while injustice is the contrary and rules those who are simple in every sense of the word and just, and they being thus ruled do what is for his advantage who is the stronger and make him happy by serving him, but themselves by no manner of means. And you must look at the matter, my simple-minded Socrates, in this way, that the just man always comes out at a disadvantage in his relation with the unjust. To begin with, in their business dealings in any joint undertaking of the two you will never find that the just man has the advantage over the unjust at the dissolution of the partnership but that he always has the worst of it. Then again, in their relations with the state, if there are direct taxes or contributions to be paid, the just man contributes more from an equal estate and the other less, and when there is a distribution the one gains much and the other nothing. And so when each holds office, apart from any other loss the just man must count on his own affairs' falling into disorder through neglect, while because of his justice he makes no profit from the state, and thereto he will displease his friends and his acquaintances by his unwillingness to serve them unjustly. But to the unjust man all the opposite advantages accrue. I mean, of course, the one I was just speaking of, the man who has the ability to overreach on a large scale. Consider this type of man, then, if you wish to judge how much more profitable it is to him personally to be unjust than to be just. And the easiest way of all to understand this matter will be to turn to the most consummate form of injustice which makes the man who has done the wrong most happy and those who are wronged and who would not themselves willingly do wrong most miserable. And this is tyranny, which both by stealth and by force takes away what belongs to others, both sacred and profane, both private and public, not little by little but at one swoop. For each several part of such wrongdoing the malefactor who fails to escape detection is fined and incurs the extreme of contumely, for temple robbers, kidnapers, burglars, swindlers, and thieves are the appellations of those who commit these several forms of injustice. But when in addition to the property of the citizens men kidnap and enslave the citizens themselves, instead of these opprobrious names they are pronounced happy and blessed not only by their fellow citizens but by all who hear the story of the man who has committed complete and entire injustice. For it is not the fear of doing but of suffering wrong that calls forth the reproaches of those who revile injustice. Thus, Socrates, injustice on a sufficiently large scale is a stronger, freer, and more masterful thing than justice, and, as I said in the beginning, it is the advantage of the stronger that is the just, while the unjust is what profits a man's self and is for his advantage.

After this Thrasymachus was minded to depart when like a bathman he had poured his speech in a sudden flood over our ears. But the company would not suffer him and were insistent that he should remain and render an account of what he had said. And I was particularly urgent and said, I am surprised at you, Thrasymachus. After hurling such a doctrine at us, can it be that you propose to depart without staying to teach us properly or learn yourself whether this thing is so or not? Do you think it a small matter that you are attempting to determine and not the entire conduct of life that for each of us would make living most worth while?

Well, do I deny it? said Thrasymachus.

You seem to, said I, or else to care nothing for us and so feel no concern whether we are going to live worse or better lives in our ignorance of what you affirm that you know. Nay, my good fellow, do your best to make the matter clear to us also—it will be no bad investment for you, any benefit that you bestow on such a company as this. For I tell you for my part that I am not convinced; neither do I think that injustice is more profitable than justice, not even if one gives it free scope and does not hinder it of its will. But, suppose, sir, a man to be unjust and to be able to act unjustly either because he is not detected or can maintain it by violence. All the same he does not convince me that it is more profitable than justice. Now it may be that there is someone else among us who feels in this way and that I am not the only one. Persuade us, then, my dear fellow, convince us satisfactorily that we are ill advised in preferring justice to injustice.

And how am I to persuade you? he said. If you are not convinced by what I just now was saying, what more can I do for you? Shall I take the argument and ram it into your head?

Heaven forbid! I said. Don't do that. But in the first place when you have said a thing stand by it, or if you shift your ground change openly and don't try to deceive us. But, as it is, you see, Thrasymachus—let us return to the previous examples—you see that while you began by taking the physician in the true sense of the word, you did not think fit afterward to be consistent and maintain with precision the notion of the true shepherd, but you apparently think that he herds his sheep in his quality of shepherd, not with regard to what is best for the sheep, but as if he were a banqueter about to be feasted with regard to the good cheer, or again with a view to the sale of them, as if he were a money-maker and not a shepherd. But the art of the shepherd surely is concerned with nothing else than how to provide what is best for that over which it is set, since its own affairs, its own best estate, are surely sufficiently provided for so long as it in nowise fails of being the shepherd's art. And in like manner I supposed that we just now were constrained to acknowledge that every form of rule in so far as it is rule considers what is best for nothing else than that which is governed and cared for by it, alike in political and private rule. Why, do you think that the rulers and holders of office in our cities—the true rulers—willingly hold office and rule?

I don't think, he said, I know right well they do.

But what of other forms of rule, Thrasymachus? Do you not perceive that no one chooses of his own will to hold the office of rule? Men demand pay, which implies that not to them will benefit accrue from their holding office but to those whom they rule. Tell me this. We ordinarily say, do we not, that each of the arts is different from others because its power or function is different? And, my dear fellow, in order that we may reach some result, don't answer counter to your real belief.

Well, yes, he said, that is what renders it different.

59

And does not each art also yield us benefit that is peculiar to itself and not general, as for example medicine health, the pilot's art safety at sea, and the other arts similarly?

Assuredly.

And does not the wage earner's art yield wages? For that is its function. Would you identify medicine and the pilot's art? Or if you please to discriminate 'precisely' as you proposed, none the more if a pilot regains his health because a sea voyage is good for him, no whit the more, I say, for this reason do you call his art medicine, do you?

Of course not, he said.

Neither, I take it, do you call wage earning medicine if a man earning wages is in health.

Surely not.

But what of this? Do you call medicine wage earning, if a man when giving treatment earns wages?

No, he said.

And did we not agree that the benefit derived from each art is peculiar to it?

So be it, he said.

Any common or general benefit that all craftsmen receive, then, they obviously derive from their common use of some further identical thing.

It seems so, he said.

And we say that the benefit of earning wages accrues to the craftsmen from their further exercise of the wage-earning art.

He assented reluctantly.

Then the benefit, the receiving of wages, does not accrue to each from his own art. But if we are to consider it 'precisely,' medicine produces health but the fee-earning art the pay, and architecture a house but the fee-earning art accompanying it the fee, and so with all the others—each performs its own task and benefits that over which it is set. But unless pay is added to it, is there any benefit which the craftsman receives from the craft?

Apparently not, he said.

Does he then bestow no benefit either when he works for nothing?

I'll say he does.

Then, Thrasymachus, is not this immediately apparent, that no art or office provides what is beneficial for itself—but as we said long ago it provides and enjoins what is beneficial to its subject, considering the advantage of that, the weaker, and not the advantage of the stronger? That was why, friend Thrasymachus, I was just now saying that no one of his own will chooses to hold rule and office and take other people's troubles in hand to straighten them out, but everybody expects pay for that, because he who is to exercise the art rightly never does what is best for himself or enjoins it when he gives commands according to the art, but what is best for the subject. That is the reason, it seems, why pay must be provided for those who are to consent to rule, either in the form of money or honor or a penalty if they refuse.

What do you mean by that, Socrates? said Glaucon. The two wages I recognize, but the penalty you speak of and described as a form of wage I don't understand.

Then, said I, you don't understand the wages of the best men for the sake of which the finest spirits hold office and rule when they consent to do so. Don't you know that to be covetous of honor and covetous of money is said to be and is a reproach?

I do, he said.

Well, then, said I, that is why the good are not willing to rule either for the sake of money or of honor. They do not wish to collect pay openly for their service of rule and be styled hirelings, nor to take it by stealth from their office and be called thieves, nor yet for the sake of honor, for they are not covetous of honor. So there must be imposed some compulsion and penalty to constrain them to rule if they are to consent to hold office. That is perhaps why to seek office oneself and not await compulsion is thought disgraceful. But the chief penalty is to be governed by someone worse if a man will not himself hold office and rule. It is from fear of this, as it appears to me, that the better sort hold office when they do, and then they go to it not in the expectation of enjoyment nor as to a good thing, but as to a necessary evil and because they are unable to turn it over to better men than themselves or to their like. For we may venture to say that, if there should be a city of good men only, immunity from office holding would be as eagerly contended for as office is now, and there it would be made plain that in very truth the true ruler does not naturally seek his own advantage but that of the ruled, so that every man of understanding would rather choose to be benefited by another than to be bothered with benefiting him. This point then I by no means concede to Thrasymachus, that justice is the advantage of the superior. But that we will reserve for another occasion. A far weightier matter seems to me Thrasymachus' present statement, his assertion that the life of the unjust man is better than that of the just. Which now do you choose, Glaucon? And which seems to you to be the truer statement?

That the life of the just man is more profitable, I say, he replied.

Did you hear, said I, all the goods that Thrasymachus just now enumerated for the life of the unjust man?

I heard, he said, but I am not convinced.

Do you wish us then to try to persuade him, supposing we can find a way, that what he says is not true?

Of course I wish it, he said.

If then we oppose him in a set speech enumerating in turn the advantages of being just and he replies and we rejoin, we shall have to count up and measure the goods listed in the respective speeches and we shall forthwith be in need of judges to decide between us. But if, as in the preceding discussion, we come to terms with one another as to what we admit in the inquiry, we shall be ourselves both judges and pleaders.

Quite so, he said.

Which method do you like better? said I.

This one, he said.

Come then, Thrasymachus, I said, go back to the beginning and answer us. You affirm that perfect and complete injustice is more profitable than justice that is complete.

I affirm it, he said, and have told you my reasons.

Tell me then how you would express yourself on this point about them. You call one of them, I presume, a virtue and the other a vice?

Of course.

Justice the virtue and injustice the vice?

It is likely, you innocent, when I say that injustice pays and justice doesn't pay.

But what then, pray?

The opposite, he replied.

What! Justice vice?

No, but a most noble simplicity or goodness of heart.

Then do you call injustice badness of heart?

No, but goodness of judgment.

Do you also, Thrasymachus, regard the unjust as intelligent and good?

Yes, if they are capable of complete injustice, he said, and are able to subject to themselves cities and tribes of men. But you probably suppose that I mean those who take purses. There is profit to be sure even in that sort of thing, he said, if it goes undetected. But such things are not worth taking into the account, but only what I just described.

I am not unaware of your meaning in that, I said, but this is what surprised me, that you should range injustice under the head of virtue and wisdom, and justice in the opposite class.

Well, I do so class them, he said.

That, said I, is a stiffer proposition, my friend, and if you are going as far as that it is hard to know what to answer. For if your position were that injustice is profitable yet you conceded it to be vicious and disgraceful as some other disputants do, there would be a chance for an argument on conventional principles. But, as it is, you obviously are going to affirm that it is honorable and strong and you will attach to it all the other qualities that we were assigning to the just, since you don't shrink from putting it in the category of virtue and wisdom.

You are a most veritable prophet, he replied.

Well, said I, I mustn't flinch from following out the logic of the inquiry, so long as I conceive you to be saying what you think. For now, Thrasymachus, I absolutely believe that you are not 'mocking' us but telling us your real opinions about the truth.

What difference does it make to you, he said, whether I believe it or not? Why don't you test the argument?

No difference, said I, but here is something I want you to tell me in addition to what you have said. Do you think the just man would want to overreach or exceed another just man?

By no means, he said. Otherwise he would not be the delightful simpleton that he is.

And would he exceed or overreach or go beyond the just action?

Not that either, he replied.

But how would he treat the unjust man—would he deem it proper and just to outdo, overreach, or go beyond him or would he not?

He would, he said, but he wouldn't be able to.

That is not my question, I said, but whether it is not the fact that the just man does not claim or wish to outdo the just man but only the unjust?

That is the case, he replied.

How about the unjust then? Does he claim to overreach and outdo the just man and the just action?

Of course, he said, since he claims to overreach and get the better of everything.

Then the unjust man will overreach and outdo also both the unjust man and the unjust action, and all his endeavor will be to get the most in everything for himself.

That is so.

Let us put it in this way, I said. The just man does not seek to take advantage of his like but of his unlike, but the unjust man of both.

Admirably put, he said.

But the unjust man is intelligent and good and the just man neither.

That, too, is right, he said.

Is it not also true, I said, that the unjust man is like the intelligent and good and the just man is not?

Of course, he said, being such he will be like to such and the other not.

Excellent. Then each is such as that to which he is like.

What else do you suppose? he said.

Very well, Thrasymachus, but do you recognize that one man is a musician and another unmusical?

I do.

Which is the intelligent and which the unintelligent?

The musician, I presume, is the intelligent and the unmusical the unintelligent.

And is he not good in the things in which he is intelligent and bad in the things in which he is unintelligent?

Yes.

And the same of the physician?

The same.

Do you think then, my friend, that any musician in the tuning of a lyre would want to overreach another musician in the tightening and relaxing of the strings or would claim and think fit to exceed or outdo him?

I do not.

But would he the unmusical man?

Of necessity, he said.

And how about the medical man? In prescribing food and drink would he want to outdo the medical man or the medical procedure?

Surely not.

But he would the unmedical man?

Yes.

Consider then with regard to all forms of knowledge and ignorance whether you think that anyone who knows would choose to do or say other or more than what another who knows would do or say, and not rather exactly what his like would do in the same action.

Why, perhaps it must be so, he said, in such cases.

But what of the ignorant man—of him who does not know? Would he not overreach or outdo equally the knower and the ignorant?

It may be.

But the one who knows is wise?

I'll say so.

And the wise is good?

I'll say so.

Then he who is good and wise will not wish to overreach his like but his unlike and opposite.

It seems so, he said.

But the bad man and the ignoramus will overreach both like and unlike?

So it appears.

And does not our unjust man, Thrasymachus, overreach both unlike and like? Did you not say that?

I did, he replied.

But the just man will not overreach his like but only his unlike?

Yes.

Then the just man is like the wise and good, and the unjust is like the bad and the ignoramus.

It seems likely.

But furthermore we agreed that each is such as that to which he is like.

Yes, we did.

Then the just man has turned out on our hands to be good and wise and the unjust man bad and ignorant.

Thrasymachus made all these admissions not as I now lightly narrate them, but with much balking and reluctance and prodigious sweating, it being summer, and it was then I beheld what I had never seen before—Thrasymachus blushing. But when we did reach our conclusion that justice is virtue and wisdom and injustice vice and ignorance, Good, said I, let this be taken as established. . . .

FROM THE *REPUBLIC*, BOOK II

. . . Nothing could please me more, said I, for on what subject would a man of sense rather delight to hold and hear discourse again and again?

That is excellent, he said, and now listen to what I said would be the first topic—the nature and origin of justice.

By nature, they say, to commit injustice is a good and to suffer it is an evil, but that the excess of evil in being wronged is greater than the excess of good in doing wrong, so that when men do wrong and are wronged by one another and taste of both, those who lack the power to avoid the one and take the other determine that it is for their profit to make a compact with one another neither to commit nor to suffer injustice, and that this is the beginning of legislation and of covenants between men, and that they name the commandment of the law the lawful and the just, and that this is the genesis and essential nature of justice—a compromise between the best, which is to do wrong with impunity, and the worst, which is to be wronged and be impotent to get one's revenge. Justice, they tell us, being midway between the two, is accepted and approved, not as a real good, but as a thing honored in the lack of vigor to do injustice, since anyone who had the power to do it and was in reality 'a man' would never make a compact with anybody neither to wrong nor to be wronged, for he would be mad. The nature, then, of justice is this and such as this, Socrates, and such are the conditions in which it originates, according to the theory.

But as for the second point, that those who practice it do so unwillingly and from want of power to commit injustice, we shall be most likely to apprehend that if we entertain some such supposition as this in thought—if we grant to both the just and the unjust license and power to do whatever they please, and then accompany them in imagination and see whither desire will conduct them. We should then catch the just man in the very act of resorting to the same conduct as the unjust man because of the self-advantage which every creature by its nature pursues as a good, while by the convention of law it is forcibly diverted to paying honor to 'equality.' The license that I mean would be most nearly such as would result from supposing them to have the power which men say once came to the ancestor of Gyges the Lydian. They relate that he was a shepherd in the service of the ruler at that time of Lydia, and that after a great deluge of rain and an earthquake the ground opened and a chasm appeared in the place where he was pasturing,

65

and they say that he saw and wondered and went down into the chasm. And the story goes that he beheld other marvels there and a hollow bronze horse with little doors, and that he peeped in and saw a corpse within, as it seemed, of more than mortal stature, and that there was nothing else but a gold ring on its hand, which he took off, and so went forth. And when the shepherds held their customary assembly to make their monthly report to the king about the flocks, he also attended, wearing the ring. So as he sat there it chanced that he turned the collet of the ring toward himself, toward the inner part of his hand, and when this took place they say that he became invisible to those who sat by him and they spoke of him as absent, and that he was amazed, and again fumbling with the ring turned the collet outward and so became visible. On noting this he experimented with the ring to see if it possessed this virtue, and he found the result to be that when he turned the collet inward he became invisible, and when outward visible, and becoming aware of this, he immediately managed things so that he became one of the messengers who went up to the king, and on coming there he seduced the king's wife and with her aid set upon the king and slew him and possessed his kingdom.

If now there should be two such rings, and the just man should put on one and the unjust the other, no one could be found, it would seem, of such adamantine temper as to persevere in justice and endure to refrain his hands from the possessions of others and not touch them, though he might with impunity take what he wished even from the market place, and enter into houses and lie with whom he pleased, and slay and loose from bonds whomsoever he would, and in all other things conduct himself among mankind as the equal of a god. And in so acting he would do no differently from the other man, but both would pursue the same course. And yet this is a great proof, one might argue, that no one is just of his own will but only from constraint, in the belief that justice is not his personal good, inasmuch as every man, when he supposes himself to have the power to do wrong, does wrong. For that there is far more profit for him personally in injustice than in justice is what every man believes, and believes truly, as the proponent of this theory will maintain. For if anyone who had got such a license within his grasp should refuse to do any wrong or lay his hands on others' possessions, he would be regarded as most pitiable and a great fool by all who took note of it, though they would praise him before one another's faces, deceiving one another because of their fear of suffering injustice. So much for this point. . . .

FROM THE *REPUBLIC*, BOOK III

. . . Consider then, said I, whether, if that is to be their character, their habitations and ways of life must not be something after this fashion. In the first place, none must possess any private property save the indispensable. Secondly, none must have any habitation or treasure house which is not open for all to enter at will. Their food, in such quantities as are needful for athletes of war sober and brave, they must receive as an agreed stipend from the other citizens as the wages of their guardianship, so measured that there shall be neither superfluity at the end of the year nor any lack. And resorting to a common mess like soldiers on campaign they will live together. Gold and silver, we will tell them, they have of the divine quality from the gods always in their souls, and they have no need of the metal of men nor does holiness suffer them to mingle and contaminate that heavenly possession with the acquisition of mortal gold, since many impious deeds have been done about the coin of the multitude, while that which dwells within them is unsullied. But for these only of all the dwellers in the city it is not lawful to handle gold and silver and to touch them nor yet to come under the same roof with them, nor to hang them as ornaments on their limbs nor to drink from silver and gold. So living they would save themselves and save their city. But whenever they shall acquire for themselves land of their own and houses and coin, they will be householders and farmers instead of guardians, and will be transformed from the helpers of their fellow citizens to their enemies and masters, and so in hating and being hated, plotting and being plotted against, they will pass their days fearing far more and rather the townsmen within than the foemen without—and then even then laying the course of near shipwreck for themselves and the state. For all these reasons, said I, let us declare that such must be the provision for our guardians in lodging and other respects and so legislate. Shall we not?

By all means, Glaucon.

For Further Reading

Plato. *The Collected Dialogues of Plato*. Edited by Edith Hamilton and Huntington Cairns (Princeton: Princeton University Press, 1961).

Plato. *The Republic of Plato*. Translated by Allan Bloom (New York: Basic Books, 1968).

Annas, Julia. *An Introduction to Plato's Republic* (Oxford: Clarendon Press, 1981).

Bloom, Allan. "An Interpretative Essay." In *The Republic of Plato*. Translated by Allan Bloom (New York: Basic Books, 1968).

Cross, R.C., and A.D. Woozley. *Plato's Republic: A Philosophical Commentary* (London: Macmillan, 1964).

Dover, K.J. *Greek Popular Morality in the Time of Plato and Aristotle* (Oxford: Blackwell, 1974).

Gouldner, Alvin W. *Enter Plato: Classical Greece and the Origins of Social Theory* (New York: Basic Books, 1965).

Irwin, Terence. *Plato's Ethics* (New York: Oxford Univ. Press, 1995).

Kraut, Richard, ed. *The Cambridge Companion to Plato* (Cambridge: Cambridge Univ. Press, 1992).

Reeve, C.D.C. *Philosopher-Kings: The Argument of Plato's* Republic (Princeton: Princeton Univ. Press, 1988).

Shell, Marc. *The Economy of Literature* (Baltimore: Johns Hopkins Univ. Press, 1978).

Vlastos, Gregory. *Plato.* 2 vols. (New York: Doubleday, 1971).

White, Nicholas P. *A Companion to Plato's* Republic (Indianapolis: Hackett, 1979).

ARISTOTLE (384–322 B.C.)

MODERN COMMENTATORS find themselves in a predicament trying to assess Aristotle's contribution to economics. Generally they identify "economics" with classical and neoclassical economics and then look to see what sort of contribution Aristotle made to either, especially to their theories of value and price. M.I. Finley criticizes those who dismiss Aristotle's contribution to economic analysis as paltry. Finley argues instead that Aristotle was not a classical or neoclassical economist *at all,* so he made *no* contribution to economic analysis. He regards Aristotle's writings to be strictly moral rather than scientific in nature. In making this judgment, however, Finley adopts the presupposition of those he criticizes: to offer an economic analysis is to contribute to one of the two leading schools of modern economics.

Aristotle's strain of economic analysis looks very different if we adopt another presupposition: any disciplined inquiry into the specific social forms of the provisioning process contributes to economic analysis. Here Aristotle's achievement is considerable, but easily overlooked. He not only violates the canons of the dominant theories, he registers a profound rejection of both the modern market economy and the methodological horizons of modern economics, against which the shadowy form of *homo economicus* is projected.

Aristotle judged natural the human need for some art of acquisition for households and cities; moreover, he recognized that this provisioning process could take a number of different forms and that those different forms were of great consequence. Against this horizon, Aristotle provides a compact account of the genesis of money and commercial forms of acquisition out of non-commercial societies. As societies grow, become more differentiated, diversify their needs, and look to neighboring peoples to supply what they lack, trade and money start up and take hold. Aristotle scrutinizes several fundamental commercial forms and weighs their human significance in a type of inquiry that does not admit of a split between science and ethics: living well, not "making a good living," is the point of acquisition. He considers the exchange of goods without or with the mediation of money, exchanges that might be called barter (C-C') and simple commodity exchange (C-M-C'); the money-making or capitalist form of exchange he calls "retail trade" (M-C-M'), and the form of exchange characteristic of interest-bearing capital (M-M') is "usury."

Aristotle sized up the fundamental problem of commodity exchange: *in terms of what* are all commodities commensurable? He tries out money and need as answers before despairing of a solution. Regarding the difference between C-C' or C-M-C' on the one hand, and M-C-M' on the other, Aristotle makes a telling observation. The former types of commercial exchange are motivated by the need for specific goods, which gives these exchanges a natural destination, whereas the point of M-C-M' is to make money, a type of exchange that knows no completion, hence the form of capital itself is charged with the vice of *pleonexia,* unbounded desiring.

Aristotle has at least three reasons for criticizing the capital form: (1) profits can only be a consequence of unfair exchanges: capitalists are cheats; (2) true wealth is limited, but moneymaking knows no limit; (3) using money to make money violates the natural purpose of money, which is to be a medium of exchange. These considerations apply all the more so to usury (M-M'), a form of exchange for which Aristotle reserves special contempt. Much less evident than his criticism of usury and the capital form generally are Aristotle's reservations regarding the commodity form as we know it. It can appear as though Aristotle simply endorses the commodity form of wealth as he seems to endorse barter and simple commodity exchange. That he does not, comes clear if we compare modern views of property rights with Aristotle's ideas about property and fellow feeling (*philia*) in a *polis*. The framework of the modern commodity form grants full ownership and use to property owners and supposes that each acts out of the narrowest self-interest, impersonally hooking up with others through the "cash nexus." By contrast, Aristotle insists: the elements of gift and reciprocity ought never be drained out of exchanges in the *polis*; property should be owned privately but its use remain responsive to common needs; and exchanges ought not completely ignore personal differences.

The hero of modern economics is *homo economicus,* that (instrumentally) rational, self-centered pursuer of goods. For Aristotle, who carefully distinguishes between natural self-love and selfishness, *homo economicus* is a twisted caricature of an actual human being. As for the subjective utility theory from which neoclassical economics springs, Aristotle's theory that pleasures and pains are neither purely subjective nor generic (without form) provides an argument powerful enough to uproot it.

FROM THE *POLITICS,* BOOK I

4 • Property is a part of the household, and the art of acquiring property is a part of the art of managing the household; for no man can live well, or indeed live at all, unless he is provided with necessaries. And as in the arts which have a definite sphere the workers must have their own proper instruments for the accomplishment of their work, so it is in the management of a household. Now instruments are of various sorts; some are living, others lifeless; in the rudder, the pilot of a ship has a lifeless, in the look-out man, a living instrument; for in the arts the servant is a kind of instrument. Thus, too, a possession is an instrument for maintaining life. And so, in the arrangement of the family, a slave is a living possession, and property a number of such instruments; and the servant is himself an instrument for instruments. For if every instrument could accomplish its own work, obeying or anticipating the will of others, like the statues of Daedalus, or the tripods of Hephaestus, which, says the poet,

> of their own accord entered the assembly of the Gods;

71

if, in like manner, the shuttle would weave and the plectrum touch the lyre, chief workmen would not want servants, nor masters slaves. Now the instruments commonly so called are instruments of production, whilst a possession is an instrument of action. From a shuttle we get something else besides the use of it, whereas of a garment or of a bed there is only the use. Further, as production and action are different in kind, and both require instruments, the instruments which they employ must likewise differ in kind. But life is action and not production . . .

8 • Let us now inquire into property generally, and into the art of getting wealth, in accordance with our usual method, for a slave has been shown to be a part of property. The first question is whether the art of getting wealth is the same as the art of managing a household or a part of it, or instrumental to it; and if the last, whether in the way that the art of making shuttles is instru-

mental to the art of weaving, or in the way that the casting of bronze is in-strumental to the art of the statuary, for they are not instrumental in the same way, but the one provides tools and the other material; and by material I mean the substratum out of which any work is made; thus wool is the mater-ial of the weaver, bronze of the statuary. Now it is easy to see that the art of household management is not identical with the art of getting wealth, for the one uses the material which the other provides. For the art which uses house-hold stores can be no other than the art of household management. There is, however, a doubt whether the art of getting wealth is a part of household management or a distinct art. If the getter of wealth has to consider whence wealth and property can be procured, but there are many sorts of property and riches, then are husbandry, and the care and provision of food in general, parts of the art of household management or distinct arts? Again, there are many sorts of food, and therefore there are many kinds of lives both of ani-mals and men; they must all have food, and the differences in their food have made differences in their ways of life. For of beasts, some are gregarious, oth-ers are solitary; they live in the way which is best adapted to sustain them, ac-cordingly as they are carnivorous or herbivorous or omnivorous: and their habits are determined for them by nature with regard to their ease and choice of food. But the same things are not naturally pleasant to all of them; and therefore the lives of carnivorous or herbivorous animals further differ among themselves. In the lives of men too there is a great difference. The laziest are shepherds, who lead an idle life, and get their subsistence without trouble from tame animals; their flocks having to wander from place to place in search of pasture, they are compelled to follow them, cultivating a sort of liv-ing farm. Others support themselves by hunting, which is of different kinds. Some, for example, are brigands, others, who dwell near lakes or marshes or rivers or a sea in which there are fish, are fishermen, and others live by the pursuit of birds or wild beasts. The greater number obtain a living from the cultivated fruits of the soil. Such are the modes of subsistence which prevail among those whose industry springs up of itself, and whose food is not ac-quired by exchange and retail trade—there is the shepherd, the husbandman, the brigand, the fisherman, the hunter. Some gain a comfortable maintenance out of two employments, eking out the deficiencies of one of them by anoth-er: thus the life of a shepherd may be combined with that of a brigand, the life of a farmer with that of a hunter. Other modes of life are similarly com-bined in any way which the needs of men may require. Property, in the sense of a bare livelihood, seems to be given by nature herself to all, both when they are first born, and when they are grown up. For some animals bring forth, together with their offspring, so much food as will last until they are able to supply themselves; of this the vermiparous or oviparous animals are an instance; and the viviparous animals have up to a certain time a supply of food for their young in themselves, which is called milk. In like manner we may infer that, after the birth of animals, plants exist for their sake, and that the other animals exist for the sake of man, the tame for use and food, the wild, if not all, at least the greater part of them, for food, and for the provision of clothing and various instruments. Now if nature makes nothing incomplete, and nothing in vain, the inference must be that she has made all animals for the sake of man. And so, from one point of view, the art of war is a natural art of acquisition, for the art of acquisition includes hunting, an art which we ought to practise against wild beasts, and against men who, though intended by nature to be governed, will not submit; for war of such a kind is naturally just.

Of the art of acquisition then there is one kind which by nature is a part of the management of a household, in so far as the art of household management must either find ready to hand, or itself provide, such things necessary to life, and useful for the community of the family or state, as can be stored. They are the elements of true riches; for the amount of property which is needed for a good life is not unlimited, although Solon in one of his poems says that

No bound to riches has been fixed for man.

But there is a boundary fixed, just as there is in the other arts; for the instruments of any art are never unlimited, either in number or size, and riches may be defined as a number of instruments to be used in a household or in a state. And so we see that there is a natural art of acquisition which is practised by managers of households and by statesmen, and the reason for this.

9 • There is another variety of the art of acquisition which is commonly and rightly called an art of wealth-getting, and has in fact suggested the notion that riches and property have no limit. Being nearly connected with the preceding, it is often identified with it. But though they are not very different, neither are they the same. The kind already described is given by nature, the other is gained by experience and art.

Let us begin our discussion of the question with the following considerations. Of everything which we possess there are two uses: both belong to the thing as such, but not in the same manner, for one is the proper, and the other the improper use of it. For example, a shoe is used for wear, and is used for exchange; both are uses of the shoe. He who gives a shoe in exchange for money or food to him who wants one, does indeed use the shoe as a shoe, but this is not its proper use, for a shoe is not made to be an object of barter. The same may be said of all possessions, for the art of exchange extends to all of them, and it arises at first from what is natural, from the circumstance that some have too little, others too much. Hence we may infer that retail trade is not a natural part of the art of getting wealth; had it been so, men would have ceased to exchange when they had enough. In the first community, indeed, which is the family, this art is obviously of no use, but it begins to be useful

73

when the society increases. For the members of the family originally had all things in common; later, when the family divided into parts, the parts shared in many things, and different parts in different things, which they had to give in exchange for what they wanted, a kind of barter which is still practised among barbarous nations who exchange with one another the necessaries of life and nothing more; giving and receiving wine, for example, in exchange for corn, and the like. This sort of barter is not part of the wealth-getting art and is not contrary to nature, but is needed for the satisfaction of men's natural wants. The other form of exchange grew, as might have been inferred, out of this one. When the inhabitants of one country became more dependent on those of another, and they imported what they needed, and exported what they had too much of, money necessarily came into use. For the various necessaries of life are not easily carried about, and hence men agreed to employ in their dealings with each other something which was intrinsically useful and easily applicable to the purposes of life, for example, iron, silver, and the like. Of this the value was at first measured simply by size and weight, but in process of time they put a stamp upon it, to save the trouble of weighing and to mark the value.

When the use of coin had once been discovered, out of the barter of necessary articles arose the other art of wealth-getting, namely, retail trade; which was at first probably a simple matter, but became more complicated as soon as men learned by experience whence and by what exchanges the greatest profit might be made. Originating in the use of coin, the art of getting wealth is generally thought to be chiefly concerned with it, and to be the art which produces riches and wealth, having to consider how they may be accumulated. Indeed, riches is assumed by many to be only a quantity of coin, because the arts of getting wealth and retail trade are concerned with coin. Others maintain that coined money is a mere sham, a thing not natural, but conventional only, because, if the users substitute another commodity for it, it is worthless, and because it is not useful as a means to any of the necessities of life, and, indeed, he who is rich in coin may often be in want of necessary food. But how can that be wealth of which a man may have a great abundance and yet perish with hunger, like Midas in the fable, whose insatiable prayer turned everything that was set before him into gold?

Hence men seek after a better notion of riches and of the art of getting wealth, and they are right. For natural riches and the natural art of wealth-getting are a different thing; in their true form they are part of the management of a household; whereas retail trade is the art of producing wealth, not in every way, but by exchange. And it is thought to be concerned with coin; for coin is the unit of exchange and the limit of it. And there is no bound to the riches which spring from this art of wealth-getting. As in the art of medicine there is no limit to the pursuit of health, and as in the other arts there is no limit to the pursuit of their several ends, for they aim at accomplishing their ends to the uttermost (but of the means there is a limit, for the end is always the limit), so, too, in this art of wealth-getting there is no limit of the end, which is riches of the spurious kind, and the acquisition of wealth. But the art of wealth-getting which consists in household management, on the other hand, has a limit; the unlimited acquisition of wealth is not its business. And, therefore, from one point of view, all riches must have a limit; nevertheless, as a matter of fact, we find the opposite to be the case; for all getters of wealth increase their hoard of coin without limit. The source of the confusion is the near connexion between the two kinds of wealth-getting; in both, the instrument is the same, although the use is different, and so they pass into one another; for each is a use of the same property, but with a difference: accumulation is the end in the one case, but there is a further end in the other. Hence some persons are led to believe that getting wealth is the object of household management, and the whole idea of their lives is that they ought either to increase their money without limit, or at any rate not to lose it. The origin of this disposition in men is that they are intent upon living only, and not upon living well; and, as their desires are unlimited, they also desire that the means of gratifying them should be without limit. Those who do aim at a good life seek the means of obtaining bodily pleasures; and, since the enjoyment of these appears to depend on property, they are absorbed in getting wealth: and so there arises the second species of wealth-getting. For, as their enjoyment is in excess, they seek an art which produces the excess of enjoyment; and, if they are not able to supply their pleasures by the art of getting wealth, they try other causes, using in turn every faculty in a manner contrary to nature. The quality of courage, for example, is not intended to make wealth, but to inspire confidence; neither is this the aim of the general's or of the physician's art; but the one aims at victory and the other at health. Nevertheless, some men turn every quality or art into a means of getting wealth; this they conceive to be the end, and to the promotion of the end they think all things must contribute.

Thus, then, we have considered the art of wealth-getting which is unnecessary, and why men want it; and also the necessary art of wealth-getting, which we have seen to be different from the other, and to be a natural part of the art of managing a household, concerned with the provision of food, not, however, like the former kind, unlimited, but having a limit.

10 • And we have found the answer to our original question, Whether the art of getting wealth is the business of the manager of a household and of the statesman or not their business?—viz. that wealth is presupposed by them. For as political science does not make men, but takes them from nature and uses them, so too nature provides them with earth or sea or the like as a source of food. At this stage begins the duty of the manager of a household, who has to order the things which nature supplies—he may be compared to the weaver who has not to make but to use wool, and to know, too, what sort of wool is

good and serviceable or bad and unserviceable. Were this otherwise, it would be difficult to see why the art of getting wealth is a part of the management of a household and the art of medicine not; for surely the members of a household must have health just as they must have life or any other necessity. The answer is that as from one point of view the master of the house and the ruler of the state have to consider about health, from another point of view not they but the physician has to; so in one way the art of household management, in another way the subordinate art, has to consider about wealth. But, strictly speaking, as I have already said, the means of life must be provided beforehand by nature; for the business of nature is to furnish food to that which is born, and the food of the offspring is always what remains over of that from which it is produced. That is why the art of getting wealth out of fruits and animals is always natural.

There are two sorts of wealth-getting, as I have said; one is a part of household management, the other is retail trade: the former is necessary and honourable, while that which consists in exchange is justly censured; for it is unnatural, and a mode by which men gain from one another. The most hated sort, and with the greatest reason, is usury, which makes a gain out of money itself, and not from the natural object of it. For money was intended to be used in exchange, but not to increase at interest. And this term interest, which means the birth of money from money, is applied to the breeding of money because the offspring resembles the parent. That is why of all modes of getting wealth this is the most unnatural.

11 • Enough has been said about the theory of wealth-getting; we will now proceed to the practical part. Such things may be studied by a free man, but will only be practised from necessity. The useful parts of wealth-getting are, first, the knowledge of live-stock—which are most profitable, and where, and how—as for example, what sort of horses or sheep or oxen or any other animals are most likely to give a return. A man ought to know which of these pay better than others, and which pay best in particular places, for some do better in one place and some in another. Secondly, husbandry, which may be either tillage or planting, and the keeping of bees and of fish, or fowl, or of any animals which may be useful to man. These are the divisions of the true or proper art of wealth-getting and come first. Of the other, which consists in exchange, the first and most important division is commerce (of which there are three kinds—ship-owning, the conveyance of goods, exposure for sale—these again differing as they are safer or more profitable), the second is usury, the third, service for hire—of this, one kind is employed in the mechanical arts, the other in unskilled and bodily labour. There is still a third sort of wealth-getting intermediate between this and the first or natural mode which is partly natural, but is also concerned with exchange, viz. the industries that make their profit from the earth, and from things growing from the earth which, although they bear no fruit, are nevertheless profitable; for example,

the cutting of timber and all mining. The art of mining itself has many branches, for there are various kinds of things dug out of the earth. Of the several divisions of wealth-getting I now speak generally; a minute consideration of them might be useful in practice, but it would be tiresome to dwell upon them at greater length now.

Those occupations are most truly arts in which there is the least element of chance; they are the meanest in which the body is most maltreated, the most servile in which there is the greatest use of the body, and the most illiberal in which there is the least need of excellence.

Works have been written upon these subjects by various persons; for example, by Chares the Parian, and Apollodorus the Lemnian, who have treated of Tillage and Planting, while others have treated of other branches; anyone who cares for such matters may refer to their writings. It would be well also to collect the scattered stories of the ways in which individuals have succeeded in amassing a fortune; for all this is useful to persons who value the art of getting wealth. There is the anecdote of Thales the Milesian and his financial scheme, which involves a principle of universal application, but is attributed to him on account of his reputation for wisdom. He was reproached for his poverty, which was supposed to show that philosophy was of no use. According to the story, he knew by his skill in the stars while it was yet winter that there would be a great harvest of olives in the coming year; so, having a little money, he gave deposits for the use of all the olive-presses in Chios and Miletus, which he hired at a low price because no one bid against him. When the harvest-time came, and many were wanted all at once and of a sudden, he let them out at any rate which he pleased, and made a quantity of money. Thus he showed the world that philosophers can easily be rich if they like, but that their ambition is of another sort. . . .

13 • Thus it is clear that household management attends more to men than to the acquisition of inanimate things, and to human excellence more than to the excellence of property which we call wealth, and to the excellence of freemen more than to the excellence of slaves. . . .

FROM THE *POLITICS,* BOOK II

1 • Our purpose is to consider what form of political community is best of all for those who are most able to realize their ideal of life. We must therefore examine not only this but other constitutions, both such as actually exist in well-governed states, and any theoretical forms which are held in esteem, so that what is good and useful may be brought to light. And let no one suppose that in seeking for something beyond them we are anxious to make a sophistical display at any cost; we only undertake this inquiry because all the constitutions which now exist are faulty.

We will begin with the natural beginning of the subject. The members of a state must either have all things or nothing in common, or some things in common and some not. That they should have nothing in common is clearly impossible, for the constitution is a community, and must at any rate have a common place—one city will be in one place, and the citizens are those who share in that one city. But should a well-ordered state have all things, as far as may be, in common, or some only and not others? For the citizens might conceivably have wives and children and property in common, as Socrates proposes in the *Republic* of Plato. Which is better, our present condition, or one conforming to the law laid down in the *Republic*?

2 • There are many difficulties in the community of women. And the principle on which Socrates rests the necessity of such an institution evidently is not established by his arguments. Further, as a means to the end which he ascribes to the state, the scheme, taken literally, is impracticable, and how we are to interpret it is nowhere precisely stated. I am speaking of the supposition from which the argument of Socrates proceeds, that it is best for the whole state to be as unified as possible. Is it not obvious that a state may at length attain such a degree of unity as to be no longer a state?—since the nature of a state is to be a plurality, and in tending to greater unity, from being a state, it becomes a family, and from being a family, an individual; for the family may be said to be more one than the state, and the individual than the family. So that we ought not to attain this greatest unity even if we could, for it would be the destruction of the state. Again, a state is not made up only of so many men, but of different kinds of men; for similars do not constitute a state. It is not like a military alliance. The usefulness of the latter depends upon its quantity even where there is no difference in quality (for mutual protection is the end aimed at), just as a greater weight depresses the scale more (in like manner, a state differs from a nation, when the nation has not its population organized in villages, but lives an Arcadian sort of life); but the elements out of which a unity is to be formed differ in kind. That is why the principle of reciprocity, as I have already remarked in the *Ethics,* is the salvation of states. Even among freemen and equals this is a principle which must be maintained, for they cannot all rule together, but must change at the end of a year or some other period of time or in some order of succession. The result is that upon this plan they all govern; just as if shoemakers and carpenters were to exchange their occupations, and the same persons did not always continue shoemakers and carpenters. And since it is better that this should be so in politics as well, it is clear that while there should be continuance of the same persons in power where this is possible, yet where this is not possible by reason of the natural equality of the citizens, and at the same time it is just that all should share in the government (whether to govern be a good thing or a bad),—in these cases this is imitated. Thus the one party rules and the others are ruled in turn, as if they were no longer the same persons. In like manner when they hold office there is a variety in the offices held. Hence it is evident that a city is not by nature one in that sense which some persons affirm; and

that what is said to be the greatest good of cities is in reality their destruction; but surely the good of things must be that which preserves them. Again, from another point of view, this extreme unification of the state is clearly not good; for a family is more self-sufficing than an individual, and a city than a family, and a city only comes into being when the community is large enough to be self-sufficing. If then self-sufficiency is to be desired, the lesser degree of unity is more desirable than the greater.

3 • But, even supposing that it were best for the community to have the greatest degree of unity, this unity is by no means proved to follow from the fact of all men saying 'mine' and 'not mine' at the same instant of time, which, according to Socrates, is the sign of perfect unity in a state. For the word 'all' is ambiguous. If the meaning be that every individual says 'mine' and 'not mine' at the same time, then perhaps the result at which Socrates aims may be in some degree accomplished; each man will call the same person his own son and the same person his own wife, and so of his property and of all that falls to his lot. This, however, is not the way in which people would speak who had their wives and children in common; they would say 'all' but not 'each'. In like manner their property would be described as belonging to them, not severally but collectively. There is an obvious fallacy in the term 'all': like some other words, 'both', 'odd', 'even', it is ambiguous, and even in abstract argument becomes a source of logical puzzles. That all persons call the same thing mine in the sense in which each does so may be a fine thing, but it is impracticable; or if the words are taken in the other sense, such a unity in no way conduces to harmony. And there is another objection to the proposal. For that which is common to the greatest number has the least care bestowed upon it. Everyone thinks chiefly of his own, hardly at all of the common interest; and only when he is himself concerned as an individual. For besides other considerations, everybody is more inclined to neglect something which he expects another to fulfil; as in families many attendants are often less useful than a few. Each citizen will have a thousand sons who will not be his sons individually, but anybody will be equally the son of anybody, and will therefore be neglected by all alike. Further, upon this principle, every one will use the word 'mine' of one who is prospering or the reverse, however small a fraction he may himself be of the whole number; the same boy will be my son, so and so's son, the son of each of the thousand, or whatever be the number of the citizens; and even about this he will not be positive; for it is impossible to know who chanced to have a child, or whether, if one came into existence, it has survived. But which is better—for each to say 'mine' in this way, making a man the same relation to two thousand or ten thousand citizens, or to use the word 'mine' as it is now used in states? For usually the same person is called by one man his own son whom another calls his own brother or cousin or kinsman—blood relation or connexion by marriage—either of himself or of some relation of his, and yet another his clans-

man or tribesman; and how much better is it to be the real cousin of somebody than to be a son after Plato's fashion! Nor is there any way of preventing brothers and children and fathers and mothers from sometimes recognizing one another; for children are born like their parents, and they will necessarily be finding indications of their relationship to one another. Geographers declare such to be the fact; they say that in part of Upper Libya, where the women are common, nevertheless the children who are born are assigned to their respective fathers on the ground of their likeness. And some women, like the females of other animals—for example, mares and cows—have a strong tendency to produce offspring resembling their parents, as was the case with the Pharsalian mare called Honest Wife.

4 • Other difficulties, against which it is not easy for the authors of such a community to guard, will be assaults and homicides, voluntary as well as involuntary, quarrels and slanders, all of which are most unholy acts when committed against fathers and mothers and near relations, but not equally unholy when there is no relationship. Moreover, they are much more likely to occur if the relationship is unknown than if it is known and, when they have occurred, the customary expiations of them can be made if the relationship is known, but not otherwise. Again, how strange it is that Socrates, after having made the children common, should hinder lovers from carnal intercourse only, but should permit love and familiarities between father and son or between brother and brother, than which nothing can be more unseemly, since even without them love of this sort is improper. How strange, too, to forbid intercourse for no other reason than the violence of the pleasure, as though the relationship of father and son or of brothers with one another made no difference.

This community of wives and children seems better suited to the husbandmen than to the guardians, for if they have wives and children in common, they will be bound to one another by weaker ties, as a subject class should be, and they will remain obedient and not rebel. In a word, the result of such a law would be just the opposite of that which good laws ought to have, and the intention of Socrates in making these regulations about women and children would defeat itself. For friendship we believe to be the greatest good of states and what best preserves them against revolutions; and Socrates particularly praises the unity of the state which seems and is said by him to be created by friendship. But the unity which he commends would be like that of the lovers in the *Symposium,* who, as Aristophanes says, desire to grow together in the excess of their affection, and from being two to become one, in which case one or both would certainly perish. Whereas in a state having women and children common, love will be diluted; and the father will certainly not say 'my son', or the son 'my father'. As a little sweet wine mingled with a great deal of water is imperceptible in the mixture, so, in this sort of community, the idea of relationship which is based upon these names will be lost; there is no reason why the so-called father should care about the son, or the son about the father, or brothers about one another. Of the two qualities which chiefly inspire regard and affection—that a thing is your own and that it is precious—neither can exist in such a state as this.

Again, the transfer of children as soon as they are born from the rank of husbandmen or of artisans to that of guardians, and from the rank of guardians into a lower rank, will be very difficult to arrange; the givers or transferrers cannot but know whom they are giving and transferring, and to whom. And the previously mentioned assaults, unlawful loves, homicides, will happen more often among them; for they will no longer call the members of the class they have left brothers, and children, and fathers, and mothers, and will not, therefore, be afraid of committing any crimes by reason of consanguinity. Touching the community of wives and children, let this be our conclusion.

5 • Next let us consider what should be our arrangements about property: should the citizens of the perfect state have their possessions in common or not? This question may be discussed separately from the enactments about women and children. Even supposing that the women and children belong to individuals, according to the custom which is at present universal, may there not be an advantage in having and using possessions in common? E.g. (1) the soil may be appropriated, but the produce may be thrown for consumption into the common stock; and this is the practice of some nations. Or (2), the soil may be common, and may be cultivated in common, but the produce divided among individuals for their private use; this is a form of common property which is said to exist among certain foreigners. Or (3), the soil and the produce may be alike common.

When the husbandmen are not the owners, the case will be different and easier to deal with; but when they till the ground for themselves the question of ownership will give a world of trouble. If they do not share equally in enjoyments and toils, those who labour much and get little will necessarily complain of those who labour little and receive or consume much. But indeed there is always a difficulty in men living together and having all human relations in common, but especially in their having common property. The partnerships of fellow-travellers are an example to the point; for they generally fall out over everyday matters and quarrel about any trifle which turns up. So with servants: we are most liable to take offence at those with whom we most frequently come into contact in daily life.

These are only some of the disadvantages which attend the community of property; the present arrangement, if improved as it might be by good customs and laws, would be far better, and would have the advantages of both systems. Property should be in a certain sense common, but, as a general rule, private; for, when everyone has a distinct interest, men will not complain of one another, and they will make more progress, because everyone will be attending to his own business. And yet by reason of goodness, and in respect of use, 'Friends', as the proverb says, 'will have all things common'. Even now there are traces of such a principle, showing that it is not impracticable, but, in well-ordered states, exists already to a certain extent and may be carried further. For, although every man has his own property, some things he will place at the disposal of his friends, while of others he shares the use with them. The Lacedaemonians, for example, use one another's slaves, and horses, and dogs, as if they were their own; and when they lack provisions on a journey, they appropriate what they find in the fields throughout the country. It is clearly better that property should be private, but the use of it common; and the special business of the legislator is to create in men this benevolent disposition. Again, how immeasurably greater is the pleasure, when a man feels a thing to be his own; for surely the love of self is a feeling implanted by nature and not given in vain, although selfishness is rightly censured; this, however, is not the mere love of self, but the love of self in excess, like the miser's love of money; for all, or almost all, men love money and other such objects in a measure. And further, there is the greatest pleasure in doing a kindness or service to friends or guests or companions, which can only be rendered when a man has private property. These advantages are lost by excessive unification of the state. The exhibition of two excellences, besides, is visibly annihilated in such a state: first, temperance towards women (for it is an honourable action to abstain from another's wife for temperance sake); secondly, liberality in the matter of property. No one, when men have all things in common, will any longer set an example of liberality or do any liberal action; for liberality consists in the use which is made of property.

Such legislation may have a specious appearance of benevolence; men readily listen to it, and are easily induced to believe that in some wonderful manner everybody will become everybody's friend—especially when someone is heard denouncing the evils now existing in states, suits about contracts, convictions for perjury, flatteries of rich men and the like, which are said to arise out of the possession of private property. These evils, however, are due not to the absence of communism but to wickedness. Indeed, we see that there is much more quarrelling among those who have all things in common, though there are not many of them when compared with the vast numbers who have private property.

Again, we ought to reckon not only the evils from which the citizens will be saved, but also the advantages which they will lose. The life which they are to lead appears to be quite impracticable. The error of Socrates must be attributed to the false supposition from which he starts. Unity there should be, both of the family and of the state, but in some respects only. For there is a point at which a state may attain such a degree of unity as to be no longer a state, or at which, without actually ceasing to exist, it will become an inferior state, like harmony passing into unison, or rhythm which has been reduced to a single foot. The state, as I was saying, is a plurality, which should be united and made into a community by education; and it is strange that the author of a system of education which he thinks will make the state virtuous, should expect to improve his citizens by regulations of this sort, and not by philosophy or by customs and laws, like those which prevail at Sparta and Crete respecting common meals, whereby the legislator has made property common. Let us remember that we should not disregard the experience of ages; in the multitude of years these things, if they were good, would certainly not have been unknown; for almost everything has been found out, although sometimes they are not put together; in other cases men do not use the knowledge which they have. Great light would be thrown on this subject if we could see such a form of government in the actual process of construction; for the legislator could not form a state at all without distributing and dividing its constituents into associations for common meals, and into phratries and tribes. But all this legislation ends only in forbidding agriculture to the guardians, a prohibition which the Lacedaemonians try to enforce already.

But, indeed, Socrates has not said, nor is it easy to decide, what in such a community will be the general form of the state. The citizens who are not guardians are the majority, and about them nothing has been determined: are the husbandmen, too, to have their property in common? Or is each individual to have his own? and are their wives and children to be individual or common? If, like the guardians, they are to have all things in common, in what do they differ from them, or what will they gain by submitting to their government? Or upon what principle would they submit, unless indeed the governing class adopt the ingenious policy of the Cretans, who give their slaves the same institutions as their own, but forbid them gymnastic exercises and the possession of arms. If, on the other hand, the inferior classes are to be like other cities in respect of marriage and property, what will be the form of the community? Must it not contain two states in one, each hostile to the other? He makes the guardians into a mere occupying garrison, while the husbandmen and artisans and the rest are real citizens. But if so the suits and quarrels, and all the evils which Socrates affirms to exist in other states, will exist equally among them. He says indeed that, having so good an education, the citizens will not need many laws, for example laws about the city or about the markets; but then he confines his education to the guardians. Again, he makes the husbandmen owners of the property upon condition of their paying a tribute. But in that case they are likely to be much more unmanageable and conceited than the Helots, or Penestae, or slaves in general. And whether community of wives and property be necessary for the lower equally with the higher class or not, and the questions akin to this, what will be the education, form of government, laws of the lower class, Socrates has nowhere determined: neither is it easy to discover this, nor is their character of small importance if the common life of the guardians is to be maintained.

83

Again, if Socrates makes the women common, and retains private property, the men will see to the fields, but who will see to the house? And who will do so if the agricultural class have both their property and their wives in common? Once more: it is absurd to argue, from the analogy of animals, that men and women should follow the same pursuits, for animals have not to manage a household. The government, too, as constituted by Socrates, contains elements of danger; for he makes the same persons always rule. And if this is often a cause of disturbance among the meaner sort, how much more among high-spirited warriors? But that the persons whom he makes rulers must be the same is evident; for the gold which the God mingles in the souls of men is not at one time given to one, at another time to another, but always to the same: as he says, God mingles gold in some, and silver in others, from their very birth; but brass and iron in those who are meant to be artisans and husbandmen. Again, he deprives the guardians even of happiness, and says that the legislator ought to make the whole state happy. But the whole cannot be happy unless most, or all, or some of its parts enjoy happiness. In this respect happiness is not like the even principle in numbers, which may exist only in the whole, but in neither of the parts; not so happiness. And if the guardians are not happy, who are? Surely not the artisans, or the common people. The Republic of which Socrates discourses has all these difficulties, and others quite as great.

For Further Reading

Aristotle. *Nicomachean Ethics.* Translated by Martin Ostward (Indianapolis: Bobbs-Merrill, 1962).

————. *The Politics of Aristotle.* Translated by Ernest Barker (Oxford: Oxford Univ. Press, 1946).

Barnes, J., M. Schofield, and R. Sorabji, eds. *Articles on Aristotle,* vol. 2: *Ethics and Politics* (New York: St. Martin's, 1977).

Booth, William James. "Politics and the Household: A Commentary on Aristotle's *Politics,* Book One," *History of Political Thought* 2 (1981): 203–226.

Castoriadis, Cornelius. "Value, Equality, Justice, Politics: From Marx to Aristotle and from Aristotle to Ourselves." In *Crossroads in the Labyrinth.* Translated by K. Soper and M. Ryle (Cambridge, Mass.: MIT Press, 1984).

Cooper, John. *Reason and Human Good in Aristotle* (Cambridge, Mass.: Harvard Univ. Press, 1975; Hackett, 1986).

Keyt, David, and Fred Miller, eds. *Essays on Aristotle's Politics* (Oxford: Blackwell, 1991).

Lewis, Thomas. "Acquisition and Anxiety: Aristotle's Case against the Market." *Canadian Journal of Economics* 11 (1978).

Meikle, Scott, "Aristotle and the Political Economy of the Polis." *Journal of Hellenic Studies* 99 (1979) 57–73.

————. "Aristotle on Equality and Market Exchange." *Journal of Hellenic Studies* 111 (1991) 193–196.

Murphy, James Bernard. *The Moral Economy of Labor: Aristotelian Themes in Economic Theory* (New Haven: Yale Univ. Press, 1993).

Nichols, Mary. *Citizens and Statesmen: A Study of Aristotle's Politics* (Lanham, Md.: Rowman and Littlefield, 1992).

Nussbaum, Martha C. *The Fragility of Goodness* (Cambridge: Cambridge Univ. Press, 1986).

———. "Nature, Function, and Capability: Aristotle on Political Distribution." *Oxford Studies in Ancient Philosophy,* suppl. vol. Edited by Julia Annas (Oxford: Clarendon Press, 1988).

Polanyi, Karl. "Aristotle Discovers the Economy." In *Trade and Market in the Early Empires: Economies in History and Theory.* Edited by K. Polanyi, E. Arensberg, and H. Pearson (Glencoe, Ill.: The Free Press, 1957).

Rorty, A.O., ed. *Essays on Aristotle's Ethics* (Berkeley: Univ. of California Press, 1980).

Soudek, Josef. "Aristotle's Theory of Exchange: An Inquiry into the Origin of Economic Analysis." *Proceedings of the American Philosophical Society* 96, no. 1 (February 1952).

Spengler, J.J. "Aristotle on Economic Imputation and Related Matters." *Southern Economic Journal* 21 (1955).

Springborg, Patricia. "Aristotle and the Problem of Needs." *History of Political Thought* 5, no. 3 (Winter 1984).

Swanson, Judith A. *The Public and the Private in Aristotle's Political Philosophy* (Ithaca, N.Y.: Cornell Univ. Press, 1994).

ST. THOMAS AQUINAS (1225–1274)

ST. THOMAS AQUINAS'S mind was an expansive meeting ground for ideas of diverse sources: the Jewish and Christian Scriptures; Catholic theology and philosophy, notably the thought of St. Augustine; the writings of the great medieval Arab philosophers, especially Ibn Rushd (Averroes) and Ibn Sina (Avicenna); and the classical Greek and Roman philosophers, most famously the one he calls "the Philosopher," Aristotle. Before turning to Aquinas's teachings on commerce, let us put in mind several Christian doctrines which not only set the horizon for Christian reflections on commerce but, some would argue, carry the seeds of modern commercial life.

There is one God, Creator of the universe and sovereign over it. The world has a beginning and an end; God's saving action in the world gives history its narrative structure. God is a person: in the Trinitarian formulation God is the perfect community of three persons in one being, and God freely enters into a loving relationship with all human beings. Humans are creatures of God who are capable of freely responding to God's love or failing to do so. In the wake of the Fall of Adam and Eve, souls are disfigured by original sin, a deep down disposition to turn away from God and choose evil. As Kant put it, we are cut from crooked wood. As the life that begins with each person is unquenchable even by death, at stake is not just earthly happiness but the disposition of each soul for eternity. Seeing one's life this way simultaneously intensifies its drama while implanting a spirit of detachment from earthly goods. The ideal of "exchange" between God and person is neither the transfer of goods of equal value by self-interested parties nor the "one-upmanship" of gift and counter-gift; it is intimate and radically free, a purely gracious mutual outpouring of love. In Christianity, then, we find a post-traditional religion, i.e., a monotheism self-consciously aspiring to universality, at whose core is an "economy" of love sharply at odds with the prestige-hungry ancient economies of gift and the calculating tit-for-tat of modern exchanges. Its doctrine of God and humanity places the freely acting and responsible person at the center of the world's stage.

In the Christian salvation story, the decisive event occurred with the life and death of Jesus of Nazareth, a person at once fully divine and human. Naturally, in thinking about ordering human societies, Christians turn to the sayings of Jesus and the New Testament authors. But the Gospels and Epistles are no *Republic* or *Politics*; though these teachings bear on political and economic life, no single, articulated model of society is found in Christian Scripture. No wonder, then, that Christian thinkers historically have drawn so heavily on non-Christian resources like Plato, Aristotle, and the Greek and Roman Stoics. While Christian practices and reflections regarding property and commerce have varied from early on, a few persistent elements are evident. The early followers of Jesus in Jerusalem lived a communal existence, but St. Paul discouraged this, and it never became normative. As the Roman Empire was declining, new forms of communal life sprang up with the early monastic movements. After Emperor Constantine's conversion, Christianity went from being a persecuted sect to the official religion of the realm, pushing Christian thinking about political life into a whole new environment. One lasting Christian theme is "stewardship": the goods of the earth are entrusted to all people to serve humanity. Charity to the poor, an early and persistent practice, is continually stressed by Christian writers. Though most early Christian writers justified the ancient practice of holding slaves, an egalitarian current may be detected. Two patristic thinkers, St. Gregory of Nyssa and St. John Chrysostom, spoke out against slavery, and St. Augustine wrote appreciatively of the value of manual labor and the work of artisans. Christian teachings on wealth evince tension between the ideal of voluntary poverty and that of using one's material possessions well, regardless of their quantity.

That two-track approach to wealth appears in the work of Aquinas, who was born into a wealthy, well-positioned family but turned in a different direction by joining the Dominicans, a religious order bound by the vow of poverty. Aquinas's arguments against making either money or material possessions one's highest good read like a page out of Aristotle's *Nicomachean Ethics*: virtue is the proper measure of wealth. Aquinas also takes up Aristotle's defense of private property, encompassing it in a theory of God's donation of earthly goods to humankind in common. Distinguishing between appropriation by the human species and private appropriation, Aquinas argues—against Locke's subsequent view—that only the former is a matter of natural law. Private property is a prudent invention of human law permissible under natural law but not dictated by it. Aquinas follows Aristotle in holding that the *use* of private property must be responsive to common needs. The modern notion of private use rights, which is tied up with the modern conceptions of commodity and capital ownership, goes against the grain of Aquinas's defense of private property. This incompatibility with modern thinking about commodities should be noted lest we slide into reading his account of just commercial practices as a medieval primer in modern business ethics.

The suppleness of Aquinas's mind in adapting his thinking to customary practices is evident in questions regarding fair trade, usury, and simony. One case of this flexibility is of special note, his treatment of making money through buying and selling, what Aristotle called "retail trade." Aquinas puts a different slant on Aristotle's judgment that "retail trade" is perverse because of the boundlessness of moneymaking. Aquinas agrees that the form of "retail trade," *taken in itself,* "has a certain debasement attaching" to it. But he stops short of branding all moneymaking as debased. "Tradesmen" are not compelled to comply with the endlessness of the capital form. Rather, the purposes to which they put their money need to be evaluated. This slight swerving from Aristotle's uncompromising rejection of "retail trade" opened moral space for fledgling capitalist operations.

FROM THE *SUMMA CONTRA GENTILES*

CHAPTER XXX
THAT MAN'S HAPPINESS DOES NOT CONSIST IN WEALTH

Hence it is evident that neither is wealth man's supreme good. For wealth is not sought except for the sake of something else: because of itself it brings us no good, but only when we use it, whether for the support of the body, or for some similar purpose. Now the supreme good is sought for its own, and not for another's sake. Therefore wealth is not man's supreme good.

Again. Man's supreme good cannot consist in the possession or preservation of things whose chief advantage for man consists in their being spent. Now the chief advantage of wealth is in its being spent; for this is its use. Therefore the possession of wealth cannot be man's supreme good.

Moreover. Acts of virtue deserve praise according as they lead to happiness. Now acts of liberality and magnificence which are concerned with money, are deserving of praise, on account of money being spent, rather than on account of its being kept: and it is from this that these virtues derive their names. Therefore man's happiness does not consist in the possession of wealth.

Besides. Man's supreme good must consist in obtaining something better than man. But man is better than wealth: since it is something directed to man's use. Therefore not in wealth does man's supreme good consist.

Further. Man's supreme good is not subject to chance. For things that happen by chance, escape the forethought of reason: whereas man has to attain his own end by means of his reason. But chance occupies the greater place in the attaining of wealth. Therefore human happiness consists not in wealth.

Moreover. This is evident from the fact that wealth is lost unwillingly. Also because wealth can come into the possession of evil persons, who, of necessity, must lack the sovereign good. Again because wealth is unstable. Other similar reasons can be gathered from the arguments given above.

CHAPTER CXXXIII
HOW POVERTY IS GOOD

In order to elucidate the truth about what we have been saying, we must form our judgement of poverty, by considering riches. External riches are necessary for the good of virtue: since by them we support the body, and help others. Now, things directed to an end must take their goodness from that end. Consequently external riches must be a good of man; not his chief, but, as it were, his secondary, good: because the end is a good principally; and other things, according as they are directed to the end. For this reason some have thought that virtues are man's greatest good, and external riches, goods of least account. Now, things directed to an end, must take their measure from the exigency of the end. Wherefore riches are good forasmuch as they serve the use of virtue: and if this measure be exceeded, so that they hinder the practice of virtue, they are no longer to be reckoned as a good but as an evil. Hence it happens that the possession of riches is good for some who use them for virtue: while to others it is an evil, because they are withdrawn thereby from virtue, through being either too anxious about them, or too much attached to them, or self-conceited about them.

Whereas, however, there are virtues of the active and of the contemplative life, both need external riches in different ways. For the contemplative virtues need them only for the support of nature: whereas the active virtues need them both for that purpose, and to support others who share the same life. Hence the contemplative life is the more perfect in that it has fewer needs. To this life indeed it would seem to belong that man occupy himself wholly with divine things: and this perfection Christ's teaching counsels to man. Consequently those who seek this perfection are content with a minimum of external riches, as much, to wit, as suffices to support nature. Hence the Apostle says (1 Tim. vi. 8): *Having food, and wherewith to be covered, with these we are content.*

Accordingly, poverty is commendable so far as it frees man from those vices in which some are enmeshed through wealth. In so far as it removes the anxiety that is occasioned by riches, it is useful to some, those namely who are disposed to occupy themselves with the better things: but it is harmful to some, who being freed from this anxiety, betake themselves to worse occupations. Hence Gregory says (6 *Moral.* xxxvii): *It often happens that people who are busy in doing well while living as men are used to live, are slain by the sword of retirement.*—In so far as poverty removes the good resulting from riches, namely the assistance of others, and one's own support, it is simply an evil: except, forasmuch as the assistance whereby one's neighbour is relieved in temporal things, may be compensated by a greater good, in that a man, through lacking wealth, can more freely give himself to the affairs of God and his soul. But the good of one's own support is so far necessary, that it cannot be compensated by any other: for man should not deprive himself of his livelihood for the sake of obtaining any other good.

Such poverty is therefore commendable when a man being freed thereby from worldly solicitude, is enabled more freely to occupy himself with divine and spiritual things; yet so as to retain the possibility of lawfully supporting himself, for which purpose not many things are needful. And according as the manner of living in a state of poverty demands less solicitude, so much the more is poverty to be commended: but not according as the poverty is greater. For poverty is not good in itself: but in so far as it frees a man from that which hinders him from being intent on spiritual things. Hence its measure of goodness depends on how far it frees man from the aforesaid obstacles.—In fact this applies to all external things in common, that they are so far good as they are serviceable to virtue, but not in themselves.

FROM THE *SUMMA THEOLOGIAE*

QUESTION 66
OF THEFT AND ROBBERY

Whether it is natural for man to possess external things?

Objection 1: It would seem that it is not natural for man to possess external things. For no man should ascribe to himself that which is God's. Now the dominion over all creatures is proper to God, according to Ps. 23:1, "The earth is the Lord's," etc. Therefore it is not natural for man to possess external things.

Objection 2: Further, Basil in expounding the words of the rich man (Lk. 12:18), "I will gather all things that are grown to me, and my goods," says [*Hom. in Luc.* xii, 18]: "Tell me: which are thine? where did you take them from and bring them into being?" Now whatever man possesses naturally, he can fittingly call his own. Therefore man does not naturally possess external things.

Objection 3: Further, according to Ambrose (*De Trin.* i [*De Fide, ad Gratianum, i, 1]) "dominion denotes power." But man has no power over external things, since he can work no change in their nature. Therefore the possession of external things is not natural to man.

On the contrary, It is written (Ps. 8:8): "Thou hast subjected all things under his feet."

I answer that, External things can be considered in two ways. First, as regards their nature, and this is not subject to the power of man, but only to the power of God Whose mere will all things obey. Secondly, as regards their use, and in this way, man has a natural dominion over external things, because, by his reason and will, he is able to use them for his own profit, as they were made on his account: for the imperfect is always for the sake of the perfect, as stated above (Q64, A1). It is by this argument that the Philosopher proves (*Polit.* i, 3) that the possession of external things is natural to man. Moreover, this natural dominion of man over other creatures, which is competent to man in respect of his reason wherein God's image resides, is shown forth in man's creation (Gn. 1:26) by the words: "Let us make man to our image and likeness: and let him have dominion over the fishes of the sea," etc.

Reply to Objection 1: God has sovereign dominion over all things: and He, according to His providence, directed certain things to the sustenance of man's body. For this reason man has a natural dominion over things, as regards the power to make use of them.

Reply to Objection 2: The rich man is reproved for deeming external things to belong to him principally, as though he had not received them from another, namely from God.

Reply to Objection 3: This argument considers the dominion over external things as regards their nature. Such a dominion belongs to God alone, as stated above.

Whether it is lawful for a man to possess a thing as his own?

Objection 1: It would seem unlawful for a man to possess a thing as his own. For whatever is contrary to the natural law is unlawful. Now according to the natural law all things are common property: and the possession of property is contrary to this community of goods. Therefore it is unlawful for any man to appropriate any external thing to himself.

Objection 2: Further, Basil in expounding the words of the rich man quoted above (A1, OBJ2), says: "The rich who deem as their own property the common goods they have seized upon, are like to those who by going beforehand to the play prevent others from coming, and appropriate to themselves what is intended for common use." Now it would be unlawful to prevent others from obtaining possession of common goods. Therefore it is unlawful to appropriate to oneself what belongs to the community.

Objection 3: Further, Ambrose says [*Serm*. lxiv, *de temp.*], and his words are quoted in the Decretals [*Dist. xlvii., Can. *Sicut hi.*]: "Let no man call his own that which is common property": and by "common" he means external things, as is clear from the context. Therefore it seems unlawful for a man to appropriate an external thing to himself.

On the contrary, Augustine says (*De Haeres.*, haer. 40): "The 'Apostolici' are those who with extreme arrogance have given themselves that name, because they do not admit into their communion persons who are married or possess anything of their own, such as both monks and clerics who in considerable number are to be found in the Catholic Church." Now the reason why these people are heretics was because severing themselves from the Church, they think that those who enjoy the use of the above things, which they themselves lack, have no hope of salvation. Therefore it is erroneous to maintain that it is unlawful for a man to possess property.

I answer that, Two things are competent to man in respect of exterior things. One is the power to procure and dispense them, and in this regard it is lawful for man to possess property. Moreover this is necessary to human life for three reasons. First because every man is more careful to procure what is for himself alone than that which is common to many or to all: since each one would shirk the labor and leave to another that which concerns the community, as happens where there is a great number of servants. Secondly, because human affairs are conducted in more orderly fashion if each man is charged with taking care of some particular thing himself, whereas there would be confusion if everyone had to look after any one thing indeterminately. Thirdly, because a more peaceful state is ensured to man if each one is contented with his own. Hence it is to be observed that quarrels arise more frequently where there is no division of the things possessed.

The second thing that is competent to man with regard to external things is their use. In this respect man ought to possess external things, not as his own, but as common, so that, to wit, he is ready to communicate them to others in their need. Hence the Apostle says (1 Tim. 6:17,18): "Charge the rich of this world . . . to give easily, to communicate to others," etc.

Reply to Objection 1: Community of goods is ascribed to the natural law, not that the natural law dictates that all things should be possessed in common and that nothing should be possessed as one's own: but because the division of possessions is not according to the natural law, but rather arose from human agreement which belongs to positive law, as stated above (Q57, AA2,3). Hence the ownership of possessions is not contrary to the natural law, but an addition thereto devised by human reason.

Reply to Objection 2: A man would not act unlawfully if by going beforehand to the play he prepared the way for others: but he acts unlawfully if by so doing he hinders others from going. In like manner a rich man does not act unlawfully if he anticipates someone in taking possession of something which at first was common property, and gives others a share: but he sins if he excludes others indiscriminately from using it. Hence Basil says (*Hom. in Luc.* xii, 18): "Why are you rich while another is poor, unless it be that you may have the merit of a good stewardship, and he the reward of patience?"

Reply to Objection 3: When Ambrose says: "Let no man call his own that which is common," he is speaking of ownership as regards use, wherefore he adds: "He who spends too much is a robber."

QUESTION 77

OF CHEATING, WHICH IS COMMITTED IN BUYING AND SELLING

We must now consider those sins which relate to voluntary commutations. First, we shall consider cheating, which is committed in buying and selling: secondly, we shall consider usury, which occurs in loans. In connection with the other voluntary commutations no special kind of sin is to be found distinct from rapine and theft.

Under the first head there are four points of inquiry:

(1) Of unjust sales as regards the price; namely, whether it is lawful to sell a thing for more than its worth?
(2) Of unjust sales on the part of the thing sold;
(3) Whether the seller is bound to reveal a fault in the thing sold?
(4) Whether it is lawful in trading to sell a thing at a higher price than was paid for it?

Whether it is lawful to sell a thing for more than its worth?

Objection 1: It would seem that it is lawful to sell a thing for more than its worth. In the commutations of human life, civil laws determine that which is just. Now according to these laws it is just for buyer and seller to deceive one another (Cod. IV, xliv, *De Rescind. Vend.* 8,15): and this occurs by the seller selling a thing for more than its worth, and the buyer buying a thing for less than its worth. Therefore it is lawful to sell a thing for more than its worth.

Objection 2: Further, that which is common to all would seem to be natural and not sinful. Now Augustine relates that the saying of a certain jester was accepted by all, "You wish to buy for a song and to sell at a premium," which agrees with the saying of Prov. 20:14, "It is naught, it is naught, saith every buyer: and when he is gone away, then he will boast." Therefore it is lawful to sell a thing for more than its worth.

Objection 3: Further, it does not seem unlawful if that which honesty demands be done by mutual agreement. Now, according to the Philosopher (*Ethic.* viii, 13), in the friendship which is based on utility, the amount of the recompense for a favor received should depend on the utility accruing to the receiver: and this utility sometimes is worth more than the thing given, for instance if the receiver be in great need of that thing, whether for the purpose of avoiding a danger, or of deriving some particular benefit. Therefore, in contracts of buying and selling, it is lawful to give a thing in return for more than its worth.

On the contrary, It is written (Mt. 7:12): "All things . . . whatsoever you would that men should do to you, do you also to them." But no man wishes to buy a thing for more than its worth. Therefore no man should sell a thing to another man for more than its worth.

I answer that, It is altogether sinful to have recourse to deceit in order to sell a thing for more than its just price, because this is to deceive one's neighbor so as to injure him. Hence Tully says (De Offic. iii, 15): "Contracts should be entirely free from double-dealing: the seller must not impose upon the bidder, nor the buyer upon one that bids against him."

But, apart from fraud, we may speak of buying and selling in two ways. First, as considered in themselves, and from this point of view, buying and selling seem to be established for the common advantage of both parties, one of whom requires that which belongs to the other, and vice versa, as the Philosopher states (Polit. i, 3). Now whatever is established for the common advantage, should not be more of a burden to one party than to another, and consequently all contracts between them should observe equality of thing and thing. Again, the quality of a thing that comes into human use is measured by the price given for it, for which purpose money was invented, as stated in Ethic. v, 5. Therefore if either the price exceed the quantity of the thing's worth, or, conversely, the thing exceed the price, there is no longer the equality of justice: and consequently, to sell a thing for more than its worth, or to buy it for less than its worth, is in itself unjust and unlawful.

Secondly we may speak of buying and selling, considered as accidentally tending to the advantage of one party, and to the disadvantage of the other: for instance, when a man has great need of a certain thing, while an other man will suffer if he be without it. In such a case the just price will depend not only on the thing sold, but on the loss which the sale brings on the seller. And thus it will be lawful to sell a thing for more than it is worth in itself, though the price paid be not more than it is worth to the owner. Yet if the one man derive a great advantage by becoming possessed of the other man's property, and the seller be not at a loss through being without that thing, the latter ought not to raise the price, because the advantage accruing to the buyer, is not due to the seller, but to a circumstance affecting the buyer. Now no man should sell what is not his, though he may charge for the loss he suffers.

On the other hand if a man find that he derives great advantage from something he has bought, he may, of his own accord, pay the seller something over and above: and this pertains to his honesty.

Reply to Objection 1: As stated above (FS, Q96, A2) human law is given to the people among whom there are many lacking virtue, and it is not given to the virtuous alone. Hence human law was unable to forbid all that is contrary to virtue; and it suffices for it to prohibit whatever is destructive of human intercourse, while it treats other matters as though they were lawful, not by approving of them, but by not punishing them. Accordingly, if without employing deceit the seller disposes of his goods for more than their worth, or the buyer obtain them for less than their worth, the law looks upon this as licit, and provides no punishment for so doing, unless the excess be too great, because then even human law demands restitution to be made, for instance if a man be deceived in regard to more than half the amount of the just price of a thing [*Cod. IV, xliv, De Rescind. Vend. 2,8].

On the other hand the Divine law leaves nothing unpunished that is contrary to virtue. Hence, according to the Divine law, it is reckoned unlawful if the equality of justice be not observed in buying and selling: and he who has received more than he ought must make compensation to him that has suffered loss, if the loss be considerable. I add this condition, because the just price of things is not fixed with mathematical precision, but depends on a kind of estimate, so that a slight addition or subtraction would not seem to destroy the equality of justice.

Reply to Objection 2: As Augustine says "this jester, either by looking into himself or by his experience of others, thought that all men are inclined to wish to buy for a song and sell at a premium. But since in reality this is wicked, it is in every man's power to acquire that justice whereby he may resist and overcome this inclination." And then he gives the example of a man who gave the just price for a book to a man who through ignorance asked a low price for it. Hence it is evident that this common desire is not from nature but from vice, wherefore it is common to many who walk along the broad road of sin.

Reply to Objection 3: In commutative justice we consider chiefly real equality. On the other hand, in friendship based on utility we consider equality of usefulness, so that the recompense should depend on the usefulness accruing, whereas in buying it should be equal to the thing bought.

Whether a sale is rendered unlawful through a fault in the thing sold?

Objection 1: It would seem that a sale is not rendered unjust and unlawful through a fault in the thing sold. For less account should be taken of the other parts of a thing than of what belongs to its substance. Yet the sale of a thing does not seem to be rendered unlawful through a fault in its substance: for instance, if a man sell instead of the real metal, silver or gold produced by some chemical process, which is adapted to all the human uses for which silver and gold are necessary, for instance in the making of vessels and the like. Much less therefore will it be an unlawful sale if the thing be defective in other ways.

Objection 2: Further, any fault in the thing, affecting the quantity, would seem chiefly to be opposed to justice which consists in equality. Now quantity is known by being measured: and the measures of things that come into human use are not fixed, but in some places are greater, in others less, as the Philosopher states (*Ethic.* v, 7). Therefore just as it is impossible to avoid defects on the part of the thing sold, it seems that a sale is not rendered unlawful through the thing sold being defective.

Objection 3: Further, the thing sold is rendered defective by lacking a fitting quality. But in order to know the quality of a thing, much knowledge is required that is lacking in most buyers. Therefore a sale is not rendered unlawful by a fault (in the thing sold).

On the contrary, Ambrose says (*De Offic.* iii, 11): "It is manifestly a rule of justice that a good man should not depart from the truth, nor inflict an unjust injury on anyone, nor have any connection with fraud."

I answer that, A threefold fault may be found pertaining to the thing which is sold. One, in respect of the thing's substance: and if the seller be aware of a fault in the thing he is selling, he is guilty of a fraudulent sale, so that the sale is rendered unlawful. Hence we find it written against certain people (Is. 1:22), "Thy silver is turned into dross, thy wine is mingled with water": because that which is mixed is defective in its substance.

Another defect is in respect of quantity which is known by being measured: wherefore if anyone knowingly make use of a faulty measure in selling, he is guilty of fraud, and the sale is illicit. Hence it is written (Dt. 25:13,14): "Thou shalt not have divers weights in thy bag, a greater and a less: neither shall there be in thy house a greater bushel and a less," and further on (Dt. 25:16): "For the Lord . . . abhorreth him that doth these things, and He hateth all injustice."

A third defect is on the part of the quality, for instance, if a man sell an unhealthy animal as being a healthy one: and if anyone do this knowingly he is guilty of a fraudulent sale, and the sale, in consequence, is illicit.

In all these cases not only is the man guilty of a fraudulent sale, but he is also bound to restitution. But if any of the foregoing defects be in the thing sold, and he knows nothing about this, the seller does not sin, because he does that which is unjust materially, nor is his deed unjust, as shown above (Q59, A2). Nevertheless he is bound to compensate the buyer, when the defect comes to his knowledge. Moreover what has been said of the seller applies equally to the buyer. For sometimes it happens that the seller thinks his goods to be specifically of lower value, as when a man sells gold instead of copper, and then if the buyer be aware of this, he buys it unjustly and is bound to restitution: and the same applies to a defect in quantity as to a defect in quality.

Reply to Objection 1: Gold and silver are costly not only on account of the usefulness of the vessels and other like things made from them, but also on account of the excellence and purity of their substance. Hence if the gold or silver produced by alchemists has not the true specific nature of gold and silver, the sale thereof is fraudulent and unjust, especially as real gold and silver can produce certain results by their natural action, which the counterfeit gold and silver of alchemists cannot produce. Thus the true metal has the property of making people joyful, and is helpful medicinally against certain maladies. Moreover real gold can be employed more frequently, and lasts longer in its condition of purity than counterfeit gold. If however real gold were to be produced by alchemy, it would not be unlawful to sell it for the genuine article, for nothing prevents art from employing certain natural causes for the production of natural and true effects, as Augustine says (De Trin. iii, 8) of things produced by the art of the demons.

Reply to Objection 2: The measures of salable commodities must needs be different in different places, on account of the difference of supply: because where there is greater abundance, the measures are wont to be larger. However in each place those who govern the state must determine the just measures of things salable, with due consideration for the conditions of place and time. Hence it is not lawful to disregard such measures as are established by public authority or custom.

Reply to Objection 3: As Augustine says (De Civ. Dei xi, 16) the price of things salable does not depend on their degree of nature, since at times a horse fetches a higher price than a slave; but it depends on their usefulness to man. Hence it is not necessary for the seller or buyer to be cognizant of the hidden qualities of the thing sold, but only of such as render the thing adapted to man's use, for instance, that the horse be strong, run well and so forth. Such qualities the seller and buyer can easily discover.

Whether the seller is bound to state the defects of the thing sold?

Objection 1: It would seem that the seller is not bound to state the defects of the thing sold. Since the seller does not bind the buyer to buy, he would seem to leave it to him to judge of the goods offered for sale. Now judgment about a thing and knowledge of that thing belong to the same person. Therefore it does not seem imputable to the seller if the buyer be deceived in his judgment, and be hurried into buying a thing without carefully inquiring into its condition.

Objection 2: Further, it seems foolish for anyone to do what prevents him carrying out his work. But if a man states the defects of the goods he has for sale, he prevents their sale: wherefore Tully (De Offic. iii, 13) pictures a man as saying: "Could anything be more absurd than for a public crier, instructed by the owner, to cry: 'I offer this unhealthy horse for sale?'" Therefore the seller is not bound to state the defects of the thing sold.

Objection 3: Further, man needs more to know the road of virtue than to know the faults of things offered for sale. Now one is not bound to offer advice to all or to tell them the truth about matters pertaining to virtue, though one should not tell anyone what is false. Much less therefore is a seller bound to tell the faults of what he offers for sale, as though he were counseling the buyer.

Objection 4: Further, if one were bound to tell the faults of what one offers for sale, this would only be in order to lower the price. Now sometimes the price would be lowered for some other reason, without any defect in the thing sold: for instance, if the seller carry wheat to a place where wheat fetches a high price, knowing that many will come after him carrying wheat; because if the buyers knew this they would give a lower price. But apparently the seller need not give the buyer this information. Therefore, in like manner, neither need he tell him the faults of the goods he is selling.

On the contrary, Ambrose says (*De Offic.* iii, 10): "In all contracts the defects of the salable commodity must be stated; and unless the seller make them known, although the buyer has already acquired a right to them, the contract is voided on account of the fraudulent action."

I answer that, It is always unlawful to give anyone an occasion of danger or loss, although a man need not always give another the help or counsel which would be for his advantage in any way; but only in certain fixed cases, for instance when someone is subject to him, or when he is the only one who can assist him. Now the seller who offers goods for sale, gives the buyer an occasion of loss or danger, by the very fact that he offers him defective goods, if such defect may occasion loss or danger to the buyer—loss, if, by reason of this defect, the goods are of less value, and he takes nothing off the price on that account—danger, if this defect either hinder the use of the goods or render it hurtful, for instance, if a man sells a lame for a fleet horse, a tottering house for a safe one, rotten or poisonous food for wholesome. Wherefore if such like defects be hidden, and the seller does not make them known, the sale will be illicit and fraudulent, and the seller will be bound to compensation for the loss incurred.

On the other hand, if the defect be manifest, for instance if a horse have but one eye, or if the goods though useless to the buyer, be useful to someone else, provided the seller take as much as he ought from the price, he is not bound to state the defect of the goods, since perhaps on account of that defect the buyer might want him to allow a greater rebate than he need. Wherefore the seller may look to his own indemnity, by withholding the defect of the goods.

Reply to Objection 1: Judgment cannot be pronounced save on what is manifest: for "a man judges of what he knows" (*Ethic.* i, 3). Hence if the defects of the goods offered for sale be hidden, judgment of them is not sufficiently left with the buyer unless such defects be made known to him. The case would be different if the defects were manifest.

Reply to Objection 2: There is no need to publish beforehand by the public crier the defects of the goods one is offering for sale, because if he were to begin by announcing its defects, the bidders would be frightened to buy, through ignorance of other qualities that might render the thing good and serviceable. Such defect ought to be stated to each individual that offers to buy: and then he will be able to compare the various points one with the other, the good with the bad: for nothing prevents that which is defective in one respect being useful in many others.

Reply to Objection 3: Although a man is not bound strictly speaking to tell everyone the truth about matters pertaining to virtue, yet he is so bound in a case when, unless he tells the truth, his conduct would endanger another man in detriment to virtue: and so it is in this case.

Reply to Objection 4: The defect in a thing makes it of less value now than it seems to be: but in the case cited, the goods are expected to be of less value at a future time, on account of the arrival of other merchants, which was not foreseen by the buyers. Wherefore the seller, since he sells his goods at the price actually offered him, does not seem to act contrary to justice through not stating what is going to happen. If however he were to do so, or if he lowered his price, it would be exceedingly virtuous on his part: although he does not seem to be bound to do this as a debt of justice.

Whether, in trading, it is lawful to sell a thing at a higher price than what was paid for it?

Objection 1: It would seem that it is not lawful, in trading, to sell a thing for a higher price than we paid for it. For Chrysostom [*Hom.* xxxviii in the *Opus Imperfectum,* falsely ascribed to St. John Chrysostom] says on Mt. 21:12: "He that buys a thing in order that he may sell it, entire and unchanged, at a profit, is the trader who is cast out of God's temple." Cassiodorus speaks in the same sense in his commentary on Ps. 70:15, "Because I have not known learning, or trading" according to another version [*The Septuagint]: "What is trade," says he, "but buying at a cheap price with the purpose of retailing at a higher price?" and he adds: "Such were the tradesmen whom Our Lord cast out of the temple." Now no man is cast out of the temple except for a sin. Therefore such like trading is sinful.

Objection 2: Further, it is contrary to justice to sell goods at a higher price than their worth, or to buy them for less than their value, as shown above (A1). Now if you sell a thing for a higher price than you paid for it, you must either have bought it for less than its value, or sell it for more than its value. Therefore this cannot be done without sin.

Objection 3: Further, Jerome says (*Ep. ad Nepot.* lii): "Shun, as you would the plague, a cleric who from being poor has become wealthy, or who, from being a nobody has become a celebrity." Now trading would not seem to be forbidden to clerics except on account of its sinfulness. Therefore it is a sin in trading, to buy at a low price and to sell at a higher price.

On the contrary, Augustine commenting on Ps. 70:15, "Because I have not known learning," [*Cf. OBJ 1] says: "The greedy tradesman blasphemes over his losses; he lies and perjures himself over the price of his wares. But these are vices of the man, not of the craft, which can be exercised without these vices." Therefore trading is not in itself unlawful.

I answer that, A tradesman is one whose business consists in the exchange of things. According to the Philosopher (*Polit.* i, 3), exchange of things is twofold; one, natural as it were, and necessary, whereby one commodity is exchanged for another, or money taken in exchange for a commodity, in order to satisfy the needs of life. Such like trading, properly speaking, does not belong to tradesmen, but rather to housekeepers or civil servants who have to provide the household or the state with the necessaries of life. The other kind of exchange is either that of money for money, or of any commodity for money, not on account of the necessities of life, but for profit, and this kind of exchange, properly speaking, regards tradesmen, according to the Philosopher (*Polit.* i, 3). The former kind of exchange is commendable because it supplies a natural need: but the latter is justly deserving of blame, because, considered in itself, it satisfies the greed for gain, which knows no limit and tends to infinity. Hence trading, considered in itself, has a certain debasement attaching thereto, in so far as, by its very nature, it does not imply a virtuous or necessary end. Nevertheless gain which is the end of trading, though not implying, by its nature, anything virtuous or necessary, does not, in itself, connote anything sinful or contrary to virtue: wherefore nothing prevents gain from being directed to some necessary or even virtuous end, and thus trading becomes lawful. Thus, for instance, a man may intend the moderate gain which he seeks to acquire by trading for the upkeep of his household, or for the assistance of the needy: or again, a man may take to trade for some public advantage, for instance, lest his country lack the necessaries of life, and seek gain, not as an end, but as payment for his labor.

Reply to Objection 1: The saying of Chrysostom refers to the trading which seeks gain as a last end. This is especially the case where a man sells something at a higher price without its undergoing any change. For if he sells at a higher price something that has changed for the better, he would seem to receive the reward of his labor. Nevertheless the gain itself may be lawfully intended, not as a last end, but for the sake of some other end which is necessary or virtuous, as stated above.

Reply to Objection 2: Not everyone that sells at a higher price than he bought is a tradesman, but only he who buys that he may sell at a profit. If, on the contrary, he buys not for sale but for possession, and afterwards, for some reason wishes to sell, it is not a trade transaction even if he sell at a profit. For he may lawfully do this, either because he has bettered the thing, or because the value of the thing has changed with the change of place or time, or on account of the danger he incurs in transferring the thing from one place to another, or again in having it carried by another. In this sense neither buying nor selling is unjust.

Reply to Objection 3: Clerics should abstain not only from things that are evil in themselves, but even from those that have an appearance of evil. This happens in trading, both because it is directed to worldly gain, which clerics should despise, and because trading is open to so many vices, since "a merchant is hardly free from sins of the lips" [★'A merchant is hardly free from negligence, and a huckster shall not be justified from the sins of the lips'] (Ecclus. 26:28). There is also another reason, because trading engages the mind too much with worldly cares, and consequently withdraws it from spiritual cares; wherefore the Apostle says (2 Tim. 2:4): "No man being a soldier to God entangleth himself with secular businesses." Nevertheless it is lawful for clerics to engage in the first mentioned kind of exchange, which is directed to supply the necessaries of life, either by buying or by selling.

QUESTION 78
OF THE SIN OF USURY

Whether it is a sin to take usury for money lent?

Objection 1: It would seem that it is not a sin to take usury for money lent. For no man sins through following the example of Christ. But Our Lord said of Himself (Lk. 19:23): "At My coming I might have exacted it," i.e. the money lent, "with usury." Therefore it is not a sin to take usury for lending money.

Objection 2: Further, according to Ps. 18:8, "The law of the Lord is unspotted," because, to wit, it forbids sin. Now usury of a kind is allowed in the Divine law, according to Dt. 23:19,20: "Thou shalt not fenerate to thy brother money, nor corn, nor any other thing, but to the stranger": nay more, it is even promised as a reward for the observance of the Law, according to Dt. 28:12: "Thou shalt fenerate★ to many nations, and shalt not borrow of any one." [★'Faeneraberis'—'Thou shalt lend upon usury.' The Douay version has simply 'lend.' The objection lays stress on the word 'faeneraberis': hence the necessity of rendering it by 'fenerate.'] Therefore it is not a sin to take usury.

Objection 3: Further, in human affairs justice is determined by civil laws. Now civil law allows usury to be taken. Therefore it seems to be lawful.

Objection 4: Further, the counsels are not binding under sin. But, among other counsels we find (Lk. 6:35): "Lend, hoping for nothing thereby." Therefore it is not a sin to take usury.

Objection 5: Further, it does not seem to be in itself sinful to accept a price for doing what one is not bound to do. But one who has money is not bound in every case to lend it to his neighbor. Therefore it is lawful for him sometimes to accept a price for lending it.

Objection 6: Further, silver made into coins does not differ specifically from silver made into a vessel. But it is lawful to accept a price for the loan of a silver vessel. Therefore it is also lawful to accept a price for the loan of a silver coin. Therefore usury is not in itself a sin.

Objection 7: Further, anyone may lawfully accept a thing which its owner freely gives him. Now he who accepts the loan, freely gives the usury. Therefore he who lends may lawfully take the usury.

On the contrary, It is written (Ex. 22:25): "If thou lend money to any of thy people that is poor, that dwelleth with thee, thou shalt not be hard upon them as an extortioner, nor oppress them with usuries."

I answer that, To take usury for money lent is unjust in itself, because this is to sell what does not exist, and this evidently leads to inequality which is contrary to justice. In order to make this evident, we must observe that there are certain things the use of which consists in their consumption: thus we consume wine when we use it for drink and we consume wheat when we use it for food. Wherefore in such like things the use of the thing must not be reckoned apart from the thing itself, and whoever is granted the use of the thing, is granted the thing itself and for this reason, to lend things of this kin is to transfer the ownership. Accordingly if a man wanted to sell wine separately from the use of the wine, he would be selling the same thing twice, or he would be selling what does not exist, wherefore he would evidently commit a sin of injustice. In like manner he commits an injustice who lends wine or wheat, and asks for double payment, viz. one, the return of the thing in equal measure, the other, the price of the use, which is called usury.

On the other hand, there are things the use of which does not consist in their consumption: thus to use a house is to dwell in it, not to destroy it. Wherefore in such things both may be granted: for instance, one man may hand over to another the ownership of his house while reserving to himself the use of it for a time, or vice versa, he may grant the use of the house, while retaining the ownership. For this reason a man may lawfully make a charge for the use of his house, and, besides this, revendicate the house from the person to whom he has granted its use, as happens in renting and letting a house.

Now money, according to the Philosopher (*Ethic.* v, 5; *Polit.* i, 3) was invented chiefly for the purpose of exchange: and consequently the proper and principal use of money is its consumption or alienation whereby it is sunk in exchange. Hence it is by its very nature unlawful to take payment for the use of money lent, which payment is known as usury: and just as a man is bound to restore other ill-gotten goods, so is he bound to restore the money which he has taken in usury.

Reply to Objection 1: In this passage usury must be taken figuratively for the increase of spiritual goods which God exacts from us, for He wishes us ever to advance in the goods which we receive from Him: and this is for our own profit not for His.

Reply to Objection 2: The Jews were forbidden to take usury from their

103

brethren, i.e. from other Jews. By this we are given to understand that to take usury from any man is evil simply, because we ought to treat every man as our neighbor and brother, especially in the state of the Gospel, whereto all are called. Hence it is said without any distinction in Ps. 14:5: "He that hath not put out his money to usury," and (Ezech. 18:8): "Who hath not taken usury [*Vulg.: 'If a man . . . hath not lent upon money, nor taken any increase . . . he is just.']." They were permitted, however, to take usury from foreigners, not as though it were lawful, but in order to avoid a greater evil, lest, to wit, through avarice to which they were prone according to Is. 56:11, they should take usury from the Jews who were worshippers of God.

Where we find it promised to them as a reward, "Thou shalt fenerate to many nations," etc., fenerating is to be taken in a broad sense for lending, as in Ecclus. 29:10, where we read: "Many have refused to fenerate, not out of wickedness," i.e. they would not lend. Accordingly the Jews are promised in reward an abundance of wealth, so that they would be able to lend to others.

Reply to Objection 3: Human laws leave certain things unpunished, on account of the condition of those who are imperfect, and who would be deprived of many advantages, if all sins were strictly forbidden and punishments appointed for them. Wherefore human law has permitted usury, not that it looks upon usury as harmonizing with justice, but lest the advantage of many should be hindered. Hence it is that in civil law [*Inst. II, iv, de Usufructu] it is stated that "those things according to natural reason and civil law which are consumed by being used, do not admit of usufruct," and that "the senate did not (nor could it) appoint a usufruct to such things, but established a quasi-usufruct," namely by permitting usury. Moreover the Philosopher, led by natural reason, says (*Polit.* i, 3) that "to make money by usury is exceedingly unnatural."

Reply to Objection 4: A man is not always bound to lend, and for this reason it is placed among the counsels. Yet it is a matter of precept not to seek profit by lending: although it may be called a matter of counsel in comparison with the maxims of the Pharisees, who deemed some kinds of usury to be lawful, just as love of one's enemies is a matter of counsel. Or again, He speaks here not of the hope of usurious gain, but of the hope which is put in man. For we ought not to lend or do any good deed through hope in man, but only through hope in God.

Reply to Objection 5: He that is not bound to lend, may accept repayment for what he has done, but he must not exact more. Now he is repaid according to equality of justice if he is repaid as much as he lent. Wherefore if he exacts more for the usufruct of a thing which has no other use but the consumption of its substance, he exacts a price of something non-existent: and so his exaction is unjust.

Reply to Objection 6: The principal use of a silver vessel is not its consumption, and so one may lawfully sell its use while retaining one's ownership of it.

104

On the other hand the principal use of silver money is sinking it in exchange, so that it is not lawful to sell its use and at the same time expect the restitution of the amount lent. It must be observed, however, that the secondary use of silver vessels may be an exchange, and such use may not be lawfully sold. In like manner there may be some secondary use of silver money; for instance, a man might lend coins for show, or to be used as security.

Reply to Objection 7: He who gives usury does not give it voluntarily simply, but under a certain necessity, in so far as he needs to borrow money which the owner is unwilling to lend without usury.

Whether it is lawful to ask for any other kind of consideration for money lent?

Objection 1: It would seem that one may ask for some other kind of consideration for money lent. For everyone may lawfully seek to indemnify himself. Now sometimes a man suffers loss through lending money. Therefore he may lawfully ask for or even exact something else besides the money lent.

Objection 2: Further, as stated in *Ethic.* v, 5, one is in duty bound by a point of honor, to repay anyone who has done us a favor. Now to lend money to one who is in straits is to do him a favor for which he should be grateful. Therefore the recipient of a loan, is bound by a natural debt to repay something. Now it does not seem unlawful to bind oneself to an obligation of the natural law. Therefore it is not unlawful, in lending money to anyone, to demand some sort of compensation as condition of the loan.

Objection 3: Further, just as there is real remuneration, so is there verbal remuneration, and remuneration by service, as a gloss says on Is. 33:15, "Blessed is he that shaketh his hands from all bribes [★Vulg.: 'Which of you shall dwell with everlasting burnings? . . . He that shaketh his hands from all bribes.']." Now it is lawful to accept service or praise from one to whom one has lent money. Therefore in like manner it is lawful to accept any other kind of remuneration.

Objection 4: Further, seemingly the relation of gift to gift is the same as of loan to loan. But it is lawful to accept money for money given. Therefore it is lawful to accept repayment by loan in return for a loan granted.

Objection 5: Further, the lender, by transferring his ownership of a sum of money removes the money further from himself than he who entrusts it to a merchant or craftsman. Now it is lawful to receive interest for money entrusted to a merchant or craftsman. Therefore it is also lawful to receive interest for money lent.

Objection 6: Further, a man may accept a pledge for money lent, the use of which pledge he might sell for a price: as when a man mortgages his land or the house wherein he dwells. Therefore it is lawful to receive interest for money lent.

Objection 7: Further, it sometimes happens that a man raises the price of his goods under guise of loan, or buys another's goods at a low figure; or raises his price through delay in being paid, and lowers his price that he may be paid the sooner. Now in all these cases there seems to be payment for a loan of money: nor does it appear to be manifestly illicit. Therefore it seems to be lawful to expect or exact some consideration for money lent.

On the contrary, Among other conditions requisite in a just man it is stated (Ezech. 18:17) that he "hath not taken usury and increase."

I answer that, According to the Philosopher (*Ethic.* iv, 1), a thing is reckoned as money "if its value can be measured by money." Consequently, just as it is a sin against justice, to take money, by tacit or express agreement, in return for lending money or anything else that is consumed by being used, so also is it a like sin, by tacit or express agreement to receive anything whose price can be measured by money. Yet there would be no sin in receiving something of the kind, not as exacting it, nor yet as though it were due on account of some agreement tacit or expressed, but as a gratuity: since, even before lending the money, one could accept a gratuity, nor is one in a worse condition through lending.

On the other hand it is lawful to exact compensation for a loan, in respect of such things as are not appreciated by a measure of money, for instance, benevolence, and love for the lender, and so forth.

Reply to Objection 1: A lender may without sin enter an agreement with the borrower for compensation for the loss he incurs of something he ought to have, for this is not to sell the use of money but to avoid a loss. It may also happen that the borrower avoids a greater loss than the lender incurs, wherefore the borrower may repay the lender with what he has gained. But the lender cannot enter an agreement for compensation, through the fact that he makes no profit out of his money: because he must not sell that which he has not yet and may be prevented in many ways from having.

Reply to Objection 2: Repayment for a favor may be made in two ways. In one way, as a debt of justice; and to such a debt a man may be bound by a fixed contract; and its amount is measured according to the favor received. Wherefore the borrower of money or any such thing the use of which is its consumption is not bound to repay more than he received in loan: and consequently it is against justice if he be obliged to pay back more. In another way a man's obligation to repayment for favor received is based on a debt of friendship, and the nature of this debt depends more on the feeling with which the favor was conferred than on the greatness of the favor itself. This debt does not carry with it a civil obligation, involving a kind of necessity that would exclude the spontaneous nature of such a repayment.

Reply to Objection 3: If a man were, in return for money lent, as though there had been an agreement tacit or expressed, to expect or exact repayment in the shape of some remuneration of service or words, it would be the same as if he expected or exacted some real remuneration, because both can be priced at a money value, as may be seen in the case of those who offer for hire the labor which they exercise by work or by tongue. If on the other hand the remuneration by service or words be given not as an obligation, but as a favor, which is not to be appreciated at a money value, it is lawful to take, exact, and expect it.

Reply to Objection 4: Money cannot be sold for a greater sum than the amount lent, which has to be paid back: nor should the loan be made with a demand or expectation of aught else but of a feeling of benevolence which cannot be priced at a pecuniary value, and which can be the basis of a spontaneous loan. Now the obligation to lend in return at some future time is repugnant to such a feeling, because again an obligation of this kind has its pecuniary value. Consequently it is lawful for the lender to borrow something else at the same time, but it is unlawful for him to bind the borrower to grant him a loan at some future time.

Reply to Objection 5: He who lends money transfers the ownership of the money to the borrower. Hence the borrower holds the money at his own risk and is bound to pay it all back: wherefore the lender must not exact more. On the other hand he that entrusts his money to a merchant or craftsman so as to form a kind of society, does not transfer the ownership of his money to them, for it remains his, so that at his risk the merchant speculates with it, or the craftsman uses it for his craft, and consequently he may lawfully demand as something belonging to him, part of the profits derived from his money.

Reply to Objection 6: If a man in return for money lent to him pledges something that can be valued at a price, the lender must allow for the use of that thing towards the repayment of the loan. Else if he wishes the gratuitous use of that thing in addition to repayment, it is the same as if he took money for lending, and that is usury, unless perhaps it were such a thing as friends are wont to lend to one another gratis, as in the case of the loan of a book.

Reply to Objection 7: If a man wish to sell his goods at a higher price than that which is just, so that he may wait for the buyer to pay, it is manifestly a case of usury: because this waiting for the payment of the price has the character of a loan, so that whatever he demands beyond the just price in consideration of this delay, is like a price for a loan, which pertains to usury. In like manner if a buyer wishes to buy goods at a lower price than what is just, for the reason that he pays for the goods before they can be delivered, it is a sin of usury; because again this anticipated payment of money has the character of a loan, the price of which is the rebate on the just price of the goods sold. On the other hand if a man wishes to allow a rebate on the just price in order that he may have his money sooner, he is not guilty of the sin of usury.

QUESTION 100
ON SIMONY

Whether simony is an intentional will to buy or sell something spiritual or connected with a spiritual thing?

Objection 1: It would seem that simony is not "an express will to buy or sell something spiritual or connected with a spiritual thing." Simony is heresy, since it is written (I, qu. i [*Can. *Eos qui per pecunias.*]): "The impious heresy of Macedonius and of those who with him impugned the Holy Ghost, is more endurable than that of those who are guilty of simony: since the former in their ravings maintained that the Holy Spirit of Father and Son is a creature and the slave of God, whereas the latter make the same Holy Spirit to be their own slave. For every master sells what he has just as he wills, whether it be his slave or any other of his possessions." But unbelief, like faith, is an act not of the will but of the intellect, as shown above (Q10, A2). Therefore simony should not be defined as an act of the will.

Objection 2: Further, to sin intentionally is to sin through malice, and this is to sin against the Holy Ghost. Therefore, if simony is an intentional will to sin, it would seem that it is always a sin against the Holy Ghost.

Objection 3: Further, nothing is more spiritual than the kingdom of heaven. But it is lawful to buy the kingdom of heaven: for Gregory says in a homily (v, *in Ev.*): "The kingdom of heaven is worth as much as you possess." Therefore simony does not consist in a will to buy something spiritual.

Objection 4: Further, simony takes its name from Simon the magician, of whom we read (Acts 8:18,19) that "he offered the apostles money" that he might buy a spiritual power, in order, to wit, "that on whomsoever he imposed his hand they might receive the Holy Ghost." But we do not read that he wished to sell anything. Therefore simony is not the will to sell a spiritual thing.

Objection 5: Further, there are many other voluntary commutations besides buying and selling, such as exchange and transaction [*A kind of legal compromise—*Oxford Dictionary*]. Therefore it would seem that simony is defined insufficiently.

Objection 6: Further, anything connected with spiritual things is itself spiritual. Therefore it is superfluous to add "or connected with spiritual things."

Objection 7: Further, according to some, the Pope cannot commit simony: yet he can buy or sell something spiritual. Therefore simony is not the will to buy or sell something spiritual or connected with a spiritual thing.

On the contrary, Gregory VII says (*Regist.* [*Caus. I, qu. i, can. *Presbyter,* qu. iii, can. *Altare*]): "None of the faithful is ignorant that buying or selling altars, tithes, or the Holy Ghost is the heresy of simony."

I answer that, As stated above (FS, Q18, A2) an act is evil generically when it bears on undue matter. Now a spiritual thing is undue matter for buying and selling for three reasons. First, because a spiritual thing cannot be appraised at any earthly price, even as it is said concerning wisdom (Prov. 3:15), "she is more precious than all riches, and all things that are desired, are not to be compared with her": and for this reason Peter, in condemning the wickedness of Simon in its very source, said (Acts 8:20): "Keep thy money to thyself to perish with thee, because thou hast thought that the gift of God may be purchased with money."

Secondly, because a thing cannot be due matter for sale if the vendor is not the owner thereof, as appears from the authority quoted (Objection 1). Now ecclesiastical superiors are not owners, but dispensers of spiritual things, according to 1 Cor. 4:1, "Let a man so account of us as of the ministers of Christ, and the dispensers of the ministers of God."

Thirdly, because sale is opposed to the source of spiritual things, since they flow from the gratuitous will of God. Wherefore Our Lord said (Mt. 10:8): "Freely have you received, freely give."

Therefore by buying or selling a spiritual thing, a man treats God and divine things with irreverence, and consequently commits a sin of irreligion.

Reply to Objection 1: Just as religion consists in a kind of protestation of faith, without, sometimes, faith being in one's heart, so too the vices opposed to religion include a certain protestation of unbelief without, sometimes, unbelief being in the mind. Accordingly simony is said to be a "heresy," as regards the outward protestation, since by selling a gift of the Holy Ghost a man declares, in a way, that he is the owner of a spiritual gift; and this is heretical. It must, however, be observed that Simon Magus, besides wishing the apostles to sell him a grace of the Holy Ghost for money, said that the world was not created by God, but by some heavenly power, as Isidore states (*Etym.* viii, 5): and so for this reason simoniacs are reckoned with other heretics, as appears from Augustine's book on heretics.

Reply to Objection 2: As stated above (Q58, A4), justice, with all its parts, and consequently all the opposite vices, is in the will as its subject. Hence simony is fittingly defined from its relation to the will. This act is furthermore described as "express," in order to signify that it proceeds from choice, which takes the principal part in virtue and vice. Nor does everyone sin against the Holy Ghost that sins from choice, but only he who chooses sin through contempt of those things whereby man is wont to be withdrawn from sin, as stated above (Q14, A1).

Reply to Objection 3: The kingdom of heaven is said to be bought when a man gives what he has for God's sake. But this is to employ the term "buying" in a wide sense, and as synonymous with merit: nor does it reach to the perfect signification of buying, both because neither "the sufferings of this time," nor any gift or deed of ours, "are worthy to be compared with the glory to come, that shall be revealed in us" (Rm. 8:18), and because merit consists chiefly, not in an outward gift, action or passion, but in an inward affection.

109

Reply to Objection 4: Simon the magician wished to buy a spiritual power in order that afterwards he might sell it. For it is written (I, qu. iii [*Can. *Salvator*]), that "Simon the magician wished to buy the gift of the Holy Ghost, in order that he might make money by selling the signs to be wrought by him." Hence those who sell spiritual things are likened in intention to Simon the magician: while those who wish to buy them are likened to him in act. Those who sell them imitate, in act, Giezi the disciple of Eliseus, of whom we read (4 Kgs. 5:20-24) that he received money from the leper who was healed: wherefore the sellers of spiritual things may be called not only "simoniacs" but also "giezites."

Reply to Objection 5: The terms "buying" and "selling" cover all kinds of non-gratuitous contracts. Wherefore it is impossible for the exchange or agency of prebends or ecclesiastical benefices to be made by authority of the parties concerned without danger of committing simony, as laid down by law [*Cap. *Quaesitum, de rerum Permutat.*; cap. *Super, de Transact.*]. Nevertheless the superior, in virtue of his office, can cause these exchanges to be made for useful or necessary reasons.

Reply to Objection 6: Even as the soul lives by itself, while the body lives through being united to the soul; so, too, certain things are spiritual by themselves, such as the sacraments and the like, while others are called spiritual, through adhering to those others. Hence (I, qu. iii, cap. *Siquis objecerit*) it is stated that "spiritual things do not progress without corporal things, even as the soul has no bodily life without the body."

Reply to Objection 7: The Pope can be guilty of the vice of simony, like any other man, since the higher a man's position the more grievous is his sin. For although the possessions of the Church belong to him as dispenser in chief, they are not his as master and owner. Therefore, were he to accept money from the income of any church in exchange for a spiritual thing, he would not escape being guilty of the vice of simony. In like manner he might commit simony by accepting from a layman moneys not belonging to the goods of the Church.

Whether it is always unlawful to give money for the sacraments?

Objection 1: It would seem that it is not always unlawful to give money for the sacraments. Baptism is the door of the sacraments, as we shall state in the TP, Q68, A6; TP, Q73, A3. But seemingly it is lawful in certain cases to give money for Baptism, for instance if a priest were unwilling to baptize a dying child without being paid. Therefore it is not always unlawful to buy or sell the sacraments.

Objection 2: Further, the greatest of the sacraments is the Eucharist, which is consecrated in the Mass. But some priests receive a prebend or money for singing masses. Much more therefore is it lawful to buy or sell the other sacraments.

Objection 3: Further, the sacrament of Penance is a necessary sacrament consisting chiefly in the absolution. But some persons demand money when absolving from excommunication. Therefore it is not always unlawful to buy or sell a sacrament.

Objection 4: Further, custom makes that which otherwise were sinful to be not sinful; thus Augustine says (*Contra Faust.* xxii, 47) that "it was no crime to have several wives, so long as it was the custom." Now it is the custom in some places to give something in the consecration of bishops, blessings of abbots, ordinations of the clergy, in exchange for the chrism, holy oil, and so forth. Therefore it would seem that it is not unlawful.

Objection 5: Further, it happens sometimes that someone maliciously hinders a person from obtaining a bishopric or some like dignity. But it is lawful for a man to make good his grievance. Therefore it is lawful, seemingly, in such a case to give money for a bishopric or a like ecclesiastical dignity.

Objection 6: Further, marriage is a sacrament. But sometimes money is given for marriage. Therefore it is lawful to sell a sacrament.

On the contrary, It is written (I, qu. i [*Can. *Qui per pecunias*]): "Whosoever shall consecrate anyone for money, let him be cut off from the priesthood."

I answer that, The sacraments of the New Law are of all things most spiritual, inasmuch as they are the cause of spiritual grace, on which no price can be set, and which is essentially incompatible with a non-gratuitous giving. Now the sacraments are dispensed through the ministers of the Church, whom the people are bound to support, according to the words of the Apostle (1 Cor. 9:13), "Know you not, that they who work in the holy place, eat the things that are of the holy place; and they that serve the altar, partake with the altar?"

Accordingly we must answer that to receive money for the spiritual grace of the sacraments, is the sin of simony, which cannot be excused by any custom whatever, since "custom does not prevail over natural or divine law" [*Cap. *Cum tanto, de Consuetud.*; cf. FS, Q97, A3]. Now by money we are to understand anything that has a pecuniary value, as the Philosopher states (*Ethic.* iv, 1). On the other hand, to receive anything for the support of those who administer the sacraments, in accordance with the statutes of the Church and approved customs, is not simony, nor is it a sin. For it is received not as a price of goods, but as a payment for their need. Hence a gloss of Augustine on 1 Tim. 5:17, "Let the priests that rule well," says: "They should look to the people for a supply to their need, but to the Lord for the reward of their ministry."

Reply to Objection 1: In a case of necessity anyone may baptize. And since nowise ought one to sin, if the priest be unwilling to baptize without being paid, one must act as though there were no priest available for the baptism. Hence the person who is in charge of the child can, in such a case, lawfully baptize it, or cause it to be baptized by anyone else. He could, however, lawfully buy the water from the priest, because it is merely a bodily element. But if it were an adult in danger of death that wished to be baptized, and the priest were unwilling to baptize him without being paid, he ought, if possible, to be baptized by someone else. And if he is unable to have recourse to another, he must by no means pay a price for Baptism, and should rather die without being baptized, because for him the baptism of desire would supply the lack of the sacrament.

Reply to Objection 2: The priest receives money, not as the price for consecrating the Eucharist, or for singing the Mass (for this would be simoniacal), but as payment for his livelihood, as stated above.

Reply to Objection 3: The money exacted of the person absolved is not the price of his absolution (for this would be simoniacal), but a punishment of a past crime for which he was excommunicated.

Reply to Objection 4: As stated above, "custom does not prevail over natural or divine law" whereby simony is forbidden. Wherefore the custom, if such there be, of demanding anything as the price of a spiritual thing, with the intention of buying or selling it, is manifestly simoniacal, especially when the demand is made of a person unwilling to pay. But if the demand be made in payment of a stipend recognized by custom it is not simoniacal, provided there be no intention of buying or selling, but only of doing what is customary, and especially if the demand be acceded to voluntarily. In all these cases, however, one must beware of anything having an appearance of simony or avarice, according to the saying of the Apostle (1 Thess. 5:22), "From all appearance of evil restrain yourselves."

Reply to Objection 5: It would be simoniacal to buy off the opposition of one's rivals, before acquiring the right to a bishopric or any dignity or prebend, by election, appointment or presentation, since this would be to use money as a means of obtaining a spiritual thing. But it is lawful to use money as a means of removing unjust opposition, after one has already acquired that right.

Reply to Objection 6: Some [*Innocent IV on Cap. *Cum in Ecclesia, de Simonia*] say that it is lawful to give money for Matrimony because no grace is conferred thereby. But this is not altogether true, as we shall state in the Third Part of the work [*XP, Q42, A3]. Wherefore we must reply that Matrimony is not only a sacrament of the Church, but also an office of nature. Consequently it is lawful to give money for Matrimony considered as an office of nature, but unlawful if it be considered as a sacrament of the Church. Hence, according to the law [*Cap. *Cum in Ecclesia, de Simonia*], it is forbidden to demand anything for the Nuptial Blessing.

Whether it is lawful to give and receive money for spiritual actions?

Objection 1: It seems that it is lawful to give and receive money for spiritual actions. The use of prophecy is a spiritual action. But something used to be given of old for the use of prophecy, as appears from 1 Kgs. 9:7,8, and 3 Kgs.

14:3. Therefore it would seem that it is lawful to give and receive money for a spiritual action.

Objection 2: Further, prayer, preaching, divine praise, are most spiritual actions. Now money is given to holy persons in order to obtain the assistance of their prayers, according to Lk. 16:9, "Make unto you friends of the mammon of iniquity." To preachers also, who sow spiritual things, temporal things are due according to the Apostle (1 Cor. 9:14). Moreover, something is given to those who celebrate the divine praises in the ecclesiastical office, and make processions: and sometimes an annual income is assigned to them. Therefore it is lawful to receive something for spiritual actions.

Objection 3: Further, science is no less spiritual than power. Now it is lawful to receive money for the use of science: thus a lawyer may sell his just advocacy, a physician his advice for health, and a master the exercise of his teaching. Therefore in like manner it would seem lawful for a prelate to receive something for the use of his spiritual power, for instance, for correction, dispensation, and so forth.

Objection 4: Further, religion is the state of spiritual perfection. Now in certain monasteries something is demanded from those who are received there. Therefore it is lawful to demand something for spiritual things.

On the contrary, It is stated (I, qu. i [*Can. *Quidquid invisibilis*]): "It is absolutely forbidden to make a charge for what is acquired by the consolation of invisible grace, whether by demanding a price or by seeking any kind of return whatever." Now all these spiritual things are acquired through an invisible grace. Therefore it is not lawful to charge a price or return for them.

I answer that, Just as the sacraments are called spiritual, because they confer a spiritual grace, so, too, certain other things are called spiritual, because they flow from spiritual grace and dispose thereto. And yet these things are obtainable through the ministry of men, according to 1 Cor. 9:7, "Who serveth as a soldier at any time at his own charges? Who feedeth the flock, and eateth not of the milk of the flock?" Hence it is simoniacal to sell or buy that which is spiritual in such like actions; but to receive or give something for the support of those who minister spiritual things in accordance with the statutes of the Church and approved customs is lawful, yet in such wise that there be no intention of buying or selling, and that no pressure be brought to bear on those who are unwilling to give, by withholding spiritual things that ought to be administered, for then there would be an appearance of simony. But after the spiritual things have been freely bestowed, then the statutory and customary offerings and other dues may be exacted from those who are unwilling but able to pay, if the superior authorize this to be done.

Reply to Objection 1: As Jerome says in his commentary on Micheas 3:9, certain gifts were freely offered to the good prophets, for their livelihood, but not as a price for the exercise of their gift of prophecy. Wicked prophets, however, abused this exercise by demanding payment for it.

Reply to Objection 2: Those who give alms to the poor in order to obtain from them the assistance of their prayers do not give with the intent of buying their prayers; but by their gratuitous beneficence inspire the poor with the mind to pray for them freely and out of charity. Temporal things are due to the preacher as means for his support, not as a price of the words he preaches. Hence a gloss on 1 Tim. 5:11, "Let the priests that rule well," says: "Their need allows them to receive the wherewithal to live, charity demands that this should be given to them: yet the Gospel is not for sale, nor is a livelihood the object of preaching: for if they sell it for this purpose, they sell a great thing for a contemptible price." In like manner temporal things are given to those who praise God by celebrating the divine office whether for the living or for the dead, not as a price but as a means of livelihood; and the same purpose is fulfilled when alms are received for making processions in funerals. Yet it is simoniacal to do such things by contract, or with the intention of buying or selling. Hence it would be an unlawful ordinance if it were decreed in any church that no procession would take place at a funeral unless a certain sum of money were paid, because such an ordinance would preclude the free granting of pious offices to any person. The ordinance would be more in keeping with the law, if it were decreed that this honor would be accorded to all who gave a certain alms, because this would not preclude its being granted to others. Moreover, the former ordinance has the appearance of an exaction, whereas the latter bears a likeness to a gratuitous remuneration.

Reply to Objection 3: A person to whom a spiritual power is entrusted is bound by virtue of his office to exercise the power entrusted to him in dispensing spiritual things. Moreover, he receives a statutory payment from the funds of the Church as a means of livelihood. Therefore, if he were to accept anything for the exercise of his spiritual power, this would imply, not a hiring of his labor (which he is bound to give, as a duty arising out of the office he has accepted), but a sale of the very use of a spiritual grace. For this reason it is unlawful for him to receive anything for any dispensing whatever, or for allowing someone else to take his duty, or for correcting his subjects, or for omitting to correct them. On the other hand it is lawful for him to receive "procurations," when he visits his subjects, not as a price for correcting them, but as a means of livelihood. He that is possessed of science, without having taken upon himself the obligation of using it for the benefit of others can lawfully receive a price for his learning or advice, since this is not a sale of truth or science, but a hiring of labor. If, on the other hand, he be so bound by virtue of his office, this would amount to a sale of the truth, and consequently he would sin grievously. For instance, those who in certain churches are appointed to instruct the clerics of that church and other poor persons, and are in receipt of an ecclesiastical benefice for so doing, are not allowed to receive anything in return, either for teaching, or for celebrating or omitting any feasts.

Reply to Objection 4: It is unlawful to exact or receive anything as price for entering a monastery: but, in the case of small monasteries, that are unable to support so many persons, it is lawful, while entrance to the monastery is free, to accept something for the support of those who are about to be received into the monastery, if its revenues are insufficient. In like manner it is lawful to be easier in admitting to a monastery a person who has proved his regard for that monastery by the generosity of his alms: just as, on the other hand, it is lawful to incite a person's regard for a monastery by means of temporal benefits, in order that he may thereby be induced to enter the monastery; although it is unlawful to agree to give or receive something for entrance into a monastery (I, qu. ii, cap. *Quam pio*).

For Further Reading

Aquinas, St. Thomas. *Summa Contra Gentiles* (Notre Dame, Ind.: Univ. of Notre Dame Press, 1975).

_____. *Readings in the* Summa Theologiae (Notre Dame, Ind.: University of Notre Dame Press, 1990). Translated by Mark D. Jordon.

Kenny, Anthony, ed. *Aquinas: A Collection of Critical Essays* (Garden City, N.Y.: Doubleday, 1969).

Kretzmann, Norman, and Eleanor Stumpf, eds. *The Cambridge Companion to Aquinas* (Cambridge: Cambridge Univ. Press, 1993).

Langholm, Odd. *Price and Value in the Aristotelian Tradition: A Study in Scholastic Economic Sources* (Bergen: Universitetsforlaget, 1979).

Margin, Christopher. *The Philosophy of Thomas Aquinas* (London: Routledge, 1988).

Nederman, Cary Joseph, and Kate Langdon Forhan, eds. *Medieval Political Theory—A Reader* (New York: Routledge, 1993).

Noonan, John T., Jr. *The Scholastic Analysis of Usury* (Cambridge, Mass.: Harvard Univ. Press, 1957).

Parel, A. "Aquinas' Theory of Property." In *Theories of Property: Aristotle to the Present.* Edited by A. Parel and T. Flanagan (Calgary: Wilfred Laurier Univ. Press, 1979).

Stark, W. "The Contained Economy: An Interpretation of Medieval Economic Thought." In *Pre-Capitalist Economic Thought: Three Modern Interpretations* (New York: Arno Press, 1972).

Weisheipl, James A. *Friar Thomas d'Aquino. His Life, Thought and Works* (Washington, D.C.: Catholic Univ. of America Press, 1983).

ST. THOMAS MORE (1478–1535)

ANYONE READING *Utopia* for the first time is bound to be brought up short by its many "dystopian" practices and by Thomas More's major reservations about the imaginary commonwealth he named "no-place." But More's *Utopia* remains an ingenious literary invention to confront us with the pitfalls of commerce and the pratfalls of certain radical alternatives to it. More sets up the depiction of Utopia in Book II with a shocking history of how the high price of sheep resulted in the ravaging and depopulating of the English countryside. Many farmers driven off once common lands by the "enclosure movement" became vagabonds who ended up branded, enslaved, or hung. As for Utopia, who would have thought it the sort of place where to learn a new trade you would have to switch families or where permission was needed to travel, a rule so strict that after two violations the penalty was enslavement?

Not surprisingly, Utopia is an island—Mandeville remarks that isolation is required for a "frugal and honest society"—but More does not let that shield him from the problem of "utopianism in one country." The Utopian solution to the prospect of hostile neighbors is to convert simple living and efficient work habits into a trade surplus huge enough to finance a mercenary military force. But what happens as technological and product innovations spiral upward in the world market? How will the Utopians keep pace and hold onto their favorable balance of trade? How would they maintain the character of their society if they transform production to cater to the ever new technologies and fickle tastes of consumer societies? How long before Utopia would be a sitting duck?

Utopia is based on a set of simple, uncompromising solutions to problems associated with money, commerce, and private property. If money is the root of all evil, pull up the root; greed and crime will shrivel for want of their object. If the invisibility Plato linked with the first coiner of money, Gyges, ends in tyranny, organize society so that everyone is "under the eyes of all"; public-spiritedness will prevail. If commerce cannot thrive without cluttering our hearts with vain desires, drive out commerce; a Spartan peace of mind will settle in. If private property unfailingly leads to inequality, insecurity, and poverty, abolish it and hold everything but husbands and wives in common; under communism "no man has anything, yet all are rich." More's reaction to his Utopia echoes Aristotle's to the republic of Plato: the communist remedy to commerce is misguided; our social problems run deeper than any distortion by commercial forms. The deeper defectiveness of human nature that Aristotle mentions is identified by More as the deadliest of the "seven deadly sins," pride.

"What is the best social order?" is a whopping, earnest question, but More's writing is playful and jesting. Like the film *Forrest Gump*, *Utopia*, with neither warning nor word to the wise, splices fiction into fact smoothly enough to keep the tease going. The central character of the book, Raphael Hythodaeus—his last name means "well-learned in nonsense"—is introduced as a traveling companion of the Portugese explorer Amerigo Vespucci, much as Gump encounters all the Vietnam and Watergate era Presidents. Hythodaeus reports his experiences with the Utopians as an actual encounter, but More has a ball pulling our leg with the details of how the Utopians try to stymie the "accursed love of gold" with a hilarious, irreverent reworking of Plato's "myth of the metals."

FROM *UTOPIA*

..."Yet surely, my dear More, to tell you candidly my heart's sentiments, it appears to me that wherever you have private property and all men measure all things by cash values, there it is scarcely possible for a commonwealth to have justice or prosperity—unless you think justice exists where all the best things flow into the hands of the worst citizens or prosperity prevails where all is divided among very few—and even they are not altogether well off, while the rest are downright wretched.

"As a result, when in my heart I ponder on the extremely wise and holy institutions of the Utopians, among whom, with very few laws, affairs are ordered so aptly that virtue has its reward, and yet, with equality of distribution, all men have abundance of all things, and then when I contrast with their policies the many nations elsewhere ever making ordinances and yet never one of them achieving good order—nations where whatever a man has acquired he calls his own private property, but where all these laws daily framed are not enough for a man to secure or to defend or even to distinguish from someone else's the goods which each in turn calls his own, a predicament readily attested by the numberless and ever new and interminable lawsuits—when I consider, I repeat, all these facts, I become more partial to Plato and less surprised at his refusal to make laws for those who rejected that legislation which gave to all an equal share in all goods.

"This wise sage, to be sure, easily foresaw that the one and only road to the general welfare lies in the maintenance of equality in all respects. I have my doubts that the latter could ever be preserved where the individual's possessions are his private property. When every man aims at absolute ownership of all the property he can get, be there never so great abundance of goods, it is all shared by a handful who leave the rest in poverty. It generally happens that the one class pre-eminently deserves the lot of the other, for the rich are greedy, unscrupulous, and useless, while the poor are well-behaved, simple, and by their daily industry more beneficial to the commonwealth than to themselves. I am fully persuaded that no just and even distribution of goods can be made and that no happiness can be found in human affairs unless private property is utterly abolished. While it lasts, there will always remain a heavy and inescapable burden of poverty and misfortunes for by far the greatest and by far the best part of mankind.

"I admit that this burden can be lightened to some extent, but I contend that it cannot be removed entirely. A statute might be made that no person should hold more than a certain amount of land and that no person should have a monetary income beyond that permitted by law. Special legislation might be passed to prevent the monarch from being overmighty and the people overweening; likewise, that public offices should not be solicited with gifts, nor be put up for sale, nor require lavish personal expenditures. Otherwise, there arise, first, the temptation to recoup one's expenses by acts of fraud and plunder and, secondly, the necessity of appointing rich men to offices which ought rather to have been administered by wise men. By this type of legislation, I maintain, as sick bodies which are past cure can be kept up by repeated medical treatments, so these evils, too, can be alleviated and made less acute. There is no hope, however, of a cure and a return to a healthy condition as long as each individual is master of his own property. Nay, while you are intent upon the cure of one part, you make worse the malady of the other parts. Thus, the healing of the one member reciprocally breeds the disease of the other as long as nothing can so be added to one as not to be taken away from another."

"But," I ventured, "I am of the contrary opinion. Life cannot be satisfactory where all things are common. How can there be a sufficient supply of goods when each withdraws himself from the labor of production? For the individual does not have the motive of personal gain and he is rendered slothful by trusting to the industry of others. Moreover, when people are goaded by want and yet the individual cannot legally keep as his own what he has gained, must there not be trouble from continual bloodshed and riot? This holds true especially since the authority of magistrates and respect for their office have been eliminated, for how there can be any place for these among men who are all on the same level I cannot even conceive." . . .

Occupations

Agriculture is the one pursuit which is common to all, both men and women, without exception. They are all instructed in it from childhood, partly by principles taught in school, partly by field trips to the farms closer to the city as if for recreation. Here they do not merely look on, but, as opportunity arises for bodily exercise, they do the actual work.

Besides agriculture (which is, as I said, common to all), each is taught one particular craft as his own. This is generally either wool-working or linen-making or masonry or metal-working or carpentry. There is no other pursuit which occupies any number worth mentioning. As for clothes, these are of one and the same pattern throughout the island and down the centuries, though there is a distinction between the sexes and between the single and married. The garments are comely to the eye, convenient for bodily movement, and fit for wear in heat and cold. Each family, I say, does its own tailoring.

Of the other crafts, one is learned by each person, and not the men only, but the women too. The latter as the weaker sex have the lighter occupations and generally work wool and flax. To the men are committed the remaining more laborious crafts. For the most part, each is brought up in his father's craft, for which most have a natural inclination. But if anyone is attracted to another occupation, he is transferred by adoption to a family pursuing that craft for which he has a liking. Care is taken not only by his father but by the authorities, too, that he will be assigned to a grave and honorable householder. Moreover, if anyone after being thoroughly taught one craft desires another also, the same permission is given. Having acquired both, he practices his choice unless the city has more need of the one than of the other.

The chief and almost the only function of the syphogrants is to manage and provide that no one sit idle, but that each apply himself industriously to his trade, and yet that he be not wearied like a beast of burden with constant toil from early morning till late at night. Such wretchedness is worse than the lot of slaves, and yet it is almost everywhere the life of workingmen—except for the Utopians. The latter divide the day and night into twenty-four equal hours and assign only six to work. There are three before noon, after which they go to dinner. After dinner, when they have rested for two hours in the afternoon, they again give three to work and finish up with supper. Counting one o'clock as beginning at midday, they go to bed about eight o'clock, and sleep claims eight hours.

The intervals between the hours of work, sleep, and food are left to every man's discretion, not to waste in revelry or idleness, but to devote the time free from work to some other occupation according to taste. These periods are commonly devoted to intellectual pursuits. For it is their custom that public lectures are daily delivered in the hours before daybreak. Attendance is compulsory only for those who have been specially chosen to devote themselves to learning. A great number of all classes, however, both males and females, flock to hear the lectures, some to one and some to another, according to their natural inclination. But if anyone should prefer to devote this time to his trade, as is the case with many minds which do not reach the level for any of the higher intellectual disciplines, he is not hindered; in fact, he is even praised as useful to the commonwealth.

After supper they spend one hour in recreation, in summer in the gardens, in winter in the common halls in which they have their meals. There they either play music or entertain themselves with conversation. Dice and that kind of foolish and ruinous game they are not acquainted with. They do play two games not unlike chess. The first is a battle of numbers in which one number plunders another. The second is a game in which the vices fight a pitched battle with the virtues. In the latter is exhibited very cleverly, to begin with, both the strife of the vices with one another and their concerted opposition to the virtues; then, what vices are opposed to what virtues, by what forces they assail them openly, by what stratagems they attack them indirectly, by what safeguards the virtues check the power of the vices, by what arts they frustrate their designs; and, finally, by what means the one side gains the victory.

But here, lest you be mistaken, there is one point you must examine more closely. Since they devote but six hours to work, you might possibly think the consequence to be some scarcity of necessities. But so far is this from being the case that the aforesaid time is not only enough but more than enough for a supply of all that is requisite for either the necessity or the convenience of living. This phenomenon you too will understand if you consider how large a part of the population in other countries exists without working. First, there are almost all the women, who constitute half the whole; or, where the women are busy, there as a rule the men are snoring in their stead. Besides, how great and how lazy is the crowd of priests and so-called religious! Add to them all the rich, especially the masters of estates, who are commonly termed

121

gentlemen and noblemen. Reckon with them their retainers—I mean, that whole rabble of good-for-nothing swashbucklers. Finally, join in the lusty and sturdy beggars who make some disease an excuse for idleness. You will certainly find far less numerous than you had supposed those whose labor produces all the articles that mortals require for daily use.

Now estimate how few of those who do work are occupied in essential trades. For, in a society where we make money the standard of everything, it is necessary to practice many crafts which are quite vain and superfluous, ministering only to luxury and licentiousness. Suppose the host of those who now toil were distributed over only as few crafts as the few needs and conveniences demanded by nature. In the great abundance of commodities which must then arise, the prices set on them would be too low for the craftsmen to earn their livelihood by their work. But suppose all those fellows who are now busied with unprofitable crafts, as well as all the lazy and idle throng, any one of whom now consumes as much of the fruits of other men's labors as any two of the workingmen, were all set to work and indeed to useful work. You can easily see how small an allowance of time would be enough and to spare for the production of all that it required by necessity or comfort (or even pleasure, provided it be genuine and natural).

The very experience of Utopia makes the latter clear. In the whole city and its neighborhood, exemption from work is granted to hardly five hundred of the total of men and women whose age and strength make them fit for work. Among them the syphogrants, though legally exempted from work, yet take no advantage of this privilege so that by their example they may the more readily attract the others to work. The same exemption is enjoyed by those whom the people, persuaded by the recommendation of the priests, have given perpetual freedom from labor through the secret vote of the syphogrants so that they may learn thoroughly the various branches of knowledge. But if any of these scholars falsifies the hopes entertained of him, he is reduced to the rank of workingman. On the other hand, not seldom does it happen that a craftsman so industriously employs his spare hours on learning and makes such progress by his diligence that he is relieved of his manual labor and advanced into the class of men of learning. It is out of this company of scholars that they choose ambassadors, priests, tranibors, and finally the governor himself, whom they call in their ancient tongue Barzanes but in their more modern language Ademus.

Nearly all the remaining populace being neither idle nor busied with useless occupations, it is easy to calculate how much good work can be produced in a very few hours. Besides the points mentioned, there is this further convenience that in most of the necessary crafts they do not require as much work as other nations. In the first place the erection or repair of buildings requires the constant labor of so many men elsewhere because what a father has built, his extravagant heir allows gradually to fall into ruin. As a result, what might

122

have been kept up at small cost, his successor is obliged to erect anew at great expense. Further, often even when a house has cost one man a large sum, another is so fastidious that he thinks little of it. When it is neglected and therefore soon becomes dilapidated, he builds a second elsewhere at no less cost. But in the land of the Utopians, where everything has its proper place and the general welfare is carefully regulated, a new home on a new site is a rare event, for not only do they promptly repair any damage, but they even take care to prevent damage. What is the result? With the minimum of labor, buildings last very long, and masons and carpenters sometimes have scarcely anything to do, except that they are set to hew out timber at home and to square and prepare stone meantime so that, if any work be required, a building may the sooner be erected.

In the matter of clothing, too, see how little toil and labor is needed. First, while at work, they are dressed unpretentiously in leather or hide, which lasts for seven years. When they go out in public, they put on a cape to hide their comparatively rough working clothes. This garment is of one color throughout the island and that the natural color. Consequently not only is much less woolen cloth needed than elsewhere, but what they have is much less expensive. On the other hand, since linen cloth is made with less labor, it is more used. In linen cloth only whiteness, in woolen cloth only cleanliness, is considered. No value is set on fineness of thread. So it comes about that, whereas elsewhere one man is not satisfied with four or five woolen coats of different colors and as many silk shirts, and the more fastidious not even with ten, in Utopia a man is content with a single cape, lasting generally for two years. There is no reason, of course, why he should desire more, for if he had them he would not be better fortified against the cold nor appear better dressed in the least.

Wherefore, seeing that they are all busied with useful trades and are satisfied with fewer products from them, it even happens that when there is an abundance of all commodities, they sometimes take out a countless number of people to repair whatever public roads are in bad order. Often, too, when there is nothing even of this kind of work to be done, they announce publicly that there will be fewer hours of work. For the authorities do not keep the citizens against their will at superfluous labor since the constitution of their commonwealth looks in the first place to this sole object: that for all the citizens, as far as the public needs permit, as much time as possible should be withdrawn from the service of the body and devoted to the freedom and culture of the mind. It is in the latter that they deem the happiness of life to consist. . . .

Utopian Travel, [etc.]

Now if any citizens conceive a desire either to visit their friends who reside in another city or to see the place itself, they easily obtain leave from their

123

syphogrants and tranibors, unless some good reason prevents them. Accordingly a party is made up and dispatched carrying a letter from the governor which bears witness to the granting of leave to travel and fixes the day of their return. A wagon is granted them with a public slave to conduct and see to the oxen, but, unless they have women in their company, they dispense with the wagon, regarding it as a burden and hindrance. Throughout their journey, though they carry nothing with them, yet nothing is lacking, for they are at home everywhere. If they stay longer than a day in any place, each practices his trade there and is entertained very courteously by workers in the same trade.

If any person gives himself leave to stray out of his territorial limits and is caught without the governor's certificate, he is treated with contempt, brought back as a runaway, and severely punished. A rash repetition of the offense entails the sentence of slavery.

If anyone is seized with the desire of exploring the country belonging to his own city, he is not forbidden to do so, provided he obtain his father's leave and his wife's consent. In any district of the country to which he comes, he receives no food until he has finished the morning share of the day's work or the labor that is usually performed there before supper. If he keep to this condition, he may go where he pleases within the territory belonging to his city. In this way he will be just as useful to the city as if he were in it.

Now you can see how nowhere is there any license to waste time, nowhere any pretext to evade work—no wine shop, no alehouse, no brothel anywhere, no opportunity for corruption, no lurking hole, no secret meeting place. On the contrary, being under the eyes of all, people are bound either to be performing the usual labor or to be enjoying their leisure in a fashion not without decency. This universal behavior must of necessity lead to an abundance of all commodities. Since the latter are distributed evenly among all, it follows, of course, that no one can be reduced to poverty or beggary.

In the senate at Amaurotum (to which, as I said before, three are sent annually from every city), they first determine what commodity is in plenty in each particular place and again where on the island the crops have been meager. They at once fill up the scarcity of one place by the surplus of another. This service they perform without payment, receiving nothing in return from those to whom they give. Those who have given out of their stock to any particular city without requiring any return from it receive what they lack from another to which they have given nothing. Thus, the whole island is like a single family.

But when they have made sufficient provision for themselves (which they do not consider complete until they have provided for two years to come, on account of the next year's uncertain crop), then they export into other countries, out of their surplus, a great quantity of grain, honey, wool, linen, timber,

124

scarlet and purple dyestuffs, hides, wax, tallow, leather, as well as livestock. Of all these commodities they bestow the seventh part on the poor of the district and sell the rest at a moderate price.

By this trade they bring into their country not only such articles as they lack themselves—and practically the only thing lacking is iron—but also a great quantity of silver and gold. This exchange has gone on day by day so long that now they have everywhere an abundance of these metals, more than would be believed. In consequence, they now care little whether they sell for ready cash or appoint a future day for payment, and in fact have by far the greatest amount out on credit. In all transactions on credit, however, they never trust private citizens but the municipal government, the legal documents being drawn up as usual. When the day for payment comes, the city collects the money due from private debtors and puts it into the treasury and enjoys the use of it until the Utopians claim payment.

The Utopians never claim payment of most of the money. They think it hardly fair to take away a thing useful to other people when it is useless to themselves. But if circumstances require that they should lend some part of it to another nation, then they call in their debts—or when they must wage war. It is for that single purpose that they keep all the treasure they possess at home: to be their bulwark in extreme peril or in sudden emergency. They use it above all to hire at sky-high rates of pay foreign mercenaries (whom they would jeopardize rather than their own citizens), being well aware that by large sums of money even their enemies themselves may be bought and sold or set to fight one another either by treachery or by open warfare.

For these military reasons they keep a vast treasure, but not as a treasure. They keep it in a way which I am really quite ashamed to reveal for fear that my words will not be believed. My fears are all the more justified because I am conscious that, had I not been there and witnessed the phenomenon, I myself should have been with difficulty induced to believe it from another's account. It needs must be almost always the rule that, as far as a thing is unlike the ways of the hearers, so far is it from obtaining their credence. An impartial judge of things, however, seeing that the rest of their institutions are so unlike ours, will perhaps wonder less that their use of silver and gold should be adapted to their way of life rather than to ours. As stated, they do not use money themselves but keep it only for an emergency, which may actually occur, yet possibly may never happen.

Meanwhile, gold and silver, of which money is made, are so treated by them that no one values them more highly than their true nature deserves. Who does not see that they are far inferior to iron in usefulness since without iron mortals cannot live any more than without fire and water? To gold and silver, however, nature has given no use that we cannot dispense with, if the folly of men had not made them valuable because they are rare. On the other

125

hand, like a most kind and indulgent mother, she has exposed to view all that is best, like air and water and earth itself, but has removed as far as possible from us all vain and unprofitable things.

If in Utopia these metals were kept locked up in a tower, it might be suspected that the governor and the senate—for such is the foolish imagination of the common folk—were deceiving the people by the scheme and they themselves were deriving some benefit therefrom. Moreover, if they made them into drinking vessels and other such skillful handiwork, then if occasion arose for them all to be melted down again and applied to the pay of soldiers, they realize that people would be unwilling to be deprived of what they had once begun to treasure.

To avoid these dangers, they have devised a means which, as it is consonant with the rest of their institutions, so it is extremely unlike our own—seeing that we value gold so much and are so careful in safeguarding it—and therefore incredible except to those who have experience of it. While they eat and drink from earthenware and glassware of fine workmanship but of little value, from gold and silver they make chamber pots and all the humblest vessels for use everywhere, not only in the common halls but in private homes also. Moreover, they employ the same metals to make the chains and solid fetters which they put on their slaves. Finally, as for those who bear the stigma of disgrace on account of some crime, they have gold ornaments hanging from their ears, gold rings encircling their fingers, gold chains thrown around their necks, and, as a last touch, a gold crown binding their temples. Thus by every means in their power they make gold and silver a mark of ill fame. In this way, too, it happens that, while all other nations bear the loss of these metals with as great grief as if they were losing their very vitals, if circumstances in Utopia ever required the removal of all gold and silver, no one would feel that he were losing as much as a penny.

They also gather pearls by the seashore and diamonds and rubies on certain cliffs. They do not look for them purposely, but they polish them when found by chance. With them they adorn little children, who in their earliest years are proud and delighted with such decorations. When they have grown somewhat older and perceive that only children use such toys, they lay them aside, not by any order of their parents, but through their own feeling of shame, just as our own children, when they grow up, throw away their marbles, rattles, and dolls.

What opposite ideas and feelings are created by customs so different from those of other people came home to me never more clearly than in the case of the Anemolian ambassadors. They arrived in Amaurotum during my stay there. Because they came to treat of important matters, the three representatives of each city had assembled before their appearance. Now all the ambassadors of neighboring nations, who had previously visited the land, were well acquainted with the manners of the Utopians and knew that they paid no respect to costly clothes but looked with contempt on silk and regarded gold as a badge of disgrace. These persons usually came in the simplest possible dress. But the Anemolians, living farther off and having had fewer dealings with them, since they heard that in Utopia all were dressed alike, and in a home-spun fashion at that, felt sure that they did not possess what they made no use of. Being more proud than wise, they determined by the grandeur of their apparel to represent the gods themselves and by their splendid adornment to dazzle the eyes of the poor Utopians.

Consequently the three ambassadors made a grand entry with a suite of a hundred followers, all in particolored clothes and most in silk. The ambassadors themselves, being noblemen at home, were arrayed in cloth of gold, with heavy gold necklaces and earrings, with gold rings on their fingers, and with strings of pearls and gems upon their caps; in fact, they were decked out with all those articles which in Utopia are used to punish slaves, to stigmatize evil-doers, or to amuse children. It was a sight worth seeing to behold their cockiness when they compared their grand clothing with that of the Utopians, who had poured out into the street to see them pass. On the other hand, it was no less delightful to notice how much they were mistaken in their sanguine expectations and how far they were from obtaining the consideration which they had hoped to get. To the eyes of all the Utopians, with the exception of the very few who for a good reason had visited foreign countries, all this gay show appeared disgraceful. They therefore bowed to the lowest of the party as to the masters but took the ambassadors themselves to be slaves because they were wearing gold chains, and passed them over without any deference whatever.

Why, you might have seen also the children who had themselves discarded gems and pearls, when they saw them attached to the caps of the ambassadors, poke and nudge their mothers and say to them:

"Look, mother, what a big booby is still wearing pearls and jewels as if he were yet a little boy!"

But the mother, also in earnest, would say:

"Hush, son, I think it is one of the ambassadors' clowns."

Others found fault with the golden chains as useless, being so slender that a slave could easily break them or, again, so loose that at his pleasure he could throw them off and escape anywhere scot-free.

After spending one or more days there, the ambassadors saw an immense quantity of gold held as cheaply and in as great contempt there as in honor among themselves. They saw, too, that more gold and silver were amassed to make the chains and fetters of one runaway slave than had made up the whole array of the three of them. They then were crestfallen and for shame put away all the finery with which they had made themselves haughtily conspicuous, especially when, after familiar talk with the Utopians, they had learned their ways and opinions.

The Utopians wonder that any mortal takes pleasure in the uncertain sparkle of a tiny jewel or precious stone when he can look at a star or even the sun itself. They wonder that anyone can be so mad as to think himself more noble on account of the texture of a finer wool, since, however fine the texture is, a sheep once wore the wool and yet all the time was nothing more than a sheep.

They wonder, too, that gold, which by its very nature is so useless, is now everywhere in the world valued so highly that man himself, through whose agency and for whose use it got this value, is priced much cheaper than gold itself. This is true to such an extent that a blockhead who has no more intelligence than a log and who is as dishonest as he is foolish keeps in bondage many wise men and good men merely for the reason that a great heap of gold coins happens to be his. Yet if some chance or some legal trick (which is as apt as chance to confound high and low) transfers it from this master to the lowest rascal in his entire household, he will surely very soon pass into the service of his former servant—as if he were a mere appendage of and addition to the coins! But much more do they wonder at and abominate the madness of persons who pay almost divine honors to the rich, to whom they neither owe anything nor are obligated in any other respect than that they are rich. Yet they know them to be so mean and miserly that they are more than sure that of all that great pile of cash, as long as the rich men live, not a single penny will ever come their way. . . .

Now I have described to you, as exactly as I could, the structure of that commonwealth which I judge not merely the best but the only one which can rightly claim the name of a commonwealth. Outside Utopia, to be sure, men talk freely of the public welfare—but look after their private interests only. In Utopia, where nothing is private, they seriously concern themselves with public affairs. Assuredly in both cases they act reasonably. For, outside Utopia, how many are there who do not realize that, unless they make some separate provision for themselves, however flourishing the commonwealth, they will themselves starve? For this reason, necessity compels them to hold that they must take account of themselves rather than of the people, that is, of others.

On the other hand, in Utopia, where everything belongs to everybody, no one doubts, provided only that the public granaries are well filled, that the individual will lack nothing for his private use. The reason is that the distribution of goods is not niggardly. In Utopia there is no poor man and no beggar. Though no man has anything, yet all are rich.

For what can be greater riches for a man than to live with a joyful and peaceful mind, free of all worries—not troubled about his food or harassed by the querulous demands of his wife or fearing poverty for his son or worrying about his daughter's dowry, but feeling secure about the livelihood and happiness of himself and his family: wife, sons, grandsons, great-grandsons, great-

great-grandsons, and all the long line of their descendants that gentlefolk anticipate? Then take into account the fact that there is no less provision for those who are now helpless but once worked than for those who are still working.

At this point I should like anyone to be so bold as to compare this fairness with the so-called justice prevalent in other nations, among which, upon my soul, I cannot discover the slightest trace of justice and fairness. What brand of justice is it that any nobleman whatsoever or goldsmith-banker or moneylender or, in fact, anyone else from among those who either do no work at all or whose work is of a kind not very essential to the commonwealth, should attain a life of luxury and grandeur on the basis of his idleness or his nonessential work? In the meantime, the common laborer, the carter, the carpenter, and the farmer perform work so hard and continuous that beasts of burden could scarcely endure it and work so essential that no commonwealth could last even one year without it. Yet they earn such scanty fare and lead such a miserable life that the condition of beasts of burden might seem far preferable. The latter do not have to work so incessantly nor is their food much worse (in fact, sweeter to their taste) nor do they entertain any fear for the future. The workmen, on the other hand, not only have to toil and suffer without return or profit in the present but agonize over the thought of an indigent old age. Their daily wage is too scanty to suffice even for the day: much less is there an excess and surplus that daily can be laid by for their needs in old age.

Now is not this an unjust and ungrateful commonwealth? It lavishes great rewards on so-called gentlefolk and banking goldsmiths and the rest of that kind, who are either idle or mere parasites and purveyors of empty pleasures. On the contrary, it makes no benevolent provision for farmers, colliers, common laborers, carters, and carpenters without whom there would be no commonwealth at all. After it has misused the labor of their prime and after they are weighed down with age and disease and are in utter want, it forgets all their sleepless nights and all the great benefits received at their hands and most ungratefully requites them with a most miserable death.

What is worse, the rich every day extort a part of their daily allowance from the poor not only by private fraud but by public law. Even before they did so it seemed unjust that persons deserving best of the commonwealth should have the worst return. Now they have further distorted and debased the right and, finally, by making laws, have palmed it off as justice. Consequently, when I consider and turn over in my mind the state of all commonwealths flourishing anywhere today, so help me God, I can see nothing else than a kind of conspiracy of the rich, who are aiming at their own interests under the name and title of the commonwealth. They invent and devise all ways and means by which, first, they may keep without fear of loss all that they have amassed by evil practices and, secondly, they may then purchase as cheaply as possible and abuse the toil and labor of all the poor. These devices become law as soon as the rich have once decreed their observance in the name of the public—that is, of the poor also!

Yet when these evil men with insatiable greed have divided up among themselves all the goods which would have been enough for all the people, how far they are from the happiness of the Utopian commonwealth! In Utopia all greed for money was entirely removed with the use of money. What a mass of troubles was then cut away! What a crop of crimes was then pulled up by the roots! Who does not know that fraud, theft, rapine, quarrels, disorders, brawls, seditions, murders, treasons, poisonings, which are avenged rather than restrained by daily executions, die out with the destruction of money? Who does not know that fear, anxiety, worries, toils, and sleepless nights will also perish at the same time as money? What is more, poverty, which alone money seemed to make poor, forthwith would itself dwindle and disappear if money were entirely done away with everywhere.

To make this assertion clearer, consider in your thoughts some barren and unfruitful year in which many thousands of men have been carried off by famine. I emphatically contend that at the end of that scarcity, if rich men's granaries had been searched, as much grain could have been found as, if it had been divided among the people killed off by starvation and disease, would have prevented anyone from feeling that meager return from soil and climate. So easily might men get the necessities of life if that blessed money, supposedly a grand invention to ease access to those necessities, was not in fact the only barrier to our getting what we need.

Even the rich, I doubt not, feel that it would be a much better state of affairs to lack no necessity than to have abundance of superfluities—to be snatched from such numerous troubles rather than to be hemmed in by great riches. Nor does it occur to me to doubt that a man's regard for his own interests or the authority of Christ our Savior—who in His wisdom could not fail to know what was best and who in His goodness would not fail to counsel what He knew to be best—would long ago have brought the whole world to adopt the laws of the Utopian commonwealth, had not one single monster, the chief and progenitor of all plagues, striven against it—I mean, Pride.

Pride measures prosperity not by her own advantages but by others' disadvantages. Pride would not consent to be made even a goddess if no poor wretches were left for her to domineer over and scoff at, if her good fortune might not dazzle by comparison with their miseries, if the display of her riches did not torment and intensify their poverty. This serpent from hell entwines itself around the hearts of men and acts like the suckfish in preventing and hindering them from entering on a better way of life.

Pride is too deeply fixed in men to be easily plucked out. For this reason, the fact that this form of a commonwealth—which I should gladly desire for all—has been the good fortune of the Utopians at least, fills me with joy. They have adopted such institutions of life as have laid the foundations of the commonwealth not only most happily, but also to last forever, as far as human prescience can forecast. At home they have extirpated the roots of ambition and factionalism, along with all the other vices. Hence there is no danger of trouble from domestic discord, which has been the only cause of ruin to the well-established prosperity of many cities. As long as harmony is preserved at home and its institutions are in a healthy state, not all the envy of neighboring rulers, though it has rather often attempted it and has always been repelled, can avail to shatter or to shake that nation.

When Raphael had finished his story, many things came to my mind which seemed very absurdly established in the customs and laws of the people described—not only in their method of waging war, their ceremonies and religion, as well as their other institutions, but most of all in that feature which is the principal foundation of their whole structure. I mean their common life and subsistence—without any exchange of money. This latter alone utterly overthrows all the nobility, magnificence, splendor, and majesty which are, in the estimation of the common people, the true glories and ornaments of the commonwealth.

I knew, however, that he was wearied with his tale, and I was not quite certain that he could brook any opposition to his views, particularly when I recalled his censure of others on account of their fear that they might not appear to be wise enough, unless they found some fault to criticize in other men's discoveries. I therefore praised their way of life and his speech and, taking him by the hand, led him in to supper. I first said, nevertheless, that there would be another chance to think about these matters more deeply and to talk them over with him more fully. If only this were some day possible!

Meanwhile, though in other respects he is a man of the most undoubted learning as well as of the greatest knowledge of human affairs, I cannot agree with all that he said. But I readily admit that there are very many features in the Utopian commonwealth which it is easier for me to wish for in our countries than to have any hope of seeing realized.

END OF BOOK TWO

THE END OF THE AFTERNOON DISCOURSE OF
RAPHAEL HYTHLODAEUS ON THE LAWS
AND CUSTOMS OF THE ISLAND OF
UTOPIA, HITHERTO KNOWN BUT
TO FEW, AS REPORTED BY THE
MOST DISTINGUISHED AND
MOST LEARNED MAN,
MR. THOMAS MORE,
CITIZEN AND SHERIFF OF LONDON
FINIS

For Further Reading

More, Thomas. *Utopia*. Edited by George M. Logan, Robert M. Adams, and Clarence Miller (Cambridge: Cambridge Univ. Press, 1995).

Baker-Smith, Dominic. *More's Utopia* (London: Harper Collins Academic, 1991).

Beresford, M. *The Lost Villages of England* (London: Lutterworth Press, 1954.

Blockmans, W.P. *Thomas More, 'Utopia' and the Aspirations of the Early Capitalist Bourgeoisie* (Rotterdam: Erasmus Universiteit, 1978).

Caspari, Fritz. *Humanism and the Social Order in Tudor England* (Chicago: Univ. of Chicago Press, 1954).

Chambers, R.W. *Thomas More*. 1935. Reprint. (Harmondsworth, England: Penguin, 1963).

Davis, J.C. *Utopia and the Ideal Society: A Study of English Utopian Writing 1516–1700* (Cambridge: Cambridge Univ. Press, 1981).

Erasmus, Desiderius. *Complete Works in English* (Toronto: Toronto Univ. Press, 1974).

_____. *The Praise of Folly*. Translated by Betty Radice with introduction by A.H.T. Levi (Hardmondsworth, England: Penguin, 1971).

Fleisher, Martin. *Radical Reform and Political Persuasion in the Life and Writings of Thomas More* (Geneva: Droz, 1973).

Hexter, J.H. *More's 'Utopia': The Biography of an Idea* (Princeton: Princeton Univ. Press, 1952).

_____. *The Vision of Politics on the Eve of the Reformation: More, Machiavelli and Seyssel* (Princeton: Princeton Univ. Press, 1972).

Kenny, Anthony. *Thomas More* (Oxford: Oxford Univ. Press, 1983).

Logan, George M., ed. *Utopia: Sir Thomas More* (New York: Cambridge Univ. Press, 1989).

_____. *The Meaning of More's "Utopia"* (Princeton: Princeton Univ. Press, 1983).

Manuel, Frank E., and Fritzie P. Manuel. *Utopian Thought in the Western World* (Oxford: Blackwell, 1979).

Marius, Richard. *Thomas More* (London: Dent, 1985.)

Starnes, Colin. *The New Republic: A Commentary on Book I of More's "Utopia" Showing Its Relation to Plato's "Republic"* (Atlantic Highlands, N.J.: Humanities Press, 1990).

Surtz, Edward, S.J. *The Praise of Pleasure: Philosophy, Education, and Communism in More's Utopia* (Cambridge, Mass.: Harvard Univ. Press, 1957).

JOHN LOCKE (1632–1704)

"IMPROVEMENT" WAS a favorite word of John Locke; improvement makes all the difference. "In the beginning all the world was *America.*" By "America" Locke meant a wasteland; only industry improves the "almost worthless materials" that nature provides. The improvement of the land, bringing it under cultivation by draining or clearing it, holds the imaginative center of Locke's use of the term. His ambition was "to be employed as an Under-Labourer in clearing Ground a little, and removing some of the Rubbish, that lies in the way to Knowledge"—but he was also impressed by scientific and technological progress outside agriculture. Locke devoted much of his *Essay concerning Human Understanding* to language precisely because speech is our common bond and "the common Conduit, whereby the Improvements of Knowledge are conveyed from one Man, and one Generation to another," and he allotted one chapter to the "Improvement of our Knowledge," a title that captures Locke's purpose well. Locke spoke of education as the "improvement" of a child's "Native Stock." His deep conviction was that God directs us to "improve the earth for the benefit of life."

Talk of improvement presupposes a measure with which to gauge it. The problem of measure proves to be one of the most urgent topics on Locke's mind: painfully aware of the jumble of conflicting human opinions, Locke sets himself the task of searching out the "Measures of the Certainty of our Knowledge." Apprehension over the fickleness of human opinion steers Locke away from placing too much confidence in it as a foundation for society. Divinely sanctioned natural law offers a fixed measure for political and economic life: "A dependent intelligent being is under the power and direction and dominion of him on whom he depends and must be for the ends appointed him by that superior being. If man were independent he could have no law but his own will no end but himself. He would be a god to himself and the satisfaction of his own will the sole measure and end of all his actions."

Locke advances three measures or bounds of property in the *Second Treatise of Government*. The first measure of private property is labor: by natural law "every man has a *property* in his own *person*," so mixing one's labor with what God has given to human beings in common makes that thing one's property. The extent of one's labor is the first measure of one's property. God's purposes give rise to two further bounds: the goods of the earth are there for the comfort and convenience of all. So the private appropriation of those goods is not to keep others from enjoying what has been given in common. A third limit holds that privately appropriated goods are not to be wasted. Curious things happen to these three measures. All three work like reversible jackets: you can turn them inside out, but *the bounds do not change*. Each of the three measures comes to accommodate more than restrain commercial tendencies.

Locke's philosophy of the person justifies the social form of pivotal importance for capitalism, wage labor: "a freeman makes himself a servant to another, by selling him, for a certain time, the service he undertakes to do, in exchange for wages he is to receive: and though this commonly puts him into the family of his master, and under the ordinary discipline thereof; yet it gives the master but a temporary power over him, and no greater than what is contained in the *contract* between them." That contract usually confers all rights to the product to the employer. This allows those who have money and do not work to amass property, thanks to the work of hired hands who themselves have no property rights to what is mixed with their labor.

It might seem as though the second measure would rule out private appropriation of the remaining common lands, but no. Locke argues that the person who improves land makes it a hundred or thousand times more valuable and must not be blocked but counted a benefactor to all. This seeming turnabout has a direct link to the wage labor issue since it is precisely the lack of access to land that can drive a person to wage labor. Locke operates with a "trickle down" theory of wealth later championed by Adam Smith:"a king of a large and fruitful territory there [in America, P.M.], feeds, lodges, and is clad worse than a day-labourer in *England.*" Everybody wins in a society of "improvers."

The prohibition against waste seems to set restrictions on private property that would block great inequalities of property and prevent the first two reversals. The invention and use of money reveals that the third lid on private property is not fastened as tightly as we might imagine: there is no limit to the private wealth we can accumulate as long as we trade our perishable goods for that imperishable store of value, money. Money knows no limit. For non-monetary goods the waste limitation might still have some bite, but who cares to police the supposed border between necessities and luxuries?

Locke's liberal rejection of labor based on personal domination in favor of wage labor, his passion for improvement, his polemical contrasting of the "useful" labors of ordinary artisans with the excesses of the gentry, all make him the perfect prophet of what Thorstein Veblen calls "the instinct of workmanship," which "disposes men to look with favor upon productive efficiency and on whatever is of human use."

FROM THE *SECOND TREATISE OF GOVERNMENT*

CHAPTER V. OF PROPERTY

25. Whether we consider natural *reason,* which tells us, that men, being once born, have a right to their preservation, and consequently to meat and drink, and such other things as nature affords for their subsistence: or *revelation,* which gives us an account of those grants God made of the world to Adam, and to Noah, and his sons, it is very clear, that God, as King David says, *Psal.* cxv. 16, "has given the earth to the children of men," given it to mankind in common. But this being supposed, it seems to some a very great difficulty how any one should ever come to have a *property* in any thing: I will not content myself to answer, that if it be difficult to make out *property,* upon a supposition, that God gave the world to Adam, and his posterity in common; it is impossible that any man, but one universal monarch, should have any property upon a supposition, that God gave the world to Adam, and his heirs in succession, exclusive of all the rest of his posterity. But I shall endeavour to shew, how men might come to have a *property* in several parts of that which God gave to mankind in common, and that without any express compact of all the commoners.

26. God, who hath given the world to men in common, hath also given them reason to make use of it to the best advantage of life, and convenience. The earth, and all that is therein, is given to men for the support and comfort of their being. And though all the fruits it naturally produces, and beasts it feeds, belong to mankind in common, as they are produced by the sponta-

neous hand of nature; and no body has originally a private dominion, exclusive of the rest of mankind, in any of them, as they are thus in their natural state: yet being given for the use of men, there must of necessity be *a means to appropriate* them some way or other, before they can be of any use, or at all beneficial to any particular man. The fruit, or venison, which nourishes the wild Indian, who knows no enclosure, and is still a tenant in common, must be his, and so his, i.e. a part of him, that another can no longer have any right to it, before it can do him any good for the support of his life.

27. Though the earth, and all inferior creatures, be common to all men, yet every man has a property in his own person: this no body has any right to but himself. The labour of his body, and the work of his hands, we may say, are properly his. Whatsoever then he removes out of the state that nature hath provided, and left it in, he hath mixed his labour with, and joined to it something that is his own, and thereby makes it his property. It being by him removed from the common state nature hath placed it in, it hath by this labour something annexed to it, that excludes the common right of other men. For this labour being the unquestionable property of the labourer, no man but he can have a right to what that is once joined to, at least where there is enough, and as good, left in common for others.

28. He that is nourished by the acorns he picked up under an oak, or the apples he gathered from the trees in the wood, has certainly appropriated them to himself. No body can deny but the nourishment is his. I ask then, when did they begin to be his? When he digested? Or when he eat? Or when he boiled? Or when he brought them home? Or when he picked them up? And it is plain, if the first gathering made them not his, nothing else could. That *labour* put a distinction between them and common: that added something to them more than nature, the common mother of all, had done; and so they became his private right. And will any one say he had no right to those acorns or apples he thus appropriated, because he had not the consent of all mankind to make them his? Was it a robbery thus to assume to himself what belonged to all in common? If such a consent as that was necessary, man had starved, notwithstanding the plenty God had given him. We see in *commons,* which remain so by compact, that it is the taking any part of what is common, and removing it out of the state nature leaves it in, which *begins the property;* without which the common is of no use. And the taking of this or that part does not depend on the express consent of all the commoners. Thus the grass my horse has bit; the turfs my servant has cut; and the ore I have digged in any place, where I have a right to them in common with others, become my *property,* without the assignation or consent of any body. The labour that was mine, removing them out of that common state they were in, hath *fixed my property* in them.

29. By making an explicit consent of every commoner necessary to any one's appropriating to himself any part of what is given in common, children

or servants could not cut the meat, which their father or master had provided for them in common, without assigning to every one his peculiar part. Though the water running in the fountain be every one's, yet who can doubt, but that in the pitcher is his only who drew it out? His *labour* hath taken it out of the hands of nature, where it was common, and belonged equally to all her children, and *hath* thereby *appropriated* it to himself.

30. Thus this law of reason makes the deer that Indian's who hath killed it; it is allowed to be his goods, who hath bestowed his labour upon it, though before it was the common right of every one. And amongst those who are counted the civilized part of mankind, who have made and multiplied positive laws to determine *property,* this original law of nature, for the *beginning of property,* in what was before common, still takes place; and by virtue thereof, what fish any one catches in the ocean, that great and still remaining common of mankind; or what ambergreise any one takes up here, is *by* the *labour* that removes it out of that common state nature left it in, *made* his *property,* who takes that pains about it. And even amongst us, the hare that any one is hunting, is thought his who pursues her during the chase. For being a beast that is still looked upon as common, and no man's private possession; whoever has employed so much *labour* about any of that kind, as to find and pursue her, has thereby removed her from the state of nature, wherein she was common, and hath *begun a property.*

31. It will perhaps be objected to this, that *if gathering the acorns, or other fruits of the earth, &c.* makes a right to them, then any one may engross as much as he will. To which I answer, Not so. The same law of nature, that does by this means give us property, does also *bound* that *property* too. "God has given us all things richly," 1 *Tim;* vi. 17, is the voice of reason confirmed by inspiration. But how far has he given it us? *To enjoy.* As much as any one can make use of to any advantage of life before it spoils, so much he may by his labour fix a property in: whatever is beyond this, is more than his share, and belongs to others. Nothing was made by God for man to spoil or destroy. And thus, considering the plenty of natural provisions there was a long time in the world, and the few spenders; and to how small a part of that provision the industry of one man could extend itself, and engross it to the prejudice of others; especially keeping within the *bounds,* set by reason, *of* what might serve for his *use*; there could be then little room for quarrels or contentions about property so established.

32. But the *chief matter of property* being now not the fruits of the earth, and the beasts that subsist on it, but the *earth it self;* as that which takes in, and carries with it all the rest: I think it is plain, that *property* in that too is acquired as the former. *As much land* as a man tills, plants, improves, cultivates, and can use the product of, so much is his *property.* He by his labour does, as it were, enclose it from the common. Nor will it invalidate his right, to say every body else has an equal title to it; and therefore he cannot appropriate, he cannot en-

close, without the consent of all his fellow commoners, all mankind. God, when he gave the world in common to all mankind, commanded man also to labour, and the penury of his condition required it of him. God and his reason commanded him to subdue the earth, i.e. improve it for the benefit of life, and therein lay out something upon it that was his own, his labour. He that, in obedience to this command of God, subdued, tilled, and sowed any part of it, thereby annexed to it something that was his *property,* which another had no title to, nor could without injury take from him.

33. Nor was this *appropriation* of any parcel of *land,* by improving it, any prejudice to any other man, since there was still enough, and as good left; and more than the yet unprovided could use. So that, in effect, there was never the less left for others because of his enclosure for himself. For he that leaves as much as another can make use of, does as good as take nothing at all. No body could think himself injured by the drinking of another man, though he took a good draught, who had a whole river of the same water left him to quench his thirst: And the case of land and water, where there is enough of both, is perfectly the same.

34. God gave the world to men in common; but since he gave it them for their benefit, and the greatest conveniences of life they were capable to draw from it, it cannot be supposed he meant it should always remain common and uncultivated. He gave it to the use of the industrious and rational, (and *labour* was to be *his title* to it) not to the fancy or covetousness of the quarrelsome and contentious. He that had as good left for his improvement, as was already taken up, needed not complain, ought not to meddle with what was already improved by another's labour: If he did, it is plain he desired the benefit of another's pains, which he had no right to, and not the ground which God had given him in common with others to labour on, and whereof there was as good left, as that already possessed, and more than he knew what to do with, or his industry could reach to.

35. It is true, in *land* that is *common* in England, or any other country, where there is plenty of people under government, who have money and commerce, no one can enclose or appropriate any part, without the consent of all his fellow-commoners: Because this is left common by compact, i.e. by the law of the land, which is not to be violated. And though it be common, in respect of some men, it is not so to all mankind, but is the joint property of this country, or this parish. Besides, the remainder, after such enclosure, would not be as good to the rest of the commoners, as the whole was when they could all make use of the whole: whereas in the beginning and first peopling of the great common of the world, it was quite otherwise. The law man was under, was rather for appropriating. God commanded, and his wants forced him to *labour.* That was his *property* which could not be taken from him wherever he had fixed it. And hence subduing or cultivating the earth, and having dominion, we see are joined together. The one gave title to the other. So that God,

by commanding to subdue, gave authority so far to *appropriate*: And the condition of human life, which requires labour and materials to work on, necessarily introduces private possessions.

36. The *measure of property* nature has well set by the extent of men's *labour, and the conveniences of life*: No man's labour could subdue or appropriate all; nor could his enjoyment consume more than a small part; so that it was impossible for any man, this way, to intrench upon the right of another, or acquire to himself a property, to the prejudice of his neighbour, who would still have room for as good, and as large a possession (after the other had taken out his) as before it was appropriated. This *measure* did confine every man's *possession* to a very moderate proportion, and such as he might appropriate to himself, without injury to any body, in the first ages of the world, when men were more in danger to be lost, by wandering from their company, in the then vast wilderness of the earth, than to be straitened for want of room to plant in. And the same measure may be allowed still without prejudice to any body, as full as the world seems. For supposing a man, or family, in the state they were at first peopling of the world by the children of Adam, or Noah; let him plant in some inland, vacant places of America, we shall find that the *possessions* he could make himself, upon the *measures* we have given, would not be very large, nor, even to this day, prejudice the rest of mankind, or give them reason to complain, or think themselves injured by this man's encroachment, though the race of men have now spread themselves to all the corners of the world, and do infinitely exceed the small number was at the beginning. Nay, the extent of *ground* is of so little value, *without labour*, that I have heard it affirmed, that in Spain itself a man may be permitted to plough, sow, and reap, without being disturbed, upon land he has no other title to, but only his making use of it. But, on the contrary, the inhabitants think themselves beholden to him, who by his industry on neglected and consequently waste land, has increased the stock of corn, which they wanted. But be this as it will, which I lay no stress on; this I dare boldly affirm, that the same *rule of propriety, (viz.)* that every man should have as much as he could make use of, would hold still in the world, without straitening any body, since there is land enough in the world to suffice double the inhabitants, had not the *invention of money,* and the tacit agreement of men to put a value on it, introduced (by consent) larger possessions, and a right to them; which, how it has done, I shall by and by shew more at large.

37. This is certain, that in the beginning, before the desire of having more than man needed had altered the intrinsic value of things, which depends only on their usefulness to the life of man; or had *agreed, that a little piece of yellow metal,* which would keep without wasting or decay, should be worth a great piece of flesh, or a whole heap of corn; though men had a right to appropriate, by their labour, each one to himself as much of the things of nature as he could use: yet this could not be much, nor to the prejudice of others,

where the same plenty was still left to those who would use the same industry. To which let me add, that he who appropriates land to himself by his labour, does not lessen, but increase the common stock of mankind. For the provisions serving to the support of human life, produced by one acre of enclosed and cultivated land, are (to speak much within compass) ten times more than those which are yielded by an acre of land of an equal richness lying waste in common. And therefore he that encloses land, and has a greater plenty of the conveniencies of life from ten acres, than he could have from an hundred left to nature, may truly be said to give ninety acres to mankind. For his labour now supplies him with provisions out of ten acres, which were by the product of an hundred lying in common. I have here rated the improved land very low, in making its product but as ten to one, when it is much nearer an hundred to one. For I ask, whether in the wild woods and uncultivated waste of America, left to nature, without any improvement, tillage, or husbandry, a thousand acres yield the needy and wretched inhabitants as many conveniencies of life, as ten acres equally fertile land do in Devonshire, where they are well cultivated?

Before the appropriation of land, he who gathered as much of the wild fruit, killed, caught, or tamed, as many of the beasts as he could; he that so employed his pains about any of the spontaneous products of nature, as any way to alter them from the state which nature put them in, *by* placing any of his *labour* on them, did thereby *acquire a propriety in them:* but if they perished, in his possession, without their due use; if the fruits rotted, or the venison putrified, before he could spend it, he offended against the common law of nature, and was liable to be punished; he invaded his neighbour's share, for he had *no right, farther than his use* called for any of them, and they might serve to afford him conveniencies of life.

38. The same *measures* governed the *possession of land* too: whatsoever he tilled and reaped, laid up and made use of, before it spoiled, that was his peculiar right; whatsoever he enclosed, and could feed, and make use of, the cattle and product was also his. But if either the grass of his inclosure rotted on the ground, or the fruit of his planting perished without gathering, and laying up, this part of the earth, notwithstanding his inclosure, was still to be looked on as waste, and might be the possession of any other. Thus at the beginning, Cain might take as much ground as he could till, and make it his own land, and yet leave enough to Abel's sheep to feed on; a few acres would serve for both their possessions. But as families increased, and industry enlarged their stocks, their *possessions enlarged* with the need of them; but yet it was commonly *without any fixed property in the ground* they made use of, till they incorporated, settled themselves together, and built cities, and then, by consent, they came in time to set out the *bounds of their distinct territories,* and agree on limits between them and their neighbours; and by laws within themselves settled the *properties* of those of the same society. For we see, that in that part of

the world which was first inhabited, and therefore like to be best peopled, even as low down as Abraham's time, they wandered with their flocks, and their herds, which was their substance, freely up and down; and this Abraham did, in a country where he was a stranger. Whence it is plain, that at least a great part of the *land lay in common;* that the inhabitants valued it not, nor claimed property in any more than they made use of. But when there was not room enough in the same place, for their herds to feed together, they by consent, as Abraham and Lot did, *Gen.* xiii. 5. separated and enlarged their pasture, where it best liked them. And for the same reason Esau went from his father, and his brother, and planted in Mount Seir, *Gen.* xxxvi. 6.

39. And thus, without supposing any private dominion, and property in Adam, over all the *world,* exclusive of all other men, which can no way be proved, nor any one's property be made out from it; but supposing the *world* given, as it was, to the children of men *in common,* we see how *labour* could make men distinct titles to several parcels of it, for their private uses; wherein there could be no doubt of right, no room for quarrel.

40. Nor is it so strange, as perhaps before consideration it may appear, that the *property of labour* should be able to over-balance the community of land. For it is *labour* indeed that *puts the difference of value* on every thing; and let any one consider what the difference is between an acre of land planted with tobacco or sugar, sown with wheat or barley, and an acre of the same land lying in common, without any husbandry upon it, and he will find, that the improvement of *labour makes* the far greater part of the value. I think it will be but a very modest computation to say, that of the *products* of the earth useful to the life of man, nine tenths are the *effects of labour:* nay, if we will rightly estimate things as they come to our use, and cast up the several expences about them, what in them is purely owing to *nature,* and what to *labour, we shall find, that in most of them ninety-nine hundredths are wholly to be put on the account of* labour.

41. There cannot be a clearer demonstration of any thing, than several nations of the Americans are of this, who are rich in land, and poor in all the comforts of life; whom nature having furnished as liberally as any other people, with the materials of plenty, i.e. a fruitful soil, apt to produce in abundance what might serve for food, raiment, and delight; yet *for want of improving it by labour,* have not one hundredth part of the conveniencies we enjoy: and a king of a large and fruitful territory there feeds, lodges, and is clad worse than a day labourer in England.

42. To make this a little clearer, let us but trace some of the ordinary provisions of life, through their several progresses, before they come to our use, and see how much they receive of their *value from human industry.* Bread, wine, and cloth, are things of daily use, and great plenty, yet notwithstanding, acorns, water, and leaves, or skins, must be our bread, drink, and cloathing, did not labour furnish us with these more useful commodities. For whatever bread is

more worth than acorns, wine than water, and *cloth* or *silk,* than leaves, skins, or moss, that is *wholly owing to labour* and *industry.* The one of these being the food and raiment which unassisted nature furnishes us with; the other, provisions which our industry and pains prepare for us, which how much they exceed the other in value, when any one hath computed, he will then see how much *labour makes the far greatest part of the value* of things we enjoy in this world: and the ground which produces the materials, is scarce to be reckoned in, as any, or, at most, but a very small part of it: so little, that even amongst us, land that is left wholly to nature, that hath no improvement of pasturage, tillage, or planting, is called, as indeed it is, *waste;* and we shall find the benefit of it amount to little more than nothing.

This shews how much numbers of men are to be preferred to largeness of dominions; and that the increase of lands, and the right of employing of them, is the great art of government: and that prince, who shall be so wise and godlike, as by established laws of liberty to secure protection and encouragement to the honest industry of mankind, against the oppression of power and narrowness of party, will quickly be too hard for his neighbours; but this by the by. To return to the argument in hand.

43. An acre of land, that bears here twenty bushels of wheat, and another in America, which, with the same husbandry, would do the like, are, without doubt, of the same natural intrinsic value: but yet the benefit mankind receives from the one in a year, is worth 5 l. and from the other possibly not worth a penny, if all the profit an Indian received from it were to be valued, and sold here; at least, I may truly say, not one thousandth. It is *labour* then which *puts the greatest part of the value upon land,* without which it would scarcely be worth any thing: it is to that we owe the greatest part of all its useful products; for all that the straw, bran, bread, of that acre of wheat, is more worth than the product of an acre of as good land, which lies waste, is all the effect of labour. For it is not barely the ploughman's pains, the reaper's and thresher's toil, and the baker's sweat is to be counted into the *bread* we eat; the labour of those who broke the oxen, who digged and wrought the iron and stones, who felled and framed the timber employed about the plough, mill, oven, or any other utensils, which are a vast number requisite to this corn, from its being seed to be sown, to its being made bread, must all be *charged on* the account of *labour,* and received as an effect of that: nature and the earth furnished only the almost worthless materials, as in themselves. It would be a strange *catalogue of things, that industry provided and made use of, about every loaf of bread,* before it came to our use, if we could trace them; iron, wood, leather, bark, timber, stone, bricks, coals, lime, cloth, dying drugs, pitch, tar, masts, ropes, and all the materials made use of in the ship, that brought any of the commodities made use of by any of the workmen, to any part of the work, all which it would be almost impossible, at least too long, to reckon up.

44. From all which it is evident, that though the things of nature are given

in common, yet man, by being master of himself, and *proprietor of his own person, and the actions or labour of it, had still in himself the great foundation of property*; and that, which made up the great part of what he applied to the support or comfort of his being, when invention and arts had improved the conveniencies of life, was perfectly his own, and did not belong in common to others.

45. Thus *labour*, in the beginning, *gave a right of property*, wherever any one was pleased to employ it upon what was common, which remained a long while the far greater part, and is yet more than mankind makes use of. Men, at first, for the most part, contented themselves with what unassisted nature offered to their necessities: and though afterwards, in some parts of the world, (where the increase of people and stock, with the *use of money*, had made land scarce, and so of some value) the several *communities* settled the bounds of their distinct territories, and by laws within themselves regulated the properties of the private men of their society, and so, by *compact* and agreement, *settled the property* which labour and industry began; and the leagues that have been made between several states and kingdoms, either expressly or tacitly disowning all claim and right to the land in the others possession, have, by common consent, given up their pretences to their natural common right, which originally they had to those countries, and so have, by *positive agreement, settled a property* amongst themselves, in distinct parts and parcels of the earth; yet there are still *great tracts of ground* to be found, which (the inhabitants thereof not having joined with the rest of mankind, in the consent of the use of their common money) *lie waste*, and are more than the people who dwell on it do, or can make use of, and so still lie in common. Though this can scarce happen amongst that part of mankind that have consented to the use of money.

46. The greatest part of *things really useful* to the life of man, and such as the necessity of subsisting made the first commoners of the world look after, as it doth the Americans now, *are* generally things of *short duration*; such as, if they are not consumed by use, will decay and perish of themselves: gold, silver, and diamonds, are things that fancy or agreement hath put the value on, more than real use, and the necessary support of life. Now of those good things which nature hath provided in common, every one had a right, (as hath been said) to as much as he could use, and property in all that he could affect with his labour; all that his *industry* could extend to, to alter from the state nature had put it in, was his. He that *gathered* a hundred bushels of acorns or apples, had thereby a *property* in them, they were his goods as soon as gathered. He was only to look, that he used them before they spoiled, else he took more than his share, and robbed others. And indeed it was a foolish thing, as well as dishonest, to hoard up more than he could make use of. If he gave away a part to any body else, so that it perished not uselessly in his possession, these he also made use of. And if he also bartered away plums, that would have rotted in a week, for nuts that would last good for his eating a whole year, he did no

143

injury; he wasted not the common stock; destroyed no part of the portion of goods that belonged to others, so long as nothing perished uselessly in his hands. Again, if he would give his nuts for a piece of metal, pleased with its colour; or exchange his sheep for shells, or wool for a sparkling pebble or a diamond, and keep those by him all his life, he invaded not the right of others, he might heap up as much of these durable things as he pleased; the *exceeding of the bounds of* his *just property* not lying in the largeness of his possession, but the perishing of any thing uselessly in it.

47. And thus *came in the use of money,* some lasting thing that men might keep without spoiling, and that by mutual consent men would take in exchange for the truly useful, but perishable supports of life.

48. And as different degrees of industry were apt to give men possessions in different proportions, so this *invention of money* gave them the opportunity to continue and enlarge them. For supposing an island, separate from all possible commerce with the rest of the world, wherein there were but an hundred families, but there were sheep, horses, and cows, with other useful animals, wholesome fruits, and land enough for corn for a hundred thousand times as many, but nothing in the island, either because of its commonness, or perishableness, fit to supply the place of *money:* What reason could any one have there to enlarge his possessions beyond the use of his family and a plentiful supply to its *consumption,* either in what their own industry produced, or they could barter for like perishable, useful commodities with others? Where there is not something, both lasting and scarce, and so valuable to be hoarded up, there men will not be apt to enlarge their *possessions of land,* were it never so rich, never so free for them to take. For I ask, what would a man value ten thousand, or an hundred thousand acres of excellent *land,* ready cultivated and well stocked too with cattle, in the middle of the inland parts of America, where he had no hopes of commerce with other parts of the world, to draw *money* to him by the sale of the product? It would not be worth the enclosing, and we should see him give up again to the wild common of nature, whatever was more than would supply the conveniencies of life to be had there for him and his family.

49. Thus in the beginning all the world was America, and more so than that is now; for no such thing as *money* was any where known. Find out something that hath the *use and value of money* amongst his neighbours, you shall see the same man will begin presently to *enlarge* his possessions.

50. But since gold and silver, being little useful to the life of man in proportion to food, raiment, and carriage, has its *value* only from the consent of men, whereof *labour* yet *makes,* in great part, the *measure,* it is plain, that men have agreed to a disproportionate and unequal *possession of the earth,* they having, by a tacit and voluntary consent, found out a way how a man may fairly possess more land than he himself can use the product of, by receiving in exchange for the overplus, gold and silver, which may be hoarded up without injury to any one; these metals not spoiling or decaying in the hands of the

possessor. This partage of things in an inequality of private possessions, men have made practicable out of the bounds of society, and without compact, only by putting a value on gold and silver, and tacitly agreeing in the use of money. For in governments, the laws regulate the right of property, and the possession of land is determined by positive constitutions.

51. And thus, I think, it is very easy to conceive, without any difficulty *how labour could at first begin a title of property* in the common things of nature, and how the spending it upon our uses bounded it. So that there could then be no reason of quarrelling about title, nor any doubt about the largeness of possession it gave. Right and conveniency went together; for as a man had a right to all he could employ his labour upon, so he had no temptation to labour for more than he could make use of. This left no room for controversy about the title, nor for encroachment on the right of others; what portion a man carved to himself, was easily seen; and it was useless, as well as dishonest, to carve himself too much, or take more than he needed.

For Further Reading

Locke, John. *The Clarendon Edition of the Works of John Locke.* Edited by Peter H. Nidditch, John W. Yolton et al. 30 vols. (Oxford: Oxford Univ. Press, 1975).

_____. *A Letter Concerning Toleration in Focus.* Edited by John Horton and Susan Mendus (New York: Routledge, 1991).

_____. *An Essay Concerning Human Understanding.* Edited by Peter H. Nidditch (Oxford: Clarendon Press, 1979).

_____. *Locke on Money.* 2 vols. Edited by Patrick Hyde Kelly (Oxford: Clarendon Press, 1991).

_____. *Essays on the Law of Nature.* Edited by W. von Leyden (Oxford: Oxford Univ. Press, 1954).

_____. *Two Tracts on Government.* Edited by Philip Abrams (Cambridge: Cambridge Univ. Press, 1967).

_____. *Two Treatises of Government.* Edited by Peter Laslett (Cambridge: Cambridge Univ. Press, 1963).

Andrew, Edward. *Shylock's Rights: A Grammar of Lockian Claims* (Toronto: Univ. of Toronto Press, 1988).

Ashcraft, Richard, ed. *John Locke: Critical Assessments.* 4 vols. (London: Routledge, 1991).

_____. *Revolutionary Politics and Locke's Two Treatises of Government* (Princeton: Princeton Univ. Press, 1986).

Ayers, Michael R. *Locke.* 2 vols. (London: Routledge, 1991).

Caffentzis, George Constantine. *Clipped Coins, Abused Words & Civil Government: John Locke's Philosophy of Money* (Brooklyn: Autonomedia, 1989).

Chappell, Vere, ed. *The Cambridge Companion to Locke* (Cambridge: Cambridge Univ. Press, 1994).

Cranston, Maurice. *John Locke: A Biography* (Oxford: Oxford Univ. Press, 1985).

Dunn, John. "From Applied Theology to Social Analysis: The Break Between John

Locke and the Scottish Enlightenment." In *Wealth and Virtue,* edited by Istvan Hont and Michael Ignatieff (Cambridge: Cambridge Univ. Press, 1983).

_____. *The Political Thought of John Locke* (Cambridge: Cambridge Univ. Press, 1969).

Fox Bourne, H.R. *The Life of John Locke.* 2 vols. Reprint of London, 1876 (Aalen: Scientia Verl., 1969).

Gough, J.W. *John Locke's Political Philosophy: Eight Studies* (Oxford: Oxford Univ. Press, 1950).

Grant, Ruth W. *John Locke's Liberalism* (Chicago: Univ. of Chicago Press, 1987).

Hundert, E.J., "Market Society and Meaning in Locke's Political Philosophy." *Journal of the History of Philosophy* 15 (1977): 33–44.

_____. "The Making of Homo Faber: John Locke between Ideology and History." *Journal of the History of Ideas* 15 (1972).

Lemos, Ramon M. "Locke's Theory of Property." *Interpretation 5* (Winter 1974).

Macpherson, D.B. *The Political Theory of Possessive Individualism: Hobbes to Locke* (Oxford: Oxford Univ. Press, 1962).

Marshall, John. *John Locke: Resistance, Religion and Responsibility* (New York: Cambridge Univ. Press, 1994).

Martin, C.B., and D.M. Armstrong, eds. *Locke and Berkeley: A Collection of Critical Essays* (Garden City, N.Y.: Doubleday, 1968).

Mitchell, Neil J. "John Locke and the Rise of Capitalism." *History of Political Economy* 18 (1986): 291–305.

Pufendorf, Samuel. *On The Law of Nature and Nations.* Translated by C.H. Oldfather and W.A. Oldfather (Oxford: Oxford Univ. Press, 1934).

_____. *The Duty of Man and Citizen* (Oxford: Oxford Univ. Press, 1927). Translated by Frank Gardner Moore.

Riley, Patrick. *Will and Political Legitimacy* (Cambridge: Harvard Univ. Press, 1982).

Rogers, G. A. J., ed. *Locke's Philosophy: Content and Context* (New York: Oxford Univ. Press, 1994).

Tarcov, Nathan. *Locke's Education for Liberty* (Chicago: Univ. of Chicago Press, 1984).

Tully, James. *A Discourse on Property: John Locke and His Adversaries* (Cambridge: Cambridge Univ. Press, 1980).

Vaughn, Karen I. *John Locke: Economist and Social Scientist* (Chicago: Univ. of Chicago Press, 1980).

Wood, Neal. *The Politics of Locke's Philosophy: A Social Study of "An Essay Concerning Human Understanding"* (Berkeley: Univ. of California Press, 1983).

_____. *John Locke and Agrarian Capitalism* (Los Angeles: Univ. of California Press, 1984).

Wootton, David. "Introduction." In *John Locke: Political Writings.* Edited by David Wootton (Harmondsworth, England: Penguin, 1993).

Yolton, John W., ed. *John Locke: Problems and Perspectives* (London: Cambridge Univ. Press, 1969).

_____. *Locke: An Introduction* (Oxford: Blackwell, 1985).

_____. *Locke Dictionary* (Oxford: Blackwell, 1993).

BERNARD MANDEVILLE (1670–1733)

THE SOUR note Bernard Mandeville sounded with *The Fable of the Bees* keeps resounding. In his caustic verse the inhabitants of a thriving beehive renounce luxury and vice for frugality and virtue, only to find their prosperity dissolve into poverty. The chorus of criticism provoked by this fable suggests Mandeville hit a nerve. Mandeville recognized that the terms on which Christianity and commerce had long accommodated one another could not withstand the gathering forces of capitalism. "Religion is one thing and Trade is another," wrote Mandeville, as if to taunt: "you can't have your cake and eat it too."

Three of the most disturbing paradoxes Mandeville examines are these. (1) An orderly society results from the manipulation of pride and shame by politicians clever enough to praise the public-spirited and shame those who ignore the public interest. The vices, and only the vices, are the building blocks of good social order. (2) Enjoyment of the "public benefits" of power, population, and prosperity requires unshackling the "private vices" of fraud, avarice, and pride. The "seven deadly sins" may mean moral ruin, but they turn out to be economic salvation. Mandeville does not put a happy face on this: if vicious conduct yields desirable outcomes, that does not absolve the vicious conduct. The fable does not vindicate modern society. (3) A thriving nation will be one where "great numbers" of the people are kept at hard work and as poor as can be without ruining them. A ready supply of cheap labor is better than any gold mine. By keeping a clear "division of labor" between the hard-working poor and the luxuriating rich, Mandeville avoids the further paradox that crops up in twentieth-century capitalism, where the same persons are counted on to work hard and consume hard.

Mandeville's writings fixed the attention of his contemporaries on the human passions. On the one hand, his knack for mocking virtue—"Pride and vanity have built more hospitals than all the Virtues together"— provoked Christian and other moralists to examine the passions anew to prove him wrong. On the other hand, Mandeville's inventory of the passions required for spiraling capitalist accumulation identified important features of capitalist development. For capitalism to take off, both the production of commodities by wage laborers and the consumption of commodities must keep growing. But how do you break down customary habits of work and consumption? How do you motivate people who work for money to work reliably and hard? And how do you stimulate ever new desires for commodities? Both prongs of Mandeville's preoccupation with human passions captured the imagination of the two greatest early advocates of the modern commercial nation, David Hume and Adam Smith. Indeed in Friedrich A. Hayek's estimation, Mandeville's greatest accomplishment was "that he made Hume possible." By meeting Mandeville halfway, Hume and Smith were able to steer clear of his immoralism: morality is a matter of taming, not eradicating, the passions. In the same stroke they discarded blocks of traditional Christian morality with derisive references to "monkish virtues," praised innocent luxury, highlighted virtues conducive to commerce (such as industriousness), and located powerful forces of moral edification in "the great scramble" of the market.

FROM *THE FABLE OF THE BEES*

FROM REMARK (L.): *WHILST LUXURY EMPLOY'D A MILLION OF THE POOR, &C.*

If every thing is to be Luxury (as in strictness it ought) that is not immediately necessary to make Man subsist as he is a living Creature, there is nothing else to be found in the World, no not even among the naked Savages; of which it is not probable that there are any but what by this time have made some Improvements upon their former manner of Living; and either in the preparation of their Eatables, the ordering of their Huts, or otherwise added something to what once sufficed them. This definition every body will say is too rigorous; I am of the same Opinion, but if we are to abate one Inch of this Severity, I am afraid we shan't know where to stop. When People tell us they only desire to keep themselves sweet and clean, there is no understanding what they would be at, if they made use of these Words in their genuine, proper, litteral Sense, they might soon be satisfy'd without much cost or trouble, if they did not want Water: But these two little adjectives are so comprehensive, especially in the Dialect of some Ladies, that no body can guess how far they may be stretcht. The Comforts of Life are likewise so various and extensive, that no body can tell what People mean by them, except he knows what sort of Life they lead. The same obscurity I observe in the words Decency and Conveniency, and I never understand them unless I am acquainted with the quality of the Persons that make use of them. People may go to Church together, and be all of one Mind as much as they please, I am apt to believe that when they pray for their daily Bread, the Bishop includes several things in that Petition which the Sexton does not think on.

By what I have said hitherto I would only shew, that if once we depart from calling every thing Luxury that is not absolutely necessary to keep a Man alive, that then there is no Luxury at all; for if the wants of Men are innumerable, then what ought to supply them has no bounds; what is call'd superfluous to some degree of People will be thought requisite to those of higher Quality; and neither the World nor the Skill of Man can produce any thing so curious or extravagant, but some most Gracious Sovereign or other, if it either eases or diverts him, will reckon it among the Necessaries of Life; not meaning every Body's Life, but that of his Sacred Person. . . .

149

FROM REMARK (Q.): FOR FRUGALLY THEY NOW LIVED ON THEIR SALARY

. . . Let us examine then what things are requisite to aggrandize and enrich a Nation. The first desirable Blessings for any Society of Men are a fertile Soil and a happy Climate, a mild Government, and more Land than People. These Things will render Man easy, loving, honest and sincere. In this Condition they may be as Virtuous as they can, without the least injury to the Publick, and consequently as happy as they please themselves. But they shall have no Arts or Sciences, or be quiet longer than their Neighbours will let them; they must be poor, ignorant, and almost wholly destitute of what we call the Comforts of Life, and all the Cardinal Virtues together won't so much as procure a tolerable Coat or a Porridge Pot among 'em: For in this State of slothful Ease and stupid Innocence, as you need not fear great Vices, so you must not expect any considerable Virtues. Man never exerts himself but when he is rous'd by his Desires: Whilst they lie dormant, and there is nothing to raise them, his Excellence and Abilities will be for ever undiscover'd, and the lumpish Machine, without the Influence of his Passions, may be justly compar'd to a huge Wind-mill without a breath of air.

Would you render a Society of Men strong and powerful, you must touch their Passions. Divide the Land, tho' there be never so much to spare, and their Possessions will make them Covetous: Rouse them, tho' but in Jest, from their Idleness with Praises, and Pride will set them to work in earnest: Teach them Trades and Handicrafts, and you'll bring Envy and Emulation among them: To encrease their Numbers, set up a variety of Manufactures, and leave no Ground uncultivated: Let Property be inviolably secured, and Priviledges equal to all Men: Suffer no body to act but what is lawful, and every body to think what he pleases; for a Country where every body may be maintained that will be employ'd, and the other Maxims are observ'd, must always be throng'd and can never want People, as long as there is any in the World. Would you have them Bold and Warlike, turn to Military Discipline, make good use of their Fear, and flatter their Vanity with Art and Assiduity: But would you moreover render them an opulent, knowing and polite Nation, teach 'em Commerce with Foreign Countries, and if possible get into the Sea, which to compass spare no Labour nor Industry, and let no difficulty de- ter you from it: Then promote Navigation, cherish the Merchant, and en- courage Trade in every Branch of it; this will bring Riches, and where they are, Arts and Sciences will soon follow, and by the help of what I have named and good Management, it is that Politicians can make a People potent, renown'd and flourishing.

But would you have a frugal and honest Society, the best Policy is to pre- serve Men in their Native Simplicity, strive not to encrease their Numbers; let them never be acquainted with Strangers or Superfluities, but remove and keep from them every thing that might raise their Desires, or improve their Understanding.

Great Wealth and Foreign Treasure will ever scorn to come among Men, unless you'll admit their inseparable Companions, Avarice and Luxury. Where Trade is considerable Fraud will intrude. To be at once well-bred and sincere, is no less than a Contradiction; and therefore whilst Man advances in Knowl- edge, and his Manners are polish'd, we must expect to see at the same time his Desires enlarg'd, his Appetites refin'd, and his Vices encreas'd.

The *Dutch* may ascribe their present Grandeur to the Virtue and Frugality of their Ancestors as they please; but what made that contemptible spot of Ground so considerable among the principal Powers of *Europe,* has been their Political Wisdom in postponing every thing to Merchandize and Navigation, the unlimited Liberty of Conscience that is enjoy'd among them, and the un- wearied Application with which they have always made use of the most ef- fectual means to encourage and increase Trade in general. . . .

Let us now, overjoy'd with this encrease of Wealth, take a view of the Con- dition the working People would be in, and reasoning from Experience, and what we daily observe of them, judge what their Behaviour would be in such a Case. Every body knows that there is a vast number of Journymen Weavers, Taylors, Clothworkers, and twenty other Handicrafts; who, if by four Days Labour in a Week they can maintain themselves, will hardly be perswaded to work the fifth; and that there are Thousands of Labouring Men of all sorts, who will, tho' they can hardly subsist, put themselves to fifty Inconveniencies, disoblige their Masters, pinch their Bellies, and run in Debt, to make Holidays. When Men shew such an extraordinary proclivity to Idleness and Pleasure, what reason have we to think that they would ever work, unless they were oblig'd to it by immediate Necessity? When we see an Artificer that cannot be drove to his Work before *Tuesday,* because the *Monday* Morning he has two Shillings left of his last Week's Pay; why should we imagine he would go to it at all, if he had fifteen or twenty Pounds in his Pocket?

What would, at this rate, become of our Manufactures? If the Merchant would send Cloth Abroad, he must make it himself, for the Clothier cannot get one Man out of twelve that used to work for him. If what I speak of was only to befal the Journeymen Shoemakers, and no body else, in less than a Twelvemonth half of us would go barefoot. The chief and most pressing use there is for Money in a Nation, is to pay the Labour of the Poor, and when there is a real Scarcity of it, those who have a great many Workmen to pay, will always feel it first; yet notwithstanding this great necessity of Coin, it would be easier, where Property was well secured, to live without Money than without Poor; for who would do the Work? For this reason the quantity of circulating Coin in a Country ought always to be proportion'd to the number of Hands that are employ'd; and the Wages of Labourers to the price of Provisions. From whence it is demonstrable, that whatever procures Plenty makes Labourers cheap, where the Poor are well managed; who as they ought to be kept from starving, so they should receive nothing worth saving. If here and there one of the lowest class by uncommon industry, and pinching his Belly, lifts himself above the Condition he was brought up in, no body ought to hinder him; Nay it is undeniably the wisest course for every Person in the Society, and for every private Family to be frugal; but it is the Intrest of all Rich Nations, that the greatest part of the Poor should almost never be Idle, and yet continually spend what they get.

All Men, as Sir *William Temple* observes very well, are more prone to Ease and Pleasure, than they are to Labour, when they are not prompted to it by Pride or Avarice, and those that get their Living by their daily Labour, are seldom powerfully influenc'd by either: So that they have nothing to stir them up to be serviceable but their Wants, which it is Prudence to relieve, but Folly to cure. The only thing then that can render the labouring Man industrious, is a moderate quantity of Money; for as too little will, according as his Temper is, either dispirit or make him Desperate, so too much will make him Insolent and Lazy.

A Man would be laugh'd at by most People, who should maintain that too much Money could undo a Nation: Yet this has been the Fate of *Spain;* to this the learned Don *Diego Savedra* ascribes the Ruin of his Country. The Fruits of the Earth in former Ages had made *Spain* so rich, that King *Lewis* XI of *France*

151

being come to the Court of *Toledo,* was astonish'd at its Splendour, and said, that he had never seen any thing to be compar'd to it, either in *Europe* or *Asia*; he that in his Travels to the *Holy Land* had run through every Province of them. In the Kingdom of *Castille* alone, (if we may believe some Writers) there were for the *Holy War* from all Parts of the World got together one hundred Thousand Foot, ten thousand Horse and sixty thousand Carriages for Baggage, which *Alonso* III maintain'd at his own Charge, and paid every Day as well Soldiers as Officers and Princes, every one according to his Rank and Dignity: Nay, down to the Reign of *Ferdinand* and *Isabella,* (who equip'd *Columbus*) and some time after, *Spain* was a fertile Country, where Trade and Manufactures flourish'd and had a knowing industrious People to boast of. But as soon as that mighty Treasure, that was obtain'd with more Hazard and Cruelty than the World till then had known, and which to come at, by the *Spaniard's* own Confession, had cost the Lives of twenty Millions of *Indians*; as soon, I say, as that Ocean of Treasure came rowling in upon them, it took away their Senses, and their Industry forsook them. The Farmer left his Plough, the Mechanick his Tools, the Merchant his Compting-house, and every body scorning to work, took his Pleasure and turn'd Gentleman. They thought they had reason to value themselves above all their Neighbours, and now nothing but the Conquest of the World would serve them.

The Consequence of this has been, that other Nations have supply'd what their own Sloth and Pride deny'd them; and when every body saw, that notwithstanding all the Prohibitions the Government could make against the Exportation of Bullion, the *Spaniard* would part with his Money, and bring it you aboard himself at the hazard of his Neck, all the World endeavour'd to work for *Spain.* Gold and Silver being by this means yearly divided and shared among all the Trading Countries, have made all Things dear, and most Nations of *Europe* Industrious, except their Owners, who ever since their mighty Acquisitions, sit with their Arms across, and wait every Year with impatience and anxiety, the arrival of their Revenues from Abroad, to pay others for what they have spent already: And thus by *too much Money,* the making of Colonies and other Mismanagements, of which it was the occasion *Spain* is from a fruitful and well peopled Country, with all its mighty Titles and Possessions, made a Barren and empty Thorough fair, thro' which Gold and Silver pass from *America* to the rest of the World, and the Nation, from a rich, acute, diligent and laborious, become a slow, idle, proud and beggarly People; so much for *Spain*: The next Country where Money may be call'd the Product is *Portugal,* and the Figure which that Kingdom with all its Gold makes in *Europe,* I think is not much to be envyed.

The great Art then to make a Nation happy, and what we call flourishing, consists in giving every body an Opportunity of being employ'd; which to compass, let a Government's first care be to promote as great a variety of Manufactures, Arts and Handicrafts, as Human Wit can invent; and the second to encourage Agriculture and Fishery in all their Branches, that the wholc Earth may be forc'd to exert itself as well as Man; for as the one is an infallible Maxim to draw vast multitudes of People into a Nation, so the other is the only Method to maintain them.

It is from this Policy, and not the trifling Regulations of Lavishness and Frugality, (which will ever take their own Course, according to the Circumstances of the People) that the Greatness and Felicity of Nations must be expected; for let the Value of Gold and Silver either rise or fall, the Enjoyment of all Societies will ever depend upon the Fruits of the Earth, and the Labour of the People; both which joyn'd together are a more certain, a more inexhaustible and a more real Treasure than the Gold of Brazil, or the Silver of *Potosi.*

For Further Reading

Mandeville, Bernard. *The Fable of the Bees.* 2 vols. Edited by F.B. Kaye (Oxford: Oxford Univ. Press, 1924).

_____. *The Fable of the Bees.* Edited with introduction by Phillip Harth (Harmondsworth, England: Penguin, 1970).

_____. *A Letter To Dion* (1732). Los Angeles: Augustan Reprint Society, Publication No. 41, 1953.

Berkeley, George. *Alciphron, or, the Minute Philosopher. Complete Works,* vol. 3. Edited by A.C. Fraser (Oxford: Clarendon Press, 1901).

Colletti, Lucio. "Mandeville, Rousseau and Smith." In *From Rousseau to Lenin* (New York: Monthly Review Press, 1972).

Goldsmith, M.M. *Private Vices, Public Benefits: Bernard Mandeville's Social and Political Thought* (Cambridge: Cambridge Univ. Press, 1985).

Hayek, Friedrich A. "Dr. Bernard Mandeville." *Proceedings of the British Academy* 52 (1966): 125-41.

Horne, Thomas A. *The Social Thought of Bernard Mandeville: Virtue and Commerce in Early Eighteenth-Century England* (New York: Columbia Univ. Press, 1978).

Hundert, E.J. *The Enlightenment's Fable: Bernard Mandeville and the Discovery of Society* (Cambridge: Cambridge Univ. Press, 1994).

Monro, Hector. *The Ambivalence of Bernard Mandeville* (London: Oxford Univ. Press, 1975).

Rosenberg, Nathan. "Mandeville and Laissez-faire." *Journal of the History of Ideas* 24 (April-June 1963).

Schneider, Louis, ed. *Paradox and Society: The Work of Bernard Mandeville* (New Brunswick, N.J.: Transaction Bks., 1987).

Viner, Jacob. "Introduction to Bernard Mandeville, A Letter to Dion." In *The Long View and the Short* (Glencoe, Ill.: Free Press, 1958).

DAVID HUME (1711–1776)

chapter 7

COMMERCE IS the social form of the provisioning process most agreeable to human nature: this is the conclusion of David Hume's philosophical and historical inquiries into the matter. Commerce's role in Hume's "natural history" of the human species marks a startling departure from the hostility or reluctant accommodation going back to Plato and Aristotle, early Christianity, and pre-commercial societies. Commerce, in Hume's view, is the great humanizing force in history. Moral considerations, joined to a host of others, weigh heavily in favor of commerce. At the close of his essay "Of Money," Hume links the spread of the commodity form to the improvement of "customs and manners" from "rustic hospitality"—a gentler phrase than Marx's "rural idiocy"—to the refined, moderate, and urbane dispositions found in commercial republics. Follow the yellow brick road from barbarism to civilization.

As announced by the title of his youthful masterwork, *A Treatise of Human*

Nature, Hume's preoccupation was puzzling out the intellectual, emotive, moral, social, and political dimensions of human nature. Hume's reflections on commerce belong to that sweeping project. Commerce is a piece of the human puzzle; fitting it in with the other pieces is Hume's task in his economic essays. Reading "Of Commerce," you cannot help but feel Hume's satisfaction: things fall into place once you give commerce its due.

While criticizing Plato's *Republic*, Aristotle asked: if the guardians of the state are denied happiness, where will we find it? Hume develops his own challenge to the Spartan conclusion that personal liberty and happiness are always at odds with the power of the state. Hume argues that a thriving commercial nation springs free of the "zero-sum game" where more wealth in private hands means less for public coffers. Prosperity strips away ancient limitations; continually expanding wealth makes citizens happy and their states mighty. Moreover, this new-found harmony of private and public interests enjoys the great advantage of conforming to the "common bent of mankind." Nonetheless, because of human laziness and hidebound ties to custom, commerce needs a jump start to get human passions pushing in the right directions. Here it was different strokes for different folks: the struggle to survive should keep the working poor hard at it—Hume ingeniously figured that a steady but moderate rate of inflation keeps wages nosed down. Filling his favored "middling ranks" called for a different strategy. Foreign trade "rouses men from indolence" both by "presenting the gayer and more opulent part of the nation with objects of luxury" and by giving merchants a taste for profits. Properly animated "with a spirit of avarice and industry, art and luxury," the middle class possesses the right composition of passions to keep commerce spiralling upward and thereby quickening "the march of the spirits," spreading happiness, advancing knowledge, softening tempers, laying down law and order, preserving liberty, and enhancing military preparedness.

A few lingering worries about commerce may be detected in Hume's writings. He warns about excessive inequalities of wealth, which encroach upon the happiness of the many, encourage political instability, and obstruct public finances. Hume detested unmixed avarice, calling it a "monstrously absurd" and chillingly "irreclaimable" passion. Only "a sense of honor and virtue" can "restrain or regulate the love of money." He relied on the resilience of commercial societies to keep reseeding that sense of honor and virtue. Though Hume endorsed the "enlargement" of our sentiments, he recognized that "the generosity of men is very limited, and that it seldom extends beyond their friends and family, or, at most, beyond their native country." Hume had just an inkling of the question: Does the global economy erode the local conditions which form identities, loyalties, and virtues? Will the commercial "enlargement" of our sentiments stretch them beyond the limits of their elasticity?

FROM *ESSAYS, MORAL, POLITICAL, AND LITERARY*

PART II

FROM ESSAY I: OF COMMERCE

...The greatness of a state, and the happiness of its subjects, how independent soever they may be supposed in some respects, are commonly allowed to be inseparable with regard to commerce; and as private men receive greater security, in the possession of their trade and riches, from the power of the public, so the public becomes powerful in proportion to the opulence and extensive commerce of private men. This maxim is true in general; though I cannot forbear thinking, that it may possibly admit of exceptions, and that we often establish it with too little reserve and limitation. There may be some circumstances, where the commerce and riches and luxury of individuals, instead of adding strength to the public, will serve only to thin its armies, and diminish its authority among the neighbouring nations. Man is a very variable being, and susceptible of many different opinions, principles, and rules of conduct. What may be true, while he adheres to one way of thinking, will be found false, when he has embraced an opposite set of manners and opinions.

The bulk of every state may be divided into *husbandmen* and *manufacturers*. The former are employed in the culture of the land; the latter work up the materials furnished by the former, into all the commodities which are necessary or ornamental to human life. As soon as men quit their savage state, where they live chiefly by hunting and fishing, they must fall into these two classes; though the arts of agriculture employ *at first* the most numerous part of the society. Time and experience improve so much these arts, that the land may easily maintain a much greater number of men, than those who are immediately employed in its culture, or who furnish the more necessary manufactures to such as are so employed.

157

If these superfluous hands apply themselves to the finer arts, which are commonly denominated the arts of *luxury,* they add to the happiness of the state; since they afford to many the opportunity of receiving enjoyments, with which they would otherwise have been unacquainted. But may not another scheme be proposed for the employment of these superfluous hands? May not the sovereign lay claim to them, and employ them in fleets and armies, to encrease the dominions of the state abroad, and spread its fame over distant nations? It is certain that the fewer desires and wants are found in the proprietors and labourers of land, the fewer hands do they employ; and consequently the superfluities of the land, instead of maintaining tradesmen and manufacturers, may support fleets and armies to a much greater extent, than where a great many arts are required to minister to the luxury of particular persons. Here therefore seems to be a kind of opposition between the greatness of the state and the happiness of the subject. A state is never greater than when all its superfluous hands are employed in the service of the public. The ease and convenience of private persons require, that these hands should be employed in their service. The one can never be satisfied, but at the expence of the other. As the ambition of the sovereign must entrench on the luxury of individuals; so the luxury of individuals must diminish the force, and check the ambition of the sovereign.

Nor is this reasoning merely chimerical; but is founded on history and experience. The republic of SPARTA was certainly more powerful than any state now in the world, consisting of an equal number of people; and this was owing entirely to the want of commerce and luxury. The HELOTES were the labourers: The SPARTANS were the soldiers or gentlemen. It is evident, that the labour of the HELOTES could not have maintained so great a number of SPARTANS, had these latter lived in ease and delicacy, and given employment to a great variety of trades and manufactures. The like policy may be remarked in ROME. And indeed, throughout all ancient history, it is observable, that the smallest republics raised and maintained greater armies, than states consisting of triple the number of inhabitants, are able to support at present. It is computed, that, in all EUROPEAN nations, the proportion between soldiers and people does not exceed one to a hundred. But we read, that the city of ROME alone, with its small territory, raised and maintained, in early times, ten legions against the LATINS. ATHENS, the whole of whose dominions was not larger than YORKSHIRE, sent to the expedition against SICILY near forty thousand men. DIONYSIUS the elder, it is said, maintained a standing army of a hundred thousand foot and ten thousand horse, besides a large fleet of four hundred sail; though his territories extended no farther than the city of SYRACUSE, about a third of the island of SICILY, and some sea-port towns and garrisons on the coast of ITALY and ILLYRICUM. It is true, the ancient armies, in time of war, subsisted much upon plunder: But did not the enemy plunder in their turn? which was a more ruinous way of levying a tax, than any other that could be devised. In short, no probable reason can be assigned for the great power of the more ancient states above the modern, but their want of commerce and luxury. Few artizans were maintained by the labour of the farmers, and therefore more soldiers might live upon it. LIVY says, that ROME, in his time, would find it difficult to raise as large an army as that which, in her early days, she sent out against the GAULS and LATINS. Instead of those soldiers who fought for liberty and empire in CAMILLUS'S time, there were, in AUGUSTUS'S days, musicians, painters, cooks, players, and tailors; and if the land was equally cultivated at both periods, it could certainly maintain equal numbers in the one profession as in the other. They added nothing to the mere necessaries of life, in the latter period more than in the former.

It is natural on this occasion to ask, whether sovereigns may not return to the maxims of ancient policy, and consult their own interest in this respect, more than the happiness of their subjects? I answer, that it appears to me, almost impossible; and that because ancient policy was violent, and contrary to the more natural and usual course of things. It is well known with what peculiar laws SPARTA was governed, and what a prodigy that republic is justly esteemed by every one, who has considered human nature as it has displayed itself in other nations, and other ages. Were the testimony of history less positive and circumstantial, such a government would appear a mere philosophical whim or fiction, and impossible ever to be reduced to practice. And though the ROMAN and other ancient republics were supported on principles somewhat more natural, yet was there an extraordinary concurrence of circumstances to make them submit to such grievous burthens. They were free states; they were small ones; and the age being martial, all their neighbours were continually in arms. Freedom naturally begets public spirit, especially in small states; and this public spirit, this *amor patriae*, must encrease, when the public is almost in continual alarm, and men are obliged, every moment, to expose themselves to the greatest dangers for its defence. A continual succession of wars makes every citizen a soldier: He takes the field in his turn: And during his service he is chiefly maintained by himself. This service is indeed equivalent to a heavy tax; yet is it less felt by a people addicted to arms, who fight for honour and revenge more than pay, and are unacquainted with gain and industry as well as pleasure. Not to mention the great equality of fortunes among the inhabitants of the ancient republics, where every field, belonging to a different proprietor, was able to maintain a family, and rendered the numbers of citizens very considerable, even without trade and manufactures.

But though the want of trade and manufactures, among a free and very martial people, may *sometimes* have no other effect than to render the public more powerful, it is certain, that, in the common course of human affairs, it will have a quite contrary tendency. Sovereigns must take mankind as they find them, and cannot pretend to introduce any violent change in their principles and ways of thinking. A long course of time, with a variety of accidents and circumstances, are requisite to produce those great revolutions, which so much diversify the face of human affairs. And the less natural any set of principles are, which support a particular society, the more difficulty will a legislator meet with in raising and cultivating them. It is his best policy to comply with the common bent of mankind, and give it all the improvements of which it is susceptible. Now, according to the most natural course of things, industry and arts and trade encrease the power of the sovereign as well as the happiness of the subjects; and that policy is violent, which aggrandizes the public by the poverty of individuals. This will easily appear from a few considerations, which will present to us the consequences of sloth and barbarity.

Where manufactures and mechanic arts are not cultivated, the bulk of the people must apply themselves to agriculture; and if their skill and industry encrease, there must arise a great superfluity from their labour beyond what suffices to maintain them. They have no temptation, therefore, to encrease their skill and industry; since they cannot exchange that superfluity for any commodities, which may serve either to their pleasure or vanity. A habit of indolence naturally prevails. The greater part of the land lies uncultivated. What is cultivated, yields not its utmost for want of skill and assiduity in the farmers. If at any time the public exigencies require, that great numbers should be employed in the public service, the labour of the people furnishes now no superfluities, by which these numbers can be maintained. The labourers cannot encrease their skill and industry on a sudden. Lands uncultivated cannot be brought into tillage for some years. The armies, mean while, must either make sudden and violent conquests, or disband for want of subsistence. A regular attack or defence, therefore, is not to be expected from such a people, and their soldiers must be as ignorant and unskilful as their farmers and manufacturers.

Every thing in the world is purchased by labour; and our passions are the only causes of labour. When a nation abounds in manufactures and mechanic arts, the proprietors of land, as well as the farmers, study agriculture as a science, and redouble their industry and attention. The superfluity, which arises from their labour, is not lost; but is exchanged with manufactures for those commodities, which men's luxury now makes them covet. By this means, land furnishes a great deal more of the necessaries of life, than what suffices for those who cultivate it. In times of peace and tranquillity, this superfluity goes to the maintenance of manufacturers, and the improvers of liberal arts. But it is easy for the public to convert many of these manufacturers into soldiers, and maintain them by that superfluity, which arises from the labour of the farmers. Accordingly we find, that this is the case in all civilized governments. When the sovereign raises an army, what is the consequence? He imposes a tax. This tax obliges all the people to retrench what is least necessary to their subsistence. Those, who labour in such commodities, must either enlist in the troops, or turn themselves to agriculture, and thereby oblige some labourers to enlist for want of business. And to consider the matter abstractedly, manufactures encrease the power of the state only as they store up so much labour, and that of a kind to which the public may lay claim, without depriving any one of the necessaries of life. The more labour, therefore, is employed beyond mere necessaries, the more powerful is any state; since the persons engaged in that labour may easily be converted to the public service. In a state without manufactures, there may be the same number of hands; but there is not the same quantity of labour, nor of the same kind. All the labour is there bestowed upon necessaries, which can admit of little or no abatement.

Thus the greatness of the sovereign and the happiness of the state are, in a great measure, united with regard to trade and manufactures. It is a violent method, and in most cases impracticable, to oblige the labourer to toil, in order to raise from the land more than what subsists himself and family. Furnish him with manufactures and commodities, and he will do it of himself. Afterwards you will find it easy to seize some part of his superfluous labour, and employ it in the public service, without giving him his wonted return. Being accustomed to industry, he will think this less grievous, than if, at once, you obliged him to an augmentation of labour without any reward. The case is the same with regard to the other members of the state. The greater is the stock of labour of all kinds, the greater quantity may be taken from the heap, without making any sensible alteration in it.

A public granary of corn, a storehouse of cloth, a magazine of arms; all these must be allowed real riches and strength in any state. Trade and industry are really nothing but a stock of labour, which, in times of peace and tranquillity, is employed for the ease and satisfaction of individuals; but in the exigencies of state, may, in part, be turned to public advantage. Could we convert a city into a kind of fortified camp, and infuse into each breast so martial a genius, and such a passion for public good, as to make every one willing to undergo the greatest hardships for the sake of the public; these affections might now, as in ancient times, prove alone a sufficient spur to industry, and support the community. It would then be advantageous, as in camps, to banish all arts and luxury; and, by restrictions on equipage and tables, make the provisions and forage last longer than if the army were loaded with a number of superfluous retainers. But as these principles are too disinterested and too difficult to support, it is requisite to govern men by other passions, and animate them with a spirit of avarice and industry, art and luxury. The camp is, in this case, loaded with a superfluous retinue; but the provisions flow in proportionably larger. The harmony of the whole is still supported; and the natural bent of the mind being more complied with, individuals, as well as the public, find their account in the observance of those maxims.

161

The same method of reasoning will let us see the advantage of *foreign* commerce, in augmenting the power of the state, as well as the riches and happiness of the subject. It encreases the stock of labour in the nation; and the sovereign may convert what share of it he finds necessary to the service of the public. Foreign trade, by its imports, furnishes materials for new manufactures; and by its exports, it produces labour in particular commodities, which could not be consumed at home. In short, a kingdom, that has a large import and export, must abound more with industry, and that employed upon delicacies and luxuries, than a kingdom which rests contented with its native commodities. It is, therefore, more powerful, as well as richer and happier. The individuals reap the benefit of these commodities, so far as they gratify the senses and appetites. And the public is also a gainer, while a greater stock of labour is, by this means, stored up against any public exigency; that is, a greater number of laborious men are maintained, who may be diverted to the public service, without robbing any one of the necessaries, or even the chief conveniencies of life.

If we consult history, we shall find, that, in most nations, foreign trade has preceded any refinement in home manufactures, and given birth to domestic luxury. The temptation is stronger to make use of foreign commodities, which are ready for use, and which are entirely new to us, than to make improvements on any domestic commodity, which always advance by slow degrees, and never affect us by their novelty. The profit is also very great, in exporting what is superfluous at home, and what bears no price, to foreign nations, whose soil or climate is not favourable to that commodity. Thus men become acquainted with the *pleasures* of luxury and the *profits* of commerce; and their *delicacy* and *industry*, being once awakened, carry them on to farther improvements, in every branch of domestic as well as foreign trade. And this perhaps is the chief advantage which arises from a commerce with strangers. It rouses men from their indolence; and presenting the gayer and more opulent part of the nation with objects of luxury, which they never before dreamed of, raises in them a desire of a more splendid way of life than what their ancestors enjoyed. And at the same time, the few merchants, who possess the secret of this importation and exportation, make great profits; and becoming rivals in wealth to the ancient nobility, tempt other adventurers to become their rivals in commerce. Imitation soon diffuses all those arts; while domestic manufactures emulate the foreign in their improvements, and work up every home commodity to the utmost perfection of which it is susceptible. Their own steel and iron, in such laborious hands, become equal to the gold and rubies of the INDIES.

When the affairs of the society are once brought to this situation, a nation may lose most of its foreign trade, and yet continue a great and powerful people. If strangers will not take any particular commodity of ours, we must cease to labour in it. The same hands will turn themselves towards some refinement in other commodities, which may be wanted at home. And there must always be materials for them to work upon; till every person in the state, who possesses riches, enjoys as great plenty of home commodities, and those in as great perfection, as he desires; which can never possibly happen. CHINA is represented as one of the most flourishing empires in the world; though it has very little commerce beyond its own territories.

It will not, I hope, be considered as a superfluous digression, if I here observe, that, as the multitude of mechanical arts is advantageous, so is the great number of persons to whose share the productions of these arts fall. A too great disproportion among the citizens weakens any state. Every person, if possible, ought to enjoy the fruits of his labour, in a full possession of all the necessaries, and many of the conveniencies of life. No one can doubt, but such an equality is most suitable to human nature, and diminishes much less from the *happiness* of the rich than it adds to that of the poor. It also augments the *power of the state*, and makes any extraordinary taxes or impositions be paid with more chearfulness. Where the riches are engrossed by a few, these must contribute very largely to the supplying of the public necessities. But when the riches are dispersed among multitudes, the burthen feels light on every shoulder, and the taxes make not a very sensible difference on any one's way of living.

Add to this, that, where the riches are in few hands, these must enjoy all the power, and will readily conspire to lay the whole burthen on the poor, and oppress them still farther, to the discouragement of all industry.

In this circumstance consists the great advantage of ENGLAND above any nation at present in the world, or that appears in the records of any story. It is true, the ENGLISH feel some disadvantages in foreign trade by the high price of labour, which is in part the effect of the riches of their artisans, as well as of the plenty of money: But as foreign trade is not the most material circumstance, it is not to be put in competition with the happiness of so many millions. And if there were no more to endear to them that free government under which they live, this alone were sufficient. The poverty of the common people is a natural, if not an infallible effect of absolute monarchy; though I doubt, whether it be always true, on the other hand, that their riches are an infallible result of liberty. Liberty must be attended with particular accidents, and a certain turn of thinking, in order to produce that effect. Lord BACON, accounting for the great advantages obtained by the ENGLISH in their wars with FRANCE, ascribes them chiefly to the superior ease and plenty of the common people amongst the former; yet the government of the two kingdoms was, at that time, pretty much alike. Where the labourers and artisans are accustomed to work for low wages, and to retain but a small part of the fruits of their labour, it is difficult for them, even in a free government, to better their condition, or conspire among themselves to heighten their wages. But even where they are accustomed to a more plentiful way of life, it is easy for the rich, in an arbitrary government, to conspire against *them*, and throw the whole burthen of the taxes on their shoulders. . . .

ESSAY II: OF REFINEMENT IN THE ARTS

Luxury is a word of an uncertain signification, and may be taken in a good as well as in a bad sense. In general, it means great refinement in the gratification of the senses; and any degree of it may be innocent or blameable, according to the age, or country, or condition of the person. The bounds between the virtue and the vice cannot here be exactly fixed, more than in other moral subjects. To imagine, that the gratifying of any sense, or the indulging of any delicacy in meat, drink, or apparel, is of itself a vice, can never enter into a head, that is not disordered by the frenzies of enthusiasm. I have, indeed, heard of a monk abroad, who, because the windows of his cell opened upon a noble prospect, made a *covenant with his eyes* never to turn that way, or receive so sensual a gratification. And such is the crime of drinking CHAMPAGNE or BURGUNDY, preferably to small beer or porter. These indulgences are only vices, when they are pursued at the expence of some virtue, as liberality or charity; in like manner as they are follies, when for them a man ruins his fortune, and reduces himself to want and beggary. Where they entrench upon no virtue, but leave ample subject whence to provide for friends, family, and every proper object of generosity or compassion, they are entirely innocent, and have in every age been acknowledged such by almost all moralists. To be entirely occupied with the luxury of the table, for instance, without any relish for the pleasures of ambition, study, or conversation, is a mark of stupidity, and is incompatible with any vigour of temper or genius. To confine one's expence entirely to such a gratification, without regard to friends or family, is an indication of a heart destitute of humanity or benevolence. But if a man reserve time sufficient for all laudable pursuits, and money sufficient for all generous purposes, he is free from every shadow of blame or reproach.

Since luxury may be considered either as innocent or blameable, one may be surprized at those preposterous opinions, which have been entertained concerning it; while men of libertine principles bestow praises even on vicious luxury, and represent it as highly advantageous to society; and on the other hand, men of severe morals blame even the most innocent luxury, and represent it as the source of all the corruptions, disorders, and factions, incident to civil government. We shall here endeavour to correct both these extremes, by proving, *first,* that the ages of refinement are both the happiest and most virtuous; *secondly,* that wherever luxury ceases to be innocent, it also ceases to be beneficial; and when carried a degree too far, is a quality pernicious, though perhaps not the most pernicious, to political society.

To prove the first point, we need but consider the effects of refinement both on *private* and on *public* life. Human happiness, according to the most received notions, seems to consist in three ingredients; action, pleasure, and indolence: And though these ingredients ought to be mixed in different proportions, according to the particular disposition of the person; yet no one ingredient can be entirely wanting, without destroying, in some measure, the relish of the whole composition. Indolence or repose, indeed, seems not of itself to contribute much to our enjoyment; but, like sleep, is requisite as an indulgence to the weakness of human nature, which cannot support an uninterrupted course of business or pleasure. That quick march of the spirits, which takes a man from himself, and chiefly gives satisfaction, does in the end exhaust the mind, and requires some intervals of repose, which, though agreeable for a moment, yet, if prolonged, beget a languor and lethargy, that destroys all enjoyment. Education, custom, and example, have a mighty influence in turning the mind to any of these pursuits; and it must be owned, that, where they promote a relish for action and pleasure, they are so far favourable to human happiness. In times when industry and the arts flourish, men are kept in perpetual occupation, and enjoy, as their reward, the occupation itself, as well as those pleasures which are the fruit of their labour. The mind acquires new vigour; enlarges its powers and faculties; and by an assiduity in honest industry, both satisfies its natural appetites, and prevents the growth of unnatural ones, which commonly spring up, when nourished by ease and idleness. Banish those arts from society, you deprive men both of action and of pleasure; and leaving nothing but indolence in their place, you even destroy the relish of indolence, which never is agreeable, but when it succeeds to labour, and recruits the spirits, exhausted by too much application and fatigue.

Another advantage of industry and of refinements in the mechanical arts, is, that they commonly produce some refinements in the liberal; nor can one be carried to perfection, without being accompanied, in some degree, with the other. The same age, which produces great philosophers and politicians, renowned generals and poets, usually abounds with skilful weavers, and ship-carpenters. We cannot reasonably expect, that a piece of woollen cloth will be wrought to perfection in a nation, which is ignorant of astronomy, or where ethics are neglected. The spirit of the age affects all the arts; and the minds of men, being once roused from their lethargy, and put into a fermentation, turn themselves on all sides, and carry improvements into every art and science. Profound ignorance is totally banished, and men enjoy the privilege of rational creatures, to think as well as to act, to cultivate the pleasures of the mind as well as those of the body.

The more these refined arts advance, the more sociable men become: nor is it possible, that, when enriched with science, and possessed of a fund of conversation, they should be contented to remain in solitude, or live with their fellow-citizens in that distant manner, which is peculiar to ignorant and barbarous nations. They flock into cities; love to receive and communicate knowledge; to show their wit or their breeding; their taste in conversation or living, in clothes or furniture. Curiosity allures the wise; vanity the foolish; and pleasure both. Particular clubs and societies are every where formed: Both sexes meet in an easy and sociable manner; and the tempers of men, as well as their behaviour, refine apace. So that, beside the improvements which they receive from knowledge and the liberal arts, it is impossible but they must feel an encrease of humanity, from the very habit of conversing together, and contributing to each other's pleasure and entertainment. Thus *industry, knowledge,* and *humanity,* are linked together by an indissoluble chain, and are found, from experience as well as reason, to be peculiar to the more polished, and, what are commonly denominated, the more luxurious ages.

Nor are these advantages attended with disadvantages, that bear any proportion to them. The more men refine upon pleasure, the less will they indulge in excesses of any kind; because nothing is more destructive to true pleasure than such excesses. One may safely affirm, that the TARTARS are

165

oftener guilty of beastly gluttony, when they feast on their dead horses, than EUROPEAN courtiers with all their refinements of cookery. And if libertine love, or even infidelity to the marriage-bed, be more frequent in polite ages, when it is often regarded only as a piece of gallantry; drunkenness, on the other hand, is much less common: A vice more odious, and more pernicious both to mind and body. And in this matter I would appeal, not only to an OVID or a PETRONIUS, but to a SENECA or a CATO. We know, that CAESAR, during CATILINE'S conspiracy, being necessitated to put into CATO'S hands a *billet-doux*, which discovered an intrigue with SERVILIA, CATO'S own sister, that stern philosopher threw it back to him with indignation; and in the bitterness of his wrath, gave him the appellation of drunkard, as a term more opprobrious than that with which he could more justly have reproached him.

But industry, knowledge, and humanity, are not advantageous in private life alone: They diffuse their beneficial influence on the *public,* and render the government as great and flourishing as they make individuals happy and prosperous. The encrease and consumption of all the commodities, which serve to the ornament and pleasure of life, are advantageous to society; because, at the same time that they multiply those innocent gratifications to individuals, they are a kind of *storehouse* of labour, which, in the exigencies of state, may be turned to the public service. In a nation, where there is no demand for such superfluities, men sink into indolence, lose all enjoyment of life, and are useless to the public, which cannot maintain or support its fleets and armies, from the industry of such slothful members.

The bounds of all the EUROPEAN kingdoms are, at present, nearly the same they were two hundred years ago: But what a difference is there in the power and grandeur of those kingdoms? Which can be ascribed to nothing but the encrease of art and industry. When CHARLES VIII. of FRANCE invaded ITALY, he carried with him about 20,000 men: Yet this armament so exhausted the nation, as we learn from GUICCIARDIN, that for some years it was not able to make so great an effort. The late king of FRANCE, in time of war, kept in pay above 400,000 men; though from MAZARINE'S death to his own, he was engaged in a course of wars that lasted near thirty years.

This industry is much promoted by the knowledge inseparable from ages of art and refinement; as, on the other hand, this knowledge enables the public to make the best advantage of the industry of its subjects. Laws, order, police, discipline; these can never be carried to any degree of perfection, before human reason has refined itself by exercise, and by an application to the more vulgar arts, at least, of commerce and manufacture. Can we expect, that a government will be well modelled by a people, who know not how to make a spinning-wheel, or to employ a loom to advantage? Not to mention, that all ignorant ages are infested with superstition, which throws the government off its bias, and disturbs men in the pursuit of their interest and happiness.

Knowledge in the arts of government naturally begets mildness and moderation, by instructing men in the advantages of humane maxims above rigour and severity, which drive subjects into rebellion, and make the return to submission impracticable, by cutting off all hopes of pardon. When the tempers of men are softened as well as their knowledge improved, this humanity appears still more conspicuous, and is the chief characteristic which distinguishes a civilized age from times of barbarity and ignorance. Factions are then less inveterate, revolutions less tragical, authority less severe, and seditions less frequent. Even foreign wars abate of their cruelty; and after the field of battle, where honour and interest steel men against compassion as well as fear, the combatants divest themselves of the brute, and resume the man.

Nor need we fear, that men, by losing their ferocity, will lose their martial spirit, or become less undaunted and vigorous in defence of their country or their liberty. The arts have no such effect in enervating either the mind or body. On the contrary, industry, their inseparable attendant, adds new force to both. And if anger, which is said to be the whetstone of courage, loses somewhat of its asperity, by politeness and refinement; a sense of honour, which is a stronger, more constant, and more governable principle, acquires fresh vigour by that elevation of genius which arises from knowledge and a good education. Add to this, that courage can neither have any duration, nor be of any use, when not accompanied with discipline and martial skill, which are seldom found among a barbarous people. The ancients remarked, that DATAMES was the only barbarian that ever knew the art of war. And PYRRHUS, seeing the ROMANS marshal their army with some art and skill, said with surprize, *These barbarians have nothing barbarous in their discipline!* It is observable, that, as the old ROMANS, by applying themselves solely to war, were almost the only uncivilized people that ever possessed military discipline; so the modern ITALIANS are the only civilized people, among EUROPEANS, that ever wanted courage and a martial spirit. Those who would ascribe this effeminacy of the ITALIANS to their luxury, or politeness, or application to the arts, need but consider the FRENCH and ENGLISH, whose bravery is as uncontestable, as their love for the arts, and their assiduity in commerce. The ITALIAN historians give us a more satisfactory reason for this degeneracy of their countrymen. They shew us how the sword was dropped at once by all the ITALIAN sovereigns; while the VENETIAN aristocracy was jealous of its subjects, the FLORENTINE democracy applied itself entirely to commerce; ROME was governed by priests, and NAPLES by women. War then became the business of soldiers of fortune, who spared one another, and to the astonishment of the world, could engage a whole day in what they called a battle, and return at night to their camp, without the least bloodshed.

What has chiefly induced severe moralists to declaim against refinement in the arts, is the example of ancient ROME, which, joining, to its poverty and

167

rusticity, virtue and public spirit, rose to such a surprizing height of grandeur and liberty; but having learned from its conquered provinces the ASIATIC luxury, fell into every kind of corruption; whence arose sedition and civil wars, attended at last with the total loss of liberty. All the LATIN classics, whom we peruse in our infancy, are full of these sentiments, and universally ascribe the ruin of their state to the arts and riches imported from the East: Insomuch that SALLUST represents a taste for painting as a vice, no less than lewdness and drinking. And so popular were these sentiments, during the later ages of the republic, that this author abounds in praises of the old rigid ROMAN virtue, though himself the most egregious instance of modern luxury and corruption; speaks contemptuously of the GRECIAN eloquence, though the most elegant writer in the world; nay, employs preposterous digressions and declamations to this purpose, though a model of taste and correctness.

But it would be easy to prove, that these writers mistook the cause of the disorders in the ROMAN state, and ascribed to luxury and the arts, what really proceeded from an ill modelled government, and the unlimited extent of conquests. Refinement on the pleasures and conveniencies of life has no natural tendency to beget venality and corruption. The value, which all men put upon any particular pleasure, depends on comparison and experience; nor is a porter less greedy of money, which he spends on bacon and brandy, than a courtier, who purchases champagne and ortolans. Riches are valuable at all times, and to all men; because they always purchase pleasures, such as men are accustomed to, and desire: Nor can any thing restrain or regulate the love of money, but a sense of honour and virtue; which, if it be not nearly equal at all times, will naturally abound most in ages of knowledge and refinement.

Of all EUROPEAN kingdoms, POLAND seems the most defective in the arts of war as well as peace, mechanical as well as liberal; yet it is there that venality and corruption do most prevail. The nobles seem to have preserved their crown elective for no other purpose, than regularly to sell it to the highest bidder. This is almost the only species of commerce, with which that people are acquainted.

The liberties of ENGLAND, so far from decaying since the improvements in the arts, have never flourished so much as during that period. And though corruption may seem to encrease of late years; this is chiefly to be ascribed to our established liberty, when our princes have found the impossibility of governing without parliaments, or of terrifying parliaments by the phantom of prerogative. Not to mention, that this corruption or venality prevails much more among the electors than the elected; and therefore cannot justly be ascribed to any refinements in luxury.

If we consider the matter in a proper light, we shall find, that a progress in the arts is rather favourable to liberty, and has a natural tendency to preserve, if not produce a free government. In rude unpolished nations, where the arts are neglected, all labour is bestowed on the cultivation of the ground; and the whole society is divided into two classes, proprietors of land, and their vassals or tenants. The latter are necessarily dependent, and fitted for slavery and subjection; especially where they possess no riches, and are not valued for their knowledge in agriculture; as must always be the case where the arts are neglected. The former naturally erect themselves into petty tyrants; and must either submit to an absolute master, for the sake of peace and order; or if they will preserve their independency, like the ancient barons, they must fall into feuds and contests among themselves, and throw the whole society into such confusion, as is perhaps worse than the most despotic government. But where luxury nourishes commerce and industry, the peasants, by a proper cultivation of the land, become rich and independent; while the tradesmen and merchants acquire a share of the property, and draw authority and consideration to that middling rank of men, who are the best and firmest basis of public liberty. These submit not to slavery, like the peasants, from poverty and meanness of spirit; and having no hopes of tyrannizing over others, like the barons, they are not tempted, for the sake of that gratification, to submit to the tyranny of their sovereign. They covet equal laws, which may secure their property, and preserve them from monarchical, as well as aristocratical tyranny.

The lower house is the support of our popular government; and all the world acknowledges, that it owed its chief influence and consideration to the encrease of commerce, which threw such a balance of property into the hands of the commons. How inconsistent then is it to blame so violently a refinement in the arts, and to represent it as the bane of liberty and public spirit!

169

To declaim against present times, and magnify the virtue of remote ancestors, is a propensity almost inherent in human nature: And as the sentiments and opinions of civilized ages alone are transmitted to posterity, hence it is that we meet with so many severe judgments pronounced against luxury, and even science; and hence it is that at present we give so ready an assent to them. But the fallacy is easily perceived, by comparing different nations that are contemporaries; where we both judge more impartially, and can better set in opposition those manners, with which we are sufficiently acquainted. Treachery and cruelty, the most pernicious and most odious of all vices, seem peculiar to uncivilized ages; and by the refined GREEKS and ROMANS were ascribed to all the barbarous nations, which surrounded them. They might justly, therefore, have presumed, that their own ancestors, so highly celebrated, possessed no greater virtue, and were as much inferior to their posterity in honour and humanity, as in taste and science. An ancient FRANK or SAXON may be highly extolled: But I believe every man would think his life or fortune much less secure in the hands of a MOOR or TARTAR, than in those of a FRENCH or ENGLISH gentleman, the rank of men the most civilized in the most civilized nations.

We come now to the *second* position which we proposed to illustrate, to wit, that, as innocent luxury, or a refinement in the arts and conveniencies of life, is advantageous to the public; so wherever luxury ceases to be innocent, it also ceases to be beneficial; and when carried a degree farther, begins to be a quality pernicious, though, perhaps, not the most pernicious, to political society.

Let us consider what we call vicious luxury. No gratification, however sensual, can of itself be esteemed vicious. A gratification is only vicious, when it engrosses all a man's expence, and leaves no ability for such acts of duty and generosity as are required by his situation and fortune. Suppose, that he correct the vice, and employ part of his expence in the education of his children, in the support of his friends, and in relieving the poor; would any prejudice result to society? On the contrary, the same consumption would arise; and that labour, which, at present, is employed only in producing a slender gratification to one man, would relieve the necessitous, and bestow satisfaction on hundreds. The same care and toil that raise a dish of peas at CHRISTMAS, would give bread to a whole family during six months. To say, that, without a vicious luxury, the labour would not have been employed at all, is only to say, that there is some other defect in human nature, such as indolence, selfishness, inattention to others, for which luxury, in some measure, provides a remedy; as one poison may be an antidote to another. But virtue, like wholesome food, is better than poisons, however corrected.

Suppose the same number of men, that are at present in GREAT BRITAIN, with the same soil and climate; I ask, is it not possible for them to be happier, by the most perfect way of life that can be imagined, and by the greatest reformation that Omnipotence itself could work in their temper and disposition? To assert, that they cannot, appears evidently ridiculous. As the land is able to maintain more than all its present inhabitants, they could never, in such a UTOPIAN state, feel any other ills than those which arise from bodily sickness; and these are not the half of human miseries. All other ills spring from some vice, either in ourselves or others; and even many of our diseases proceed from the same origin. Remove the vices, and the ills follow. You must only take care to remove all the vices. If you remove part, you may render the matter worse. By banishing *vicious* luxury, without curing sloth and an indifference to others, you only diminish industry in the state, and add nothing to men's charity or their generosity. Let us, therefore, rest contented with asserting, that two opposite vices in a state may be more advantageous than either of them alone; but let us never pronounce vice in itself advantageous. Is it not very inconsistent for an author to assert in one page, that moral distinctions are inventions of politicians for public interest; and in the next page maintain, that vice is advantageous to the public? And indeed it seems upon any system of morality, little less than a contradiction in terms, to talk of a vice, which is in general beneficial to society.

I thought this reasoning necessary, in order to give some light to a philosophical question, which has been much disputed in ENGLAND. I call it a *philosophical* question, not a *political* one. For whatever may be the consequence of such a miraculous transformation of mankind, as would endow them with every species of virtue, and free them from every species of vice; this concerns not the magistrate, who aims only at possibilities. He cannot cure every vice by substituting a virtue in its place. Very often he can only cure one vice by another; and in that case, he ought to prefer what is least pernicious to society. Luxury, when excessive, is the source of many ills; but is in general preferable to sloth and idleness, which would commonly succeed in its place, and are more hurtful both to private persons and to the public. When sloth reigns, a mean uncultivated way of life prevails amongst individuals, without society, without enjoyment. And if the sovereign, in such a situation, demands the service of his subjects, the labour of the state suffices only to furnish the necessaries of life to the labourers, and can afford nothing to those who are employed in the public service.

For Further Reading

Hume, David. *A Treatise of Human Nature.* Edited by P.H. Nidditch (Oxford: Oxford Univ. Press, 1978).

_____. *Essays: Moral, Political and Literary.* Edited by Eugene F. Miller (Indianapolis: Liberty Classics, 1985).

_____. *Dialogues Concerning Natural Religion.* Edited by Richard Popkin (Indianapolis: Hackett, 1980).

_____. *Writings on Economics.* Edited and introduction by Eugene Rotwein (Madison, Wis.: Univ. of Wisconsin Press, 1970).

Ardal, P.S. *Passion and Value in Hume's Treatise* (Edinburgh: Edinburgh Univ. Press, 1966).

Baier, Annette C. *A Progress of Sentiments: Reflections on Hume's* Treatise (Cambridge: Harvard Univ. Press, 1991).

Chappell.V.C., ed. *Hume* (New York: Doubleday, 1966).

Deleuze, Gilles. *Empiricism and Subjectivity, an Essay on Hume's Theory of Human Nature* (New York: Columbia Univ. Press, 1991).

Ferguson, Adam. *An Essay on the History of Civil Society.* Edited by Duncan Forbes (Edinburgh: Edinburgh Univ. Press, 1966).

Forbes, Duncan. *Hume's Philosophical Politics* (Cambridge: Cambridge Univ. Press, 1975).

Harrison, Jonathan. *Hume's Theory of Justice* (Oxford: Clarendon Press, 1981).

Hayek, Friedrich A. "The Legal and Political Philosophy of David Hume." In *Studies in Philosophy, Politics and Economics* (New York: Clarion, 1967).

Kettler, David. *The Social and Political Thought of Adam Ferguson* (Columbus: Ohio State Univ. Press, 1965).

Kydd, Rachael. *Reason and Conduct in Hume's* Treatise (London: Oxford Univ. Press, 1946).

Jones, Peter, ed. *The Science of Man in the Scottish Enlightenment* (Edinburgh: Edinburgh Univ. Press, 1990).

Livingston, Donald W. *Hume's Philosophy of Common Life* (Chicago: Univ. of Chicago Press, 1984).

Livingston, Donald W., and James T. King, eds. *Hume: A Reevaluation* (New York: Fordham Univ. Press, 1976).

Mackie, J.L. *Hume's Moral Theory* (London: Routledge, 1985).

McGee, Robert W. "The Economic Thought of David Hume." *Hume Studies* 15 (April 1989).

Miller, David. *Philosophy and Ideology in Hume's Political Thought* (Oxford: Clarendon Press, 1981).

Moore, James. "Hume's Theory of Justice and Property." *Political Studies* 24 (1976): 103-19.

Mossner, Ernest Campbell. *The Life of David Hume.* 2nd ed. (Oxford: Clarendon Press, 1980).

Norton, David Fate. *David Hume: Common Sense Moralist, Sceptical Metaphysician* (Princeton: Princeton Univ. Press, 1982).

Norton, D.F., N. Capaldi, and W.L. Robison, eds. *McGill Hume Studies* (San Diego, Calif.: Austin Hill Press, 1979).

Phillipson, Nicholas. *Hume* (London: Weidenfeld and Nicolson, 1989).

Siebert, Donald T. *The Moral Animus of David Hume* (Newark: Univ. of Delaware Press, 1990).

Smith, Norman Kemp. *The Philosophy of David Hume* (New York: Garland, 1983).

Stroud, Barry. *Hume* (New York: Routledge, 1977).

Whelan, Frederick G. *Order and Artifice in Hume's Political Philosophy* (Princeton: Princeton Univ. Press, 1985).

ADAM SMITH (1723–1790)

chapter 8

ADAM SMITH did not always succeed in properly conceptualizing modern commercial forms, but that did not keep him from being a brilliant, if uneasy, advocate of capitalism. Smith's four stages of human history bear some resemblance to Aristotle's forms of acquisition, but Smith's narration ends on quite a different note: commercial, that is capitalist, society is the highest and final stage of social evolution. In a commercial society, as a rule, goods and services take the commodity form, labor takes the form of wage labor, and the economic initiative lies with capitalists, or "undertakers." Sensing the interconnectedness of these forms, Smith simultaneously defends the capital form, the generalization of the commodity form, wage labor, and the nearly absolute use rights of private property owners. As the title of his famous book *The Wealth of Nations* suggests, capitalism's main draw for Smith was its remarkable capacity to generate "that universal opulence which extends itself to the lowest ranks of the people." Smith believed, as had Locke, that, even if the resulting abundance was divided into preposterously unequal portions, the rising tide of wealth would lift the laboring poor of commercial societies—"that is, the great body of the people"—to heights of material comfort unimaginable to the rulers of "rude" societies. Further benefits of commerce, he said, were its tendencies to make society orderly and well governed.

"Unintended consequences" is our dull revision of "the invisible hand," Smith's memorable phrase that appears but once in *The Wealth of Nations*. With it he crystallized a notion dear to Mandeville and Hume that settled into German Idealism by way of Kant's historical essays, eventually reminted by Hegel as the "cunning of reason." No one intends the happy consequences of commerce. On the contrary, narrow self-interest, without trace of benevolence, motivates all participants in "the great scramble." Smith strives to quiet Mandeville's jeers about "private vices, public benefits" by criticizing as unduly rigorous his standard of virtue and by morally rehabilitating the desire for approval. But we are left wondering: Would a strictly self-seeking person care whether or not an "invisible hand" responds to the needs of others? And if narrow self-interest directs our daily business, what would be the consequences were Smith right that "the understandings of the greater part of men are necessarily formed by their ordinary employments"?

What made the upsurge of wealth in commercial societies possible? wonders Smith. He wastes no time in supplying his answer, the detailed division of labor (as illustrated by the pin factory). For all the weight Smith places on the division of labor, however, it is curious that it causes increased productivity in part by leading to new inventions. In retrospect, it appears that scientific and technological innovation, not the division of labor, is chiefly responsible for increased productivity. For Smith, though the division of labor is the great benefactor to the "common stock," it nonetheless harbors a dilemma that exceeds the coping mechanisms of untrammeled capitalism. In vivid language, Smith probes the tendency of the division of labor to leave workers "mutilated and deformed." In his film *Modern Times,* Charlie Chaplin illustrates Smith's point for anyone who has not experienced it first hand. If this degradation were not bad enough, Smith worries that human beings reduced to such proportions are easy marks for troublemakers ready to stir up "the most dreadful disorders." Since educated workers are better disposed to respect their "superiors," prudence dictates that the government impose and partially finance public education.

In the division of labor Smith recognized not only the engine of untold wealth but an epochal transformation of the character of property. As labor is increasingly divided, people become more and more dependent upon strangers. How can we reliably get these strangers to supply us with what we want? For Smith, the only plausible answer to this question involved appealing to their self-interest. Aristotle and Aquinas favored private property precisely because they saw how inelastic are our sentiments, how futile to oppose the natural urge to love what is ours. Still, they qualified their endorsement by holding out for the "common use" of private property. This slippery reservation impedes the spread of the commodity form and, as Smith was keen to point out, discourages enterprising capitalists. Pitched battles were fought during the 17th and 18th centuries over the rights of the poor to grain they needed but could not afford to purchase. On another plane of conflict, natural law theorists like Hugo Grotius and Samuel Pufendorf were squeezing the Thomistic theory of private property. Their innovations restricted or eliminated the space for appealing to the common good to justify the appropriation of private property. Smith came down squarely on the side of insuring private use rights and treating grain like any other commodity, arguing that in the long run this would best serve the interests of the poor. The world to which the "common use" doctrine belonged was losing ground to one where we depend upon unknown others for our daily bread.

In Smith we find both acute observations of commercial forms and failures to distinguish between a thing's physical properties and its social form. One of Smith's reasons for thinking that the commerce of the towns improves the country turns on the salutary effects of commerce on merchants: "the habits, besides of order, economy and attention, to which mercantile business naturally forms a merchant, render him much fitter to execute, with profit and success, any project of improvement." When merchants buy land in the country, expect improvements to rural life. Smith's history of the decline of the British barons is a gem; it demonstrates the phenomenon of "unintended consequences" as it traces the power of a new social form of wealth. Smith reveals how the political power of the barons depended upon the form their wealth took, namely, agricultural rents with which they treated a company of retainers to their "rustic hospitality." As foreign commodities became increasingly available, however, the barons cashed their agricultural surpluses to purchase the "trinkets and baubles" that dragged them down. No longer able to support legions of dependents, the barons witnessed their power slip away— not an outcome they had in mind.

Smith's notions of "productive" and "unproductive" labor blur the distinction between wealth in general and the particular social form of wealth that is capital. From the sound of the words one would think that "productive" labor results in wealth of whatever sort while "unproductive" labor fails to do so. But Smith defines productive labor as labor that exchanges with capital to produce wealth that has the specific social form of commodity capital, i.e., a commodity whose sale brings a profit. This exposes a crucial feature of the modern enthusiasm for "industry"; it actually pertains to a peculiar social form of labor, the type employed to reap profits. Mixing matters up more, Smith draws the distinction a second way, supposing it is equivalent to the first. "Productive" labor produces something lasting; it stocks up labor that could be used later. "Unproductive" labor is service labor; it leaves nothing

175

enduring behind. One definition is in terms of a social form, capital; the second is in terms of physical properties. Smith wrongly thinks they amount to the same thing. For a singer may be hired by a profitmaking nightclub and be productive without leaving any lasting object, while a servant's labor in making a table for an employer's domestic use is unproductive though it results in something lasting. It is characteristic of Smith to provide incisive accounts of the effects of modern commerce but also to mishandle the conceptual determination of commercial forms.

FROM *THE WEALTH OF NATIONS*

BOOK I

Of the Causes of Improvement in the productive Powers of Labour, and of the Order according to which its Produce is naturally distributed among the different Ranks of the People.

CHAPTER I

OF THE DIVISION OF LABOUR

The greatest improvement in the productive powers of labour, and the greater part of the skill, dexterity, and judgment with which it is any where directed, or applied, seem to have been the effects of the division of labour.

The effects of the division of labour, in the general business of society, will be more easily understood, by considering in what manner it operates in some particular manufactures. It is commonly supposed to be carried furthest in some very trifling ones; not perhaps that it really is carried further in them than in others of more importance: but in those trifling manufactures which are destined to supply the small wants of but a small number of people, the whole number of workmen must necessarily be small; and those employed in every different branch of the work can often be collected into the same workhouse, and placed at once under the view of the spectator. In those great manufactures, on the contrary, which are destined to supply the great wants of the great body of the people, every different branch of the work employs so great a number of workmen, that it is impossible to collect them all into the same workhouse. We can seldom see more, at one time, than those employed in one single branch. Though in such manufactures, therefore, the work may really be divided into a much greater number of parts, than in those of a more trifling nature, the division is not near so obvious, and has accordingly been much less observed.

To take an example, therefore, from a very trifling manufacture; but one in which the division of labour has been very often taken notice of, the trade of the pin-maker; a workman not educated to this business (which the division of labour has rendered a distinct trade), nor acquainted with the use of the machinery employed in it (to the invention of which the same division of labour has probably given occasion), could scarce, perhaps, with his utmost industry, make one pin in a day, and certainly could not make twenty. But in the way in which this business is now carried on, not only the whole work is a peculiar trade, but it is divided into a number of branches, of which the greater part are likewise peculiar trades. One man draws out the wire, another straights it, a third cuts it, a fourth points it, a fifth grinds it at the top for receiving the head; to make the head requires two or three distinct operations; to put it on, is a peculiar business, to whiten the pins is another; it is even a trade by itself to put them into the paper; and the important business of making a pin is, in this manner, divided into about eighteen distinct operations, which, in some manufactories, are all performed by distinct hands, though in others the same man will sometimes perform two or three of them. I have seen a small manufactory of this kind where ten men only were employed, and where some of them consequently performed two or three distinct operations. But though they were very poor, and therefore but indifferently accommodated with the necessary machinery, they could, when they exerted themselves, make among them about twelve pounds of pins in a day. There are in a pound upwards of four thousand pins of a middling size. Those ten persons, therefore, could make among them upwards of forty-eight thousand pins in a day. Each person, therefore, making a tenth part of forty-eight thousand pins, might be considered as making four thousand eight hundred pins in a day. But if they had all wrought separately and independently, and without any of them having been educated to this peculiar business, they certainly could not each of them have made twenty, perhaps not one pin in a day; that is, certainly, not the two hundred and fortieth, perhaps not the four thousand eight hundredth part of what they are at present capable of performing, in consequence of a proper division and combination of their different operations.

177

In every other art and manufacture, the effects of the division of labour are similar to what they are in this very trifling one; though, in many of them, the labour can neither be so much subdivided, nor reduced to so great a simplicity of operation. The division of labour, however, so far as it can be introduced, occasions, in every art, a proportionable increase of the productive powers of labour. The separation of different trades and employments from one another, seems to have taken place, in consequence of this advantage. This separation too is generally carried furthest in those countries which enjoy the highest degree of industry and improvement; what is the work of one man in a rude state of society, being generally that of several in an improved one. In every improved society, the farmer is generally nothing but a farmer; the manufacturer, nothing but a manufacturer. The labour too which is necessary to produce any one complete manufacture, is almost always divided among a great number of hands. How many different trades are employed in each branch of the linen and woollen manufactures, from the growers of the flax and the wool, to the bleachers and smoothers of the linen, or to the dyers and dressers of the cloth! The nature of agriculture, indeed, does not admit of so many subdivisions of labour, nor of so complete a separation of one business from another, as manufactures. It is impossible to separate so entirely, the business of the grazier from that of the corn-farmer, as the trade of the carpenter is commonly separated from that of the smith. The spinner is almost always a distinct person from the weaver; but the ploughman, the harrower, the sower of the seed, and the reaper of the corn, are often the same. The occasions for those different sorts of labour returning with the different seasons of the year, it is impossible that one man should be constantly employed in any one of them. This impossibility of making so complete and entire a separation of all the different branches of labour employed in agriculture, is perhaps the reason why the improvement of the productive powers of labour in this art, does not always keep pace with their improvement in manufactures. The most opulent nations, indeed, generally excel all their neighbours in agriculture as well as in manufactures; but they are commonly more distinguished by their superiority in the latter than in the former. Their lands are in general better cultivated, and having more labour and expence bestowed upon them, produce more in proportion to the extent and natural fertility of the ground. But this superiority of produce is seldom much more than in proportion to the superiority of labour and expence. In agriculture, the labour of the rich country is not always much more productive than that of the poor; or, at least, it is never so much more productive, as it commonly is in manufactures. The corn of the rich country, therefore, will not always, in the same degree of goodness, come cheaper to market than that of the poor. The corn of Poland, in the same degree of goodness, is as cheap as that of France, notwithstanding the superior opulence and improvement of the latter country. The corn of France is, in the corn provinces, fully as good, and in most years nearly about the same price with the corn of England, though, in opulence and improvement, France is perhaps inferior to England. The corn-lands of England, however, are better cultivated than those of France, and the corn-lands of France are said to be much better cultivated than those of Poland. But though the poor country, notwithstanding the inferiority of its cultivation, can, in some measure, rival the rich in the cheapness and goodness of its corn, it can pretend to no such competition in its manufactures; at least if those manufactures suit the soil, climate, and situation of the rich country. The silks of France are better and cheaper than those of England, because the silk manufacture, at least under the present high duties upon the importation of raw silk, does not so well suit the climate of England as that of France. But the hard-ware and the coarse woollens of England are beyond all comparison superior to those of France, and much cheaper too in the same degree of goodness. In Poland there are said to be scarce any manufactures of any kind, a few of those coarser household manufactures excepted, without which no country can well subsist.

178

This great increase of the quantity of work, which, in consequence of the division of labour, the same number of people are capable of performing, is owing to three different circumstances; first, to the increase of dexterity in every particular workman; secondly, to the saving of the time which is commonly lost in passing from one species of work to another; and lastly, to the invention of a great number of machines which facilitate and abridge labour, and enable one man to do the work of many.

First, the improvement of the dexterity of the workman necessarily increases the quantity of the work he can perform; and the division of labour, by reducing every man's business to some one simple operation, and by making this operation the sole employment of his life, necessarily increases very much the dexterity of the workman. A common smith, who, though accustomed to handle the hammer, has never been used to make nails, if upon some particular occasion he is obliged to attempt it, will scarce, I am assured, be able to make above two or three hundred nails in a day, and those too very bad ones. A smith who has been accustomed to make nails, but whose sole or principal business has not been that of a nailer, can seldom with his utmost diligence make more than eight hundred or a thousand nails in a day. I have seen several boys under twenty years of age who had never exercised any other trade but that of making nails, and who, when they exerted themselves, could make, each of them, upwards of two thousand three hundred nails in a day. The making of a nail, however, is by no means one of the simplest operations. The same person blows the bellows, stirs or mends the fire as there is occasion, heats the iron, and forges every part of the nail: In forging the head too he is obliged to change his tools. The different operations into which the making of a pin, or of a metal button, is subdivided, are all of them much more simple, and the dexterity of the person, of whose life it has been the sole business to perform them, is usually much greater. The rapidity with which some of the operations of those manufactures are performed, exceeds what the human hand could, by those who had never seen them, be supposed capable of acquiring.

Secondly, the advantage which is gained by saving the time commonly lost in passing from one sort of work to another, is much greater than we should at first view be apt to imagine it. It is impossible to pass very quickly from one kind of work to another, that is carried on in a different place, and with quite different tools. A country weaver, who cultivates a small farm, must lose a good deal of time in passing from his loom to the field, and from the field to his loom. When the two trades can be carried on in the same workhouse, the loss of time is no doubt much less. It is even in this case, however, very considerable. A man commonly saunters a little in turning his hand from one sort of employment to another. When he first begins the new work he is seldom very keen and hearty; his mind, as they say, does not go to it, and for some time he rather trifles than applies to good purpose. The habit of sauntering

179

and of indolent careless application, which is naturally, or rather necessarily acquired by every country workman who is obliged to change his work and his tools every half hour, and to apply his hand in twenty different ways almost every day of his life; renders him almost always slothful and lazy, and incapable of any vigorous application even on the most pressing occasions. Independent, therefore, of his deficiency in point of dexterity, this cause alone must always reduce considerably the quantity of work which he is capable of performing.

Thirdly, and lastly, every body must be sensible how much labour is facilitated and abridged by the application of proper machinery. It is unnecessary to give any example. I shall only observe, therefore, that the invention of all those machines by which labour is so much facilitated and abridged, seems to have been originally owing to the division of labour. Men are much more likely to discover easier and readier methods of attaining any object, when the whole attention of their minds is directed towards that single object, than when it is dissipated among a great variety of things. But in consequence of the division of labour, the whole of every man's attention comes naturally to be directed towards some one very simple object. It is naturally to be expected, therefore, that some one or other of those who are employed in each particular branch of labour should soon find out easier and readier methods of performing their own particular work, wherever the nature of it admits of such improvement. A great part of the machines made use of in those manufactures in which labour is most subdivided, were originally the inventions of common workmen, who, being each of them employed in some very simple operation, naturally turned their thoughts towards finding out easier and readier methods of performing it. Whoever has been much accustomed to visit such manufactures, must frequently have been shewn very pretty machines, which were the inventions of such workmen, in order to facilitate and quicken their own particular part of the work. In the first fire-engines, a boy was constantly employed to open and shut alternately the communication between the boiler and the cylinder, according as the piston either ascended or descended. One of those boys, who loved to play with his companions, observed that, by tying a string from the handle of the valve which opened this communication to another part of the machine, the valve would open and shut without his assistance, and leave him at liberty to divert himself with his play-fellows. One of the greatest improvements that has been made upon this machine, since it was first invented, was in this manner the discovery of a boy who wanted to save his own labour.

All the improvements in machinery, however, have by no means been the inventions of those who had occasion to use the machines. Many improvements have been made by the ingenuity of the makers of the machines, when to make them became the business of a peculiar trade; and some by that of those who are called philosophers or men of speculation, whose trade it is not to do any thing, but to observe every thing; and who, upon that account, are often capable of combining together the powers of the most distant and dissimilar objects. In the progress of society, philosophy or speculation becomes, like every other employment, the principal or sole trade and occupation of a particular class of citizens. Like every other employment too, it is subdivided into a great number of different branches, each of which affords occupation to a peculiar tribe or class of philosophers; and this subdivision of employment in philosophy, as well as in every other business, improves dexterity, and saves time. Each individual becomes more expert in his own peculiar branch, more work is done upon the whole, and the quantity of science is considerably increased by it.

It is the great multiplication of the productions of all the different arts, in consequence of the division of labour, which occasions, in a well-governed society, that universal opulence which extends itself to the lowest ranks of the people. Every workman has a great quantity of his own work to dispose of beyond what he himself has occasion for; and every other workman being exactly in the same situation, he is enabled to exchange a great quantity of his own goods for a great quantity, or, what comes to the same thing, for the price of a great quantity of theirs. He supplies them abundantly with what they have occasion for, and they accommodate him as amply with what he has occasion for, and a general plenty diffuses itself through all the different ranks of the society.

Observe the accommodation of the most common artificer or day-labourer in a civilized and thriving country, and you will perceive that the number of people of whose industry a part, though but a small part, has been employed in procuring him this accommodation, exceeds all computation. The woollen coat, for example, which covers the day-labourer, as coarse and rough as it may appear, is the produce of the joint labour of a great multitude of workmen. The shepherd, the sorter of the wool, the wool-comber or carder, the dyer, the scribbler, the spinner, the weaver, the fuller, the dresser, with many others, must all join their different arts in order to complete even this homely production. How many merchants and carriers, besides, must have been employed in transporting the materials from some of those workmen to others who often live in a very distant part of the country! how much commerce and navigation in particular, how many ship-builders, sailors, sail-makers, rope-makers, must have been employed in order to bring together the different drugs made use of by the dyer, which often come from the remotest corners of the world! What a variety of labour too is necessary in order to produce the tools of the meanest of those workmen! To say nothing of such complicated machines as the ship of the sailor, the mill of the fuller, or even the loom of the weaver, let us consider only what a variety of labour is requisite in order to form that very simple machine, the shears with which the shepherd clips the wool. The miner, the builder of the furnace for smelt-

181

ing the ore, the feller of the timber, the burner of the charcoal to be made use of in the smelting-house, the brick-maker, the brick-layer, the workmen who attend the furnace, the mill-wright, the forger, the smith, must all of them join their different arts in order to produce them. Were we to examine, in the same manner, all the different parts of his dress and household furniture, the coarse linen shirt which he wears next his skin, the shoes which cover his feet, the bed which he lies on, and all the different parts which compose it, the kitchen-grate at which he prepares his victuals, the coals which he makes use of for that purpose, dug from the bowels of the earth, and brought to him perhaps by a long sea and a long land carriage, all the other utensils of his kitchen, all the furniture of his table, the knives and forks, the earthen or pewter plates upon which he serves up and divides his victuals, the different hands employed in preparing his bread and his beer, the glass window which lets in the heat and the light, and keeps out the wind and the rain, with all the knowledge and art requisite for preparing that beautiful and happy invention, without which these northern parts of the world could scarce have afforded a very comfortable habitation, together with the tools of all the different work-men employed in producing those different conveniencies; if we examine, I say, all these things, and consider what a variety of labour is employed about each of them, we shall be sensible that without the assistance and co-opera-tion of many thousands, the very meanest person in a civilized country could not be provided, even according to, what we very falsely imagine, the easy and simple manner in which he is commonly accommodated. Compared, in-deed, with the more extravagant luxury of the great, his accommodation must no doubt appear extremely simple and easy; and yet it may be true, per-haps, that the accommodation of an European prince does not always so much exceed that of an industrious and frugal peasant, as the accommodation of the latter exceeds that of many an African king, the absolute master of the lives and liberties of ten thousand naked savages.

CHAPTER II

OF THE PRINCIPLE WHICH GIVES OCCASION TO THE DIVISION OF LABOUR

This division of labour, from which so many advantages are derived, is not originally the effect of any human wisdom, which foresees and intends that general opulence to which it gives occasion. It is the necessary, though very slow and gradual, consequence of a certain propensity in human nature which has in view no such extensive utility; the propensity to truck, barter, and exchange one thing for another.

Whether this propensity be one of those original principles in human na-ture, of which no further account can be given; or whether, as seems more probable, it be the necessary consequence of the faculties of reason and speech, it belongs not to our present subject to enquire. It is common to all men, and to be found in no other race of animals, which seem to know neither this nor any other species of contracts. Two greyhounds, in running down the same hare, have sometimes the appearance of acting in some sort of concert. Each turns her towards his companion, or endeavours to intercept her when his companion turns her towards himself. This, however, is not the effect of any contract, but of the accidental concurrence of their passions in the same object at that particular time. Nobody ever saw a dog make a fair and deliberate exchange of one bone for another with another dog. Nobody ever saw one animal by its gestures and natural cries signify to another, this is mine, that yours; I am willing to give this for that. When an animal wants to obtain something either of a man or of another animal, it has no other means of persuasion but to gain the favour of those whose service it requires. A puppy fawns upon its dam, and a spaniel endeavours by a thousand attractions to engage the attention of its master who is at dinner, when it wants to be fed by him. Man sometimes uses the same arts with his brethren, and when he has no other means of engaging them to act according to his inclinations, endeavours by every servile and fawning attention to obtain their good will. He has not time, however, to do this upon every occasion. In civilized society he stands at all times in need of the co-operation and assistance of great multitudes, while his whole life is scarce sufficient to gain the friendship of a few persons. In almost every other race of animals each individual, when it is grown up to maturity, is entirely independent, and in its natural state has occasion for the assistance of no other living creature. But man has almost constant occasion for the help of his brethren, and it is in vain for him to expect it from their benevolence only. He will be more likely to prevail if he can interest their self-love in his favour, and shew them that it is for their own advantage to do for him what he requires of them. Whoever offers to another a bargain of any kind, proposes to do this. Give me that which I want, and you shall have this which you want, is the meaning of every such offer; and it is in this manner that we obtain from one another the far greater part of those good offices which we stand in need of. It is not from the benevolence of the butcher, the brewer, or the baker, that we expect our dinner, but from their regard to their own interest. We address ourselves, not to their humanity but to their self-love, and never talk to them of our own necessities but of their advantages. Nobody but a beggar chuses to depend chiefly upon the benevolence of his fellow-citizens. Even a beggar does not depend upon it entirely. The charity of well-disposed people, indeed, supplies him with the whole fund of his subsistence. But though this principle ultimately provides him with all the necessaries of life which he has occasion for, it neither does nor can provide him with them as he has occasion for them. The greater part of his occasional wants are supplied in the same manner as those of other people, by treaty, by barter, and by purchase. With the money which one man gives him he purchases food. The old cloaths which another bestows upon him he exchanges for other old cloaths which suit him better, or for lodging,

183

or for food, or for money, with which he can buy either food, cloaths, or lodging, as he has occasion.

As it is by treaty, by barter, and by purchase, that we obtain from one another the greater part of those mutual good offices which we stand in need of, so it is this same trucking disposition which originally gives occasion to the division of labour. In a tribe of hunters or shepherds a particular person makes bows and arrows, for example, with more readiness and dexterity than any other. He frequently exchanges them for cattle or for venison with his companions; and he finds at last that he can in this manner get more cattle and venison, than if he himself went to the field to catch them. From a regard to his own interest, therefore, the making of bows and arrows grows to be his chief business, and he becomes a sort of armourer. Another excels in making the frames and covers of their little huts or moveable houses. He is accustomed to be of use in this way to his neighbours, who reward him in the same manner with cattle and with venison, till at last he finds it his interest to dedicate himself entirely to this employment, and to become a sort of house-carpenter. In the same manner a third becomes a smith or a brazier; a fourth a tanner or dresser of hides or skins, the principal part of the clothing of savages. And thus the certainty of being able to exchange all that surplus part of the produce of his own labour, which is over and above his own consumption, for such parts of the produce of other men's labour as he may have occasion for, encourages every man to apply himself to a particular occupation, and to cultivate and bring to perfection whatever talent or genius he may possess for that particular species of business.

184

The difference of natural talents in different men is, in reality, much less than we are aware of; and the very different genius which appears to distinguish men of different professions, when grown up to maturity, is not upon many occasions so much the cause, as the effect of the division of labour. The difference between the most dissimilar characters, between a philosopher and a common street porter, for example, seems to arise not so much from nature, as from habit, custom, and education. When they came into the world, and for the first six or eight years of their existence, they were, perhaps, very much alike, and neither their parents nor playfellows could perceive any remarkable difference. About that age, or soon after, they come to be employed in very different occupations. The difference of talents comes then to be taken notice of, and widens by degrees, till at last the vanity of the philosopher is willing to acknowledge scarce any resemblance. But without the disposition to truck, barter, and exchange, every man must have procured to himself every necessary and conveniency of life which he wanted. All must have had the same duties to perform, and the same work to do, and there could have been no such difference of employment as could alone give occasion to any great difference of talents.

As it is this disposition which forms that difference of talents, so remarkable among men of different professions, so it is this same disposition which renders that difference useful. Many tribes of animals acknowledged to be all of the same species, derive from nature a much more remarkable distinction of genius, than what, antecedent to custom and education, appears to take place among men. By nature a philosopher is not in genius and disposition half so different from a street porter, as a mastiff is from a greyhound, or a greyhound from a spaniel, or this last from a shepherd's dog. Those different tribes of animals, however, though all of the same species, are of scarce any use to one another. The strength of the mastiff is not in the least supported either by the swiftness of the greyhound, or by the sagacity of the spaniel, or by the docility of the shepherd's dog. The effects of those different geniuses and talents, for want of the power or disposition to barter and exchange, cannot be brought into a common stock, and do not in the least contribute to the better accommodation and conveniency of the species. Each animal is still obliged to support and defend itself, separately and independently, and derives no sort of advantage from that variety of talents with which nature has distinguished its fellows. Among men, on the contrary, the most dissimilar geniuses are of use to one another; the different produces of their respective talents, by the general disposition to truck, barter, and exchange, being brought, as it were, into a common stock, where every man may purchase whatever part of the produce of other men's talents he has occasion for.

BOOK II

Of the Nature, Accumulation, and Employment of Stock

CHAPTER III

OF THE ACCUMULATION OF CAPITAL, OR OF PRODUCTIVE AND UNPRODUCTIVE LABOUR

There is one sort of labour which adds to the value of the subject upon which it is bestowed: there is another which has no such effect. The former, as it produces a value, may be called productive; the latter, unproductive labour. Thus the labour of a manufacturer adds, generally, to the value of the materials which he works upon, that of his own maintenance, and of his master's profit. The labour of a menial servant, on the contrary, adds to the value of nothing. Though the manufacturer has his wages advanced to him by his master, he, in reality, costs him no expence, the value of those wages being generally restored, together with a profit, in the improved value of the subject upon which his labour is bestowed. But the maintenance of a menial servant never is restored. A man grows rich by employing a multitude of manufacturers: he grows poor, by maintaining a multitude of menial servants. The labour of the latter, however, has its value, and deserves its reward as well as that of the former. But the labour of the manufacturer fixes and realizes itself in some particular subject or vendible commodity, which lasts for some time at least after that labour is past. It is, as it were, a certain quantity of labour stocked and stored up to be employed, if necessary, upon some other occasion. That subject, or what is the same thing, the price of that subject, can afterwards, if necessary, put into motion a quantity of labour equal to that which had originally produced it. The labour of the menial servant, on the contrary, does not fix or realize itself in any particular subject or vendible commodity. His services generally perish in the very instant of their performance, and seldom leave any trace or value behind them, for which an equal quantity of service could afterwards be procured.

The labour of some of the most respectable orders in the society is, like that of menial servants, unproductive of any value, and does not fix or realize itself in any permanent subject, or vendible commodity, which endures after that labour is past, and for which an equal quantity of labour could afterwards be procured. The sovereign, for example, with all the officers both of justice and war who serve under him, the whole army and navy, are unproductive labourers. They are the servants of the public, and are maintained by a part of the annual produce of the industry of other people. Their service, how honourable, how useful, or how necessary soever, produces nothing for which an equal quantity of service can afterwards be procured. The protection, security, and defence of the commonwealth, the effect of their labour this year, will not purchase its protection, security, and defence for the year to come. In the same class must be ranked, some both of the gravest and most important, and some of the most frivolous professions: churchmen, lawyers, physicians, men of letters of all kinds; players, buffoons, musicians, opera-singers, opera-dancers, &c. The labour of the meanest of these has a certain value, regulated by the very same principles which regulate that of every other sort of labour; and that of the noblest and most useful, produces nothing which could afterwards purchase or procure an equal quantity of labour. Like the declamation of the actor, the harangue of the orator, or the tune of the musician, the work of all of them perishes in the very instant of its production.

Both productive and unproductive labourers, and those who do not labour at all, are all equally maintained by the annual produce of the land and labour of the country. This produce, how great soever, can never be infinite, but must have certain limits. According, therefore, as a smaller or greater proportion of it is in any one year employed in maintaining unproductive hands, the more in the one case and the less in the other will remain for the productive, and the next year's produce will be greater or smaller accordingly; the whole annual produce, if we except the spontaneous productions of the earth, being the effect of productive labour.

Though the whole annual produce of the land and labour of every country, is, no doubt, ultimately destined for supplying the consumption of its inhabitants, and for procuring a revenue to them; yet when it first comes either from the ground, or from the hands of the productive labourers, it naturally divides itself into two parts. One of them, and frequently the largest, is, in the first place, destined for replacing a capital, or for renewing the provisions, materials, and finished work, which had been withdrawn from a capital; the other for constituting a revenue either to the owner of this capital, as the profit of his stock; or to some other person, as the rent of his land. Thus, of the produce of land, one part replaces the capital of the farmer; the other pays his profit and the rent of the landlord; and thus constitutes a revenue both to the owner of this capital, as the profits of his stock; and to some other person, as the rent of his land. Of the produce of a great manufactory, in the same manner, one part, and that always the largest, replaces the capital of the undertaker of the work; the other pays his profit, and thus constitutes a revenue to the owner of this capital.

That part of the annual produce of the land and labour of any country which replaces a capital, never is immediately employed to maintain any but productive hands. It pays the wages of productive labour only. That which is immediately destined for constituting a revenue either as profit or as rent, may maintain indifferently either productive or unproductive hands.

Whatever part of his stock a man employs as a capital, he always expects is to be replaced to him with a profit. He employs it, therefore, in maintaining productive hands only; and after having served in the function of a capital to him, it constitutes a revenue to them. Whenever he employs any part of it in maintaining unproductive hands of any kind, that part is, from that moment, withdrawn from his capital, and placed in his stock reserved for immediate consumption.

Unproductive labourers, and those who do not labour at all, are all maintained by revenue; either, first, by that part of the annual produce which is originally destined for constituting a revenue to some particular persons, either as the rent of land or as the profits of stock; or, secondly, by that part which, though originally destined for replacing a capital and for maintaining productive labourers only, yet when it comes into their hands, whatever part of it is over and above their necessary subsistence, may be employed in maintaining indifferently either productive or unproductive hands. Thus, not only the great landlord or the rich merchant, but even the common workman, if his wages are considerable, may maintain a menial servant; or he may sometimes go to a play or a puppet-show, and so contribute his share towards maintaining one set of unproductive labourers; or he may pay some taxes, and thus help to maintain another set, more honourable and useful, indeed, but equally unproductive. No part of the annual produce, however, which had been originally destined to replace a capital, is ever directed towards maintaining unproductive hands, till after it has put into motion its full complement of productive labour, or all that it could put into motion in the way in which it was employed. The workman must have earned his wages by work done, before he can employ any part of them in this manner. That part too is generally but a small one. It is his spare revenue only, of which productive labourers have seldom a great deal. They generally have some, however; and in the payment of taxes the greatness of their number may compensate, in some measure, the smallness of their contribution. The rent of land and the profits of stock are every-where, therefore, the principal sources from which unproductive hands derive their subsistence. These are the two sorts of revenue of which the owners have generally most to spare. They might both maintain indifferently either productive or unproductive hands. They seem, however, to have some predilection for the latter. The expence of a great lord feeds generally more idle than industrious people. The rich merchant, though with his capital he maintains industrious people only, yet by his expence, that is, by the employment of his revenue, he feeds commonly the very same sort as the great lord.

The proportion, therefore, between the productive and unproductive hands, depends very much in every country upon the proportion between that part of the annual produce, which, as soon as it comes either from the ground or from the hands of the productive labourers, is destined for replacing a capital, and that which is destined for constituting a revenue, either as rent, or as profit. This proportion is very different in rich from what it is in poor countries.

Thus, at present, in the opulent countries of Europe, a very large, frequently the largest portion of the produce of the land, is destined for replacing the capital of the rich and independent farmer; the other for paying his profits, and the rent of the landlord. But anciently, during the prevalency of the feudal government, a very small portion of the produce was sufficient to replace the capital employed in cultivation. It consisted commonly in a few wretched cattle, maintained altogether by the spontaneous produce of uncultivated land, and which might, therefore, be considered as a part of that spontaneous produce. It generally too belonged to the landlord, and was by him advanced to the occupiers of the land. All the rest of the produce properly belonged to him too, either as rent for his land, or as profit upon this paultry capital. The occupiers of land were generally bondmen, whose persons and effects were equally his property. Those who were not bondmen were tenants at will, and though the rent which they paid was often nominally little more than a quit-rent, it really amounted to the whole produce of the land. Their lord could at all times command their labour in peace, and their service in war. Though they lived at a distance from his house, they were equally dependent upon him as his retainers who lived in it. But the whole produce of the land undoubtedly belongs to him, who can dispose of the labour and service of all those whom it maintains. In the present state of Europe, the share of the landlord seldom exceeds a third, sometimes not a fourth part of the whole produce of the land. The rent of land, however, in all the improved parts of the country, has been tripled and quadrupled since those ancient times; and this third or fourth part of the annual produce is, it seems, three or four times greater than the whole had been before. In the progress of improvement, rent, though it increases in proportion to the extent, diminishes in proportion to the produce of the land. . . .

BOOK III
Of the Different Progress of Opulence in Different Nations

CHAPTER I
OF THE NATURAL PROGRESS OF OPULENCE

The great commerce of every civilized society, is that carried on between the inhabitants of the town and those of the country. It consists in the exchange of rude for manufactured produce, either immediately, or by the intervention of money, or of some sort of paper which represents money. The country supplies the town with the means of subsistence, and the materials of manufacture. The town repays this supply by sending back a part of the manufactured produce to the inhabitants of the country. The town, in which there neither is nor can be any reproduction of substances, may very properly be said to gain its whole wealth and subsistence from the country. We must not, however, upon this account, imagine that the gain of the town is the loss of the country. The gains of both are mutual and reciprocal, and the division of labour is in this, as in all other cases, advantageous to all the different persons employed in the various occupations into which it is subdivided. The inhabitants of the country purchase of the town a greater quantity of manufactured goods, with the produce of a much smaller quantity of their own labour, than they must have employed had they attempted to prepare them themselves. The town affords a market for the surplus produce of the country, or what is over and above the maintenance of the cultivators, and it is there that the inhabitants of the country exchange it for something else which is in demand among them. The greater the number and revenue of the inhabitants of the town, the more extensive is the market which it affords to those of the country; and the more extensive that market, it is always the more advantageous to a great number. The corn which grows within a mile of the town, sells there for the same price with that which comes from twenty miles distance. But the price of the latter must generally, not only pay the expence of raising and bringing it to market, but afford too the ordinary profits of agriculture to the farmer. The proprietors and cultivators of the country, therefore, which lies in the neighbourhood of the town, over and above the ordinary profits of agriculture, gain, in the price of what they sell, the whole value of the carriage of the like produce that is brought from more distant parts, and they save, besides, the whole value of this carriage in the price of what they buy. Compare the cultivation of the lands in the neighbourhood of any considerable town, with that of those which lie at some distance from it, and you will easily satisfy yourself how much the country is benefited by the commerce of the town. Among all the absurd speculations that have been propagated concerning the balance of trade, it has never been pretended that either the country loses by its commerce with the town, or the town by that with the country which maintains it.

As subsistence is, in the nature of things, prior to conveniency and luxury,

189

so the industry which procures the former, must necessarily be prior to that which ministers to the latter. The cultivation and improvement of the country, therefore, which affords subsistence, must, necessarily, be prior to the increase of the town, which furnishes only the means of conveniency and luxury. It is the surplus produce of the country only, or what is over and above the maintenance of the cultivators, that constitutes the subsistence of the town, which can therefore increase only with the increase of this surplus produce. The town, indeed, may not always derive its whole subsistence from the country in its neighbourhood, or even from the territory to which it belongs, but from very distant countries; and this, though it forms no exception from the general rule, has occasioned considerable variations in the progress of opulence in different ages and nations. . . .

According to the natural course of things, therefore, the greater part of the capital of every growing society is, first, directed to agriculture, afterwards to manufactures, and last of all to foreign commerce. This order of things is so very natural, that in every society that had any territory, it has always, I believe, been in some degree observed. Some of their lands must have been cultivated before any considerable towns could be established, and some sort of coarse industry of the manufacturing kind must have been carried on in those towns, before they could well think of employing themselves in foreign commerce.

But though this natural order of things must have taken place in some degree in every such society, it has, in all the modern states of Europe, been, in many respects, entirely inverted. The foreign commerce of some of their cities has introduced all their finer manufactures, or such as were fit for distant sale; and manufactures and foreign commerce together, have given birth to the principal improvements of agriculture. The manners and customs which the nature of their original government introduced, and which remained after that government was greatly altered, necessarily forced them into this unnatural and retrograde order.

CHAPTER IV

HOW THE COMMERCE OF THE TOWNS CONTRIBUTED TO THE
IMPROVEMENT OF THE COUNTRY

The increase and riches of commercial and manufacturing towns, contributed to the improvement and cultivation of the countries to which they belonged, in three different ways.

First, by affording a great and ready market for the rude produce of the country, they gave encouragement to its cultivation and further improvement. This benefit was not even confined to the countries in which they were situated, but extended more or less to all those with which they had any dealings. To all of them they afforded a market for some part either of their rude or manufactured produce, and consequently gave some encouragement to the industry and improvement of all. Their own country, however, on account of its neighbourhood, necessarily derived the greatest benefit from this market. Its rude produce being charged with less carriage, the traders could pay the growers a better price for it, and yet afford it as cheap to the consumers as that of more distant countries.

Secondly, the wealth acquired by the inhabitants of cities was frequently employed in purchasing such lands as were to be sold, of which a great part would frequently be uncultivated. Merchants are commonly ambitious of becoming country gentlemen, and when they do, they are generally the best of all improvers. A merchant is accustomed to employ his money chiefly in profitable projects; whereas a mere country gentleman is accustomed to employ it chiefly in expence. The one often sees his money go from him and return to him again with a profit: the other, when once he parts with it, very seldom expects to see any more of it. Those different habits naturally affect their temper and disposition in every sort of business. A merchant is commonly a bold; a country gentleman, a timid undertaker. The one is not afraid to lay out at once a large capital upon the improvement of his land, when he has a probable prospect of raising the value of it in proportion to the expence. The other, if he has any capital, which is not always the case, seldom ventures to employ it in this manner. If he improves at all, it is commonly not with a capital, but with what he can save out of his annual revenue. Whoever has had the fortune to live in a mercantile town situated in an unimproved country, must have frequently observed how much more spirited the operations of merchants were in this way, than those of mere country gentlemen. The habits, besides, of order, œconomy and attention, to which mercantile business naturally forms a merchant, render him much fitter to execute, with profit and success, any project of improvement.

Thirdly, and lastly, commerce and manufactures gradually introduced order and good government, and with them, the liberty and security of individuals, among the inhabitants of the country, who had before lived almost in a continual state of war with their neighbours, and of servile dependency upon their superiors. This, though it has been the least observed, is by far the most important of all their effects. Mr. Hume is the only writer who, so far as I know, has hitherto taken notice of it.

In a country which has neither foreign commerce, nor any of the finer manufactures, a great proprietor, having nothing for which he can exchange the greater part of the produce of his lands which is over and above the maintenance of the cultivators, consumes the whole in rustic hospitality at home. If this surplus produce is sufficient to maintain a hundred or a thousand men, he can make use of it in no other way than by maintaining a hundred or a thousand men. He is at all times, therefore, surrounded with a multitude of retainers and dependants, who having no equivalent to give in return for their maintenance, but being fed entirely by his bounty, must obey him, for the same reason that soldiers must obey the prince who pays them. Before the extension of commerce and manufactures in Europe, the hospitality of the rich and the great, from the sovereign down to the smallest baron, exceeded every thing which in the present times we can easily form a notion of. West-minster hall was the dining-room of William Rufus, and might frequently, perhaps, not be too large for his company. It was reckoned a piece of magnif-icence in Thomas Becket, that he strowed the floor of his hall with clean hay or rushes in the season, in order that the knights and squires, who could not get seats, might not spoil their fine clothes when they sat down on the floor to eat their dinner. The great earl of Warwick is said to have entertained every day at his different manors, thirty thousand people; and though the number here may have been exaggerated, it must, however, have been very great to admit of such exaggeration. A hospitality nearly of the same kind was exer-cised not many years ago in many different parts of the highlands of Scotland. It seems to be common in all nations to whom commerce and manufactures are little known. I have seen, says Doctor Pocock, an Arabian chief dine in the streets of a town where he had come to sell his cattle, and invite all passen-gers, even common beggars, to sit down with him and partake of his banquet.

The occupiers of land were in every respect as dependent upon the great proprietor as his retainers. Even such of them as were not in a state of villan-age, were tenants at will, who paid a rent in no respect equivalent to the sub-sistence which the land afforded them. A crown, half a crown, a sheep, a lamb, was some years ago in the highlands of Scotland a common rent for lands which maintained a family. In some places it is so at this day; nor will money at present purchase a greater quantity of commodities there than in other places. In a country where the surplus produce of a large estate must be con-sumed upon the estate itself, it will frequently be more convenient for the proprietor, that part of it be consumed at a distance from his own house, pro-vided they who consume it are as dependent upon him as either his retainers or his menial servants. He is thereby saved from the embarrassment of either too large a company or too large a family. A tenant at will, who possesses land sufficient to maintain his family for little more than a quit-rent, is as depen-dent upon the proprietor as any servant or retainer whatever, and must obey him with as little reserve. Such a proprietor, as he feeds his servants and re-tainers at his own house, so he feeds his tenants at their houses. The subsis-tence of both is derived from his bounty, and its continuance depends upon his good pleasure.

Upon the authority which the great proprietors necessarily had in such a state of things over their tenants and retainers, was founded the power of the ancient barons. They necessarily became the judges in peace, and the leaders in war, of all who dwelt upon their estates. They could maintain order and execute the law within their respective demesnes, because each of them could there turn the whole force of all the inhabitants against the injustice of any one. No other person had sufficient authority to do this. The king in particular had not. In those ancient times he was little more than the greatest proprietor in his dominions, to whom, for the sake of common defence against their common enemies, the other great proprietors paid certain respects. To have enforced payment of a small debt within the lands of a great proprietor, where all the inhabitants were armed and accustomed to stand by one another, would have cost the king, had he attempted it by his own authority, almost the same effort as to extinguish a civil war. He was, therefore, obliged to abandon the administration of justice through the greater part of the country, to those who were capable of administering it; and for the same reason to leave the command of the country militia to those whom that militia would obey.

It is a mistake to imagine that those territorial jurisdictions took their origin from the feudal law. Not only the highest jurisdictions both civil and criminal, but the power of levying troops, of coining money, and even that of making bye-laws for the government of their own people, were all rights possessed allodially by the great proprietors of land several centuries before even the name of the feudal law was known in Europe. The authority and jurisdiction of the Saxon lords in England, appear to have been as great before the conquest, as that of any of the Norman lords after it. But the feudal law is not supposed to have become the common law of England till after the conquest. That the most extensive authority and jurisdictions were possessed by the great lords in France allodially, long before the feudal law was introduced into that country, is a matter of fact that admits of no doubt. That authority and those jurisdictions all necessarily flowed from the state of property and manners just now described. Without remounting to the remote antiquities of either the French or English monarchies, we may find in much later times many proofs that such effects must always flow from such causes. It is not thirty years ago since Mr. Cameron of Lochiel, a gentleman of Lochabar in Scotland, without any legal warrant whatever, not being what was then called a lord of regality, nor even a tenant in chief, but a vassal of the duke of Argyle, and without being so much as a justice of peace, used, notwithstanding, to exercise the highest criminal jurisdiction over his own people. He is said to have done so with great equity, though without any of the formalities of justice; and it is not improbable that the state of that part of the country at that time made it necessary for him to assume this authority in order to maintain the public peace. That gentleman, whose rent never exceeded five hundred pounds a year, carried, in 1745, eight hundred of his own people into the rebellion with him.

The introduction of the feudal law, so far from extending, may be regarded as an attempt to moderate the authority of the great allodial lords. It established a regular subordination, accompanied with a long train of services and duties, from the king down to the smallest proprietor. During the minority of

193

the proprietor, the rent, together with the management of his lands, fell into the hands of his immediate superior, and, consequently, those of all great proprietors into the hands of the king, who was charged with the maintenance and education of the pupil, and who, from his authority as guardian, was supposed to have a right of disposing of him in marriage, provided it was in a manner not unsuitable to his rank. But though this institution necessarily tended to strengthen the authority of the king, and to weaken that of the great proprietors, it could not do either sufficiently for establishing order and good government among the inhabitants of the country; because it could not alter sufficiently that state of property and manners from which the disorders arose. The authority of government still continued to be, as before, too weak in the head and too strong in the inferior members, and the excessive strength of the inferior members was the cause of the weakness of the head. After the institution of feudal subordination, the king was as incapable of restraining the violence of the great lords as before. They still continued to make war according to their own discretion, almost continually upon one another, and very frequently upon the king; and the open country still continued to be a scene of violence, rapine, and disorder.

But what all the violence of the feudal institutions could never have effected, the silent and insensible operation of foreign commerce and manufactures gradually brought about. These gradually furnished the great proprietors with something for which they could exchange the whole surplus produce of their lands, and which they could consume themselves without sharing it either with tenants or retainers. All for ourselves, and nothing for other people, seems, in every age of the world, to have been the vile maxim of the masters of mankind. As soon, therefore, as they could find a method of consuming the whole value of their rents themselves, they had no disposition to share them with any other persons. For a pair of diamond buckles perhaps, or for something as frivolous and useless, they exchanged the maintenance, or what is the same thing, the price of the maintenance of a thousand men for a year, and with it the whole weight and authority which it could give them. The buckles, however, were to be all their own, and no other human creature was to have any share of them; whereas in the more ancient method of expence they must have shared with at least a thousand people. With the judges that were to determine the preference, this difference was perfectly decisive; and thus, for the gratification of the most childish, the meanest and the most sordid of all vanities, they gradually bartered their whole power and authority.

In a country where there is no foreign commerce, nor any of the finer manufactures, a man of ten thousand a year cannot well employ his revenue in any other way than in maintaining, perhaps, a thousand families, who are all of them necessarily at his command. In the present state of Europe, a man of ten thousand a year can spend his whole revenue, and he generally does so, without directly maintaining twenty people, or being able to command more than ten footmen not worth the commanding. Indirectly, perhaps, he maintains as great or even a greater number of people than he could have done by the ancient method of expence. For though the quantity of precious productions for which he exchanges his whole revenue be very small, the number of workmen employed in collecting and preparing it, must necessarily have been very great. Its great price generally arises from the wages of their labour, and the profits of all their immediate employers. By paying that price he indirectly pays all those wages and profits, and thus indirectly contributes to the maintenance of all the workmen and their employers. He generally contributes, however, but a very small proportion to that of each, to very few perhaps a tenth, to many not a hundredth, and to some not a thousandth, nor even a ten thousandth part of their whole annual maintenance. Though he contributes, therefore, to the maintenance of them all, they are all more or less independent of him, because generally they can all be maintained without him.

When the great proprietors of land spend their rents in maintaining their tenants and retainers, each of them maintains entirely all his own tenants and all his own retainers. But when they spend them in maintaining tradesmen and artificers, they may, all of them taken together, perhaps, maintain as great, or, on account of the waste which attends rustic hospitality, a greater number of people than before. Each of them, however, taken singly, contributes often but a very small share to the maintenance of any individual of this greater number. Each tradesman or artificer derives his subsistence from the employment, not of one, but of a hundred or a thousand different customers. Though in some measure obliged to them all, therefore, he is not absolutely dependent upon any one of them.

The personal expence of the great proprietors having in this manner gradually increased, it was impossible that the number of their retainers should not as gradually diminish, till they were at last dismissed altogether. The same cause gradually led them to dismiss the unnecessary part of their tenants. Farms were enlarged, and the occupiers of land, notwithstanding the complaints of depopulation, reduced to the number necessary for cultivating it, according to the imperfect state of cultivation and improvement in those times. By the removal of the unnecessary mouths, and by exacting from the farmer the full value of the farm, a greater surplus, or what is the same thing, the price of a greater surplus, was obtained for the proprietor, which the merchants and manufacturers soon furnished him with a method of spending upon his own person in the same manner as he had done the rest. The same cause continuing to operate, he was desirous to raise his rents above what his lands, in the actual state of their improvement, could afford. His tenants could agree to this upon one condition only, that they should be secured in their possession, for such a term of years as might give them time to recover with profit whatever they should lay out in the further improvement of the land.

195

The expensive vanity of the landlord made him willing to accept of this condition; and hence the origin of long leases.

Even a tenant at will, who pays the full value of the land, is not altogether dependent upon the landlord. The pecuniary advantages which they receive from one another, are mutual and equal, and such a tenant will expose neither his life nor his fortune in the service of the proprietor. But if he has a lease for a long term of years, he is altogether independent; and his landlord must not expect from him even the most trifling service beyond what is either expressly stipulated in the lease, or imposed upon him by the common and known law of the country.

The tenants having in this manner become independent, and the retainers being dismissed, the great proprietors were no longer capable of interrupting the regular execution of justice, or of disturbing the peace of the country. Having sold their birth-right, not like Esau for a mess of pottage in time of hunger and necessity, but in the wantonness of plenty, for trinkets and baubles, fitter to be the play-things of children than the serious pursuits of men, they became as insignificant as any substantial burgher or tradesman in a city. A regular government was established in the country as well as in the city, nobody having sufficient power to disturb its operations in the one, any more than in the other.

It does not, perhaps, relate to the present subject, but I cannot help remarking it, that very old families, such as have possessed some considerable estate from father to son for many successive generations, are very rare in commercial countries. In countries which have little commerce, on the contrary, such as Wales or the highlands of Scotland, they are very common. The Arabian histories seem to be all full of genealogies, and there is a history written by a Tartar Khan, which has been translated into several European languages, and which contains scarce any thing else; a proof that ancient families are very common among those nations. In countries where a rich man can spend his revenue in no other way than by maintaining as many people as it can maintain, he is not apt to run out, and his benevolence it seems is seldom so violent as to attempt to maintain more than he can afford. But where he can spend the greatest revenue upon his own person, he frequently has no bounds to his expence, because he frequently has no bounds to his vanity, or to his affection for his own person. In commercial countries, therefore, riches, in spite of the most violent regulations of law to prevent their dissipation, very seldom remain long in the same family. Among simple nations, on the contrary, they frequently do without any regulations of law: for among nations of shepherds, such as the Tartars and Arabs, the consumable nature of their property necessarily renders all such regulations impossible.

A revolution of the greatest importance to the public happiness, was in this manner brought about by two different orders of people, who had not the least intention to serve the public. To gratify the most childish vanity was the sole motive of the great proprietors. The merchants and artificers, much less ridiculous, acted merely from a view to their own interest, and in pursuit of their own pedlar principle of turning a penny wherever a penny was to be got. Neither of them had either knowledge or foresight of that great revolution which the folly of the one, and the industry of the other, was gradually bringing about.

It is thus that through the greater part of Europe the commerce and manufactures of cities, instead of being the effect, have been the cause and occasion of the improvement and cultivation of the country. . . .

BOOK V

Of the Revenue of the Sovereign or Commonwealth

CHAPTER I

OF THE EXPENCES OF THE SOVEREIGN OR COMMONWEALTH

ARTICLE II *OF THE EXPENCE OF THE INSTITUTIONS FOR THE EDUCATION OF YOUTH*

. . . In the progress of the division of labour, the employment of the far greater part of those who live by labour, that is, of the great body of the people, comes to be confined to a few very simple operations, frequently to one or two. But the understandings of the greater part of men are necessarily formed by their ordinary employments. The man whose whole life is spent in performing a few simple operations, of which the effects too are, perhaps, always the same, or very nearly the same, has no occasion to exert his understanding, or to exercise his invention in finding out expedients for removing difficulties which never occur. He naturally loses, therefore, the habit of such exertion, and generally becomes as stupid and ignorant as it is possible for a human creature to become. The torpor of his mind renders him, not only incapable of relishing or bearing a part in any rational conversation, but of conceiving any generous, noble, or tender sentiment, and consequently of forming any just judgment concerning many even of the ordinary duties of private life. Of the great and extensive interests of his country he is altogether incapable of judging; and unless very particular pains have been taken to render him otherwise, he is equally incapable of defending his country in war. The uniformity of his stationary life naturally corrupts the courage of his mind, and makes him regard with abhorrence the irregular, uncertain, and adventurous life of a soldier. It corrupts even the activity of his body, and renders him incapable of exerting his strength with vigour and perseverance, in any other employment than that to which he has been bred. His dexterity at his own particular trade seems, in this manner, to be acquired at the expence of his intellectual, social, and martial virtues. But in every improved and civilized society this is the state into which the labouring poor, that is, the great body of the people, must necessarily fall, unless government takes some pains to prevent it.

It is otherwise in the barbarous societies, as they are commonly called, of hunters, of shepherds, and even of husbandmen in that rude state of husbandry which precedes the improvement of manufactures, and the extension of foreign commerce. In such societies the varied occupations of every man oblige every man to exert his capacity, and to invent expedients for removing difficulties which are continually occurring. Invention is kept alive, and the mind is not suffered to fall into that drowsy stupidity, which, in a civilized society, seems to benumb the understanding of almost all the inferior ranks of people. In those barbarous societies, as they are called, every man, it has already been observed, is a warrior. Every man too is in some measure a statesman, and can form a tolerable judgment concerning the interest of the society, and the conduct of those who govern it. How far their chiefs are good judges in peace, or good leaders in war, is obvious to the observation of almost every single man among them. In such a society indeed, no man can well acquire that improved and refined understanding, which a few men sometimes possess in a more civilized state. Though in a rude society there is a good deal of variety in the occupations of every individual, there is not a great deal in those of the whole society. Every man does, or is capable of doing, almost every thing which any other man does, or is capable of doing. Every man has a considerable degree of knowledge, ingenuity, and invention; but scarce any man has a great degree. The degree, however, which is commonly possessed, is generally sufficient for conducting the whole simple business of the society. In a civilized state, on the contrary, though there is little variety in the occupations of the greater part of individuals, there is an almost infinite variety in those of the whole society. These varied occupations present an almost infinite variety of objects to the contemplation of those few, who, being attached to no particular occupation themselves, have leisure and inclination to examine the occupations of other people. The contemplation of so great a variety of objects necessarily exercises their minds in endless comparisons and combinations, and renders their understandings, in an extraordinary degree, both acute and comprehensive. Unless those few, however, happen to be placed in some very particular situations, their great abilities, though honourable to themselves, may contribute very little to the good government or happiness of their society. Notwithstanding the great abilities of those few, all the nobler parts of the human character may be, in a great measure, obliterated and extinguished in the great body of the people.

The education of the common people requires, perhaps, in a civilized and commercial society, the attention of the public more than that of people of some rank and fortune. People of some rank and fortune are generally eighteen or nineteen years of age before they enter upon that particular business, profession, or trade, by which they propose to distinguish themselves in the world. They have before that full time to acquire, or at least to fit themselves for afterwards acquiring, every accomplishment which can recommend them to the public esteem, or render them worthy of it. Their parents or guardians are generally sufficiently anxious that they should be so accomplished, and are, in most cases, willing enough to lay out the expence which is necessary for that purpose. If they are not always properly educated, it is seldom from the want of expence laid out upon their education; but from the improper application of that expence. It is seldom from the want of masters; but from the negligence and incapacity of the masters who are to be had, and from the difficulty, or rather from the impossibility which there is, in the present state of things, of finding any better. The employments too in which people of some rank or fortune spend the greater part of their lives, are not, like those of the common people, simple and uniform. They are almost all of them extremely complicated, and such as exercise the head more than the hands. The understandings of those who are engaged in such employments can seldom grow torpid for want of exercise. The employments of people of some rank and fortune, besides, are seldom such as harass them from morning to night. They generally have a good deal of leisure, during which they may perfect themselves in every branch either of useful or ornamental knowledge of which they may have laid the foundation, or for which they may have acquired some taste in the earlier part of life.

It is otherwise with the common people. They have little time to spare for education. Their parents can scarce afford to maintain them even in infancy. As soon as they are able to work, they must apply to some trade by which they can earn their subsistence. That trade too is generally so simple and uniform as to give little exercise to the understanding; while, at the same time, their labour is both so constant and so severe, that it leaves them little leisure and less inclination to apply to, or even to think of any thing else.

But though the common people cannot, in any civilized society, be so well instructed as people of some rank and fortune, the most essential parts of education, however, to read, write, and account, can be acquired at so early a period of life, that the greater part even of those who are to be bred to the lowest occupations, have time to acquire them before they can be employed in those occupations. For a very small expence the public can facilitate, can encourage, and can even impose upon almost the whole body of the people, the necessity of acquiring those most essential parts of education.

The public can facilitate this acquisition by establishing in every parish or district a little school, where children may be taught for a reward so moderate, that even a common labourer may afford it; the master being partly, but not wholly paid by the public; because, if he was wholly, or even principally paid by it, he would soon learn to neglect his business. In Scotland the establishment of such parish schools has taught almost the whole common people to read, and a very great proportion of them to write and account. In England the establishment of charity schools has had an effect of the same kind, though not so universally, because the establishment is not so universal. If in those little schools the books, by which the children are taught to read, were a little more instructive than they commonly are; and if, instead of a little smattering of Latin, which the children of the common people are sometimes taught there, and which can scarce ever be of any use to them; they were instructed in the elementary parts of geometry and mechanics, the literary education of this rank of people would perhaps be as complete as it can be. There is scarce a common trade which does not afford some opportunities of applying to it the principles of geometry and mechanics, and which would not therefore gradually exercise and improve the common people in those principles, the necessary introduction to the most sublime as well as to the most useful sciences.

The public can encourage the acquisition of those most essential parts of education by giving small premiums, and little badges of distinction, to the children of the common people who excel in them.

The public can impose upon almost the whole body of the people the necessity of acquiring those most essential parts of education, by obliging every man to undergo an examination or probation in them before he can obtain the freedom in any corporation, or be allowed to set up any trade either in a village or town corporate.

It was in this manner, by facilitating the acquisition of their military and gymnastic exercises, by encouraging it, and even by imposing upon the whole body of the people the necessity of learning those exercises, that the Greek and Roman republics maintained the martial spirit of their respective citizens. They facilitated the acquisition of those exercises by appointing a certain place for learning and practising them, and by granting to certain masters the privilege of teaching in that place. Those masters do not appear to have had either salaries or exclusive privileges of any kind. Their reward consisted altogether in what they got from their scholars; and a citizen who had learnt his exercises in the public Gymnasia, had no sort of legal advantage over one who had learnt them privately, provided the latter had learnt them equally well. Those republics encouraged the acquisition of those exercises, by bestowing little premiums and badges of distinction upon those who excelled in them. To have gained a prize in the Olympic, Isthmian or Nemæan games gave illustration, not only to the person who gained it, but to his whole family and kindred. The obligation which every citizen was under to serve a certain number of years, if called upon, in the armies of the republic, sufficiently imposed the necessity of learning those exercises without which he could not be fit for that service.

That in the progress of improvement the practice of military exercises, unless government takes proper pains to support it, goes gradually to decay, and, together with it, the martial spirit of the great body of the people, the example of modern Europe sufficiently demonstrates. But the security of every society must always depend, more or less, upon the martial spirit of the great body of the people. In the present times, indeed, that martial spirit alone, and unsupported by a well-disciplined standing army, would not, perhaps, be sufficient for the defence and security of any society. But where every citizen had the spirit of a soldier, a smaller standing army would surely be requisite. That spirit, besides, would necessarily diminish very much the dangers to liberty, whether real or imaginary, which are commonly apprehended from a standing army. As it would very much facilitate the operations of that army against a foreign invader, so it would obstruct them as much if unfortunately they should ever be directed against the constitution of the state.

The ancient institutions of Greece and Rome seem to have been much more effectual, for maintaining the martial spirit of the great body of the people, than the establishment of what are called the militias of modern times. They were much more simple. When they were once established, they executed themselves, and it required little or no attention from government to maintain them in the most perfect vigour. Whereas to maintain, even in tolerable execution, the complex regulations of any modern militia, requires the continual and painful attention of government, without which they are constantly falling into total neglect and disuse. The influence, besides, of the ancient institutions was much more universal. By means of them the whole body of the people was completely instructed in the use of arms. Whereas it is but a very small part of them who can ever be so instructed by the regulations of any modern militia; except, perhaps, that of Switzerland. But a coward, a man incapable either of defending or of revenging himself, evidently wants one of the most essential parts of the character of a man. He is as much mutilated and deformed in his mind as another is in his body, who is either deprived of some of its most essential members, or has lost the use of them. He is evidently the more wretched and miserable of the two; because happiness and misery, which reside altogether in the mind, must necessarily depend more upon the healthful or unhealthful, the mutilated or entire state of the mind, than upon that of the body. Even though the martial spirit of the people were of no use towards the defence of the society, yet to prevent that sort of mental mutilation, deformity, and wretchedness, which cowardice necessarily involves in it, from spreading themselves through the great body of the people, would still deserve the most serious attention of government; in the same manner as it would deserve its most serious attention to prevent a leprosy or any other loathsome and offensive disease, though neither mortal nor dangerous, from spreading itself among them; though, perhaps, no other public good might result from such attention besides the prevention of so great a public evil.

The same thing may be said of the gross ignorance and stupidity which, in a civilized society, seem so frequently to benumb the understandings of all the inferior ranks of people. A man without the proper use of the intellectual faculties of a man, is, if possible, more contemptible than even a coward, and

201

seems to be mutilated and deformed in a still more essential part of the character of human nature. Though the state was to derive no advantage from the instruction of the inferior ranks of people, it would still deserve its attention that they should not be altogether uninstructed. The state, however, derives no inconsiderable advantage from their instruction. The more they are instructed, the less liable they are to the delusions of enthusiasm and superstition, which, among ignorant nations, frequently occasion the most dreadful disorders. An instructed and intelligent people besides, are always more decent and orderly than an ignorant and stupid one. They feel themselves, each individually more respectable, and more likely to obtain the respect of their lawful superiors, and they are therefore more disposed to respect those superiors. They are more disposed to examine, and more capable of seeing through, the interested complaints of faction and sedition, and they are, upon that account, less apt to be misled into any wanton or unnecessary opposition to the measures of government. In free countries, where the safety of government depends very much upon the favourable judgment which the people may form of its conduct, it must surely be of the highest importance that they should not be disposed to judge rashly or capriciously concerning it.

For Further Reading

Smith, Adam. *The Theory of Moral Sentiments.* Edited by D.D. Raphael and A.L. Macfie (Oxford: Oxford Univ. Press, 1980).

_____. *An Inquiry into the Nature and Causes of The Wealth of Nations.* 2 vols. Edited by R.H. Campbell, A.S. Skinner, and W.B. Todd (Indianapolis: Liberty Classics, 1981).

_____. *An Inquiry Into the Nature and Causes of The Wealth of Nations* (Indianapolis: Hackett, 1993).

Campbell, Thomas D. *Adam Smith's Science of Morals* (London: George Allen and Unwin, 1971).

Foley, Vernard. *The Social Physics of Adam Smith* (Lafayette, Ind.: Purdue Univ. Press, 1976).

Haakonssen, Knud. *The Science of a Legislator: The Natural Jurisprudence of David Hume and Adam Smith* (Cambridge: Cambridge Univ. Press, 1981).

Lindgren, J. Ralph. *The Social Philosophy of Adam Smith* (The Hague: Martinus Nijhoff, 1973).

Macfie, A.L. *The Individual in Society: Papers on Adam Smith* (London: Allen and Unwin, 1967).

Minowitz, Peter. *Profits, Priests, and Princes: Adam Smith's Emancipation of Economics from Politics and Religion* (Stanford, Calif.: Stanford Univ. Press, 1993).

Rae, John. *Life of Adam Smith* (New York: Augustus M. Kelly, 1965).

Raphael, D.D. *Adam Smith* (Oxford: Oxford Univ. Press, 1985).

Reisman, D.A. *Adam Smith's Sociological Economics* (New York: Barnes and Noble, 1976).

Robertson, J. "Scottish Political Economy Beyond the Civic Tradition: Government and Economic Development in the 'Wealth of Nations'." *History of Political Thought* 4 (Winter 1983).

Samuels, Warren J. "The Political Economy of Adam Smith." *Ethics* 87 (April 77).

Skinner, A.S., and Thomas Wilson, eds. *Essays on Adam Smith* (Oxford: Oxford Univ. Press, 1976).

Werhane, Patricia H. "Freedom, Commodification, and the Alienation of Labor in Adam Smith's 'Wealth of Nations'." *Philosophical Forum* (Summer 1991).

_____. "The Role of Self-Interest in Adam Smith's 'Wealth of Nations'." *Journal of Philosophy* 86 (Nov. 1989).

Winch, Donald. *Adam Smith's Politics: An Essay in Historiographic Revision* (Cambridge: Cambridge Univ. Press, 1978).

JAMES MADISON (1751–1836)

chapter 9

THE POLITICAL tradition of classical republicanism, which James Madison adapted to commercial conditions, stretches back to Periclean Athens and pre-imperial Rome. Its original theoretical statement is Aristotle's defense, in the *Politics*, of a mixed form of government, a "polity," designed to foster civic virtue and overcome problems he found with monarchy, aristocracy, and democracy. In fifteenth-century Florence, Machiavelli renewed republican thought, and it figured prominently in seventeenth- and eighteenth-century Europe and North America. The upsurge of commerce in that latter period, however, posed grave challenges to republican politics: (1) commerce thrives on luxury and narrow self-interest; republicanism calls for sensible morals and public spirit; (2) the division of labor specializes social roles, notably that of the soldier; the republican ideal was the versatile citizen soldier; (3) commerce shifts power from landed property owners to merchants, manufacturers, and financiers, whose dependence upon money and markets makes their property and personal identity insecure; republican virtue counts on stability of property and person; (4) the geographical expansion of trade means that small regions are dependent on outside suppliers; republicanism calls for a compact, independent nation; (5) commerce favors liberty but beyond that has little idea of what is the good for human beings; the purpose of a republic is not only to secure liberty but to promote virtue, which involves a definite conception of proper human functioning; (6) commerce tends to create great inequalities of wealth; republicans warn against the political instability they bring about; (7) commerce creates conflicting economic groups, in Madison's words, "different classes, activated by different sentiments and views," and expects them to operate from self-interest; the republican solution to economic differences relies on individuals committing themselves to the public good.

What propels Madison's contributions to *The Federalist Papers* and the American Constitution is his conviction, one shared with David Hume, that an expansive, commercial republic can prosper. To solve the problem of factions—and he cites commerce as their "most common and durable source"—Madison devises a liberal synthesis of commercial and republican elements marked chiefly by its formalism. Madison drops both the classical aspiration that republican life cultivate virtue and the traditional reliance on individuals making the public good their own. Sounding like Locke, Madison asserts that the first duty of government is to protect the "faculties" of its citizens; as differences in "faculties" lead to differences in property, these too must be secured. Because reason is directed by self-love, differences of property so influence "the sentiments and views of the respective proprietors" as to make interest-based factions second nature. The classical "virtue solution" to factions flies in the face of human nature; at best, the bad effects of factions can be blocked by a political "invisible hand." The *form* of the republic will have to look after justice and the public good, since on their own the republic's incurably splintered inhabitants cannot be expected to rise to the task.

Questions left for Madison's brilliant constitutional amalgam include these: (1) If a commercial society is a capitalist one, how can the joint interests of capitalists fail to become a filter for governmental action? (2) Can politics afford to be as inept at promoting public spirit as the marketplace? (3) What if capitalism undermines the Lockean theory of property without violating the rules of the game? What if protecting capitalist property rights shields a new system of exploitation? (4) What if, as a consequence of world trade, the commercial factions that matter most exceed the bounds of even an expansive republic? (5) What if commercial societies are dominated impersonally by the peculiar social form of their provisioning processes, capital? How will the republic's resources for blockading factions address that?

206

FROM *THE FEDERALIST PAPERS*

NUMBER X

THE SAME SUBJECT CONTINUED.

Among the numerous advantages promised by a well constructed union, none deserves to be more accurately developed than its tendency to break and control the violence of faction. The friend of popular governments, never finds himself so much alarmed for their character and fate, as when he contemplates their propensity to this dangerous vice. He will not fail therefore to set a due value on any plan which, without violating the principles to which he is attached, provides a proper cure for it. The instability, injustice and confusion introduced into the public councils, have in truth been the mortal diseases under which popular governments have every where perished; as they continue to be the favorite and fruitful topics from which the adversaries to liberty derive their most specious declamations. The valuable improvements made by the American constitutions on the popular models, both ancient and modern, cannot certainly be too much admired; but it would be an unwarrantable partiality, to contend that they have as effectually obviated the danger on this side as was wished and expected. Complaints are every where heard from our most considerate and virtuous citizens, equally the friends of public and private faith, and of public and personal liberty; that [our] governments are too unstable; that the public good is disregarded in the conflicts of rival parties; and that measures are too often decided, not according to the rules of justice, and the rights of the minor party; but by the superior force of an interested and over-bearing majority. However anxiously we may wish that these complaints had no foundation, the evidence of known facts will not permit us to deny that they are in some degree true. It will be found indeed, on a candid review of our situation, that some of the distresses under which we labor, have been erroneously charged on the operation of our governments; but it will be found, at the same time, that other causes will not alone account for many of our heaviest misfortunes; and particularly, for that prevailing and increasing distrust of public engagements, and alarm for private rights, which are echoed from one end of the continent to the other. These must be chiefly, if not wholly, effects of the unsteadiness and injustice, with which a factious spirit has tainted our public [administration.]

By a faction I understand a number of citizens, whether amounting to a majority or minority of the whole, who are united and actuated by some common impulse of passion, or of interest, adverse to the rights of other citizens or to the permanent and aggregate interests of the community.

There are two methods of curing the mischiefs of faction: the one, by removing its causes; the other, by controling its effects.

There are again two methods of removing the causes of faction: the one by destroying the liberty which is essential to its existence, the other, by giving to every citizen the same opinions, the same passions, and the same interests.

It could never be more truly said than of the first remedy, that it is worse than the disease. Liberty is to faction, what air is to fire, an aliment without which it instantly expires. But it could not be a less folly to abolish liberty, which is essential to political life, because it nourishes faction, than it would be to wish the annihilation of air, which is essential to animal life, because it imparts to fire its destructive agency.

The second expedient is as impracticable, as the first would be unwise. As long as the reason of man continues fallible, and he is at liberty to exercise it, different opinions will be formed. As long as the connection subsists between his reason and his self-love, his opinions and his passions will have a reciprocal influence on each other; and the former will be objects to which the latter will attach themselves. The diversity in the faculties of men from which the rights of property originate, is not less an insuperable obstacle to [an] uniformity of interests. The protection of these faculties is the first object of government. From the protection of different and unequal faculties of acquiring property, the possession of different degrees and kinds of property immediately results: and from the influence of these on the sentiments and views of the respective proprietors, ensues a division of the society into different interests and parties.

The latent causes of faction are thus sown in the nature of man; and we see them every where brought into different degrees of activity, according to the different circumstances of civil society. A zeal for different opinions concerning religion, concerning government and many other points, as well of speculation as of practice; an attachment to different leaders ambitiously contending for pre-eminence and power; or to persons of other descriptions whose fortunes have been interesting to the human passions, have in turn divided mankind into parties, inflamed them with mutual animosity, and rendered them much more disposed to vex and oppress each other, than to co-operate for their common good. So strong is this propensity of mankind to fall into mutual animosities, that where no substantial occasion presents itself, the most frivolous and fanciful distinctions have been sufficient to kindle their unfriendly passions, and excite their most violent conflicts. But the most common and durable source of factions, has been the various and unequal distribution of property. Those who hold, and those who are without property, have ever formed distinct interests in society. Those who are creditors, and those who are debtors, fall under a like discrimination. A landed interest, a manufacturing interest, a mercantile interest, a monied interest, with many lesser interests, grow up of necessity in civilized nations, and divide them into different classes, actuated by different sentiments and views. The regulation of these various and interfering interests forms the principal task of modern legislation, and involves the spirit of party and faction in the necessary and ordinary operations of government.

No man is allowed to be a judge in his own cause; because his interest would certainly bias his judgment, and, not improbably, corrupt his integrity. With equal, nay with greater reason, a body of men, are unfit to be both judges and parties, at the same time; yet, what are many of the most important acts of legislation, but so many judicial determinations, not indeed concerning the rights of single persons, but concerning the rights of large bodies of citizens; and what are the different classes of legislators, but advocates and parties to the causes which they determine? Is a law proposed concerning private debts? It is a question to which the creditors are parties on one side, and the debtors on the other. Justice ought to hold the balance between them. Yet the parties are and must be themselves the judges; and the most numerous party, or, in other words, the most powerful faction must be expected to prevail. Shall domestic manufactures be encouraged, and in what degree, by restrictions on foreign manufactures? are questions which would be differently decided by the landed and the manufacturing classes; and probably by neither, with a sole regard to justice and the public good. The apportionment of taxes on the various descriptions of property, is an act which seems to require the most exact impartiality; yet, there is perhaps no legislative act in which greater opportunity and temptation are given to a predominant party, to trample on the rules of justice. Every shilling with which they over-burden the inferior number, is a shilling saved to their own pockets.

It is in vain to say, that enlightened statesmen will be able to adjust these clashing interests, and render them all subservient to the public good. Enlightened statesmen will not always be at [the] helm: Nor, in many cases, can such an adjustment be made at all, without taking into view indirect and remote considerations, which will rarely prevail over the immediate interest which one party may find in disregarding the rights of another, or the good of the whole.

The inference to which we are brought, is, that the *causes* of faction cannot be removed; and that relief is only to be sought in the means of controling its *effects*.

If a faction consists of less than a majority, relief is supplied by the republican principle, which enables the majority to defeat its sinister views by regular vote: It may clog the administration, it may convulse the society; but it will be unable to execute and mask its violence under the forms of the constitution. When a majority is included in a faction, the form of popular government on the other hand enables it to sacrifice to its ruling passion or interest, both the public good and the rights of other citizens. To secure the public good, and private rights against the danger of such a faction, and at the same time to preserve the spirit and the form of popular government, is then the great object to which our enquiries are directed. Let me add that it is the

209

great desideratum, by which alone this form of government can be rescued from the opprobrium under which it has so long labored, and be recommended to the esteem and adoption of mankind.

By what means is this object attainable? Evidently by one of two only. Either the existence of the same passion or interest in a majority at the same time must be prevented; or the majority, having such co-existent passion or interest, must be rendered, by their number and local situation, unable to concert and carry into effect schemes of oppression. If the impulse and the opportunity be suffered to coincide, we well know that neither moral nor religious motives can be relied on as an adequate control. They are not found to be such on the injustice and violence of individuals, and lose their efficacy in proportion to the number combined together; that is, in proportion as their efficacy becomes needful.

From this view of the subject, it may be concluded, that a pure democracy, by which I mean a society consisting of a small number of citizens, who assemble and administer the government in person, can admit of no cure for the mischiefs of faction. A common passion or interest will, in almost every case, be felt by a majority of the whole; a communication and concert results from the form of government itself; and there is nothing to check the inducements to sacrifice the weaker party, or an obnoxious individual. Hence it is, that such democracies have ever been spectacles of turbulence and contention; have ever been found incompatible with personal security or the rights of property; and have in general been as short in their lives, as they have been violent in their deaths. Theoretic politicians, who have patronized this species of government, have erroneously supposed, that by reducing mankind to a perfect equality in their political rights, they would, at the same time, be perfectly equalized and assimilated in their possessions, their opinions, and their passions.

A republic, by which I mean a government in which the scheme of representation takes place, opens a different prospect, and promises the cure for which we are seeking. Let us examine the points in which it varies from pure democracy, and we shall comprehend both the nature of the cure, and the efficacy which it must derive from the union.

The two great points of difference between a democracy and a republic are, first, the delegation of the government, in the latter, to a small number of citizens elected by the rest: secondly, the greater number of citizens and greater sphere of country, over which the latter may be extended.

The effect of the first difference is, on the one hand to refine and enlarge the public views, by passing them through the medium of a chosen body of citizens, whose wisdom may best discern the true interest of their country, and whose patriotism and love of justice, will be least likely to sacrifice it to temporary or partial considerations. Under such a regulation, it may well happen that the public voice pronounced by the representatives of the people,

210

will be more consonant to the public good, than if pronounced by the people themselves convened for the purpose. On the other hand, the effect may be inverted. Men of factious tempers, of local prejudices, or of sinister designs, may by intrigue, by corruption or by other means, first obtain the suffrages, and then betray the interests of the people. The question resulting is, whether small or extensive republics are most favorable to the election of proper guardians of the public weal: and it is clearly decided in favor of the latter by two obvious considerations.

In the first place it is to be remarked that however small the republic may be, the representatives must be raised to a certain number, in order to guard against the cabals of a few; and that however large it may be, they must be limited to a certain number, in order to guard against the confusion of a multitude. Hence the number of representatives in the two cases, not being in proportion to that of the constituents, and being proportionally greatest in the small republic, it follows, that if the proportion of fit characters, be not less, in the large than in the small republic, the former will present a greater option, and consequently a greater probability of a fit choice.

In the next place, as each representative will be chosen by a greater number of citizens in the large than in the small republic, it will be more difficult for unworthy candidates to practise with success the vicious arts, by which elections are too often carried; and the suffrages of the people being more free, will be more likely to centre on men who possess the most attractive merit, and the most diffusive and established characters.

It must be confessed, that in this, as in most other cases, there is a mean, on both sides of which inconveniencies will be found to lie. By enlarging too much the number of electors, you render the representative too little acquainted with all their local circumstances and lesser interests; as by reducing it too much, you render him unduly attached to these, and too little fit to comprehend and pursue great and national objects. The federal constitution forms a happy combination in this respect; the great and aggregate interests being referred to the national, the local and particular, to the state legislatures.

The other point of difference is, the greater number of citizens and extent of territory which may be brought within the compass of republican, than of democratic government; and it is this circumstance principally which renders factious combinations less to be dreaded in the former, than in the latter. The smaller the society, the fewer probably will be the distinct parties and interests composing it, the fewer the distinct parties and interests, the more frequently will a majority be found of the same party; and the smaller the number of individuals composing a majority, and the smaller the compass within which they are placed, the more easily will they concert and execute their plans of oppression. Extend the sphere, and you take in a greater variety of parties and interests; you make it less probable that a majority of the whole will have a common motive to invade the rights of other citizens; or if such a common

211

motive exists, it will be more difficult for all who feel it to discover their own strength, and to act in unison with each other. Besides other impediments, it may be remarked, that where there is a consciousness of unjust or dishonorable purposes, communication is always checked by distrust, in proportion to the number whose concurrence is necessary.

Hence it clearly appears, that the same advantage, which a republic has over a democracy, in controling the effects of faction, is enjoyed by a large over a small republic—is enjoyed by the union over the states composing it. Does this advantage consist in the substitution of representatives, whose enlightened views and virtuous sentiments render them superior to local prejudices, and to schemes of injustice? It will not be denied, that the representation of the union will be most likely to possess these requisite endowments. Does it consist in the greater security afforded by a greater variety of parties, against the event of any one party being able to outnumber and oppress the rest? In an equal degree does the encreased variety of parties, comprised within the union, encrease this security. Does it, in fine, consist in the greater obstacles opposed to the concert and accomplishment of the secret wishes of an unjust and interested majority? Here, again, the extent of the union gives it the most palpable advantage.

The influence of factious leaders may kindle a flame within their particular states, but will be unable to spread a general conflagration through the other states: A religious sect, may degenerate into a political faction in a part of the confederacy; but the variety of sects dispersed over the entire face of it, must secure the national councils against any danger from that source: A rage for paper money, for an abolition of debts, for an equal division of property, or for any other improper or wicked project, will be less apt to pervade the whole body of the union, than a particular member of it; in the same proportion as such a malady is more likely to taint a particular county or district, than an entire state.

In the extent and proper structure of the union, therefore, we behold a republican remedy for the diseases most incident to republican government. And according to the degree of pleasure and pride, we feel in being republicans, ought to be our zeal in cherishing the spirit, and supporting the character of federalists.

PUBLIUS.

For Further Reading

Kramnick, Isaac, ed. *James Madison, Alexander Hamilton, and John Jay: The Federalist Papers* (Harmondsworth, England: Penguin Books, 1987).

Adair, Douglass. *Fame and the Founding Fathers: Essays by Douglass Adair.* Edited by Trevor Cobourn. (New York: W.W. Norton, 1974).

Banning, Lance. *The Sacred Fire of Liberty: James Madison and the Founding of the Federal Republic* (Ithaca, N.Y.: Cornell Univ. Press, 1995).

Beard, Charles A. *An Economic Interpretation of the Constitution* (New York: Macmillan, 1913).

_____. *The Enduring Federalist* (New York: Doubleday, 1948).

Burns, James McGregor. *The Deadlock of Democracy* (Englewood Cliffs, N.J.: Prentice-Hall, 1963).

_____. *Uncommon Sense* (New York: Harper and Row, 1972).

Carey, George W. *The Federalist: Design for a Constitutional Republic* (Urbana: Univ. of Illinois Press, 1989).

Cooke, Jacob E. *Introduction to The Federalist* (Middletown, Conn.: Wesleyan Univ. Press, 1961).

Dahl, Robert. *Preface to Democratic Theory* (Chicago: Univ. of Chicago Press, 1956).

Epstein, David F. *The Political Theory of "The Federalist"* (Chicago: Univ. of Chicago Press, 1984).

Mace, George. *Locke, Hobbes, and "The Federalist Papers"* (Carbondale: Univ. of Southern Illinois Press, 1979).

Matson, Cathy D., and Peter S. Onuf, eds. *A Union of Interests: Political and Economic Thought in Revolutionary America* (Lawrence: Univ. of Kansas Press, 1993).

Matthews, Richard. *If Men Were Angels: James Madison and the Heartless Empire of Reason* (Lawrence, Kans.: Univ. Press of Kansas: 1995).

Montesquieu, Baron de. *Considerations on the Causes of the Greatness of the Romans and their Decline*. Translated by David Lowenthal (Ithaca, N.Y.: Cornell Univ. Press, 1968).

_____. *The Spirit of the Laws*. Translated by Anne Cohler, Basia Miller, and Harold Stone (Cambridge: Cambridge Univ. Press, 1989).

Scanlon, James P. "'The Federalist' and Human Nature," *Review of Politics* 21 (Oct. 1959).

Tocqueville, Alexis de. *Democracy in America*. Translated by George Lawrence (New York: Doubleday, 1969).

Wills, Garry. *Explaining America* (Garden City, N.Y.: Doubleday, 1981).

Wood, Gordon. *The Creation of the American Republic* (Chapel Hill: Univ. of North Carolina Press, 1969).

213

FRIEDRICH SCHILLER (1759–1805)

chapter 10

THE DIVISION of labor that lifts humanity out of stifling poverty shatters individuals. Friedrich Schiller reconciles himself to this paradox posed by Adam Smith and extends its logic to encompass the destinies of reason, nature, and political life. But fragmentation does not have the last word. Schiller puts his hope in a future where divisions give way to wholeness, believing that civilization possesses the resources to heal its self-inflicted wounds. By generalizing Smith's paradox into a wider model, Schiller brings into view a history of interaction between philosophy and political economy during the modern period. That interplay was especially pronounced in British theorists such as Locke, Berkeley, Hutcheson, Hume, and Smith, who made a deep impression on Schiller's mentor, Immanuel Kant. And Schiller's generalization of the division of labor was an important springboard for Hegel's philosophy, of which the young Karl Marx could write: "Hegel shares the standpoint of the modern national economists. He grasps *labor* as the essence, as the self-confirming essence of man." For all the attention that labor and the division of labor receive from Smith, Schiller, and Hegel, however, they never adequately think through the *social form* of labor in a commercial society.

Struggling with severe depression, the young John Stuart Mill might have found in Schiller's description of the painful but necessary "spirit of abstraction" a precise diagnosis of his condition: it "stifles the fire at which the heart should have warmed itself and the imagination been kindled." Fragmentation results when analytical distinctions drawn by the mind are imposed on reality. Conceding that the intellect's powers of abstraction cannot be kept on a leash, Schiller turns to concrete, sensuous manifestations of freedom; he looks to beauty and play for a recovery of wholeness. There, sense and reason, matter and form, put an end to their strife. As he writes in the fourteenth of the letters composing *On the Aesthetic Education of Man,* the play impulse "endeavors to receive according as it would have produced, and to produce according as the senses strive to receive." This earthly hope impressed Karl Marx, and Schiller's aesthetic model of liberation influenced Herbert Marcuse, an important figure for the "New Left" radicals of the 1960s.

FROM *ON THE AESTHETIC EDUCATION OF MAN: IN A SERIES OF LETTERS*

SIXTH LETTER

1. Have I not perhaps been too hard on our age in the picture I have just drawn? That is scarcely the reproach I anticipate. Rather a different one: that I have tried to make it prove too much. Such a portrait, you will tell me, does indeed resemble mankind as it is today; but does it not also resemble any people caught up in the process of civilization, since all of them, without exception, must fall away from Nature by the abuse of Reason before they can return to her by the use of Reason?

2. Closer attention to the character of our age will, however, reveal an astonishing contrast between contemporary forms of humanity and earlier ones, especially the Greek. The reputation for culture and refinement, on which we otherwise rightly pride ourselves *vis-à-vis* humanity in its merely natural state, can avail us nothing against the natural humanity of the Greeks. For they were wedded to all the delights of art and all the dignity of wisdom, without however, like us, falling a prey to their seduction. The Greeks put us to shame not only by a simplicity to which our age is a stranger; they are at the same time our rivals, indeed often our models, in those very excellences with which we are wont to console ourselves for the unnaturalness of our manners. In fullness of form no less than of content, at once philosophic and creative, sensitive and energetic, the Greeks combined the first youth of imagination with the manhood of reason in a glorious manifestation of humanity.

3. At that first fair awakening of the powers of the mind, sense and intellect

did not as yet rule over strictly separate domains; for no dissension had as yet provoked them into hostile partition and mutual demarcation of their frontiers. Poetry had not as yet coquetted with wit, nor speculation prostituted itself to sophistry. Both of them could, when need arose, exchange functions, since each in its own fashion paid honour to truth. However high the mind might soar, it always drew matter lovingly along with it; and however fine and sharp the distinctions it might make, it never proceeded to mutilate. It did indeed divide human nature into its several aspects, and project these in magnified form into the divinities of its glorious pantheon; but not by tearing it to pieces; rather by combining its aspects in different proportions, for in no single one of their deities was humanity in its entirety ever lacking. How different with us Moderns! With us too the image of the human species is projected in magnified form into separate individuals—but as fragments, not in different combinations, with the result that one has to go the rounds from one individual to another in order to be able to piece together a complete image of the species. With us, one might almost be tempted to assert, the various faculties appear as separate in practice as they are distinguished by the psychologist in theory, and we see not merely individuals, but whole classes of men, developing but one part of their potentialities, while of the rest, as in stunted growths, only vestigial traces remain.

4. I do not underrate the advantages which the human race today, considered as a whole and weighed in the balance of intellect, can boast in the face of what is best in the ancient world. But it has to take up the challenge in serried ranks, and let whole measure itself against whole. What individual Modern could sally forth and engage, man against man, with an individual Athenian for the prize of humanity?

5. Whence this disadvantage among individuals when the species as a whole is at such an advantage? Why was the individual Greek qualified to be the representative of his age, and why can no single Modern venture as much? Because it was from all-unifying Nature that the former, and from the all-dividing Intellect that the latter, received their respective forms.

6. It was civilization itself which inflicted this wound upon modern man. Once the increase of empirical knowledge, and more exact modes of thought, made sharper divisions between the sciences inevitable, and once the increasingly complex machinery of State necessitated a more rigorous separation of ranks and occupations, then the inner unity of human nature was severed too, and a disastrous conflict set its harmonious powers at variance. The intuitive and the speculative understanding now withdrew in hostility to take up positions in their respective fields, whose frontiers they now began to guard with jealous mistrust; and with this confining of our activity to a particular sphere we have given ourselves a master within, who not infrequently ends by suppressing the rest of our potentialities. While in the one a riotous imagination ravages the hard-won fruits of the intellect, in another the spirit

217

of abstraction stifles the fire at which the heart should have warmed itself and the imagination been kindled.

7. This disorganization, which was first started within man by civilization and learning, was made complete and universal by the new spirit of government. It was scarcely to be expected that the simple organization of the early republics should have survived the simplicity of early manners and conditions; but instead of rising to a higher form of organic existence it degenerated into a crude and clumsy mechanism. That polypoid character of the Greek States, in which every individual enjoyed an independent existence but could, when need arose, grow into the whole organism, now made way for an ingenious clock-work, in which, out of the piecing together of innumerable but lifeless parts, a mechanical kind of collective life ensued. State and Church, laws and customs, were now torn asunder; enjoyment was divorced from labour, the means from the end, the effort from the reward. Everlastingly chained to a single little fragment of the Whole, man himself develops into nothing but a fragment; everlastingly in his ear the monotonous sound of the wheel that he turns, he never develops the harmony of his being, and instead of putting the stamp of humanity upon his own nature, he becomes nothing more than the imprint of his occupation or of his specialized knowledge. But even that meagre, fragmentary participation, by which individual members of the State are still linked to the Whole, does not depend upon forms which they spontaneously prescribe for themselves (for how could one entrust to their freedom of action a mechanism so intricate and so fearful of light and enlightenment?); it is dictated to them with meticulous exactitude by means of a formulary which inhibits all freedom of thought. The dead letter takes the place of living understanding, and a good memory is a safer guide than imagination and feeling.

8. When the community makes his office the measure of the man; when in one of its citizens it prizes nothing but memory, in another a mere tabularizing intelligence, in a third only mechanical skill; when, in the one case, indifferent to character, it insists exclusively on knowledge, yet is, in another, ready to condone any amount of obscurantist thinking as long as it is accompanied by a spirit of order and law-abiding behavior; when, moreover, it insists on special skills being developed with a degree of intensity which is only commensurate with its readiness to absolve the individual citizen from developing himself in extensity—can we wonder that the remaining aptitudes of the psyche are neglected in order to give undivided attention to the one which will bring honour and profit? True, we know that the outstanding individual will never let the limits of his occupation dictate the limits of his activity. But a mediocre talent will consume in the office assigned him the whole meagre sum of his powers, and a man has to have a mind above the ordinary if, without detriment to his calling, he is still to have time for the chosen pursuits of his leisure. Moreover, it is rarely a recommendation in the eyes of the State if

a man's powers exceed the tasks he is set, or if the higher needs of the man of parts constitute a rival to the duties of his office. So jealously does the State insist on being the sole proprietor of its servants that it will more easily bring itself (and who can blame it?) to share its man with the Cytherean, than with the Uranian, Venus.

9. Thus little by little the concrete life of the Individual is destroyed in order that the abstract idea of the Whole may drag out its sorry existence, and the State remains for ever a stranger to its citizens since at no point does it ever make contact with their feeling. Forced to resort to classification in order to cope with the variety of its citizens, and never to get an impression of humanity except through representation at second hand, the governing section ends up by losing sight of them altogether, confusing their concrete reality with a mere construct of the intellect; while the governed cannot but receive with indifference laws which are scarcely, if at all, directed to them as persons. Weary at last of sustaining bonds which the State does so little to facilitate, positive society begins (this has long been the fate of most European States) to disintegrate into a state of primitive morality, in which public authority has become but one party more, to be hated and circumvented by those who make authority necessary, and only obeyed by such as are capable of doing without it.

10. With this twofold pressure upon it, from within and from without, could humanity well have taken any other course than the one it actually took? In its striving after inalienable possessions in the realm of ideas, the spirit of speculation could do no other than become a stranger to the world of sense, and lose sight of matter for the sake of form. The practical spirit, by contrast, enclosed within a monotonous sphere of material objects, and within this uniformity still further confined by formulas, was bound to find the idea of an unconditioned Whole receding from sight, and to become just as impoverished as its own poor sphere of activity. If the former was tempted to model the actual world on a world conceivable by the mind, and to exalt the subjective conditions of its own perceptual and conceptual faculty into laws constitutive of the existence of things, the latter plunged into the opposite extreme of judging all experience whatsoever by one particular fragment of experience, and of wanting to make the rules of its own occupation apply indiscriminately to all others. The one was bound to become the victim of empty subtilties, the other of narrow pedantry; for the former stood too high to discern the particular, the latter too low to survey the Whole. But the damaging effects of the turn which mind thus took were not confined to knowledge and production; it affected feeling and action no less. We know that the sensibility of the psyche depends for its intensity upon the liveliness, for its scope upon the richness, of the imagination. The preponderance of the analytical faculty must, however, of necessity, deprive the imagination of its energy and warmth, while a more restricted sphere of objects must reduce its

wealth. Hence the abstract thinker very often has a cold heart, since he dissects his impressions, and impressions can move the soul only as long as they remain whole; while the man of practical affairs often has a narrow heart, since his imagination, imprisoned within the unvarying confines of his own calling, is incapable of extending itself to appreciate other ways of seeing and knowing.

11. It was part of my procedure to uncover the disadvantageous trends in the character of our age and the reasons for them, not to point out the advantages which Nature offers by way of compensation. I readily concede that, little as individuals might benefit from this fragmentation of their being, there was no other way in which the species as a whole could have progressed. With the Greeks, humanity undoubtedly reached a maximum of excellence, which could neither be maintained at that level nor rise any higher. Not maintained, because the intellect was unavoidably compelled by the store of knowledge it already possessed to dissociate itself from feeling and intuition in an attempt to arrive at exact discursive understanding; not rise any higher, because only a specific degree of clarity is compatible with a specific fullness and warmth. This degree the Greeks had attained; and had they wished to proceed to a higher stage of development, they would, like us, have had to surrender their wholeness of being and pursue truth along separate paths.

12. If the manifold potentialities in man were ever to be developed, there was no other way but to pit them one against the other. This antagonism of faculties and functions is the great instrument of civilization—but it is only the instrument; for as long as it persists, we are only on the way to becoming civilized. Only through individual powers in man becoming isolated, and arrogating to themselves exclusive authority, do they come into conflict with the truth of things, and force the Common Sense, which is otherwise content to linger with indolent complacency on outward appearance, to penetrate phenomena in depth. By pure thought usurping authority in the world of sense, while empirical thought is concerned to subject the usurper to the conditions of experience, both these powers develop to their fullest potential, and exhaust the whole range of their proper sphere. And by the very boldness with which, in the one case, imagination allows her caprice to dissolve the existing world-order, she does, in the other, compel Reason to rise to the ultimate sources of knowing, and invoke the law of Necessity against her.

13. One-sidedness in the exercise of his powers must, it is true, inevitably lead the individual into error; but the species as a whole to truth. Only by concentrating the whole energy of our mind into a single focal point, contracting our whole being into a single power, do we, as it were, lend wings to this individual power and lead it, by artificial means, far beyond the limits which Nature seems to have assigned to it. Even as it is certain that all individuals taken together would never, with the powers of vision granted them

by Nature alone, have managed to detect a satellite of Jupiter which the tele-scope reveals to the astronomer, so it is beyond question that human powers of reflection would never have produced an analysis of the Infinite or a Cri-tique of Pure Reason, unless, in the individuals called to perform such feats, Reason had separated itself off, disentangled itself, as it were, from all matter, and by the most intense effort of abstraction armed their eyes with a glass for peering into the Absolute. But will such a mind, dissolved as it were into pure intellect and pure contemplation, ever be capable of exchanging the rigorous bonds of logic for the free movement of the poetic faculty, or of grasping the concrete individuality of things with a sense innocent of preconceptions and faithful to the object? At this point Nature sets limits even to the most uni-versal genius, limits which he cannot transcend; and as long as philosophy has to make its prime business the provision of safeguards against error, truth will be bound to have its martyrs.

14. Thus, however much the world as a whole may benefit through this fragmentary specialization of human powers, it cannot be denied that the in-dividuals affected by it suffer under the curse of this cosmic purpose. Athletic bodies can, it is true, be developed by gymnastic exercises; beauty only through the free and harmonious play of the limbs. In the same way the key-ing up of individual functions of the mind can indeed produce extraordinary human beings; but only the equal tempering of them all, happy and complete human beings. And in what kind of relation would we stand to either past or future ages, if the development of human nature were to make such sacrifice necessary? We would have been the serfs of mankind; for several millenia we would have done slaves' work for them, and our mutilated nature would bear impressed upon it the shameful marks of this servitude. And all this in order that a future generation might in blissful indolence attend to the care of its moral health, and foster the free growth of its humanity!

15. But can Man really be destined to miss himself for the sake of any pur-pose whatsoever? Should Nature, for the sake of her own purposes, be able to rob us of a completeness which Reason, for the sake of hers, enjoins upon us? It must, therefore, be wrong if the cultivation of individual powers involves the sacrifice of wholeness. Or rather, however much the law of Nature tends in that direction, it must be open to us to restore by means of a higher Art the totality of our nature which the arts themselves have destroyed.

For Further Reading

Schiller, Friedrich. *On the Aesthetic Education of Man, In A Series of Letters.* Translated by Reginald Snell (New York: F. Ungar, 1965).
_____. *Essays.* Edited by Walter Hinderer and Daniel O. Dahlstrom (New York: Con-tinuum, 1993).
_____. *Naive and Sentimental Poetry, and On The Sublime.* Translated by Julius A. Elias (New York: F. Ungar, 1967).

Hinderer, Walter. "Aspects of Schiller's Philosophy of Art." In *Philosophy and Art*. Edited by Daniel Dahlstrom (Washington: Catholic Univ. Press, 1991).

Ives, Margaret C. *The Analogue of Harmony: Some Reflections on Schiller's Philosophical Essays* (Pittsburgh: Duquesne Univ. Press, 1970).

Kain, Philip J. *Schiller, Hegel, and Marx: State, Society, and the Aesthetic Ideal of Ancient Greece* (Montreal: McGill Univ. Press, 1982).

Miller, Ronald Duncan. *Schiller and the Ideal of Freedom* (Harrogate, England: Duchy Press, 1959).

Regin, Deric. *Freedom and Dignity: The Historical and Philosophical Thought of Schiller* (The Hague: Martinus Nijhoff, 1965).

Reiner, Hans. *Duty and Inclination: The Fundamentals of Morality Discussed and Redefined With Special Regard to Kant and Schiller* (Boston: Martinus Nijhoff, 1983).

Sharpe, Lesley. *Friedrich Schiller: Drama, Thought and Politics* (New York: Cambridge Univ. Press, 1991).

Simmons, John D. *Friedrich Schiller* (Boston: Twayne, 1981).

G.W.F. HEGEL (1770–1831)

HEGEL ORDERS his thinking on commercial society under the heading of "civil society," the second of three topics (with family and state) in the section of the *Philosophy of Right* devoted to "ethical life" (*Sittlichkeit*). Hegel comprehends the free market not as natural or morally indifferent but as constituting the ethical pivot of the modern world, since he believes that only a commercial society can secure human freedom. Hegel is no defender of *gemeinschaft* (community) against *gesellschaft* (impersonal society). Though he calls "civil society" a "second family," Hegel, like Schiller, accepts the troubling fragmentations of modern life as necessary to bring about a freedom truer and more precious than any imagined by the Greeks. Only the commercial form of the provisioning process respects the central ethical principle of the modern world, "the principle of self-sufficient particularity," i.e., individual liberty. As Christianity is, for Hegel, the origin of this radical notion of personal freedom, the true Christian economy turns out to be a commercial one.

Readers who think of a commercial society simply as the play of personal preferences are pulled up short by Hegel's assertion that universality pertains as much to "civil society" as do the self-centered wants of particular persons. In a commercial society needs make up a system, a network of all-round dependence on strangers; my needs involve both countless others whom I depend upon to supply me with goods and their anonymous needs for what I bring to the market. Prices wield the power of the universal. Concisely, Hegel shows how in "civil society" needs, work, goods, and human relations all take definite and interrelated forms characterized by abstraction, differentiation, "refinement," and impersonal recognition of others. Hegel knows that the provisioning process always has a specific social form and how much that form matters.

The "system of needs," or commercial trade and industry, does not stand alone for Hegel. Not only does commerce presuppose abstract right, morality, the family, and the state, even within "civil society" the market depends upon the "administration of justice" to secure property and contracts, and the shortcomings of the market need to be offset by what Hegel calls "the police and corporations." While Hegel largely lets the "invisible hand" of the market see to the provisioning process, he does not trust it to assure the liberty, welfare, and proper recognition of all members of civil society.

For a staunch defender of the free market and an advocate of reconciliation, Hegel leaves us remarkably ill at ease with commercial life. The whole sphere of "free" trade is actually a realm of necessity wherein particular persons are buffeted about by the coercive power of "the universal," prices. The "unconscious necessity" of the "invisible hand," whereby in providing for ourselves we provide for others, is an ethical conundrum; for Hegel, we need to be "knowing and thinking" in ethical life. Relatedly, commercial societies fail to assure their members recognition as contributing, rather than self-absorbed, members of society. And without proper recognition, the well of self-respect runs dry. Extravagances mushroom as poor substitutes for real recognition and self-esteem. Though demands for economic equality strike Hegel as simple-minded, the distribution of wealth in commercial societies tends to become so imbalanced as to afford "a spectacle of extravagance and misery as well as of the physical and ethical corruption common to both." Worse, the degrading poverty of many drives down wages and tips the scales more heavily in favor of the rich, turning both rich and "rabble" into loose cannons. "Welfare" is a bad solution to poverty because, without work, its recipients lack the ordinary basis of respect; "workfare" is no solution since, for Hegel, "overproduction" is the original problem. Against this backdrop, the prospect that workers whose labor has been reduced to mechanical motions will be replaced by machines offers little solace. Solving the problems of "overproduction" and "surplus population" by foreign trade and colonization must—bar-

224

ring world wars or extensive space ventures—eventually run up against global limits. Our "second family" seems to be badly dysfunctional.

SECTION 2

CIVIL SOCIETY

§ 182

The concrete person who, as a *particular* person, as a totality of needs and a mixture of natural necessity and arbitrariness, is his own end, is *one principle* of civil society. But this particular person stands essentially in *relation* [*Beziehung*] to other similar particulars, and their relation is such that each asserts itself and gains satisfaction through the others, and thus at the same time through the exclusive *mediation* of the form of *universality,* which is *the second principle.*

Addition (H,G). Civil society is the [stage of] difference [*Differenz*] which intervenes between the family and the state, even if its full development [*Ausbildung*] occurs later than that of the state; for as difference, it presupposes the state, which it must have before it as a self-sufficient entity in order to subsist [*bestehen*] itself. Besides, the creation of civil society belongs to the modern world, which for the first time allows all determinations of the Idea to attain their rights. If the state is represented as a unity of different persons, as a unity which is merely a community [of interests], this applies only to the determination of civil society. Many modern exponents of constitutional law have been unable to offer any view of the state but this. In civil society, each individual is his own end, and all else means nothing to him. But he cannot accomplish the full extent of his ends without reference to others; these others are therefore means to the end of the particular [person]. But through its reference to others, the particular end takes on the form of universality, and gains satisfaction by simultaneously satisfying the welfare of others. Since particularity is tied to the condition of universality, the whole [of civil society] is the sphere [*Boden*] of mediation in which all individual characteristics [*Einzelheiten*], all aptitudes, and all accidents of birth and fortune are liberated, and where the waves of all passions surge forth, governed only by the reason which shines through them. Particularity, limited by universality, is the only standard by which each particular [person] promotes his welfare.

225

§ 183

The selfish end in its actualization, conditioned in this way by universality, establishes a system of all-round interdependence, so that the subsistence [*Subsistenz*] and welfare of the individual [*des Einzelnen*] and his rightful existence [*Dasein*] are interwoven with, and grounded on, the subsistence, welfare, and rights of all, and have actuality and security only in this context.—One may regard this system in the first instance as the *external state*, the *state of necessity* and *of the understanding*.

§ 184

When it is divided in this way, the Idea gives a *distinct existence* [*Dasein*] to its *moments*—to *particularity* it gives the right to develop and express itself in all directions, and to universality the right to prove itself both as the ground and necessary form of particularity, and as the power behind it and its ultimate end.—It is the system of ethical life, lost in its extremes, which constitutes the abstract moment of the *reality* of the Idea, which is present here only as the *relative totality* and *inner necessity* of this external *appearance*.

Addition (H). Here, the ethical is lost in its extremes, and the immediate unity of the family has disintegrated into a plurality. Reality here is externality, the dissolution of the concept, the self-sufficiency of its liberated and existent moments. Although particularity and universality have become separated in civil society, they are nevertheless bound up with and conditioned by each other. Although each appears to do precisely the opposite of the other and imagines that it can exist only by keeping the other at a distance, each nevertheless has the other as its condition. Thus, most people regard the payment of taxes, for example, as an infringement of their particularity, as a hostile element prejudicial to their own ends; but however true this may *appear,* the particularity of their own ends cannot be satisfied without the universal, and a country in which no taxes were paid could scarcely distinguish itself in strengthening its particular interests [*Besonderheit*]. It might likewise appear that the universal would do better to absorb the strength of the particular, as described, for example, in Plato's *Republic;* but this again is only apparent, for the two exist solely through and for one another and are transformed into one another. In furthering my end, I further the universal, and this in turn furthers my end.

§ 185

Particularity in itself [*für sich*], on the one hand indulging itself in all directions as it satisfies its needs, contingent arbitrariness, and subjective caprice, destroys itself and its substantial concept in the act of enjoyment; on the other hand, as infinitely agitated and continually dependent on external contingency and arbitrariness and at the same time limited by the power of universality, the satisfaction of both necessary and contingent needs is itself contingent. In these opposites and their complexity, civil society affords a spectacle of extravagance and misery as well as of the physical and ethical corruption common to both.

> The self-sufficient development of particularity (cf. Remarks to § 124) is the moment which appears in the states of the ancient world as an influx of ethical corruption and as the ultimate reason [*Grund*] for their downfall. These states, some of which were based on the patriarchal and religious principle and others

on the principle of a more spiritual, though simpler, ethical life, but all of which were based on *original* natural intuition, could not withstand the division which arose within the latter as self-consciousness became infinitely reflected into itself. As this reflection began to emerge, first as a disposition and then in actuality, they succumbed to it, because the simple principle on which they were still based lacked the truly infinite power which resides solely in that unity which allows the *opposition* within reason [*Vernunft*] *to develop to its full strength,* and has overcome it so as to preserve itself within it and *wholly contain it within itself.* — Plato, in his *Republic*, presents the substance of ethical life in its ideal *beauty* and *truth;* but he cannot come to terms with the principle of self-sufficient particularity, which had suddenly overtaken Greek ethical life in his time, except by setting up his purely substantial state in opposition to it and completely excluding it [from this state], from its very beginnings in *private property* (see Remarks to § 46) and the *family* to its subsequent development [*Ausbildung*] as the arbitrary will of individuals and their choice of social position [*des Standes*], etc. This deficiency also explains why the great *substantial* truth of his *Republic* is imperfectly understood, and why it is usually regarded as a dream of abstract thought, as what is indeed often called an *ideal.* The principle of the *self-sufficient and inherently infinite personality* of the individual [*des Einzelnen*], the principle of subjective freedom, which arose in an inward form in the *Christian* religion and in an external form (which was therefore linked with abstract universality) in the *Roman* world, is denied its right in that merely substantial form of the actual spirit [in Plato's *Republic*]. This principle is historically later than the Greek world, and the philosophical reflection which can fathom these depths is likewise later than the substantial Idea of Greek philosophy.

227

Addition (H). Particularity in itself [*für sich*] is boundless [*maßlos*] extravagance, and the forms of this extravagance are themselves boundless. Through their representations [*Vorstellungen*] and reflections, human beings expand their desires, which do not form a closed circle like animal instinct, and extend them to false [*schlechte*] infinity. But on the other hand, deprivation and want are likewise boundless, and this confused situation can be restored to harmony only through the forcible intervention of the state. Although Plato's state sought to exclude particularity, this is of no help, because such help would contradict the infinite right of the Idea to allow particularity its freedom. It was primarily in the Christian religion that the right of subjectivity arose, along with the infinity of being-for-itself; and in this situation, the totality must also be endowed with sufficient strength to bring particularity into harmony with the ethical unity.

§ 186

But in the very act of developing itself independently [*für sich*] to totality, the principle of particularity passes over into *universality*, and only in the latter does it have its truth and its right to positive actuality. This unity is not that of ethical identity, because at this level of division (see § 184), the two principles are self-sufficient; and for the same reason, it is present not as *freedom*, but as the *necessity* whereby the *particular* must rise to the *form of universality* and seek and find its subsistence in this form.

§ 187

Individuals, as citizens of this state, are *private persons* who have their own interest as their end. Since this end is mediated through the universal, which thus appears to the individuals as a *means*, they can attain their end only in so far as they themselves determine their knowledge, volition, and action in a universal way and make themselves *links* in the chain of this *continuum* [*Zusammenhang*]. In this situation, the interest of the Idea, which is not present in the consciousness of these members of civil society as such, is the *process* whereby their individuality [*Einzelheit*] and naturalness are raised, both by natural necessity and by their arbitrary needs, *to formal freedom* and formal *universality of knowledge and volition*, and subjectivity is *educated* in its particularity.

> The ideas [*Vorstellungen*] of the *innocence* of the state of nature and of the ethical simplicity of uncultured [*ungebildeter*] peoples imply that *education* [*Bildung*] will be regarded as something purely *external* and associated with corruption. On the other hand, if one believes that needs, their satisfaction, the pleasures and comforts of individual [*partikularen*] life, etc. are *absolute* ends, education will be regarded as merely a *means* to these ends. Both of these views show a lack of familiarity with the nature of spirit and with the end of reason. Spirit attains its actuality only through internal division, by imposing this limitation and finitude upon itself in [the shape of] natural needs and the continuum [*Zusammenhang*] of this external necessity, and, *in the very process of adapting itself to these* limitations, by overcoming them and gaining its *objective* existence [*Dasein*] within them. The end of reason is consequently neither the natural ethical simplicity referred to above, nor, as particularity develops, the pleasures as such which are attained through education. Its end is rather to work to eliminate *natural simplicity,* whether as passive selflessness or as barbarism of knowledge and volition—i.e. to eliminate the *immediacy* and *individuality* [*Einzelheit*] in which spirit is immersed, so that this externality may take on the rationality *of which it is capable,* namely the *form of universality or of the understanding.* Only in this way is the spirit *at home and with itself* in this externality as such. Its freedom thus has an existence [*Dasein*] within the latter; and, in this element, which, *in itself,* is alien to its determination of freedom, the spirit becomes *for itself,* and has to do only with what it has impressed its seal upon and *produced* itself.—By this very means, the *form of universality* comes into existence [*Existenz*] for itself in thought, the only form which is a worthy element for the existence [*Existenz*] of the Idea. *Education,* in its absolute determination, is therefore *liberation* and *work* towards a higher liberation; it is the absolute transition to the infinitely subjective substantiality of ethical life, which is no longer immediate and natural, but spiritual and at the same time raised to the shape of universality. Within the subject, this liberation is the *hard work* of opposing mere subjectivity of conduct, of opposing the immediacy

228

of desire as well as the subjective vanity of feeling [*Empfindung*] and the arbitrariness of caprice. The fact that it is such hard work accounts for some of the disfavour which it incurs. But it is through this work of education that the subjective will attains *objectivity* even within itself, that objectivity in which alone it is for its part worthy and capable of being the *actuality* of the Idea.—Furthermore, this form of universality to which particularity has worked its way upwards and cultivated [*heraufgebildet*] itself, i.e. the form of the understanding, ensures at the same time that particularity becomes the genuine *being-for-itself* of individuality [*Einzelheit*]; and, since it is from particularity that universality receives both the content which fills it and its infinite self-determination, particularity is itself present in ethical life as free subjectivity which has infinite being-for-itself. This is the level at which it becomes plain that *education* is an immanent moment of the absolute, and that it has infinite value.

Addition (H). By educated people, we may understand in the first place those who do everything as others do it and who do not flaunt their particular characteristics [*Partikularität*], whereas it is precisely these characteristics which the uneducated display, since their behaviour is not guided by the universal aspects of its object [*Gegenstand*]. Similarly, in his relations with others, the uneducated man can easily cause offence, for he simply lets himself go and does not reflect on the feelings [*Empfindungen*] of others. He does not wish to hurt others, but his conduct is not in harmony with his will. Thus, education irons out particularity to make it act in accordance with the nature of the thing [*Sache*]. True originality, by which the [universal] thing is produced, requires true education, whereas false originality assumes tasteless forms which occur only to the uneducated.

§ 188

Civil society contains the following three moments:

A. The mediation of *need* and the satisfaction of the individual [*des Einzelnen*] through his work and through the work and satisfaction of the needs of all the others—the system of *needs*.

B. The actuality of the universal of *freedom* contained therein, the protection of property through the *administration of justice*.

C. Provisions against the contingency which remains present in the above systems, and care for the particular interest as a *common* interest, by means of the *police* and the *corporation*.

A. The System of Needs

§ 189

Particularity, in its primary determination as that which is opposed to the universal of the will in general (see § 60), is *subjective need,* which attains its objectivity, i.e. its *satisfaction*, by means of (a) external things [*Dinge*], which are likewise the *property* and product of the needs and *wills* of others and of (b) activity and work, as the mediation between the two aspects. The end of subjective need is the satisfaction of subjective *particularity*, but in the relation [*Beziehung*] between this and the needs and free arbitrary will of others, *universality* asserts itself, and the resultant manifestation [*Scheinen*] of rationality in the sphere of finitude is *the understanding*. This is the chief aspect which must be considered here, and which itself constitutes the conciliatory element within this sphere.

> *Political economy* is the science which begins with the above viewpoints but must go on to explain mass relationships and mass movements in their qualitative and quantitative determinacy and complexity.—This is one of the sciences which have originated in the modern age as their element [*Boden*]. The development of science is of interest in showing how *thought* extracts from the endless multitude of details with which it is initially confronted the simple principles of the thing [*Sache*], the understanding which works within it and controls it (see Smith, Say, and Ricardo).—To recognize, in the sphere of needs, this manifestation [*Scheinen*] of rationality which is present in the thing [*Sache*] and active within it has, on the one hand, a conciliatory effect; but conversely, this is also the field in which the understanding, with its subjective ends and moral opinions, gives vent to its discontent and moral irritation.

Addition (H,G). There are certain universal needs, such as food, drink, clothing, etc., and how these are satisfied depends entirely on contingent circumstances. The soil is more or less fertile in different places, the years are more or less productive, one man is industrious and the other lazy. But this proliferation of arbitrariness generates universal determinations from within itself, and this apparently scattered and thoughtless activity is subject to a necessity which arises of its own accord. To discover the necessity at work here is the object [*Gegenstand*] of political economy, a science which does credit to thought because it finds the laws underlying a mass of contingent occurrences. It is an interesting spectacle to observe here how all the interconnections have repercussions on others, how the particular spheres fall into groups, influence others, and are helped or hindered by these. This interaction, which is at first sight incredible since everything seems to depend on the arbitrary will of the individual [*des Einzelnen*], is particularly worthy of note; it bears a resemblance to the planetary system, which presents only irregular movements to the eye, yet whose laws can nevertheless be recognized.

a. The Nature of Needs and their Satisfaction

§ 190

The ways and means by which the *animal* can satisfy its needs are limited in scope, and its needs are likewise limited. Though sharing this dependence, the *human being* is at the same time able to transcend it and to show his universality, first by *multiplying* his needs and means [of satisfying them], and secondly by *dividing* and *differentiating* the concrete need into individual parts and aspects which then become different needs, *particularized* and hence *more abstract*.

In right, the object [*Gegenstand*] is the *person;* at the level of morality, it is the *subject,* in the family, the *family-member,* and in civil society in general, the *citizen* (in the sense of *bourgeois*). Here, at the level of needs (cf. Remarks to § 123), it is that concretum *of representational thought* which we call *the human being;* this is the first, and in fact the only occasion on which we shall refer to *the human being* in this sense.

Addition (H). The animal is a particular entity [*ein Partikulares*] which has its instinct and the means of satisfying it, means whose bounds cannot be exceeded. There are insects which are tied to a specific plant, and other animals whose sphere is wider and which can live in different climates; but there is always a limiting factor in comparison with the sphere which is open to the human being. The need for food and clothing, the necessity of renouncing raw food and of making it fit to eat and destroying its natural immediacy, means that the human being's life is less comfortable than that of the animal—as indeed it ought to be, since man is a spiritual being. The understanding, which can grasp distinctions, brings multiplicity into these needs; and since taste and utility become criteria of judgement, the needs themselves are also affected by them. In the end, it is no longer need but opinion which has to be satisfied, and it is a distinctive feature of education that it resolves the concrete into its particulars. The very multiplication of needs has a restraining influence on desire, for if people make use of many things, the pressure to obtain any one of these which they might need is less strong, and this is a sign that necessity [*die Not*] in general is less powerful.

231

§ 191

In the same way, the *means* employed by particularized needs, and in general the ways in which these are satisfied, are *divided* and *multiplied* so that they in turn become relative ends and abstract needs. It is an infinite process of multiplication which is in equal measure a *differentiation* of these determinations and a *judgement* on the suitability of the means to their ends—i.e. [a process of] *refinement*.

Addition (H). What the English call 'comfortable' is something utterly inexhaustible; its ramifications are infinite, for every comfort in turn reveals its less comfortable side, and the resulting inventions are endless. A need is therefore created not so much by those who experience it directly as by those who seek to profit from its emergence.

§ 192

Needs and means, as existing in reality [*als reelles Dasein*], become a *being* [*Sein*] for *others* by whose needs and work their satisfaction is mutually conditioned. That abstraction which becomes a quality of both needs and means (see § 191) also becomes a determination of the mutual relations [*Beziehung*] between individuals. This universality, as the *quality of being recognized*, is the moment which makes isolated and abstract needs, means, and modes of satisfaction into *concrete*, i.e. *social* ones.

Addition (H). The fact that I have to fit in with other people brings the form of universality into play at this point. I acquire my means of satisfaction from others and must accordingly accept their opinions. But at the same time, I am compelled to produce means whereby others can be satisfied. Thus, the one plays into the hands of the other and is connected with it. To this extent, everything particular [*alles Partikulare*] takes on a social character; in the manner of dress and times of meals, there are certain conventions which one must accept, for in such matters, it is not worth the trouble to seek to display one's own insight, and it is wisest to act as others do.

§ 193

This moment thus becomes a particular end-determinant for the means themselves and their ownership, and also for the way in which needs are satisfied. In addition, it immediately involves the requirement of *equality* in this respect with others. On the one hand, the need for this equality, together with *imitation* as the process whereby people make themselves like others, and on the other hand the need of *particularity* (which is likewise present here) to assert itself through some distinctive quality, themselves become an actual source of the multiplication and expansion of needs.

§ 194

Within social needs, as a combination of immediate or natural needs and the spiritual needs of *representational thought* [*Vorstellung*], the spiritual needs, as the universal, predominate. This social moment accordingly contains the aspect of *liberation*, because the strict natural necessity of need is concealed and man's relation is to *his own opinion*, which is universal, and to a necessity imposed by himself alone, instead of simply to an external necessity, to inner contingency, and to *arbitrariness*.

The notion [*Vorstellung*] that, in relation to his needs, man lived in *freedom* in a so-called state of nature in which he had only so-called natural needs of a simple kind and in which, to satisfy these, he employed only those means with which a contingent nature immediately provided him—this notion, even if we disregard the moment of liberation which is present in work (and which will be discussed below), is mistaken. For a condition in which natural needs as such were immediately satisfied would merely be one in which spirituality was immersed in nature, and hence a condition of savagery and unfreedom; whereas freedom consists solely in the reflection of the spiritual into itself, its distinction from the natural, and its reflection upon the latter.

§ 195

This liberation is *formal,* because the particularity of the ends remains the basic content. The tendency of the social condition towards an indeterminate multiplication and specification of needs, means, and pleasures—i.e. *luxury*—a tendency which, like the distinction between natural and educated needs, has no limits [*Grenzen*], involves an equally infinite increase in dependence and want. These are confronted with a material which offers infinite resistance, i.e. with external means whose particular character is that they are the property of the free will [of others] and are therefore absolutely unyielding.

Addition (H). Diogenes, in his whole character as a Cynic, is in fact merely a product of the social life of Athens, and what determined him was the opinion against which his entire way of life reacted. His way of life was therefore not independent, but merely a consequence of these social conditions, and itself an unprepossessing product of luxury. Where, on the one hand, luxury is at its height, want and depravity are equally great on the other, and Cynicism is then evoked by the opposite extreme of refinement.

b. The Nature of Work

§ 196

233

The mediation whereby appropriate and *particularized* means are acquired and prepared for similarly *particularized* needs is *work.* By the most diverse processes, work specifically applies to these numerous ends the material which is immediately provided by nature. This process of formation gives the means their value and appropriateness, so that man, as a consumer, is chiefly concerned with *human* products, and it is human effort which he consumes.

Addition (H). There are few immediate materials which do not need to be processed: even air has to be earned—inasmuch as it has to be heated—and perhaps water is unique in that it can be drunk as it is found. It is by the sweat and labour of human beings that man obtains the means to satisfy his needs.

§ 197

The variety of determinations and objects [*Gegenstände*] which are worthy of interest is the basis from which *theoretical education* develops. This involves not only a variety of representations [*Vorstellungen*] and items of knowledge [*Kenntnissen*], but also an ability to form such representations [*des Vorstellens*] and pass from one to the other in a rapid and versatile manner, to grasp complex and general relations [*Beziehungen*], etc.—it is the education of the understanding in general, and therefore also includes language.—*Practical educa-*

tion through work consists in the self-perpetuating need and *habit of being occupied* in one way or another, in the *limitation of one's activity* to suit both the nature of the material in question and, in particular, the arbitrary will of others, and in a habit, acquired through this discipline, of *objective* activity and *universally applicable* skills.

Addition (H). The barbarian is lazy and differs from the educated man in his dull and solitary brooding, for practical education consists precisely in the need and habit of being occupied. The clumsy man always produces something other than what he intended, because he is not in control of his own actions. But a worker can be described as skilled if he produces the thing [*Sache*] as it ought to be, and if, in his subjective actions, he encounters no resistance to the end he is pursuing.

§ 198

The universal and objective aspect of work consists, however, in that [process of] *abstraction* which confers a specific character on means and needs and hence also on production, so giving rise to the *division of labour*. Through this division, the work of the individual [*des Einzelnen*] becomes *simpler*, so that his skill at his abstract work becomes greater, as does the volume of his output. At the same time, this abstraction of skill and means makes the *dependence* and *reciprocity* of human beings in the satisfaction of their other needs complete and entirely necessary. Furthermore, the abstraction of production makes work increasingly *mechanical*, so that the human being is eventually able to step aside and let a *machine* take his place.

c. Resources [and Estates]

§ 199

In this dependence and reciprocity of work and the satisfaction of needs, *subjective selfishness* turns into a *contribution towards the satisfaction of the needs of everyone else*. By a dialectical movement, the particular is mediated by the universal so that each individual, in earning, producing, and enjoying on his own account [*für sich*], thereby earns and produces for the enjoyment of others. This necessity which is inherent in the interlinked dependence of each on all now appears to each individual in the form of *universal and permanent resources* (see § 170) in which, through his education and skill, he has an opportunity to share; he is thereby assured of his livelihood, just as the universal resources are maintained and augmented by the income which he earns through his work.

§ 200

The *possibility of sharing* in the universal resources—i.e. of holding *particular* resources—is, however, *conditional* upon one's own immediate basic assets (i.e. capital) on the one hand, and upon one's skill on the other; the latter in turn is itself conditioned by the former, but also by contingent circumstances whose variety gives rise to *differences* in the *development* of natural physical and mental [*geistigen*] aptitudes which are already unequal in themselves [*für sich*]. In this sphere of particularity, these differences manifest themselves in every direction and at every level, and, in conjunction with other contingent and arbitrary circumstances, necessarily result in *inequalities in the resources and skills* of individuals.

> The spirit's objective *right of particularity*, which is contained within the Idea, does not cancel out [*nicht aufhebt*] the inequality of human beings in civil society—an inequality posited by nature, which is the element of inequality—but in fact produces it out of the spirit itself and raises it to an inequality of skills, resources, and even of intellectual and moral education. To oppose this right with a demand for *equality* is characteristic of the empty understanding, which mistakes this abstraction and *obligation* of its own for the real and the rational. This sphere of particularity imagines that it is universal, but in its merely relative identity with the universal, it retains both natural and arbitrary particularity, and hence the remnants of the state of nature. In addition, that reason which is immanent in the system of human needs and their movement articulates this system into an organic whole composed of different elements (see § 201).

§ 201

The infinitely varied means and their equally infinite and intertwined movements of reciprocal production and exchange *converge*, by virtue of the universality inherent in their content, and become *differentiated* into *universal masses*. In consequence, the whole complex [*Zusammenhang*] evolves into *particular systems* of needs, with their corresponding means, varieties of work, modes of satisfaction, and theoretical and practical education—into systems to which individuals are separately assigned, i.e. into different *estates*.

Addition (H). The manner in which the universal resources are shared depends on every particular characteristic of the individuals concerned; but the universal differences into which civil society is particularized are necessary in character. While the family is the primary basis of the state, the estates are the second. The latter are of special importance, because private persons, despite their selfishness, find it necessary to have recourse to others. This is accordingly the root which links selfishness with the universal, i.e. with the state, which must take care to ensure that this connection is a firm and solid one.

§ 202

The estates are determined, in accordance with *the concept,* as the *substantial* or immediate estate, the reflecting or *formal* estate, and lastly, the *universal* estate.

§ 203

(a) The *substantial* estate has its resources in the natural products of the *soil* which it cultivates—soil which is capable of being exclusively private property, and which requires not just indeterminate exploitation, but formation of an objective kind. Given the association of work and acquisition with fixed *individual* seasons, and the dependence of the yield on the varying character of natural processes, the end to which need is directed in this case becomes that of *provision* for the future. But because of the conditions to which it is subject, this provision retains the character of a [mode of] subsistence [*Subsistenz*] in which reflection and the will of the individual play a lesser role, and thus its substantial disposition in general is that of an immediate ethical life based on the family relationship and on trust.

The proper beginning and original foundation of states has rightly been equated with the introduction of *agriculture* and of *marriage*. For the former principle brings with it the cultivation of the soil, and in consequence exclusively private property (cf. Remarks to § 170), and it reduces the nomadic life of savages, who seek their livelihood in constant movement, to the tranquillity of civil law [*Privatrecht*] and the secure satisfaction of needs. This is accompanied by the restriction [*Beschränkung*] of sexual love to marriage, and the marriage bond is in turn extended to become a *lasting* and inherently [*in sich*] universal union, while need becomes *care for the family* and possession becomes *family property*. Security, consolidation, lasting satisfaction of needs, etc.—qualities by which these institutions primarily recommend themselves—are nothing but forms of universality and shapes assumed by rationality, the absolute and ultimate end, as it asserts itself in these objects [*Gegenständen*].—What can be more interesting in this connection than the ingenious and learned *explanations* which my highly esteemed friend, Herr Creuzer, has given of the *agrarian* festivals, images, and shrines of the ancients (especially in the fourth volume of his *Mythology and Symbolism*)? In the consciousness of the ancients, the introduction of agriculture and of the institutions associated with it were divine acts, and they were accordingly treated with religious veneration. A further consequence, which also occurs in the other estates, is that the substantial character of this estate entails modifications with regard to civil law—especially to the administration of justice—and likewise with regard to education and instruction and also to religion; these modifications do *not* affect the *substantial content*, but only its *form* and the *development of reflection*.

Addition (H). In our times, the [agricultural] economy, too, is run in a reflective manner, like a factory, and it accordingly takes on a character like that of the second estate and opposed to its own character of naturalness. Nevertheless, this first estate will always retain the patriarchal way of life and the substantial disposition associated with it. The human being reacts here with immediate feeling [*Empfindung*] as he accepts what he receives; he thanks God for it and lives in faith and confidence that this goodness will continue. What he receives is enough for him; he uses it up, for it will be replenished. This is a simple disposition which is not concerned with the acquisition of wealth; it may also be described as that of the *old nobility*, which consumed whatever it had. In this estate, the main part is played by nature, and human industry is subordinate to it. In the second estate, however, it is the understanding itself which is essential, and the products of nature can be regarded only as raw materials.

§ 204

(b) The *estate of trade and industry* [*Stand des Gewerbes*] has the task of *giving form* to natural products, and it relies for its livelihood on its *work,* on *reflection* and the understanding, and essentially on its mediation of the needs and work of others. What it produces and enjoys, it owes chiefly to *itself* and to its own activity.—Its business is in turn subdivided into work performed in a relatively concrete manner in response to individual [*einzelne*] needs and at the request of individuals [*Einzelner*] (*the estate of craftsmanship*); more abstract work of mass production which supplies individual needs but is more universally in demand (*the estate of manufacturers*); and the business of exchanging separate commodities [*Mittel*] for one another, chiefly through the universal means of exchange, namely money, in which the abstract value of all goods is actualized (*the estate of commerce*).

Addition (H). In the estate of trade and industry, the individual [*Individuum*] has to rely on himself, and this feeling of selfhood is intimately connected with the demand for a condition in which right is upheld. The sense of freedom and order has therefore arisen mainly in towns. The first estate, on the other hand, has little need to think for itself: what it gains is an alien gift, a gift of nature. This feeling of dependence is fundamental to it, and may easily be coupled with a willingness to accept whatever may befall it at the hands of other people. The first estate is therefore more inclined to subservience, the second estate to freedom.

237

§ 205

(c) The *universal estate* has *the universal interests* of society as its business. It must therefore be exempted from work for the direct satisfaction of its needs, either by having private resources, or by receiving an indemnity from the state which calls upon its services, so that the private interest is satisfied through working for the universal.

§ 206

On the one hand, the *estates*, as particularity become objective to itself, are divided in this way into different general categories in accordance with the concept. But on the other hand, the question of which particular estate the *individual* will belong to is influenced by his natural disposition, birth, and circumstances, although the ultimate and essential determinant is *subjective opinion* and the *particular arbitrary will,* which are accorded their right, their merit, and their honour in this sphere. Thus, what happens in this sphere through *inner necessity* is at the same time *mediated by the arbitrary will,* and for the subjective consciousness, it has the shape of being the product of its own will.

In this respect, too, in relation to the principle of particularity and subjective arbitrariness, a difference emerges between the political life of east and west, and of the ancient and modern worlds. In the former, the division of the whole into estates came about *objectively and of its own accord,* because it is rational *in itself;* but the principle of subjective particularity was at the same time denied its rights, as when, for example, the allocation of individuals to specific estates was left to the rulers, as in Plato's *Republic* (Book III, p. 320, Zweibrücken edition, Vol. VI [415 a-d]), or to birth *alone,* as in the *Indian caste-system.* Thus subjective particularity, excluded from the organization of the whole and not reconciled within it, consequently shows itself—since it likewise appears as an essential moment—as a hostile element, as a corruption of the social order (see Remarks to § 185). It either overthrows the latter, as in the Greek states and in the Roman Republic; or if the social order survives as a ruling power—or perhaps as a religious authority—it appears as inner corruption and complete degeneration, as was to some extent the case in Sparta and as is now entirely the case in India.—But if it is supported by the objective order, conforming to the latter and at the same time retaining its rights, subjective particularity becomes the sole animating principle of civil society and of the development of intellectual activity, merit, and honour. The recognition and right according to which all that is rationally necessary in civil society and in the state should at the same time come into effect *through the mediation of the arbitrary will* is the more precise definition [*Bestimmung*] of what is primarily meant by the universal idea [*Vorstellung*] of *freedom* (see § 121).

§ 207

The individual attains actuality only by entering into *existence* [*Dasein*] in general, and hence into *determinate particularity;* he must accordingly limit himself *exclusively* to one of the *particular* spheres of need. The ethical disposition within this system is therefore that of *rectitude* and the *honour of one's estate,* so that each individual, by a process of self-determination, makes himself a member of one of the moments of civil society through his activity, diligence, and skill, and supports himself in this capacity; and only through this mediation with the universal does he simultaneously provide for himself and gain *recognition* in his own eyes [*Vorstellung*] and in the eyes of others.—*Morality* has its proper place in this sphere, where reflection on one's own actions and the ends of welfare and of particular needs are dominant, and where contingency in the satisfaction of the latter makes even contingent and individual help into a duty.

Initially—i.e. especially in youth—the individual balks at the notion [*Vorstellung*] of committing himself to a particular estate, and regards this as a limitation imposed on his universal determination and as a purely *external* necessity. This is a consequence of abstract thinking, which stops short at the universal and so does not reach actuality; it does not recognize that the concept, in order to exist, must first of all enter into the distinction between the concept and its reality, and hence into determinacy and particularity (see § 7), and that only thus can abstract thinking attain actuality and ethical objectivity.

Addition (H). When we say that a human being must be *somebody* [*etwas*], we mean that he must belong to a particular estate; for being somebody means that he has substantial being. A human being with no estate is merely a private person and does not possess actual universality. On the other hand, the individual [*der Einzelne*] in his particularity may see himself as the universal and believe that he would be lowering himself if he became a member of an estate. This is the false notion [*Vorstellung*] that, if something attains an existence [*Dasein*] which is necessary to it, it is thereby limiting and surrendering itself.

§ 208

The principle of this system of needs, as that of the personal [*eigene*] particularity of knowledge and volition, contains within itself that universality which has being *in and for itself,* i.e. the universality of *freedom*, but only *abstractly* and hence as the *right of property*. Here, however, this right is present no longer merely *in itself,* but in its valid actuality as the *protection of property* through the *administration of justice....*

§ 229

In the administration of justice, civil society, in which the Idea has lost itself in particularity and split up into the division between inward and outward, returns to its *concept*, to the unity of the universal which has being in itself with subjective particularity (although the particularity in question is that of the individual case, and the universal is that of *abstract right*). The actualization of this unity in its extension to the entire range of particularity, first as a relative union, constitutes the determination of the *police*; and secondly, as a limited but concrete totality, it constitutes the *corporation*.

Addition (H). In civil society, universality is merely necessity. As far as needs are concerned, right as such is the only fixed point. But this right, which is only a limited sphere, relates solely to the protection of what I possess; welfare is something external to right as such. Nevertheless, this welfare is an essential determination in the system of needs. Hence the universal, which in the first instance is merely right, has to be extended over the entire field of particularity. Justice is a major factor in civil society: good laws will cause the state to flourish, and free ownership is a fundamental condition of its success. But since I am completely involved in particularity, I have a right to demand that, within this context, my particular welfare should also be promoted. Account should be taken of my welfare, of my particularity, and this is the task of the police and the corporation.

C. The Police and the Corporation

§ 230

In the *system of needs*, the livelihood and welfare of each individual [*jedes Einzelnen*] are a *possibility* whose actualization is conditioned by the individual's own arbitrary will and particular nature, as well as by the objective system of needs. Through the administration of justice, *infringements* of property or personality are annulled. But the right *which is actually present in particularity* means not only that *contingencies* which interfere with this or that end should be *cancelled* [*aufgehoben*] and that the *undisturbed security* of *persons* and *property* should be guaranteed, but also that the livelihood and welfare of individuals should be *secured*—i.e. that *particular welfare* should be *treated as a right* and duly *actualized*.

a. The Police

§ 231

In so far as the principle by which this or that end is governed is still that of the particular will, that authority [*Macht*] of the universal which guarantees security remains, on the one hand, primarily limited to the sphere of *contingencies*, and on the other, it remains an *external order*.

§ 232

Apart from crimes which the universal authority [*Macht*] must prevent or bring to justice—i.e. contingency in the shape of arbitrary evil—the permissible arbitrariness of inherently [*für sich*] rightful actions and of the private use of property also has external relations [*Beziehungen*] with other individuals [*Einzelne*], as well as with other public arrangements designed to further a common end. Through this universal aspect, private actions become a contingent matter which passes out of my control [*Gewalt*] and which can wrong or harm other people or actually does so.

§ 233

There is admittedly only a possibility that harm may be done. But the fact that no harm is done is, as a contingency, likewise no more than that. This is the aspect of *wrong* which is inherent in such actions, and which is consequently the ultimate reason [*Grund*] for penal justice as implemented by the police.

§ 234

The relations [*Beziehungen*] of external existence [*Dasein*] fall within the infinite of the understanding; consequently, no boundary is present *in itself* between what is harmful and what is harmless (even with regard to crime), between what is suspicious and what is not suspicious, or between what should be prohibited or kept under surveillance and what should be exempted from prohibitions, surveillance and suspicion, inquiry and accountability. The more precise determinations will depend on custom, the spirit of the rest of the constitution, prevailing conditions, current emergencies, etc.

Addition (H). No fixed determinations are possible here, and no absolute boundaries can be drawn. Everything here is personal; subjective opinion comes into play, and the spirit of the constitution and current dangers will determine the more precise circumstances. In times of war, for example, various things which are otherwise harmless must be regarded as harmful. Because of these aspects of contingency and arbitrary personality, the police takes on a certain character of *maliciousness*. When reflection is highly developed, the police may tend to draw everything it can into its sphere of influence, for it is possible to discover some potentially harmful aspect in everything. On such occasions, the police may proceed very pedantically and disrupt the ordinary life of individuals. But however troublesome this may be, no objective boundary line can be drawn here.

§ 235

In the indeterminate multiplication and interdependence of daily needs, the *procurement* and *exchange of means* to satisfy these (a process on whose unimpeded continuance everyone relies) and the need to make the requisite inquiries and negotiations as short as possible give rise to aspects of common interest in which the business *of one* is at the same time carried out on behalf of *all*; they also give rise to means and arrangements which may be of use to the community. These *universal functions* and arrangements *of public utility* require oversight and advance provision on the part of the public authority [*Macht*].

§ 236

The differing interests of producers and consumers may come into collision with each other, and even if, *on the whole,* their correct relationship re-establishes itself automatically, its adjustment also needs to be consciously regulated by an agency which stands above both sides. The right to regulate individual matters in this way (e.g. by deciding the value of the commonest necessities of life) is based on the fact that, when commodities in completely universal everyday use are publicly marketed, they are offered not so much to a particular individual [*Individuum*] as such, as to the individual in a universal sense, i.e. to the public; and the task of upholding the public's right not to be cheated and of inspecting market commodities may, as a common concern, be entrusted to a public authority [*Macht*].—But the main reason why some universal provision and direction are necessary is that large branches of industry are dependent on external circumstances and remote combinations whose full implications cannot be grasped by the individuals [*Individuen*] who are tied to these spheres by their occupation.

At the opposite extreme to freedom of trade and commerce in civil society are public arrangements to provide for and determine the work of everyone. These included, for example, the building of the pyramids in ancient times, and other enormous works in Egypt and Asia which were undertaken for public ends, and in which the work of the individual [*des Einzelnen*] was not mediated by his par-

241

ticular arbitrary will and particular interest. This interest invokes the freedom of trade and commerce against regulation from above; but the more blindly it immerses itself in its selfish ends, the more it requires such regulation to bring it back to the universal, and to moderate and shorten the duration of those dangerous convulsions to which its collisions give rise, and which should return to equilibrium by a process of unconscious necessity.

Addition (H). The aim of oversight and provisions on the part of the police is to mediate between the individual [*Individuum*] and the universal possibility which is available for the attainment of individual ends. The police should provide for street-lighting, bridge-building, the pricing of daily necessities, and public health. Two main views are prevalent on this subject. One maintains that the police should have oversight over everything, and the other maintains that the police should have no say in such matters, since everyone will be guided in his actions by the needs of others. The individual [*der Einzelne*] must certainly have a right to earn his living in this way or that; but on the other hand, the public also has a right to expect that necessary tasks will be performed in the proper manner. Both viewpoints must be satisfied, and the freedom of trade should not be such as to prejudice the general good.

§ 237

Now even if the possibility exists for individuals to share in the universal resources, and even if this possibility is guaranteed by the public authority [*Macht*], it remains—apart from the fact that such a guarantee must always be incomplete—open to contingencies of a subjective kind. This is increasingly the case the more it takes such conditions as skill, health, capital, etc. for granted.

§ 238

Initially, the family is the substantial whole whose task it is to provide for this particular aspect of the individual, both by giving him the means and skills he requires in order to earn his living from the universal resources, and by supplying his livelihood and maintenance in the event of his incapacity to look after himself. But civil society tears the individual [*Individuum*] away from family ties, alienates the members of the family from one another, and recognizes them as self-sufficient persons. Furthermore, it substitutes its own soil for the external inorganic nature and paternal soil from which the individual [*der Einzelne*] gained his livelihood, and subjects the existence [*Bestehen*] of the whole family itself to dependence on civil society and to contingency. Thus, the individual [*Individuum*] becomes a *son of civil society*, which has as many claims upon him as he has rights in relation to it.

Addition (H). Admittedly, the family must provide food for its individual members [*Einzelnen*], but in civil society, the family is subordinate and merely

242

lays the foundations; its effectiveness is no longer so comprehensive. Civil society, on the other hand, is the immense power which draws people to itself and requires them to work for it, to owe everything to it, and to do everything by its means. Thus, if a human being is to be a member of civil society, he has rights and claims in relation to it, just as he had in relation to his family. Civil society must protect its members and defend their rights, just as the individual [*der Einzelne*] owes a duty to the rights of civil society.

§ 239

In this character as a *universal family*, civil society has the duty and right, in the face of *arbitrariness* and contingency on the part of *the parents*, to supervise and influence the *education* [*Erziehung*] of children in so far as this has a bearing on their capacity to become members of society, and particularly if this education is to be completed not by the parents themselves, but by others. In so far as communal arrangements can be made for this purpose, it is likewise incumbent upon civil society to make them.

Addition (H,G). It is difficult to draw a boundary here between the rights of parents and those of civil society. As far as education is concerned, parents usually consider that they have complete freedom and can do whatever they please. With all public education, the main opposition usually comes from the parents, and it is they who protest and speak out about teachers and institutions because their own preference goes against them. Nevertheless, society has a right to follow its own tested views on such matters, and to compel parents to send their children to school, to have them vaccinated, etc. The controversies which have arisen in France between the demands for freedom of instruction (i.e. for parental choice) and for state supervision are relevant in this context.

243

§ 240

In the same way, society has the duty and right to act as guardian on behalf of those who destroy the security of their own and their family's livelihood by their extravagance, and to implement their end and that of society in their place.

Addition (G). In Athens, the law obliged every citizen to give an account of his means of support; the view nowadays is that this is a purely private matter. On the one hand, it is true that every individual has an independent existence [*ist jedes Individuum für sich*]; but on the other, the individual is also a member of the system of civil society, and just as every human being has a right to demand a livelihood from society, so also must society protect him against himself. It is not just starvation which is at stake here; the wider viewpoint is the need to prevent a rabble from emerging. Since civil society is obliged to feed its members, it also has the right to urge them to provide for their own livelihood.

§ 241

Not only arbitrariness, however, but also contingent physical factors and circumstances based on external conditions (see § 200) may reduce individuals to poverty. In this condition, they are left with the needs of civil society and yet—since society has at the same time taken from them the natural means of acquisition (see § 217), and also dissolves [*aufhebt*] the bond of the family in its wider sense as a kinship group (see § 181)—they are more or less deprived of all the advantages of society, such as the ability to acquire skills and education in general, as well as of the administration of justice, health care, and often even of the consolation of religion. For the poor, the universal authority [*Macht*] takes over the role of the family with regard not only to their immediate deficiencies, but also to the disposition of laziness, viciousness, and the other vices to which their predicament and sense of wrong give rise.

§ 242

The subjective aspect of poverty, and in general of every kind of want to which all individuals are exposed, even in their natural environment, also requires *subjective* help, both with regard to the *particular* circumstances and with regard to *emotion* and *love*. This is a situation in which, notwithstanding all universal arrangements, *morality* finds plenty to do. But since this help, both in itself [*für sich*] and in its effects, is dependent on contingency, society endeavours to make it less necessary by identifying the universal aspects of want and taking steps to remedy them.

244

> The contingent character of almsgiving and charitable donations (e.g. for burning lamps before the images of saints, etc.) is supplemented by public poorhouses, hospitals, streetlighting, etc. Charity still retains enough scope for action, and it is mistaken if it seeks to restrict the alleviation of want to the *particularity* of emotion and the *contingency* of its own disposition and knowledge [*Kenntnis*], and if it feels injured and offended by universal rulings and precepts of an *obligatory* kind. On the contrary, public conditions should be regarded as all the more perfect the less there is left for the individual to do by himself [*für sich*] in the light of his own particular opinion (as compared with what is arranged in a universal manner).

§ 243

When the activity of civil society is unrestricted, it is occupied internally with *expanding its population and industry*.—On the one hand, as the association [*Zusammenhang*] of human beings through their needs is *universalized*, and with it the ways in which means of satisfying these needs are devised and made available, the *accumulation of wealth* increases; for the greatest profit is derived from this twofold universality. But on the other hand, the *specialization* [*Vereinzelung*] and *limitation* of particular work also increase, as do likewise the *dependence* and *want* of the class which is tied to such work; this in turn leads to an inability to feel and enjoy the wider freedoms, and particularly the spiritual advantages, of civil society.

§ 244

When a large mass of people sinks below the level of a certain standard of living—which automatically regulates itself at the level necessary for a member of the society in question—that feeling of right, integrity [*Rechtlichkeit*], and honour which comes from supporting oneself by one's own activity and work is lost. This leads to the creation of a *rabble*, which in turn makes it much easier for disproportionate wealth to be concentrated in a few hands.

Addition (G). The lowest level of subsistence [*Subsistenz*], that of the rabble, defines itself automatically, but this minimum varies greatly between different peoples. In England, even the poorest man believes he has his rights; this differs from what the poor are content with in other countries. Poverty in itself does not reduce people to a rabble; a rabble is created only by the disposition associated with poverty, by inward rebellion against the rich, against society, the government, etc. It also follows that those who are dependent on contingency become frivolous and lazy, like the *lazzaroni* of Naples, for example. This in turn gives rise to the evil that the rabble do not have sufficient honour to gain their livelihood through their own work, yet claim that they have a right to receive their livelihood. No one can assert a right against nature, but within the conditions of society hardship at once assumes the form of a wrong inflicted on this or that class. The important question of how poverty can be remedied is one which agitates and torments modern societies especially.

245

§ 245

If the direct burden [of support] were to fall on the wealthier class, or if direct means were available in other public institutions (such as wealthy hospitals, foundations, or monasteries) to maintain the increasingly impoverished mass at its normal standard of living, the livelihood of the needy would be ensured without the mediation of work; this would be contrary to the principle of civil society and the feeling of self-sufficiency and honour among its individual members. Alternatively, their livelihood might be mediated by work (i.e. by the opportunity to work) which would increase the volume of production; but it is precisely in overproduction and the lack of a proportionate number of consumers who are themselves productive that the evil [*Übel*] consists [*besteht*], and this is merely exacerbated by the two expedients in question. This shows that, despite an *excess of wealth*, civil society is *not wealthy enough*—i.e. its own distinct resources are not sufficient—to prevent an excess of poverty and the formation of a rabble.

The example of *England* permits us to study these phenomena [*Erscheinungen*] on a large scale, especially the results achieved by poor-rates, boundless donations, and equally limitless private charity, and above all by the abolition [*Aufheben*] of the corporations. There (especially in Scotland), it has emerged that the most direct means of dealing with poverty, and particularly with the renunciation of shame and honour as the subjective bases of society and with the laziness and extravagance which give rise to a rabble, is to leave the poor to their fate and direct them to beg from the public.

§ 246

This inner dialectic of society drives it—or in the first instance *this specific society*—to go beyond its own confines and look for consumers, and hence the means it requires for subsistence [*Subsistenz*], in other nations [*Völkern*] which lack those means of which it has a surplus or which generally lag behind it in creativity, etc.

§ 247

Just as the earth, the firm and *solid ground*, is a precondition of the principle of family life, so is the *sea* the natural element for industry, whose relations with the external world it enlivens. By exposing the pursuit of gain to danger, industry simultaneously rises above it; and for the ties of the soil and the limited circles of civil life with its pleasures and desires, it substitutes the element of fluidity, danger, and destruction. Through this supreme medium of communication, it also creates trading links between distant countries, a legal [*rechtlichen*] relationship which gives rise to contracts; and at the same time, such trade [*Verkehr*] is the greatest educational asset [*Bildungsmittel*] and the source from which commerce derives its world-historical significance.

Rivers are *not natural boundaries*, which they have been taken to represent in modern times. On the contrary, both they and the oceans link human beings together. It is also inaccurate on Horace's part to say:

> deus *abscidit*
> Prudens Oceano dissociabili
> Terras

This can be seen not only from the fact that river basins are inhabited by a single tribe or people, but also, for example, from the relations which existed in former times between Greece, Ionia, and Magna Graecia, between Brittany and Britain, between Denmark and Norway, Sweden, Finland, Livonia, etc.; it is also particularly clear when we contrast this with the lesser degree of contact between the inhabitants of coastal territories and those of the interior.—But in order to appreciate what an educational asset is present in the link with the sea, one should compare the relationship to the sea of those nations in which creativity has flourished with those which have shunned navigation and which, like the Egyptians and Indians, have stagnated internally and sunk into the most appalling and miserable superstition; one should likewise note how all great and enterprising nations push their way to the sea.

§ 248

This extended link also supplies the means necessary for *colonization*—whether sporadic or systematic—to which the fully developed civil society is driven, and by which it provides part of its population with a return to the family principle in a new country, and itself with a new market and sphere of industrial activity.

Addition G). Civil society is driven to establish colonies. The increase of population alone has this effect; but a particular factor is the emergence of a mass of people who cannot gain satisfaction for their needs by their work when production exceeds the needs of consumers. Sporadic colonization is found particularly in Germany. The colonists move to America or Russia and retain no links with their home country, to which they are consequently of no service. The second variety of colonization, quite different from the first, is systematic. It is initiated by the state, which is aware of the proper way of carrying it out and regulates it accordingly. This mode of colonization was frequently employed by the ancients, especially the Greeks. Hard work was not the concern [*Sache*] of the Greek citizen, whose activity was directed rather towards public affairs [*öffentlichen Dingen*]. Accordingly, whenever the population grew to a point at which it could become difficult to provide for it, the young people were sent off to a new region, which was either specifically chosen or left to be discovered by chance. In more recent times, colonies have not been granted the same rights as the inhabitants of the mother country, and this situation has resulted in wars and eventual independence, as the history of the English and Spanish colonies shows. The liberation of colonies itself proves to be of the greatest advantage to the mother state, just as the emancipation of slaves is of the greatest advantage to the master.

§ 249

What the police provides for in the first instance is the actualization and preservation of the universal which is contained within the particularity of civil society, [and it does so] as *an external order and arrangement* for the protection and security of the masses of particular ends and interests which have their subsistence [*Bestehen*] in this universal; as the higher guiding authority, it also provides for those interests which extend beyond the society in question (see § 246). In accordance with the Idea, particularity itself makes this universal, which is present in its immanent interests, the end and object [*Gegenstand*] of its will and activity, with the result that *the ethical returns* to civil society as an immanent principle; this constitutes the determination of the *corporation*.

b. The Corporation

§ 250

The *agricultural estate,* in view of the substantiality of its natural and family life, has within itself, in immediate form, the concrete universal in which it lives. The *universal estate,* by definition [*in seiner Bestimmung*], has the universal for itself as its basis and as the end of its activity. The intermediate estate, i.e. the estate of trade and industry, is essentially concerned with the particular, and the corporation is therefore specially characteristic of it.

§ 251

The work performed by civil society is divided into different branches according to its particular nature. Since the inherent likeness of such particulars, as the quality *common* to them all, comes into existence [*Existenz*] in the association, the *selfish* end which pursues its own particular interest comprehends [*faßt*] and expresses itself at the same time as a universal end; and the member of civil society, in accordance with his *particular skill,* is a member of a corporation whose universal end is therefore wholly *concrete,* and no wider in scope than the end inherent in the trade which is the corporation's proper business and interest.

§ 252

By this definition [*Bestimmung*], the corporation has the right, under the supervision of the public authority [*Macht*], to look after its own interests within its enclosed sphere, to admit members in accordance with their objective qualification of skill and rectitude and in numbers determined by the universal context, to protect its members against particular contingencies, and to educate others so as to make them eligible for membership. In short, it has the right to assume the role of a *second* family for its members, a role which must remain more indeterminate in the case of civil society in general, which is more remote from individuals and their particular requirements.

> The tradesman [*Gewerbsmann*] is distinct from the day labourer, as he is from someone who is prepared to perform an occasional [*einzelnen*] contingent service. The former, who is—or wishes to become—a *master,* is a member of an association not for occasional contingent gain, but for the *whole* range and universality of his particular livelihood.—*Privileges,* in the sense of rights of a branch of civil society which constitutes a corporation, are distinct from privileges proper in the etymological sense, in that the latter are contingent exceptions to the universal law, whereas the former are no more than legally fixed determinations which lie in the *particular nature* of an essential branch of society itself.

§ 253

In the corporation, the family not only *has* its firm basis in that its livelihood is *guaranteed*—i.e. it has secure *resources* (see § 170)—on condition of its [possessing a certain] *capability*, but the two [i.e. livelihood and capability] are also *recognized*, so that the member of a corporation has no need to demonstrate his competence and his regular income and means of support—i.e. the fact that he *is somebody*—by any further *external evidence*. In this way, it is also recognized that he belongs to a whole which is itself a member of society in general, and that he has an interest in, and endeavours to promote, the less selfish end of this whole. Thus, he has *his honour in his estate*.

As a guarantor of resources, the institution of the corporation corresponds to the introduction of agriculture and private property in another sphere (see Remarks to § 203).—When complaints are made about that luxury and love of extravagance of the professional [*gewerbetreibenden*] classes which is associated with the creation of a rabble (see § 244), we must not overlook, in addition to the other causes [of this phenomenon] (e.g. the increasingly mechanical nature of work), its ethical basis as implied in what has been said above. If the individual [*der Einzelne*] is not a member of a legally recognized [*berechtigten*] corporation (and it is only through legal recognition that a community becomes a corporation), he is without the *honour of belonging to an estate*, his isolation reduces him to the selfish aspect of his trade, and his livelihood and satisfaction lack stability. He will accordingly try to gain *recognition* through the external manifestations of success in his trade, and these are without limit [*unbegrenzt*], because it is impossible for him to live in a way appropriate to his estate if his estate does not exist; for a community can *exist* in civil society only if it is legally constituted and recognized. Hence no way of life of a more general kind appropriate to such an estate can be devised.—Within the corporation, the help which poverty receives loses its contingent and unjustly [*mit Unrecht*] humiliating character, and wealth, in fulfilling the duty it owes to its association, loses the ability to provoke arrogance in its possessor and envy in others; rectitude also receives the true recognition and honour which are due to it.

249

§ 254

In the corporation, the so-called *natural right* to practise one's skill and thereby earn what there is to earn is limited only to the extent that, in this context, the skill is rationally determined. That is, it is freed from personal opinion and contingency, from its danger to oneself and others, and is recognized, guaranteed, and at the same time raised to a conscious activity for a common end.

§ 255

The *family is* the first *ethical* root of the state; the *corporation* is the second, and it is based in civil society. The former contains the moments of subjective particularity and objective universality in *substantial* unity; but in the latter, these moments, which in civil society are at first divided into the *internally reflected* particularity of need and satisfaction and abstract legal [*rechtlichen*] universality, are inwardly united in such a way that particular welfare is present as a right and is actualized within this union.

The sanctity of marriage and the honour attaching to the corporation are the two moments round which the disorganization of civil society revolves.

Addition (H).When the corporations were abolished [*aufgehoben*] in recent times, it was with the intention that the individual [*der Einzelne*] should look after himself. But even if we accept this, the corporation does not affect the individual's obligation to earn his living. In our modern states, the citizens have only a limited share in the universal business of the state; but it is necessary to provide ethical man with a universal activity in addition to his private end. This universal [activity], which the modern state does not always offer him, can be found in the corporation. We saw earlier that, in providing for himself, the individual [*das Individuum*] in civil society is also acting for others. But this unconscious necessity is not enough; only in the corporation does it become a knowing and thinking [part of] ethical life. The corporation, of course, must come under the higher supervision of the state, for it would otherwise become ossified and set in its ways, and decline into a miserable guild system. But the corporation in and for itself is not an enclosed guild; it is rather a means of giving the isolated trade an ethical status, and of admitting it to a circle in which it gains strength and honour.

§ 256

250

The end of the corporation, which is limited and finite, has its truth in the *end which is universal* in and for itself and in the absolute actuality of this end. So likewise do the separation and relative identity which were present in the external organization of the police. The sphere of civil society thus passes over into the state.

The town is the seat of civil trade and industry, of self-absorbed and divisive [*vereinzelnden*] reflection, of individuals who mediate their own self-preservation in relation to other legal [*rechtlichen*] persons. The country is the seat of an ethical life based on nature and the family. Town and country—these constitute in general the two ideal moments from which the state *emerges* as their true *ground*.— This development of immediate ethical life through the division of civil society and on to the state, which is shown to be their true ground, is the *scientific proof* of the concept of the state, a proof which only a development of this kind can furnish.—Since the state appears as the *result* of the development of the scientific concept in that it turns out to be the *true* ground [of this development], the *mediation* and semblance already referred to are likewise *superseded* by *immediacy*. In actuality, therefore, the *state* in general is in fact the *primary* factor; only within the state does the family first develop into civil society, and it is the idea of the state itself which divides into these two moments. In the development of civil society, the ethical substance takes on its *infinite* form, which contains within itself the following two moments: (1) infinite *differentiation* to the point at which the *inward being* [*Insichsein*] of self-consciousness attains being-for-itself and (2) the form of *universality* which is present in education, the form of *thought* whereby the spirit is objective and actual to itself as an *organic* totality in laws and *institutions*, i.e. in its own will as *thought*.

For Further Reading

Hegel, Georg Wilhelm Friedrich. *Hegel's Political Writings*. Translated by T.M. Knox (Oxford: Clarendon Press, 1964).

———. *Phenomenology of Spirit*. Translated by A.V. Miller (Oxford: Oxford Univ. Press, 1971).

———. *The Philosophy of Mind*. Translated by A.V. Miller (Oxford: Clarendon Press, 1977).

———. *The Philosophy of Right*. Translated by T.M. Knox (Oxford: Clarendon Press, 1952).

Avineri, Shlomo. *Hegel's Theory of the Modern State* (Cambridge: Cambridge Univ. Press, 1972).

Beiser, Frederick, C., ed. *The Cambridge Companion to Hegel* (Cambridge: Cambridge Univ. Press, 1993).

Berry, Christopher J. *Hume, Hegel and Human Nature* (The Hague: Martinus Nijhoff, 1982).

Colletti, Lucio. *Marxism and Hegel*. Translated by L. Garner (London:Verso, 1979).

Cullen, Bernard. *Hegel's Social and Political Thought* (New York: St. Martin's, 1979).

Dickey, Laurence. *Hegel: Religion, Economics, and the Politics of Spirit, 1770–1807* (New York: Cambridge Univ. Press, 1987).

Harris, H.S. *Hegel's Development Toward the Sunlight 1770–1801* (Oxford: Clarendon Press, 1972).

———. *Hegel's Development: Night Thoughts (Jena, 1801–1806)* (Oxford: Clarendon Press, 1983).

Hinchman, Lew. *Hegel's Critique of the Enlightenment* (Tampa: Univ. of Florida Press, 1984).

d'Hondt, Jacques. *Hegel in his Time*. Translated by J. Burbidge (Lewiston, N.Y.: Broadview, 1988).

Hyppolite, Jean. *Studies on Marx and Hegel*. Translated by J. O'Neill (New York: Harper and Row, 1969).

Inwood, M. J. *Hegel* (London: Routledge, 1983).

Kelly, George Armstrong. *Idealism, Politics and History: Sources of Hegelian Thought* (Cambridge: Cambridge Univ. Press, 1969).

———. *Hegel's Retreat from Eleusis* (Princeton: Princeton Univ. Press, 1978).

Kojève, Alexander. *Introduction to the Reading of Hegel*. Translated by J.H. Nichols (New York: Basic Books, 1969).

Kolb, David. *The Critique of Pure Modernity: Hegel, Heidegger, and After* (Chicago: Univ. of Chicago Press, 1986).

Löwith, Karl. *From Hegel to Nietzsche*. Translated by David F. Green (New York: Doubleday, 1967).

Lukács, George. *The Young Hegel*. Translated by Rodney Livingstone (Cambridge, Mass.: MIT Press, 1975).

MacIntyre, Alasdair, ed. *Hegel: A Collection of Critical Essays* (Garden City, N.Y.: Doubleday, 1972).

Maker, William, ed. *Hegel on Economics and Freedom* (Macon: Mercer Univ. Press, 1987).

Marcuse, Herbert. *Reason and Revolution: Hegel and the Rise of Social Theory* (Boston: Beacon Press, 1960).

Marx, Karl. *Critique of Hegel's Philosophy of Right.* Translated by J.O'Malley (Cambridge: Cambridge Univ. Press, 1970).

Mitias, Michael. *The Moral Foundation of the State in Hegel's 'Philosophy of Right'* (Amsterdam: Rodopi, 1984).

O'Brien, George Dennis. *Hegel on Reason and History* (Chicago: Univ. of Chicago Press, 1975).

Pelczynski, Z., ed. *Hegel's Political Philosophy: Problems and Perspectives* (Cambridge: Cambridge Univ. Press, 1971).

_____., ed. *The State and Civil Society: Studies in Hegel's Political Philosophy* (Cambridge: Cambridge Univ. Press, 1984).

Pippin, Robert. *Hegel's Idealism: The Satisfactions of Self-Consciousness* (Cambridge: Cambridge Univ. Press, 1989).

Plant, Raymond. *Hegel, An Introduction.* 2nd ed. (Oxford: Blackwell, 1983).

Riedel, Manfred. *Between Tradition and Revolution* (Cambridge: Cambridge Univ. Press, 1984).

Ritter, Joachim. *Hegel and the French Revolution* (Cambridge, MA.: MIT Press, 1982).

Rose, Gillian R. *Hegel Contra Sociology* (Atlantic Highlands, N.J.: Humanities Press, 1981).

Shklar, Judith. *Freedom and Independence: A Study of the Political Ideas of Hegel's 'Phenomenology of Mind'* (Cambridge: Cambridge Univ. Press, 1976).

Singer, Peter. *Hegel* (Oxford: Oxford Univ. Press, 1983).

Smith, Steven B. *Hegel's Critique of Liberalism: Rights in Context* (Chicago: Univ. of Chicago Press, 1989).

Steinberger, Peter. *Logic and Politics: Hegel's "Philosophy of Right"* (New Haven: Yale University Press, 1988).

Taylor, Charles. *Hegel* (Cambridge: Cambridge Univ. Press, 1975).

_____. *Hegel and Modern Society* (Cambridge: Cambridge Univ. Press, 1979).

Verene, Donald Philip, ed. *Hegel's Social and Political Thought* (Atlantic Highlands, N.J.: Humanities Press, 1980).

Waszek, Norbert. *The Scottish Enlightenment and Hegel's Account of Civil Society* (Boston: Kluwer Academic Publishers, 1988).

KARL MARX (1818–1883)

chapter 12

"THUS THERE has been history, but there is no longer any." Marx here offers not his own view but the conclusion of classical political economy. To show that history remains open and that even commercial societies may someday pass, Marx undertook a "critique of political economy." Most political economists treated "economic" forms such as the commodity, money, wage-labor, capital, and profit, as "as much a self-evident necessity imposed by nature as productive labor itself." Marx's project was to dismantle the picture of the modern commercial "economy" as "disembedded" in the sense of being free of any particular social form. The provisioning process always has a determinate social form, Marx insisted, and the forms mistaken to be natural by political economy are actually specific to capitalism. Moreover, in analyzing the "value form" Marx revealed how money conceals the social form of capitalism, whereby he *explained* how political economy comes to slur general with socially determinate categories.

"The Fetishism of Commodities," the famous closing section of *Capital's* first chapter, is largely a commentary on the thorny section preceding it, "The Form of Value or Exchange Value," for it is the *form* of value that gives rise to the fetishism. The fetishism of commodities is not about consumers swooning over possessions; it marks the bizarre fact that commodities appear not to be social at all, only because their social form pops up as a thing, money. As *values* capable of being redeemed for other goods, commodities are more than useful items; they pack social power—they have clout. This fetishistic investment of things with social power takes its most blinding form with money. Imagine the perplexity that would be aroused in a noncommercial society if cash were offered for a meal. To understand this "fetishism" we have to clear our minds of the thought that Marx's theory of value is a version of the classical, Ricardian "labor theory of value." Where Ricardo suggests that any labor creates value, in Marx's theory, value refers to the specific social form of labor and its products under capitalism. This is a far cry from the classical labor theory of value.

Capital's beginning sentence introduces the book's topic as the wealth of *capitalist* nations. Capitalist societies are commercial societies: their wealth comes in the commodity form. Since the generalized commodity form is a particular social form of wealth, Marx keeps to his insight that wealth and its creation always have a determinate social form—it is futile to study the wealth of a nation in abstraction from the social form of that wealth. A commodity, the unit of commercial wealth, is something useful that has an exchange value. There is nothing socially determinate about use value (though useful goods may be affected by specific social forms; consider crowns and monarchies); wealth of whichever social form must be useful in this general sense. So, the social form of the commodity lies in its exchange value. But the exchange value of a commodity is a sum of money. So we come to this: the social form of wealth in capitalist societies is a thing, money! In the remainder of his first chapter, Marx explores what gives rise to this cockeyed result.

He works in two phases: first, he arrives at the notion of *value* by examining *exchange value,* reopening Aristotle's failed inquiry into what makes all commodities commensurable. He distinguishes between *concrete* and *abstract* labor, concluding that the value of a good, what gets expressed by its exchange value, is the amount of "socially necessary" abstract labor congealed in it. This concept of "socially necessary" abstract labor takes the rest of *Capital* to unpack; among the many factors determining what counts as "socially necessary" are the upkeep of equipment, the duration of the production and merchandizing processes, and demand. Second, Marx asks a question political economists never raised: why is labor represented by the exchange value of a commodity and labor time by the magnitude of that exchange value? His examination of the "form of value" gives his answer. It comes to this: the kind of labor that creates value, "socially necessary" abstract labor, is not the sort that can stand alone: what would congealed abstract labor look like? Value itself cannot appear directly, so it lacks an observable fixed measure. Value appears only in the polar expression of exchange value: x commodity A = y commodity B. That commodity B embodies, in the only way possible, the value of commodity A results in these oddities of the "equivalent form": 1) though B is a concrete use-value, it embodies something wholly abstract, value; 2) though the labor that produces B is concrete, B embodies human labor in the abstract; and 3) though the labor that produces B is private, B embodies "socially necessary" labor. Exchange-value, ultimately money, embodies value in this topsy turvy manner because of what value is, namely, the peculiarly asocial social form of labor in capitalism, whereby the social mediation of particular labors occurs not directly, as in feudalism or a "community of free individuals," but through the pricing and sale of commodities.

Marx meant *Capital* to be a devastating critique of liberalism. He presents the sphere of generalized commodity circulation, the marketplace where buyers and sellers freely exchange goods and money, as the liberal's Eden of "Freedom, Equality, Property and Bentham." But the "fetishism of commodities" reveals how even this realm harbors a profound alienation, wherein the interaction of products and prices lords over us all. Hegel had already recognized the "system of needs" as coercive, and Smith's "invisible hand" conceded this point even as it strove to take the sting out of it. Seconding Hegel in saying that commercial society promotes the free or detached individual, Marx takes a swipe at the "unencumbered self" of the marketplace. He argues that commercial societies, being necessarily capitalist, are two-faced: the cheerful bustle of commodity circulation cannot be torn from the dismal aspect of capitalist production. New pitfalls enter the picture with capital. The notion—so attractive to liberalism—that the commercial scramble lacks an organizing goal is, according to Marx, false. In truth, the "free" market means the impersonal domination of its participants by the endless aim of capital accumulation. Ownership of the means of production enables capitalists *as a class* to exploit wage laborers *as a class*—"it's not personal, it's business"—extracting surplus value from them as a condition of employment without needing to violate the liberal rules of the marketplace. Even when the rules of simple commodity circulation are observed, the Lockean principle reverses itself: property flows to those who hold capital; those who work settle for wages. And the vaunted freedom of the market turns toward domination and subordination as buyer and seller shift into the workplace roles of capitalist and wage laborer.

Though *Capital's* critique is targeted primarily at classical political economy—the marginal utility approach of neoclassical economics arrives on the scene later—Marx pulls the rug out from utility theory's *purely subjective* conception of usefulness. The present translation, unfortunately, obscures the point; it reads: "utility is not a thing of air. Being limited by the physical properties of the commodity, it has no existence apart from that commodity." *Use-*

fulness is "not a thing of air"; *utility*, which purports to be purely subjective (that is, to exist apart from the commodity), is.

FROM *CAPITAL*, VOLUME I

BOOK I.

CAPITALIST PRODUCTION.

PART I.

COMMODITIES AND MONEY.

CHAPTER I. COMMODITIES.

Section 1.—The Two Factors of a Commodity: Use-Value and Value
(The Substance of Value and the Magnitude of Value).

The wealth of those societies in which the capitalist mode of production prevails, presents itself as "an immense accumulation of commodities," its unit being a single commodity. Our investigation must therefore begin with the analysis of a commodity.

A commodity is, in the first place, an object outside us, a thing that by its properties satisfies human wants of some sort or another. The nature of such wants, whether, for instance, they spring from the stomach or from fancy, makes no difference. Neither are we here concerned to know how the object satisfies these wants, whether directly as means of subsistence, or indirectly as means of production.

Every useful thing, as iron, paper, &c., may be looked at from the two points of view of quality and quantity. It is an assemblage of many properties, and may therefore be of use in various ways. To discover the various use of things is the work of history. So also is the establishment of socially-recognised standards of measure for the quantities of these useful objects. The diversity of these measures has its origin partly in the diverse nature of the objects to be measured, partly in convention.

The utility of a thing makes it a use-value. But this utility is not a thing of air. Being limited by the physical properties of the commodity, it has no existence apart from that commodity. A commodity, such as iron, corn, or a diamond, is therefore, so far as it is a material thing, a use-value, something useful. This property of a commodity is independent of the amount of labour required to appropriate its useful qualities. When treating of use-value, we always assume to be dealing with definite quantities, such as dozens of watches, yards of linen, or tons of iron. The use-values of commodities furnish the material for a special study, that of the commercial knowledge of commodities. Use-values become a reality only by use or consumption: they also constitute the substance of all wealth, whatever may be the social form of that wealth. In the form of society we are about to consider, they are, in addition, the material depositories of exchange value.

Exchange value, at first sight, presents itself as a quantitative relation, as the proportion in which values in use of one sort are exchanged for those of another sort, a relation constantly changing with time and place. Hence exchange value appears to be something accidental and purely relative, and consequently an intrinsic value, *i.e.*, an exchange value that is inseparably connected with, inherent in commodities, seems a contradiction in terms. Let us consider the matter a little more closely.

A given commodity, *e.g.,* a quarter of wheat is exchanged for x blacking, y silk, or z gold, &c.—in short, for other commodities in the most different proportions. Instead of one exchange value, the wheat has, therefore, a great many. But since x blacking, y silk, or z gold, &c., each represent the exchange value of one quarter of wheat, x blacking, y silk, z gold, &c., must as exchange values be replaceable by each other, or equal to each other. Therefore, first: the valid exchange values of a given commodity express something equal; secondly, exchange value, generally, is only the mode of expression, the phenomenal form, of something contained in it, yet distinguishable from it.

Let us take two commodities, *e.g.* , corn and iron. The proportions in which they are exchangeable, whatever those proportions may be, can always be represented by an equation in which a given quantity of corn is equated to some quantity of iron: *e.g.*, 1 quarter corn = x cwt. iron. What does this equation tell us? It tells us that in two different things—in 1 quarter of corn and x cwt. of iron, there exists in equal quantities something common to both. The two things must therefore be equal to a third, which in itself is neither the one nor the other. Each of them, so far as it is exchange value, must therefore be reducible to this third.

257

A simple geometrical illustration will make this clear. In order to calculate and compare the areas of rectilinear figures, we decompose them into triangles. But the area of the triangle itself is expressed by something totally different from its visible figure, namely, by half the product of the base into the altitude. In the same way the exchange values of commodities must be capable of being expressed in terms of something common to them all, of which thing they represent a greater or less quantity.

This common "something" cannot be either a geometrical, a chemical, or any other natural property of commodities. Such properties claim our attention only in so far as they affect the utility of those commodities, make them use-values. But the exchange of commodities is evidently an act characterised by a total abstraction from use-value. Then one use value is just as good as another, provided only it be present in sufficient quantity. Or, as old Barbon says, "one sort of wares are as good as another, if the values be equal. There is no difference or distinction in things of equal value. . . An hundred pounds' worth of lead or iron, is of as great value as one hundred pounds' worth of silver or gold." As use-values, commodities are, above all, of different qualities, but as exchange values they are merely different quantities, and consequently do not contain an atom of use-value.

If then we leave out of consideration the use-value of commodities, they have only one common property left, that of being products of labour. But even the product of labour itself has undergone a change in our hands. If we make abstraction from its use-value, we make abstraction at the same time from the material elements and shapes that make the product a use-value; we see in it no longer a table, a house, yarn, or any other useful thing. Its existence as a material thing is put out of sight. Neither can it any longer be regarded as the product of the labour of the joiner, the mason, the spinner, or of any other definite kind of productive labour. Along with the useful qualities of the products themselves, we put out of sight both the useful character of the various kinds of labour embodied in them, and the concrete forms of that labour; there is nothing left but what is common to them all; all are reduced to one and the same sort of labour, human labour in the abstract.

Let us now consider the residue of each of these products; it consists of the same unsubstantial reality in each, a mere congelation of homogeneous human labour, of labour-power expended without regard to the mode of its expenditure. All that these things now tell us is, that human labour-power has been expended in their production, that human labor is embodied in them. When looked at as crystals of this social substance, common to them all, they are—Values.

We have seen that when commodities are exchanged, their exchange value manifests itself as something totally independent of their use-value. But if we abstract from their use-value, there remains their Value as defined above. Therefore, the common substance that manifests itself in the exchange value of commodities, whenever they are exchanged, is their value. The progress of our investigation will show that exchange value is the only form in which the value of commodities can manifest itself or be expressed. For the present, however, we have to consider the nature of value independently of this, its form.

A use-value, or useful article, therefore, has value only because human labour in the abstract has been embodied or materialised in it. How, then, is the magnitude of this value to be measured? Plainly, by the quantity of the value-creating substance, the labour, contained in the article. The quantity of labour, however, is measured by its duration, and labour-time in its turn finds its standard in weeks, days, and hours.

Some people might think that if the value of a commodity is determined by the quantity of labour spent on it, the more idle and unskilful the labourer, the more valuable would his commodity be, because more time would be required in its production. The labour, however, that forms the substance of value, is homogeneous human labour, expenditure of one uniform labour-power. The total labour-power of society, which is embodied in the sum total of the values of all commodities produced by that society, counts here as one homogeneous mass of human labour-power, composed though it be of innumerable individual units. Each of these units is the same as any other, so far as it has the character of the average labour-power of society, and takes effect as such; that is, so far as it requires for producing a commodity, no more time than is needed on an average, no more than is socially necessary. The labour-time socially necessary is that required to produce an article under the normal conditions of production, and with the average degree of skill and intensity prevalent at the time. The introduction of power looms into England probably reduced by one half the labour required to weave a given quantity of yarn into cloth. The hand-loom weavers, as a matter of fact, continued to require the same time as before; but for all that, the product of one hour of their labour represented after the change only half an hour's social labour, and consequently fell to one-half its former value.

We see then that that which determines the magnitude of the value of any article is the amount of labour socially necessary, or the labour-time socially necessary for its production. Each individual commodity, in this connexion, is to be considered as an average sample of its class. Commodities, therefore, in which equal quantities of labour are embodied, or which can be produced in the same time, have the same value. The value of one commodity is to the value of any other, as the labour-time necessary for the production of the one is to that necessary for the production of the other. "As values, all commodities are only definite masses of congealed labour-time."

The value of a commodity would therefore remain constant, if the labour-time required for its production also remained constant. But the latter changes with every variation in the productiveness of labour. This productiveness is determined by various circumstances, amongst others, by the average amount of skill of the workmen, the state of science, and the degree of its practical application, the social organisation of production, the extent and capabilities of the means of production, and by physical conditions. For example, the same amount of labour in favourable seasons is embodied in 8 bushels of corn, and in unfavourable, only in four. The same labour extracts from rich mines more metal than from poor mines. Diamonds are of very rare occurrence on the earth's surface, and hence their discovery costs, on an average, a great deal of labour-time. Consequently much labour is represented in a small compass. Jacob doubts whether gold has ever been paid for at its full value. This applies still more to diamonds. According to Eschwege, the total produce of the Brazilian diamond mines for the eighty years, ending in 1823, had not realised the price of one-and-a-half years' average produce of the sugar and coffee plantations of the same country, although the diamonds cost much more labour, and therefore represented more value. With richer mines, the same quantity of labour would embody itself in more diamonds and their value would fall. If we could succeed at a small expenditure of labour, in converting carbon into diamonds, their value might fall below that of bricks. In general, the greater the productiveness of labour, the less is the labour-time

259

required for the production of an article, the less is the amount of labour crystallised in that article, and the less is its value; and *vice versa,* the less the productiveness of labour, the greater is the labour-time required for the production of an article, and the greater is its value. The value of a commodity, therefore, varies directly as the quantity, and inversely as the productiveness, of the labour incorporated in it.

A thing can be a use-value, without having value. This is the case whenever its utility to man is not due to labour. Such are air, virgin soil, natural meadows, &c. A thing can be useful, and the product of human labour, without being a commodity. Whoever directly satisfies his wants with the produce of his own labour, creates, indeed, use-values, but not commodities. In order to produce the latter, he must not only produce use-values, but use-values for others, social use-values. Lastly, nothing can have value, without being an object of utility. If the thing is useless, so is the labour contained in it; the labour does not count as labour, and therefore creates no value.

Section 2.—The Twofold Character of the Labour Embodied in Commodities.

At first sight a commodity presented itself to us as a complex of two things—use-value and exchange-value. Later on, we saw also that labour, too, possesses the same two-fold nature; for, so far as it finds expression in value, it does not possess the same characteristics that belong to it as a creator of use-values. I was the first to point out and to examine critically this two-fold nature of the labour contained in commodities. As this point is the pivot on which a clear comprehension of political economy turns, we must go more into detail.

Let us take two commodities such as a coat and 10 yards of linen, and let the former be double the value of the latter, so that, if 10 yards of linen = W, the coat = 2W.

The coat is a use-value that satisfies a particular want. Its existence is the result of a special sort of productive activity, the nature of which is determined by its aim, mode of operation, subject, means, and result. The labour, whose utility is thus represented by the value in use of its product, or which manifests itself by making its product a use-value, we call useful labour. In this connexion we consider only its useful effect.

As the coat and the linen are two qualitatively different use-values, so also are the two forms of labour that produce them, tailoring and weaving. Were these two objects not qualitatively different, not produced respectively by labour of different quality, they could not stand to each other in the relation of commodities. Coats are not exchanged for coats, one use-value is not exchanged for another of the same kind.

To all the different varieties of values in use there correspond as many different kinds of useful labour, classified according to the order, genus, species, and variety to which they belong in the social division of labour. This division of labour is a necessary condition for the production of commodities, but it does not follow conversely, that the production of commodities is a necessary condition for the division of labour. In the primitive Indian community there is social division of labour, without production of commodities. Or, to take an example nearer home, in every factory the labour is divided according to a system, but this division is not brought about by the operatives mutually exchanging their individual products. Only such products can become commodities with regard to each other, as result from different kinds of labour, each kind being carried on independently and for the account of private individuals.

To resume, then: In the use-value of each commodity there is contained useful labour, *i.e.*, productive activity of a definite kind and exercised with a definite aim. Use-values cannot confront each other as commodities, unless the useful labour embodied in them is qualitatively different in each of them. In a community, the produce of which in general takes the form of commodities, *i.e.*, in a community of commodity producers, this qualitative difference between the useful forms of labour that are carried on independently by individual producers, each on their own account, develops into a complex system, a social division of labour.

Anyhow, whether the coat be worn by the tailor or by his customer, in either case it operates as a use-value. Nor is the relation between the coat and the labour that produced it altered by the circumstance that tailoring may have become a special trade, an independent branch of the social division of labour. Wherever the want of clothing forced them to it, the human race made clothes for thousands of years, without a single man becoming a tailor. But coats and linen, like every other element of material wealth that is not the spontaneous produce of nature, must invariably owe their existence to a special productive activity, exercised with a definite aim, an activity that appropriates particular nature-given materials to particular human wants. So far therefore as labour is a creator of use-value, is useful labour, it is a necessary condition, independent of all forms of society, for the existence of the human race; it is an eternal nature-imposed necessity, without which there can be no material exchanges between man and Nature, and therefore no life.

The use-values, coat, linen, &c., *i.e.*, the bodies of commodities, are combinations of two elements—matter and labour. If we take away the useful labour expended upon them, a material substratum is always left, which is furnished by Nature without the help of man. The latter can work only as Nature does, that is by changing the form of matter. Nay more, in this work of changing the form he is constantly helped by natural forces. We see, then, that labour is not the only source of material wealth, of use-values produced by labour. As William Petty puts it, labour is its father and the earth its mother.

261

Let us now pass from the commodity considered as a use-value to the value of commodities.

By our assumption, the coat is worth twice as much as the linen. But this is a mere quantitative difference, which for the present does not concern us. We bear in mind, however, that if the value of the coat is double that of 10 yds. of linen, 20 yds. of linen must have the same value as one coat. So far as they are values, the coat and the linen are things of a like substance, objective expressions of essentially identical labour. But tailoring and weaving are, qualitatively, different kinds of labour. There are, however, states of society in which one and the same man does tailoring and weaving alternately, in which case these two forms of labour are mere modifications of the labour of the same individual, and not special and fixed functions of different persons; just as the coat which our tailor makes one day, and the trousers which he makes another day, imply only a variation in the labour of one and the same individual. Moreover, we see at a glance that, in our capitalist society, a given portion of human labour is, in accordance with the varying demand, at one time supplied in the form of tailoring, at another in the form of weaving. This change may possibly not take place without friction, but take place it must.

Productive activity, if we leave out of sight its special form, viz., the useful character of the labour, is nothing but the expenditure of human labour-power. Tailoring and weaving, though qualitatively different productive activities, are each a productive expenditure of human brains, nerves, and muscles, and in this sense are human labour. They are but two different modes of expending human labour-power. Of course, this labour-power, which remains the same under all its modifications, must have attained a certain pitch of development before it can be expended in a multiplicity of modes. But the value of a commodity represents human labour in the abstract, the expenditure of human labour in general. And just as in society, a general or a banker plays a great part, but mere man, on the other hand, a very shabby part, so here with mere human labour. It is the expenditure of simple labour-power, *i.e.,* of the labour-power which, on an average, apart from any special development, exists in the organism of every ordinary individual. Simple average labour, it is true, varies in character in different countries and at different times, but in a particular society it is given. Skilled labour counts only as simple labour intensified, or rather, as multiplied simple labour, a given quantity of skilled being considered equal to a greater quantity of simple labour. Experience shows that this reduction is constantly being made. A commodity may be the product of the most skilled labour, but its value, by equating it to the product of simple unskilled labour, represents a definite quantity of the latter labour alone. The different proportions in which different sorts of labour are reduced to unskilled labour as their standard, are established by a social process that goes on behind the backs of the producers, and, consequently, appear to be fixed by custom. For simplicity's sake we shall henceforth account every kind

262

of labour to be unskilled, simple labour; by this we do no more than save ourselves the trouble of making the reduction.

Just as, therefore, in viewing the coat and linen as values, we abstract from their different use-values, so it is with the labour represented by those values: we disregard the difference between its useful forms, weaving and tailoring. As the use-values, coat and linen, are combinations of special productive activities with cloth and yarn, while the values, coat and linen, are, on the other hand, mere homogeneous congelations of indifferentiated labour, so the labour embodied in these latter values does not count by virtue of its productive relation to cloth and yarn, but only as being expenditure of human labour-power. Tailoring and weaving are necessary factors in the creation of the use-values, coat and linen, precisely because these two kinds of labour are of different qualities; but only in so far as abstraction is made from their special qualities, only in so far as both possess the same quality of being human labour, do tailoring and weaving form the substance of the values of the same articles.

Coats and linen, however, are not merely values, but values of definite magnitude, and according to our assumption, the coat is worth twice as much as the ten yards of linen. Whence this difference in their values? It is owing to the fact that the linen contains only half as much labour as the coat, and consequently, that in the production of the latter, labour-power must have been expended during twice the time necessary for the production of the former.

While, therefore, with reference to use-value, the labour contained in a commodity counts only qualitatively, with reference to value it counts only quantitatively, and must first be reduced to human labour pure and simple. In the former case, it is a question of How and What, in the latter of How much? How long a time? Since the magnitude of the value of a commodity represents only the quantity of labour embodied in it, it follows that all commodities, when taken in certain proportions, must be equal in value.

263

If the productive power of all the different sorts of useful labour required for the production of a coat remains unchanged, the sum of the values of the coat produced increases with their number. If one coat represents x days' labour, two coats represent 2x days' labour, and so on. But assume that the duration of the labour necessary for the production of a coat becomes doubled or halved. In the first case, one coat is worth as much as two coats were before; in the second case, two coats are only worth as much as one was before, although in both cases one coat renders the same service as before, and the useful labour embodied in it remains of the same quality. But the quantity of labour spent on its production has altered.

An increase in the quantity of use-values is an increase of material wealth. With two coats two men can be clothed, with one coat only one man. Nevertheless, an increased quantity of material wealth may correspond to a simultaneous fall in the magnitude of its value. This antagonistic movement has its origin in the two-fold character of labour. Productive power has reference, of course, only to labour of some useful concrete form; the efficacy of any special productive activity during a given time being dependent on its productiveness. Useful labour becomes, therefore, a more or less abundant source of products, in proportion to the rise or fall of its productiveness. On the other hand, no change in this productiveness affects the labour represented by value. Since productive power is an attribute of the concrete useful forms of labour, of course it can no longer have any bearing on that labour, so soon as we make abstraction from those concrete useful forms. However then productive power may vary, the same labour, exercised during equal periods of time, always yields equal amounts of value. But it will yield, during equal periods of time, different quantities of values in use; more, if the productive power rise, fewer, if it fall. The same change in productive power, which increases the fruitfulness of labour, and, in consequence, the quantity of use-values produced by that labour, will diminish the total value of this increased quantity of use-values, provided such change shorten the total labour-time necessary for their production; and *vice versa*.

On the one hand all labour is, speaking physiologically, an expenditure of human labour-power, and in its character of identical abstract human labour, it creates and forms the value of commodities. On the other hand, all labour is the expenditure of human labour-power in a special form and with a definite aim, and in this, its character of concrete useful labour, it produces use-values.

264

Section 3.—The Form of Value or Exchange Value.

Commodities come into the world in the shape of use-values, articles, or goods, such as iron, linen, corn, &c. This is their plain, homely, bodily form. They are, however, commodities, only because they are something twofold, both objects of utility, and, at the same time, depositories of value. They manifest themselves therefore as commodities, or have the form of commodities, only in so far as they have two forms, a physical or natural form, and a value form.

The reality of the value of commodities differs in this respect from Dame Quickly, that we don't know "where to have it." The value of commodities is the very opposite of the coarse materiality of their substance, not an atom of matter enters into its composition. Turn and examine a single commodity, by itself, as we will. Yet in so far as it remains an object of value, it seems impossible to grasp it. If, however, we bear in mind that the value of commodities has a purely social reality, and that they acquire this reality only in so far as they are expressions or embodiments of one identical social substance, viz., human labour, it follows as a matter of course, that value can only manifest itself in the social relation of commodity to commodity. In fact we started from exchange value, or the exchange relation of commodities, in order to get at the value that lies hidden behind it. We must now return to this form under which value first appeared to us.

Every one knows, if he knows nothing else, that commodities have a value form common to them all, and presenting a marked contrast with the varied bodily forms of their use-values. I mean their money form. Here, however, a task is set us, the performance of which has never yet even been attempted by *bourgeois* economy, the task of tracing the genesis of this money form, of developing the expression of value implied in the value relation of commodities, from its simplest, almost imperceptible outline, to the dazzling money form. By doing this we shall, at the same time, solve the riddle presented by money.

The simplest value relation is evidently that of one commodity to some one other commodity of a different kind. Hence the relation between the values of two commodities supplies us with the simplest expression of the value of a single commodity.

A. Elementary or Accidental Form of Value.

x commodity A = y commodity B, or
x commodity A is worth y commodity B.
20 yards of linen = 1 coat, or
20 yards of linen are worth 1 coat.

1. The Two Poles of the Expression of Value: Relative Form and Equivalent Form.

The whole mystery of the form of value lies hidden in this elementary form. Its analysis, therefore, is our real difficulty.

265

Here two different kinds of commodities (in our example the linen and the coat), evidently play two different parts. The linen expresses its value in the coat; the coat serves as the material in which that value is expressed. The former plays an active, the latter a passive, part. The value of the linen is represented as relative value, or appears in relative form. The coat officiates as equivalent, or appears in equivalent form.

The relative form and the equivalent form are two intimately connected, mutually dependent and inseparable elements of the expression of value; but, at the same time, are mutually exclusive, antagonistic extremes—*i.e.,* poles of the same expression. They are allotted respectively to the two different commodities brought into relation by that expression. It is not possible to express the value of linen in linen. 20 yards of linen = 20 yards of linen is no expression of value. On the contrary, such an equation merely says that 20 yards of linen are nothing else than 20 yards of linen, a definite quantity of the use-value linen. The value of the linen can therefore be expressed only relatively—*i.e.,* in some other commodity. The relative form of the value of the linen pre-supposes, therefore, the presence of some other commodity—here the coat—under the form of an equivalent. On the other hand, the commodity that figures as the equivalent cannot at the same time assume the relative form. That second commodity is not the one whose value is expressed. Its function is merely to serve as the material in which the value of the first commodity is expressed.

No doubt, the expression 20 yards of linen = 1 coat, or 20 yards of linen are worth 1 coat, implies the opposite relation: 1 coat = 20 yards of linen, or 1 coat is worth 20 yards of linen. But in that case, I must reverse the equation, in order to express the value of the coat relatively; and, so soon as I do that, the linen becomes the equivalent instead of the coat. A single commodity cannot, therefore, simultaneously assume, in the same expression of value, both forms. The very polarity of these forms makes them mutually exclusive.

Whether, then, a commodity assumes the relative form, or the opposite equivalent form, depends entirely upon its accidental position in the expression of value—that is, upon whether it is the commodity whose value is being expressed or the commodity in which value is being expressed.

2. The Relative Form of Value.

(a.) The nature and import of this form.

In order to discover how the elementary expression of the value of a commodity lies hidden in the value relation of two commodities, we must, in the first place, consider the latter entirely apart from its quantitative aspect. The usual mode of procedure is generally the reverse, and in the value relation nothing is seen but the proportion between definite quantities of two different sorts of commodities that are considered equal to each other. It is apt to be forgotten that the magnitudes of different things can be compared quantitatively, only when those magnitudes are expressed in terms of the same unit. It is only as expressions of such a unit that they are of the same denomination, and therefore commensurable.

Whether 20 yards of linen = 1 coat or = 20 coats or = x coats—that is, whether a given quantity of linen is worth few or many coats, every such statement implies that the linen and coats, as magnitudes of value, are expressions of the same unit, things of the same kind. Linen = coat is the basis of the equation.

But the two commodities whose identity of quality is thus assumed, do not play the same part. It is only the value of the linen that is expressed. And how? By its reference to the coat as its equivalent, as something that can be exchanged for it. In this relation the coat is the mode of existence of value, is value embodied, for only as such is it the same as the linen. On the other hand, the linen's own value comes to the front, receives independent expression, for it is only as being value that it is comparable with the coat as a thing of equal value, or exchangeable with the coat. To borrow an illustration from chemistry, butyric acid is a different substance from propyl formate. Yet both are made up of the same chemical substances, carbon (C), hydrogen (H), and oxygen (O),

266

and that, too, in like proportions—namely, $C_4H_8O_2$. If now we equate butyric acid to propyl formate, then, in the first place, propyl formate would be, in this relation, merely a form of existence of $C_4H_8O_2$; and in the second place, we should be stating that butyric acid also consists of $C_4H_8O_2$. Therefore, by thus equating the two substances, expression would be given to their chemical composition, while their different physical forms would be neglected.

If we say that, as values, commodities are mere congelations of human labour, we reduce them by our analysis, it is true, to the abstraction, value; but we ascribe to this value no form apart from their bodily form. It is otherwise in the value relation of one commodity to another. Here, the one stands forth in its character of value by reason of its relation to the other.

By making the coat the equivalent of the linen, we equate the labour embodied in the former to that in the latter. Now, it is true that the tailoring, which makes the coat, is concrete labour of a different sort from the weaving which makes the linen. But the act of equating it to the weaving, reduces the tailoring to that which is really equal in the two kinds of labour, to their common character of human labour. In this roundabout way, then, the fact is expressed, that weaving also, in so far as it weaves value, has nothing to distinguish it from tailoring, and, consequently, is abstract human labour. It is the expression of equivalence between different sorts of commodities that alone brings into relief the specific character of value-creating labour, and this it does by actually reducing the different varieties of labour embodied in the different kinds of commodities to their common quality of human labour in the abstract.

There is, however, something else required beyond the expression of the specific character of the labour of which the value of the linen consists. Human labour-power in motion, or human labour, creates value, but is not itself value. It becomes value only in its congealed state, when embodied in the form of some object. In order to express the value of the linen as a congelation of human labour, that value must be expressed as having objective existence, as being a something materially different from the linen itself, and yet a something common to the linen and all other commodities. The problem is already solved.

When occupying the position of equivalent in the equation of value, the coat ranks qualitatively as the equal of the linen, as something of the same kind, because it is value. In this position it is a thing in which we see nothing but value, or whose palpable bodily form represents value. Yet the coat itself, the body of the commodity, coat, is a mere use-value. A coat as such no more tells us it is value, than does the first piece of linen we take hold of. This shows that when placed in value relation to the linen, the coat signifies more than when out of that relation, just as many a man strutting about in a gorgeous uniform counts for more than when in mufti.

In the production of the coat, human labour-power, in the shape of tailor-

267

ing, must have been actually expended. Human labour is therefore accumulated in it. In this aspect the coat is a depository of value, but though worn to a thread, it does not let this fact show through. And as equivalent of the linen in the value equation, it exists under this aspect alone, counts therefore as embodied value, as a body that is value. *A*, for instance, cannot be "your majesty" to *B*, unless at the same time majesty in *B*'s eyes assumes the bodily form of *A*, and, what is more, with every new father of the people, changes its features, hair, and many other things besides.

Hence, in the value equation, in which the coat is the equivalent of the linen, the coat officiates as the form of value. The value of the commodity linen is expressed by the bodily form of the commodity coat, the value of one by the use-value of the other. As a use-value, the linen is something palpably different from the coat; as value, it is the same as the coat, and now has the appearance of a coat. Thus the linen acquires a value form different from its physical form. The fact that it is value, is made manifest by its equality with the coat, just as the sheep's nature of a Christian is shown in his resemblance to the Lamb of God.

We see, then, all that our analysis of the value of commodities has already told us, is told us by the linen itself, so soon as it comes into communication with another commodity, the coat. Only it betrays its thoughts in that language with which alone it is familiar, the language of commodities. In order to tell us that its own value is created by labour in its abstract character of human labour, it says that the coat, in so far as it is worth as much as the linen, and therefore is value, consists of the same labour as the linen. In order to inform us that its sublime reality as value is not the same as its buckram body, it says that value has the appearance of a coat, and consequently that so far as the linen is value, it and the coat are as like as two peas. We may here remark, that the language of commodities has, besides Hebrew, many other more or less correct dialects. The German "werthsein," to be worth, for instance, expresses in a less striking manner than the Romance verbs "valere," "valer," "valoir," that the equating of commodity B to commodity A, is commodity A's own mode of expressing its value. Paris vaut bien une messe.

By means, therefore, of the value relation expressed in our equation, the bodily form of commodity B becomes the value form of commodity A, or the body of commodity B acts as a mirror to the value of commodity A. By putting itself in relation with commodity B, as value in *propriâ personâ*, as the matter of which human labour is made up, the commodity A converts the value in use, B, into the substance in which to express its, A's, own value. The value of A, thus expressed in the use-value of B, has taken the form of relative value. . . .

3. The Equivalent Form of Value.

We have seen that commodity A (the linen), by expressing its value in the use-value of a commodity differing in kind (the coat), at the same time im-

268

presses upon the latter a specific form of value, namely that of the equivalent. The commodity linen manifests its quality of having a value by the fact that the coat, without having assumed a value form different from its bodily form, is equated to the linen. The fact that the latter therefore has a value is expressed by saying that the coat is directly exchangeable with it. Therefore, when we say that a commodity is in the equivalent form, we express the fact that it is directly exchangeable with other commodities.

When one commodity, such as a coat, serves as the equivalent of another, such as linen, and coats consequently acquire the characteristic property of being directly exchangeable with linen, we are far from knowing in what proportion the two are exchangeable. The value of the linen being given in magnitude, that proportion depends on the value of the coat. Whether the coat serves as the equivalent and the linen as relative value, or the linen as the equivalent and the coat as relative value, the magnitude of the coat's value is determined, independently of its value form, by the labour time necessary for its production. But whenever the coat assumes in the equation of value, the position of equivalent, its value acquires no quantitative expression; on the contrary, the commodity coat now figures only as a definite quantity of some article.

For instance, 40 yards of linen are worth—what? 2 coats. Because the commodity coat here plays the part of equivalent, because the use-value coat, as opposed to the linen, figures as an embodiment of value, therefore a definite number of coats suffices to express the definite quantity of value in the linen. Two coats may therefore express the quantity of value of 40 yards of linen, but they can never express the quantity of their own value. A superficial observation of this fact, namely, that in the equation of value, the equivalent figures exclusively as a simple quantity of some article, of some use-value, has misled Bailey, as also many others, both before and after him, into seeing, in the expression of value, merely a quantitative relation. The truth being, that when a commodity acts as equivalent, no quantitative determination of its value is expressed.

The first peculiarity that strikes us, in considering the form of the equivalent, is this: use-value becomes the form of manifestation, the phenomenal form of its opposite, value.

The bodily form of the commodity becomes its value form. But, mark well, that this *quid pro quo* exists in the case of any commodity B, only when some other commodity A enters into a value relation with it, and then only within the limits of this relation. Since no commodity can stand in the relation of equivalent to itself, and thus turn its own bodily shape into the expression of its own value, every commodity is compelled to choose some other commodity for its equivalent, and to accept the use-value, that is to say, the bodily shape of that other commodity as the form of its own value.

One of the measures that we apply to commodities as material substances, as use-values, will serve to illustrate this point. A sugar-loaf being a body, is heavy, and therefore has weight: but we can neither see nor touch this weight. We then take various pieces of iron, whose weight has been determined beforehand. The iron, as iron, is no more the form of manifestation of weight, than is the sugar-loaf. Nevertheless, in order to express the sugar-loaf as so much weight, we put it into a weight-relation with the iron. In this relation, the iron officiates as a body representing nothing but weight. A certain quantity of iron therefore serves as the measure of the weight of the sugar, and represents, in relation to the sugar-loaf, weight embodied, the form of manifestation of weight. This part is played by the iron only within this relation, into which the sugar or any other body, whose weight has to be determined, enters with the iron. Were they not both heavy, they could not enter into this relation, and the one could therefore not serve as the expression of the weight of the other. When we throw both into the scales, we see in reality, that as weight they are both the same, and that, therefore, when taken in proper proportions, they have the same weight. Just as the substance iron, as a measure of weight, represents in relation to the sugar-loaf weight alone, so, in our expression of value, the material object, coat, in relation to the linen, represents value alone.

Here, however, the analogy ceases. The iron, in the expression of the weight of the sugar-loaf, represents a natural property common to both bodies, namely their weight; but the coat in the expression of value of the linen, represents a non-natural property of both, something purely social, namely, their value.

Since the relative form of value of a commodity—the linen, for example—expresses the value of that commodity, as being something wholly different from its substance and properties, as being, for instance, coat-like, we see that this expression itself indicates that some social relation lies at the bottom of it. With the equivalent form it is just the contrary. The very essence of this form is that the material commodity itself—the coat—just as it is, expresses value, and is endowed with the form of value by Nature itself. Of course this holds good only so long as the value relation exists, in which the coat stands in the position of equivalent to the linen. Since, however, the properties of a thing are not the result of its relations to other things, but only manifest themselves in such relations, the coat seems to be endowed with its equivalent form, its property of being directly exchangeable, just as much by Nature as it is endowed with the property of being heavy, or the capacity to keep us warm. Hence the enigmatical character of the equivalent form which escapes the notice of the bourgeois political economist, until this form, completely developed, confronts him in the shape of money. He then seeks to explain away the mystical character of gold and silver, by substituting for them less dazzling commodities, and by reciting, with ever renewed satisfaction, the catalogue of all possible commodities which at one time or another have played the part of equivalent. He has not the least suspicion that the most simple expression of value, such as 20 yds. of linen = 1 coat, already propounds the riddle of the equivalent form for our solution.

The body of the commodity that serves as the equivalent, figures as the materialization of human labour in the abstract and is at the same time the product of some specifically useful concrete labour. This concrete labour becomes, therefore, the medium for expressing abstract human labour. If on the one hand the coat ranks as nothing but the embodiment of abstract human labour, so, on the other hand, the tailoring which is actually embodied in it, counts as nothing but the form under which that abstract labour is realised. In the expression of value of the linen, the utility of the tailoring consists, not in making clothes, but in making an object, which we at once recognise to be Value, and therefore to be a congelation of labour, but of labour indistinguishable from that realised in the value of the linen. In order to act as such a mirror of value, the labour of tailoring must reflect nothing besides its own abstract quality of being human labour generally.

In tailoring, as well as in weaving, human labour-power is expended. Both, therefore, possess the general property of being human labour, and may, therefore, in certain cases, such as in the production of value, have to be considered under this aspect alone. There is nothing mysterious in this. But in the expression of value there is a complete turn of the tables. For instance, how is the fact to be expressed that weaving creates the value of the linen, not by virtue of being weaving, as such, but by reason of its general property of being human labour? Simply by opposing to weaving that other particular form of concrete labour (in this instance tailoring), which produces the equivalent of the product of weaving. Just as the coat in its bodily form became a direct expression of value, so now does tailoring, a concrete form of labour, appear as the direct and palpable embodiment of human labour generally.

Hence, the second peculiarity of the equivalent form is, that concrete labour becomes the form under which its opposite, abstract human labour, manifests itself.

But because this concrete labour, tailoring in our case, ranks as, and is directly identified with, undifferentiated human labour, it also ranks as identical with any other sort of labor, and therefore with that embodied in linen. Consequently, although, like all other commodity-producing labour, it is the labour of private individuals, yet, at the same time, it ranks as labour directly social in its character. This is the reason why it results in a product directly exchangeable with other commodities. We have then a third peculiarity of the Equivalent form, namely, that the labour of private individuals takes the form of its opposite, labour directly social in its form.

The two latter peculiarities of the Equivalent form will become more intelligible if we go back to the great thinker who was the first to analyse so

271

many forms, whether of thought, society, or nature, and amongst them also the form of value. I mean Aristotle.

In the first place, he clearly enunciates that the money form of commodities is only the further development of the simple form of value—*i.e.,* of the expression of the value of one commodity in some other commodity taken at random; for he says

5 beds = 1 house (κλίναι πέντε ἀντὶ οἰκίας) is not to be distinguished from 5 beds = so much money. (κλίναι πέντε ἀντὶ . . . ὅσου ἁι πέντε κλίναι)

He further sees that the value relation which gives rise to this expression makes it necessary that the house should qualitatively be made the equal of the bed, and that, without such an equalization, these two clearly different things could not be compared with each other as commensurable quantities. "Exchange," he says, "cannot take place without equality, and equality not without commensurability" (οὔτ' ἰσότης μὴ οὔσης συμμετρίας). Here, however, he comes to a stop, and gives up the further analysis of the form of value. "It is, however, in reality, impossible (τῇ μὲν οὖν ἀληθείᾳ ἀδύνατον), that such unlike things can be commensurable"—*i.e.,* qualitatively equal. Such an equalisation can only be something foreign to their real nature, consequently only "a make-shift for practical purposes."

Aristotle therefore, himself, tells us, what barred the way to his further analysis; it was the absence of any concept of value. What is that equal something, that common substance, which admits of the value of the beds being expressed by a house? Such a thing, in truth, cannot exist, says Aristotle. And why not? Compared with the beds, the house does represent something equal to them, in so far as it represents what is really equal, both in the beds and the house. And that is—human labour.

There was, however, an important fact which prevented Aristotle from seeing that, to attribute value to commodities, is merely a mode of expressing all labour as equal human labour, and consequently as labour of equal quality. Greek society was founded upon slavery, and had, therefore, for its natural basis, the inequality of men and of their labour powers. The secret of the expression of value, namely, that all kinds of labour are equal and equivalent, because, and so far as they are human labour in general, cannot be deciphered, until the notion of human equality has already acquired the fixity of a popular prejudice. This, however, is possible only in a society in which the great mass of the produce of labour takes the form of commodities, in which, consequently, the dominant relation between man and man, is that of owners of commodities. The brilliancy of Aristotle's genius is shown by this alone, that he discovered, in the expression of the value of commodities, a relation of equality. The peculiar conditions of the society in which he lived, alone prevented him from discovering what, "in truth," was at the bottom of this equality.

4. The Elementary Form of Value Considered as a Whole. The elementary form of value of a commodity is contained in the equation, expressing its value relation to another commodity of a different kind, or in its exchange relation to the same. The value of commodity A is qualitatively expressed by the fact that commodity B is directly exchangeable with it. Its value is quantitively expressed by the fact, that a definite quantity of B is exchangeable with a definite quantity of A. In other words, the value of a commodity obtains independent and definite expression, by taking the form of exchange value. When, at the beginning of this chapter, we said, in common parlance, that a commodity is both a use-value and an exchange value, we were, accurately speaking, wrong. A commodity is a use-value or object of utility, and a value. It manifests itself as this two-fold thing, that it is, as soon as its value assumes an independent form—viz., the form exchange value. It never assumes this form when isolated, but only when placed in a value or exchange relation with another commodity of a different kind. When once we know this, such a mode of expression does no harm; it simply serves as an abbreviation.

Our analysis has shown, that the form or expression of the value of a commodity originates in the nature of value, and not that value and its magnitude originate in the mode of their expression as exchange value. . . .

A close scrutiny of the expression of the value of A in terms of B, contained in the equation expressing the value relation of A to B, has shown us that, within that relation, the bodily form of A figures only as a use-value, the bodily form of B only as the form or aspect of value. The opposition or contrast existing internally in each commodity between use-value and value, is, therefore, made evident externally by two commodities being placed in such relation to each other, that the commodity whose value it is sought to express, figures directly as a mere use-value, while the commodity in which that value is to be expressed, figures directly as mere exchange value. Hence the elementary form of value of a commodity is the elementary form in which the contrast contained in that commodity, between use-value and value, becomes apparent.

Every product of labour is, in all states of society, a use-value; but it is only at a definite historical epoch in a society's development that such product becomes a commodity, viz., at the epoch when the labour spent on the production of a useful article becomes expressed as one of the objective qualities of that article, *i.e.,* as its value. It therefore follows that the elementary value-form is also the primitive form under which a product of labour appears historically as a commodity, and that the gradual transformation of such products into commodities, proceeds *pari passu* with the development of the value-form.

We perceive, at first sight, the deficiencies of the elementary form of value: it is a mere germ, which must undergo a series of metamorphoses before it can ripen into the Price-form. . . .

273

Section 4.—The Fetishism of Commodities and the Secret Thereof.

A commodity appears, at first sight, a very trivial thing, and easily understood. Its analysis shows that it is, in reality, a very queer thing, abounding in metaphysical subtleties and theological niceties. So far as it is a value in use, there is nothing mysterious about it, whether we consider it from the point of view that by its properties it is capable of satisfying human wants, or from the point that those properties are the product of human labour. It is as clear as noonday, that man, by his industry, changes the forms of the materials furnished by Nature, in such a way as to make them useful to him. The form of wood, for instance, is altered, by making a table out of it. Yet, for all that, the table continues to be that common, every-day thing, wood. But, so soon as it steps forth as a commodity, it is changed into something transcendent. It not only stands with its feet on the ground, but, in relation to all other commodities, it stands on its head, and evolves out of its wooden brain grotesque ideas, far more wonderful than "table-turning" ever was.

The mystical character of commodities does not originate, therefore, in their use-value. Just as little does it proceed from the nature of the determining factors of value. For, in the first place, however varied the useful kinds of labour, or productive activities, may be, it is a physiological fact, that they are functions of the human organism, and that each such function, whatever may be its nature or form, is essentially the expenditure of human brain, nerves, muscles, &c. Secondly, with regard to that which forms the ground-work for the quantitative determination of value, namely, the duration of that expenditure, or the quantity of labour, it is quite clear that there is a palpable difference between its quantity and quality. In all states of society, the labour-time that it costs to produce the means of subsistence must necessarily be an object of interest to mankind, though not of equal interest in different stages of development. And lastly, from the moment that men in any way work for one another, their labour assumes a social form.

Whence, then, arises the enigmatical character of the product of labour, so soon as it assumes the form of commodities? Clearly from this form itself. The equality of all sorts of human labour is expressed objectively by their products all being equally values; the measure of the expenditure of labour-power by the duration of that expenditure, takes the form of the quantity of value of the products of labour; and finally, the mutual relations of the producers, within which the social character of their labour affirms itself, take the form of a social relation between the products.

A commodity is therefore a mysterious thing, simply because in it the social character of men's labour appears to them as an objective character stamped upon the product of that labour; because the relation of the producers to the sum total of their own labour is presented to them as a social relation, existing not between themselves, but between the products of their labour. This is the reason why the products of labour become commodities, social things whose qualities are at the same time perceptible and imperceptible by the senses. In the same way the light from an object is perceived by us not as the subjective excitation of our optic nerve, but as the objective form of something outside the eye itself. But, in the act of seeing, there is at all events, an actual passage of light from one thing to another, from the external object to the eye. There is a physical relation between physical things. But it is different with commodities. There, the existence of the things *qua* commodities, and the value relation between the products of labour which stamps them as commodities, have absolutely no connexion with their physical properties and with the material relations arising therefrom. There it is a definite social relation between men, that assumes, in their eyes, the fantastic form of a relation between things. In order, therefore, to find an analogy, we must have recourse to the mist-enveloped regions of the religious world. In that world the productions of the human brain appear as independent beings endowed with life, and entering into relation both with one another and the human race. So it is in the world of commodities with the products of men's hands. This I call the Fetishism which attaches itself to the products of labour, so soon as they are produced as commodities, and which is therefore inseparable from the production of commodities.

This Fetishism of commodities has its origin, as the foregoing analysis has already shown, in the peculiar social character of the labour that produces them.

As a general rule, articles of utility become commodities, only because they are products of the labour of private individuals or groups of individuals who carry on their work independently of each other. The sum total of the labour of all these private individuals forms the aggregate labour of society. Since the producers do not come into social contact with each other until they exchange their products, the specific social character of each producer's labour does not show itself except in the act of exchange. In other words, the labour of the individual asserts itself as a part of the labour of society, only by means of the relations which the act of exchange establishes directly between the products, and indirectly, through them, between the producers. To the latter, therefore, the relations connecting the labour of one individual with that of the rest appear, not as direct social relations between individuals at work, but as what they really are, material relations between persons and social relations between things. It is only by being exchanged that the products of labour acquire, as values, one uniform social status, distinct from their varied forms of existence as objects of utility. This division of a product into a useful thing and a value becomes practically important, only when exchange has acquired such an extension that useful articles are produced for the purpose of being exchanged, and their character as values has therefore to be taken into account, beforehand, during production. From this moment the labour of the individual producer acquires socially a two-fold character. On the one hand, it must, as a definite useful kind of labour, satisfy a definite social want, and thus hold its place as part and parcel of the collective labour of all, as a branch of a social division of labour that has sprung up spontaneously. On the other hand, it can satisfy the manifold wants of the individual producer himself, only in so far as the mutual exchangeability of all kinds of useful private labour is an established social fact, and therefore the private useful labour of each producer ranks on an equality with that of all others. The equalisation of the most different kinds of labour can be the result only of an abstraction from their inequalities, or of reducing them to their common denominator, viz., expenditure of human labour power or human labour in the abstract. The two-fold social character of the labour of the individual appears to him, when reflected in his brain, only under those forms which are impressed upon that labour in everyday practice by the exchange of products. In this way, the character that his own labour possesses of being socially useful takes the form of the condition, that the product must be not only useful, but useful for others, and the social character that his particular labour has of being the equal of all other particular kinds of labour, takes the form that all the physically different articles that are the products of labour, have one common quality, viz, that of having value.

Hence, when we bring the products of our labour into relation with each other as values, it is not because we see in these articles the material receptacles of homogeneous human labour. Quite the contrary: whenever, by an exchange, we equate as values our different products, by that very act, we also equate, as human labour, the different kinds of labour expended upon them. We are not aware of this, nevertheless we do it. Value, therefore, does not stalk about with a label describing what it is. It is value, rather, that converts every product into a social hieroglyphic. Later on, we try to decipher the hieroglyphic, to get behind the secret of our own social products; for to stamp an object of utility as a value, is just as much a social product as language. The recent scientific discovery, that the products of labour, so far as they are values, are but material expressions of the human labour spent in their production, marks, indeed, an epoch in the history of the development of the human race, but, by no means, dissipates the mist through which the social character of labour appears to us to be an objective character of the products themselves. The fact, that in the particular form of production with which we are dealing, viz., the production of commodities, the specific social character of private labour carried on independently, consists in the equality of every kind of that labour, by virtue of its being human labour, which character, therefore, assumes in the product the form of value—this fact appears to the producers, notwithstanding the discovery above referred to, to be just as real and final, as the fact, that, after the discovery by science of the component gases of air, the atmosphere itself remained unaltered.

What, first of all, practically concerns producers when they make an exchange, is the question, how much of some other product they get for their own? in what proportions the products are exchangeable? When these proportions have, by custom, attained a certain stability, they appear to result from the nature of the products, so that, for instance, one ton of iron and two ounces of gold appear as naturally to be of equal value as a pound of gold and a pound of iron in spite of their different physical and chemical qualities appear to be of equal weight. The character of having value, when once impressed upon products, obtains fixity only by reason of their acting and reacting upon each other as quantities of value. These quantities vary continually, independently of the will, foresight and action of the producers. To them, their own social action takes the form of the action of objects, which rule the producers instead of being ruled by them. It requires a fully developed production of commodities before, from accumulated experience alone, the scientific conviction springs up, that all the different kinds of private labour, which are carried on independently of each other, and yet as spontaneously developed branches of the social division of labour, are continually being reduced to the quantitative proportions in which society requires them. And why? Because, in the midst of all the accidental and ever fluctuating exchange-relations between the products, the labour-time socially necessary for their production forcibly asserts itself like an over-riding law of Nature. The law of gravity thus asserts itself when a house falls about our ears. The determination of the magnitude of value by labour-time is therefore a secret, hidden under the apparent fluctuations in the relative values of commodities. Its discovery, while removing all appearance of mere accidentality from the determination of the magnitude of the values of products, yet in no way alters the mode in which that determination takes place.

277

Man's reflections on the forms of social life, and consequently, also, his scientific analysis of those forms, take a course directly opposite to that of their actual historical development. He begins, post festum, with the results of the process of development ready to hand before him. The characters that stamp products as commodities, and whose establishment is a necessary preliminary to the circulation of commodities, have already acquired the stability of natural, self-understood forms of social life, before man seeks to decipher, not their historical character, for in his eyes they are immutable, but their meaning. Consequently it was the analysis of the prices of commodities that alone led to the determination of the magnitude of value, and it was the common expression of all commodities in money that alone led to the establishment of their characters as values. It is, however, just this ultimate money-form of the world of commodities that actually conceals, instead of disclosing, the social character of private labour, and the social relations between the individual producers. When I state that coats or boots stand in a relation to linen, because it is the universal incarnation of abstract human labour, the absurdity of the statement is self-evident. Nevertheless, when the producers of coats and boots compare those articles with linen, or, what is the same thing, with gold or silver, as the universal equivalent, they express the relation between their own private labour and the collective labour of society in the same absurd form.

The categories of bourgeois economy consist of such like forms. They are forms of thought expressing with social validity the conditions and relations of a definite, historically determined mode of production, viz., the production of commodities. The whole mystery of commodities, all the magic and necromancy that surrounds the products of labour as long as they take the form of commodities, vanishes therefore, so soon as we come to other forms of production.

Since Robinson Crusoe's experiences are a favorite theme with political economists, let us take a look at him on his island. Moderate though he be, yet some few wants he has to satisfy, and must therefore do a little useful work of various sorts, such as making tools and furniture, taming goats, fishing and hunting. Of his prayers and the like we take no account, since they are a source of pleasure to him, and he looks upon them as so much recreation. In spite of the variety of his work, he knows that his labour, whatever its form, is but the activity of one and the same Robinson, and consequently, that it consists of nothing but different modes of human labour. Necessity itself compels him to apportion his time accurately between his different kinds of work. Whether one kind occupies a greater space in his general activity than another, depends on the difficulties, greater or less as the case may be, to be overcome in attaining the useful effect aimed at. This our friend Robinson soon learns by experience, and having rescued a watch, ledger, and pen and ink from the wreck, commences, like a true-born Briton, to keep a set of books. His stock-book contains a list of the objects of utility that belong to him, of the operations necessary for their production; and lastly, of the labour time that definite quantities of these objects have, on an average, cost him. All the relations between Robinson and the objects that form this wealth of his own creation, are here so simple and clear as to be intelligible without exertion, even to Mr. Sedley Taylor. And yet those relations contain all that is essential to the determination of value.

Let us now transport ourselves from Robinson's island bathed in light to the European middle ages shrouded in darkness. Here, instead of the independent man, we find everyone dependent, serfs and lords, vassals and suzerains, laymen and clergy. Personal dependence here characterises the social relations of production just as much as it does the other spheres of life organised on the basis of that production. But for the very reason that personal dependence forms the groundwork of society, there is no necessity for labour and its products to assume a fantastic form different from their reality. They take the shape, in the transactions of society, of services in kind and payments in kind. Here the particular and natural form of labour, and not, as in a society based on production of commodities, its general abstract form is the immediate social form of labour. Compulsory labour is just as properly measured by time, as commodity-producing labour; but every serf knows that what he expends in the service of his lord, is a definite quantity of his own personal labour-power. The tithe to be rendered to the priest is more matter of fact than his blessing. No matter, then, what we may think of the parts played by the different classes of people themselves in this society, the social relations between individuals in the performance of their labour, appear at all events as their own mutual personal relations, and are not disguised under the shape of social relations between the products of labour.

For an example of labour in common or directly associated labour, we have no occasion to go back to that spontaneously developed form which we find on the threshold of the history of all civilised races. We have one close at hand in the patriarchal industries of a peasant family, that produces corn, cattle, yarn, linen, and clothing for home use. These different articles are, as regards the family, so many products of its labour, but as between themselves, they are not commodities. The different kinds of labour, such as tillage, cattle tending, spinning, weaving and making clothes, which result in the various products, are in themselves, and such as they are, direct social functions, because functions of the family, which, just as much as a society based on the production of commodities, possesses a spontaneously developed system of division of labour. The distribution of the work within the family, and the regulation of the labour-time of the several members, depend as well upon differences of age and sex as upon natural conditions varying with the seasons. The labour-power of each individual, by its very nature, operates in this case merely as a definite portion of the whole labour-power of the family, and therefore, the measure of the expenditure of individual labour-power by its duration, appears here by its very nature as a social character of their labour.

Let us now picture to ourselves, by way of change, a community of free individuals, carrying on their work with the means of production in common, in which the labour-power of all the different individuals is consciously applied as the combined labour-power of the community. All the characteristics of Robinson's labour are here repeated, but with this difference, that they are social, instead of individual. Everything produced by him was exclusively the result of his own personal labour, and therefore simply an object of use for himself. The total product of our community is a social product. One portion serves as fresh means of production and remains social. But another portion is consumed by the members as means of subsistence. A distribution of this portion amongst them is consequently necessary. The mode of this distribution will vary with the productive organisation of the community, and the degree of historical development attained by the producers. We will assume, but merely for the sake of a parallel with the production of commodities, that the share of each individual producer in the means of subsistence is determined by his labour-time. Labour-time would, in that case, play a double part. Its apportionment in accordance with a definite social plan maintains the proper proportion between the different kinds of work to be done and the various wants of the community. On the other hand, it also serves as a measure of the portion of the common labour borne by each individual, and of his share in the part of the total product destined for individual consumption. The social relations of the individual producers, with regard both to their labour and to its products, are in this case perfectly simple and intelligible, and that with regard not only to production but also to distribution.

The religious world is but the reflex of the real world. And for a society based upon the production of commodities, in which the producers in general enter into social relations with one another by treating their products as commodities and values, whereby they reduce their individual private labour to the standard of homogeneous human labour—for such a society, Christianity with its *cultus* of abstract man, more especially in its bourgeois developments, Protestantism, Deism, &c., is the most fitting form of religion. In the ancient Asiatic and other ancient modes of production, we find that the conversion of products into commodities, and therefore the conversion of men into producers of commodities, holds a subordinate place, which, however, increases in importance as the primitive communities approach nearer and nearer to their dissolution. Trading nations, properly so called, exist in the ancient world only in its interstices, like the gods of Epicurus in the Intermundia, or like Jews in the pores of Polish society. Those ancient social organisms of production are, as compared with bourgeois society, extremely simple and transparent. But they are founded either on the immature development of man individually, who has not yet severed the umbilical cord that unites him with his fellowmen in a primitive tribal community, or upon direct relations of subjection. They can arise and exist only when the development of the productive power of labour has not risen beyond a low stage, and when, therefore, the social relations within the sphere of material life, between man and man, and between man and Nature, are correspondingly narrow. This narrowness is reflected in the ancient worship of Nature, and in the other elements of the popular religions. The religious reflex of the real world can, in any case, only then finally vanish, when the practical relations of everyday life offer to man none but perfectly intelligible and reasonable relations with regard to his fellowmen and to Nature.

The life-process of society, which is based on the process of material production, does not strip off its mystical veil until it is treated as production by freely associated men, and is consciously regulated by them in accordance with a settled plan. This, however, demands for society a certain material groundwork or set of conditions of existence which in their turn are the spontaneous product of a long and painful process of development.

Political economy has indeed analysed, however incompletely, value and its magnitude, and has discovered what lies beneath these forms. But it has never once asked the question why labour is represented by the value of its product and labour time by the magnitude of that value.[1] These formulae, which bear it stamped upon them in unmisteakable letters that they belong to a state of society, in which the process of production has the mastery over man, instead of being controlled by him, such formulae appear to the bourgeois intellect to be as much a self-evident necessity imposed by Nature as productive labour itself. Hence forms of social production that preceded the bourgeois form, are treated by the bourgeoisie in much the same way as the Fathers of the Church treated pre-Christian religions.[2]

To what extent some economists are misled by the Fetishism inherent in commodities, or by the objective appearance of the social characteristics of labour, is shown, amongst other ways, by the dull and tedious quarrel over the part played by Nature in the formation of exchange value. Since exchange value is a definite social manner of expressing the amount of labour bestowed upon an object, Nature has no more to do with it, than it has in fixing the course of exchange.

The mode of production in which the product takes the form of a commodity, or is produced directly for exchange, is the most general and most embryonic form of bourgeois production. It therefore makes its appearance at an early date in history, though not in the same predominating and characteristic manner as now-a-days. Hence its Fetish character is comparatively easy to be seen through. But when we come to more concrete forms, even this appearance of simplicity vanishes. Whence arose the illusions of the monetary system? To it gold and silver, when serving as money, did not represent a social relation between producers, but were natural objects with strange social properties. And modern economy, which looks down with such disdain on the monetary system, does not its superstition come out as clear as noon-day, whenever it treats of capital? How long is it since economy discarded the physiocratic illusion, that rents grow out of the soil and not out of society?

But not to anticipate, we will content ourselves with yet another example relating to the commodity-form. Could commodities themselves speak, they would say: Our use-value may be a thing that interests men. It is no part of us as objects. What, however, does belong to us as objects, is our value. Our natural intercourse as commodities proves it. In the eyes of each other we are nothing but exchange values. Now listen how those commodities speak through the mouth of the economist. "Value"—(*i.e.*, exchange-value) "is a property of things, riches"—(*i.e.*, use-value) "of man. Value, in this sense, necessarily implies exchanges, riches do not." "Riches" (use-value) "are the attribute of men, value is the attribute of commodities. A man or a community is rich, a pearl or a diamond is valuable. . . A pearl or a diamond is valuable" as a pearl or diamond. So far no chemist has ever discovered exchange value either in a pearl or a diamond. The economical discoverers of this chemical element, who by-the-by lay special claim to critical acumen, find however that the use-value of objects belongs to them independently of their material properties, while their value, on the other hand, forms a part of them as objects. What confirms them in this view, is the peculiar circumstances that the use-value of objects is realised without exchange, by means of a direct relation between the objects and man, while, on the other hand, their value is realised only by exchange, that is, by means of a social process. Who fails here to call to mind our good friend, Dogberry, who informs neighbour Seacoal, that, "To be a well-favoured man is the gift of fortune; but reading and writing comes by Nature."

PART II.

THE TRANSFORMATION OF MONEY INTO CAPITAL.

CHAPTER IV.

THE GENERAL FORMULA FOR CAPITAL.

The circulation of commodities is the starting point of capital. The production of commodities, their circulation, and that more developed form of their circulation called commerce, these form the historical groundwork from which it rises. The modern history of capital dates from the creation in the 16th century of a world-embracing commerce and a world-embracing market.

If we abstract from the material substance of the circulation of commodities, that is, from the exchange of the various use-values, and consider only the economic forms produced by this process of circulation, we find its final result to be money: this final product of the circulation of commodities is the first form in which capital appears.

As a matter of history, capital, as opposed to landed property, invariably takes the form at first of money; it appears as moneyed wealth, as the capital of the merchant and of the usurer. But we have no need to refer to the origin of capital in order to discover that the first form of appearance of capital is money. We can see it daily under our very eyes. All new capital, to commence with, comes on the stage, that is, on the market, whether of commodities, labour, or money, even in our days, in the shape of money that by a definite process has to be transformed into capital.

The first distinction we notice between money that is money only, and money that is capital, is nothing more than a difference in their form of circulation.

The simplest form of the circulation of commodities is C—M—C, the transformation of commodities into money, and the change of the money back again into commodities; or selling in order to buy. But alongside of this form we find another specifically different form: M—C—M, the transformation of money into commodities, and the change of commodities back again into money; or buying in order to sell. Money that circulates in the latter manner is thereby transformed into, becomes capital, and is already potentially capital.

Now let us examine the circuit M—C—M a little closer. It consists, like the other, of two antithetical phases. In the first phase, M—C, or the purchase, the money is changed into a commodity. In the second phase, C—M, or the sale, the commodity is changed back again into money. The combination of these two phases constitutes the single movement whereby money is exchanged for a commodity, and the same commodity is again exchanged for money; whereby a commodity is bought in order to be sold, or, neglecting the distinction in form between buying and selling, whereby a commodity is bought with money, and then money is bought with a commodity. The result, in which the phases of the process vanish, is the exchange of money for money, M—M. If I purchase 2000 lbs. of cotton for £100, and resell the 2000 lbs. of cotton for £110, I have, in fact, exchanged £100 for £110, money for money.

Now it is evident that the circuit M—C—M would be absurd and without meaning if the intention were to exchange by this means two equal sums of money, £100 for £100. The miser's plan would be far simpler and surer; he sticks to his £100 instead of exposing it to the dangers of circulation. And yet, whether the merchant who has paid £100 for his cotton sells it for £110, or lets it go for £100, or even £50, his money has, at all events, gone through a characteristic and original movement, quite different in kind from that which it goes through in the hands of the peasant who sells corn, and with the money thus set free buys clothes. We have therefore to examine first the distinguishing characteristics of the forms of the circuits M—C—M and C—M—C, and in doing this the real difference that underlies the mere difference of form will reveal itself. . . .

The circuit C—M—C comes completely to an end, so soon as the money brought in by the sale of one commodity is abstracted again by the purchase of another.

If, nevertheless, there follows a reflux of money to its starting point, this can only happen through a renewal or repetition of the operation. If I sell a quarter of corn for £3, and with this £3 buy clothes, the money, so far as I am concerned, is spent and done with. It belongs to the clothes merchant. If I now sell a second quarter of corn, money indeed flows back to me, not however as a sequel to the first transaction, but in consequence of its repetition. The money again leaves me, so soon as I complete this second transaction by a fresh purchase. Therefore, in the circuit C—M—C, the expenditure of money has nothing to do with its reflux. On the other hand, in M—C—M, the reflux of the money is conditioned by the very mode of its expenditure. Without this reflux, the operation fails, or the process is interrupted and incomplete, owing to the absence of its complementary and final phase, the sale.

283

The circuit C—M—C starts with one commodity, and finishes with another, which falls out of circulation and into consumption. Consumption, the satisfaction of wants, in one word, use-value, is its end and aim. The circuit M—C—M, on the contrary, commences with money and ends with money. Its leading motive, and the goal that attracts it, is therefore mere exchange value.

In the simple circulation of commodities, the two extremes of the circuit have the same economic form. They are both commodities, and commodities of equal value. But they are also use-values differing in their qualities, as, for example, corn and clothes. The exchange of products, of the different materials in which the labour of society is embodied, forms here the basis of the movement. It is otherwise in the circulation M—C—M, which at first sight appears purposeless, because tautological. Both extremes have the same economic form. They are both money, and therefore are not qualitatively different use-values; for money is but the converted form of commodities, in which their particular use-values vanish. To exchange £100 for cotton, and then this same cotton again for £100, is merely a roundabout way of exchanging money for money, the same for the same, and appears to be an operation just as purposeless as it is absurd. One sum of money is distinguishable from another only by its amount. The character and tendency of the process M—C—M, is therefore not due to any qualitative difference between its extremes, both being money, but solely to their quantitative difference. More money is withdrawn from circulation at the finish than was thrown into it at the start. The cotton that was bought for £100 is perhaps resold for £100+£10 or £110. The exact form of this process is therefore M—C—M′, where M′=M+△M=the original sum advanced, plus an increment. This increment or excess over the original value I call "surplus-value." The value originally advanced, therefore, not only remains intact while in circulation, but adds to itself a surplus-value or expands itself. It is this movement that converts it into capital.

Of course it is also possible, that in C—M—C, the two extremes C—C, say corn and clothes, may represent different quantities of value. The farmer may sell his corn above its value, or may buy the clothes at less than their value. He may, on the other hand, "be done" by the clothes merchant. Yet, in the form of circulation now under consideration, such differences in value are purely accidental. The fact that the corn and the clothes are equivalents, does not deprive the process of all meaning, as it does in M—C—M. The equivalence of their values is rather a necessary condition to its normal course.

The repetition or renewal of the act of selling in order to buy, is kept within bounds by the very object it aims at, namely, consumption or the satisfaction of definite wants, an aim that lies altogether outside the sphere of circulation. But when we buy in order to sell, we, on the contrary, begin and end with the same thing, money, exchange-value; and thereby the movement becomes interminable. No doubt, M becomes M+△M, £100 become £110. But when viewed in their qualitative aspect alone, £110 are the same as £100, namely money; and considered quantitatively, £110 is, like £100, a sum of definite and limited value. If now, the £110 be spent as money, they cease to play their part. They are no longer capital. Withdrawn from circulation, they become petrified into a hoard, and though they remained in that state till doomsday, not a single farthing would accrue to them. If, then, the expansion of value is once aimed at, there is just the same inducement to augment the value of the £110 as that of the £100; for both are but limited expressions for exchange-value, and therefore both have the same vocation to approach, by quantitative increase, as near as possible to absolute wealth. Momentarily, indeed, the value originally advanced, the £100 is distinguishable from the surplus value of £10 that is annexed to it during circulation; but the distinction vanishes immediately. At the end of the process, we do not receive with one hand the original £100, and with the other, the surplus-value of £10. We simply get a value of £110, which is in exactly the same condition and fitness for commencing the expanding process, as the original £100 was. Money ends the movement only to begin it again. Therefore, the final result of every separate circuit, in which a purchase and consequent sale are completed, forms of itself the starting point of a new circuit. The simple circulation of commodities—selling in order to buy—is a means of carrying out a purpose unconnected with circulation, namely, the appropriation of use-values, the satisfaction of wants. The circulation of money as capital is, on the contrary, an end in itself, for the expansion of value takes place only within this constantly renewed movement. The circulation of capital has therefore no limits.[3] Thus the conscious representative of this movement, the possessor of money becomes a capitalist. His person, or rather his pocket, is the point from which the money starts and to which it returns. The expansion of value, which is the objective basis or main-spring of the circulation M—C—M, becomes his subjective aim, and it is only in so far as the appropriation of ever more and more wealth in the abstract becomes the sole motive of his operations, that he functions as a capitalist, that is, as capital personified and endowed with consciousness and a will. Use-values must therefore never be looked upon as the real aim of the capitalist; neither must the profit on any single transaction. The restless never-ending process of profit-making alone is what he aims at. This boundless greed after riches, this passionate chase after exchange-value, is common to the capitalist and the miser; but while the miser is merely a capitalist gone mad, the capitalist is a rational miser. The never-ending augmentation of exchange-value, which the miser strives after, by seeking to save his money from circulation, is attained by the more acute capitalist, by constantly throwing it afresh into circulation.

The independent form, *i.e.*, the money-form, which the value of commodities assumes in the case of simple circulation, serves only one purpose, namely, their exchange, and vanishes in the final result of the movement. On the other hand, in the circulation M—C—M, both the money and the commodity represent only different modes of existence of value itself, the money its general mode, and the commodity its particular, or, so to say, disguised mode. It is constantly changing from one form to the other without thereby becoming lost, and thus assumes an automatically active character. If now we take in turn each of the two different forms which self-expanding value successively assumes in the course of its life, we then arrive at these two propositions: Capital is money: Capital is commodities. In truth, however, value is here the active factor in a process, in which, while constantly assuming the form in turn of money and commodities, it at the same time changes in magnitude, differentiates itself by throwing off surplus-value from itself; the original value, in other words, expands spontaneously. For the movement, in the course of which it adds surplus value, is its own movement, its expansion, therefore, is automatic expansion. Because it is value, it has acquired the occult quality of being able to add value to itself. It brings forth living offspring, or, at the least, lays golden eggs.

Value, therefore, being the active factor in such a process, and assuming at one time the form of money, at another that of commodities, but through all these changes preserving itself and expanding, it requires some independent form, by means of which its identity may at any time be established. And this form it possesses only in the shape of money. It is under the form of money that value begins and ends, and begins again, every act of its own spontaneous generation. It began by being £100, it is now £110, and so on. But the money itself is only one of the two forms of value. Unless it takes the form of some commodity, it does not become capital. There is here no antagonism, as in the case of hoarding, between the money and commodities. The capitalist knows that all commodities, however scurvy they may look, or however badly they may smell, are in faith and in truth money, inwardly circumcised Jews, and what is more, a wonderful means whereby out of money to make more money.

In simple circulation, C—M—C, the value of commodities attained at the most a form independent of their use-values, *i.e.*, the form of money; but that same value now in the circulation M—C—M, or the circulation of capital, suddenly presents itself as an independent substance, endowed with a motion of its own, passing through a life-process of its own, in which money and commodities are mere forms which it assumes and casts off in turn. Nay, more: instead of simply representing the relations of commodities, it enters now, so to say, into private relations with itself. It differentiates itself as original value from itself as surplus-value; as the father differentiates himself from himself quâ the son, yet both are one and of one age: for only by the surplus value of £10 does the £100 originally advanced become capital, and so soon as this takes place, so soon as the son, and by the son, the father, is begotten, so soon does their difference vanish, and they again become one, £110.

Value therefore now becomes value in process, money in process, and, as such, capital. It comes out of circulation, enters into it again, preserves and multiplies itself within its circuit, comes back out of it with expanded bulk, and begins the same round ever afresh. M—M´, money which begets money, such is the description of Capital from the mouths of its first interpreters, the Mercantilists.

Buying in order to sell, or, more accurately, buying in order to sell dearer, M—C—M´, appears certainly to be a form peculiar to one kind of capital alone, namely, merchants' capital. But industrial capital too is money, that is changed into commodities, and by the sale of these commodities, is reconverted into more money. The events that take place outside the sphere of circulation, in the interval between the buying and selling, do not affect the form of this movement. Lastly, in the case of interest-bearing capital, the circulation M—C—M´ appears abridged. We have its result without the intermediate stage, in the form M—M´, "en style lapidaire" so to say, money that is worth more money, value that is greater than itself.

M—C—M´ is therefore in reality the general formula of capital as it appears prima facie within the sphere of circulation. . . .

CHAPTER VI.
THE BUYING AND SELLING OF LABOUR-POWER.

The change of value that occurs in the case of money intended to be converted into capital, cannot take place in the money itself, since in its function of means of purchase and of payment, it does no more than realise the price of the commodity it buys or pays for; and, as hard cash, it is value petrified, never varying. Just as little can it originate in the second act of circulation, the re-sale of the commodity, which does no more than transform the article from its bodily form back again into its money-form. The change must, therefore, take place in the commodity bought by the first act, M—C, but not in its value, for equivalents are exchanged, and the commodity is paid for at its full value. We are, therefore, forced to the conclusion that the change originates in the use-value, as such, of the commodity, *i.e.*, in its consumption. In order to be able to extract value from the consumption of a commodity, our friend, Moneybags, must be so lucky as to find, within the sphere of circulation, in the market, a commodity, whose use-value possesses the peculiar property of being a source of value, whose actual consumption, therefore, is itself an embodiment of labour, and, consequently, a creation of value. The possessor of money does find on the market such a special commodity in capacity for labour or labour-power.

By labour-power or capacity for labour is to be understood the aggregate

287

of those mental and physical capabilities existing in a human being, which he exercises whenever he produces a use-value of any description.

But in order that our owner of money may be able to find labour-power offered for sale as a commodity, various conditions must first be fulfilled. The exchange of commodities of itself implies no other relations of dependence than those which result from its own nature. On this assumption, labour-power can appear upon the market as a commodity only if, and so far as, its possessor, the individual whose labour-power it is, offers it for sale, or sells it, as a commodity. In order that he may be able to do this, he must have it at his disposal, must be the untrammelled owner of his capacity for labour, *i.e.*, of his person. He and the owner of money meet in the market, and deal with each other as on the basis of equal rights, with this difference alone, that one is buyer, the other seller; both, therefore, equal in the eyes of the law. The continuance of this relation demands that the owner of the labour-power should sell it only for a definite period, for if he were to sell it rump and stump, once for all, he would be selling himself, converting himself from a free man into a slave, from an owner of a commodity into a commodity. He must constantly look upon his labour-power as his own property, his own commodity, and this he can only do by placing it at the disposal of the buyer temporarily, for a definite period of time. By this means alone can he avoid renouncing his rights of ownership over it.[4]

The second essential condition to the owner of money finding labour-power in the market as a commodity is this—that the labourer instead of being in the position to sell commodities in which his labour is incorporated, must be obliged to offer for sale as a commodity that very labour-power, which exists only in his living self.

In order that a man may be able to sell commodities other than labour-power, he must of course have the means of production, as raw material, implements, &c. No boots can be made without leather. He requires also the means of subsistence. Nobody—not even "a musician of the future" can live upon future products, or upon use-values in an unfinished state; and ever since the first moment of his appearance on the world's stage, man always has been, and must still be a consumer, both before and while he is producing. In a society where all products assume the form of commodities, these commodities must be sold after they have been produced; it is only after their sale that they can serve in satisfying the requirements of their producer. The time necessary for their sale is superadded to that necessary for their production.

For the conversion of his money into capital, therefore, the owner of money must meet in the market with the free labourer, free in the double sense, that as a free man he can dispose of his labour-power as his own commodity, and that on the other hand he has no other commodity for sale, is short of everything necessary for the realisation of his labour-power.

The question why this free labourer confronts him in the market, has no interest for the owner of money, who regards the labour market as a branch of the general market for commodities. And for the present it interests us just as little. We cling to the fact theoretically, as he does practically. One thing, however, is clear—nature does not produce on the one side owners of money or commodities, and on the other men possessing nothing but their own labour-power. This relation has no natural basis, neither is its social basis one that is common to all historical periods. It is clearly the result of a past historical development, the product of many economical revolutions, of the extinction of a whole series of older forms of social production.

So, too, the economical categories, already discussed by us, bear the stamp of history. Definite historical conditions are necessary that a product may become a commodity. It must not be produced as the immediate means of subsistence of the producer himself. Had we gone further, and inquired under what circumstances all, or even the majority of products take the form of commodities, we should have found that this can only happen with production of a very specific kind, capitalist production. Such an inquiry, however, would have been foreign to the analysis of commodities. Production and circulation of commodities can take place, although the great mass of the objects produced are intended for the immediate requirements of their producers, are not turned into commodities, and consequently social production is not yet by a long way dominated in its length and breadth by exchange-value, the appearance of products as commodities presupposed such a development of the social division of labour, that the separation of use-value from exchange-value, a separation which first begins with barter, must already have been completed. But such a degree of development is common to many forms of society, which in other respects present the most varying historical features. On the other hand, if we consider money, its existence implies a definite stage in the exchange of commodities. The particular functions of money which it performs, either as the mere equivalent of commodities, or as means of circulation, or means of payment, as hoard or as universal money, point, according to the extent and relative preponderance of the one function or the other, to very different stages in the process of social production. Yet we know by experience that a circulation of commodities relatively primitive, suffices for the production of all these forms. Otherwise with capital. The historical conditions of its existence are by no means given with the mere circulation of money and commodities. It can spring into life, only when the owner of the means of production and subsistence meets in the market with the free labourer selling his labour-power. And this one historical condition comprises a world's history. Capital therefore, announces from its first appearance a new epoch in the process of social production.[5]

We must now examine more closely this peculiar commodity, labour-power. Like all others it has a value. How is that value determined?

The value of labour-power is determined, as in the case of every other

289

commodity, by the labour-time necessary for the production, and consequently also the reproduction, of this special article. So far as it has value, it represents no more than a definite quantity of the average labour of society incorporated in it. Labour-power exists only as a capacity, or power of the living individual. Its production consequently presupposes his existence. Given the individual, the production of labour-power consists in his reproduction of himself or his maintenance. For his maintenance he requires a given quantity of the means of subsistence. Therefore the labour-time requisite for the production of labour-power reduces itself to that necessary for the production of those means of subsistence; in other words, the value of labour-power is the value of the means of subsistence necessary for the maintenance of the labourer. Labour-power, however, becomes a reality only by its exercise; it sets itself in action only by working. But thereby a definite quantity of human muscle, nerve, brain, &c., is wasted, and these require to be restored. This increased expenditure demands a larger income. If the owner of labour-power works to-day, to-morrow he must again be able to repeat the same process in the same conditions as regards health and strength. His means of subsistence must therefore be sufficient to maintain him in his normal state as a labouring individual. His natural wants, such as food, clothing, fuel, and housing, vary according to the climatic and other physical conditions of his country. On the other hand, the number and extent of his so-called necessary wants, as also the modes of satisfying them, are themselves the product of historical development, and depend therefore to a great extent on the degree of civilisation of a country, more particularly on the conditions under which, and consequently on the habits and degree of comfort in which, the class of free labourers has been formed. In contradistinction therefore to the case of other commodities, there enters into the determination of the value of labour-power a historical and moral element. Nevertheless, in a given country, at a given period, the average quantity of the means of subsistence necessary for the labourer is practically known. . . .

We now know how the value paid by the purchaser to the possessor of this peculiar commodity, labour-power, is determined. The use-value which the former gets in exchange, manifests itself only in the actual usufruct, in the consumption of the labour-power. The money owner buys everything necessary for this purpose, such as raw material, in the market, and pays for it at its full value. The consumption of labour-power is at one and the same time the production of commodities and of surplus value. The consumption of labour-power is completed, as in the case of every other commodity, outside the limits of the market or of the sphere of circulation. Accompanied by Mr. Money-bags and by the possessor of labour-power, we therefore take leave for a time of this noisy sphere, where everything takes place on the surface and in view of all men, and follow them both into the hidden abode of production, on whose threshold there stares us in the face "No admittance except on business." Here we shall see, not only how capital produces, but how capital is produced. We shall at last force the secret of profit making.

This sphere that we are deserting, within whose boundaries the sale and purchase of labour-power goes on, is in fact a very Eden of the innate rights of man. There alone rule Freedom, Equality, Property and Bentham. Freedom, because both buyer and seller of a commodity, say of labour-power, are constrained only by their own free will. They contract as free agents, and the agreement they come to, is but the form in which they give legal expression to their common will. Equality, because each enters into relation with the other, as with a simple owner of commodities, and they exchange equivalent for equivalent. Property, because each disposes only of what is his own. And Bentham, because each looks only to himself. The only force that brings them together and puts them in relation with each other, is the selfishness, the gain and the private interests of each. Each looks to himself only, and no one troubles himself about the rest, and just because they do so, do they all, in accordance with the pre-established harmony of things, or under the auspices of an all-shrewd providence, work together to their mutual advantage, for the common weal and in the interest of all.

On leaving this sphere of simple circulation or of exchange of commodities, which furnishes the "Free-trader Vulgaris" with his views and ideas, and with the standard by which he judges a society based on capital and wages, we think we can perceive a change in the physiognomy of our dramatis personæ. He, who before was the money owner, now strides, in front as capitalist; the possessor of labour-power follows as his labourer. The one with an air of importance, smirking, intent on business; the other, timid and holding back, like one who is bringing his own hide to market and has nothing to expect but—a hiding.

291

Notes

1. It is one of the chief failings of classical economy that it has never succeeded, by means of its analysis of commodities, and, in particular, of their value, in discovering that form under which value becomes exchange-value. Even Adam Smith and Ricardo, the best representatives of the school, treat the form of value as a thing of no importance, as having no connexion with the inherent nature of commodities. The reason for this is not solely because their attention is entirely absorbed in the analysis of the magnitude of value. It lies deeper. The value form of the product of labour is not only the most abstract, but is also the most universal form, taken by the product in bourgeois production, and stamps that production as a particular species of social production, and thereby gives it its special historical character. If we then treat this mode of production as one eternally fixed by Nature for every state of society, we necessarily overlook that which is the differentia specifica of the value-form, and consequently of the commodity-form, and of its further developments, money-form, capital-form, &c. We consequently find that economists, who are thoroughly agreed as to labor time

being the measure of the magnitude of value, have the most strange and contradictory ideas of money, the perfected form of the general equivalent. . . .

2. "The economists have a singular manner of proceeding. There are for them only two kinds of institutions, those of art and those of nature. Feudal institutions are artificial institutions, those of the bourgeoisie are natural institutions. In this they resemble the theologians, who also establish two kinds of religion. Every religion but their own is an invention of men, while their own religion is an emanation of God. . . . Thus there has been history, but there is no longer any" (Karl Marx, *The Poverty of Philosophy*). . . .

—I seize this opportunity of shortly answering an objection taken by a German paper in America, to my work, *Critique of Political Economy* (1859). In the estimation of that paper, my view that each special mode of production and the social relations corresponding to it, in short, that the economic structure of society, is the real basis on which the juridical and political superstructure is raised, and to which definite social forms of thought correspond; that the mode of production determines the character of the social, political, and intellectual life generally, all this is very true for our own times, in which material interests preponderate, but not for the middle ages, in which Catholicism, nor for Athens and Rome, where politics, reigned supreme. In the first place it strikes one as an odd thing for any one to suppose that these well-worn phrases about the middle ages and the ancient world are unknown to anyone else. This much, however, is clear, that the middle ages could not live on Catholicism, nor the ancient world on politics. On the contrary, it is the mode in which they gained a livelihood that explains why here politics, and there Catholicism, played the chief part. For the rest, it requires but a slight acquaintance with the history of the Roman republic, for example, to be aware that its secret history is the history of its landed property. On the other hand, Don Quixote long ago paid the penalty for wrongly imagining that knight errantry was compatible with all economical forms of society.

3. Aristotle opposes Œconomic to Chrematistic. He starts from the former. So far as it is the art of gaining a livelihood, it is limited to procuring those articles that are necessary to existence, and useful either to a household or the state. "True wealth (ὁ ἀνληθινὸς πλοῦτος) consists of such values in use; for the quantity of possessions of this kind, capable of making life pleasant, is not unlimited. There is, however, a second mode of acquiring things, to which we may by preference and with correctness give the name of Chrematistic, and in this case, there appear to be no limits to riches and possessions. Trade (ἡ καπηλικὴ is literally retail trade, and Aristotle takes this kind because in it values in use predominate) does not in its nature belong to Chrematistic, for here the exchange has reference only to what is necessary to themselves (the buyer or seller)." Therefore, as he goes on to show, the original form of trade was barter, but with the extension of the latter, there arose the necessity for money. On the discovery of money, barter of necessity developed into καπηλικὴ, into trading in commodities, and this again, in opposition to its original tendency, grew into Chrematistic, into the art of making money. Now Chrematistic is distinguishable from Œconomic in this way, that "in the case of Chrematistic, circulation is the source of riches (ποιητικὴ χρημάτων . . . διὰ χρημάτων διαβολῆς). And it appears to revolve about money, for money is the beginning and end of this kind of exchange (τὸ γὰρ νόμισμα στοιχεῖον καὶ πέρας τῆς ἀλλαγῆς ἐστίν). Therefore also riches, such as Chre-

matistic strives for, are unlimited. Just as every art that is not a means to an end, but an end in itself, has no limit to its aims, because it seeks constantly to approach nearer and nearer to that end, while those arts that pursue means to an end, are not boundless, since the goal itself imposes a limit upon them, so with Chrematistic, there are no bounds to its aims, these aims being absolute wealth. Œconomic not Chrematistic has a limit . . . the object of the former is something different from money, of the latter the augmentation of money. . . . By confounding these two forms, which overlap each other, some people have been led to look upon the preservation and increase of money ad infinitum as the end and aim of Œconomic." (Aristotles De Rep. edit. Bekker. lib. I. c. 8, 9. passim.)

4. Hence legislation in various countries fixes a maximum for labor-contracts. Wherever free labor is the rule, the laws regulate the mode of terminating this contract. . .

"I may make over to another the use, for a limited time, of my particular bodily and mental aptitudes and capabilities; because, in a consequence of this restriction, they are impressed with a character of alienation with regard to me as a whole. But by the alienation of all my labor-time and the whole of my work, I should be converting the substance itself, in other words, my general activity and reality, my person, into the property of another." (Hegel, "Philosophie des Rechts." Berlin, 1840, p. 104 # 67.)

5. The capitalist epoch is therefore characterised by this, that labour-power takes in the eyes of the labourer himself the form of a commodity which is his property; his labour consequently becomes wage labour. On the other hand, it is only from this moment that the produce of labour universally becomes a commodity.

For Further Reading

Marx, Karl. *Capital, A Critique of Political Economy*. 3 vols. Translated by Ben Fowke et al. (Harmondsworth, England: Penguin, 1976-1981).

_____. *Collected Works*. Translated by Richard Dixon et al. (New York: International Publishers, 1975).

_____. *Grundrisse*. Translated by Martin Nicolaus (Harmondsworth, England: Penguin, 1973).

_____. *Karl Marx: Texts on Method*. Edited by Terrell Carver (Oxford: Blackwell, 1975).

_____. *Theories of Surplus Value*. 3 vols. Translated by Jack Cohen and S.W. Ryazanskaya (Moscow: Progress Publishers, 1971).

Althusser, Louis. *For Marx*. Translated by Ben Brewster (London: Verso, 1977).

_____, and Etienne Balibar. *Reading Capital* (London: New Left Books, 1977).

Arthur, Chris J. *Dialectics of Labour* (Oxford: Blackwell, 1986).

Avineri, Shlomo. *The Social and Political Thought of Karl Marx* (Cambridge Univ. Press, 1968).

Ball, Terence, and James Farr, eds. *After Marx* (Cambridge: Cambridge Univ. Press, 1984).

Böhm-Bawerk, Eugen von. *Karl Marx and the Close of His System* (New York: Augustus M. Kelly, 1975).

Bologh, Roslyn Wallach. *Dialectical Phenomenology: Marx's Method* (Boston: Routledge, 1980).

Bottomore, Tom, et al., eds. *A Dictionary of Marxist Thought* (Cambridge: Harvard Univ. Press, 1983).

Bubner, Rüdiger. *Essays in Hermeneutics and Critical Theory.* Translated by Eric Matthews (New York: Columbia Univ. Press, 1988).

Buchanan, Allen E. *Marx and Justice: The Radical Critique of Liberalism* (Totowa, N.J.: Rowman and Littlefield, 1982).

Carver, Terrell. *The Cambridge Companion to Marx* (Cambridge: Cambridge Univ. Press, 1991).

Cohen, G.A. *Karl Marx's Theory of History: A Defense* (Princeton: Princeton Univ. Press, 1978).

Eldred, Michael, and M. Roth. *A Guide to Marx's "Capital"* (London: CSE Books, 1978).

Elson, Diane, ed. *Value: The Representation of Labor in Capitalism* (Atlantic Highlands, N.J.: Humanities Press, 1979).

Elster, Jon. *Making Sense of Marx* (Cambridge: Cambridge Univ. Press, 1985).

Fine, Ben, and Laurence Harris. *Rereading "Capital"* (London: Macmillan, 1979).

Foley, Duncan K. *Understanding "Capital": Marx's Economic Theory* (Cambridge: Harvard Univ. Press, 1986).

Gould, Carol. *Marx's Social Ontology* (Cambridge: MIT Press, 1978).

Harvey, David. *The Limits to Capital* (Chicago: Univ. of Chicago Press, 1982).

Heilbroner, Robert. *Marxism: For and Against* (New York: Norton, 1980).

Heller, Agnes. *The Theory of Need in Marx* (New York: St Martin's, 1976).

Kain, Philip J. *Marx and Modern Political Theory* (Lanham, Md.: Roman and Littlefield, 1993).

Kolakowski, Leszek. *Main Currents in Marxism.* 3 vols. Translated by P.S. Falla (Oxford: Oxford Univ. Press, 1981).

Lukes, Steven. *Marxism and Morality* (Oxford: Clarendon Press, 1985).

Mattick, Paul. *Marx and Keynes: The Limits of the Mixed Economy* (Boston: Porter Sargent, 1969).

McCarthy, George E. *Dialectics and Decadence: Echoes of Antiquity in Marx and Nietzsche* (Savage, Md.: Rowman and Littlefield, 1994).

_____. *Marx and the Ancients: Classical Ethics, Social Justice and Nineteenth-Century Political Economy* (Savage, Md.: Rowman and Littlefield, 1990).

McLellan, David. *Karl Marx: His Life and Thought* (New York: Harper and Row, 1973).

Meikle, Scott. *Essentialism in the Thought of Karl Marx* (London: Duckworth, 1985).

Miller, Richard W. *Analyzing Marx: Morality, Power and History* (Princeton: Princeton Univ. Press, 1984).

Mosley, Fred, ed. *Marx's Method in "Capital": A Reexamination* (Atlantic Highlands, N.J.: Humanities Press, 1993).

Murray, Patrick. *Marx's Theory of Scientific Knowledge* (Atlantic Highlands, N.J.: Humanities Press, 1988).

Nicholson, Linda. "Feminism and Marx: Interacting Kinship with the Economic." *Praxis International* (1986): 367–380.

Ollman, Bertell. *Alienation: Marx's Conception of Man in Capitalist Society* (London: Cambridge Univ. Press, 1971).

Pashukanis, Evgeny B. *Law and Marxism: A General Theory*. Translated by Barbara Einhorn (London: Ink Links, 1978).

Peffer, Rodney G. *Marxism, Morality, and Social Justice* (Princeton: Princeton Univ. Press, 1990).

Pilling, Geoffrey. *Marx's "Capital": Philosophy and Political Economy* (London: Routledge, 1980).

Postone, Moishe. *Time, Labor, and Social Domination* (Cambridge: Cambridge Univ. Press, 1993).

Resnick, Stephan A., and Richard D. Wolff. *Knowledge and Class: A Marxian Critique of Political Economy* (Chicago: Univ. of Chicago Press, 1987).

Roemer, John. *A General Theory of Exploitation and Class* (Cambridge: Harvard Univ. Press, 1982).

Rosdolsky, Roman. *The Making of Marx's "Capital"* (London: Pluto Press, 1977).

Rubin, I.I. *Essays on Marx's Theory of Value* (Detroit: Black and Red, 1972).

Sayer, Derek. *Marx's Method: Ideology, Science, and Critique in "Capital"* (Atlantic Highlands, N.J.: Humanities Press, 1979).

_____. *The Violence of Abstraction* (Oxford: Blackwell, 1987).

Smith, Tony. *The Logic of Marx's "Capital"* (Albany: State University of New York Press, 1990).

Steedman, Ian. *Marx After Sraffa* (London: New Left Books, 1977).

Sweezy, Paul. *The Theory of Capitalist Development* (New York: Monthly Review Press, 1968).

Williams, Michael, ed. *Value, Social Form and the State* (New York: St. Martin's, 1988).

Wolff, Robert Paul. *Moneybags Must Be So Lucky* (Amherst: Univ. of Massachusetts Press, 1988).

Wood, Allen W. *Karl Marx* (London: Routledge, 1981).

JOHN STUART MILL (1806–1873)

chapter 13

THE LIBERALISM of John Stuart Mill involves quite a switch from that of John Locke or Adam Smith. Locke's liberalism begins with the God-given, inalienable "property" we have in our own person, from which further property rights naturally flow. Smith's liberal defense of free trade and private property also has roots in natural law theory, but it comes wrapped in his judgment that modern capitalism deserves approval for its capacity to spread wealth and order. Mill's endorsement of liberalism rests on Bentham's utilitarian principles, hence it must be cashed out in terms of the happiness it returns to individuals. The route from Mill's "greatest happiness" principle to conclusions favoring free trade, limited government, and the protection of private property is longer and less certain than the argumentative paths Locke and Smith follow.

A further consideration, beyond the point that Mill's liberalism is grounded in utilitarian rather than natural law principles, increases the possibility that

Mill's principles will lead away from classical liberalism toward government activism and checks on the rights of property owners, that is, toward "liberalism" in its current political sense, social democracy, or even socialism. For the point of Karl Marx's jibe at Jeremy Bentham, "To know what is useful for a dog, one must investigate the nature of dogs. This nature is not itself deducible from the principle of utility" (*Capital* I, 758–759), was not lost on Mill. Mill thickens Benthamite utilitarianism—it may be wondered whether the altered version remains utilitarian—by assessing what actually is good for beings with our nature. It is on the basis of particular judgments of that sort that Mill concludes that individuality and the free exercise of diverse human faculties must be numbered among the chief human goods. This provides him ample, indeed fresh, reasons to defend liberty, but not necessarily as classical liberals construe it.

Mill's controversial doctrine that while the production of wealth "partakes of the character of physical truths," the distribution of wealth "is a matter of human institutions solely," swept aside objections of classical economics to interfering with the market. His insights into the paradoxes of collective action gave him further reasons not to rely entirely on the free market to bring about the greatest happiness. For example, government action was required to avoid "free rider" problems faced by market economies: How could workers ever succeed in reducing the length of the work day without the compulsion of law? or Who would undertake costly scientific research if not the government?

Evidence of the world-making power of 19th-century capitalism keeps showing up in Mill's writings. Democracy was on the increase, which brought the new threat to liberty of the "tyranny of the majority." The rise of "mass society" and "public opinion" posed a *social,* not political, threat to liberty that gripped Mill in this irony: commercial freedoms were unleashing homogenizing forces that endangered the "variety of situations" needed to cultivate individuality. "Joint-stock" companies were forming. Demand for large-scale scientific and technological research was soaring. The early organization of the modern working class and the experimentation with cooperative and socialistic ideas signaled the shift in the lines of class conflict from "commons" against lords toward wage laborers confronting capitalists. Massive unemployment (or "surplus population") posed gigantic welfare problems and fueled colonization schemes to relieve them. Outrage at the plight of children in their homes and at work was building, as was distress at cruelty to animals. And voices challenging the subjugation of women were making themselves heard.

Mill's moral and political ideas were shaped over his adult life in collaboration with Harriet Taylor, whom he married after a friendship of twenty years. His writings do plead for numerous "liberal" causes: recognizing women's rights, providing easy access to birth control and divorce, prohibiting cruelty to animals, publicly funding education and assistance to the poor, protecting consumers, taxing rents and inheritances, acknowledging the rights of workers to organize and establish cooperatives, and establishing the goal of a "no growth" economy.

FROM THE *PRINCIPLES OF POLITICAL ECONOMY*

CHAPTER XI

OF THE GROUNDS AND LIMITS OF THE LAISSER–FAIRE OR NON–INTERFERENCE PRINCIPLE

§ 1. We have now reached the last part of our undertaking; the discussion, so far as suited to this treatise (that is, so far as it is a question of principle, not detail) of the limits of the province of government: the question, to what objects governmental intervention in the affairs of society may or should extend, over and above those which necessarily appertain to it. No subject has been more keenly contested in the present age: the contest, however, has chiefly taken place round certain select points, with only flying excursions into the rest of the field. Those indeed who have discussed any particular question of government interference, such as state education (spiritual or secular), regulation of hours of labour, a public provision for the poor, &c., have often dealt largely in general arguments, far outstretching the special application made of them, and have shown a sufficiently strong bias either in favour of letting things alone, or in favour of meddling; but have seldom declared, or apparently decided in their own minds, how far they would carry either principle. The supporters of interference have been content with asserting a general right and duty on the part of government to intervene, wherever its intervention would be useful: and when those who have been called the *laisser-faire* school have attempted any definite limitation of the province of government, they have usually restricted it to the protection of person and property against force and fraud; a definition to which neither they nor any one else can deliberately adhere, since it excludes, as has been shown in a preceding chapter, some of the most indispensable and unanimously recognised of the duties of government.

Without professing entirely to supply this deficiency of a general theory, on a question which does not, as I conceive, admit of any universal solution, I shall attempt to afford some little aid towards the resolution of this class of questions as they arise, by examining, in the most general point of view in which the subject can be considered, what are the advantages, and what the evils or inconveniences, of government interference.

We must set out by distinguishing between two kinds of intervention by the government, which, though they may relate to the same subject, differ widely in their nature and effects, and require, for their justification, motives of a very different degree of urgency. The intervention may extend to controlling the free agency of individuals. Government may interdict all persons from doing certain things; or from doing them without its authorization; or may prescribe to them certain things to be done, or a certain manner of doing things which it is left optional with them to do or to abstain from. This is the *authoritative* interference of government. There is another kind of intervention which is not authoritative: when a government, instead of issuing a command and enforcing it by penalties, adopts the course so seldom resorted to by governments, and of which such important use might be made, that of giving advice, and promulgating information; or when, leaving individuals free to use their own means of pursuing any object of general interest, the government, not meddling with them, but not trusting the object solely to their care, establishes, side by side with their arrangements, an agency of its own for a like purpose. Thus, it is one thing to maintain a Church Establishment, and another to refuse toleration to other religions, or to persons professing no religion. It is one thing to provide schools or colleges, and another to require that no person shall act as an instructor of youth without a government licence. There might be a national bank, or a government manufactory, without any monopoly against private banks and manufactories. There might be a post-office, without penalties against the conveyance of letters by other means. There may be a corps of government engineers for civil purposes, while the profession of a civil engineer is free to be adopted by every one. There may be public hospitals, without any restriction upon private medical or surgical practice.

§ 2. It is evident, even at first sight, that the authoritative form of government intervention has a much more limited sphere of legitimate action than the other. It requires a much stronger necessity to justify it in any case; while there are large departments of human life from which it must be unreservedly and imperiously excluded. Whatever theory we adopt respecting the foundation of the social union, and under whatever political institutions we live, there is a circle around every individual human being, which no government, be it that of one, of a few, or of the many, ought to be permitted to overstep: there is a part of the life of every person who has come to years of discretion, within which the individuality of that person ought to reign uncontrolled either by any other individual or by the public collectively. That there is, or ought to be, some space in human existence thus entrenched around, and sacred from authoritative intrusion, no one who professes the smallest regard to human freedom or dignity will call in question: the point to be determined is, where the limit should be placed; how large a province of human life this reserved territory should include. I apprehend that it ought to include all that part which concerns only the life, whether inward or outward, of the individual, and does not affect the interests of others, or affects them only through the moral influence of example. With respect to the domain of the inward consciousness, the thoughts and feelings, and as much of external conduct as is personal only, involving no consequences, none at least of a painful or injurious kind, to other people; I hold that it is allowable in all, and in the more thoughtful and cultivated often a duty, to assert and promulgate, with all the force they are capable of, their opinion of what is good or bad, admirable or contemptible, but not to compel others to conform to that opinion; whether the force used is that of extra-legal coercion, or exerts itself by means of the law.

Even in those portions of conduct which do affect the interest of others, the onus of making out a case always lies on the defenders of legal prohibitions. It is not a merely constructive or presumptive injury to others, which will justify the interference of law with individual freedom. To be prevented from doing what one is inclined to, or from acting according to one's own judgment of what is desirable, is not only always irksome, but always tends, *pro tanto*, to starve the development of some portion of the bodily or mental faculties, either sensitive or active; and unless the conscience of the individual goes freely with the legal restraint, it partakes, either in a great or in a small degree, of the degradation of slavery. Scarcely any degree of utility, short of absolute necessity, will justify a prohibitory regulation, unless it can also be made to recommend itself to the general conscience; unless persons of ordinary good intentions either believe already, or can be induced to believe, that the thing prohibited is a thing which they ought not to wish to do.

It is otherwise with governmental interferences which do not restrain individual free agency. When a government provides means for fulfilling a certain end, leaving individuals free to avail themselves of different means if in their opinion preferable, there is no infringement of liberty, no irksome or degrading restraint. One of the principal objections to government interference is then absent. There is, however, in almost all forms of government agency, one thing which is compulsory; the provision of the pecuniary means. These are derived from taxation; or, if existing in the form of an endowment derived from public property, they are still the cause of as much compulsory taxation as the sale or the annual proceeds of the property would enable to be dispensed with. And the objection necessarily attaching to compulsory contributions, is almost always greatly aggravated by the expensive precautions and onerous restrictions, which are indispensable to prevent evasion of a compulsory tax.

§ 3. A second general objection to government agency, is that every increase of the functions devolving on the government is an increase of its power, both in the form of authority, and still more, in the indirect form of influence. The importance of this consideration, in respect to political freedom, has in general been quite sufficiently recognised, at least in England; but many, in latter times, have been prone to think that limitation of the powers of the government is only essential when the government itself is badly constituted; when it does not represent the people, but is the organ of a class, or

301

coalition of classes: and that a government of sufficiently popular constitution might be trusted with any amount of power over the nation, since its power would be only that of the nation over itself. This might be true, if the nation, in such cases, did not practically mean a mere majority of the nation, and if minorities were only capable of oppressing, but not of being oppressed. Experience, however, proves that the depositaries of power who are mere delegates of the people, that is of a majority, are quite as ready (when they think they can count on popular support) as any organs of oligarchy, to assume arbitrary power, and encroach unduly on the liberty of private life. The public collectively is abundantly ready to impose, not only its generally narrow views of its interests, but its abstract opinions, and even its tastes, as laws binding upon individuals. And the present civilization tends so strongly to make the power of persons acting in masses the only substantial power in society, that there never was more necessity for surrounding individual independence of thought, speech, and conduct, with the most powerful defences, in order to maintain that originality of mind and individuality of character, which are the only source of any real progress, and of most of the qualities which make the human race much superior to any herd of animals. Hence it is no less important in a democratic than in any other government, that all tendency on the part of public authorities to stretch their interference, and assume a power of any sort which can easily be dispensed with, should be regarded with unremitting jealousy. Perhaps this is even more important in a democracy than in any other form of political society; because where public opinion is sovereign, an individual who is oppressed by the sovereign does not, as in most other states of things, find a rival power to which he can appeal for relief, or, at all events, for sympathy. . . .

§ 6. I have reserved for the last place one of the strongest of the reasons against the extension of government agency. Even if the government could comprehend within itself, in each department, all the most eminent intellectual capacity and active talent of the nation, it would not be the less desirable that the conduct of a large portion of the affairs of the society should be left in the hands of the persons immediately interested in them. The business of life is an essential part of the practical education of a people; without which, book and school instruction, though most necessary and salutary, does not suffice to qualify them for conduct, and for the adaptation of means to ends. Instruction is only one of the desiderata of mental improvement; another, almost as indispensable, is a vigorous exercise of the active energies; labour, contrivance, judgment, self-control: and the natural stimulus to these is the difficulties of life. This doctrine is not to be confounded with the complacent optimism, which represents the evils of life as desirable things, because they call forth qualities adapted to combat with evils. It is only because the difficulties exist, that the qualities which combat with them are of any value. As practical beings it is our business to free human life from as many as possible of its difficulties, and not to keep up a stock of them as hunters preserve game, for the exercise of pursuing it. But since the need of active talent and practical judgment in the affairs of life can only be diminished, and not, even on the most favourable supposition, done away with, it is important that those endowments should be cultivated not merely in a select few, but in all, and that the cultivation should be more varied and complete than most persons are able to find in the narrow sphere of their merely individual interests. A people among whom there is no habit of spontaneous action for a collective interest—who look habitually to their government to command or prompt them in all matters of joint concern—who expect to have everything done for them, except what can be made an affair of mere habit and routine—have their faculties only half developed; their education is defective in one of its most important branches.

Not only is the cultivation of the active faculties by exercise, diffused through the whole community, in itself one of the most valuable of national possessions: it is rendered, not less, but more, necessary, when a high degree of that indispensable culture is systematically kept up in the chiefs and func-tionaries of the state. There cannot be a combination of circumstances more dangerous to human welfare, than that in which intelligence and talent are maintained at a high standard within a governing corporation, but starved and discouraged outside the pale. Such a system, more completely than any other, embodies the idea of despotism, by arming with intellectual superiori-ty as an additional weapon, those who have already the legal power. It ap-proaches as nearly as the organic difference between human beings and other animals admits, to the government of sheep by their shepherd, without any-thing like so strong an interest as the shepherd has in the thriving condition of the flock. The only security against political slavery, is the check main-tained over governors, by the diffusion of intelligence, activity, and public spirit among the governed. Experience proves the extreme difficulty of per-manently keeping up a sufficiently high standard of those qualities; a difficul-ty which increases, as the advance of civilization and security removes one af-ter another of the hardships, embarrassments, and dangers against which indi-viduals had formerly no resource but in their own strength, skill, and courage. It is therefore of supreme importance that all classes of the community, down to the lowest, should have much to do for themselves; that as great a demand should be made upon their intelligence and virtue as it is in any respect equal to; that the government should not only leave as far as possible to their own faculties the conduct of whatever concerns themselves alone, but should suf-fer them, or rather encourage them, to manage as many as possible of their joint concerns by voluntary co-operation; since this discussion and manage-ment of collective interests is the great school of that public spirit, and the great source of that intelligence of public affairs, which are always regarded as the distinctive character of the public of free countries.

303

A democratic constitution, not supported by democratic institutions in detail, but confined to the central government, not only is not political freedom, but often creates a spirit precisely the reverse, carrying down to the lowest grade in society the desire and ambition of political domination. In some countries the desire of the people is for not being tyrannized over, but in others it is merely for an equal chance to everybody of tyrannizing. Unhappily this last state of the desires is fully as natural to mankind as the former, and in many of the conditions even of civilized humanity, is far more largely exemplified. In proportion as the people are accustomed to manage their affairs by their own active intervention, instead of leaving them to the government, their desires will turn to repelling tyranny, rather than to tyrannizing: while in proportion as all real initiative and direction resides in the government, and individuals habitually feel and act as under its perpetual tutelage, popular institutions develop in them not the desire of freedom, but an unmeasured appetite for place and power; diverting the intelligence and activity of the country from its principal business, to a wretched competition for the selfish prizes and the petty vanities of office.

§ 7. The preceding are the principal reasons, of a general character, in favour of restricting to the narrowest compass the intervention of a public authority in the business of the community: and few will dispute the more than sufficiency of these reasons, to throw, in every instance, the burthen of making out a strong case, not on those who resist, but on those who recommend, government interference. *Laisser-faire*, in short, should be the general practice: every departure from it, unless required by some great good, is a certain evil. . . .

We have observed that, as a general rule, the business of life is better performed when those who have an immediate interest in it are left to take their own course, uncontrolled either by the mandate of the law or by the meddling of any public functionary. The persons, or some of the persons, who do the work, are likely to be better judges than the government, of the means of attaining the particular end at which they aim. Were we to suppose, what is not very probable, that the government has possessed itself of the best knowledge which had been acquired up to a given time by the persons most skilled in the occupation; even then, the individual agents have so much stronger and more direct an interest in the result, that the means are far more likely to be improved and perfected if left to their uncontrolled choice. But if the workman is generally the best selector of means, can it be affirmed with the same universality, that the consumer, or person served, is the most competent judge of the end? Is the buyer always qualified to judge of the commodity? If not, the presumption in favour of the competition of the market does not apply to the case; and if the commodity be one, in the quality of which society has much at stake, the balance of advantages may be in favour of some mode and degree of intervention, by the authorized representatives of the collective interest of the state.

§ 8. Now, the proposition that the consumer is a competent judge of the commodity, can be admitted only with numerous abatements and exceptions. He is generally the best judge (though even this is not true universally) of the material objects produced for his use. These are destined to supply some physical want, or gratify some taste or inclination, respecting which wants or inclinations there is no appeal from the person who feels them; or they are the means and appliances of some occupation, for the use of the persons engaged in it, who may be presumed to be judges of the things required in their own habitual employment. But there are other things, of the worth of which the demand of the market is by no means a test; things of which the utility does not consist in ministering to inclinations, nor in serving the daily uses of life, and the want of which is least felt where the need is greatest. This is peculiarly true of those things which are chiefly useful as tending to raise the character of human beings. The uncultivated cannot be competent judges of cultivation. Those who most need to be made wiser and better, usually desire it least, and if they desired it, would be incapable of finding the way to it by their own lights. It will continually happen, on the voluntary system, that, the end not being desired, the means will not be provided at all, or that, the persons requiring improvement having an imperfect or altogether erroneous conception of what they want, the supply called forth by the demand of the market will be anything but what is really required. Now any well-intentioned and tolerably civilized government may think, without presumption, that it does or ought to possess a degree of cultivation above the average of the community which it rules, and that it should therefore be capable of offering better education and better instruction to the people, than the greater number of them would spontaneously demand. Education, therefore, is one of those things which it is admissible in principle that a government should provide for the people. The case is one to which the reasons of the non-interference principle do not necessarily or universally extend.

305

With regard to elementary education, the exception to ordinary rules may, I conceive, justifiably be carried still further. There are certain primary elements and means of knowledge, which it is in the highest degree desirable that all human beings born into the community should acquire during childhood. If their parents, or those on whom they depend, have the power of obtaining for them this instruction, and fail to do it, they commit a double breach of duty, towards the children themselves, and towards the members of the community generally, who are all liable to suffer seriously from the consequences of ignorance and want of education in their fellow-citizens. It is therefore an allowable exercise of the powers of government, to impose on parents the legal obligation of giving elementary instruction to children. This, however, cannot fairly be done, without taking measures to insure that such instruction shall be always accessible to them, either gratuitously or at a trifling expense.

It may indeed be objected that the education of children is one of those expenses which parents, even of the labouring class, ought to defray; that it is desirable that they should feel it incumbent on them to provide by their own means for the fulfilment of their duties, and that by giving education at the cost of others, just as much as by giving subsistence, the standard of necessary wages is proportionally lowered, and the springs of exertion and self-restraint in so much relaxed. This argument could, at best, be only valid if the question were that of substituting a public provision for what individuals would otherwise do for themselves; if all parents in the labouring class recognised and practised the duty of giving instruction to their children at their own expense. But inasmuch as parents do not practise this duty, and do not include education among those necessary expenses which their wages must provide for, therefore the general rate of wages is not high enough to bear those expenses, and they must be borne from some other source. And this is not one of the cases in which the tender of help perpetuates the state of things which renders help necessary. Instruction, when it is really such, does not enervate, but strengthens as well as enlarges the active faculties: in whatever manner acquired, its effect on the mind is favourable to the spirit of independence: and when, unless had gratuitously, it would not be had at all, help in this form has the opposite tendency to that which in so many other cases makes it objectionable; it is help towards doing without help.

In England, and most European countries, elementary instruction cannot be paid for, at its full cost, from the common wages of unskilled labour, and would not if it could. The alternative, therefore, is not between government and private speculation, but between a government provision and voluntary charity: between interference by government, and interference by associations of individuals, subscribing their own money for the purpose, like the two great School Societies. It is, of course, not desirable that anything should be done by funds derived from compulsory taxation, which is already sufficiently well done by individual liberality. How far this is the case with school instruction, is, in each particular instance, a question of fact. The education provided in this country on the voluntary principle has of late been so much discussed, that it is needless in this place to criticise it minutely, and I shall merely express my conviction, that even in quantity it is, and is likely to remain, altogether insufficient, while in quality, though with some slight tendency to improvement, it is never good except by some rare accident, and generally so bad as to be little more than nominal. I hold it therefore the duty of the government to supply the defect, by giving pecuniary support to elementary schools, such as to render them accessible to all the children of the poor, either freely, or for a payment too inconsiderable to be sensibly felt.

One thing must be strenuously insisted on; that the government must claim no monopoly for its education, either in the lower or in the higher branches; must exert neither authority nor influence to induce the people to resort to its teachers in preference to others, and must confer no peculiar advantages on those who have been instructed by them. Though the government teachers will probably be superior to the average of private instructors, they will not embody all the knowledge and sagacity to be found in all instructors taken together, and it is desirable to leave open as many roads as possible to the desired end. It is not endurable that a government should, either *de jure* or *de facto*, have a complete control over the education of the people. To possess such a control, and actually exert it, is to be despotic. A government which can mould the opinions and sentiments of the people from their youth upwards, can do with them whatever it pleases. Though a government, therefore, may, and in many cases ought to, establish schools and colleges, it must neither compel nor bribe any person to come to them; nor ought the power of individuals to set up rival establishments, to depend in any degree upon its authorization. It would be justified in requiring from all the people that they shall possess instruction in certain things, but not in prescribing to them how or from whom they shall obtain it.

§ 9. In the matter of education, the intervention of government is justifiable, because the case is not one in which the interest and judgment of the consumer are a sufficient security for the goodness of the commodity. Let us now consider another class of cases, where there is no person in the situation of a consumer, and where the interest and judgment to be relied on are those of the agent himself; as in the conduct of any business in which he is exclusively interested, or in entering into any contract or engagement by which he himself is to be bound.

307

The ground of the practical principle of non-interference must here be, that most persons take a juster and more intelligent view of their own interest, and of the means of promoting it, than can either be prescribed to them by a general enactment of the legislature, or pointed out in the particular case by a public functionary. The maxim is unquestionably sound as a general rule; but there is no difficulty in perceiving some very large and conspicuous exceptions to it. These may be classed under several heads.

First:—The individual who is presumed to be the best judge of his own interests may be incapable of judging or acting for himself; may be a lunatic, an idiot, an infant: or though not wholly incapable, may be of immature years and judgment. In this case the foundation of the *laisser-faire* principle breaks down entirely. The person most interested is not the best judge of the matter, nor a competent judge at all. Insane persons are everywhere regarded as proper objects of the care of the state. In the case of children and young persons, it is common to say, that though they cannot judge for themselves, they have their parents or other relatives to judge for them. But this removes the question into a different category; making it no longer a question whether the government should interfere with individuals in the direction of their own conduct and interests, but whether it should leave absolutely in their power the conduct and interests of somebody else. Parental power is as susceptible of abuse as any other power, and is, as a matter of fact, constantly abused. If laws do not succeed in preventing parents from brutally ill-treating, and even from murdering their children, far less ought it to be presumed that the interests of children will never be sacrificed, in more commonplace and less revolting ways, to the selfishness or the ignorance of their parents. Whatever it can be clearly seen that parents ought to do or forbear for the interest of children, the law is warranted, if it is able, in compelling to be done or forborne, and is generally bound to do so. To take an example from the peculiar province of political economy; it is right that children, and young persons not yet arrived at maturity, should be protected, so far as the eye and hand of the state can reach, from being over-worked. Labouring for too many hours in the day, or on work beyond their strength, should not be permitted to them, for if permitted it may always be compelled. Freedom of contract, in the case of children, is but another word for freedom of coercion. Education also, the best which circumstances admit of their receiving, is not a thing which parents or relatives, from indifference, jealousy, or avarice, should have it in their power to withhold.

The reasons for legal intervention in favour of children, apply not less strongly to the case of those unfortunate slaves and victims of the most brutal part of mankind, the lower animals. It is by the grossest misunderstanding of the principles of liberty, that the infliction of exemplary punishment on ruffianism practised towards these defenceless creatures, has been treated as a meddling by government with things beyond its province; an interference with domestic life. The domestic life of domestic tyrants is one of the things which it is the most imperative on the law to interfere with; and it is to be regretted that metaphysical scruples respecting the nature and source of the authority of government, should induce many warm supporters of laws against cruelty to animals, to seek for a justification of such laws in the incidental consequences of the indulgence of ferocious habits to the interests of human beings, rather than in the intrinsic merits of the case itself. What it would be the duty of a human being, possessed of the requisite physical strength, to prevent by force if attempted in his presence, it cannot be less incumbent on society generally to repress. The existing laws of England on the subject are chiefly defective in the trifling, often almost nominal, maximum, to which the penalty even in the worst cases is limited.

Among those members of the community whose freedom of contract ought to be controlled by the legislature for their own protection, on account (it is said) of their dependent position, it is frequently proposed to include women: and in the existing Factory Acts, their labour, in common with that of young persons, has been placed under peculiar restrictions. But the classing together, for this and other purposes, of women and children, appears to me both indefensible in principle and mischievous in practice. Children below a certain age *cannot* judge or act for themselves; up to a considerably greater age they are inevitably more or less disqualified for doing so; but women are as capable as men of appreciating and managing their own concerns, and the only hindrance to their doing so arises from the injustice of their present social position. When the law makes everything which the wife acquires, the property of the husband, while by compelling her to live with him it forces her to submit to almost any amount of moral and even physical tyranny which he may choose to inflict, there is some ground for regarding every act done by her as done under coercion: but it is the great error of reformers and philanthropists in our time, to nibble at the consequences of unjust power, instead of redressing the injustice itself. If women had as absolute a control as men have, over their own persons and their own patrimony or acquisitions, there would be no plea for limiting their hours of labouring for themselves, in order that they might have time to labour for the husband, in what is called, by the advocates of restriction, *his* home. Women employed in factories are the only women in the labouring rank of life whose position is not that of slaves and drudges; precisely because they cannot easily be compelled to work and earn wages in factories against their will. For improving the condition of women, it should, on the contrary, be an object to give them the readiest access to independent industrial employment, instead of closing, either entirely or partially, that which is already open to them.

§ 10. A second exception to the doctrine that individuals are the best judges of their own interest, is when an individual attempts to decide irrevocably now, what will be best for his interest at some future and distant time. The presumption in favour of individual judgment is only legitimate, where the judgment is grounded on actual, and especially on present, personal experience; not where it is formed antecedently to experience, and not suffered to be reversed even after experience has condemned it. When persons have bound themselves by a contract, not simply to do some one thing, but to continue doing something for ever or for a prolonged period, without any power of revoking the engagement, the presumption which their perseverance in that course of conduct would otherwise raise in favour of its being advantageous to them, does not exist; and any such presumption which can be grounded on their having voluntarily entered into the contract, perhaps at an early age, and without any real knowledge of what they undertook, is commonly next to null. The practical maxim of leaving contracts free, is not applicable without great limitations in case of engagements in perpetuity; and the law should be extremely jealous of such engagements; should refuse its sanction to them, when the obligations they impose are such as the contracting party cannot be a competent judge of; if it ever does sanction them, it should take every possible security for their being contracted with foresight and deliberation; and in compensation for not permitting the parties themselves to revoke their engagement, should grant them a release from it, on a sufficient case being made out before an impartial authority. These considerations are eminently applicable to marriage, the most important of all cases of engagement for life.

§ 11. The third exception which I shall notice, to the doctrine that government cannot manage the affairs of individuals as well as the individuals themselves, has reference to the great class of cases in which the individuals can only manage the concern by delegated agency, and in which the so-called private management is, in point of fact, hardly better entitled to be called management by the persons interested, than administration by a public officer. Whatever, if left to spontaneous agency, can only be done by joint-stock associations, will often be as well, and sometimes better done, as far as the actual work is concerned, by the state. Government management is, indeed, proverbially jobbing, careless, and ineffective, but so likewise has generally been joint-stock management. The directors of a joint-stock company, it is true, are always shareholders; but also the members of a government are invariably taxpayers; and in the case of directors, no more than in that of governments, is their proportional share of the benefits of good management, equal to the interest they may possibly have in mismanagement, even without reckoning the interest of their ease. It may be objected, that the shareholders, in their collective character, exercise a certain control over the directors, and have almost always full power to remove them from office. Practically, however, the difficulty of exercising this power is found to be so great, that it is hardly ever exercised except in cases of such flagrantly unskilful, or, at least, unsuccessful management, as would generally produce the ejection from office of managers appointed by the government. Against the very ineffectual security afforded by meetings of shareholders, and by their individual inspection and inquiries, may be placed the greater publicity and more active discussion and comment, to be expected in free countries with regard to affairs in which the general government takes part. The defects, therefore, of government management, do not seem to be necessarily much greater, if necessarily greater at all, than those of management by joint-stock.

The true reasons in favour of leaving to voluntary associations all such things as they are competent to perform, would exist in equal strength if it were certain that the work itself would be as well or better done by public officers. These reasons have been already pointed out: the mischief of overloading the chief functionaries of government with demands on their attention, and diverting them from duties which they alone can discharge, to objects which can be sufficiently well attained without them; the danger of unnecessarily swelling the direct power and indirect influence of government, and multiplying occasions of collision between its agents and private citizens; and the inexpediency of concentrating in a dominant bureaucracy, all the skill and experience in the management of large interests, and all the power of organized action, existing in the community; a practice which keeps the citizens in a relation to the government like that of children to their guardians, and is a main cause of the inferior capacity for political life which has hitherto characterized the over-governed countries of the Continent, whether with or without the forms of representative government.

But although, for these reasons, most things which are likely to be even tolerably done by voluntary associations, should, generally speaking, be left to them; it does not follow that the manner in which those associations perform their work should be entirely uncontrolled by the government. There are many cases in which the agency, of whatever nature, by which a service is performed, is certain, from the nature of the case, to be virtually single; in which a practical monopoly, with all the power it confers of taxing the community, cannot be prevented from existing. I have already more than once adverted to the case of the gas and water companies, among which, though perfect freedom is allowed to competition, none really takes place, and practically they are found to be even more irresponsible, and unapproachable by individual complaints, than the government. There are the expenses without the advantages of plurality of agency; and the charge made for services which cannot be dispensed with, is, in substance, quite as much compulsory taxation as if imposed by law; there are few householders who make any distinction between their "water rate" and their other local taxes. In the case of these particular services, the reasons preponderate in favour of their being performed, like the paving and cleansing of the streets, not certainly by the general government of the state, but by the municipal authorities of the town, and the expense defrayed, as even now it in fact is, by a local rate. But in the many analogous cases which it is best to resign to voluntary agency, the community needs some other security for the fit performance of the service than the interest of the managers; and it is the part of government, either to subject the business to reasonable conditions for the general advantage, or to retain such power over it, that the profits of the monopoly may at least be obtained for the public. This applies to the case of a road, a canal, or a railway. These are always, in a great degree, practical monopolies; and a government which concedes such monopoly unreservedly to a private company, does much the same thing as if it allowed an individual or an association to levy any tax they chose, for their own benefit, on all the malt produced in the country, or on all the cotton imported into it. To make the concession for a limited time is generally justifiable, on the principle which justifies patents for inventions: but the state should either reserve to itself a reversionary property in such public works, or should retain, and freely exercise, the right of fixing a maximum of fares and charges, and, from time to time, varying that maximum. It is perhaps necessary to remark, that the state may be the proprietor of canals or railways without itself working them; and that they will almost always be better worked by means of a company, renting the railway or canal for a limited period from the state.

§ 12. To a fourth case of exception I must request particular attention, it being one to which, as it appears to me, the attention of political economists has not yet been sufficiently drawn. There are matters in which the interference of law is required, not to overrule the judgment of individuals respecting their own interest, but to give effect to that judgment: they being unable to give effect to it except by concert, which concert again cannot be effectual unless it receives validity and sanction from the law. For illustration, and without prejudging the particular point, I may advert to the question of diminishing the hours of labour. Let us suppose, what is at least supposable, whether it be the fact or not—that a general reduction of the hours of factory labour, say from ten to nine, would be for the advantage of the work-people: that they would receive as high wages, or nearly as high, for nine hours' labour as they receive for ten. If this would be the result, and if the operatives generally are convinced that it would, the limitation, some may say, will be adopted spontaneously. I answer, that it will not be adopted unless the body of operatives bind themselves to one another to abide by it. A workman who refused to work more than nine hours while there were others who worked ten, would either not be employed at all, or if employed, must submit to lose one-tenth of his wages. However convinced, therefore, he may be that it is the interest of the class to work short time, it is contrary to his own interest to set the example, unless he is well assured that all or most others will follow it. But suppose a general agreement of the whole class: might not this be effectual without the sanction of law? Not unless enforced by opinion with a rigour practically equal to that of law. For however beneficial the observance of the regulation might be to the class collectively, the immediate interest of every individual would lie in violating it: and the more numerous those were who adhered to the rule, the more would individuals gain by departing from it. If nearly all restricted themselves to nine hours, those who chose to work for ten would gain all the advantages of the restriction, together with the profit of infringing it; they would get ten hours' wages for nine hours' work, and an hour's wages besides. I grant that if a large majority adhered to the nine hours, there would be no harm done: the benefit would be, in the main, secured to the class, while those individuals who preferred to work harder and earn more, would have an opportunity of doing so. This certainly would be the state of things to be wished for; and assuming that a reduction of hours without any diminution of wages could take place without expelling the commodity from some of its markets—which is in every particular instance a question of fact, not of principle—the manner in which it would be most desirable that this effect should be brought about, would be by a quiet change in the general custom of the trade; short hours becoming, by spontaneous choice, the general practice, but those who chose to deviate from it having the fullest liberty to do so. Probably, however, so many would prefer the ten hours' work on the improved terms, that the limitation could not be maintained as a general practice: what some did from choice, others would soon be obliged to do from necessity, and those who had chosen long hours for the sake of increased wages, would be forced in the end to work long hours for no greater wages than before. Assuming then that it really would be the interest of each to work only nine hours if he could be assured that all others would do the same, there might be no means of their attaining this object but by converting their supposed mutual agreement into an engagement under penalty, by consenting to have it enforced by law. I am not expressing any opinion in favour of such an enactment, which has never in this country been demanded, and which I certainly should not, in present circumstances, recommend: but it serves to exemplify the manner in which classes of persons may need the assistance of law, to give effect to their deliberate collective opinion of their own interest, by affording to every individual a guarantee that his competitors will pursue the same course, without which he cannot safely adopt it himself. . . .

§ 13. Fifthly; the argument against government interference grounded on the maxim that individuals are the best judges of their own interest, cannot apply to the very large class of cases, in which those acts of individuals with which the government claims to interfere, are not done by those individuals for their own interest, but for the interest of other people. This includes, among other things, the important and much agitated subject of public charity. Though individuals should, in general, be left to do for themselves whatever it can reasonably be expected that they should be capable of doing, yet when they are at any rate not to be left to themselves, but to be helped by other people, the question arises whether it is better that they should receive this help exclusively from individuals, and therefore uncertainly and casually, or by systematic arrangements, in which society acts through its organ, the state.

This brings us to the subject of Poor Laws; a subject which would be of very minor importance if the habits of all classes of the people were temperate and prudent, and the diffusion of property satisfactory; but of the greatest moment in a state of things so much the reverse of this, in both points, as that which the British islands present.

Apart from any metaphysical considerations respecting the foundation of morals or of the social union, it will be admitted to be right that human beings should help one another; and the more so, in proportion to the urgency of the need: and none needs help so urgently as one who is starving. The claim to help, therefore, created by destitution, is one of the strongest which can exist; and there is *primâ facie* the amplest reason for making the relief of so extreme an exigency as certain to those who require it, as by any arrangements of society it can be made.

On the other hand, in all cases of helping, there are two sets of consequences to be considered; the consequences of the assistance itself, and the consequences of relying on the assistance. The former are generally beneficial, but the latter, for the most part, injurious; so much so, in many cases, as greatly to outweigh the value of the benefit. And this is never more likely to happen than in the very cases where the need of help is the most intense. There are few things for which it is more mischievous that people should rely on the habitual aid of others, than for the means of subsistence, and unhappily there is no lesson which they more easily learn. The problem to be solved is therefore one of peculiar nicety as well as importance; how to give the greatest amount of needful help, with the smallest encouragement to undue reliance on it.

Energy and self-dependence are, however, liable to be impaired by the absence of help, as well as by its excess. It is even more fatal to exertion to have no hope of succeeding by it, than to be assured of succeeding without it. When the condition of any one is so disastrous that his energies are paralyzed by discouragement, assistance is a tonic, not a sedative: it braces instead of deadening the active faculties: always provided that the assistance is not such as to dispense with self-help, by substituting itself for the person's own labour, skill, and prudence, but is limited to affording him a better hope of attaining success by those legitimate means. This accordingly is a test to which all plans of philanthropy and benevolence should be brought, whether intended for the benefit of individuals or of classes, and whether conducted on the voluntary or on the government principle.

In so far as the subject admits of any general doctrine or maxim, it would appear to be this—that if assistance is given in such a manner that the condition of the person helped is as desirable as that of the person who succeeds in doing the same thing without help, the assistance, if capable of being previously calculated on, is mischievous: but if, while available to everybody, it leaves to every one a strong motive to do without it if he can, it is then for the most part beneficial. This principle, applied to a system of public charity, is that of the Poor Law of 1834. If the condition of a person receiving relief is made as eligible as that of the labourer who supports himself by his own exertions, the system strikes at the root of all individual industry and self-government; and, if fully acted up to, would require as its supplement an organized system of compulsion, for governing and setting to work like cattle, those who had been removed from the influence of the motives that act on human beings. But if, consistently with guaranteeing all persons against absolute want, the condition of those who are supported by legal charity can be kept considerably less desirable than the condition of those who find support for themselves, none but beneficial consequences can arise from a law which renders it impossible for any person, except by his own choice, to die from insufficiency of food. That in England at least this supposition can be realized, is proved by the experience of a long period preceding the close of the last century, as well as by that of many highly pauperized districts in more recent times, which have been dispauperized by adopting strict rules of poor-law administration, to the great and permanent benefit of the whole labouring class. There is probably no country in which, by varying the means suitably to the character of the people, a legal provision for the destitute might not be made compatible with the observance of the conditions necessary to its being innocuous.

Subject to these conditions, I conceive it to be highly desirable, that the certainty of subsistence should be held out by law to the destitute able-bodied, rather than that their relief should depend on voluntary charity. In the first place, charity almost always does too much or too little: it lavishes its bounty in one place, and leaves people to starve in another. Secondly, since the state must necessarily provide subsistence for the criminal poor while undergoing punishment, not to do the same for the poor who have not offended is to give a premium on crime. And lastly, if the poor are left to individual charity, a vast amount of mendicity is inevitable. What the state may and should abandon to private charity, is the task of distinguishing between one case of real necessity and another. Private charity can give more to the more deserving. The state must act by general rules. It cannot undertake to discriminate between the deserving and the undeserving indigent. It owes no more than subsistence to the first, and can give no less to the last. What is said about the injustice of a law which has no better treatment for the merely unfortunate poor than for the ill-conducted, is founded on a misconception of the province of law and public authority. The dispensers of public relief have no business to be inquisitors. Guardians and overseers are not fit to be trusted to give or withhold other people's money according to their verdict on the morality of the person soliciting it; and it would show much ignorance of the ways of mankind to suppose that such persons, even in the almost impossible case of their being qualified, will take the trouble of ascertaining and sifting the past conduct of a person in distress, so as to form a rational judgment on it. Private charity can make these distinctions; and in bestowing its own money, is entitled to do so according to its own judgment. It should understand that this is its peculiar and appropriate province, and that it is commendable or the contrary, as it exercises the function with more or less discernment. But the administrators of a public fund ought not to be required to do more for anybody, than that minimum which is due even to the worst. If they are, the indulgence very speedily becomes the rule, and refusal the more or less capricious or tyrannical exception.

[The remainder of the chapter is omitted.]

For Further Reading

Mill, John Stuart. *Autobiography.* Edited by John Robson. (New York: Penguin, 1982).
_____. *Chapters on Socialism* (New York: American Book Exchange, 1880).
_____. *On Liberty.* Edited by Elizabeth Rapaport. (Indianapolis: Hackett, 1978).

315

_____. *Principles of Political Economy.* Edited by J.M Robson. (Toronto: Univ. of Toronto Press: 1977).

_____. *The Subjection of Women.* Edited by Susan Moller Okin. (Indianapolis: Hackett, 1988).

_____. *Utilitarianism and Other Essays* (New York: Penguin, 1987).

Arneson, Richard J. "Prospects for Community in a Market Economy." *Political Theory* 9 (May 1981): 207–227.

Cowling, M. *Mill and Liberalism.* 2nd ed. (Cambridge: Cambridge Univ. Press, 1990).

Cranston, Maurice. *John Stuart Mill* (London: Longmans, Green, 1958).

Duncan, Graeme C. *Marx and Mill: Two Views of Social Conflict and Social Harmony* (Cambridge: Cambridge Univ. Press, 1973).

Gray, John. *Mill On Liberty: A Defence* (London: Routledge, 1983).

Halèvy, Elie. *The Growth of Philosophical Radicalism.* Translated by Mary Morris (Boston: Beacon Press, 1955).

Hamburger, Joseph. *Intellectuals in Politics: John Stuart Mill and the Philosophic Radicals* (New Haven, Conn.: Yale Univ. Press, 1965).

Himmelfarb, Gertrude. *On Liberty and Liberalism: The Case of John Stuart Mill* (New York: Knopf, 1974).

McCloskey, J.J. *John Stuart Mill: A Critical Study* (London: Macmillan, 1971).

Rees, John C. *John Stuart Mill's "On Liberty"* (New York: Oxford Univ. Press, 1985).

Robson, John M. *The Improvement of Mankind* (London: Routledge, 1968).

Robson, John M., and Michael Laine, eds. *James and John Stuart Mill* (Toronto: Univ. of Toronto Press, 1976).

Ryan, Alan, ed. *The Philosophy of John Stuart Mill.* 2nd ed. (London: Macmillan, 1987).

Schneewind, J.B., ed. *Mill: A Collection of Critical Essays* (Garden City, N.Y.: Anchor Books, 1968).

Skorupski, John. *John Stuart Mill* (New York: Routledge, 1989).

THORSTEIN VEBLEN (1857–1929)

chapter 14

IN NUMBERING pride the deadliest of the seven sins, Christianity acknowledged the urgency of the human passions for reputation and self-esteem. With grating phrases like "pecuniary emulation," "invidious comparison," and "conspicuous consumption," Thorstein Veblen recast the pursuit of wealth as a struggle for recognition no less than for survival or comfort. Veblen situated modern consumption among predatory patriarchal cultures, for which the paradigm of wealth is the captive woman, a "trophy" testifying to her captor's prowess. With the gradual development of less barbaric tests, wealth changes its form but still ranks people through invidious comparisons of predatory power.

In commercial society, money measures superiority. One's reputation depends on a fluctuating standard of pecuniary decency; to rise in esteem means to get ahead in financial terms and make it public. Wealth becomes a fetish that confers honor (which may explain why Veblen's "conspicuous consumption" is often confused with Marx's different concept of the "fetishism of commodities"). The satisfactions of status, unlike matters of livelihood or convenience, hinge on the other's situation; to increase one person's standing deflates another's. Insofar as consumer satisfaction feeds off invidious comparison, a rising "standard of living" provides no additional net gain. For capitalism, this "status treadmill" is a godsend that gives wings to endless accumulation. It compensates for the "value treadmill," whereby productivity increases distributed across competing businesses mean more products but not necessarily more profits.

As money becomes the arbiter of success, and lavish expenditure becomes the most traveled route to reputation, the Aristotelian distinction between "use value" and "exchange value" requires rethinking. Aristotle's assumption that use value is independent of exchange value breaks down when the (apparent or actual) expensiveness of a commodity figures into its desirability. "Pecuniary institutions induce pecuniary habits of thought which affect men's discrimination outside of pecuniary matters": our taste in food, cars, clothes—even shopping centers and occupations, gender roles and college degrees. These pecuniary rankings are no less consequential for our self-regard.

Veblen's attention to "pecuniary habits" signaled a fundamental criticism of the leading schools of economic thought, classical and neoclassical economics. Veblen subjected marginal utility (neoclassical) theory to several different criticisms that return to points made earlier by David Hume. (1) "Though men be much governed by interest; yet even interest itself, and all human affairs, are entirely governed by *opinion*," Hume wrote. Veblen argued that utility theory's hedonism falsified human desires precisely by abstracting from their social determination by "opinion." He insisted: "a theoretical account of the phenomena of this life must be drawn in these terms in which the phenomena occur"; in commercial societies, the pecuniary determination of human needs, interests, and practices *belongs to the phenomena*. In neoclassical economics, institutional phenomena (and social forms) are "taken for granted, denied, or explained away." (2) Writing in the wake of Darwin, Veblen renews Hume's "natural history" approach to economic institutions with his call for an "evolutionary economics." Failure to treat its object as inherently social reduced neoclassical economics to a strictly static theory, incapable of addressing developmental issues. (3) Though notorious for criticizing ordinary notions of causality, David Hume reasoned according to efficient causes at almost every turn. Veblen argues that neoclassical theory is "rationalist," not only in ignoring the social and historical character of human conduct but also in appealing to the rational purposes (reasons) of economic agents, rather than efficient causes, to explain behavior. So Veblen labeled neoclassical economics "teleological" and classified it as a type of archaic, "animistic" thinking.

318

With a mind to explain the evolution of economic practices, Veblen added the notion of "process" to the contrast between obsolete "teleological" reasoning and the appeal to cause and effect. A "third way" of explanation seemed called for, since Veblen joined American philosophers like William James and Charles Sanders Peirce in criticizing the simple-minded hedonism and associationist psychology they found in classical British empiricism. However, Veblen could not sort through the matted scientific, metaphysical, and moral implications of such a third way. Instead, he wriggled in the straightjacket of positivism's insistence on efficient causes and its dismissal of making intelligent value judgments. How seriously can one take Veblen's protestations that his accounts of conspicuous waste or the use of women and servants as "chattel" in "vicarious conspicuous leisure" intend no value judgments? Theodor Adorno turned to the word "spleen" to capture Veblen's turbulent, tongue-in-cheek positivism.

Veblen's bewilderment over values drove his technocratic proposal for reforming commerce. Keenly aware of the difference between wealth and money, Veblen sharply distinguished between the *industrial* and the *pecuniary* dimensions of modern business and looked to the day when engineers, not entrepreneurs, would be in charge. The industrial dimension pertains to his hobby-horse, "the instinct of workmanship," which, with good Lockean sensibilities, abhors waste. Waste is what fails the test of impersonal usefulness, "usefulness as seen from the point of view of the generically human." By eliminating "unfree" labor and separating being a worker from being subjugated, modern commerce spurs the "instinct of workmanship." But the unfettered spirit of efficient work runs up against the imperatives of pecuniary accumulation. Veblen saw through capitalism's claim to be "natural," yet ironically, in his rage against pecuniary display, he clutched at the impossible capitalist fantasy: an economic order that is "generically human."

319

FROM *THE THEORY OF THE LEISURE CLASS*

CHAPTER II

PECUNIARY EMULATION

In the sequence of cultural evolution the emergence of a leisure class coincides with the beginning of ownership. This is necessarily the case, for these two institutions result from the same set of economic forces. In the inchoate phase of their development they are but different aspects of the same general facts of social structure.

It is as elements of social structure—conventional facts—that leisure and ownership are matters of interest for the purpose in hand. An habitual neglect of work does not constitute a leisure class; neither does the mechanical fact of use and consumption constitute ownership. The present inquiry, therefore, is not concerned with the beginning of indolence, nor with the beginning of the appropriation of useful articles to individual consumption. The point in question is the origin and nature of a conventional leisure class on the one hand and the beginnings of individual ownership as a conventional right or equitable claim on the other hand.

The early differentiation out of which the distinction between a leisure and a working class arises is a division maintained between men's and women's work in the lower stages of barbarism. Likewise the earliest form of ownership is an ownership of the women by the able bodied men of the community. The facts may be expressed in more general terms, and truer to the import of the barbarian theory of life, by saying that it is an ownership of the woman by the man.

There was undoubtedly some appropriation of useful articles before the custom of appropriating women arose. The usages of existing archaic communities in which there is no ownership of women is warrant for such a view. In all communities the members, both male and female, habitually appropriate to their individual use a variety of useful things; but these useful things are not thought of as owned by the person who appropriates and consumes them. The habitual appropriation and consumption of certain slight personal effects goes on without raising the question of ownership; that is to say, the question of a conventional, equitable claim to extraneous things.

The ownership of women begins in the lower barbarian stages of culture, apparently with the seizure of female captives. The original reason for the seizure and appropriation of women seems to have been their usefulness as trophies. The practice of seizing women from the enemy as trophies, gave rise to a form of ownership-marriage, resulting in a household with a male head. This was followed by an extension of slavery to other captives and inferiors, besides women, and by an extension of ownership-marriage to other women than those seized from the enemy. The outcome of emulation under the circumstances of a predatory life, therefore, has been on the one hand a form of marriage resting on coercion, and on the other hand the custom of ownership. The two institutions are not distinguishable in the initial phase of their development; both arise from the desire of the successful men to put their prowess in evidence by exhibiting some durable result of their exploits. Both also minister to that propensity for mastery which pervades all predatory communities. From the ownership of women the concept of ownership extends itself to include the products of their industry, and so there arises the ownership of things as well as of persons.

In this way a consistent system of property in goods is gradually installed. And although in the latest stages of the development, the serviceability of goods for consumption has come to be the most obtrusive element of their value, still, wealth has by no means yet lost its utility as a honorific evidence of the owner's prepotence.

Wherever the institution of private property is found, even in a slightly developed form, the economic process bears the character of a struggle between men for the possession of goods. It has been customary in economic theory, and especially among those economists who adhere with least faltering to the body of modernised classical doctrines, to construe this struggle for wealth as being substantially a struggle for subsistence. Such is, no doubt, its character in large part during the earlier and less efficient phases of industry. Such is also its character in all cases where the "niggardliness of nature" is so strict as to afford but a scanty livelihood to the community in return for strenuous and unremitting application to the business of getting the means of subsistence. But in all progressing communities an advance is presently made beyond this early stage of technological development. Industrial efficiency is presently carried to such a pitch as to afford something appreciably more than a bare livelihood to those engaged in the industrial process. It has not been unusual for economic theory to speak of the further struggle for wealth on this new industrial basis as a competition for an increase of the comforts of life,—primarily for an increase of the physical comforts which the consumption of goods affords.

The end of acquisition and accumulation is conventionally held to be the consumption of the goods accumulated—whether it is consumption directly by the owner of the goods or by the household attached to him and for this purpose identified with him in theory. This is at least felt to be the economically legitimate end of acquisition, which alone it is incumbent on the theory to take account of. Such consumption may of course be conceived to serve the consumer's physical wants—his physical comfort—or his so-called higher wants—spiritual, aesthetic, intellectual, or what not; the latter class of wants being served indirectly by an expenditure of goods, after the fashion familiar to all economic readers.

But it is only when taken in a sense far removed from its naïve meaning that consumption of goods can be said to afford the incentive from which accumulation invariably proceeds. The motive that lies at the root of ownership is emulation; and the same motive of emulation continues active in the further development of the institution to which it has given rise and in the development of all those features of the social structure which this institution of ownership touches. The possession of wealth confers honour; it is an invidious distinction. Nothing equally cogent can be said for the consumption of goods, nor for any other conceivable incentive to acquisition, and especially not for any incentive to the accumulation of wealth.

It is of course not to be overlooked that in a community where nearly all goods are private property the necessity of earning a livelihood is a powerful and ever-present incentive for the poorer members of the community. The need of subsistence and of an increase of physical comfort may for a time be the dominant motive of acquisition for those classes who are habitually employed at manual labour, whose subsistence is on a precarious footing, who

321

possess little and ordinarily accumulate little; but it will appear in the course of the discussion that even in the case of these impecunious classes the predominance of the motive of physical want is not so decided as has sometimes been assumed. On the other hand, so far as regards those members and classes of the community who are chiefly concerned in the accumulation of wealth, the incentive of subsistence or of physical comfort never plays a considerable part. Ownership began and grew into a human institution on grounds unrelated to the subsistence minimum. The dominant incentive was from the outset the invidious distinction attaching to wealth, and, save temporarily and by exception, no other motive has usurped the primacy at any later stage of the development.

Property set out with being booty held as trophies of the successful raid. So long as the group had departed but little from the primitive communal organisation, and so long as it still stood in close contact with other hostile groups, the utility of things or persons owned lay chiefly in an invidious comparison between their possessor and the enemy from whom they were taken. The habit of distinguishing between the interests of the individual and those of the group to which he belongs is apparently a later growth. Invidious comparison between the possessor of the honorific booty and his less successful neighbours within the group was no doubt present early as an element of the utility of the things possessed, though this was not at the outset the chief element of their value. The man's prowess was still primarily the group's prowess, and the possessor of the booty felt himself to be primarily the keeper of the honour of his group. This appreciation of exploit from the communal point of view is met with also at later stages of social growth, especially as regards the laurels of war.

But so soon as the custom of individual ownership begins to gain consistency, the point of view taken in making the invidious comparison on which private property rests will begin to change. Indeed, the one change is but the reflex of the other. The initial phase of ownership, the phase of acquisition by naïve seizure and conversion, begins to pass into the subsequent stage of an incipient organisation of industry on the basis of private property (in slaves); the horde develops into a more or less self-sufficing industrial community; possessions then come to be valued not so much as evidence of successful foray, but rather as evidence of the prepotence of the possessor of these goods over other individuals within the community. The invidious comparison now becomes primarily a comparison of the owner with the other members of the group. Property is still of the nature of trophy, but, with the cultural advance, it becomes more and more a trophy of successes scored in the game of ownership carried on between the members of the group under the quasi-peaceable methods of nomadic life.

Gradually, as industrial activity further displaces predatory activity in the community's everyday life and in men's habits of thought, accumulated prop-

322

erty more and more replaces trophies of predatory exploit as the conventional exponent of prepotence and success. With the growth of settled industry,
therefore, the possession of wealth gains in relative importance and effectiveness as a customary basis of repute and esteem. Not that esteem ceases to be
awarded on the basis of other, more direct evidence of prowess; not that successful predatory aggression or warlike exploit ceases to call out the approval
and admiration of the crowd, or to stir the envy of the less successful competitors; but the opportunities for gaining distinction by means of this direct
manifestation of superior force grow less available both in scope and frequency. At the same time opportunities for industrial aggression, and for the accumulation of property by the quasi-peaceable methods of nomadic industry,
increase in scope and availability. And it is even more to the point that property now becomes the most easily recognised evidence of a reputable degree
of success as distinguished from heroic or signal achievement. It therefore becomes the conventional basis of esteem. Its possession in some amount becomes necessary in order to any reputable standing in the community. It becomes indispensable to accumulate, to acquire property, in order to retain
one's good name. When accumulated goods have in this way once become
the accepted badge of efficiency, the possession of wealth presently assumes
the character of an independent and definitive basis of esteem. The possession
of goods, whether acquired aggressively by one's own exertion or passively by
transmission through inheritance from others, becomes a conventional basis
of reputability. The possession of wealth, which was at the outset valued simply as an evidence of efficiency, becomes, in popular apprehension, itself a
meritorious act. Wealth is now itself intrinsically honourable and confers honour on its possessor. By a further refinement, wealth acquired passively by
transmission from ancestors or other antecedents presently becomes even
more honorific than wealth acquired by the possessor's own effort; but this
distinction belongs at a later stage in the evolution of the pecuniary culture
and will be spoken of in its place.

Prowess and exploit may still remain the basis of award of the highest popular esteem, although the possession of wealth has become the basis of common place reputability and of a blameless social standing. The predatory instinct and the consequent approbation of predatory efficiency are deeply ingrained in the habits of thought of those peoples who have passed under the
discipline of a protracted predatory culture. According to popular award, the
highest honours within human reach may, even yet, be those gained by an
unfolding of extraordinary predatory efficiency in war, or by a quasi-predato-
ry efficiency in statecraft; but for the purposes of a commonplace decent
standing in the community these means of repute have been replaced by the
acquisition and accumulation of goods. In order to stand well in the eyes of
the community, it is necessary to come up to a certain, somewhat indefinite,
conventional standard of wealth; just as in the earlier predatory stage it is nec-

essary for the barbarian man to come up to the tribe's standard of physical endurance, cunning, and skill at arms. A certain standard of wealth in the one case, and of prowess in the other, is a necessary condition of reputability, and anything in excess of this normal amount is meritorious.

Those members of the community who fall short of this, somewhat indefinite, normal degree of prowess or of property suffer in the esteem of their fellow-men; and consequently they suffer also in their own esteem, since the usual basis of self-respect is the respect accorded by one's neighbours. Only individuals with an aberrant temperament can in the long run retain their self-esteem in the face of the disesteem of their fellows. Apparent exceptions to the rule are met with, especially among people with strong religious convictions. But these apparent exceptions are scarcely real exceptions, since such persons commonly fall back on the putative approbation of some supernatural witness of their deeds.

So soon as the possession of property becomes the basis of popular esteem, therefore, it becomes also a requisite to that complacency which we call self-respect. In any community where goods are held in severalty it is necessary, in order to his own peace of mind, that an individual should possess as large a portion of goods as others with whom he is accustomed to class himself; and it is extremely gratifying to possess something more than others. But as fast as a person makes new acquisitions, and becomes accustomed to the resulting new standard of wealth, the new standard forthwith ceases to afford appreciably greater satisfaction than the earlier standard did. The tendency in any case is constantly to make the present pecuniary standard the point of departure for a fresh increase of wealth; and this in turn gives rise to a new standard of sufficiency and a new pecuniary classification of one's self as compared with one's neighbours. So far as concerns the present question, the end sought by accumulation is to rank high in comparison with the rest of the community in point of pecuniary strength. So long as the comparison is distinctly unfavourable to himself, the normal, average individual will live in chronic dissatisfaction with his present lot; and when he has reached what may be called the normal pecuniary standard of the community, or of his class in the community, this chronic dissatisfaction will give place to a restless straining to place a wider and ever-widening pecuniary interval between himself and this average standard. The invidious comparison can never become so favourable to the individual making it that he would not gladly rate himself still higher relatively to his competitors in the struggle for pecuniary reputability.

In the nature of the case, the desire for wealth can scarcely be satiated in any individual instance, and evidently a satiation of the average or general desire for wealth is out of the question. However widely, or equally, or "fairly," it may be distributed, no general increase of the community's wealth can make any approach to satiating this need, the ground of which is the desire of every one to excel every one else in the accumulation of goods. If, as is sometimes assumed, the incentive to accumulation were the want of subsistence or of physical comfort, then the aggregate economic wants of a community might conceivably be satisfied at some point in the advance of industrial efficiency; but since the struggle is substantially a race for reputability on the basis of an invidious comparison, no approach to a definitive attainment is possible.

What has just been said must not be taken to mean that there are no other incentives to acquisition and accumulation than this desire to excel in pecuniary standing and so gain the esteem and envy of one's fellow-men. The desire for added comfort and security from want is present as a motive at every stage of the process of accumulation in a modern industrial community; although the standard of sufficiency in these respects is in turn greatly affected by the habit of pecuniary emulation. To a great extent this emulation shapes the methods and selects the objects of expenditure for personal comfort and decent livelihood.

Besides this, the power conferred by wealth also affords a motive to accumulation. That propensity for purposeful activity and that repugnance to all futility of effort which belong to man by virtue of his character as an agent do not desert him when he emerges from the naïve communal culture where the dominant note of life is the unanalysed and undifferentiated solidarity of the individual with the group with which his life is bound up. When he enters upon the predatory stage, where self-seeking in the narrower sense becomes the dominant note, this propensity goes with him still, as the pervasive trait that shapes his scheme of life. The propensity for achievement and the repugnance to futility remain the underlying economic motive. The propensity changes only in the form of its expression and in the proximate objects to which it directs the man's activity. Under the régime of individual ownership the most available means of visibly achieving a purpose is that afforded by the acquisition and accumulation of goods; and as the self-regarding antithesis between man and man reaches fuller consciousness, the propensity for achievement—the instinct of workmanship—tends more and more to shape itself into a straining to excel others in pecuniary achievement. Relative success, tested by an invidious pecuniary comparison with other men, becomes the conventional end of action. The currently accepted legitimate end of effort becomes the achievement of a favourable comparison with other men; and therefore the repugnance to futility to a good extent coalesces with the incentive of emulation. It acts to accentuate the struggle for pecuniary reputability by visiting with a sharper disapproval all shortcoming and all evidence of shortcoming in point of pecuniary success. Purposeful effort comes to mean, primarily, effort directed to or resulting in a more creditable showing of accumulated wealth. Among the motives which lead men to accumulate wealth, the primacy, both in scope and intensity, therefore, continues to belong to this motive of pecuniary emulation.

In making use of the term "invidious," it may perhaps be unnecessary to

325

remark, there is no intention to extol or depreciate, or to commend or deplore any of the phenomena which the word is used to characterise. The term is used in a technical sense as describing a comparison of persons with a view to rating and grading them in respect of relative worth or value—in an aesthetic or moral sense—and so awarding and defining the relative degrees of complacency with which they may legitimately be contemplated by themselves and by others. An invidious comparison is a process of valuation of persons in respect of worth.

CHAPTER IV

CONSPICUOUS CONSUMPTION

. . .Conspicuous consumption of valuable goods is a means of reputability to the gentleman of leisure. As wealth accumulates on his hands, his own unaided effort will not avail to sufficiently put his opulence in evidence by this method. The aid of friends and competitors is therefore brought in by resorting to the giving of valuable presents and expensive feasts and entertainments. Presents and feasts had probably another origin than that of naïve ostentation, but they acquired their utility for this purpose very early, and they have retained that character to the present; so that their utility in this respect has now long been the substantial ground on which these usages rest. Costly entertainments, such as the potlatch or the ball, are peculiarly adapted to serve this end. The competitor with whom the entertainer wishes to institute a comparison is, by this method, made to serve as a means to the end. He consumes vicariously for his host at the same time that he is a witness to the consumption of that excess of good things which his host is unable to dispose of single-handed, and he is also made to witness his host's facility in etiquette. . . .

With the disappearance of servitude, the number of vicarious consumers attached to any one gentleman tends, on the whole, to decrease. The like is of course true, and perhaps in a still higher degree, of the number of dependents who perform vicarious leisure for him. In a general way, though not wholly nor consistently, these two groups coincide. The dependent who was first delegated for these duties was the wife, or the chief wife; and, as would be expected, in the later development of the institution, when the number of persons by whom these duties are customarily performed gradually narrows, the wife remains the last. In the higher grades of society a large volume of both these kinds of service is required; and here the wife is of course still assisted in the work by a more or less numerous corps of menials. But as we descend the social scale, the point is presently reached where the duties of vicarious leisure and consumption devolve upon the wife alone. In the communities of the Western culture, this point is at present found among the lower middle class.

And here occurs a curious inversion. It is a fact of common observation that in this lower middle class there is no pretence of leisure on the part of the head of the household. Through force of circumstances it has fallen into disuse. But the middle-class wife still carries on the business of vicarious leisure, for the good name of the household and its master. In descending the social scale in any modern industrial community, the primary fact—the conspicuous leisure of the master of the household—disappears at a relatively high point. The head of the middle-class household has been reduced by economic circumstances to turn his hand to gaining a livelihood by occupations which often partake largely of the character of industry, as in the case of the ordinary business man of to-day. But the derivative fact—the vicarious leisure and consumption rendered by the wife, and the auxiliary vicarious performance of leisure by menials—remains in vogue as a conventionality which the demands of reputability will not suffer to be slighted. It is by no means an uncommon spectacle to find a man applying himself to work with the utmost assiduity, in order that his wife may in due form render for him that degree of vicarious leisure which the common sense of the time demands.

The leisure rendered by the wife in such cases is, of course, not a simple manifestation of idleness or indolence. It almost invariably occurs disguised under some form of work or household duties or social amenities, which prove on analysis to serve little or no ulterior end beyond showing that she does not and need not occupy herself with anything that is gainful or that is of substantial use. As has already been noticed under the head of manners, the greater part of the customary round of domestic cares to which the middle-class housewife gives her time and effort is of this character. Not that the results of her attention to household matters, of a decorative and mundificatory character, are not pleasing to the sense of men trained in middle-class proprieties; but the taste to which these effects of household adornment and tidiness appeal is a taste which has been formed under the selective guidance of a canon of propriety that demands just these evidences of wasted effort. The effects are pleasing to us chiefly because we have been taught to find them pleasing. There goes into these domestic duties much solicitude for a proper combination of form and colour, and for other ends that are to be classed as aesthetic in the proper sense of the term; and it is not denied that effects having some substantial aesthetic value are sometimes attained. Pretty much all that is here insisted on is that, as regards these amenities of life, the housewife's efforts are under the guidance of traditions that have been shaped by the law of conspicuously wasteful expenditure of time and substance. If beauty or comfort is achieved,—and it is a more or less fortuitous circumstance if they are,—they must be achieved by means and methods that commend themselves to the great economic law of wasted effort. The more reputable, "presentable" portion of middle-class household paraphernalia are, on the one hand, items of conspicuous consumption, and on the other hand, apparatus for putting in evidence the vicarious leisure rendered by the housewife.

The requirement of vicarious consumption at the hands of the wife continues in force even at a lower point in the pecuniary scale than the require-

327

ment of vicarious leisure. At a point below which little if any pretence of wasted effort, in ceremonial cleanness and the like, is observable, and where there is assuredly no conscious attempt at ostensible leisure, decency still requires the wife to consume some goods conspicuously for the reputability of the household and its head. So that, as the latter-day outcome of this evolution of an archaic institution, the wife, who was at the outset the drudge and chattel of the man, both in fact and in theory,—the producer of goods for him to consume,—has become the ceremonial consumer of goods which he produces. But she still quite unmistakably remains his chattel in theory; for the habitual rendering of vicarious leisure and consumption is the abiding mark of the unfree servant.

This vicarious consumption practised by the household of the middle and lower classes can not be counted as a direct expression of the leisure-class scheme of life, since the household of this pecuniary grade does not belong within the leisure class. It is rather that the leisure-class scheme of life here comes to an expression at the second remove. The leisure class stands at the head of the social structure in point of reputability; and its manner of life and its standards of worth therefore afford the norm of reputability for the community. The observance of these standards, in some degree of approximation, becomes incumbent upon all classes lower in the scale. In modern civilized communities the lines of demarcation between social classes have grown vague and transient, and wherever this happens the norm of reputability imposed by the upper class extends its coercive influence with but slight hindrance down through the social structure to the lowest strata. The result is that the members of each stratum accept as their ideal of decency the scheme of life in vogue in the next higher stratum, and bend their energies to live up to that ideal. On pain of forfeiting their good name and their self-respect in case of failure, they must conform to the accepted code, at least in appearance.

The basis on which good repute in any highly organised industrial community ultimately rests is pecuniary strength; and the means of showing pecuniary strength, and so of gaining or retaining a good name, are leisure and a conspicuous consumption of goods. Accordingly, both of these methods are in vogue as far down the scale as it remains possible; and in the lower strata in which the two methods are employed, both offices are in great part delegated to the wife and children of the household. Lower still, where any degree of leisure, even ostensible, has become impracticable for the wife, the conspicuous consumption of goods remains and is carried on by the wife and children. The man of the household also can do something in this direction, and indeed, he commonly does; but with a still lower descent into the levels of indigence—along the margin of the slums—the man, and presently also the children, virtually cease to consume valuable goods for appearances, and the woman remains virtually the sole exponent of the household's pecuniary decency. No class of society, not even the most abjectly poor, foregoes all customary conspicuous consumption. The last items of this category of consumption are not given up except under stress of the direst necessity. Very much of squalor and discomfort will be endured before the last trinket or the last pretence of pecuniary decency is put away. There is no class and no country that has yielded so abjectly before the pressure of physical want as to deny themselves all gratification of this higher or spiritual need. . . .

The use of the term "waste" is in one respect an unfortunate one. As used in the speech of everyday life the word carries an undertone of deprecation. It is here used for want of a better term that will adequately describe the same range of motives and of phenomena, and it is not to be taken in an odious sense, as implying an illegitimate expenditure of human products or of human life. In the view of economic theory the expenditure in question is no more and no less legitimate than any other expenditure. It is here called "waste" because this expenditure does not serve human life or human well-being on the whole, not because it is waste or misdirection of effort or expenditure as viewed from the standpoint of the individual consumer who chooses it. If he chooses it, that disposes of the question of its relative utility to him, as compared with other forms of consumption that would not be deprecated on account of their wastefulness. Whatever form of expenditure the consumer chooses, or whatever end he seeks in making his choice, has utility to him by virtue of his preference. As seen from the point of view of the individual consumer, the question of wastefulness does not arise within the scope of economic theory proper. The use of the word "waste" as a technical term, therefore, implies no deprecation of the motives or of the ends sought by the consumer under this canon of conspicuous waste.

But it is, on other grounds, worth noting that the term "waste" in the language of everyday life implies deprecation of what is characterised as wasteful. This common-sense implication is itself an outcropping of the instinct of workmanship. The popular reprobation of waste goes to say that in order to be at peace with himself the common man must be able to see in any and all human effort and human enjoyment an enhancement of life and well-being on the whole. In order to meet with unqualified approval, any economic fact must approve itself under the test of impersonal usefulness—usefulness as seen from the point of view of the generically human. Relative or competitive advantage of one individual in comparison with another does not satisfy the economic conscience, and therefore competitive expenditure has not the approval of this conscience.

In strict accuracy nothing should be included under the head of conspicuous waste but such expenditure as is incurred on the ground of an invidious pecuniary comparison. But in order to bring any given item or element in under this head it is not necessary that it should be recognised as waste in this sense by the person incurring the expenditure. It frequently happens that an

329

element of the standard of living which set out with being primarily wasteful, ends with becoming, in the apprehension of the consumer, a necessary of life; and it may in this way become as indispensable as any other item of the consumer's habitual expenditure. As items which sometimes fall under this head, and are therefore available as illustrations of the manner in which this principle applies, may be cited carpets and tapestries, silver table service, waiter's services, silk hats, starched linen, many articles of jewellery and of dress. The indispensability of these things after the habit and the convention have been formed, however, has little to say in the classification of expenditures as waste or not waste in the technical meaning of the word. The test to which all expenditure must be brought in an attempt to decide that point is the question whether it serves directly to enhance human life on the whole—whether it furthers the life process taken impersonally. For this is the basis of award of the instinct of workmanship, and that instinct is the court of final appeal in any question of economic truth or adequacy. It is a question as to the award rendered by a dispassionate common sense. The question is, therefore, not whether, under the existing circumstances of individual habit and social custom, a given expenditure conduces to the particular consumer's gratification or peace of mind; but whether, aside from acquired tastes and from the canons of usage and conventional decency, its result is a net gain in comfort or in the fulness of life. Customary expenditure must be classed under the head of waste in so far as the custom on which it rests is traceable to the habit of making an invidious pecuniary comparison—in so far as it is conceived that it could not have become customary and prescriptive without the backing of this principle of pecuniary reputability or relative economic success.

It is obviously not necessary that a given object of expenditure should be exclusively wasteful in order to come in under the category of conspicuous waste. An article may be useful and wasteful both, and its utility to the consumer may be made up of use and waste in the most varying proportions. Consumable goods, and even productive goods, generally show the two elements in combination, as constituents of their utility; although, in a general way, the element of waste tends to predominate in articles of consumption, while the contrary is true of articles designed for productive use. Even in articles which appear at first glance to serve for pure ostentation only, it is always possible to detect the presence of some, at least ostensible, useful purpose; and on the other hand, even in special machinery and tools contrived for some particular industrial process, as well as in the rudest appliances of human industry, the traces of conspicuous waste, or at least of the habit of ostentation, usually become evident on a close scrutiny. It would be hazardous to assert that a useful purpose is ever absent from the utility of any article or of any service, however obviously its prime purpose and chief element is conspicuous waste; and it would be only less hazardous to assert of any primarily useful product that the element of waste is in no way concerned in its value, immediately or remotely.

For Further Reading

Veblen, Thorstein. *The Engineers and the Price System* (New Brunswick, N.J.: Transaction Bks., 1983).

_____. *The Instinct of Workmanship and the State of the Industrial Arts* (New Brunswick, N.J.: Transaction Bks., 1990).

_____. *The Place of Science in Modern Civilisation, and other Essays* (New Brunswick, N.J.: Transaction Bks., 1990).

_____. *The Theory of Business Enterprise* (New Brunswick, N.J.: Transaction Bks., 1978).

Adorno, Theodor. "Veblen's Attack on Culture." In *Prisms* (Cambridge: MIT Press, 1982).

Commons, R. *Institutional Economics* (New York: Macmillan, 1934).

Diggins, John P. *The Bard of Savagery: Thorstein Veblen and Modern Social Theory* (Hassocks, England: Harvester Press, 1978).

Dorfman, Joseph. *Thorstein Veblen and His America* (New York: Viking, 1934).

Dos Passos, John. *The Big Money* (New York: Harcourt, Brace, 1936).

Lerner, Max. *The Portable Veblen* (New York: Viking Press, 1950).

Riesman, David. *Thorstein Veblen; A Critical Interpretation* (New York: Seabury Press, 1960).

Tilman, Rick. *Thorstein Veblen and His Critics, 1891–1963: Conservative, Liberal, and Radical Perspectives* (Princeton: Princeton Univ. Press, 1992).

GEORG SIMMEL (1858–1918)

chapter 15

SOUL AND form preoccupied Georg Simmel. The soul's form-giving capacity is the source of its tragic dialectic: "life can express itself and realize its freedom only through forms; yet forms must necessarily suffocate life and obstruct freedom." Human association is likewise dialectical. We are always within social roles and always outside them: no actual person is just a banker, an aunt, a waiter. The personal is never completely swallowed up by the social; neither can the alienation of the individual from fixed social forms be overcome: "life is always in latent opposition to the form." Social forms, then, are not just something "out there"; they matter all the way down to the depths of our souls, determining our manners of thinking, perceiving, feeling, desiring. This allows Simmel to enter a detail of life through a phenomenological inquiry and brilliantly illumine the whole.

Money and the money economy held Simmel's attention as no other phenomena; money was for him the prime example of a social form submerging the form-givers, the individuals composing modern society. Money is the "frightful leveler—it hollows out the core of things, their peculiarities, their specific values and their uniqueness and incomparability in a way which is beyond repair." Questions about goods in a money economy always come down to "How much?" The subjective correlate to money's hollowing of things is what Simmel calls the blasé attitude: the indifference of those who expect nothing new. Faced with the vapidness of commodities, the fugitive family in the film *Running on Empty* allowed only found or homemade objects as birthday gifts. Calculation, precision, punctuality, the reduction of quality to quantity all flow from money to shape a culture of "intellectualism" and rationalization, the phenomena that engrossed Max Weber. Under the rule of money, persons are channeled into acting as buyers and sellers, social roles remarkable for their impersonality. The blasé attitude, in other words, defines feelings for persons as well as for goods: impersonality has personal effects.

Not all those effects are bad, Simmel thinks. The impersonality of money, along with modern urban life, opens space for individual freedom. Despite his grim account of money, Simmel never idealizes the narrow circles of pre-commercial communities. To Simmel, *gemeinschaft* means too many watchful eyes. The anonymity of a commercial city allows individuals to break free from customary expectations. He identifies two types of freedom congenial to commerce and city life: "freedom from" past restraints on individual choices and the cultivation of individuality—a favorite theme of the nineteenth century.

If we piece this picture together, serious conundrums for consumers arise. Where the money economy takes hold, our search for satisfaction increasingly turns to the world of commodities. But the more the money form seeps through, the less distinctive goods seem and the less they are able to satisfy. This falling rate of satisfaction is compounded by the blasé attitude that dulls the consumer's sense of self. Because the division of labor fragments our work, and the enormous "objective culture" overwhelms us, the pressure to establish an identity puts great weight upon what we buy. This is welcomed by the marketplace, where sellers are eager to ply us with products and services. How often is the new line introduced to meet "your special needs"? But how likely are we to express individuality by stringing together the right purchases?

Simmel can be faulted for paying too little attention to the relations between the money economy and capitalism. Max Weber made such a criticism, as did Karl Mannheim, who complained that Simmel "had abstracted, in a completely unhistorical manner, the capitalistic money form from its capitalistic background and imputed the characteristic structural change to 'money as such.'" Nonetheless, since capitalism presupposes and continually reproduces the money economy, Simmel's analysis of the powers of money, properly qualified, keeps its bite.

334

Simmel observed a new tendency in the dialectic of spirit, one linked to cultural modernism and postmodernism: "life...would like to puncture not only this or that form, but form *as such,* and to absorb the form in its immediacy." Against traditionalist defenders of forms, Simmel affirms the "life" he finds here, yet he resolves that there is no escaping the tragic inevitability of the soul's form-giving power.

This new tendency followed from a new level of reflection on the opposition between "life" and "form." Just as modern political economy focused attention on labor's role in the creation of wealth, modern philosophy made us heed how the mind bestows form. The critique of anthropomorphism is one of the most familiar arguments in modern thought; it reinterprets properties once attributed to objects as our projections onto the world. For example, Aristotelian claims about "natural place" or natural purposes are "seen through" as false objectifications of human dispositions or purposes. Form gets construed as *purely subjective,* an interpretation resonating with classical political economy's assertion that human labor (in abstraction from nature) is the *sole* source of value, and again with neoclassical economics' assumption that utility is something *purely subjective.* (That both Simmel and Weber adopted neoclassical economics was of great consequence to the emerging discipline of sociology.) Kant christened this turnabout in thinking the "Copernican revolution," and Simmel's philosophy of form radicalized it with the notion of multiple, subjectively constituted world views (*Weltanschauungen*) or paradigms. How can these subjective perspectives make any claims that are not arbitrary and alienating?

335

Simmel leaves us with an unhappy choice: either rebel against form as such, the postmodern path, or agree with him that spirit's life is tragic. Yet these options may rest on an untenable, subjectivistic doctrine of form. Given money's capacity to hollow out the essence of things, we may wonder whether Simmel's own fateful doctrine of form is an intellectual offspring of the money economy.

"THE METROPOLIS AND MENTAL LIFE"

The deepest problems of modern life flow from the attempt of the individual to maintain the independence and individuality of his existence against the sovereign powers of society, against the weight of the historical heritage and the external culture and technique of life. This antagonism represents the most modern form of the conflict which primitive man must carry on with nature for his own bodily existence. The eighteenth century may have called for liberation from all the ties which grew up historically in politics, in religion, in morality and in economics in order to permit the original natural virtue of man, which is equal in everyone, to develop without inhibition; the nineteenth century may have sought to promote, in addition to man's freedom, his individuality (which is connected with the division of labor) and his achievements which make him unique and indispensable but which at the same time make him so much the more dependent on the complementary activity of others; Nietzsche may have seen the relentless struggle of the individual as the prerequisite for his full development, while Socialism found the same thing in the suppression of all competition—but in each of these the same fundamental motive was at work, namely the resistance of the individual to being levelled, swallowed up in the social-technological mechanism. When one inquires about the products of the specifically modern aspects of contemporary life with reference to their inner meaning—when, so to speak, one examines the body of culture with reference to the soul, as I am to do concerning the metropolis today—the answer will require the investigation of the relationship which such a social structure promotes between the individual aspects of life and those which transcend the existence of single individuals. It will require the investigation of the adaptations made by the personality in its adjustment to the forces that lie outside of it.

The psychological foundation, upon which the metropolitan individuality is erected, is the intensification of emotional life due to the swift and continuous shift of external and internal stimuli. Man is a creature whose existence is dependent on differences, i.e., his mind is stimulated by the difference between present impressions and those which have preceded. Lasting impressions, the slightness in their differences, the habituated regularity of their course and contrasts between them, consume, so to speak, less mental energy than the rapid telescoping of changing images, pronounced differences within what is grasped at a single glance, and the unexpectedness of violent stimuli. To the extent that the metropolis creates these psychological conditions—with every crossing of the street, with the tempo and multiplicity of economic, occupational and social life—it creates in the sensory foundations of mental life, and in the degree of awareness necessitated by our organization as creatures dependent on differences, a deep contrast with the slower, more habitual, more smoothly flowing rhythm of the sensory-mental phase of small town and rural existence. Thereby the essentially intellectualistic character of the mental life of the metropolis becomes intelligible as over against that of the small town which rests more on feelings and emotional relationships. These latter are rooted in the unconscious levels of the mind and develop most readily in the steady equilibrium of unbroken customs. The locus of reason, on the other hand, is in the lucid, conscious upper strata of the mind and it is the most adaptable of our inner forces. In order to adjust itself to the shifts and contradictions in events, it does not require the disturbances and inner upheavals which are the only means whereby more conservative personalities are able to adapt themselves to the same rhythm of events. Thus the metropolitan type—which naturally takes on a thousand individual modifications—creates a protective organ for itself against the profound disruption with which the fluctuations and discontinuities of the external milieu threaten it. Instead of reacting emotionally, the metropolitan type reacts primarily in a rational manner, thus creating a mental predominance through the intensification of consciousness, which in turn is caused by it. Thus the reaction of the metropolitan person to those events is moved to a sphere of mental activity which is least sensitive and which is furthest removed from the depths of the personality.

This intellectualistic quality which is thus recognized as a protection of the inner life against the domination of the metropolis, becomes ramified into numerous specific phenomena. The metropolis has always been the seat of money economy because the many-sidedness and concentration of commercial activity have given the medium of exchange an importance which it could not have acquired in the commercial aspects of rural life. But money economy and the domination of the intellect stand in the closest relationship to one another. They have in common a purely matter-of-fact attitude in the treatment of persons and things in which a formal justice is often combined with an unrelenting hardness. The purely intellectualistic person is indifferent to all things personal because, out of them, relationships and reactions develop which are not to be completely understood by purely rational methods—just as the unique element in events never enters into the principle of money. Money is concerned only with what is common to all, i.e., with the exchange value which reduces all quality and individuality to a purely quantitative level. All emotional relationships between persons rest on their individuality, whereas intellectual relationships deal with persons as with numbers, that is, as with elements which, in themselves, are indifferent, but which are of interest only insofar as they offer something objectively perceivable. It is in this very manner that the inhabitant of the metropolis reckons with his merchant, his customer, and with his servant, and frequently with the persons with whom he is thrown into obligatory association. These relationships stand in distinct contrast with the nature of the smaller circle in which the inevitable knowledge of individual characteristics produces, with an equal inevitability, an emotional tone in conduct, a sphere which is beyond the mere objective weighting of tasks performed and payments made. What is essential here as regards the economic-psychological aspect of the problem is that in less advanced cultures production was for the customer who ordered the product so that the producer and the purchaser knew one another. The modern city, however, is supplied almost exclusively by production for the market, that is, for entirely unknown purchasers who never appear in the actual field of vision of the producers themselves. Thereby, the interests of each party acquire a relentless matter-of-factness, and its rationally calculated economic egoism need not fear any divergence from its set path because of the imponderability of personal relationships. This is all the more the case in the money economy which dominates the metropolis in which the last remnants of domestic production and direct barter of goods have been eradicated and in

337

which the amount of production on direct personal order is reduced daily. Furthermore, this psychological intellectualistic attitude and the money economy are in such close integration that no one is able to say whether it was the former that effected the latter or *vice versa*. What is certain is only that the form of life in the metropolis is the soil which nourishes this interaction most fruitfully, a point which I shall attempt to demonstrate only with the statement of the most outstanding English constitutional historian to the effect that through the entire course of English history London has never acted as the heart of England but often as its intellect and always as its money bag.

In certain apparently insignificant characters or traits of the most external aspects of life are to be found a number of characteristic mental tendencies. The modern mind has become more and more a calculating one. The calculating exactness of practical life which has resulted from a money economy corresponds to the ideal of natural science, namely that of transforming the world into an arithmetical problem and of fixing every one of its parts in a mathematical formula. It has been [the, P.M.] money economy which has thus filled the daily life of so many people with weighing, calculating, enumerating and the reduction of qualitative values to quantitative terms. Because of the character of calculability which money has there has come into the relationships of the elements of life a precision and a degree of certainty in the definition of the equalities and inequalities and an unambiguousness in agreements and arrangements, just as externally this precision has been brought about through the general diffusion of pocket watches. It is, however, the conditions of the metropolis which are cause as well as effect for this essential characteristic. The relationships and concerns of the typical metropolitan resident are so manifold and complex that, especially as a result of the agglomeration of so many persons with such differentiated interests, their relationships and activities intertwine with one another into a many-membered organism. In view of this fact, the lack of the most exact punctuality in promises and performances would cause the whole to break down into an inextricable chaos. If all the watches in Berlin suddenly went wrong in different ways even only as much as an hour, its entire economic and commercial life would be derailed for some time. Even though this may seem more superficial in its significance, it transpires that the magnitude of distances results in making all waiting and the breaking of appointments an ill-afforded waste of time. For this reason the technique of metropolitan life in general is not conceivable without all of its activities and reciprocal relationships being organized and coordinated in the most punctual way into a firmly fixed framework of time which transcends all subjective elements. But here too there emerge those conclusions which are in general the whole task of this discussion, namely, that every event, however restricted to this superficial level it may appear, comes immediately into contact with the depths of the soul, and that the most banal externalities are, in the last analysis, bound up with the fi-

338

nal decisions concerning the meaning and the style of life. Punctuality, calculability, and exactness, which are required by the complications and extensiveness of metropolitan life are not only most intimately connected with its capitalistic and intellectualistic character but also color the content of life and are
conducive to the exclusion of those irrational, instinctive, sovereign human
traits and impulses which originally seek to determine the form of life from
within instead of receiving it from the outside in a general, schematically precise form. Even though those lives which are autonomous and characterized
by these vital impulses are not entirely impossible in the city, they are, none
the less, opposed to it *in abstracto*. It is in the light of this that we can explain
the passionate hatred of personalities like Ruskin and Nietzsche for the metropolis—personalities who found the value of life only in unschematized individual expressions which cannot be reduced to exact equivalents and in
whom, on that account, there flowed from the same source as did that hatred,
the hatred of the money economy and of the intellectualism of existence.

The same factors which, in the exactness and the minute precision of the
form of life, have coalesced into a structure of the highest impersonality, have,
on the other hand, an influence in a highly personal direction. There is perhaps no psychic phenomenon which is so unconditionally reserved to the
city as the blasé outlook. It is at first the consequence of those rapidly shifting
stimulations of the nerves which are thrown together in all their contrasts and
from which it seems to us the intensification of metropolitan intellectuality
seems to be derived. On that account it is not likely that stupid persons who
have been hitherto intellectually dead will be blasé. Just as an immoderately
sensuous life makes one blasé because it stimulates the nerves to their utmost
reactivity until they finally can no longer produce any reaction at all, so, less
harmful stimuli, through the rapidity and the contradictoriness of their shifts,
force the nerves to make such violent responses, tear them about so brutally
that they exhaust their last reserves of strength and, remaining in the same
milieu, do not have time for new reserves to form. This incapacity to react to
new stimulation with the required amount of energy constitutes in fact that
blasé attitude which every child of a large city evinces when compared with
the products of the more peaceful and more stable milieu.

Combined with this physiological source of the blasé metropolitan attitude there is another which derives from a money economy. The essence of
the blasé attitude is an indifference toward the distinctions between things.
Not in the sense that they are not perceived, as is the case of mental dullness,
but rather that the meaning and the value of the distinctions between things,
and therewith of the things themselves, are experienced as meaningless. They
appear to the blasé person in a homogeneous, flat and gray color with no one
of them worthy of being preferred to another. This psychic mood is the correct subjective reflection of a complete money economy to the extent that
money takes the place of all the manifoldness of things and expresses all qual-

itative distinctions between them in the distinction of "how much." To the extent that money, with its colorlessness and its indifferent quality, can become a common denominator of all values it becomes the frightful leveler—it hollows out the core of things, their peculiarities, their specific values and their uniqueness and incomparability in a way which is beyond repair. They all float with the same specific gravity in the constantly moving stream of money. They all rest on the same level and are distinguished only by their amounts. In individual cases this coloring, or rather this de-coloring of things, through their equation with money, may be imperceptibly small. In the relationship, however, which the wealthy person has to objects which can be bought for money, perhaps indeed in the total character which, for this reason, public opinion now recognizes in these objects, it takes on very considerable proportions. This is why the metropolis is the seat of commerce and it is in it that the purchasability of things appears in quite a different aspect than in simpler economies. It is also the peculiar seat of the blasé attitude. In it is brought to a peak, in a certain way, that achievement in the concentration of purchasable things which stimulates the individual to the highest degree of nervous energy. Through the mere quantitative intensification of the same conditions this achievement is transformed into its opposite, into this peculiar adaptive phenomenon—the blasé attitude—in which the nerves reveal their final possibility of adjusting themselves to the content and the form of metropolitan life by renouncing the response to them. We see that the self-preservation of certain types of personalities is obtained at the cost of devaluing the entire objective world, ending inevitably in dragging the personality downward into a feeling of its own valuelessness.

Whereas the subject of this form of existence must come to terms with it for himself, his self-preservation in the face of the great city requires of him a no less negative type of social conduct. The mental attitude of the people of the metropolis to one another may be designated formally as one of reserve. If the unceasing external contact of numbers of persons in the city should be met by the same number of inner reactions as in the small town, in which one knows almost every person he meets and to each of whom he has a positive relationship, one would be completely atomized internally and would fall into an unthinkable mental condition. Partly this psychological circumstance and partly the privilege of suspicion which we have in the face of the elements of metropolitan life (which are constantly touching one another in fleeting contact) necessitates in us that reserve, in consequence of which we do not know by sight neighbors of years standing and which permits us to appear to small-town folk so often as cold and uncongenial. Indeed, if I am not mistaken, the inner side of this external reserve is not only indifference but more frequently than we believe, it is a slight aversion, a mutual strangeness and repulsion which, in a close contact which has arisen any way whatever, can break out into hatred and conflict. The entire inner organization of such a type of extended commercial life rests on an extremely varied structure of sympathies, indifferences and aversions of the briefest as well as of the most enduring sort. This sphere of indifference is, for this reason, not as great as it seems superficially. Our minds respond, with some definite feeling, to almost every impression emanating from another person. The unconsciousness, the transitoriness and the shift of these feelings seem to raise them only into indifference. Actually this latter would be as unnatural to us as immersion into a chaos of unwished-for suggestions would be unbearable. From these two typical dangers of metropolitan life we are saved by antipathy which is the latent adumbration of actual antagonism since it brings about the sort of distanciation and deflection without which this type of life could not be carried on at all. Its extent and its mixture, the rhythm of its emergence and disappearance, the forms in which it is adequate—these constitute, with the simplified motives (in the narrower sense) an inseparable totality of the form of metropolitan life. What appears here directly as dissociation is in reality only one of the elementary forms of socialization.

This reserve with its overtone of concealed aversion appears once more, however, as the form or the wrappings of a much more general psychic trait of the metropolis. It assures the individual of a type and degree of personal freedom to which there is no analogy in other circumstances. It has its roots in one of the great developmental tendencies of social life as a whole; in one of the few for which an approximately exhaustive formula can be discovered. The most elementary stage of social organization which is to be found historically, as well as in the present, is this: a relatively small circle almost entirely closed against neighboring foreign or otherwise antagonistic groups but which has however within itself such a narrow cohesion that the individual member has only a very slight area for the development of his own qualities and for free activity for which he himself is responsible. Political and familial groups began in this way as do political and religious communities; the self-preservation of very young associations requires a rigorous setting of boundaries and a centripetal unity and for that reason it cannot give room to freedom and the peculiarities of inner and external development of the individual. From this stage social evolution proceeds simultaneously in two divergent but none the less corresponding directions. In the measure that the group grows numerically, spatially, and in the meaningful content of life, its immediate inner unity and the definiteness of its original demarcation against others are weakened and rendered mild by reciprocal interactions and interconnections. And at the same time the individual gains a freedom of movement far beyond the first jealous delimitation, and gains also a peculiarity and individuality to which the division of labor in groups, which have become larger, gives both occasion and necessity. However much the particular conditions and forces of the individual situation might modify the general scheme, the state and Christianity, guilds and political parties and innumerable other

341

groups have developed in accord with this formula. This tendency seems, to me, however to be quite clearly recognizable also in the development of individuality within the framework of city life. Small town life in antiquity as well as in the Middle Ages imposed such limits upon the movements of the individual in his relationships with the outside world and on his inner independence and differentiation that the modern person could not even breathe under such conditions. Even today the city dweller who is placed in a small town feels a type of narrowness which is very similar. The smaller the circle which forms our environment and the more limited the relationships which have the possibility of transcending the boundaries, the more anxiously the narrow community watches over the deeds, the conduct of life and the attitudes of the individual and the more will a quantitative and qualitative individuality tend to pass beyond the boundaries of such a community.

The ancient *polis* seems in this regard to have had a character of a small town. The incessant threat against its existence by enemies from near and far brought about that stern cohesion in political and military matters, that supervision of the citizen by other citizens, and that jealousy of the whole toward the individual whose own private life was repressed to such an extent that he could compensate himself only by acting as a despot in his own household. The tremendous agitation and excitement, and the unique colorfulness of Athenian life is perhaps explained by the fact that a people of incomparably individualized personalities were in constant struggle against the incessant inner and external oppression of a de-individualizing small town. This created an atmosphere of tension in which the weaker were held down and the stronger were impelled to the most passionate type of self-protection. And with this there blossomed in Athens, what, without being able to define it exactly, must be designated as "the general human character" in the intellectual development of our species. For the correlation, the factual as well as the historical validity of which we are here maintaining, is that the broadest and the most general contents and forms of life are intimately bound up with the most individual ones. Both have a common prehistory and also common enemies in the narrow formations and groupings, whose striving for self-preservation set them in conflict with the broad and general on the outside, as well as the freely mobile and individual on the inside. Just as in feudal times the "free" man was he who stood under the law of the land, that is, under the law of the largest social unit, but he was unfree who derived his legal rights only from the narrow circle of a feudal community—so today in an intellectualized and refined sense the citizen of the metropolis is "free" in contrast with the trivialities and prejudices which bind the small town person. The mutual reserve and indifference, and the intellectual conditions of life in large social units are never more sharply appreciated in their significance for the independence of the individual than in the dense crowds of the metropolis because the bodily closeness and lack of space make intellectual distance really perceivable for the first time. It is obviously only the obverse of this freedom that, under certain circumstances, one never feels as lonely and as deserted as in this metropolitan crush of persons. For here, as elsewhere, it is by no means necessary that the freedom of man reflect itself in his emotional life only as a pleasant experience.

It is not only the immediate size of the area and population which, on the basis of world-historical correlation between the increase in the size of the social unit and the degree of personal inner and outer freedom, makes the metropolis the locus of this condition. It is rather in transcending this purely tangible extensiveness that the metropolis also becomes the seat of cosmopolitanism. Comparable with the form of the development of wealth—(beyond a certain point property increases in ever more rapid progression as out of its own inner being)—the individual's horizon is enlarged. In the same way, economic, personal and intellectual relations in the city (which are its ideal reflection), grow in a geometrical progression as soon as, for the first time, a certain limit has been passed. Every dynamic extension becomes a preparation not only for a similar extension but rather for a larger one and from every thread which is spun out of it there continue, growing as out of themselves, an endless number of others. This may be illustrated by the fact that within the city the "unearned increment" of ground rent, through a mere increase in traffic, brings to the owner profits which are self-generating. At this point the quantitative aspects of life are transformed qualitatively. The sphere of life of the small town is, in the main, enclosed within itself. For the metropolis it is decisive that its inner life is extended in a wave-like motion over a broader national or international area. Weimar was no exception because its significance was dependent upon individual personalities and died with them, whereas the metropolis is characterised by its essential independence even of the most significant individual personalities; this is rather its antithesis and it is the price of independence which the individual living in it enjoys. The most significant aspect of the metropolis lies in this functional magnitude beyond its actual physical boundaries and this effectiveness reacts upon the latter and gives to it life, weight, importance and responsibility. A person does not end with limits of his physical body or with the area to which his physical activity is immediately confined but embraces, rather, the totality of meaningful effects which emanates from him temporally and spatially. In the same way the city exists only in the totality of the effects which transcend their immediate sphere. These really are the actual extent in which their existence is expressed. This is already expressed in the fact that individual freedom, which is the logical historical complement of such extension, is not only to be understood in the negative sense as mere freedom of movement and emancipation from prejudices and philistinism. Its essential characteristic is rather to be found in the fact that the particularity and incomparability which ultimately every person possesses in some way is actually ex-

343

pressed, giving form to life. That we follow the laws of our inner nature—and this is what freedom is—becomes perceptible and convincing to us and to others only when the expressions of this nature distinguish themselves from others; it is our irreplaceability by others which shows that our mode of existence is not imposed upon us from the outside.

Cities are above all the seat of the most advanced economic division of labor. They produce such extreme phenomena as the lucrative vocation of the *quatorzieme* in Paris. These are persons who may be recognized by shields on their houses and who hold themselves ready at the dinner hour in appropriate costumes so they can be called upon on short notice in case thirteen persons find themselves at the table. Exactly in the measure of its extension the city offers to an increasing degree the determining conditions for the division of labor. It is a unit which, because of its large size, is receptive to a highly diversified plurality of achievements while at the same time the agglomeration of individuals and their struggle for the customer forces the individual to a type of specialized accomplishment in which he cannot be so easily exterminated by the other. The decisive fact here is that in the life of a city, struggle with nature for the means of life is transformed into a conflict with human beings and the gain which is fought for is granted, not by nature, but by man. For here we find not only the previously mentioned source of specialization but rather the deeper one in which the seller must seek to produce in the person to whom he wishes to sell ever new and unique needs. The necessity to specialize one's product in order to find a source of income which is not yet exhausted and also to specialize a function which cannot be easily supplanted is conducive to differentiation, refinement and enrichment of the needs of the public which obviously must lead to increasing personal variation within this public.

All this leads to the narrower type of intellectual individuation of mental qualities to which the city gives rise in proportion to its size. There is a whole series of causes for this. First of all there is the difficulty of giving one's own personality a certain status within the framework of metropolitan life. Where quantitative increase of value and energy has reached its limits, one seizes on qualitative distinctions, so that, through taking advantage of the existing sensitivity to differences, the attention of the social world can, in some way, be won for oneself. This leads ultimately to the strangest eccentricities, to specifically metropolitan extravagances of self-distanciation, of caprice, of fastidiousness, the meaning of which is no longer to be found in the content of such activity itself but rather in its being a form of "being different"—of making oneself noticeable. For many types of persons these are still the only means of saving for oneself, through the attention gained from others, some sort of self-esteem and the sense of filling a position. In the same sense there operates an apparently insignificant factor which in its effects however is perceptibly cumulative, namely, the brevity and rarity of meetings which are allotted to each individual as compared with social intercourse in a small city. For here we find the attempt to appear to-the-point, clear-cut and individual with extraordinarily greater frequency than where frequent and long association assures to each person an unambiguous conception of the other's personality.

This appears to me to be the most profound cause of the fact that the metropolis places emphasis on striving for the most individual forms of personal existence—regardless of whether it is always correct or always successful. The development of modern culture is characterised by the predominance of what one can call the objective spirit over the subjective; that is, in language as well as in law, in the technique of production as well as in art, in science as well as in the objects of domestic environment, there is embodied a sort of spirit [*Geist*], the daily growth of which is followed only imperfectly and with an even greater lag by the intellectual development of the individual. If we survey for instance the vast culture which during the last century has been embodied in things and in knowledge, in institutions and comforts, and if we compare them with the cultural progress of the individual during the same period—at least in the upper classes—we would see a frightful difference in rate of growth between the two which represents, in many points, rather a regression of the culture of the individual with reference to spirituality, delicacy and idealism. This discrepancy is in essence the result of the success of the growing division of labor. For it is this which requires from the individual an ever more one-sided type of achievement which, at its highest point, often permits his personality as a whole to fall into neglect. In any case this overgrowth of objective culture has been less and less satisfactory for the individual. Perhaps less conscious than in practical activity and in the obscure complex of feelings which flow from him, he is reduced to a negligible quantity. He becomes a single cog as over against the vast overwhelming organization of things and forces which gradually take out of his hands everything connected with progress, spirituality and value. The operation of these forces results in the transformation of the latter from a subjective form into one of purely objective existence. It need only be pointed out that the metropolis is the proper arena for this type of culture which has outgrown every personal element. Here in buildings and in educational institutions, in the wonders and comforts of space-conquering technique, in the formations of social life and in the concrete institutions of the State is to be found such a tremendous richness of crystallizing, depersonalized cultural accomplishments that the personality can, so to speak, scarcely maintain itself in the face of it. From one angle life is made infinitely more easy in the sense that stimulations, interests, and the taking up of time and attention, present themselves from all sides and carry it in a stream which scarcely requires any individual efforts for its ongoing. But from another angle, life is composed more and more of these impersonal cultural elements and existing goods and values which seek to suppress

345

peculiar personal interests and incomparabilities. As a result, in order that this most personal element be saved, extremities and peculiarities and individualizations must be produced and they must be over-exaggerated merely to be brought into the awareness even of the individual himself. The atrophy of individual culture through the hypertrophy of objective culture lies at the root of the bitter hatred which the preachers of the most extreme individualism, in the footsteps of Nietzsche, directed against the metropolis. But it is also the explanation of why indeed they are so passionately loved in the metropolis and indeed appear to its residents as the saviors of their unsatisfied yearnings.

When both of these forms of individualism which are nourished by the quantitative relationships of the metropolis, i.e., individual independence and the elaboration of personal peculiarities, are examined with reference to their historical position, the metropolis attains an entirely new value and meaning in the world history of the spirit. The eighteenth century found the individual in the grip of powerful bonds which had become meaningless—bonds of a political, agrarian, guild and religious nature—delimitations which imposed upon the human being at the same time an unnatural form and for a long time an unjust inequality. In this situation arose the cry for freedom and equality—the belief in the full freedom of movement of the individual in all his social and intellectual relationships which would then permit the same noble essence to emerge equally from all individuals as Nature had placed it in them and as it had been distorted by social life and historical development. Alongside of this liberalistic ideal there grew up in the nineteenth century from Goethe and the Romantics, on the one hand, and from the economic division of labor on the other, the further tendency, namely, that individuals who had been liberated from their historical bonds sought now to distinguish themselves from one another. No longer was it the "general human quality" in every individual but rather his qualitative uniqueness and irreplaceability that now became the criteria of his value. In the conflict and shifting interpretations of these two ways of defining the position of the individual within the totality is to be found the external as well as the internal history of our time. It is the function of the metropolis to make a place for the conflict and for the attempts at unification of both of these in the sense that its own peculiar conditions have been revealed to us as the occasion and the stimulus for the development of both. Thereby they attain a quite unique place, fruitful with an inexhaustible richness of meaning in the development of the mental life. They reveal themselves as one of those great historical structures in which conflicting life-embracing currents find themselves with equal legitimacy. Because of this, however, regardless of whether we are sympathetic or antipathetic with their individual expressions, they transcend the sphere in which a judge-like attitude on our part is appropriate. To the extent that such forces have been integrated, with the fleeting existence of a single cell, into the root

346

as well as the crown of the totality of historical life to which we belong—it is our task not to complain or to condone but only to understand.

For Further Reading

Simmel, Georg. *Essays on Interpretation in Social Science.* Translated and edited with an introduction by G. Oakes (Totowa, N.J.: Roman and Littlefield, 1980).

_____. *Georg Simmel: On Women, Sexuality, and Love* (New Haven: Yale Univ. Press, 1984).

_____. *On Individuality and Social Forms.* Edited and with introduction by D.N. Levine. (Chicago: Univ. of Chicago Press, 1971).

_____. *The Philosophy of Money.* Translated by T. Bottomore and D. Frisby with an introduction by D. Frisby (London: Routledge, 1978).

_____. *The Problems of the Philosophy of History.* Translated, edited and with an introduction by G. Oakes (New York: Free Press, 1977).

Coser, Lewis A., ed. *Georg Simmel* (Englewood Cliffs, N.J.: Prentice-Hall, 1965).

_____. "Georg Simmel" in *Masters of Sociological Thought* (New York: Harcourt Brace Jovanovich, 1971).

Frankel, S.H. *Money: Two Philosophies* (Oxford: Blackwell, 1977).

Frisby, David. *Fragments of Modernity: Georg Simmel, Siegfried Kracauer, Walter Benjamin* (London: Heinemann, 1985).

_____. *Georg Simmel* (New York: Methuen, 1984).

Levine, D.N. *Simmel and Parsons: Two Approaches to the Study of Society* (New York: Arno Press, 1980).

Mayntz, Renate. "Simmel." In *International Encyclopedia of the Social Sciences* 14. Edited by D.L. Sills. (New York: Macmillan, 1968).

O'Neill, John. "On Simmel's 'Sociological Apriorites'." In *Sociology as a Skin Trade* (London: Heinemann, 1976).

Spykman, Nicholas J. *The Sociological Theory of Georg Simmel* (New York: Atherton Press, 1966).

Weber, M. "George Simmel as Sociologist," *Social Research* 39 (1972): 155–63.

Weingartner, Rudolph H. *Experience and Culture, The Philosophy of Georg Simmel* (Middletown, Conn.: Wesleyan Univ. Press, 1962).

Weinstein, Deena and Michael A. *Postmodern(ized) Simmel* (New York: Routledge, 1993).

Wolff, Kurt H. "Georg Simmel." In *Trying Sociology: Beyond the Sociology of Knowledge* (Lanham, Md.: Univ. Press of America, 1983).

347

MAX WEBER (1864–1920)

chapter 16

"NOT SUMMER'S bloom lies ahead of us, but rather the polar night of icy darkness and hardness." Max Weber's bleak forecast for the future of capitalism still grips us. His thesis that Calvinism's work ethic provided the proper passions to launch modern capitalism is common knowledge. Rarely heard is Weber's further observation that capitalism discards Protestant piety like a set of training wheels: "the religious root of modern economic humanity is dead; today the concept of the calling is a *caput mortuum* in the world." Without recourse to religion, the "immense cosmos" of capitalism now overwhelms individuals and compels them to conform to its rules and expectations. Modern capitalism clamps down on the space that allowed traditional profitmakers not to get lost in the whirlwind of capital accumulation, the space Aquinas counted on. Yet this capitalist cosmos, where "material goods have gained . . . an inexorable power over the lives of men as at no period in history," looks attractive compared with the grimmer prospect of complete bureaucratic rationalization. At least capitalism has the spontaneity of markets and entrepreneurs. Capitalism—"the most fateful force in modern life"—spawns yet a broader upheaval of culture from *traditionalism* to *rationalization*. Here lies a graver challenge for Marxism, as for us all.

A remarkable student of diverse cultures, Weber was struck by the distinctiveness of the rationality that emerged in the West in modern times. This rationality spans a wide range of cultural and scientific developments and is anchored in the *rational capital accounting* that spreads with modern capitalism. Just as rationality can be found around the globe and throughout history, profit making and greed are commonplace. What Weber notices is the relationship between the rationality that develops in the West and the peculiarities of *modern capitalism,* including the odd motivation it promotes. What distinguishes the "spirit of capitalism" from ordinary greed is the sense of a *duty* to accumulate money as an end in itself. Weber traces this attitude back to the "Protestant ethic" of hard work. The emptiness or formal character of capitalist rationality is kin to this blank command to toil endlessly. Weber makes clear that it is also bound up with the existence of private property and wage labor: "Exact calculation—the basis of everything else—is only possible on a basis of free labor." At least for its entry onto center stage, formal rationality is indebted to capitalism. But, like utility theory, formal rationality can turn against capitalism and attempt to subject its disorderly institutions and politics to technical and bureaucratic reorganization. Would driving "social engineering" into the marrow of capitalism doom the reform program? Just how beholden to capital is formal rationality?

350

Capitalist rationalization splits off *formal* rationality, which is "value-free" and does not set ultimate ends, from *substantive* rationality, which claims to determine ends. For Plato and Aristotle, reason determines the best ways to live, and limits pecuniary values. In modern times, this substantive reason is stripped of its claim to be reason at all. Weber's tale of Western rationality ends in irony: at its most developed, reason tells us nothing about what we ought to do or how to live. Instead, reason simply serves as instrument to the arbitrary values or preferences that guide us. Reason calculates the best way to reach goals whose merits it is unable to judge. These agonizing consequences Weber accepted stoically, surrendering to the positivist claim that "a logical gulf" separates the scientific realm of facts ("is") from the realm of irrational values ("ought"). Yet his actual account of the genesis of modern reason leaves us wondering whether that reason's sterility stems from logic or the capitalist form of the provisioning process.

FROM *THE PROTESTANT ETHIC AND THE SPIRIT OF CAPITALISM*

"THE SPIRIT OF CAPITALISM"

. . . "Remember, that *time* is money. He that can earn ten shillings a day by his labour, and goes abroad, or sits idle, one half of that day, though he spends but sixpence during his diversion or idleness, ought not to reckon *that* the only expense; he has really spent, or rather thrown away, five shillings besides.

"Remember, that *credit* is money. If a man lets his money lie in my hands after it is due, he gives me the interest, or so much as I can make of it during that time. This amounts to a considerable sum where a man has good and large credit, and makes good use of it.

"Remember, that money is of the prolific, generating nature. Money can beget money, and its offspring can beget more, and so on. Five shillings turned is six, turned again it is seven and threepence, and so on, till it becomes a hundred pounds. The more there is of it, the more it produces ever turning, so that the profits rise quicker and quicker. He that kills a breeding-sow, destroys all her offspring to the thousandth generation. He that murders a crown, destroys all that it might have produced, even scores of pounds."

"Remember this saying, *The good paymaster is lord of another man's purse.* He that is known to pay punctually and exactly to the time he promises, may at any time, and on any occasion, raise all the money his friends can spare. This is sometimes of great use. After industry and frugality, nothing contributes more to the raising of a young man in the world than punctuality and justice in all his dealings; therefore never keep borrowed money an hour beyond the time you promised, lest a disappointment shut up your friend's purse for ever.

"The most trifling actions that affect a man's credit are to be regarded. The sound of your hammer at five in the morning, or eight at night, heard by a creditor, makes him easy six months longer; but if he sees you at a billiard-table, or hears your voice at a tavern, when you should be at work, he sends for his money the next day; demands it, before he can receive it, in a lump.

"It shows, besides, that you are mindful of what you owe; it makes you appear a careful as well as an honest man, and that still increases your credit.

"Beware of thinking all your own that you possess, and of living accordingly. It is a mistake that many people who have credit fall into. To prevent this, keep an exact account for some time both of your expenses and your income. If you take the pains at first to mention particulars, it will have this good effect: you will discover how wonderfully small, trifling expenses mount up to large sums, and will discern what might have been, and may for the future be saved, without occasioning any great inconvenience."

"For six pounds a year you may have the use of one hundred pounds, provided you are a man of known prudence and honesty.

"He that spends a groat a day idly, spends idly above six pounds a year, which is the price for the use of one hundred pounds.

"He that wastes idly a groat's worth of his time per day, one day with another, wastes the privilege of using one hundred pounds each day.

"He that idly loses five shillings' worth of time, loses five shillings, and might as prudently throw five shillings into the sea.

"He that loses five shillings, not only loses that sum, but all the advantage that might be made by turning it in dealing, which by the time a young man becomes old, will amount to a considerable sum of money."

It is Benjamin Franklin who preaches to us in these sentences, the same which Ferdinand Kürnberger satirizes in his clever and malicious *Picture of American Culture* as the supposed confession of faith of the Yankee. That it is the spirit of capitalism which here speaks in characteristic fashion, no one will doubt, however little we may wish to claim that everything which could be understood as pertaining to that spirit is contained in it. Let us pause a moment to consider this passage, the philosophy of which Kürnberger sums up in the words, "They make tallow out of cattle and money out of men". The peculiarity of this philosophy of avarice appears to be the ideal of the honest man of recognized credit, and above all the idea of a duty of the individual toward the increase of his capital, which is assumed as an end in itself. Truly what is here preached is not simply a means of making one's way in the world, but a peculiar ethic. The infraction of its rules is treated not as foolishness but as forgetfulness of duty. That is the essence of the matter. It is not mere business astuteness, that sort of thing is common enough, it is an ethos. *This* is the quality which interests us.

When Jacob Fugger, in speaking to a business associate who had retired and who wanted to persuade him to do the same, since he had made enough money and should let others have a chance, rejected that as pusillanimity and answered that "he (Fugger) thought otherwise, he wanted to make money as long as he could", the spirit of his statement is evidently quite different from that of Franklin. What in the former case was an expression of commercial daring and a personal inclination morally neutral, in the latter takes on the character of an ethically coloured maxim for the conduct of life. The concept spirit of capitalism is here used in this specific sense, it is the spirit of modern capitalism. For that we are here dealing only with Western European and American capitalism is obvious from the way in which the problem was stated. Capitalism existed in China, India, Babylon, in the classic world, and in the Middle Ages. But in all these cases, as we shall see, this particular ethos was lacking.

Now, all Franklin's moral attitudes are coloured with utilitarianism. Honesty is useful, because it assures credit; so are punctuality, industry, frugality, and that is the reason they are virtues. A logical deduction from this would be that where, for instance, the appearance of honesty serves the same purpose, that would suffice, and an unnecessary surplus of this virtue would evidently appear to Franklin's eyes as unproductive waste. And as a matter of fact, the story in his autobiography of his conversion to those virtues, or the discussion of the value of a strict maintenance of the appearance of modesty, the assiduous belittlement of one's own deserts in order to gain general recognition later, confirms this impression. According to Franklin, those virtues, like all others, are only in so far virtues as they are actually useful to the individual, and

352

the surrogate of mere appearance is always sufficient when it accomplishes the end in view. It is a conclusion which is inevitable for strict utilitarianism. The impression of many Germans that the virtues professed by Americanism are pure hypocrisy seems to have been confirmed by this striking case. But in fact the matter is not by any means so simple. Benjamin Franklin's own character, as it appears in the really unusual candidness of his autobiography, belies that suspicion. The circumstance that he ascribes his recognition of the utility of virtue to a divine revelation which was intended to lead him in the path of righteousness, shows that something more than mere garnishing for purely egocentric motives is involved.

In fact, the *summum bonum* of this ethic, the earning of more and more money, combined with the strict avoidance of all spontaneous enjoyment of life, is above all completely devoid of any eudæmonistic, not to say hedonistic, admixture. It is thought of so purely as an end in itself, that from the point of view of the happiness of, or utility to, the single individual, it appears entirely transcendental and absolutely irrational. Man is dominated by the making of money, by acquisition as the ultimate purpose of his life. Economic acquisition is no longer subordinated to man as the means for the satisfaction of his material needs. This reversal of what we should call the natural relationship, so irrational from a naïve point of view, is evidently as definitely a leading principle of capitalism as it is foreign to all peoples not under capitalistic influence. At the same time it expresses a type of feeling which is closely connected with certain religious ideas. If we thus ask, *why* should "money be made out of men", Benjamin Franklin himself, although he was a colourless deist, answers in his autobiography with a quotation from the Bible, which his strict Calvinistic father drummed into him again and again in his youth: "Seest thou a man diligent in his business? He shall stand before kings" (Prov. xxii. 29). The earning of money within the modern economic order is, so long as it is done legally, the result and the expression of virtue and proficiency in a calling; and this virtue and proficiency are, as it is now not difficult to see, the real Alpha and Omega of Franklin's ethic, as expressed in the passages we have quoted, as well as in all his works without exception.

And in truth this peculiar idea, so familiar to us to-day, but in reality so little a matter of course, of one's duty in a calling, is what is most characteristic of the social ethic of capitalistic culture, and is in a sense the fundamental basis of it. It is an obligation which the individual is supposed to feel and does feel towards the content of his professional activity, no matter in what it consists, in particular no matter whether it appears on the surface as a utilization of his personal powers, or only of his material possessions (as capital).

Of course, this conception has not appeared only under capitalistic conditions. On the contrary, we shall later trace its origins back to a time previous to the advent of capitalism. Still less, naturally, do we maintain that a conscious acceptance of these ethical maxims on the part of the individuals, entrepreneurs or laborers, in modern capitalistic enterprises, is a condition of the further existence of present-day capitalism. The capitalistic economy of the present day is an immense cosmos into which the individual is born, and which presents itself to him, at least as an individual, as an unalterable order of things in which he must live. It forces the individual, in so far as he is involved in the system of market relationships, to conform to capitalistic rules of action. The manufacturer who in the long run acts counter to these norms, will just as inevitably be eliminated from the economic scene as the worker who cannot or will not adapt himself to them will be thrown into the streets without a job.

Thus the capitalism of to-day, which has come to dominate economic life, educates and selects the economic subjects which it needs through a process of economic survival of the fittest. But here one can easily see the limits of the concept of selection as a means of historical explanation. In order that a manner of life so well adapted to the peculiarities of capitalism could be selected at all, i.e. should come to dominate others, it had to originate somewhere, and not in isolated individuals alone, but as a way of life common to whole groups of men. This origin is what really needs explanation. Concerning the doctrine of the more naïve historical materialism, that such ideas originate as a reflection or superstructure of economic situations, we shall speak more in detail below. At this point it will suffice for our purpose to call attention to the fact without doubt, in the country of Benjamin Franklin's birth (Massachusetts), the spirit of capitalism (in the sense we have attached to it) was present before the capitalistic order. There were complaints of a peculiarly calculating sort of profit-seeking in New England, as distinguished from other parts of America, as early as 1632. It is further undoubted that capitalism remained far less developed in some of the neighboring colonies, the later Southern States of the United States of America, in spite of the fact that these latter were founded by large capitalists for business motives, while the New England colonies were founded by preachers and seminary graduates with the help of small bourgeois, craftsmen and yeomen, for religious reasons. In this case the causal relation is certainly the reverse of that suggested by the materialistic standpoint.

But the origin and history of such ideas is much more complex than the theorists of the superstructure suppose. The spirit of capitalism, in the sense in which we are using the term, had to fight its way to supremacy against a whole world of hostile forces. A state of mind such as that expressed in the passages we have quoted from Franklin, and which called forth the applause of a whole people, would both in ancient times and in the Middle Ages have been proscribed as the lowest sort of avarice and as an attitude entirely lacking in self-respect. It is, in fact, still regularly thus looked upon by all those social groups which are least involved in or adapted to modern capitalistic conditions. This is not wholly because the instinct of acquisition was in those

354

times unknown or undeveloped, as has often been said. Nor because the *auri sacra fames*, the greed for gold, was then, or now, less powerful outside of bourgeois capitalism than within its peculiar sphere, as the illusions of modern romanticists are wont to believe. The difference between the capitalistic and precapitalistic spirits is not to be found at this point. The greed of the Chinese Mandarin, the old Roman aristocrat, or the modern peasant, can stand up to any comparison. And the *auri sacra fames* of a Neapolitan cab-driver or *barcaiuolo*, and certainly of Asiatic representatives of similar trades, as well as of the craftsmen of southern European or Asiatic countries, is, as anyone can find out for himself, very much more intense, and especially more unscrupulous than that of, say, an Englishman in similar circumstances.

The universal reign of absolute unscrupulousness in the pursuit of selfish interests by the making of money has been a specific characteristic of precisely those countries whose bourgeois-capitalistic development, measured according to Occidental standards, has remained backward. As every employer knows, the lack of *coscienziosità* of the laborers of such countries, for instance Italy as compared with Germany, has been, and to a certain extent still is, one of the principal obstacles to their capitalistic development. Capitalism cannot make use of the labor of those who practice the doctrine of undisciplined *liberum arbitrium*, any more than it can make use of the business man who seems absolutely unscrupulous in his dealings with others, as we can learn from Franklin. Hence the difference does not lie in the degree of development of any impulse to make money. The *auri sacra fames* is as old as the history of man. But we shall see that those who submitted to it without reserve as a uncontrolled impulse, such as the Dutch sea-captain who "would go through hell for gain, even though he scorched his sails", were by no means the representatives of that attitude of mind from which the specifically modern capitalistic spirit as a mass phenomenon is derived, and that is what matters. At all periods of history, wherever it was possible, there has been ruthless acquisition, bound to no ethical norms whatever. Like war and piracy, trade has often been unrestrained in its relations with foreigners and those outside the group. The double ethic has permitted here what was forbidden in dealings among brothers.

Capitalistic acquisition as an adventure has been at home in all types of economic society which have known trade with the use of money and which have offered it opportunities, through *commenda*, farming of taxes, State loans, financing of wars, ducal courts and office-holders. Likewise the inner attitude of the adventurer, which laughs at all ethical limitations, has been universal. Absolute and conscious ruthlessness in acquisition has often stood in the closest connection with the strictest conformity to tradition. Moreover, with the breakdown of tradition and the more or less complete extension of free economic enterprise, even to within the social group, the new thing has not generally been ethically justified and encouraged, but only tolerated as a fact. And

355

this fact has been treated either as ethically indifferent or reprehensible, but unfortunately unavoidable. This has not only been the normal attitude of all ethical teachings, but, what is more important, also that expressed in the practical action of the average man of pre-capitalistic times, pre-capitalistic in the sense that the rational utilization of capital in a permanent enterprise and the rational capitalistic organization of labour had not yet become dominant forces in the determination of economic activity. Now just this attitude was one of the strongest inner obstacles which the adaptation of men to the conditions of an ordered bourgeois-capitalistic economy has encountered everywhere.

The most important opponent with which the spirit of capitalism, in the sense of a definite standard of life claiming ethical sanction, has had to struggle, was that type of attitude and reaction to new situations which we may designate as traditionalism. In this case also every attempt at a final definition must be held in abeyance. On the other hand, we must try to make the provisional meaning clear by citing a few cases. We will begin from below, with the laborers.

One of the technical means which the modern employer uses in order to secure the greatest possible amount of work from his men is the device of piece-rates. In agriculture, for instance, the gathering of the harvest is a case where the greatest possible intensity of labour is called for, since, the weather being uncertain, the difference between high profit and heavy loss may depend on the speed with which the harvesting can be done. Hence a system of piece-rates is almost universal in this case. And since the interest of the employer in a speeding-up of harvesting increases with the increase of the results and the intensity of the work, the attempt has again and again been made, by increasing the piece-rates of the workmen, thereby giving them an opportunity to earn what is for them a very high wage, to interest them in increasing their own efficiency. But a peculiar difficulty has been met with surprising frequency: raising the piece-rates has often had the result that not more but less has been accomplished in the same time, because the worker reacted to the increase not by increasing but by decreasing the amount of his work. A man, for instance, who at the rate of 1 mark per acre mowed 2½ acres per day and earned 2½ marks, when the rate was raised to 1.25 marks per acre mowed, not 3 acres, as he might easily have done, thus earning 3.75 marks, but only 2 acres, so that he could still earn the 2½ marks to which he was accustomed. The opportunity of earning more was less attractive than that of working less. He did not ask: how much can I earn in a day if I do as much work as possible? but: how much must I work in order to earn the wage, 2½ marks, which I earned before and which takes care of my traditional needs? This is an example of what is here meant by traditionalism. A man does not "by nature" wish to earn more and more money, but simply to live as he is accustomed to live and to earn as much as is necessary for that purpose. Wherever modern capitalism has begun its work of increasing the productivity of human labor by increasing its intensity, it has encountered the immensely stubborn resistance of this leading trait of pre-capitalistic labor. And to-day it encounters it the more, the more backward (from a capitalistic point of view) the labouring forces are with which it has to deal.

Another obvious possibility, to return to our example, since the appeal to the acquisitive instinct through higher wage-rates failed, would have been to try the opposite policy, to force the worker by reduction of his wage-rates to work harder to earn the same amount than he did before. Low wages and high profits seem even to-day to a superficial observer to stand in correlation; everything which is paid out in wages seems to involve a corresponding reduction of profits. That road capitalism has taken again and again since its beginning. For centuries it was an article of faith, that low wages were productive, i.e. that they increased the material results of labor so that, as Pieter de la Cour, on this point, as we shall see, quite in the spirit of the old Calvinism, said long ago, the people only work because and so long as they are poor.

But the effectiveness of this apparently so efficient method has its limits. Of course the presence of a surplus population which it can hire cheaply in the labor market is a necessity for the development of capitalism. But though too large a reserve army may in certain cases favour its quantitative expansion, it checks its qualitative development, especially the transition to types of enterprise which make more intensive use of labor. Low wages are by no means identical with cheap labor. From a purely quantitative point of view the efficiency of labor decreases with a wage which is physiologically insufficient, which may in the long run even mean a survival of the unfit. The present-day average Silesian mows, when he exerts himself to the full, little more than two-thirds as much land as the better paid and nourished Pomeranian or Mecklenburger, and the Pole, the further East he comes from, accomplishes progressively less than the German. Low wages fail even from a purely business point of view wherever it is a question of producing goods which require any sort of skilled labor, or the use of expensive machinery which is easily damaged, or in general wherever any great amount of sharp attention or of initiative is required. Here low wages do not pay, and their effect is the opposite of what was intended. For not only is a developed sense of responsibility absolutely indispensable, but in general also an attitude which, at least during working hours, is freed from continual calculations of how the customary wage may be earned with a maximum of comfort and a minimum of exertion. Labour must, on the contrary, be performed as if it were an absolute end in itself, a calling. But such an attitude is by no means a product of nature. It cannot be evoked by low wages or high ones alone, but can only be the product of a long and arduous process of education. To-day, capitalism, once in the saddle, can recruit its laboring force in all industrial countries with comparative ease. In the past this was in every case an extremely difficult problem. And even to-day it could probably not get along without the sup-

357

port of a powerful ally along the way, which, as we shall see below, was at hand at the time of its development.

What is meant can again best be explained by means of an example. The type of backward traditional form of labor is to-day very often exemplified by women workers, especially unmarried ones. An almost universal complaint of employers of girls, for instance German girls, is that they are almost entirely unable and unwilling to give up methods of work inherited or once learned in favor of more efficient ones, to adapt themselves to new methods, to learn and to concentrate their intelligence, or even to use it at all. Explanations of the possibility of making work easier, above all more profitable to themselves, generally encounter a complete lack of understanding. Increases of piece-rates are without avail against the stone wall of habit. In general it is other-wise, and that is a point of no little importance from our view-point, only with girls having a specifically religious, especially a Pietistic, background. One often hears, and statistical investigation confirms it, that by far the best chances of economic education are found among this group. The ability of mental concentration, as well as the absolutely essential feeling of obligation to one's job, are here most often combined with a strict economy which cal-culates the possibility of high earnings, and a cool self-control and frugality which enormously increase performance. This provides the most favourable foundation for the conception of labour as an end in itself, as a calling which is necessary to capitalism: the chances of overcoming traditionalism are great-est on account of the religious upbringing. This observation of present-day capitalism in itself suggests that it is worth while to ask how this connection of adaptability to capitalism with religious factors may have come about in the days of the early development of capitalism. For that they were even then present in much the same form can be inferred from numerous facts. For in-stance, the dislike and the persecution which Methodist workmen in the eighteenth century met at the hands of their comrades were not solely nor even principally the result of their religious eccentricities, England had seen many of those and more striking ones. It rested rather, as the destruction of their tools, repeatedly mentioned in the reports, suggests, upon their specific willingness to work as we should say to-day.

However, let us again return to the present, and this time to the entrepre-neur, in order to clarify the meaning of traditionalism in his case.

Sombart, in his discussions of the genesis of capitalism, has distinguished between the satisfaction of needs and acquisition as the two great leading principles in economic history. In the former case the attainment of the goods necessary to meet personal needs, in the latter a struggle for profit free from the limits set by needs, have been the ends controlling the form and di-rection of economic activity. What he calls the economy of needs seems at first glance to be identical with what is here described as economic tradition-alism. That may be the case if the concept of needs is limited to traditional needs. But if that is not done, a number of economic types which must be considered capitalistic according to the definition of capital which Sombart gives in another part of his work, would be excluded from the category of acquisitive economy and put into that of needs economy. Enterprises, namely, which are carried on by private entrepreneurs by utilizing capital (money or goods with a money value) to make a profit, purchasing the means of production and selling the product, i.e. undoubted capitalistic enterprises, may at the same time have a traditionalistic character. This has, in the course even of modern economic history, not been merely an occasional case, but rather the rule, with continual interruptions from repeated and increasingly powerful conquests of the capitalistic spirit. To be sure the capitalistic form of an enterprise and the spirit in which it is run generally stand in some sort of adequate relationship to each other, but not in one of necessary interdependence. Nevertheless, we provisionally use the expression spirit of (modern) capitalism to describe that attitude which seeks profit rationally and systematically in the manner which we have illustrated by the example of Benjamin Franklin. This, however, is justified by the historical fact that that attitude of mind has on the one hand found its most suitable expression in capitalistic enterprise, while on the other the enterprise has derived its most suitable motive force from the spirit of capitalism.

But the two may very well occur separately. Benjamin Franklin was filled with the spirit of capitalism at a time when his printing business did not differ in form from any handicraft enterprise. And we shall see that at the beginning of modern times it was by no means the capitalistic entrepreneurs of the commercial aristocracy, who were either the sole or the predominant bearers of the attitude we have here called the spirit of capitalism. It was much more the rising strata of the lower industrial middle classes. Even in the nineteenth century its classical representatives were not the elegant gentlemen of Liverpool and Hamburg, with their commercial fortunes handed down for generations, but the self-made parvenus of Manchester and Westphalia, who often rose from very modest circumstances. As early as the sixteenth century the situation was similar; the industries which arose at that time were mostly created by parvenus.

The management, for instance, of a bank, a wholesale export business, a large retail establishment, or of a large putting-out enterprise dealing with goods produced in homes, is certainly only possible in the form of a capitalistic enterprise. Nevertheless, they may all be carried on in a traditionalistic spirit. In fact, the business of a large bank of issue cannot be carried on in any other way. The foreign trade of whole epochs has rested on the basis of monopolies and legal privileges of strictly traditional character. In retail trade— and we are not here talking of the small men without capital who are continually crying out for Government aid—the revolution which is making an end of the old traditionalism is still in full swing. It is the same development which broke up the old putting-out system, to which modern domestic labour is related only in form. How this revolution takes place and what is its significance may, in spite of the fact these things are so familiar, be again brought out by a concrete example.

Until about the middle of the past century the life of a putter-out was, at least in many of the branches of the Continental textile industry, what we should to-day consider very comfortable. We may imagine its routine some-what as follows: The peasants came with their cloth, often (in the case of linen) principally or entirely made from raw material which the peasant him-self had produced, to the town in which the putter-out lived, and after a care-ful, often official, appraisal of the quality, received the customary price for it. The putter-out's customers, for markets any appreciable distance away, were middlemen, who also came to him, generally not yet following samples, but seeking traditional qualities, and bought from his warehouse, or, long before delivery, placed orders which were probably in turn passed on to the peasants. Personal canvassing of customers took place, if at all, only at long intervals. Otherwise correspondence sufficed, though the sending of samples slowly gained ground. The number of business hours was very moderate, perhaps five to six a day, sometimes considerably less; in the rush season, where there was one, more. Earnings were moderate; enough to lead a respectable life and in good times to put away a little. On the whole, relations among competitors were relatively good, with a large degree of agreement on the fundamentals of business. A long daily visit to the tavern, with often plenty to drink, and a congenial circle of friends, made life comfortable and leisurely.

The form of organization was in every respect capitalistic; the entrepre-neur's activity was of a purely business character; the use of capital, turned over in the business, was indispensable; and finally, the objective aspect of the economic process, the book-keeping, was rational. But it was traditionalistic business, if one considers the spirit which animated the entrepreneur: the tra-ditional manner of life, the traditional rate of profit, the traditional amount of work, the traditional manner of regulating the relationships with labour, and the essentially traditional circle of customers and the manner of attracting new ones. All these dominated the conduct of the business, were at the basis, one may say, of the *ethos* of this group of business men.

Now at some time this leisureliness was suddenly destroyed, and often en-tirely without any essential change in the form of organization, such as the transition to a unified factory, to mechanical weaving, etc. What happened was, on the contrary, often no more than this: some young man from one of the putting-out families went out into the country, carefully chose weavers for his employ, greatly increased the rigour of his supervision of their work, and thus turned them from peasants into laborers. On the other hand, he would begin to change his marketing methods by so far as possible going directly to the fi-nal consumer, would take the details into his own hands, would personally so-licit customers, visiting them every year, and above all would adapt the quality of the product directly to their needs and wishes. At the same time he began to introduce the principle of low prices and large turnover. There was repeated what everywhere and always is the result of such a process of rationalization: those who would not follow suit had to go out of business. The idyllic state collapsed under the pressure of a bitter competitive struggle, respectable fortunes were made, and not lent out at interest, but always reinvested in the business. The old leisurely and comfortable attitude toward life gave way to a hard frugality in which some participated and came to the top, because they did not wish to consume but to earn, while others who wished to keep on with the old ways were forced to curtail their consumption.

And, what is most important in this connection, it was not generally in such cases a stream of new money invested in the industry which brought about this revolution—in several cases known to me the whole revolutionary process was set in motion with a few thousands of capital borrowed from relations—but the new spirit, the spirit of modern capitalism, had set to work. The question of the motive forces in the expansion of modern capitalism is not in the first instance a question of the origin of the capital sums which were available for capitalistic uses, but, above all, of the development of the spirit of capitalism. Where it appears and is able to work itself out, it produces its own capital and monetary supplies as the means to its ends, but the reverse is not true. Its entry on the scene was not generally peaceful. A flood of mistrust, sometimes of hatred, above all of moral indignation, regularly opposed itself to the first innovator. Often—I know of several cases of the sort—regular legends of mysterious shady spots in his previous life have been produced. It is very easy not to recognize that only an unusually strong character could save an entrepreneur of this new type from the loss of his temperate self-control and from both moral and economic shipwreck. Furthermore, along with clarity of vision and ability to act, it is only by virtue of very definite and highly developed ethical qualities that it has been possible for him to command the absolutely indispensable confidence of his customers and workmen. Nothing else could have given him the strength to overcome the innumerable obstacles, above all the infinitely more intensive work which is demanded of the modern entrepreneur. But these are ethical qualities of quite a different sort from those adapted to the traditionalism of the past.

And, as a rule, it has been neither dare-devil and unscrupulous speculators, economic adventurers such as we meet at all periods of economic history, nor simply great financiers who have carried through this change, outwardly so inconspicuous, but nevertheless so decisive for the penetration of economic life with the new spirit. On the contrary, they were men who had grown up in the hard school of life, calculating and daring at the same time, above all temperate and reliable, shrewd and completely devoted to their business, with strictly bourgeois opinions and principles.

361

One is tempted to think that these personal moral qualities have not the slightest relation to any ethical maxims, to say nothing of religious ideas, but that the essential relation between them is negative. The ability to free oneself from the common tradition, a sort of liberal enlightenment, seems likely to be the most suitable basis for such a business man's success. And to-day that is generally precisely the case. Any relationship between religious beliefs and conduct is generally absent, and where any exists, at least in Germany, it tends to be of the negative sort. The people filled with the spirit of capitalism to-day tend to be indifferent, if not hostile, to the Church. The thought of the pious boredom of paradise has little attraction for their active natures; religion appears to them as a means of drawing people away from labour in this world. If you ask them what is the meaning of their restless activity, why they are never satisfied with what they have, thus appearing so senseless to any purely worldly view of life, they would perhaps give the answer, if they know any at all: "to provide for my children and grand-children". But more often and, since that motive is not peculiar to them, but was just as effective for the traditionalist, more correctly, simply: that business with its continuous work has become a necessary part of their lives. That is in fact the only possible motivation, but it at the same time expresses what is, seen from the view-point of personal happiness, so irrational about this sort of life, where a man exists for the sake of his business, instead of the reverse.

Of course, the desire for the power and recognition which the mere fact of wealth brings plays its part. When the imagination of a whole people has once been turned toward purely quantitative bigness, as in the United States, this romanticism of numbers exercises an irresistible appeal to the poets among business men. Otherwise it is in general not the real leaders, and especially not the permanently successful entrepreneurs, who are taken in by it. In particular, the resort to entailed estates and the nobility, with sons whose conduct at the university and in the officers' corps tries to cover up their social origin; as has been the typical history of German capitalistic parvenu families, is a product of later decadence. The ideal type of the capitalistic entrepreneur, as it has been represented even in Germany by occasional outstanding examples, has no relation to such more or less refined climbers. He avoids ostentation and unnecessary expenditure, as well as conscious enjoyment of his power, and is embarrassed by the outward signs of the social recognition which he receives. His manner of life is, in other words, often, and we shall have to investigate the historical significance of just this important fact, distinguished by a certain ascetic tendency, as appears clearly enough in the sermon of Franklin which we have quoted. It is, namely, by no means exceptional, but rather the rule, for him to have a sort of modesty which is essentially more honest than the reserve which Franklin so shrewdly recommends. He gets nothing out of his wealth for himself, except the irrational sense of having done his job well.

But it is just that which seems to the pre-capitalistic man so incomprehensible and mysterious, so unworthy and contemptible. That anyone should be able to make it the sole purpose of his life-work, to sink into the grave weighed down with a great material load of money and goods, seems to him explicable only as a product of a perverse instinct, the *auri sacra fames*.

At present under our individualistic political, legal, and economic institutions, with the forms of organization and general structure which are peculiar to our economic order, this spirit of capitalism might be understandable, as has been said, purely as a result of adaptation. The capitalistic system so needs this devotion to the calling of making money, it is an attitude toward material goods which is so well suited to that system, so intimately bound up with the conditions of survival in the economic struggle for existence, that there can to-day no longer be any question of a necessary connection of that acquisitive manner of life with any single *Weltanschauung*. In fact, it no longer needs the support of any religious forces, and feels the attempts of religion to influence economic life, in so far as they can still be felt at all, to be as much an unjustified interference as its regulation by the State. In such circumstances men's commercial and social interests do tend to determine their opinions and attitudes. Whoever does not adapt his manner of life to the conditions of capitalistic success must go under, or at least cannot rise. But these are phenomena of a time in which modern capitalism has become dominant and has become emancipated from its old supports.

For Further Reading

Weber, Max. *Max Weber: Economy and Society; An Outline of Interpretive Sociology*, 2 vols. Edited by Guenther Roth and Claus Wittich (Berkeley: Univ. of California Press, 1978).

_____. *From Max Weber. Essays in Sociology*. Translated and edited by H. H. Gerth and C. Wright Mills (New York: Oxford Univ. Press, 1946).

_____. *General Economic History* (New Brunswick, N.J.: Transaction Bks., 1981).

_____. *Political Writings: Max Weber*. Edited by Peter Lassman and Ronald Speirs (New York: Cambridge Univ. Press, 1994).

_____. *The Protestant Ethic and the Spirit of Capitalism* (New York: Scribner's, 1958). Translated by Talcott Parsons.

Bendix, Reinhard. *Max Weber: An Intellectual Portrait* (Garden City: N.Y.: Doubleday, 1960).

Collins, Randall. *Max Weber* (Beverly Hills, Calif.: Sage, 1986).

Dronberger, Ilse. *The Political Thought of Max Weber* (New York: Irvington, 1971).

Giddens, Anthony. *Politics and Sociology in the Thought of Max Weber* (London: Macmillan, 1972).

Glassman, Ronald M., and V. Murvar, eds. *Max Weber's Political Sociology: A Pessimistic Vision of a Rationalized World* (Westport, Conn.: Greenwood, 1984).

Habermas, Jürgen. *Theory of Communicative Action,* vol. 1 (Boston, Mass.: Beacon Press, 1984).

Hennis, Wilhelm. *Max Weber, Essays in Reconstruction* (London: Allen and Unwin, 1988).

Schluchter, Wolfgang. *The Rise of Western Rationalism, Max Weber's Developmental History*. Translated with an introduction by Guenther Roth (Berkeley: Univ. of California Press, 1981).

Sica, Alan. *Weber, Irrationality, and Social Order* (Berkeley: Univ. of California Press, 1988).

Turner, Stephen P., and Regis A. Factor. *Max Weber and the Dispute Over Reason and Value* (London: Routledge, 1984).

Weber, Marianne. *Max Weber: A Biography* (New Brunswick, N.J.: Transaction Bks., 1988).

Whimster, Sam, and Scott Lash, eds. *Max Weber, Rationality and Modernity* (London: Allen and Unwin, 1987).

Wiley, Norbert, ed. *The Marx-Weber Debate* (Newbury Park, Calif.: Sage, 1987).

MARCEL MAUSS (1872–1950)

chapter 17

SOCIAL SOLIDARITY preoccupied Marcel Mauss and his famous uncle, teacher, and collaborator, Émile Durkheim. For both, a society's morality varies with its form of solidarity; a society lacking solidarity is no society at all. In *The Division of Labor,* Durkheim distinguished between the cramped "mechanical solidarity" of traditional societies having little division of labor and the looser, liberating "organic solidarity" of commercial societies with distinct occupations. Though persistent social injustices troubled Durkheim, he regarded the modern division of labor as a source of both personal fulfill-ment and social solidarity respectful of individuals—not a greedy "free-for-all." As Mary Douglas observes, Mauss's "theory of the gift is a theory of hu-man solidarity." Mauss boldly proposes that obligatory, mutual gift-giving can organize a (non-market) society no less than commodity exchange coordi-nates commercial life. Mauss makes us speak cautiously of barter in tradition-al contexts lest we project the commodity form onto the gift mode of exchange. After Mauss, Adam Smith's "natural propensity to truck and barter" smells even fishier.

What can explain our desire—or apparent desire—for gifts that come without strings or conditions? Are we exhausted by the daily grind where everything has its price? Are we lured by the Christian theology of grace, God's freely given gift? Mauss's *The Gift* is a slap in the face to anyone expecting evidence of such giving. No, the "gifts" in these societies resemble a gangster's "favors" or the patronage of a big city political boss: they create dependence and oblige others to offer "countergifts." Giving, as well as ritual destruction of wealth, brings honor; receiving confers disgrace—quite a different take on "it is better to give than to receive"! Lavish countergifts humiliate rather than meet interest payments. Mauss's gifts bind.

Though put forward as an account of "primitive" practices, Mauss's theory of the gift is directed to the present in several ways. (1) It reinforces Durkheim's critique of utilitarianism and neoclassical economics by showing how social solidarity determines individual consciousness (*conscience*) and "economic" exchanges. (2) It offers clues to present-day practices such as the wedding reception—our feeble attempt at a wedding feast—and suggests that traces of gift exchange pervade commercial society (a point explored by Veblen). (3) It could defend demands for guaranteed pensions, health care, or unemployment benefits as appropriate "countergifts" or compensation for a worker's toil—though a bureaucratic welfare state bears no likeness to a traditional "pot luck." These political trappings of Mauss's theory of the gift are the perfect foil for Friedrich A. Hayek's complaint that interfering with the market in the name of "social justice" squanders the hard-won disciplines of liberalism and sinks us back into "the emotions of tribal society."

FROM *THE GIFT*

II

CONCLUSIONS FOR ECONOMIC SOCIOLOGY AND POLITICAL ECONOMY

These facts not only throw light upon our morality and help to direct our ideals. In their light, we can analyse better the most general economic facts, and even this analysis helps us dimly to perceive better organizational procedures applicable in our societies.

Several times we have seen how far this whole economy of the exchange-through-gift lay outside the bounds of the so-called natural economy, that of utilitarianism. All these very considerable phenomena of the economic life of all peoples—let us say, to fix things firmly in our minds, that they represent fittingly the great Neolithic civilization—and all these important vestiges of those traditions in societies close to our own, or of our own customs, fall outside the schemes normally put forward by those rare economists who have wished to compare the various types of known economies. We therefore add our own repeated observations to those of Malinowski, who has devoted an entire study to "exploding" current doctrines concerning "primitive" economy.

From this there follows a very solid chain of facts: the notion of value functions in these societies. Very large surpluses, speaking in absolute terms, are amassed. They are often expended to no avail, with comparatively enormous luxury, which is in no way commercial. These are the signs of wealth, and kinds of money are exchanged. Yet the whole of this very rich economy is still filled with religious elements. Money still possesses its magical power and is still linked to the clan or to the individual. The various economic activities, for example the market, are suffused with rituals and myths. They retain a ceremonial character that is obligatory and effective. They are full of rituals and rights. In this light we can already reply to the question that Durkheim posed concerning the religious origin of the notion of economic value. The facts also answer a host of questions concerning the forms and reasons behind what we so ineptly term exchange, the "barter," the *permutation* of useful things, that, in the wake of the prudent Romans, who were themselves following Aristotle, an *a priori* economic history places at the origin of the division of labour. It is indeed something other than utility that circulates in societies of all kinds, most of which are already fairly enlightened. The clans, the generations, and the sexes generally—because of the many different relationships to which the contracts give rise—are in a perpetual state of economic ferment and this state of excitement is very far from being materialistic. It is far less prosaic than our buying and selling, our renting of services, or the games we play on the Stock Exchange.

However, we can go even farther than we have gone up to now. One can dissolve, jumble up together, colour and define differently the principal notions that we have used. The terms that we have used—present and gift—are not themselves entirely exact. We shall, however, find no others. These concepts of law and economics that it pleases us to contrast: liberty and obligation; liberality, generosity, and luxury, as against savings, interest, and utility—it would be good to put them into the melting pot once more. We can only give the merest indications on this subject. Let us choose, for example, the Trobriand Islands. There they still have a complex notion that inspires all the economic acts we have described. Yet this notion is neither that of the free, purely gratuitous rendering of total services, nor that of production and exchange purely interested in what is useful. It is a sort of hybrid that flourished.

Malinowski has made a serious attempt at classifying, from the point of view of motives of self-interest and disinterestedness, all the transactions that he noted among the Trobriand Islanders. He gradates them between the pure gift and pure barter after bargaining has taken place. This classification is in reality inapplicable. Thus, according to Malinowski, the type of pure gift would

367

be the gift between man and wife. But, in our view, precisely one of the most important facts reported by Malinowski and one that throws a brilliant light upon all sexual relationships throughout humanity, consists of comparing the *mapula*, the "constant" payment made by the man to his wife, as a kind of salary for sexual services rendered. Likewise the presents made to the chief are a tribute paid; the distributions of food (*sagali*) are rewards for work or rituals performed, for example, in the case of funeral vigils. All in all, just as these gifts are not freely given, they are also not really disinterested. They already represent for the most part total counter-services, not only made with a view to paying for services or things, but also to maintaining a profitable alliance, one that cannot be rejected. Such, for example, is the alliance between tribes of fishermen and tribes of farmers or potterymakers. Now, this is a general fact. We have met it, for example, in the Maori and Tsimshian areas, etc. We can therefore see where this force resides. It is one that is both mystical and practical, one that ties clans together and at the same time divides them, that divides their labour, and at the same time constrains them to carry out exchange. Even in these societies, the individual and the group, or rather the subgroup, have always felt they had a sovereign right to refuse a contract. It is this that gives the stamp of generosity to this circulation of goods. On the other hand they normally had neither the right to, nor any interest in refusing. It is this that makes these distant societies nevertheless related to our own.

The use of money might suggest other reflections. The *vaygu'a* of the Trobriands, bracelets and necklaces, just as the copper objects of the American Northwest or the *wampun* of the Iroquois, are both riches, signs of wealth, and means of exchange and of payment, but also things that must be given, or even destroyed. However, these are still pledges linked to the persons that use them, and these pledges bind them. Since, on the other hand, they already serve as indicators of money, one has an interest in giving them away so as to be able to possess yet other objects, by transforming them into goods or services that, in their turn, can be transformed again into money. One might really say that the Trobriand or Tsimshian, although far removed from him, proceeds like the capitalist who knows how to dispose of his ready cash at the right time, in order to reconstitute at a later date this mobile form of capital. Self-interest and disinterestedness likewise explain this form of the circulation of wealth and that of the archaic circulation of the signs of wealth that ensue.

Even pure destruction of wealth does not signify that complete detachment that one might believe to be found in it. Even these acts of greatness are not without egoism. The purely sumptuary form of consumption (which is almost always exaggerated and often purely destructive), in which considerable amounts of goods that have taken a long time to amass are suddenly given away or even destroyed, particularly in the case of the potlatch, give such institutions the appearance of representing purely lavish expenditure and childish prodigality. In effect, and in reality, not only are useful things given away and rich foods consumed to excess, but one even destroys for the pleasure of destroying. For example, the Tsimshian, Tlingit, and Haïda chiefs throw these copper objects and money into the water. The Kwakiutl chiefs smash them, as do those of the tribes allied to them. But the reason for these gifts and frenetic acts of wealth consumption is in no way disinterested, particularly in societies that practise the potlatch. Between chiefs and their vassals, between vassals and their tenants, through such gifts a hierarchy is established. To give is to show one's superiority, to be more, to be higher in rank, *magister.* To accept without giving in return, or without giving more back, is to become client and servant, to become small, to fall lower (*minister*).

The magic ritual of the *kula* called the *mwasila* is full of formulas and symbols that demonstrate that the potential contracting party seeks above all this advantage of social superiority—one might almost say brute superiority. Thus, having cast a spell over the betel nut that they are going to use with their partners, after having cast a spell over the chief, his comrades, their pigs, the necklaces, then the head and its orifices, plus everything that is brought there, the *pari,* the opening gifts, etc. . . . after having cast a spell over all these, the magician sings, not without exaggeration:

> I topple the mountain, the mountain moves, the mountain crumbles away, etc.
> . . . My charm goes to the summit of the Dobu mountain. . . . My boat is going to sink . . . etc. My fame is like that of the lightning. My tread is like that of the flying witch doctors, the Tudududu.

369

To be the first, the most handsome, the luckiest, the strongest, and wealthiest—this is what is sought after, and how it is obtained. Later, the chief gives proof of his *mana* by redistributing what he has just received to his vassals and relations. He sustains his rank among the chiefs by giving back bracelets for necklaces, hospitality for visits, etc. In this case riches are from every viewpoint as much a means of retaining prestige as something useful. Yet are we sure that it is any different in our own society, and that even with us riches are not above all a means of lording it over our fellow men?

Let us now put to the test the other notion that we have just opposed to that of the gift and disinterestedness: the notion of interest, of the individual search after what is useful. This does not present itself either as it functions in our own minds. If some equivalent reason animates the Trobriand or American Indian chiefs, the Andaman clans, etc., or once motivated generous Hindus, and Germanic or Celtic nobles, as regards their gifts and expenditure, it is not the cold reasoning of the merchant, the banker, and the capitalist. In those civilizations they are concerned with their own interest, but in a different way from our own age. They hoard, but in order to spend, to place under an obligation, to have their own "liege men." On the other hand, they carry on exchange, but it is above all in luxury articles, ornaments or clothes, or things that are consumed immediately, as at feasts. They repay with interest, but this is in order to humiliate the person initially making the gift or exchange, and not only to recompense him for loss caused to him by "deferred consumption." There is self-interest, but this self-interest is only analogous to what allegedly sways us.

A relatively amorphous and disinterested economic system exists within subgroups, that regulates the life of the Australian clans or those of North America (the East and the Prairies). On the other hand there exists also the individualistic and purely self-interested economy that our own societies have experienced at least in part, as soon as it was discovered by the Semitic and Greek peoples. Between these two types there is an entire and immensely gradated series of institutions and economic events, and this series is not governed by the economic rationalism whose theory we are so willing to propound.

The very word "interest" is itself recent, originally an accounting technique: the Latin word *interest* was written on account books against the sums of interest that had to be collected. In ancient systems of morality of the most epicurean kind it is the good and pleasurable that is sought after, and not material utility. The victory of rationalism and mercantilism was needed before the notions of profit and the individual, raised to the level of principles, were introduced. One can almost date—since Mandeville's *The Fable of the Bees*—the triumph of the notion of individual interest. Only with great difficulty and the use of periphrasis can these two words be translated into Latin, Greek, or Arabic. Even those who wrote classical Sanskrit, who used the word *artha,* fairly close to our own idea of interest, had a different idea of it from our own, as they did for other categories of action. The sacred books of classical India already divide human activities up as follows: law (*dharma*), interest (*artha*), desire (*kama*). But above all it is a matter of *political* self-interest—that of the king and the Brahmins, of the ministers, in the kingdom and in each caste. The considerable literature of the *Niticastra* is not concerned with economics.

It is our western societies who have recently made man an "economic animal." But we are not yet all creatures of this genus. Among the masses and the elites in our society purely irrational expenditure is commonly practised. It is still characteristic of a few of the fossilized remnants of our aristocracy. *Homo oeconomicus* is not behind us, but lies ahead, as does the man of morality and duty, the man of science and reason. For a very long time man was something different, and he has not been a machine for very long, made complicated by a calculating machine.

Moreover, happily we are still somewhat removed from this constant, icy, utilitarian calculation. We need to carry out an analysis in depth, with statistics, as Halbwachs has done for the working classes, of our own consumption and expenditure, we of the western middle class. How many needs do we satisfy? And how many inclinations do we not satisfy whose ultimate purpose is not that of utility? How much of his income does or can the rich man allocate to his personal utilitarian needs? His expenditure on luxury, on art, on outrageous things, on servants—do not these make him resemble the nobles of former times or the barbarian chiefs whose customs we have described?

Is it good that this should be so? That is a different question. It is perhaps good that there are other means of spending or exchanging than pure expenditure. In our view, however, it is not in the calculation of individual needs that the method for an optimum economy is to be found. I believe that we must remain something other than pure financial experts, even in so far as we wish to increase our own wealth, whilst becoming better accountants and managers. The brutish pursuit of individual ends is harmful to the ends and the peace of all, to the rhythm of their work and joys—and rebounds on the individual himself.

As we have just seen, already important sections of society, associations of our capitalist firms themselves, are seeking as bodies to group their employees together. Moreover, all syndicalist groupings, whether of employers or wage-earners, claim they are defending and representing the general interest as fervently as the individual interest of their members or even their corporations. These fine speeches, it is true, are adorned with many metaphors. However, we must state that not only morality and philosophy, but even public opinion and political economy itself, are beginning to elevate themselves to this 'social' level. We sense that we cannot make men work well unless they are sure of being fairly paid throughout their life for work they have fairly carried out, both for others and for themselves. The producer who carries on exchange feels once more—he has always felt it, but this time he does so acutely—that he is exchanging more than a product of hours of working time, but that he is giving something of himself—his time, his life. Thus he wishes to be rewarded, even if only moderately, for this gift. To refuse him this reward is to make him become idle or less productive.

371

Perhaps we may point out a conclusion that is both sociological and practical. The famous Sourate LXIV, 'mutual disappointment' (the Last Judgement) given to Mahomet at Mecca, says of God:

15. Your wealth and your children are your temptation, whilst God holds in reserve a magnificent reward.

16. Fear God with all your might; listen and obey, give alms (*sadaqa*) in your own interest. He who is on his guard against his avarice will be happy.

17. If you make a generous loan to God, he will pay you back double; he will forgive you because he is grateful and longsuffering.

18. He knows things visible and invisible, he is the one powerful and wise.

Substitute for the name of Allah that of society and the occupational grouping, or put together all three names, if you are religious. Replace the concept of alms by that of co-operation, of a task done or service rendered for others. You will then have a fairly good idea of the kind of economy that is at present laboriously in gestation. We see it already functioning in certain economic groupings, and in the hearts of the masses, who possess, very often better than their leaders, a sense of their own interests, and of the common interest.

Perhaps by studying these obscure aspects of social life we shall succeed in throwing a little light upon the path that our nations must follow, both in their morality and in their economy.

For Further Reading

Mauss, Marcel. "A Category of the Human Mind." In *The Category of the Person: Anthropology, Philosophy, History*. Edited by Michael Carrithers (Cambridge: Cambridge Univ. Press, 1985).

_____. *Sociology and Psychology: Essays* (London: Routledge, 1979).

_____, and Émile Durkheim. *Primitive Classification* (Chicago: Univ. of Chicago Press, 1963). Translated by Rodney Needham.

_____, and Henri Hubert. *Sacrifice: Its Nature and Function* (Chicago: Univ. of Chicago Press, 1964).

Bataille, Georges. *The Accursed Share*. Translated by Robert Hurley (New York: Zone Books, 1988).

Blau, Peter. *Exchange and Power in Social Life* (New York: Wiley, 1964).

Carrithers, Michael, Steven Collins, and Steven Lukes, eds. *The Category of the Person: Anthropology, Philosophy, History* (Cambridge: Cambridge Univ. Press, 1985).

Derrida, Jacques. *Given Time: I. Counterfeit Money*. Translated by Peggy Kamuf (Chicago: Univ. of Chicago Press, 1991).

Goody, Jack, and S.J. Tambiah, *Bridewealth and Dowry* (London: Cambridge Univ. Press, 1973).

Hyde, Lewis. *The Gift: Imagination and the Erotic Life of Property* (New York: Vintage, 1983).

Malinowski, Bronislaw. *Argonauts of the Western Pacific* (London: Routledge, 1922).

Sahlins, Marshall. *Stone Age Economics* (Chicago: Aldine, 1972).

Titmuss, Richard. *The Gift Relationship: From Human Blood to Social Policy* (New York: Pantheon, 1971).

GEORGES BATAILLE (1897–1962)

chapter 18

HOMOGENEITY, INSTRUMENTALISM, and egoism, three shadows cast by capitalism, repulsed Georges Bataille. Utilitarianism, as Bataille construed it, unites all three and poses a greater threat than capitalism itself. Bourgeois society issues in a "universal meanness," and "the bourgeois are incapable of concealing a sordid face, a face so rapacious and lacking in nobility, so frighteningly small, that all human life, upon seeing it, seems degraded." Utilitarianism likewise forms the horizon of socialist proposals to spur production by abolishing private property. Revolted by this "disenchanted" world, Bataille turned to the sacred, the paradigm of the heteronomous or "other." Against the pinch-penny fixation on means, Bataille exuded the vocabulary of pure ends: "glory," "(pure) sacrifice," "play," "exuberance," "extravagance," "luxury." Against the egoism of utilitarianism Bataille set the solidarity of a sacred community rooted in ecstatic group experience, sacrifice, and ritual.

Émile Durkheim, likewise dead set against utilitarianism, had merged the topics of heterogeneity and solidarity in his book *The Elementary Forms of Religious Life*. There he argued that the origins of social solidarity lie in transfiguring experiences of the sacred that break away from the routine. Ritual reenactments of these originary events renew contact with the sacred and sustain solidarity. By contrast, the utilitarian debasement of culture leaves it dull as lead. Bataille and his associates in the independent "College of Sociology" sought a "leftist sacred" as an alternative both to utilitarianism and to fascist efforts to spiritualize society. However, they inherited from Durkheim these troublesome questions: Is sociology of religion a viable point of departure for resacralization? How does one insist on the sacred sources of social solidarity while skeptically regarding such sources as arbitrary?

Though not an economist, Bataille claimed to make a "Copernican revolution" in economics by distinguishing between "general economy" and "restricted economy." Attention usually focuses on the "restricted economy," i.e., the production and conservation of wealth in the battle with scarcity. "General economy" widens the perspective to emphasize the excessiveness of organic life. The deepest "economic" problems we face, and the ones most revealing of our destiny, according to Bataille, are how to dispense excess wealth and spend free time. Adam Smith's prizing of "productive" over "unproductive" labor exemplifies the mentality Bataille finds so short-sighted. Not that Bataille ignores the problems of scarcity—he proposes, for example, that the United States massively share its wealth with India. But, for him, the accent falls on expenditure, not acquisition. Failure to give excess its due makes it a curse that we undergo—often in the stupidity of war or the rat race for status—rather than a joyful undertaking. Bataille figured that the carrying capacity of the biosphere would soon halt the funnelling of excess into new growth and would bring us face to face with our earthly destiny.

Mauss's book on the gift inspired Bataille's reversal of economic discourse, making scarcity revolve around excess. From Mauss he learned with dismay that, despite their show of disinterestedness, gifts and sacrifice were not pure bestowal but devices for converting wealth into rank: "It [gift exchange] places the value, the prestige and the truth of life in the negation of the servile use of possessions, but at the same time it makes a servile use of this negation." Against the "servile" pursuits of our "crooked wills," Bataille sets the beatific example of the sun, whose pure, unrequited release of energy is the source of all earthly excess. Plato's sun in his allegory of the cave was also the primal source, but it stood for the Good; Bataille's sun is Spinozan; it stands for Glory, exuberant freedom beyond good and evil. According to the doctrine on human beings that is wrapped up in Bataille's "general economics," we are bound for a glory to which the dismal science of the "restricted economy" is oblivious.

Bataille, like Veblen, highlights the economics of luxury, identifies the use of luxury to attain social rank, and despises the waste of wealth on social climbing. But the two are of wildly divergent minds. Both recognize that actual goods cannot be sorted into the useful and the luxurious; nevertheless, the distinction between pure usefulness and pure expenditure figures prominently for each. But where Veblen wants us to cut out the childish squandering of resources on status-seeking and follow our nose for the strictly useful, Bataille, echoing Schiller and Nietzsche, wants us to grow up and play.

FROM *THE ACCURSED SHARE*

THEORY OF "POTLATCH"

1. The paradox of the "gift" reduced to the "acquisition" of a "power."

Since the publication of Marcel Mauss's *The Gift,* the institution of potlatch has been the object of a sometimes dubious interest and curiosity. Potlatch enables one to perceive a connection between religious behaviors and economic ones. Nevertheless, one would not be able to find laws in common between these two types of behavior—if by economy one understood a conventional set of human activities, and not the general economy in its irreducible movement. It would be futile, as a matter of fact, to consider the economic aspects of potlatch without first having formulated the viewpoint defined by *general economy.*[1] There would be no potlatch if, in a general sense, the ultimate problem concerned the acquisition and not the dissipation of useful wealth.

The study of this strange yet familiar institution (a good many of our behaviors are reducible to the laws of potlatch; they have the same significance as it does) has a privileged place in general economy. If there is within us, running through the space we inhabit, a movement of energy that we use, but that is not reducible to its utility (which we are impelled by reason to seek), we can disregard it; but we can also adapt our activity to its completion outside us. The solution of the problem thus posed calls for an action in two contrary directions: We need on the one hand to go beyond the narrow limits within which we ordinarily remain, and on the other hand somehow bring our going-beyond back within our limits. The problem posed is that of the expenditure of the surplus. We need to give away, lose or destroy. But the gift would be senseless (and so we would never decide to give) if it did not take on the meaning of an acquisition. Hence *giving* must become *acquiring a power.* Gift-giving has the virtue of a surpassing of the subject who gives, but in exchange for the object given, the subject appropriates the surpassing: He regards his virtue, that which he had the capacity for, as an asset, as a *power* that he now possesses. He enriches himself with a contempt for riches, and what he proves to be miserly of is in fact his generosity.

But he would not be able by himself to acquire a power constituted by a relinquishment of power: If he destroyed the object in solitude, in silence, no sort of *power* would result from the act; there would not be anything for the

375

subject but a separation from power without any compensation. But if he destroys the object in front of another person or if he gives it away, the one who gives has actually acquired, in the other's eyes, the power of giving or destroying. He is now rich for having made use of wealth in the manner its essence would require: He is rich for having ostentatiously consumed what is wealth only if it is consumed. But the wealth that is actualized in the potlatch, *in consumption for others,* has no real existence except insofar as the other is changed by the consumption. In a sense, authentic consumption ought to be solitary, but then it would not have the completion that the action it has on the other confers on it. And this action that is brought to bear on others is precisely what constitutes the gift's power, which one acquires from the fact of *losing.* The exemplary virtue of the potlatch is given in this possibility for man to grasp what eludes him, to combine the limitless movements of the universe with the limit that belongs to him.

2. *The apparent absurdity of gifts.*

But "you can't have your cake and eat it too," the saying goes.

It is contradictory to try to be unlimited and limited at the same time, and the result is comedy: The gift does not mean anything from the standpoint of general economy; there is dissipation only for the giver.

Moreover, it turns out that the giver has only apparently lost. Not only does he have the power over the recipient that the gift has bestowed on him, but the recipient is obligated to nullify that power by repaying the gift. The rivalry even entails the return of a greater gift: In order to *get even* the giver must not only redeem himself, but he must also impose the "power of the gift" on his rival in turn. In a sense the presents are repaid *with interest.* Thus the gift is the opposite of what it seemed to be: To give is obviously to lose, but the loss apparently brings a profit to the one who sustains it.

In reality, this absurdly contradictory aspect of potlatch is misleading. The first giver *suffers* the apparent gain resulting from the difference between his presents and those given to him in return. The one who repays only has the feeling of acquiring—a power—and of outdoing. Actually, as I have said, the ideal would be that a potlatch could not be repaid. The benefit in no way corresponds to the desire for gain. On the contrary, receiving prompts one— and obliges one—to give more, for it it is necessary to remove the resulting obligation.

3. *The acquisition of rank.*

Doubtless potlatch is not reducible to the desire to lose, but what it brings to the giver is not the inevitable increase of return gifts; it is the rank *which it confers on the one who has the last word.*

Prestige, glory and rank should not be confused with *power.* Or if prestige is *power,* this is insofar as power itself escapes the considerations of force or right to which it is ordinarily reduced. It must be said, further, that the identity of the power and the ability to lose is fundamental. Numerous factors stand in the way, interfere and finally prevail, but, all things considered, neither force nor right is the *human basis* of the differentiated value of individuals. As the surviving practices make clear, *rank* varies decisively according to an individual's capacity for giving. The animal factor (the capacity for defeating an adversary in a fight) is itself subordinated, by and large, to the value of giving. To be sure, this is the ability to appropriate a position or possessions, but it is also the fact of a man's having staked his whole being. Moreover, the gift's aspect of an appeal to animal force is brought out in fights for a common cause, to which the fighter gives himself. *Glory,* the consequence of a superiority, is itself something different from an ability to take another's place and seize his possessions: It expresses a movement of senseless frenzy, of measureless expenditure of energy, which the fervor of combat presupposes. Combat is glorious in that it is always beyond calculation at some moment. But the meaning of warfare and glory is poorly grasped if it is not related in part to the acquisition of *rank* through a reckless expenditure of vital resources, of which potlatch is the most legible form.

4. The first basic laws.

But if it is true that potlatch remains the opposite of a rapine, of a profitable exchange or, generally speaking, of an appropriation of possessions, acquisition is nonetheless its ultimate purpose. Because the movement it structures differs from ours, it appears stranger to us, and so it is more capable of revealing what usually escapes our perception, and what it shows us is our basic ambiguity. One can deduce the following laws from it. Of course man is not definable once and for all and these laws operate differently—their effects are even neutralized—at different stages of history, but basically they never cease to reveal a decisive play of forces:

> *a surplus of resources, which societies have constantly at their disposal at certain points, at certain times, cannot be the object of a complete appropriation (it cannot be usefully employed; it cannot be employed for the growth of the productive forces), but the squandering of this surplus itself becomes an object of appropriation;*
>
> *what is appropriated in the squander is the prestige it gives to the squanderer (whether an individual or a group), which is acquired by him as a possession and which determines his rank;*
>
> *conversely, rank in society (or the rank of one society among others) can be appropriated in the same way as a tool or a field; if it is ultimately a source of profit, the principle of it is nevertheless determined by a resolute squandering of resources that in theory could have been acquired.*

5. Ambiguity and contradiction.

While the resources he controls are reducible to quantities of energy, man is not always able to set them aside for a growth that cannot be endless or, above all, continual. He must waste the excess, but he remains eager to acquire even when he does the opposite, and so he makes waste itself an object of acquisition. Once the resources are dissipated, there remains the prestige *acquired* by the one who wastes. The waste is an ostentatious squandering to this end, with a view to a superiority over others that he attributes to himself by this means. But he misuses the negation he makes of the utility of the resources he wastes, bringing into contradiction not only himself but man's entire existence. The latter thus enters into an ambiguity where it remains: It places the value, the prestige and the truth of life in the negation of the servile use of possessions, but at the same time it makes a servile use of this negation. On the one hand, in the useful and graspable thing it discerns that which, being necessary to it, can be used for its growth (or its subsistence), but if strict necessity ceases to bind it, this "useful thing" cannot entirely answer to its wishes. Consequently, it calls for that which cannot be grasped, for the useless employment of oneself, of one's possessions, for *play,* but it attempts to grasp that which it wished to be *ungraspable,* to *use* that whose *utility* it denied. It is not enough for our left hand not to know what the right hand gives: Clumsily, it tries to take it back.

Rank is entirely the effect of this crooked will. In a sense, *rank* is the opposite of a thing: What founds it is sacred, and the general ordering of ranks is given the name of *hierarchy*. It is the stubborn determination to treat as a disposable and usable *thing* that whose essence is sacred, that which is completely removed from the profane utilitarian sphere, where the hand—unscrupulously and for servile ends—raises the hammer and nails the timber. But ambiguity encumbers the profane operation just as it empties desire's vehemence of its meaning and changes it into an apparent comedy.

This compromise given in our nature heralds those linked series of deceptions, exploitations and manias that give a temporal order to the apparent unreason of history. Man is necessarily in a mirage, his very reflection mystifies him, so intent is he on grasping the ungraspable, on using transports of lost hatred as tools. *Rank,* where loss is changed into acquisition, corresponds to the activity of the intellect, which reduces the objects of thought to *things*. In point of fact, the contradiction of potlatch is revealed not only throughout history, but more profoundly in the operations of thought. Generally, in sacrifice or in potlatch, in action (in history) or in contemplation (in thought), what we seek is always this semblance—which by definition we cannot grasp—that we vainly call the poetry, the depth or the intimacy of passion. We are necessarily deceived since we want to grasp this shadow.

We could not reach the final object of knowledge without the dissolution of knowledge, which aims to reduce its object to the condition of subordinated and managed things. The ultimate problem of knowledge is the same as that of consumption. No one can both know and not be destroyed; no one can both consume wealth and increase it.

6. Luxury and extreme poverty.

But if the demands of the life of beings (or groups) detached from life's immensity defines an interest to which every operation is referred, the *general* movement of life is nevertheless accomplished beyond the demands of individuals. Selfishness is finally disappointed. It seems to prevail and to lay down a definitive boundary, but it is surpassed in any case. No doubt the rivalries of individuals among themselves take away the multitude's ability to be overrun by the global exuberance of energy. The weak are fleeced, exploited by the strong, who pay them with flagrant lies. But this cannot change the overall results, where individual interest is mocked, and where *the lies of the rich are changed into truth*.

In the end, with the possibility of growth or of acquisition reaching its limit at a certain point, *energy*, the object of greed of every isolated individual, is necessarily liberated—truly liberated under the cover of lies. Definitively, men lie; they do their best to relate this liberation to interest, but this liberation carries them further. Consequently, in a sense they lie in any case. As a rule the individual accumulation of resources is doomed to destruction. The individuals who carry out this destruction do not truly possess this wealth, *this rank*. Under primitive conditions, wealth is always analogous to stocks of munitions, which so clearly express the annihilation, not the possession of wealth. But this image is just as accurate if it is a matter of expressing the equally ludicrous truth of *rank:* It is an explosive charge. The man of high rank is originally only an explosive individual (all men are explosive, but he is explosive in a privileged way). Doubtless he tries to prevent, or at least delay the explosion. Thus he lies to himself by derisively taking his wealth and his power for something that they are not. If he manages to enjoy them peacefully, it is at the cost of a misunderstanding of himself, of his real nature. He lies at the same time to all the others, before whom on the contrary he maintains the affirmation of a truth (his explosive nature), from which he tries to escape. Of course, he will be engulfed in these lies: *Rank* will be reduced to a commodity of exploitation, a shameless source of profits. This poverty cannot in any way interrupt the movement of exuberance.

Indifferent to intentions, to reticences and lies, slowly or suddenly, the movement of wealth exudes and consumes the resources of energy. This often seems strange, but not only do these resources suffice; if they cannot be completely consumed productively a surplus usually remains, which must be annihilated. At first sight, potlatch appears to carry out this consumption badly. The destruction of riches is not its rule: They are ordinarily given away and the loss in the operation is reduced to that of the giver: The aggregate of riches is preserved. But this is only an appearance. If potlatch rarely results in acts similar in every respect to sacrifice, it is nonetheless *the complementary form of an institution whose meaning is in the fact that it withdraws wealth from productive consumption.* In general, sacrifice withdraws useful products from profane circulation; in principle the gifts of potlatch liberate objects that are useless from the start. The industry of archaic luxury is the basis of potlatch; obviously, this industry squanders resources represented by the quantities of available human labor. Among the Aztecs, they were "cloaks, petticoats, precious blouses"; or "richly coloured feathers . . . cut stones, shells, fans, shell paddles . . . wild animal skins worked and ornamented with designs." In the American Northwest, canoes and houses are destroyed, and dogs or slaves are slaughtered: These are useful riches. Essentially the gifts are objects of luxury (elsewhere the gifts of food are pledged from the start to the useless consumption of feasts).

One might even say that potlatch is the specific manifestation, the meaningful form of luxury. Beyond the archaic forms, luxury has actually retained the functional value of potlatch, creative of *rank.* Luxury still determines the rank of the one who displays it, and there is no exalted rank that does not require a display. But the petty calculations of those who enjoy luxury are surpassed in every way. In wealth, what shines through the defects extends the brilliance of the sun and provokes passion. It is not what is imagined by those who have reduced it to their *poverty;* it is the return of life's immensity to the truth of exuberance. This truth destroys those who have taken it for what it is not; the least that one can say is that the present forms of wealth make a shambles and a human mockery of those who think they own it. In this respect, present-day society is a huge counterfeit, where this *truth* of wealth has underhandedly slipped into *extreme poverty.* The true luxury and the real potlatch of our times falls to the poverty stricken, that is, to the individual who lies down and scoffs. A genuine luxury requires the complete contempt for riches, the somber indifference of the individual who refuses work and makes his life on the one hand an infinitely ruined splendor, and on the other, a silent insult to the laborious lie of the rich. Beyond a military exploitation, a religious mystification and a capitalist misappropriation, henceforth no one can rediscover the meaning of wealth, the explosiveness that it heralds, unless it is in the splendor of rags and the somber challenge of indifference. One might say, finally, that the lie destines life's exuberance to revolt.

Notes

1. Let me indicate here that the studies whose results I am publishing here came out of my reading of the *Essai sur le don.* To begin with, reflection on potlatch led me to formulate the laws of *general economy.* But it may be of interest to mention a special difficulty that I was hard put to resolve. The general principles that I introduced, which enable one to interpret a large number of facts, left irreducible elements in the

potlatch, which in my mind remained the origin of those facts. Potlatch cannot be unilaterally interpreted as a consumption of riches. It is only recently that I have been able to reduce the difficulty, and give the principles of "general economy" a rather ambiguous foundation. What it comes down to is that a squandering of energy is always the opposite of a thing, but it enters into consideration only once it has entered into the order of things, once it has been changed into a *thing*.

For Further Reading

Bataille, Georges. *Theory of Religion.* Translated by Robert Hurley (New York: Zone Books, 1988).

_____. *Visions of Excess: Selected Writings 1927–1939.* Translated by Allan Stoekl (Manchester: Manchester Univ. Press, 1985).

Gill, Carolyn Bailey. *Bataille: Writing the Sacred* (London: Routledge, 1995).

Habermas, Jürgen. "Between Eroticism and General Economics: Georges Bataille." In *The Philosophical Discourse of Modernity* (Oxford: Polity Press, 1987). Translated by Frederick Lawrence.

Hollier, Denis. *Against Architecture: The Writings of Georges Bataille* (Cambridge: MIT Press, 1989).

Land, Nick. *The Taste for Annihilation: Georges Bataille and Violent Nihilism* (London: Routledge, 1992).

Pefanis, Julian. *Heterology and the Postmodern: Bataille, Baudrillard, and Lyotard* (Durham, N.C.: Duke Univ. Press, 1991).

Richardson, Michael. *Georges Bataille* (London: Routledge, 1994).

Richman, Michele. *Beyond the Gift: Reading Georges Bataille* (Baltimore, Md.: Johns Hopkins University Press, 1982).

SIMONE WEIL (1909–1943)

chapter 19

"NOTHING IS made to man's measure," warns Simone Weil. The gigantic prevails in twentieth-century economies, technologies, state bureaucracies, media, wars. With such disproportion between glass-eyed collective powers and human individuals comes a dizzying sense of unreality. Thought is for Weil a human's "supreme dignity," and she trusts its power when trained against force, but the conditions for real thought and action are being crowded out. Factory work dispirits and dumbs workers down; financial power brokering overwhelms entrepreneurial ingenuity; the sciences are unfathomable labyrinths; the popular press degrades language and stokes public opinion, that "monstrous nothing," as Kierkegaard termed it; war and the mobilization for war endanger human existence. If the scale of things is all wrong, what can right it? What can overcome these enormities but countervailing forces just as immense and oppressive? wonders Weil, despairing of the "political illusion." The demise of industrialized commercial life is inevitable: Weil imagines a "motor-car launched at full speed and driverless across broken country"—only the timing of the wreck remains in doubt.

Though Weil sympathized deeply with the workers under capitalism, associated with various radicals (including a leader of the Russian Revolution, Leon Trotsky), and held Karl Marx in high regard, she was an early and forceful critic of Marxism, Russian Communism, and Marx. Albert Camus considered Weil the most incisive social analyst since Marx, and her ideas resound in the thought of recent French post-Marxists from Jacques Ellul to Cornelius Castoriadis. The technological and organizational transformations wrought by industrial capitalism—what Marx termed the real subsumption of production under capital—profoundly alter the terms of revolutionary change. Weil charged that under these new conditions the Marxist focus—class, exploitation (the expropriation of surplus-value), and private property—overlooks too much.

Weil considers ways in which capitalism does not prepare the way for a life of greater liberty and equality. The oppression of wage earners depends more on the organization of the factory than on its private ownership. The separation of mental from manual labor becomes routine, and, independently of property relations, the specialization of knowledge makes prospects poor for overcoming that separation. Weil concludes that the liberty and equality sought by socialists presuppose "a preliminary transformation in the realm of production and in the realm of culture." To end production that is driven by profit while preserving the shambles of working life misses the boat. Marx's thoughtlessness regarding the emergence of communism from capitalism galled Weil. Why, she demanded, should we expect slaves to establish freedom? Why should we count on technical progress to eliminate oppressive labor? How long will our energy sources hold out? Why should we assume that we will discover cheap replacements once non-renewable energy sources are tapped out? Weil charged that, at these points, Marx fell back on a secular form of Providence: the "religion of the productive forces." Without reaching conclusions, she posed questions sufficiently pointed as to cast doubt upon Marx's project.

Simone Weil's brief life overlapped two World Wars, the Russian Revolution, the deepest economic crisis in the history of modern capitalism, and the rise of Fascism. For Weil, the combined developments of the concentration of industry, the power of fictional capital (credit), and invasive publicity doomed the market's capacity to self-regulate. Anticipating what Guy Debord and Jean Baudrillard would call, respectively, "the society of the spectacle" and "hyperreality," Weil wrote: "everything takes place in the realm of opinion, and almost of fiction, by means of speculation and publicity." As economic life falls more and more under the grip of the state, it becomes increasingly a matter of competition for power in the international arena, with military buildup swelling the power of the state.

FROM *OPPRESSION AND LIBERTY*

FROM "SKETCH OF CONTEMPORARY SOCIAL LIFE"

It is impossible to imagine anything more contrary to this ideal than the form which modern civilization has assumed in our day, at the end of a development lasting several centuries. Never has the individual been so completely delivered up to a blind collectivity, and never have men been less capable, not only of subordinating their actions to their thoughts, but even of thinking. Such terms as oppressors and oppressed, the idea of classes—all that sort of thing is near to losing all meaning, so obvious are the impotence and distress of all men in face of the social machine, which has become a machine for breaking hearts and crushing spirits, a machine for manufacturing irresponsibility, stupidity, corruption, slackness and, above all, dizziness. The reason for this painful state of affairs is perfectly clear. We are living in a world in which nothing is made to man's measure; there exists a monstrous discrepancy between man's body, man's mind and the things which at the present time constitute the elements of human existence; everything is disequilibrium. There is not a single category, group or class of men that is altogether exempt from this destructive disequilibrium, except perhaps for a few isolated patches of more primitive life; and the younger generation, who have grown and are growing up in it, inwardly reflect the chaos surrounding them more than do their elders. This disequilibrium is essentially a matter of quantity. Quantity is changed into quality, as Hegel said, and in particular a mere difference in quantity is sufficient to change what is human into what is inhuman. From the abstract point of view quantities are immaterial, since you can arbitrarily change the unit of measurement; but from the concrete point of view certain units of measurement are given and have hitherto remained invariable, such as the human body, human life, the year, the day, the average quickness of human thought. Present-day life is not organized on the scale of all these things; it has been transported into an altogether different order of magnitude, as though man were trying to raise it to the level of the forces of outside nature while neglecting to take his own nature into account. If we add that, to all appearances, the economic system has exhausted its constructive capacity and is beginning to be able to function only by undermining little by little its own material foundations, we shall perceive in all its simplicity the veritable essence of the bottomless misery that forms the lot of the present generations.

In appearance, nearly everything nowadays is carried out methodically; science is king, machinery invades bit by bit the entire field of labour, statistics take on a growing importance, and over one-sixth of the globe the central authority is trying to regulate the whole of social life according to plans. But in reality methodical thought is progressively disappearing, owing to the fact that the mind finds less and less matter on which to bite. Mathematics by itself forms too vast and too complex a whole to be embraced by one mind; *a*

385

fortiori the whole formed by mathematics and the natural sciences; *a fortiori* the whole formed by science and its applications; and, on the other hand, everything is too intimately connected for the mind to be able really to grasp partial concepts. Now everything that the individual becomes powerless to control is seized upon by the collectivity. Thus science has now been for a long time—and to an ever-increasing extent—a collective enterprise. Actually, new results are always, in fact, the work of specific individuals; but, save perhaps for rare exceptions, the value of any result depends on such a complex set of interrelations with past discoveries and possible future researches that even the mind of the inventor cannot embrace the whole. Consequently, new discoveries, as they go on accumulating, take on the appearance of enigmas, after the style of too thick a glass which ceases to be transparent. *A fortiori* practical life takes on a more and more collective character, and the individual as such a more and more insignificant place in it. Technical progress and mass production reduce manual workers more and more to a passive role; in increasing proportion and to an ever greater extent they arrive at a form of labour that enables them to carry out the necessary movements without understanding their connection with the final result. On the other hand, an industrial concern has become something too vast and too complex for any one man to be able to grasp it fully; and furthermore, in all spheres, the men who occupy key posts in social life are in charge of matters which are far beyond the compass of any single human mind. As for the general body of social life, it depends on so many factors, each of which is impenetrably obscure and which are tangled up in inextricable relations with one another, that it would never even occur to anyone to try to understand its mechanism. Thus the social function most essentially connected with the individual, that which consists in co-ordinating, managing, deciding, is beyond any individual's capacity and becomes to a certain extent collective and, as it were, anonymous.

To the very extent to which what is systematic in contemporary life escapes the control of the mind, its regularity is established by things which constitute the equivalent of what collective thought would be if the collectivity did think. The cohesiveness of science is ensured by means of signs; namely, on the one hand, by words or ready-made phrases whose use is stretched beyond the meanings originally contained in them, on the other hand, by algebraic calculations. In the sphere of labour, the things which take upon themselves the essential functions are machines. The thing which relates production to consumption and governs the exchange of products is money. Finally, where the function of co-ordination and management is too heavy for the mind and intelligence of one man, it is entrusted to a curious machine, whose parts are men, whose gears consist of regulations, reports and statistics, and which is called bureaucratic organization. All these blind things imitate the effort of thought to the life. Just the mechanism of algebraic calculation has led more than once to what might be called a new idea, except that the content of such pseudo-ideas is no more than that of relations between signs; and algebra is often marvellously apt to transform a series of experimental results into laws, with a disconcerting ease reminding one of the fantastic transformations one sees in motion-picture cartoons. Automatic machines seem to offer the model for the intelligent, faithful, docile and conscientious worker. As for money, economists have long been convinced that it possesses the virtue of establishing harmonious relations between the various economic functions. And bureaucratic machines almost reach the point of taking the place of leaders. Thus, in all spheres, thought, the prerogative of the individual, is subordinated to vast mechanisms which crystallize collective life, and that is so to such an extent that we have almost lost the notion of what real thought is. The efforts, the labours, the inventions of beings of flesh and blood whom time introduces in successive waves to social life only possess social value and effectiveness on condition that they become in their turn crystallized in these huge mechanisms. The inversion of the relation between means and ends—an inversion which is to a certain extent the law of every oppressive society—here becomes total or nearly so, and extends to nearly everything. The scientist does not use science in order to manage to see more clearly into his own thinking, but aims at discovering results that will go to swell the present volume of scientific knowledge. Machines do not run in order to enable men to live, but we resign ourselves to feeding men in order that they may serve the machines. Money does not provide a convenient method for exchanging products; it is the sale of goods which is a means for keeping money in circulation. Lastly, organization is not a means for exercising a collective activity, but the activity of a group, whatever it may be, is a means for strengthening organization. Another aspect of the same inversion consists in the fact that signs, words and algebraic formulas in the field of knowledge, money and credit symbols in economic life, play the part of realities of which the actual things themselves constitute only the shadows, exactly as in Hans Andersen's tale in which the scientist and his shadow exchanged roles; this is because signs constitute the material of social relations, whereas the perception of reality is something individual. The dispossession of the individual in favour of the collectivity is not, indeed, absolute, and it cannot become so; but it is hard to imagine how it could go much farther than at present. The power and concentration of armaments place all human lives at the mercy of the central authority. As a result of the vast extension of exchange, the majority of men cannot procure for themselves the greater part of what they consume save through the medium of society and in return for money; the peasants themselves are today to a large extent under this obligation to buy. And as big industry is a system of collective production, a great many men are forced, in order that their hands may come into contact with the material of work, to go through a collectivity which swallows them up and pins them down to a more or less servile task; when it rejects them, the

387

strength and skill of their hands remain useless. The very peasants, who hitherto had managed to escape this wretched condition, have been reduced to it of late over one-sixth of the globe. Such a stifling state of affairs certainly provokes here and there an individualistic reaction; art, and especially literature, bears the marks of it; but since, owing to objective conditions, this reaction cannot impinge on either the sphere of thought or that of action, it remains bottled up in the play of the inner consciousness or in dreams of adventure and gratuitous acts, in other words, it never leaves the realm of shadows; and everything leads one to suppose that even this shadowy reaction is doomed to disappear almost completely.

When man reaches this degree of enslavement, judgments of value can only be based, whatever the particular field may be, on a purely external criterion; language does not possess any term so foreign to thought as properly to express something so devoid of meaning; but we may say that this criterion is constituted by efficiency, provided we thereby understand successes obtained in a vacuum. Even a scientific concept is not valued according to its content, which may be completely unintelligible, but according to the opportunities it provides for co-ordinating, abbreviating, summarizing. In the economic field, an undertaking is judged, not according to the real utility of the social functions it fulfils, but according to its growth so far and the speed with which it is developing; and the same is true of everything. Thus judgment of values is as it were entrusted to material objects instead of to the mind. The efficacy of efforts of whatever kind must always, it is true, be verified by thought, for, generally speaking, all verification proceeds from the mind; but thought has been reduced to such a subordinate role that one may say, by way of simplification, that the function of verification has passed from thought to things. But this excessive complication of all theoretical and practical activities which has thus dethroned thought, finally, when still further aggravated, comes to render the verification exercised by things in its turn imperfect and almost impossible. Everything is then blind. Thus it is that, in the sphere of science, the excessive accumulation of materials of every kind produces such chaos that the time seems to be approaching when any system will appear arbitrary. The chaos existing in economic life is still far more patent. In the actual carrying out of work, the subordination of irresponsible slaves to leaders overwhelmed by the mass of things to attend to, and, incidentally, themselves to a large extent irresponsible, is the cause of faulty workmanship and countless acts of negligence; this evil, which was first of all restricted to the big industrial undertakings, has now spread to the countryside wherever the peasants are enslaved after the manner of the industrial workers, that is to say, in Soviet Russia. The tremendous extension of credit prevents money from playing its regulating role so far as concerns commercial exchanges and the relationships between the various branches of production; and it would be useless to try to remedy this by doses of statistics. The parallel extension of speculation ends up by rendering the prosperity of industries independent, to a large extent, of their good functioning; the reason being that the capital increase brought about by the actual production of each of them counts less and less as compared with the constant supply of fresh capital. In short, in all spheres, success has become something almost arbitrary; it seems more and more to be the work of pure chance; and as it constituted the sole rule in all branches of human activity, our civilization is invaded by an ever-increasing disorder, and ruined by a waste in proportion to that disorder. This transformation is taking place at the very moment when the sources of profit on which the capitalist economy formerly drew for its prodigious development are becoming less and less plentiful, and when the technical conditions of work are themselves imposing a rapidly decreasing tempo on the improvement of industrial equipment.

So many profound changes have been taking place almost unbeknownst to us, and yet we are living in a period when the very axis of the social system is as it were in process of heeling over. Throughout the rise of the industrial system social life found itself oriented in the direction of construction. The industrial equipment of the planet was the supreme battle-ground on which the struggle for power was waged. To increase the size of an undertaking faster than its competitors, and that by means of its own resources—such was, broadly speaking, the aim and object of economic activity. Saving was the rule of economic life; consumption was restricted as much as possible, not only that of the workers, but also that of the capitalists themselves, and, in general, all expenditure connected with other things than industrial equipment. The supreme mission of governments was to preserve peace at home and abroad. The bourgeoisie were under the impression that this state of things would go on indefinitely, for the greater happiness of humanity; but it could not go on indefinitely in this way. Nowadays, the struggle for power, while preserving to a certain extent the same outward appearance, has entirely changed in character. The formidable increase in the part capital plant plays in undertakings, if compared with that of living labour, the rapid decrease in the rate of profit which has resulted, the ever-increasing amount of overhead expenses, waste, leakage, the lack of any regulating device for adjusting the various branches of production to one another—everything prevents social activity from still having as its pivot the development of the undertaking by turning profits into capital. It seems as though the economic struggle has ceased to be a form of competition in order to become a sort of war. It is no longer so much a question of properly organizing the work as of squeezing out the greatest possible amount of available capital scattered about in society by marketing shares, and then of squeezing out the greatest possible amount of money from everywhere by marketing products; everything takes place in the realm of opinion, and almost of fiction, by means of speculation and publicity. Since credit is the key to all economic success, saving is replaced by the

389

maddest forms of expenditure. The term property has almost ceased to have any meaning; the ambitious man no longer thinks of being owner of a business and running it at a profit, but of causing the widest possible sector of economic activity to pass under his control. In a word, if we attempt to characterize, albeit in vague and summary fashion, this almost impenetrably obscure transformation, it is now a question in the struggle for economic power far less of building up than of conquering; and since conquest is destructive, the capitalist system, though remaining outwardly pretty much the same as it was fifty years ago, is wholly turned towards destruction. The means employed in the economic struggle—publicity, lavish display of wealth, corruption, enormous capital investments based almost entirely on credit, marketing of useless products by almost violent methods, speculations with the object of ruining rival concerns—all these tend to undermine the foundations of our economic life far more than to broaden them.

But all that is little enough compared with two related phenomena which are beginning to appear clearly and to cause a tragic threat to weigh upon the life of everyone; namely, on the one hand, the fact that the State tends more and more, and with an extraordinary rapidity, to become the center of economic and social life, and, on the other hand, the subordination of economic to military interests. If one tries to analyse these phenomena in detail, one is held up by an almost inextricable web of reciprocal causes and effects; but the general trend is clear enough. It is quite natural that the increasingly bureaucratic nature of economic activity should favour the development of the power of the State, which is the bureaucratic organization *par excellence*. The profound change in the economic struggle operates in the same direction; the State is incapable of constructing, but owing to the fact that it concentrates in its hands the most powerful means of coercion, it is brought, as it were, by its very weight gradually to become the central element when it comes to conquering and destroying. Finally, seeing that the extraordinary complication of exchange and credit operations prevents money henceforth from sufficing to co-ordinate economic life, a semblance of bureaucratic co-ordination has to make up for it; and the central bureaucratic organization, which is the State machine, must naturally be led sooner or later to take the main hand in this co-ordination. The pivot around which revolves social life, thus transformed, is none other than preparation for war. Seeing that the struggle for power is carried out by conquest and destruction, in other words by a diffused economic war, it is not surprising that actual war should come to occupy the foreground. And since war is the recognized form of the struggle for power when the competitors are States, every increase in the State's grip on economic life has the effect of orienting industrial life yet a little farther towards preparation for war; while, conversely, the ever increasing demands occasioned by preparation for war help day by day to bring the all-round economic and social activities of each country more and more into subjection to the authority of the central power. It seems fairly clear that contemporary humanity tends pretty well everywhere towards a totalitarian form of social organization—to use the term which the national socialists have made fashionable—that is to say, towards a system in which the State power comes to exercise sovereign sway in all spheres, even, indeed above all, in that of thought. Russia presents us with an almost perfect example of such a system, for the greater misfortune of the Russian people; other countries will only be able to approach it, short of upheavals similar to that of October 1917; but it seems inevitable that all of them will approach it more or less in the course of the coming years. This development will only give disorder a bureaucratic form, and still further increase confusion, waste and misery. Wars will bring in their train a frantic consumption of raw materials and capital equipment, a crazy destruction of wealth of all kinds that previous generations have bequeathed us. When chaos and destruction have reached the limit beyond which the very functioning of the economic and social organization becomes materially impossible, our civilization will perish; and humanity, having gone back to a more or less primitive level of existence and to a social life dispersed into much smaller collectivities, will set out again along a new road which it is quite impossible for us to predict.

To imagine that we can switch the course of history along a different track by transforming the system through reforms or revolutions, to hope to find salvation in a defensive or offensive action against tyranny and militarism—all that is just day-dreaming. There is nothing on which to base even attempts. Marx's assertion that the régime would produce its own gravediggers is cruelly contradicted every day; and one wonders, incidentally, how Marx could ever have believed that slavery could produce free men. Never yet in history has a régime of slavery fallen under the blows of the slaves. The truth is that, to quote a famous saying, slavery degrades man to the point of making him love it; that liberty is precious only in the eyes of those who effectively possess it; and that a completely inhuman system, as ours is, far from producing beings capable of building up a human society, models all those subjected to it—oppressed and oppressors alike—according to its own image. Everywhere, in varying degrees, the impossibility of relating what one gives to what one receives has killed the feeling for sound workmanship, the sense of responsibility, and has developed passivity, neglect, the habit of expecting everything from outside, the belief in miracles. Even in the country, the feeling of a deep-seated bond between the land which sustains the man and the man who works the land has to a large extent been obliterated since the taste for speculation, the unpredictable rises and falls in currencies and prices have got countryfolk into the habit of turning their eyes towards the towns. The worker has not the feeling of earning his living as a producer; it is merely that the undertaking keeps him enslaved for long hours every day and allows him each week a sum of money which gives him the magic power of conjuring up at a moment's notice ready-made products, exactly as the rich do. The presence of innumerable unemployed, the cruel necessity of having to beg for a job, make wages appear less as wages than as alms. As for the unemployed themselves, the fact that they are involuntary parasites, and poverty-stricken into the bargain, does not make them any the less parasites. Generally speaking, the relation between work done and money earned is so hard to grasp that it appears as almost accidental, so that labour takes on the aspect of servitude, money that of a favour. The so-called governing classes are affected by the same passivity as all the others, owing to the fact that, snowed under as they are by an avalanche of inextricable problems, they long since gave up governing. One would look in vain, from the highest down to the lowest rungs of the social ladder, for a class of men among whom the idea could one day spring up that they might, in certain circumstances, have to take in hand the destinies of society; the harangues of the fascists could alone give the illusion of this, but they are empty.

As always happens, mental confusion and passivity leave free scope to the imagination. On all hands one is obsessed by a representation of social life which, while differing considerably from one class to another, is always made up of mysteries, occult qualities, myths, idols and monsters; each one thinks that power resides mysteriously in one of the classes to which he has no access, because hardly anybody understands that it resides nowhere, so that the dominant feeling everywhere is that dizzy fear which is always brought about by loss of contact with reality. Each class appears from the outside as a nightmare object. In circles connected with the working-class movement, dreams are haunted by mythological monsters called Finance, Industry, Stock Exchange, Bank, etc.; the bourgeois dream about other monsters which they call ringleaders, agitators, demagogues; the politicians regard the capitalists as supernatural beings who alone possess the key to the situation, and *vice versa;* each nation regards its neighbours as collective monsters inspired by a diabolical perversity. One could go on developing this theme indefinitely. In such a situation, any log whatever can be looked upon as king and take the place of one up to a certain point thanks to that belief alone; and this is true, not merely in the case of men in general, but also in that of the governing classes. Nothing is easier, for that matter, than to spread any myth whatsoever throughout a whole population. We must not be surprised, therefore, at the appearance of "totalitarian" régimes unprecedented in history. It is often said that force is powerless to overcome thought; but for this to be true, there must be thought. Where irrational opinions hold the place of ideas, force is all-powerful. It is quite unfair to say, for example, that fascism annihilates free thought; in reality it is the lack of free thought which makes it possible to impose by force official doctrines entirely devoid of meaning. Actually, such a régime even manages considerably to increase the general stupidity, and there is little hope for the generations that will have grown up under the conditions which it creates. Nowadays, every attempt to turn men into brutes finds powerful means at its disposal. On the other hand, one thing is impossible, even were you to dispose of the best of public platforms, and that is to diffuse clear ideas, correct reasoning and sensible views on any wide scale.

It is no good expecting help to come from men; and even were it otherwise, men would none the less be vanquished in advance by the natural power of things. The present social system provides no means of action other than machines for crushing humanity; whatever may be the intentions of those who use them, these machines crush and will continue to crush as long as they exist. With the industrial convict prisons constituted by the big factories, one can only produce slaves and not free workers, still less workers who would form a dominant class. With guns, aeroplanes, bombs, you can spread death, terror, oppression, but not life and liberty. With gas masks, air-raid shelters and air-raid warnings, you can create wretched masses of panic-stricken human beings, ready to succumb to the most senseless forms of terror and to welcome with gratitude the most humiliating forms of tyranny, but not citizens. With the popular press and the wireless, you can make a whole people swallow with their breakfast or their supper a series of ready-made and, by the same token, absurd opinions—for even sensible views become deformed and falsified in minds which accept them unthinkingly; but you cannot with the aid of these things arouse so much as a gleam of thought. And without factories, without arms, without the popular press you can do nothing against those who possess all these things. The same applies to everything. The powerful means are oppressive, the non-powerful means remain inoperative. Each time that the oppressed have tried to set up groups able to exercise a real influence, such groups, whether they went by the name of parties or unions, have reproduced in full within themselves all the vices of the system which they claimed to reform or abolish, namely, bureaucratic organization, reversal of the relationship between means and ends, contempt for the individual, separation between thought and action, the mechanization of thought itself, the exploitation of stupidity and lies as means of propaganda, and so on.

The only possibility of salvation would lie in a methodical co-operation between all, strong and weak, with a view to accomplishing a progressive decentralization of social life; but the absurdity of such an idea strikes one immediately. Such a form of co-operation is impossible to imagine, even in dreams, in a civilization that is based on competition, on struggle, on war. Apart from some such co-operation, there is no means of stopping the blind trend of the social machine towards an increasing centralization, until the machine itself suddenly jams and flies into pieces. What weight can the hopes and desires of those who are not at the control levers carry, when, reduced to the most tragic impotence, they find themselves the mere playthings of blind

393

and brutish forces? As for those who exercise economic or political authority, harried as they are incessantly by rival ambitions and hostile powers, they cannot work to weaken their own authority without condemning themselves almost certainly to being deprived of it. The more they feel themselves to be animated by good intentions, the more they will be brought, even despite themselves, to endeavour to extend their authority in order to increase their ability to do good; which amounts to oppressing people in the hope of liberating them, as Lenin did. It is quite patently impossible for decentralization to be initiated by the central authority; to the very extent to which the central authority is exercised, it brings everything else under its subjection. Generally speaking, the idea of enlightened despotism, which has always had a utopian flavour about it, is in our day completely absurd. Faced with problems whose variety and complexity are infinitely beyond the range of great as of limited minds, no despot in the world can possibly be enlightened. Though a few men may hope, by dint of honest and methodical thinking, to perceive a few gleams in this impenetrable darkness, those whom the cares and responsibilities of authority deprive of both leisure and liberty of mind are certainly not of that number.

In such a situation, what can those do who still persist, against all eventualities, in honouring human dignity both in themselves and in others? Nothing, except endeavour to introduce a little play into the cogs of the machine that is grinding us down; seize every opportunity of awakening a little thought wherever they are able; encourage whatever is capable, in the sphere of politics, economics or technique, of leaving the individual here and there a certain freedom of movement amid the trammels cast around him by the social organization. That is certainly something, but it does not go very far. On the whole, our present situation more or less resembles that of a party of absolutely ignorant travellers who find themselves in a motor-car launched at full speed and driverless across broken country. When will the smash-up occur after which it will be possible to consider trying to construct something new? Perhaps it is a matter of a few decades, perhaps of centuries. There are no data enabling one to fix a probable lapse of time. It seems, however, that the material resources of our civilization are not likely to become exhausted for some considerable time, even allowing for wars; and, on the other hand, as centralization, by abolishing all individual initiative and all local life, destroys by its very existence everything which might serve as a basis for a different form of organization, one may suppose that the present system will go on existing up to the extreme limit of possibility. To sum up, it seems reasonable to suppose that the generations which will have to face the difficulties brought about by the collapse of the present system have yet to be born. As for the generations now living, they are perhaps, of all those that have followed each other in the course of human history, the ones which will have had to shoulder the maximum of imaginary responsibilities and the minimum of real ones. Once this situation is fully realized, it leaves a marvellous freedom of mind. . . .

For Further Reading

Weil, Simone. *Gravity and Grace.* Translated by Arthur Wills with an introduction by Gustave Thibon (London: Routledge, 1952).

_____. *The Iliad or the Poem of Force.* Translated by Mary McCarthy.

_____. *Lectures on Philosophy* (Cambridge: Cambridge Univ. Press, 1978). Translated by Hugh Price (Wallingford, Pa: Pendle Hill, 1956).

_____. *The Need for Roots.* Translated by Arthur F. Wills (Boston: Beacon Press, 1952).

_____. *On Science, Necessity, and Love of God.* Edited by Richard Rees (London: Oxford Univ. Press, 1968).

_____. *Oppression and Liberty.* Translated by Arthur Wills and John Petrie (Amherst: Univ. of Massachusetts Press, 1973).

_____. *The Simone Weil Reader.* Edited by George A. Panichas (New York: David McKay Company, 1977).

_____. *Waiting for God.* Translated by Emma Craufurd (New York: Harper, 1951).

Bell, Richard H., ed. *Simone Weil's Philosophy of Culture* (New York: Cambridge Univ. Press, 1993).

Blum, Larry. *A Truer Liberty: Simone Weil and Marxism* (New York: Routledge, 1989).

Coles, Robert. *Simone Weil: A Modern Pilgrimage* (New York: Addison-Wesley, 1987).

Dietz, Mary G. *Between the Human and the Divine: The Political Thought of Simone Weil* (Totowa, N.J.: Rowman and Littlefield, 1988).

Dunaway, John M. *Simone Weil* (Boston: Twayne Publishers, 1984).

Hellman, John. *Simone Weil: An Introduction to Her Thought* (Waterloo: Wilfrid Laurier Univ. Press, 1982).

McFarland, Dorothy. *Simone Weil* (New York: F. Ungar, 1983).

Nevin, Thomas R. *Simone Weil: Portrait of a Self-Exiled Jew* (Chapel Hill: Univ. of North Carolina Press, 1991).

Petrement, Simone. *Simone Weil: A Life.* Translated by Raymond Rosenthal (New York: Pantheon, 1976).

Pierce, Roy. *Contemporary French Political Thought* (New York: Oxford Univ. Press, 1966).

Rees, Richard. *Simone Weil, A Sketch for a Portrait* (Carbondale: Southern Illinois Univ. Press, 1966).

White, George Abbott, ed. *Simone Weil, Interpretation of a Life* (Amherst: Univ. of Mass. Press, 1981).

Winch, Peter. *Simone Weil: "The Just Balance"* (New York: Cambridge Univ. Press, 1989).

FRIEDRICH A. HAYEK (1899–1992)

chapter 20

PLATO AND all others who organize the just society around the Good would be bewildered by the notion that *refraining from* organizing a polity around a visible common good is what makes a just society possible. Yet that notion, according to Friedrich Hayek, is "perhaps the greatest discovery mankind ever made." For Plato, the light of the Good guides us away from the slippery slope leading to despotism. Hayek reversed Plato's thought. According to Hayek, the truth is this: insisting on visible common purposes sends us down the sure road to totalitarianism. Demands for "social justice" (or socialism) ignore this remarkable truth and the difficult moral discipline it demands, and arouse the narrow, easier sentiments of "tribal societies" that are rooted in particular emotional attachments rather than abstract rational principles. To Hayek, social justice and solidarity were no more than smoke screens for special interests and parochial purposes. Hayek did not deny the power of the solidarity fostered by shared values, but he insisted that for liberty's sake an "open society" must not pander to this solidarity.

In David Hume, the great liberal conservative, Hayek found a congenial ancestor. Hume was stubbornly anti-rationalist in his moral, legal, and political theories. His "natural history" approach to the evolution of human beliefs, sentiments, and institutions expounded the notion that these developments are, in the phrase of his fellow Scotsman Adam Ferguson, "the result of human action but not of human design." Hume's politics stressed the protection of individual liberties and private property in accordance with time-honored general rules, and he was an enthusiastic advocate for the refinements brought on by modern commercial life. Like Hume, Hayek rooted his individualism in a social and political theory of liberty rather than an asocial, rationalistic conception of the individual as *homo economicus*. For Hayek, the market and liberal society were public proving grounds where individual desires and ideas could be tested and refined—not places where private preferences and opinions were simply revealed.

Hayek linked his criticisms of *constructivist rationalism* and his evolutionary defense of *spontaneous order* with his attacks on social justice and socialist planning. What bears the weight in those attacks, however, are several reasoned judgments: that sticking to abstract general rules (such as those protecting private property) proves beneficial over the long haul; that the information required for economic planning or distribution based on desert is unattainable in a modern, complex society; or that interventions in pursuit of social justice violate the basic canon of justice that the same principles be universally applied. "Rationalists" like Kant, Hegel, and Marx agree with Hayek that liberty and reason have an evolutionary natural history, yet this history need not displace reason as the standard of criticism.

Several difficulties surround Hayek's case for a liberal commercial society organized by the free market and general rules securing the liberty of individuals. (1) If no common purpose whatsoever is served by liberal commercial society, what can be said on its behalf? Hayek does not acknowledge the several interrelated purposes that do enter into his endorsement of liberal commercial life. What appeal would his writings have in abstraction from their reference to tolerance, justice, liberty, the creation of wealth, and the growth of knowledge? (2) In Karl Polanyi's terminology, Hayek is claiming that only the "disembedded" economy, precisely by setting aside all visible common purposes, can be a just economy. But according to Karl Marx, the notion that such economies lack an organizing purpose is only an illusion; an "invisible" purpose, inherent in liberal society, prevails. Moreover, that hidden, organizing purpose is not justice, liberty, the creation of wealth, or the growth of knowledge—though each of these could be by-products—but the impersonal project of endlessly accumulating capital. This common purpose often enough subordinates individuals to *irrational* constraints that are "the result of human action but not of human design." (3) Modern society purports to promote the growth of knowledge, including knowledge of what is good for human beings. If such knowledge of the good exceeds our grasp, how intelligible is modern society? If such knowledge has been achieved, why should society refrain from judging and acting on the basis of it?

FROM *LAW, LEGISLATION AND LIBERTY*

FROM "THE DISCIPLINE OF ABSTRACT RULES AND THE EMOTIONS OF THE TRIBAL SOCIETY"

> Liberalism—it is well to recall this today—is the supreme form of generosity; it is the right which the majority concedes to minorities and hence it is the noblest cry that has ever resounded on this planet. It announces the determination to share existence with the enemy; more than that, with an enemy which is weak. It was incredible that the human species should have arrived at so noble an attitude, so paradoxical, so refined, so anti-natural. Hence it is not to be wondered at that this same humanity should soon appear anxious to get rid of it. It is a discipline too difficult and complex to take firm root on Earth.
>
> José Ortega y Gasset*

The pursuit of unattainable goals may prevent the achievement of the possible

It is not enough to recognize that 'social justice' is an empty phrase without determinable content. It has become a powerful incantation which serves to support deep-seated emotions that are threatening to destroy the Great Society. Unfortunately it is not true that if something cannot be achieved, it can do no harm to strive for it.[1] Like chasing any mirage it is likely to produce results which one would have done much to avoid if one had foreseen them. Many desirable aims will be sacrificed in the vain hope of making possible what must forever elude our grasp.

We live at present under the governance of two different and irreconcilable conceptions of what is right; and after a period of ascendancy of conceptions which have made the vision of an Open Society possible, we are relapsing rapidly into the conceptions of the tribal society from which we had been slowly emerging. We had hoped that with the defeat of the European dictators we had banished the threat of the totalitarian state; but all we have achieved was to put down the first flare-up of a reaction which is slowly spreading everywhere. Socialism is simply a re-assertion of that tribal ethics whose gradual weakening had made an approach to the Great Society possible. The submergence of classical liberalism under the inseparable forces of socialism and nationalism is the consequence of a revival of those tribal sentiments.

Most people are still unwilling to face the most alarming lesson of modern history: that the greatest crimes of our time have been committed by governments that had the enthusiastic support of millions of people who were guided by moral impulses. It is simply not true that Hitler or Mussolini, Lenin or Stalin, appealed only to the worst instincts of their people: they also appealed to some of the feelings which also dominate contemporary democracies. Whatever disillusionment the more mature supporters of these movements may have experienced as they came to see the effects of the policies they had supported, there can be no doubt that the rank and file of the communist, national-socialist or fascist movements contained many men and women inspired by ideals not very different from those of some of the most influential social philosophers in the Western countries. Some of them certainly believed that they were engaged in the creation of a just society in which the needs of the most deserving or 'socially most valuable' would be better cared for. They were led by a desire for a visible common purpose which is our inheritance from the tribal society and which we still find breaking through everywhere.

The causes of the revival of the organizational thinking of the tribe

One reason why in recent times we have seen a strong revival of organizational thinking and a decline in the understanding of the operation of the market order is that an ever growing proportion of the members of society work as members of large organizations and find their horizon of comprehension limited to what is required by the internal structure of such organizations. While the peasant and the independent craftsman, the merchant and the journeyman, were familiar with the market and, even if they did not understand its operation, had come to accept its dictates as the natural course of things, the growth of big enterprise and of the great administrative bureaucracies has brought it about that an ever increasing part of the people spend their whole working life as members of large organizations, and are led to think wholly in terms of the requirements of the organizational form of life. Even though in the pre-industrial society the great majority also spent most of their lives within the familial organization which was the unit of all economic activity,[2] the heads of the households saw society as a network of family units connected by the markets.

Today organizational thinking increasingly dominates the activities of many of the most powerful and influential figures of modern society, the organizers themselves.[3] The modern improvements in the technique of organization, and the consequent increase of the range of particular tasks which can be performed by means of large-scale organization far beyond what was possible before, have created the belief that there are no limits to what organization can achieve. Most people are no longer aware of the extent to which the more comprehensive order of society on which depends the very success of the organizations within it is due to ordering forces of an altogether different kind.

The other main reason for the growing dominance of organizational thinking is that the success of the deliberate creation of new rules for purpo-

400

sive organizations has in many respects been so great, that men no longer recognize that the more comprehensive order within which the organizations operate rests on a different type of rules which have not been invented with a definite foreseen purpose in mind, but are the product of a process of trial and error in the course of which more experience has been accumulated than any living person is aware of.

The immoral consequences of morally inspired efforts

Though in the long perspective of Western civilization the history of law is a history of a gradual emergence of rules of just conduct capable of universal application, its development during the last hundred years has become increasingly one of the destruction of justice by 'social justice', until even some students of jurisprudence have lost sight of the original meaning of 'justice'. We have seen how the process has mainly taken the form of a replacement of the rules of just conduct by those rules of organization which we call public law (a 'subordinating law'), a distinction which some socialist lawyers are trying hard to obliterate.[4] In substance this has meant that the individual is no longer bound only by rules which confine the scope of his private actions, but has become increasingly subject to the commands of authority. The growing technological possibilities of control, together with the presumed moral superiority of a society whose members serve the same hierarchy of ends, have made this totalitarian trend appear under a moral guise. It is indeed the concept of 'social justice' which has been the Trojan Horse through which totalitarianism has entered.

401

The values which still survive from the small end-connected groups whose coherence depended upon them, are, however, not only different from, but often incompatible with, the values which make possible the peaceful coexistence of large numbers in the Open Society. The belief that while we pursue the new ideal of this Great Society in which all human beings are regarded as equal, we can also preserve the different ideals of the small closed society, is an illusion. To attempt it leads to the destruction of the Great Society.

The possibility of men living together in peace and to their mutual advantage without having to agree on common concrete aims, and bound only by abstract rules of conduct,[5] was perhaps the greatest discovery mankind ever made. The 'capitalist' system which grew out of this discovery no doubt did not fully satisfy the ideals of liberalism, because it grew up while legislators and governments did not really understand the *modus operandi* of the market, and largely in spite of the policies actually pursued.[6] Capitalism as it exists today in consequence undeniably has many remediable defects that an intelligent policy of freedom ought to correct. A system which relies on the spontaneous ordering forces of the market, once it has reached a certain level of wealth, is also by no means incompatible with government providing, outside the market, some security against severe deprivation. But the attempt to secure to each what he is thought to deserve, by imposing upon all a system of common concrete ends towards which their efforts are directed by authority, as socialism aims to do, would be a retrograde step that would deprive us of the utilization of the knowledge and aspirations of millions, and thereby of the advantages of a free civilization. Socialism is not based merely on a different system of ultimate values from that of liberalism, which one would have to respect even if one disagreed; it is based on an intellectual error which makes its adherents blind to its consequences. This must be plainly said because the emphasis on the alleged difference of the ultimate values has become the common excuse of the socialists for shirking the real intellectual issue. The pretended difference of the underlying value judgments has become a protective cloak used to conceal the faulty reasoning underlying the socialist schemes.

In the Great Society 'social justice' becomes a disruptive force

Not only is it impossible for the Great Society to maintain itself while enforcing rules of 'social' or distributive justice; for its preservation it is also necessary that no particular groups holding common views about what they are entitled to should be allowed to enforce these views by preventing others to offer their services at more favourable terms. Though common interests of those whose position is affected by the same circumstances are likely to produce strong common opinions about what they deserve, and will provide a motive for common action to achieve their ends, any such group action to secure a particular income or position for its members creates an obstacle to the integration of the Great Society and is therefore anti-social in the true sense of this word. It must become a divisive force because it produces not a reconciliation of, but a conflict between, the interests of the different groups. As the active participants in the struggle for 'social justice' well know, it becomes in practice a struggle for power of organized interests in which arguments of justice serve merely as pretexts.

The chief insight we must hold on to is that not always when a group of people have strong views about what they regard as their claims in justice does this mean that there exists (or can be found) a corresponding rule which, if universally applied, would produce a viable order. It is a delusion to believe that whenever a question is represented as one of justice it must be possible to discover a rule capable of universal application which will decide that question.[7] Nor does the fact that a law endeavours to meet somebody's claim for justice prove that it is a rule of just conduct.

All groups whose members pursue the same or parallel aims will develop common views about what is right for members of those groups. Such views, however, will be right only for all those who pursue the same aims, but may be wholly incompatible with any principles by which such a group can be integrated into the overall order of society. The producers of any particular commodity or service who all aim at a good remuneration for their efforts will regard as unjust the action of any fellow producer who tends to reduce the incomes of the others. Yet it will be precisely the kind of actions by some members of the group that the rest regard as harmful which will fit the activities of the members of the group into the overall pattern of the Great Society and thereby benefit all.

It is certainly in itself not unjust if a barber in one city receives $3 for a haircut while in another city only $2 is paid for the same work. But it would clearly be unjust if the barbers in the first prevented any from the second city from improving their position by offering their services in the first for, say, $2.50 and thus, while improving their position, lowering the income of the first group. Yet it is precisely against such efforts that established groups are to-day permitted to combine in defence of their established position. The rule 'do nothing which will decrease the income of the members of your own group' will often be regarded as an obligation of justice toward one's fellow members. But it cannot be accepted as a rule of just conduct in a Great Society where it will conflict with the general principles on which the activities of that society are co-ordinated. The other members of that society will have every interest and moral right to prevent the enforcement of such a rule that the members of a special group regard as just, because the principles of integration of the Great Society demand that the action of some of those occupied in a particular manner should often lead to a reduction of the incomes of their fellows. This is precisely the virtue of competition. The conceptions of group justice would often proscribe all effective competition as unjust— and many of the 'fair competition' demands aim in effect at little less.

It is probably true that in any group whose members know that their prospects depend on the same circumstances, views will develop that represent as unjust all conduct of any member which harms the others; and there will in consequence arise a desire to prevent such conduct. But by any outsider it will rightly be regarded as unjust if any member of such a group is prevented by his fellows from offering him more advantageous terms than the rest of the group are willing to offer. And the same is true when some 'interloper' who before was not recognized as a member of the group is made to conform to the standards of the group as soon as his efforts compete with theirs.

The important fact which most people are reluctant to admit, yet which is probably true in most instances, is that, though the pursuit of the selfish aims of the individual will usually lead him to serve the general interest, the collective actions of organized groups are almost invariably contrary to the general interest. What in fact leads to the condemnation as anti-social of that pursuit of individual interests which contributes to the general interest, and to the commendation as 'social' of the subservience to those sectional interests which destroy the overall order, are sentiments which we have inherited from earlier forms of society. The use of coercion in this kind of 'social justice', meaning the interests of the particular group to which the individual belongs, will thus always mean the creation of particular preserves of special groups united against the outsiders—interest groups which exist because they are allowed to use force or pressure on government for the benefit of their members. But, however much the members of such groups may agree among themselves that what they want is just, there exists no principle which could make it appear as just to the outsider. Yet today, if such a group is only large enough, its representation of the demands of its members as just is commonly accepted as one view of justice which must be taken into account in ordering the whole, even though it does not rest on any principle which could be generally applied.

From the care of the most unfortunate to the protection of vested interests

We must not lose sight, however, of the fact that at the beginning of the striving for 'social justice' stood the laudable desire to abolish destitution, and that the Great Society has brilliantly succeeded in abolishing poverty in the absolute sense.[8] Nobody capable of useful work need today lack food and shelter in the advanced countries, and for those incapable of themselves earning enough these necessities are generally provided outside the market. Poverty in the relative sense must of course continue to exist outside of any completely egalitarian society: so long as there exists inequality, somebody must be the bottom of the scale. But the abolition of absolute poverty is not helped by the endeavour to achieve 'social justice'; in fact, in many of the countries in which absolute poverty is still an acute problem, the concern with 'social justice' has become one of the greatest obstacles to the elimination of poverty. In the West the rise of the great masses to tolerable comfort has been the effect of the general growth of wealth and has been merely slowed down by measures interfering with the market mechanism. It has been this market mechanism which has created the increase of aggregate income, which also has made it possible to provide outside the market for the support of those unable to earn enough. But the attempts to 'correct' the results of the market in the direction of 'social justice' have probably produced more injustice in the form of new privileges, obstacles to mobility and frustration of efforts than they have contributed to the alleviation of the lot of the poor.

This development is a consequence of the circumstance that the appeal to 'social justice' that was originally made on behalf of the most unfortunate was taken up by many other groups whose members felt that they did not get as much as they thought that they deserved, and particularly by those groups who felt threatened in their present positions. As a demand that political action should assign to the members of any group the position which in some sense it deserved, 'social justice' is irreconcilable with the ideal that coercion should be used only to enforce the same rules of just conduct which all could take into account in making their plans. Yet when those claims were first admitted in favour of groups with whose misfortune everybody sympathized, the floodgates were opened to the demand by all who found their relative position threatened that their position be protected by government action. Misfortune, however, cannot create a claim for protection against risks which all have had to run in order to attain the position they occupy. The very language in current use which at once labels as a 'social problem' anything which causes dissatisfaction of any group, and suggests that it is the duty of the legislature to do something about such 'social injustice', has turned the conception of 'social justice' into a mere pretext for claims for privileges by special interests.

Those who turn with indignation against a conception of justice which failed, e.g., to prevent 'the rapidly proceeding up-rooting of the peasantry which commenced already after the Napoleonic wars, or the decline of the artisanry after the middle of the century, or the pauperization of the wage labourers'[9] wholly misconceive what can be achieved by enforcement of rules of just conduct in a world of free men who reciprocally serve each other for their own benefit and to whom nobody assigns tasks or allocates benefits. Since today we can probably even feed the numbers to which mankind has grown only thanks to the intensive utilization of dispersed knowledge which is made possible by the market—not to speak of maintaining that level of comfort which the great majority has reached in some parts of the world—it certainly would not be just to exempt some from the necessity of accepting a less favourable position than they had already attained if an unforeseen turn of events diminishes the value of their services to the rest. However sorry we may be for those who, through no fault of their own but as a result of unforeseeable developments, find themselves in a reduced position, this does not mean that we can have both the progressive increase in the level of general wealth on which the future improvement of the conditions of the great masses depends and no such recurrent declines of the position of some groups.

'Social justice' has in practice become simply the slogan used by all groups whose status tends to decline—by the farmer, the independent craftsman, the coalminer, the small shopkeeper, the clerical worker and a considerable part of the old 'middle class', rather than the industrial workers on whose behalf it was first raised but who have in general been the beneficiaries of recent developments. That the appeal to justice by such groups frequently succeeds in mobilizing the sympathy of many who regard the traditional hierarchy of society as a natural one, and who resent the ascent of new types to that middle position to which once the bare capacity to read and write gave access, does not show that such demands have any connection with generally applicable rules of just conduct.

In the existing political order such claims will in fact be met only when such groups are large enough to count politically and especially when it is possible to organize their members for common action. We shall see later that only some but not all such interests can be thus organized, and that in consequence the resulting advantages can be achieved only by some and will harm the rest. Yet the more organizations of interests are used for this purpose, the more necessary does it become for each group to organize for pressure on government, since those who fail to do so will be left out in the cold. Thus the conception of 'social justice' has resulted in the assurance by government of an appropriate income to particular groups, which has made the progressive organization of all such 'interests' inevitable. But the protection of expectations which such assurance involves cannot possibly be granted to all in any but a stationary society. The only just principle is therefore to concede this privilege to none.

At one time this argument would have had to be directed chiefly against the trade unions, since they were the first of such groups who succeeded in clothing their demands with the aura of legitimacy (and in being allowed to use coercion for their enforcement) by representing them as a requirement of 'social justice'. But though it was initially the use in the service of relatively poor and unfortunate groups that made discrimination in their favour appear justifiable, such discrimination served as the thin end of the wedge by which the principle of equality under the law was destroyed. It is now simply those who are numerically strong, or can readily be organized to withhold essential services, who gain in the process of political bargaining which governs legislation in contemporary democracy. But the particular absurdities which will arise when a democracy attempts to determine the distribution of incomes by majority vote will occupy us further only in the third volume of the present work.

Attempts to 'correct' the order of the market lead to its destruction

The predominant view today appears to be that we should avail ourselves in the main of the ordering forces of the market, indeed must in a great measure do so, but should 'correct' its results where they are flagrantly unjust. Yet so long as the earnings of particular individuals or groups are not determined by the decision of some agency, no particular distribution of incomes can be meaningfully described as more just than another. If we want to make it substantively just, we can do so only by replacing the whole spontaneous order by an organization in which the share of each is fixed by some central authority. In other words, 'corrections' of the distribution brought about in a spontaneous process by particular acts of interference can never be just in the sense of satisfying a rule equally applicable to all. Every single act of this kind will give rise to demands by others to be treated on the same principle; and these demands can be satisfied only if all incomes are thus allocated.

The current endeavour to rely on a spontaneous order corrected according to principles of justice amounts to an attempt to have the best of two worlds which are mutually incompatible. Perhaps an absolute ruler, wholly indepen- dent of public opinion, might confine himself to mitigating the hardships of the more unfortunate ones by isolated acts of intervention and let a sponta- neous order determine the positions of the rest. And it is certainly possible to take entirely out of the market process those who cannot adequately maintain themselves on the market and support them by means set aside for the pur- pose. For a person at the beginning of an uncertain career, and for his chil- dren, it might even be perfectly rational to agree that all should insure for a minimum of sustenance in such an eventuality. But a government dependent on public opinion, and particularly a democracy, will not be able to confine such attempts to supplement the market to the mitigation of the lot of the poorest. Whether it intends to let itself be guided by principles or not, it is in fact, if it has the power to do so, certain to be driven on by the principles im- plicit in the precedents it sets. By the measures it takes it will produce opin- ions and set standards which will force it to continue on the course on which it has embarked.

It is possible to 'correct' an order only by assuring that the principles on which it rests are consistently applied, but not by applying to some part of the whole principles which do not apply to the rest. As it is the essence of justice that the same principles are universally applied, it requires that government assist particular groups only in conditions in which it is prepared to act on the same principle in all similar instances.

407

The revolt against the discipline of abstract rules

The rise of the ideal of impersonal justice based on formal rules has been achieved in a continuous struggle against those feelings of personal loyalty which provide the basis of the tribal society but which in the Great Society must not be allowed to influence the use of the coercive powers of govern- ment. The gradual extension of a common order of peace from the small group to ever larger communities has involved constant clashes between the demands of sectional justice based on common visible purposes and the re- quirements of a universal justice equally applicable to the stranger and to the member of the group.[10] This has caused a constant conflict between emotions deeply ingrained in human nature through millennia of tribal existence and the demands of abstract principles whose significance nobody fully grasped. Human emotions are attached to concrete objects, and the emotions of jus- tice in particular are still very much connected with the visible needs of the group to which each person belongs—the needs of the trade or profession, of the clan or the village, the town or the country to which each belongs. Only a mental reconstruction of the overall order of the Great Society enables us to comprehend that the deliberate aim at concrete common purposes, which to most people still appears as more meritorious and superior to blind obedience to abstract rules, would destroy that larger order in which all human beings count alike.

As we have already seen, much that will be truly social in the small end-connected group because it is conducive to the coherence of the working order of that society, will be anti-social from the point of view of the Great Society. The demand for 'social justice' is indeed an expression of revolt of the tribal spirit against the abstract requirements of the coherence of the Great Society with no such visible common purpose. It is only by extending the rules of just conduct to the relations with all other men, and at the same time depriving of their obligatory character those rules which cannot be universally applied, that we can approach a universal order of peace which might integrate all mankind into a single society.

While in the tribal society the condition of internal peace is the devotion of all members to some common visible purposes, and therefore to the will of somebody who can decide what at any moment these purposes are to be and how they are to be achieved, the Open Society of free men becomes possible only when the individuals are constrained only to obey the abstract rules that demarcate the domain of the means that each is allowed to use for his purposes. So long as any particular ends, which in a society of any size must always be the ends of some particular persons or group, are regarded as a justification of coercion, there must always arise conflicts between groups with different interests. Indeed, so long as particular purposes are the foundation of political organization, those whose purposes are different are inevitably enemies; and it is true that in such a society politics necessarily is dominated by the friend-enemy relation.[11] Rules of just conduct can become the same for all only when particular ends are not regarded as justification for coercion (apart from such special passing circumstances as war, rebellion or natural catastrophes).

The morals of the open and of the closed society

The process we are describing is closely associated with, and indeed a necessary consequence of, the circumstance that in an extensive market order the producers are led to serve people without knowing of their individual needs. Such an order which relies on people working with the effect of satisfying the wants of people of whom they do not know presupposes and requires somewhat different moral views, from one in which people serve visible needs. The indirect guidance by an expected monetary return, operating as an indicator of the requirements of others, demanded new moral conceptions which do not prescribe particular aims but rather general rules limiting the range of permitted actions.

It did become part of the ethos of the Open Society that it was better to invest one's fortune in instruments making it possible to produce more at smaller costs than to distribute it among the poor, or to cater for the needs of thousands of unknown people rather than to provide for the needs of a few known neighbours. These views, of course, did not develop because those who first acted upon them understood that they thus conferred greater benefits on their fellows, but because the groups and societies which acted in this way prospered more than others; it became in consequence gradually the recognized moral duty of the 'calling' to do so. In its purest form this ethos regards it as the prime duty to pursue a self-chosen end as effectively as possible without paying attention to the role it plays in the complex network of human activities. It is the view which is now commonly but somewhat misleadingly described as the Calvinist ethic—misleading because it prevailed already in the mercantile towns of medieval Italy and was taught by the Spanish Jesuits long before Calvin.[12]

We still esteem doing good only if it is done to benefit specific known needs of known people, and regard it as really better to help one starving man we know than to relieve the acute need of a hundred men we do not know; but in fact we generally are doing most good by pursuing gain. It was somewhat misleading, and did his cause harm, when Adam Smith gave the impression as if the significant difference were that between the egoistic striving for gain and the altruistic endeavour to meet known needs. The aim for which the successful entrepreneur wants to use his profits may well be to provide a hospital or an art gallery for his home town. But quite apart from the question of what he wants to do with his profits after he has earned them, he is led to benefit more people by aiming at the largest gain than he could if he concentrated on the satisfaction of the needs of known persons. He is led by the invisible hand of the market to bring the succour of modern conveniences to the poorest homes he does not even know.[13]

It is true, however, that the moral views underlying the Open Society were long confined to small groups in a few urban localities, and have come generally to govern law and opinion in the Western world so comparatively recently that they are often still felt to be artificial and unnatural in contrast to the intuitive, and in part perhaps even instinctive, sentiments inherited from the older tribal society. The moral sentiments which made the Open Society possible grew up in the towns, the commercial and trading centres, while the feelings of the large numbers were still governed by the parochial sentiments and the xenophobic and fighting attitudes governing the tribal group.[14] The rise of the Great Society is far too recent an event to have given man time to shed the results of a development of hundreds of thousands of years, and not to regard as artificial and inhuman those abstract rules of conduct which often conflict with the deeply ingrained instincts to let himself be guided in action by perceived needs.

The resistance against the new morals of the Open Society was strengthened also by the realization that it not only indefinitely enlarged the circle of other people in relation to whom one had to obey moral rules, but that this

extension of the scope of the moral code necessarily brought with itself a reduction of its content. If the enforceable duties towards all are to be the same,
the duties towards none can be greater than the duties towards all—except
where special natural or contractual relations exist. There can be a general
obligation to render assistance in case of need towards a circumscribed group
of fellow-men, but not towards men in general. The moral progress by which
we have moved towards the Open Society, that is, the extension of the obligation to treat alike, not only the members of our tribe but persons of ever
wider circles and ultimately all men, had to be bought at the price of an at-
tenuation of the enforceable duty to aim deliberately at the well-being of the
other members of the same group. When we can no longer know the others
or the circumstances under which they live, such a duty becomes a psychological and intellectual impossibility. Yet the disappearance of these specific
duties leaves an emotional void by depriving men both of satisfying tasks and
the assurance of support in case of need.[15]

It would therefore not be really surprising if the first attempt of man to
emerge from the tribal into an open society should fail because man is not yet
ready to shed moral views developed for the tribal society; or, as Ortega y
Gasset wrote of classical liberalism in the passage placed at the head of this
chapter, it is not to be wondered that 'humanity should soon appear anxious
to get rid of . . . so noble an attitude, so paradoxical, so refined, so anti-natural
. . . a discipline too difficult and complex to take firm root on earth.' At a time
when the great majority are employed in organizations and have little opportunity to learn the morals of the market, their intuitive craving for a more humane and personal morals corresponding to their inherited instincts is quite
likely to destroy the Open Society.

It should be realized, however, that the ideals of socialism (or of 'social justice') which in such a position prove so attractive, do not really offer a new
moral but merely appeal to instincts inherited from an earlier type of society.
They are an atavism, a vain attempt to impose upon the Open Society the
morals of the tribal society which, if it prevails, must not only destroy the
Great Society but would also greatly threaten the survival of the large numbers to which some three hundred years of a market order have enabled
mankind to grow.

Similarly the people who are described as alienated or estranged from a society based on the market order are not the bearers of a new moral but the
non-domesticated or un-civilized who have never learnt the rules of conduct
on which the Open Society is based, but want to impose upon it their instinctive, 'natural' conceptions derived from the tribal society. What especially
most of the members of the New Left do not appear to see is that equal treatment of all men which they also demand is possible only under a system in
which individual actions are restricted merely by formal rules rather than
guided by their known effects.

The Rousseauesque nostalgia for a society guided, not by learnt moral rules which can be justified only by a rational insight into the principles on which this order is based, but by the unreflected 'natural' emotions deeply grounded on millennia of life in the small horde, leads thus directly to the demand for a socialist society in which authority ensures that visible 'social justice' is done in a manner which gratifies natural emotions. In this sense, however, of course all culture is unnatural and, though undesigned, still artificial because relying on obedience to learnt rules rather than on natural instincts. This conflict between what men still feel to be natural emotions and the discipline of rules required for the preservation of the Open Society is indeed one of the chief causes of what has been called the 'fragility of liberty': all attempts to model the Great Society on the image of the familiar small group, or to turn it into a community by directing the individuals towards common visible purposes, must produce a totalitarian society.

The old conflict between loyalty and justice

The persistent conflict between tribal morals and universal justice has manifested itself throughout history in a recurrent clash between the sense of loyalty and that of justice. It is still loyalty to such particular groups as those of occupation or class as well as those of clan, nation, race or religion which is the greatest obstacle to a universal application of rules of just conduct. Only slowly and gradually do those general rules of conduct towards all fellow men come to prevail over the special rules which allowed the individual to harm the stranger if it served the interest of his group. Yet while only this process has made possible the rise of the Open Society, and offers the distant hope of a universal order of peace, current morals do not yet wholeheartedly approve this development; indeed, there has in recent times taken place a retreat from positions which had already been largely achieved in the Western World.

411

If in the distant past perhaps altogether inhuman demands were sometimes made in the name of formal justice, as when in ancient Rome the father was praised who as a magistrate unflinchingly condemned his son to death, we have learned to avoid the gravest of such conflicts, and in general to reduce the requirements of formal justice to what is compatible with our emotions. The advance of justice continued until recent times as a progressive ascendancy of the general rules of just conduct applying to our relations to any fellow member of society over the special rules serving the needs of particular groups. It is true that this development in some measure stopped at national frontiers; but most nations were of such a size that it still brought about a progressive replacement of the rules of the purpose-connected organization by the rules of the spontaneous order of an Open Society.

The main resistance to this development was due to its requiring a predominance of abstract rational principles over those emotions that are evoked by the particular and the concrete, or the predominance of conclusions derived from abstract rules, whose significance was little understood, over the spontaneous response to the perception of concrete effects which touched the lives and conditions of those familiar to us. This does not mean that those rules of conduct which refer to special personal relations have lost their importance for the functioning of the Great Society. It merely means that, since in a society of free men the membership in such special groups will be voluntary, there must also be no power of enforcing the rules of such groups. It is in such a free society that a clear distinction between the moral rules which are not enforced and the rules of law which are enforced becomes so important. If the smaller groups are to be integrated into the more comprehensive order of society at large, it must be through the free movement of individuals between groups into which they may be accepted if they submit to their rules.

The small group in the Open Society

The revolt against the abstractness of the rules we are required to obey in the Great Society, and the predilection for the concrete which we feel to be human, are thus merely a sign that intellectually and morally we have not yet fully matured to the needs of the impersonal comprehensive order of mankind. To submit comprehendingly to those rules which have made the approach to the Open Society possible and which we have obeyed so long as we attributed them to the command of a higher personal authority, and not to blame some imagined personal agent for any misfortune that we encounter, evidently requires a degree of insight into the working of a spontaneous order which few persons have yet attained.

412

Even moral philosophers often appear simply to wallow in the emotions inherited from the tribal society without examining their compatibility with the aspirations of the universal humanism that they also champion. Most people indeed will watch with regret the decline of the small group in which a limited number of persons were connected by many personal ties, and the disappearance of certain sentiments connected with it. But the price we have to pay for the achievement of the Great Society in which all human beings have the same claims on us is that these claims must be reduced to the avoidance of harmful actions and cannot include positive duties. The individual's free choice of his associates will in general have the effect that for different purposes he will be acting with different companions and that none of these connections will be compulsory. This presupposes that none of these small groups has power to enforce its standards on any unwilling person.

The savage in us still regards as good what was good in the small group but what the Great Society must not only refrain from enforcing but cannot even allow particular groups to enforce. A peaceful Open Society is possible only if it renounces the method of creating solidarity that is most effective in the small group, namely acting on the principle that 'if people are to be in harmony, then let them strive for some common end'. This is the conception of creating coherence which leads straight to the interpretation of all politics as a matter of friend–enemy relations. It is also the device which has been effectively employed by all dictators.

Except when the very existence of a free society is threatened by an enemy, it must deny itself what in many respects is still the strongest force making for cohesion, the common visible purpose. It must bid farewell, so far as the use of coercion is concerned, to the use of some of the strong moral emotions which still stand us in good stead in the small group and which, though still needed within the small groups from which the Great Society is built up, must result in tension and conflict if enforced in the Great Society.

The conception through which the atavistic craving for visible common purposes which so well served the needs of the small group today chiefly expresses itself is that of 'social justice'. It is incompatible with the principles on which the Great Society rests and indeed the opposite of those forces making for its coherence which can truly be called 'social'. Our innate instincts are here in conflict with the rules of reason we have learned, a conflict we can resolve only by limiting coercion to what is required by abstract rules and by abstaining from enforcing what can be justified only by the desire for particular results.

The kind of abstract order on which man has learnt to rely and which has enabled him peacefully to co-ordinate the efforts of millions, unfortunately cannot be based on such feelings as love which constituted the highest virtue in the small group. Love is a sentiment which only the concrete evokes, and the Great Society has become possible through the individual's efforts being guided not by the aim of helping particular other persons, but the confinement of the pursuit of their purposes by abstract rules.

The importance of voluntary associations

It would be a sad misunderstanding of the basic principles of a free society if it were concluded that, because they must deprive the small group of all coercive powers, they do not attach great value to voluntary action in the small groups. In restricting all coercion to the agencies of government and confining its employment to the enforcement of general rules, these principles aim at reducing all coercion as much as possible and leaving as much as possible to voluntary efforts. The mischievous idea that all public needs should be satisfied by compulsory organization and that all the means that the individuals are willing to devote to public purposes should be under the control of government, is wholly alien to the basic principles of a free society. The true liberal must on the contrary desire as many as possible of those 'particular societies within the state', voluntary organizations between the individual and government, which the false individualism of Rousseau and the French Revolution wanted to suppress; but he wants to deprive them of all exclusive and compulsory powers. Liberalism is not individualistic in the 'everybody for himself' sense, though necessarily suspicious of the tendency of organizations to arrogate exclusive rights for their members. . . .

Notes

*José Ortega y Gasset, *The Revolt of the Masses* (London, 1932), p. 83.

1. This is surprisingly maintained by such an acute thinker as Michael Polanyi with regard to central planning in *The Logic of Liberty* (London, 1951), p. 111: 'How can central economic planning, if it is utterly incapable of achievement, be a danger to liberty as it is widely assumed to be?' It may well be impossible to achieve what the planners intend and yet the attempt to realize their intentions do much harm.

2. Cf. Peter Laslett, *The World we Have Lost* (London and New York, 1965).

3. See W. H. Whyte, *The Organization Man* (New York, 1957).

4. See Martin Bullinger, *Oeffentliches Recht und Privatrecht* (Stuttgart, 1968).

5. In the present connection we revert to the term 'abstract rule' in order to stress that the rules of just conduct do not refer to specific purposes and that the resulting order is what Sir Karl Popper has called an 'abstract society'.

6. Cf. Adam Smith, *Wealth of Nations,* ed. Cannan, vol. II, p. 43:

> The natural effort of every individual to better his own condition, where suffered to exert itself with freedom and security, is so powerful a principle, that it is alone, and without any assistance, not only capable of carrying on the society to wealth and prosperity, but of surmounting a hundred impertinent obstructions with which the folly of human laws too often encumbers its operations; though the effect of these obstructions is always more or less either to encroach upon its freedom, or to diminish its security.

7. C. Perelman, *Justice* (New York, 1967), p. 20: 'A form of behavior or a human judgement can be termed just only if it can be subjected to rules or criteria.'

8. Since it is frequently ignored that this was both the aim and the achievement of classical liberalism, two statements from the middle of the last century deserve to be quoted. N. W. Senior (cited by L. C. Robbins, *The Theory of Economic Policy,* London, 1952, p. 140) wrote in 1848: 'To proclaim that no man, whatever his vices or even his crimes, shall die of hunger or cold, is a promise that in the state of civilization of England, or of France, can be performed not merely with safety but with advantage, because the gift of mere subsistence may be subjected to conditions which no one will voluntarily accept.' In the same year the German constitutional lawyer Moritz Mohl, as representative to the German Constitutional Assembly at Frankfurt, could maintain (*Stenographischer Bericht über die Verhandlungen der Deutschen konstituierenden Nationalversammlung zu Frankfurt a.M.,* ed., Franz Wigard, Leipzig, 1949, vol. 7, p. 5109) that 'es gibt in Deutschland, meines Wissens, nicht einen einzigen Staat, in welchem nicht positive, ganz bestimmte Gesetze beständen, welche verhindern, dass jemand verhungere. In allen deutschen Gesetzgebungen, die mir bekannt sind, ist die Gemeinde gehalten, den, der sich nicht selbst erhalten kann, zu erhalten.'

9. Cf. Franz Beyerle, 'Der andere Zugang zum Naturrecht', *Deutsche Rechtswissenschaft,* 1939, p. 20: 'Zeitlos und unbekümmert um die eigene Umwelt hat sie [die Pandektenlehre] keine einzige soziale Krise ihrer Zeit erkannt und geistig aufgefan-

gen. Weder die rasch fortschreitende Entwurzelung des Bauerntums, die schon nach den napoleonischen Kriegen einsetzte, noch das Absinken der handwerklichen Existenzen nach der Jahrhundertmitte, noch endlich die Verelendung der Lohnarbeiterschaft.' From the number of times this statement by a distinguished teacher of private law has been quoted in the current German literature it seems to express a widely held view.

10. J.-J. Rousseau has clearly seen that what in his sense of the 'general will' may be just for a particular group, may not be so for a more comprehensive society. Cf. *The Political Writings of J.-J. Rousseau,* ed. E. E. Vaughan (Cambridge, 1915), vol. I, p. 243: 'Pour les membres de l'association, c'est une volonté générale; pour la grande société, c'est une volonté particulière, qui très souvent se trouve droite au premier égard, et vicieuse au second.' But to the positivist interpretation of justice which identifies it with the commands of some legitimate authority, it comes inevitably to be thought that, as e.g. E. Forsthoff, *Lehrbuch des Verwaltungsrechts* (eighth ed., Munich, 1961, vol. I, p. 66) maintains, 'any question of a just order is a question of law'. But this 'orientation on the idea of justice', as this view has been curiously called, is certainly not sufficient to turn a command into a rule of just conduct unless by that phrase is meant, not merely that the rule satisfies somebody's claim for just treatment, but that the rule satisfies the Kantian test of universal applicability.

11. This is the main thesis of Carl Schmitt, *Der Begriff des Politischen* (Berlin, 1932). Cf. the comment on it by J. Huizinga quoted on p. 71 of vol. I of the present work.

12. See note 15 to chapter 9 above.

13. The constructivist prejudice which still makes so many socialists scoff at the 'miracle' that the unguided pursuit of their own interests by the individuals should produce a beneficial order is of course merely the reverse form of that dogmatism which opposed Darwin on the ground that the existence of order in organic nature was proof of intelligent design.

14. Cf. H. B. Acton, *The Morals of Markets* (London, 1971).

15. Cf. Bertrand de Jouvenel, *Sovereignty* (London and Chicago, 1957), p. 136: 'We are thus driven to three conclusions. The first is that the small society, the milieu in which man is first found, retains for him an infinite attraction; the next, that he undoubtedly goes to it to renew his strength; but, the last, that any attempt to graft the same features on a large society is utopian and leads to tyranny'; to which the author adds in a footnote: 'In this respect Rousseau (*Rousseau Juge de Jean-Jaques,* Third Dialogue) displayed a wisdom which his disciples missed: 'His object could not be to recall populous countries and large states to their primitive simplicity, but only to check, if possible, the progress of those whom smallness and situation had preserved from the same headlong rush to the perfection of society and the deterioration of the species.'

For Further Reading

Hayek, Friedrich A. *The Constitution of Liberty* (Chicago: Univ of Chicago Press, 1960).

———. *New Studies in Philosophy, Politics, Economics and the History of Ideas* (London: Routledge, 1978).

———. *The Road to Serfdom.* Introduction by Milton Friedman (Chicago: Univ. of Chicago Press, 1994).

Antonio, Robert J. "Reason and History in Hayek." *Critical Review* (1987): 58–73.

Blaug, Mark. "Hayek Revisited." *Critical Review* 23, no. 3 (1993): 249–264.

Burczak, Theodore A. "The Postmodern Moments of F. A. Hayek's Economics." *Economics and Philosophy* 10, no.1 (April 1994).

Gray, John. *Hayek on Liberty* (Oxford: Blackwell, 1984).

Heath, Eugene. "Rules, Functions, and Invisible Hand: 'An Interpretation of Hayek's Social Theory.'" *Philosophy of Social Science* 22, no.1 (1992): 28-45.

Hodgson, Geoffrey R. "Hayek's Theory of Cultural Evolution: An Evaluation in the Light of Vanberg's Critique." *Economics and Philosophy* (1991): 67–82.

Kley, Roland. *Hayek's Social and Political Thought* (New York: Oxford Univ. Press, 1994).

Livingston, Donald W. "Hayek as Humean." *Critical Review 5,* no.2 (1991): 159–177.

O'Neill, John. "Markets, Socialism, and Information: A Reformulation of a Marxian Objection to the Market." *Social Philosophy and Policy 6* (1989): 200–210.

Popper, Karl. *The Open Society and Its Enemies.* 5th ed. revised (Princeton: Princeton Univ. Press, 1971).

———. *The Poverty of Historicism* (London: Routledge, 1957).

Rowland, Barbara M. *Ordered Liberty and the Constitutional Framework: The Political Thought of Friedrich A. Hayek* (Westport: Greenwood Press, 1987).

416

HANNAH ARENDT (1906–1975)

chapter 21

THE FUTILITY of housekeeping appalled Hannah Arendt. For the monotonous round of chores—food to cook, corners to mop, repairs to make, bills to pay—reveals the futility of animal life, and more generally, of transient existence. In the private space of the household, "man existed . . . not as a truly human being but only as a specimen of the animal species man-kind." Arendt associated labor with housekeeping, the process of providing for material necessities, and she sharply contrasted it with the two truly human types of activity, *work* and *action*. Work overreaches nature and furnishes a *world* of artifacts, a durable home for distinctively human life in common. Action occurs in the public sphere between plural human beings; in contrast to *behavior*, it is a consummately free, though worldly, activity capable of "beginning something anew" and conferring glory and immortality. In work and action humans make a redemptive stand against the futility of labor and animal life. Against this horizon, the course Arendt saw modern commercial life taking could hardly have been more ominous. A defining trait of modernity for Arendt is the loss of worldly, public spaces that follows from the outbreak of "the social." With the rise of "the social," the transitory concerns of house-keeping and *animal laborans* sop up all our attention and energy. Consumption, comfort, needs, lifestyle, privacy, and security absorb us; we lack the time or the disposition for the give and take of political involvement and debates. For Arendt, even at our best we are satyrs, half human, half goat. At our worst, we sink into herd animals under the onslaught of "the social."

The spiraling accumulation of wealth brings about the "rise of the social." These developments signal an end to *property,* which Arendt contrasts with *wealth.* Property has to do with private place, with being situated in a world; wealth is modern and uncannily abstracts from locale and situation—wealth is uncreaturely. The "irresistible tendency to grow, to devour the older realms of the political and private as well as the more recently established sphere of intimacy," which is characteristic of "the social," has many dire consequences. As the "enlightened" critique of anthropomorphism runs amok, and our world—now cleverly "seen through" as just another "worldview"—collapses, all that remains to hold us together are the generic, animal concerns of the life cycle. With the demise of a common, meaningful world, individuals are homeless and incapable of action. Disconnected from the past, their sense of reality breaks down—no wonder that social statistics and "behavioral" sciences crop up with the culmination of "the social" in mass society. Likewise, the renewal of Epicurean philosophy in utility theories is to be expected: when "worldly values" lose their hold, the resources of moral philosophy shrink to what we experience in common with animals: pleasure and pain. As preoccupation with the life process intrudes into the public sphere, surrogates of "the social": bureaucracy, "pure administration," "rule by nobody," replace real politics.

Under the headings of "the rise of the social" and "the loss of the world," Arendt addresses what Karl Polanyi termed "the great transformation" that resulted in the "disembedded" modern commercial economy intent solely on growth. Dismayed at this perceived victory of "wealth" as an end in itself, Arendt unsuspectingly supported the erroneous notion that wealth can exist without having a determinate social form. Labor, as she thought of it, was devoid of social form; it was simply brutish. Likewise, she kept referring to natural "necessities" as the target of labor's activities, missing Mandeville's point that the idea of purely natural necessities is out of place when the issue is *human* needs. That we labor out of necessity does not entail that there is any set of natural necessities we labor to produce. Arendt failed to recognize that the apparent unworldliness and naturalness of the "disembedded" economy was itself the result of the peculiar social form of modern commercial life. Rethinking the "rise of the social" along these lines suggests: (1) that modernity is not so much a worldless animal kingdom as it is a highly formal world in-

habited by those "unencumbered selves" we call persons and (2) that the focus of a commercial economy is not on natural necessities but on those needs
for which we seek satisfaction through the consumption of wealth in the
commodity form. For Arendt, modern commerce tramples down the very
demarcations (between the private and public spheres) that set human off
from animal life. The trouble with this chilling diagnosis lies in its faulty diag-
nostic categories; its power is suggested by Theodor Adorno's remark "Only
the exaggerations are true."

FROM *THE HUMAN CONDITION*

THE RISE OF THE SOCIAL

The emergence of society—the rise of housekeeping, its activities, problems,
and organizational devices—from the shadowy interior of the household into
the light of the public sphere, has not only blurred the old borderline between private and political, it has also changed almost beyond recognition the
meaning of the two terms and their significance for the life of the individual
and the citizen. Not only would we not agree with the Greeks that a life
spent in the privacy of "one's own" (*idion*), outside the world of the common,
is "idiotic" by definition, or with the Romans to whom privacy offered but a
temporary refuge from the business of the *res publica*; we call private today a
sphere of intimacy whose beginnings we may be able to trace back to late
Roman, though hardly to any period of Greek antiquity, but whose peculiar
manifoldness and variety were certainly unknown to any period prior to the
modern age.

419

This is not merely a matter of shifted emphasis. In ancient feeling the priv-
ative trait of privacy, indicated in the word itself, was all-important; it meant
literally a state of being deprived of something, and even of the highest and
most human of man's capacities. A man who lived only a private life, who like
the slave was not permitted to enter the public realm, or like the barbarian
had chosen not to establish such a realm, was not fully human. We no longer
think primarily of deprivation when we use the word "privacy," and this is
partly due to the enormous enrichment of the private sphere through modern individualism. However, it seems even more important that modern privacy is at least as sharply opposed to the social realm—unknown to the ancients who considered its content a private matter—as it is to the political,
properly speaking. The decisive historical fact is that modern privacy in its
most relevant function, to shelter the intimate, was discovered as the opposite
not of the political sphere but of the social, to which it is therefore more
closely and authentically related.

The first articulate explorer and to an extent even theorist of intimacy was
Jean-Jacques Rousseau who, characteristically enough, is the only great author still frequently cited by his first name alone. He arrived at his discovery

through a rebellion not against the oppression of the state but against society's unbearable perversion of the human heart, its intrusion upon an innermost region in man which until then had needed no special protection. The intimacy of the heart, unlike the private household, has no objective tangible place in the world, nor can the society against which it protests and asserts itself be localized with the same certainty as the public space. To Rousseau, both the intimate and the social were, rather, subjective modes of human existence, and in his case, it was as though Jean-Jacques rebelled against a man called Rousseau. The modern individual and his endless conflicts, his inability either to be at home in society or to live outside it altogether, his ever-changing moods and the radical subjectivism of his emotional life, was born in this rebellion of the heart. The authenticity of Rousseau's discovery is beyond doubt, no matter how doubtful the authenticity of the individual who was Rousseau. The astonishing flowering of poetry and music from the middle of the eighteenth century until almost the last third of the nineteenth, accompanied by the rise of the novel, the only entirely social art form, coinciding with a no less striking decline of all the more public arts, especially architecture, is sufficient testimony to a close relationship between the social and the intimate.

The rebellious reaction against society during which Rousseau and the Romanticists discovered intimacy was directed first of all against the leveling demands of the social, against what we would call today the conformism inherent in every society. It is important to remember that this rebellion took place before the principle of equality, upon which we have blamed conformism since Tocqueville, had had the time to assert itself in either the social or the political realm. Whether a nation consists of equals or non-equals is of no great importance in this respect, for society always demands that its members act as though they were members of one enormous family which has only one opinion and one interest. Before the modern disintegration of the family, this common interest and single opinion was represented by the household head who ruled in accordance with it and prevented possible disunity among the family members.[1] The striking coincidence of the rise of society with the decline of the family indicates clearly that what actually took place was the absorption of the family unit into corresponding social groups. The equality of the members of these groups, far from being an equality among peers, resembles nothing so much as the equality of household members before the despotic power of the household head, except that in society, where the natural strength of one common interest and one unanimous opinion is tremendously enforced by sheer number, actual rule exerted by one man, representing the common interest and the right opinion, could eventually be dispensed with. The phenomenon of conformism is characteristic of the last stage of this modern development.

It is true that one-man, monarchical rule, which the ancients stated to be the organizational device of the household, is transformed in society—as we know it today, when the peak of the social order is no longer formed by the royal household of an absolute ruler—into a kind of no-man rule. But this nobody, the assumed one interest of society as a whole in economics as well as the assumed one opinion of polite society in the salon, does not cease to rule for having lost its personality. As we know from the most social form of government, that is, from bureaucracy (the last stage of government in the nation-state just as one-man rule in benevolent despotism and absolutism was its first), the rule by nobody is not necessarily no-rule; it may indeed, under certain circumstances, even turn out to be one of its cruelest and most tyrannical versions.

It is decisive that society, on all its levels, excludes the possibility of action, which formerly was excluded from the household. Instead, society expects from each of its members a certain kind of behavior, imposing innumerable and various rules, all of which tend to "normalize" its members, to make them behave, to exclude spontaneous action or outstanding achievement. With Rousseau, we find these demands in the salons of high society, whose conventions always equate the individual with his rank within the social framework. What matters is this equation with social status, and it is immaterial whether the framework happens to be actual rank in the half-feudal society of the eighteenth century, title in the class society of the nineteenth, or mere function in the mass society of today. The rise of mass society, on the contrary, only indicates that the various social groups have suffered the same absorption into one society that the family units had suffered earlier; with the emergence of mass society, the realm of the social has finally, after several centuries of development, reached the point where it embraces and controls all members of a given community equally and with equal strength. But society equalizes under all circumstances, and the victory of equality in the modern world is only the political and legal recognition of the fact that society has conquered the public realm, and that distinction and difference have become private matters of the individual.

This modern equality, based on the conformism inherent in society and possible only because behavior has replaced action as the foremost mode of human relationship, is in every respect different from equality in antiquity, and notably in the Greek city-states. To belong to the few "equals" (*homoioi*) meant to be permitted to live among one's peers; but the public realm itself, the *polis*, was permeated by a fiercely agonal spirit, where everybody had constantly to distinguish himself from all others, to show through unique deeds or achievements that he was the best of all (*aien aristeuein*).[2] The public realm, in other words, was reserved for individuality; it was the only place where men could show who they really and inexchangeably were. It was for the sake of this chance, and out of love for a body politic that made it possible to them all, that each was more or less willing to share in the burden of jurisdiction, defense, and administration of public affairs.

It is the same conformism, the assumption that men behave and do not act with respect to each other, that lies at the root of the modern science of economics, whose birth coincided with the rise of society and which, together with its chief technical tool, statistics, became the social science par excellence. Economics—until the modern age a not too important part of ethics and politics and based on the assumption that men act with respect to their economic activities as they act in every other respect[3]—could achieve a scientific character only when men had become social beings and unanimously followed certain patterns of behavior, so that those who did not keep the rules could be considered to be asocial or abnormal.

The laws of statistics are valid only where large numbers or long periods are involved, and acts or events can statistically appear only as deviations or fluctuations. The justification of statistics is that deeds and events are rare occurrences in everyday life and in history. Yet the meaningfulness of everyday relationships is disclosed not in everyday life but in rare deeds, just as the significance of a historical period shows itself only in the few events that illuminate it. The application of the law of large numbers and long periods to politics or history signifies nothing less than the wilful obliteration of their very subject matter, and it is a hopeless enterprise to search for meaning in politics or significance in history when everything that is not everyday behavior or automatic trends has been ruled out as immaterial.

However, since the laws of statistics are perfectly valid where we deal with large numbers, it is obvious that every increase in population means an increased validity and a marked decrease of "deviation." Politically, this means that the larger the population in any given body politic, the more likely it will be the social rather than the political that constitutes the public realm. The Greeks, whose city-state was the most individualistic and least conformable body politic known to us, were quite aware of the fact that the *polis,* with its emphasis on action and speech, could survive only if the number of citizens remained restricted. Large numbers of people, crowded together, develop an almost irresistible inclination toward despotism, be this the despotism of a person or of majority rule; and although statistics, that is, the mathematical treatment of reality, was unknown prior to the modern age, the social phenomena which make such treatment possible—great numbers, accounting for conformism, behaviorism, and automatism in human affairs—were precisely those traits which, in Greek self-understanding, distinguished the Persian civilization from their own.

The unfortunate truth about behaviorism and the validity of its "laws" is that the more people there are, the more likely they are to behave and the less likely to tolerate non-behavior. Statistically, this will be shown in the leveling out of fluctuation. In reality, deeds will have less and less chance to stem the tide of behavior, and events will more and more lose their significance, that is, their capacity to illuminate historical time. Statistical uniformity is by no means a harmless scientific ideal; it is the no longer secret political ideal of a society which, entirely submerged in the routine of everyday living, is at peace with the scientific outlook inherent in its very existence.

The uniform behavior that lends itself to statistical determination, and therefore to scientifically correct prediction, can hardly be explained by the liberal hypothesis of a natural "harmony of interests," the foundation of "classical" economics; it was not Karl Marx but the liberal economists themselves who had to introduce the "communistic fiction," that is, to assume that there is one interest of society as a whole which with "an invisible hand" guides the behavior of men and produces the harmony of their conflicting interests.[4] The difference between Marx and his forerunners was only that he took the reality of conflict, as it presented itself in the society of his time, as seriously as the hypothetical fiction of harmony; he was right in concluding that the "socialization of man" would produce automatically a harmony of all interests, and was only more courageous than his liberal teachers when he proposed to establish in reality the "communistic fiction" underlying all economic theories. What Marx did not—and, at his time, could not—understand was that the germs of communistic society were present in the reality of a national household, and that their full development was not hindered by any class-interest as such, but only by the already obsolete monarchical structure of the nation-state. Obviously, what prevented society from smooth functioning was only certain traditional remnants that interfered and still influenced the behavior of "backward" classes. From the viewpoint of society, these were merely disturbing factors in the way of a full development of "social forces"; they no longer corresponded to reality and were therefore, in a sense, much more "fictitious" than the scientific "fiction" of one interest.

A complete victory of society will always produce some sort of "communistic fiction," whose outstanding political characteristic is that it is indeed ruled by an "invisible hand," namely, by nobody. What we traditionally call state and government gives place here to pure administration—a state of affairs which Marx rightly predicted as the "withering away of the state," though he was wrong in assuming that only a revolution could bring it about, and even more wrong when he believed that this complete victory of society would mean the eventual emergence of the "realm of freedom."[5]

To gauge the extent of society's victory in the modern age, its early substitution of behavior for action and its eventual substitution of bureaucracy, the rule of nobody, for personal rulership, it may be well to recall that its initial science of economics, which substitutes patterns of behavior only in this rather limited field of human activity, was finally followed by the all-comprehensive pretension of the social sciences which, as "behavioral sciences," aim to reduce man as a whole, in all his activities, to the level of a conditioned and behaving animal. If economics is the science of society in its early stages, when it could impose its rules of behavior only on sections of the population and on parts of their activities, the rise of the "behavioral sciences" indicates clearly the final stage of this development, when mass society has devoured all strata of the nation and "social behavior" has become the standard for all regions of life.

Since the rise of society, since the admission of household and housekeeping activities to the public realm, an irresistible tendency to grow, to devour the older realms of the political and private as well as the more recently established sphere of intimacy, has been one of the outstanding characteristics of the new realm. This constant growth, whose no less constant acceleration we can observe over at least three centuries, derives its strength from the fact that through society it is the life process itself which in one form or another has been channeled into the public realm. The private realm of the household was the sphere where the necessities of life, of individual survival as well as of continuity of the species, were taken care of and guaranteed. One of the characteristics of privacy, prior to the discovery of the intimate, was that man existed in this sphere not as a truly human being but only as a specimen of the animal species man-kind. This, precisely, was the ultimate reason for the tremendous contempt held for it by antiquity. The emergence of society has changed the estimate of this whole sphere but has hardly transformed its nature. The monolithic character of every type of society, its conformism which allows for only one interest and one opinion, is ultimately rooted in the one-ness of man-kind. It is because this one-ness of man-kind is not fantasy and not even merely a scientific hypothesis, as in the "communistic fiction" of classical economics, that mass society, where man as a social animal rules supreme and where apparently the survival of the species could be guaranteed on a world-wide scale, can at the same time threaten humanity with extinction.

Perhaps the clearest indication that society constitutes the public organization of the life process itself may be found in the fact that in a relatively short time the new social realm transformed all modern communities into societies of laborers and jobholders; in other words, they became at once centered around the one activity necessary to sustain life. (To have a society of laborers, it is of course not necessary that every member actually be a laborer or worker—not even the emancipation of the working class and the enormous potential power which majority rule accords to it are decisive here—but only that all members consider whatever they do primarily as a way to sustain their own lives and those of their families.) Society is the form in which the fact of mutual dependence for the sake of life and nothing else assumes public significance and where the activities connected with sheer survival are permitted to appear in public.

Whether an activity is performed in private or in public is no means a matter of indifference. Obviously, the character of the public realm must change in accordance with the activities admitted into it, but to a large extent the activity itself changes its own nature too. The laboring activity, though under all circumstances connected with the life process in its most elementary, biological sense, remained stationary for thousands of years, imprisoned in the eternal recurrence of the life process to which it was tied. The admission of labor to public stature, far from eliminating its character as a process—which one might have expected, remembering that bodies politic have always been designed for permanence and their laws always understood as limitations imposed upon movement—has, on the contrary, liberated this process from its circular, monotonous recurrence and transformed it into a swiftly progressing development whose results have in a few centuries totally changed the whole inhabited world.

The moment laboring was liberated from the restrictions imposed by its banishment into the private realm—and this emancipation of labor was not a consequence of the emancipation of the working class, but preceded it—it was as though the growth element inherent in all organic life had completely overcome and overgrown the processes of decay by which organic life is checked and balanced in nature's household. The social realm, where the life process has established its own public domain, has let loose an unnatural growth, so to speak, of the natural; and it is against this growth, not merely against society but against a constantly growing social realm, that the private and intimate, on the one hand, and the political (in the narrower sense of the word), on the other, have proved incapable of defending themselves.

What we described as the unnatural growth of the natural is usually considered to be the constantly accelerated increase in the productivity of labor. The greatest single factor in this constant increase since its inception has been the organization of laboring, visible in the so-called division of labor, which preceded the industrial revolution; even the mechanization of labor processes, the second greatest factor in labor's productivity, is based upon it. Inasmuch as the organizational principle itself clearly derives from the public rather than the private realm, division of labor is precisely what happens to the laboring activity under conditions of the public realm and what could never have happened in the privacy of the household.[6] In no other sphere of life do we appear to have attained such excellence as in the revolutionary transformation of laboring, and this to the point where the verbal significance of the word itself (which always had been connected with hardly bearable "toil and trouble," with effort and pain and, consequently, with a deformation of the human body, so that only extreme misery and poverty could be its source), has begun to lose its meaning for us.[7] While dire necessity made labor indispensable to sustain life, excellence would have been the last thing to expect from it. . . .

Notes

1. This is well illustrated by a remark of Seneca, who, discussing the usefulness of highly educated slaves (who know all the classics by heart) to an assumedly rather ig-

norant master, comments: "What the household knows the master knows" (*Ep.* 27. 6, quoted from Barrow, *Slavery in the Roman Empire,* p. 61).

2. *Aien aristeuein kai hypeirochon emmenai allōn* ("always to be the best and to rise above others") is the central concern of Homer's heroes (*Iliad* vi. 208), and Homer was "the educator of Hellas."

3. "The conception of political economy as primarily a 'science' dates only from Adam Smith" and was unknown not only to antiquity and the Middle Ages, but also to canonist doctrine, the first "complete and economic doctrine" which "differed from modern economics in being an 'art' rather than a 'science'" (W. J. Ashley, *op. cit.,* pp. 379 ff.). Classical economics assumed that man, in so far as he is an active being, acts exclusively from self-interest and is driven by only one desire, the desire for acquisition. Adam Smith's introduction of an "invisible hand to promote an end which was no part of [anybody's] intention" proves that even this minimum of action with its uniform motivation still contains too much unpredictable initiative for the establishment of a science. Marx developed classical economics further by substituting group or class interests for individual and personal interests and by reducing these class interests to two major classes, capitalists and workers, so that he was left with one conflict, where classical economics had seen a multitude of contradictory conflicts. The reason why the Marxian economic system is more consistent and coherent, and therefore apparently so much more "scientific" than those of his predecessors, lies primarily in the construction of "socialized man," who is even less an acting being than the "economic man" of liberal economics.

4. That liberal utilitarianism, and not socialism, is "forced into an untenable 'communistic fiction' about the unity of society" and that "the communist fiction [is] implicit in most writings on economics" constitutes one of the chief theses of Myrdal's brilliant work (*op. cit.,* pp. 54 and 150). He shows conclusively that economics can be a science only if one assumes that one interest pervades society as a whole. Behind the "harmony of interests" stands always the "communistic fiction" of one interest, which may then be called welfare or commonwealth. Liberal economists consequently were always guided by a "communistic" ideal, namely, by "interest of society as a whole" (pp. 194–95). The crux of the argument is that this "amounts to the assertion that society must be conceived as a single subject. This, however, is precisely what cannot be conceived. If we tried, we would be attempting to abstract from the essential fact that social activity is the result of the intentions of several individuals" (154). [The reference is to Gunnar Myrdal, *The Political Element in the Development of Economic Theory,* trans. by Paul Streeten (London: Routledge and Paul, 1953.]

5. For a brilliant exposition of this usually neglected aspect of Marx's relevance for modern society, see Siegfried Landshut, "Die Gegenwart im Lichte der Marxschen Lehre," *Hamburger Jahrbuch für Wirtschafts- und Gesellschaftspolitik,* Vol. I (1956).

6. Here and later I apply the term "division of labor" only to modern labor conditions where one activity is divided and atomized into innumerable minute manipulations, and not to the "division of labor" given in professional specialization. The latter can be so classified only under the assumption that society must be conceived as one single subject, the fulfilment of whose needs are then subdivided by "an invisible hand" among its members. The same holds true, *mutatis mutandis,* for the odd notion of a division of labor between the sexes, which is even considered by some writers to

426

be the most original one. It presumes as its single subject man-kind, the human species, which has divided its labors among men and women. Where the same argument is used in antiquity (see, for instance, Xenophon *Oeconomicus* vii. 22), emphasis and meaning are quite different. The main division is between a life spent indoors, in the household, and a life spent outside, in the world. Only the latter is a life fully worthy of man, and the notion of equality between man and woman, which is a necessary assumption for the idea of division of labor, is of course entirely absent (cf. n. 81). Antiquity seems to have known only professional specialization, which assumedly was predetermined by natural qualities and gifts. Thus work in the gold mines, which occupied several thousand workers, was distributed according to strength and skill. See J.-P. Vernant, "Travail et nature dans la Grèce ancienne," *Journal de psychologie normale et pathologique,* Vol. LII, No. 1 (January–March, 1955).

7. All the European words for "labor," the Latin and English *labor,* the Greek *ponos,* the French *travail,* the German *Arbeit,* signify pain and effort and are also used for the pangs of birth. *Labor* has the same etymological root as *labare* ("to stumble under a burden"); *ponos* and *Arbeit* have the same etymological roots as "poverty" (*penia* in Greek and *Armut* in German). Even Hesiod, currently counted among the few defenders of labor in antiquity, put *ponon alginoenta* ("painful labor") as first of the evils plaguing man (*Theogony* 226). For the Greek usage, see G. Herzog-Hauser, "*Ponos,*" in Pauly-Wissowa. The German *Arbeit* and *arm* are both derived from the Germanic *arbma-,* meaning lonely and neglected, abandoned. Se Kluge/Götze, *Etymologisches Wöterbuch* (1951). In medieval German, the word is used to translate *labor, tribulatio, persecutio, adversitas, malum*(see Klara Vontobel, *Das Arbeitsethos des deutschen Protestantismus* [Dissertation, Bern, 1946]).

427

For Further Reading

Arendt, Hannah. *Between Past and Future: Eight Exercises in Political Thought* (New York: Viking, 1961).

———. *Hannah Arendt: Lectures on Kant's Political Philosophy.* Edited by Ronald Beiner (Chicago: Univ. of Chicago Press, 1989).

———. *The Human Condition* (Chicago: Univ. of Chicago Press, 1958).

———. *The Life of the Mind.* 2 vols. (New York: Harcourt Brace World, 1977–78).

———. *On Revolution* (New York: Viking, 1963),

———. *On Violence* (New York: Harcourt Brace World, 1970).

———. *Origins of Totalitarianism* (New York: Harcourt Brace, 1951).

Bernauer, James W., ed. *Amor Mundi* (Dordrecht: Nijhoff, 1987).

Bradshaw, Leah. *Acting and Thinking: The Political Thought of Hannah Arendt* (Toronto: Univ. of Toronto Press, 1989).

Canovan, Margaret. *Hannah Arendt: A Reinterpretation of Her Political Thought* (New York: Cambridge Univ. Press, 1992).

Disch, Lisa Jane. *Hannah Arendt and the Limits of Philosophy* (Ithaca, N.Y.: Cornell Univ. Press, 1994).

Gottsegen, Michael G. *The Political Thought of Hannah Arendt* (Albany: State Univ. of New York Press, 1994).

Habermas, Jürgen. *Philosophical-Political Profiles* (Cambridge: MIT Press, 1983).

Hinchman, Lewis P., and Sandra K. Hinchman, eds. *Hannah Arendt: Critical Essays* (Albany: State University of New York Press, 1994).

Lefort, Claude. *Democracy and Political Theory*. Translated by David Macey (Minneapolis: Univ. of Minnesota Press, 1988).

May, Derwent. *Hannah Arendt* (New York: Penguin, 1986).

Passerin d'Entrêves, Maurizio. *The Political Philosophy of Hannah Arendt* (New York: Routledge, 1994).

Young-Bruehl, Elisabeth. *Hannah Arendt: For Love of the World* (New Haven: Yale Univ. Press, 1982).

DANIEL BELL (1919–   )

chapter 22

CULTURE IS the realm where a person or group acquires a moral and aesthetic identity, a mode of perceiving, judging, and acting in the world. Our cheap substitute for culture, "lifestyle," marks the phenomenon most troubling to Daniel Bell: in industrial societies, we have stopped making sense together. The shared meaning missing from modernism and spurned by postmodernism make them, for Bell, not so much peculiar cultural forms as scavengers feeding off the remains of culture. Change becomes our sole expectation. Proteus, the mythical character who could assume any shape but had none to call his own, is for Bell the model of the modern self. Following Émile Durkheim, Bell sees the fundamental social crisis in the industrial world as religious: the solidarity once sustained by the Protestant, and specifically Puritan, values of hard work, abstinence, and sobriety has been eaten away by the combined forces of modernism and consumerism.

There is irony in the timing of this collapse of shared religious values. For, according to Bell, *industrial* societies governed by the market and individualistic practices are giving way to *postindustrial* societies, where the state and other non-market forces play a greater role. The state that intervenes and regulates economic growth is no mere "watchman" but one that opens the door to a "sociologizing mode" of governance. Potentially, the needs of the community are increasingly fit topics for political deliberation. Yet just when industrial capitalism pushes toward an expanded "public household" and a more deliberately social direction, we lack the needed "public philosophy" and sensibilities to revive communal life.

Bell wants to refute the Marxist insistence on the primacy of the mode of production while he gives a conservative twist to the Marxist notion of capitalism's contradictions. But he fluctuates between insisting on the autonomy and *avant garde* status of modern "culture," and arguing that the consumerism dating from the "Roaring Twenties" replaced the Protestant work ethic and Puritan strictness with the "fun morality." Likewise, Bell swings between talk of a "radical disjuncture" between consumer hedonism and the capitalist "social structure," and the judgment that maintaining the Puritan temper would choke the "new capitalism." Just how capitalism generates cultural contradictions remains uncertain with Bell. He shifts between identifying capitalism narrowly with *industrial production* and broadly with the full sweep of enterprises that includes finance and merchandising. Only the latter conception, which better represents the encompassing reality of capital, suggests the notion of a cultural contradiction: industrial capitalism still needs "hard workers," but selling mass-produced commodities calls for plenty of "big spenders." Still, we might wonder whether a "work hard, party hard" mentality actually threatens capitalism with any psychological or existential contradiction.

In fact, as Jean Baudrillard observes, the Protestant work ethic and the consumerist "fun morality" agree in their abstractness and compulsiveness. Hard work, instinctual restraint, and fixation on an ever higher "standard of living" are not, by themselves, impressive values. Bell's sympathy for the Protestant work ethic is curious in light of Max Weber's account of it as: (1) inimical to traditional forms of economic life; (2) destined to be replaced by a flatter, secular work ethic once industrial capitalism got on its feet; and (3) deeply irrational from the standpoint of any traditional or substantive standard of values. The radicals of the 1960s, whom Bell was quick to dismiss, rightly sensed that the Protestant work ethic was part of the problem with values in capitalist society. The search for a substantive measure of wealth to root a "postindustrial" public philosophy surely leads elsewhere than back to Benjamin Franklin.

FROM "THE CULTURAL CONTRADICTIONS OF CAPITALISM"

The relationship between a civilization's socioeconomic structure and its culture is perhaps the most complicated of all problems for the sociologist. A nineteenth century tradition, one deeply impregnated with Marxist conceptions, held that changes in social structure determined man's imaginative reach. An earlier vision of man—as *homo pictor*, the symbol-producing animal, rather than as *homo faber*, the tool-making animal—saw him as a creature uniquely able to prefigure what he would later "objectify" or construct in reality. It thus ascribed to the realm of culture the initiative for change. Whatever the truth of these older arguments about the past, today culture has clearly become supreme; what is played out in the imagination of the artist foreshadows, however dimly, the social reality of tomorrow.

Culture has become supreme for two complementary reasons. First, culture has become the most dynamic component of our civilization, outreaching the dynamism of technology itself. There is now in art—as there has increasingly been for the past hundred years—a dominant impulse towards the new and the original, a self-conscious search for future forms and sensations, so that *the idea* of change and novelty overshadows the dimensions of actual change. And secondly, there has come about, in the last fifty years or so, a legitimation of this cultural impulse. Society now accepts this role for the imagination, rather than—as in the past—seeing it as establishing a norm and affirming a moral-philosophic tradition against which the new could be measured and (more often than not) censured. Indeed, society has done more than passively accept—it has provided a market which eagerly gobbles up the new, because it believes it to be superior in value to all older forms. Thus, our culture has an unprecedented mission: it is an official, ceaseless searching for a new sensibility.

It is true, of course, that the idea of change dominates the modern economy and modern technology as well. But changes in the economy and technology are constrained by available resources and financial cost. In politics, too, innovation is constrained by existing institutional structures, by the veto power of contending groups, and to some extent by tradition. But the changes in expressive symbols and forms, difficult as it may be for the mass of people to absorb them readily, meet no resistance in the realm of culture itself.

What is singular about this "tradition of the new" (as Harold Rosenberg has called it) is that it allows art to be unfettered, to break down all genres and to explore all modes of experience and sensation. Fantasy today has few costs (is *anything* deemed bizarre or opprobrious today?) other than the risk of individual madness. And even madness, in the writings of such social theorists as Michel Foucault and R. D. Laing, is now conceived to be a superior form of truth! The new sensibilities, and the new styles of behavior associated with them, are created by small coteries which are devoted to exploring the new; and because the new has value in and of itself, and meets with so little resistance, the new sensibility and its behavior-styles diffuse rapidly, transforming the thinking and actions of larger masses of people.

Along with this emphasis on the new has come the ideology, self-consciously accepted by the artist, that art will lead the way, will serve as the *avant-garde*. Now the very idea of an *avant-garde*—an advance assault team—indicates that modern art or culture would never permit itself to serve as a "reflection" of an underlying social structure, but rather would open the way to something radically new. In fact, as we shall see, the very idea of an *avant-garde*, once its legitimacy is accepted, serves to institutionalize the primacy of culture in the fields of manners, morals, and ultimately politics.

The first major formulation of this conception of the *avant-garde* was by the man who, ironically, has come to serve as the symbol of technocratic rule, Henri de Saint-Simon. For all his vision of the engineer as the driving force of the new society, Saint-Simon knew that men were in want of inspiration, that Christianity itself was worn out, and that a new cult was needed. He found this new cult in the cult of art itself. The artist would reveal to society the glorious future, exciting men with the prospect of a new civilization. In a dialogue between an artist and a scientist Saint-Simon gave the phrase its modern *cultural*—rather than its earlier military—meaning:

> It is we, artists, who will serve you as *avant-garde:* the power of the arts is in fact most immediate and most rapid. When we wish to spread new ideas among men, we inscribe them on marble or on canvas; . . . and in that way above all we exert an electric and victorious influence. We address ourselves to the imagination and to the sentiments of mankind, we should therefore always exercise the liveliest and the most decisive action. . . .

> What a most beautiful destiny for the arts, that of exercising over society a positive power, a true priestly function, and of marching forcefully in the van of all the intellectual faculties in the epoch of their greatest development! This is the duty of artists and their mission. . . .

The commonplace observation that today there is no longer a significant *avant-garde*—that there is no longer a radical tension between a new art which shocks and a society that is shocked—merely signifies that the *avant-garde* has won its victory. A society given over entirely to innovation, in the joyful acceptance of change, has in fact institutionalized an *avant-garde* and charged it—perhaps to its own eventual dismay—with constantly turning up something new. In effect, "culture" has been given a blank check, and its primacy in generating social change has been firmly acknowledged.

This changeover creates a new and peculiar set of historic tensions in the society. The social structure today is ruled by an economic principle of rationality, defined in terms of efficiency in the allocation of resources; the culture, in contrast, is prodigal, promiscuous, dominated by an antirational, anti-intellectual temper. The character structure inherited from the nineteenth century—with its emphasis on self-discipline, delayed gratification, restraint—is still relevant to the demands of the social structure; but it clashes sharply with the culture, where such bourgeois values have been completely rejected—in part, as we shall see, and paradoxically, because of the workings of the capitalist economic system itself. . . .

III

We come to an extraordinary sociological puzzle. A single cultural temper, mood, movement—its very amorphousness or protean nature precludes a single encapsulating term—has persisted for more than a century and a quarter, nourishing renewed and sustained attacks on the social structure. Perhaps the most inclusive term for this cultural temper is *modernism:* the self-willed effort of a style and sensibility to remain in the forefront of "advancing consciousness." What is the nature, then, of this sentiment that, antedating even Marxism, has been attacking bourgeois society and has been able to sustain such a program? Why has it so captured the artistic imagination that it can preserve itself through generations, and have fresh appeal for each new cohort of the intelligentsia?

Modernism pervades all the arts. Yet if one looks at the individual examples, there seems to be no single unifying principle. It includes the new syntax of Mallarme, the dislocation of forms of Cubism, the stream of consciousness in Virginia Woolf or Joyce, the atonality of Berg. Each of these, as it first appeared, was "difficult" to understand. In fact, as a number of writers have suggested, original difficulty is a sign of a modernist movement. It is willfully opaque, works with unfamiliar forms, is self-consciously experimental, and seeks deliberately to disturb the audience—to shock it, shake it up, even to transform it as if in a religious conversion. This very difficulty is clearly one source of its appeal to initiates, for esoteric knowledge—like the special formula of the magi or the hermeticism of ancient priests—gives one an enhanced sense of power over the vulgar and unenlightened.

Modernism is a response to two social changes in the nineteenth century, one on the level of sense perception of the social environment, the other of consciousness about the self. In the everyday world of sense impressions, there was a disorientation of the sense of space and time derived from the new awareness of motion and speed, light, and sound, which came from the revolutions in communication and transport. The crisis in self-consciousness arose from the loss of religious certitude, of belief in an afterlife, in heaven or hell, and the new consciousness of an immutable boundary beyond life and the nothingness of death. In effect, these were two new ways of experiencing the world and often the artist himself was never wholly aware of the sources of disorientation in the social environment which had shaken up the world and made it seem as if there were only pieces. Yet he had to reassemble these pieces in a new way.

For the second half of the nineteenth century, then, an ordered world was a chimera. What was suddenly real, in molding the sense perception of an environment, was movement and flux. A radical change in the nature of es-

433

thetic perception had suddenly occurred. If one asks, in esthetic terms, how modern man differs from the Greeks in experiencing sensations or emotions, the answer would have to do not with the basic human feelings, such as friendship, love, fear, cruelty, and aggression, which are common to all ages, but with the temporal-spatial dislocation of motion and height. In the nineteenth century, for the first time in history, men could travel faster than on foot or on an animal, and gain a different sense of changing landscape, a succession of images, the blur of motion, which he had never before experienced. Or one could, first in a balloon and later in a plane, rise thousands of feet in the sky and see topographical patterns that the ancients had never known.

What was true of the physical world was equally true of the social. With the growth of numbers and density in the cities, there was greater interaction among persons, a syncretism of experience that provided a sudden openness to new styles of life—a geographical and social mobility—that had never been available before. In the canvases of art, the subjects were no longer the mythological creatures of the past or the stillness of nature, but the promenade and the *plage,* the bustle of city life, and the brilliance of night life in an urban environment transformed by electric light. It is this response to movement, space, and change which provided the new syntax of art and the dislocation of traditional forms.

In the classical premodern view, art was essentially contemplative; the viewer or spectator held "power" over the experience by keeping his esthetic distance from it. In modernism, the intention is to "overwhelm" the spectator so that the art product itself—through the foreshortening of perspective in painting, or the "sprung rhythm" of a Hopkins in poetry—imposes itself on the spectator in its own terms. In modernism, genre becomes an archaic conception whose distinctions are ignored in the flux of experience. In all this, there is an "eclipse of distance," so that the spectator loses control and becomes subject to the intentions of the artist. The very structural forms are organized to provide immediacy, simultaneity, envelopment of experience. Power has moved from the spectator, who could contemplate the picture, the sculpture, or the story, to the artist, who brings the viewer into his own field of action. The eclipse of distance provides a stylistic unity, a common syntax for painting, poetry, narrative, music, and becomes a common structural component—a formal element—across all the arts.

All of this was reflected in the explosive burst of artistic energy in the forty years before World War I. In the Impressionists' experiments with light, the capture of motion by the Futurists, the spatial dislocation of form in Cubism, then a bit later in the anti-art of Dadaism—in which everyday objects and "readymades" are pasted together on a canvas—one sees the bewildering succession of efforts to catch the swiftness of change through new kinds of painting. The modernist effort to capture this flux gives full meaning, I think, to Irving Howe's citation of Virginia Woolf's gnomic remark: "On or about December 1910, human nature changed." As Howe comments, in this there is a "frightening discontinuity between the traditional past and the shaken present . . . the line of history has been bent, perhaps broken."

In making this break, in the emphasis on the *absolute present,* both artist and spectator are forced to make and remake themselves anew each moment. With the repudiation of unbroken continuity, and the belief that the future is in the present, one loses the classical sense of wholeness or completeness. The fragment replaces the whole: one finds a new esthetic in the broken torso, the isolated hand, the primitive grimace, the figure cut by the frame. And in the mingling and jostling of styles, the very idea of genre and boundary, of principles appropriate to a genre, is abandoned. One might say, in fact, that esthetic disaster itself becomes an esthetic.

Enter Nothingness and Self

The sense of movement and change—the upheaval in the mode of confronting the world—established vivid new conventions and forms by which people judged their sense perceptions and experience. But more subtly, the awareness of change prompted a deeper crisis in the human spirit, the fear of nothingness. The decline of religion, and especially of belief in an immortal soul, provoked a momentous break with the centuries-old conception of an unbridgeable chasm between the human and the divine. Men now sought to cross that gulf and, as Faust, the first modern, put it, attain "godlike knowledge," to "prove in man the stature of a god" or else confess his "kinship with the worm."

As a consequence of this superhuman effort, in the nineteenth century, the sense of the self comes to the fore. The individual comes to be considered as unique, with singular aspirations, and life assumes a greater sanctity and preciousness. The enhancement of the single life becomes a value for its own sake. Economic meliorism, anti-slavery sentiment, women's rights, the end of child labor and cruel punishments became the social issues of the day. But in a deeper metaphysical sense, this spiritual enterprise became the basis for the idea that men could go beyond necessity, that they would no longer be constrained by nature but could arrive—in Hegel's phrase—at the end of history, in the kingdom of perfect freedom. The "unhappy consciousness" of which Hegel wrote is the realization of a divine power and status which man must strive to achieve. The deepest nature of modern man, the secret of his soul as revealed by the modern metaphysic, is that he seeks to reach out beyond himself; knowing that negativity—death—is finite, he refuses to accept it. Behind the chiliasm of modern man, is the megalomania of self-infinitization. In consequence, the modern hubris is the refusal to accept limits, the insistence on continually reaching out; and the modern world proposes a destiny that is always *beyond*—beyond morality, beyond tragedy, beyond culture.[1]

The Triumph of Will

In Western consciousness there has always been tension between the rational and the nonrational, between reason and will, between reason and instinct, as the driving forces of man. A basic triadic distinction was made by Plato, who divided the soul into the rational, the spirited, and the appetitive. But whatever the specific distinctions, rational judgment was traditionally thought to be superior in the hierarchy, and this order dominated Western culture for almost two millennia.

Modernism dirempts this hierarchy. It is the triumph of the spirited, of the will. In Hobbes and Rousseau, intelligence is a slave to the passions. In Hegel, the will is the necessary component of knowing. In Nietzsche, the will is fused with the esthetic mode, in which knowledge derives most directly ("apprehended, not ascertained," as he says in the first line of *The Birth of Tragedy*) from intoxication and dream. And if the esthetic experience alone is to justify life, then morality is suspended and desire has no limit. Anything is possible in this quest of the self to explore its relation to sensibility.

The emphasis of modernism is on the present, or on the future, but never on the past. Yet when one is cut off from the past, one cannot escape the final sense of nothingness that the future then holds. Faith is no longer possible, and art, or nature, or impulse can erase the self only momentarily in the intoxication or frenzy of the Dionysian act. But intoxication always passes and there is the cold morning after, which arrives inexorably with the break of day. This inescapable eschatalogical anxiety leads inevitably to the feeling—the black thread of modernist thought—that each person's own life is at the end of time. The sense of an ending, the feeling that one is living in an apocalyptic age, is, as Frank Kermode has observed, "as endemic to what we call modernism as apocalyptic utopianism is to political revolution. . . . Its recurrence is a feature of our cultural tradition."[2]

In discussing modernism, the categories of "left" and "right" make little sense. Modernism, as Thomas Mann phrased it, cultivates "a sympathy for the abyss." Nietzsche and Yeats, Pound and Wyndham Lewis were politically far to the right. Gide was a pagan, Malraux a revolutionist. But whatever the political stripe, the modern movement has been united by rage against the social order as the first cause, and a belief in the apocalypse as the final cause. It is this trajectory which provides the permanent appeal and the permanent radicalism of that movement.

IV

Traditional modernism, in Frank Kermode's term, sought to substitute for religion or morality an esthetic justification of life; to create a work of art, to be a work of art—this alone provided meaning in man's effort to transcend himself. But in going back to art, as is evident in Nietzsche, the very search for the roots of self moves the quest of modernism from art to psychology: from the product to the producer, from the object to the psyche.

In the 1960's, a powerful current of post-modernism has developed which has carried the logic of modernism to its farthest reaches. In the theoretical writings of Norman O. Brown and Michel Foucault, in the novels of William Burroughs, Jean Genet, and to some extent Norman Mailer, and in the porno-pop culture that is now all about us, one sees a logical culmination of modernist intentions.

There are several dimensions to the post-modernist mood. Thus, against the esthetic justification for life, post-modernism has completely substituted the instinctual. Impulse and pleasure alone are real and life-affirming; all else is neurosis and death. Moreover, traditional modernism, no matter how daring, played out its impulses in the imagination, within the constraints of art. Whether demonic or murderous, the fantasies were expressed through the ordering principle of esthetic form. Art, therefore, even though subversive of society, still ranged itself on the side of order and, implicitly, of a rationality of form, if not of content. Post-modernism overflows the vessels of art. It tears down the boundaries and insists that *acting out,* rather than making distinctions, is the way to gain knowledge. The "happening" and the "environment," the "street" and the "scene," are the proper arena for life.

Extraordinarily, none of this is in itself completely new. There has always been an esoteric tradition within all Western religion which has sanctioned participation in secret rites of release, debauch, and total freedom for those— the "gnostics"—who have been initiated into secret sects through secret knowledge. Gnosticism, in its intellectual formulations has provided the justification for the attacks on restraints that every society has imposed on its members. Yet in the past, this knowledge was kept hermetic, its members were secretive. What is most striking about post-modernism is that what was once maintained as esoteric is now proclaimed as ideology, and what was once the property of an aristocracy of the spirit is now turned into the democratic property of the mass. The gnostic mode has always beat against the historic, psychological taboos of civilization. That assault has now been made the platform of a widespread cultural movement.

437

The post-modern temper, looked at as a set of loosely associated doctrines, itself goes in two directions. One is philosophical, a kind of negative Hegelianism. Michel Foucault, who is now very much "in," sees man as a short-lived historical incarnation, "a trace on the sand," to be washed away by the waves. The "ruined and pest-ridden cities of man called "soul" and "being" will be "deconstructed." It is no longer the decline of the West, but the end of all civilization. Much of this is modish, a play of words pushing a thought to an absurd logicality. Like the angry playfulness of Dada or Surrealism, it will probably be remembered, if at all, as a footnote to cultural history.

But the post-modern temper, moving in another direction, does carry a much more significant implication. It provides the doctrinal spearhead for an onslaught on the values and motivational patterns of "ordinary" behavior, in the name of liberation, eroticism, freedom of impulse, and the like. It is this, dressed up in more popular form, which is the real importance of the post-modernist doctrine. For it means that a crisis of middle-class values is at hand.

Death of the Bourgeois

The bourgeois world-view—rationalistic, matter-of-fact, pragmatic; neither magical, mystical, nor romantic; emphasizing work and function; concerned with restraint and order in morals and conduct—had by the mid-nineteenth-century come to dominate, not only the social structure (the organization of the economy), but also the culture, especially the religious order and the educational system which instilled "appropriate" motivation in the child. It reigned triumphant everywhere, opposed only in the realm of culture by those who disdained its un-heroic and anti-tragic mood, as well as its orderly attitude towards time.

The last hundred years has seen an effort by anti-bourgeois culture to achieve *autonomy* from the social structure, first by a denial of bourgeois values in the realm of art, and second by carving out enclaves where the bohemian and the *avant-gardist* could live a contrary style of life. By the turn of the century the *avant-garde* had succeeded in establishing a "life-space" of its own, and by 1910—1930 it was on the offensive against traditional culture.

Today, in both doctrine and life-style, the anti-bourgeois has won. This triumph means that, in the culture today, antinomianism and anti-institutionalism rule. In the realm of art, on the level of esthetic doctrine, no one opposes the idea of boundless experiment, of unfettered freedom, of unconstrained sensibility, of impulse being superior to order, of the imagination being immune to merely rational criticism. There is no longer an *avant-garde*, because no one in our post-modern culture is on the side of order or tradition. There exists only a desire for the new.

The traditional bourgeois organization of life—its rationalism and sobriety—no longer has any defenders in the culture, nor does it have any established system of culture meanings or stylistic forms with any intellectual or cultural respectability. To assume, as some social critics do, that the technocratic mentality dominates the cultural order is to fly in the face of every bit of evidence at hand. What we have today is a radical disjunction of culture and social structure, and it is such disjunctions which historically have paved the way for more direct social revolutions.

In two fundamental ways, that revolution has already begun. First, the autonomy of culture, achieved in art, now passes over into the arena of life. The post-modernist temper demands that what was previously played out in fantasy and imagination must be acted out in life as well. There is no distinction between art and life. Anything permitted in art is permitted in life as well.

Second, the life-style once practiced by a small *cénacle*, whether the cool life-mask of a Baudelaire or the hallucinatory rage of a Rimbaud, is now copied by a "many"—a minority in the society to be sure, but nonetheless large in number—and dominates the cultural scene. This change of scale gives the culture of the 1960's its special power, plus the fact that a bohemian life-style once limited to a tiny elite is now acted out on the giant screen of the mass media. Woodstock—both the event and the movie—gives us a clear sense of what's happening.

The combination of these two changes adds up to the beginning of a major onslaught by the "culture" against the "social structure." When such attacks were launched before—say André Breton's surrealistic proposal in the early 1930's that the Towers of Notre Dame be replaced by an enormous glass cruet, one of the bottles filled with blood, the other with sperm, the church itself becoming a sexual school for virgins—they were understood as heavy-handed japes, perpetrated by the licensed "fools" of society. But the rise of a hip-drug-rock culture on a popular level, and the "new sensibility" of black-mass ritual and violence in the arena of culture, are a set of cultural actions that undermine the social structure itself by striking at the motivational and psychic-reward system which has sustained it. In this sense, the culture of the 1960's has a new and perhaps distinctive historic meaning.

V

Changes in cultural *ideas* have an immanence and autonomy because they develop from an internal logic at work with a cultural tradition. In this sense, new ideas and forms derive out of a kind of dialogue with, or rebellion against, previous ideas and forms. But changes in cultural *practice and life-styles* necessarily interact with social structure, since works of art, accoutrements, records, films, and plays are bought and sold in the market. The market is where social structure and culture cross. Changes in culture—particularly the emergence of new life-styles—are made possible, not only by changes in sensibility, but by shifts in the social structure itself. One can see this most readily, in the contemporary instance, in the development of new buying habits in a high consumption economy and the resultant erosion of the Protestant Ethic and the Puritan Temper, the two codes which once sustained the traditional value system of our society. It is the breakup of this ethic and temper, owing as much to changes in social structure as in the culture, that has undercut the beliefs and legitimations that sanctioned work and reward in American society. It is the transformation and the lack of any rooted new ethic, that is responsible, in good part, for the sense of disorientation and dismay that marks the public mood today.

The "Protestant Ethic" and the "Puritan Temper" were codes that emphasized work, sobriety, frugality, sexual restraint, and a forbidding attitude toward life. They defined the nature of moral conduct and social respectability.

The post-modernist culture of the 1960's has been interpreted, because it calls itself a "counterculture," as defying the Protestant Ethic, heralding the end of Puritanism, and mounting a final attack on bourgeois values. This is too facile. The Protestant Ethic and the Puritan Temper, as social facts, were eroded long ago, and they linger on as pale ideologies, used more by moralists to admonish and by sociologists to mythologize than as behavioral realities. The breakup of the traditional bourgeois value system, in fact, was brought about by the bourgeois economic system—by the free market, to be precise.

From the Protestant Ethic to the Psychedelic Bazaar

The Protestant Ethic and the Puritan Temper in the United States were the world view of an agrarian, small-town, mercantile, and artisan way of life. In the United States, as Page Smith reminds us "if we except the family and the church, the basic form of social organization up to the early decades of the twentieth century was the small town."[3] The life and character of American society were shaped by the small town—and especially by its religions. The erosion of traditional (i.e., smalltown) American values took place on two levels. In the realm of culture and ideas, a withering attack on small-town life as constricting and banal was first organized, in the period between 1910 and 1920, by the Young Intellectuals, a self-consciously defined group, including such figures as Van Wyck Brooks and Harold Stearns, who sought a new and more inclusive vision of American culiture. This attack was sustained in the journalistic criticism of H. L. Mencken and in the sketches and novels of Sherwood Anderson and Sinclair Lewis.

But a more fundamental transformation was occurring in the social structure itself. There was, first, the enormous expansion of the cities in response to industrialism. Equally important, if not more so, was the change in the motivations and rewards of the system itself. The rising wealth of the plutocracy, becoming evident in the Gilded Age, meant that work and accumulation were no longer ends in themselves (though they were still crucial to a John D. Rockefeller or an Andrew Carnegie) but means to consumption and display. Status and its badges, not work and the election of God, became the mark of success.

This is a familiar process of social history, with the rise of new classes, though in the past it was military predators whose scions went from spartan to sybaritic living. Because the parvenu classes could distance themselves from the rest of society, such social changes often developed independently of changes in the lives of the classes below. But the real social revolution in modern society came in the 1920's, when the rise of mass production and high consumption began to transform the life of the middle class itself. In effect the Protestant Ethic as a social reality and a life-style for the middle class was replaced by a materialistic hedonism, and the Puritan Temper by a psychological eudaemonism.

440

But bourgeois society, justified and propelled as it had been in its earliest energies by these older ethics, could not easily admit to the change. It promoted a hedonistic way of life furiously—one has only to look at the transformation of advertising in the 1920's—but could not justify it. It lacked a new religion or a value system to replace the old, and the result was a disjunction.

The "new capitalism"—the phrase was used in the 1920's—continued to demand a Protestant Ethic in the area of production—that is, in the realm of work—but to stimulate a demand for pleasure and play in the area of consumption. The disjunction was bound to widen. The spread of urban life, with its variety of distractions and multiple stimuli; the new roles of women, created by the expansion of office jobs and the freer social and sexual contacts; the rise of a national culture through motion pictures and radio—all contributed to a loss of social authority on the part of the older value system.

The Puritan Ethic might be described most simply by the phrase "delayed gratification," and by restraint in gratification. It is, of course, the Malthusian injunction for prudence in a world of scarcity. But the claim of the American economic system was that it had introduced abundance, and the nature of abundance is to encourage prodigality rather than prudence. The "higher standard of living," not work as an end in itself, then becomes the engine of change. The glorification of plenty, rather than the bending to niggardly nature, becomes the justification of the system. But all of this was highly incongruent with the theological and sociological foundations of nineteenth century Protestantism, which was in turn the foundation of the American value system.

441

The Abdication of the Corporate Class

The ultimate support for any social system is the acceptance by the population of a moral justification of authority. The older justifications of bourgeois society lay in the defense of private property, which itself was justified on the grounds, elaborated by Locke, that one infused one's own labor into property. But the "new capitalism" of the twentieth century has lacked such moral grounding, and in periods of crisis it has either fallen back on the traditional value assertions, which have been increasingly incongruent with social reality, or it has been ideologically impotent.

It is in this context that one can see the weakness of corporate capitalism in trying to deal with some of the major political dilemmas of the century. Political—and value—conflicts in the United States can be looked at from two different perspectives. From one, there have been economic and class issues which divided farmer and banker, worker and employer, and led to the functional and interest-group conflicts which were especially sharp in the 1930's. Along a different sociological axis, one can see the politics of the 1920's, and to some extent that of the 1950's within the framework of "tradition" versus "modernity," with the rural, small-town Protestant intent on defending his historic values against the cosmopolitan liberal interested in reform and social welfare. The issues here are not primarily economic but sociocultural. The traditionalist defends fundamentalist religion, censorship, stricter divorce, and anti-abortion laws; the modernist is for secular rationality, freer personal relations, tolerance of sexual deviance, and the like. These represent the political side of cultural issues, and to the extent that culture is the symbolic expression, and justification of experience, this is the realm of symbolic or expressive politics.

In this respect, the great symbolic issue of American politics was Prohibition. It was the major—and almost the last—effort by small-town and traditionalist forces to impose a specific value, the prohibition of liquor, on the rest of the society; and, initially, of course, the traditionalists won. In a somewhat different sense, McCarthyism in the 1950's represented an effort by some traditionalist forces to impose a uniform political morality on the society through conformity to one ideology of Americanism and a virulent form of anti-Communism.

Now, the curious fact is that the "new capitalism" of abundance, which emerged in the 1920's, has never been able to define its view of these cultural-political issues, as it had of the economic-political conflicts. Given its split character, it could not do so. Its values derive from the traditionalist past, and its language is the archaism of the Protestant Ethic. Its technology and dynamism, however, derive from the spirit of modernity—the spirit of perpetual innovation, and of the creation of new "needs" on the installment plan. The one thing that would utterly destroy the "new capitalism" is the serious practice of "deferred gratification."

When members of the corporate class have taken a stand on cultural-political issues, they have often divided on geographical lines. Midwesterners, or Texans, or those coming from small-town backgrounds, display traditionalist attitudes; Easterners, or products of Ivy League schools, are more liberal. More recently, the division has been based on education and age rather than region. But the singular fact remains. The new capitalism was primarily responsible for transforming the society, and in the process undermined the Puritan Temper, but it was never able to develop successfully a new ideology congruent with the change, and it used—and often was trapped by—the older language of Protestant values.

The forces of modernity, which had taken the lead against the traditionalists on these social and cultural issues, have been a *melange* of intellectuals, professors, welfare and reform-minded individuals (though, paradoxically, the prohibition movement at its inception was allied with the reformers against the evils of industrialism and city life), joined, for political reasons, by labor leaders and ethnic politicians who represented urban forces. The dominant philosophy has been liberalism, which included a critique of the inequalities and social costs generated by capitalism.

The fact that the corporate economy has no unified value system of its own, or still mouthed a flaccid version of Protestant virtues, meant that liberalism could go ideologically unchallenged. In the realm of culture, and of cultural-social issues—of political philosophy, in short—the corporate class had abdicated. The important consideration is that, *as an ideology,* liberalism had become dominant over these past decades.

VI

From a *cultural* point of view, the politics of the 1920's to 1960's was a struggle between tradition and modernity. In the 1960's a new cultural style appeared. Call it psychedelic or call it, as its own protagonists have, a "counter-culture." It announced a strident opposition to bourgeois values and to the traditional codes of American life. "The bourgeoisie," we are told, "is obsessed by greed; its sex life is insipid and prudish; its family patterns are debased; its slavish conformities of dress and grooming are degrading; its mercenary routinization of life is intolerable. . . ."[4]

What is quixotic about such pronouncements is the polemical and ideological caricature of a set of codes that had been trampled on long ago—beginning sixty years earlier, with the Young Intellectuals. Yet such a caricature is necessary to make the new counter-culture seem more daring and revolutionary than it is. The new sensibility, with its emphasis on psychedelic experience, sexual freedom, apocalyptic moods and the like, thinks of itself as being against "bourgeois" culture. But in truth, bourgeois culture vanished long ago. What the counter-culture embodies is an extension of the tendencies initiated sixty years ago by political liberalism and modernist culture, and represents, in effect, a split in the camp of modernism. For it now seeks to take the preachments of personal freedom, extreme experience ("kicks," and "the high") and sexual experimentation, to a point in *life-style* that the liberal culture—which would approve of such ideas in *art and imagination*—is not prepared to go. Yet liberalism finds itself uneasy to say why. It approves a basic permissiveness, but cannot with any certainty define the bounds. And this is its dilemma. In culture, as well as in politics, liberalism is now up against the wall.

443

Liberalism also finds itself in disarray in an arena where it had joined in support of capitalism—in the economy. The economic philosophy of American liberalism had been rooted in the idea of growth. One forgets that in the late 1940's and 1950's Walter Reuther, Leon Keyserling, and other liberals had attacked the steel companies and much of American industry for being unwilling to expand capacity and had urged the government to set target growth figures. Cartelization, monopoly, and the restriction of production had been historic tendencies of capitalism. The Eisenhower administration consciously chose price stability over growth. It was the liberal economists who instilled in the society the policy of the conscious planning of growth through government inducements (e.g., investment credits, which industry, at first, did not want) and government investment. The idea of potential GNP and the concept of "short-fall"—the posting of a mark of what the economy at full utilization of resources could achieve compared to the actual figure— was introduced in the Council of Economic Advisors by the liberals. The idea of growth has become so fully absorbed as an economic ideology that one re- alizes no longer, as I said, how much of a liberal innovation it was.

The liberal answer to social problems such as poverty was that growth would provide the resources to raise the incomes of the poor.[5] The thesis that growth was necessary to finance public services was the center of John Ken- neth Galbraith's book *The Affluent Society.*

And yet, paradoxically, it is the very idea of economic growth that is now coming under attack—and from liberals. Affluence is no longer seen as an an- swer. Growth is held responsible for the spoliation of the environment, the voracious use of natural resources, the crowding in the recreation areas, the densities in the city, and the like. One finds, startlingly, the idea of zero eco- nomic growth—or John Stuart Mill's idea of the "stationary state"—now proposed as a serious goal of government policy. Just as the counter-culture rejects the traditional problem-solving pragmatism of American politics, it now also rejects the newer, liberal policy of economic growth as a positive goal for the society. But without a commitment to economic growth, what is the *raison d'etre* of capitalism?

Two Crises

American society faces a number of crises. Some are more manifest—the alienation of the young, the militancy of the blacks, the crisis of confidence created by the Vietnam war. Some are structural—the creation of a national society, a communal society, and a post-industrial phase—which are rework- ing the occupational structure and the social arrangements of the society.[6] These are all aspects of a political torment in the social system. Yet these crises, I believe, are manageable (not solvable; what problems are?) if the polit- ical leadership is intelligent and determined. The resources are present (or will be, once the Vietnam war is ended) to relieve many of the obvious tensions and to finance the public needs of the society. The great need here is *time,* for the social changes which are required (a decent welfare and income mainte- nance system for the poor, the reorganization of the universities, the control of the environment) can only be handled within the space of a decade or more. It is the demand for "instant solutions" which, in this respect, is the source of political trouble.

But the deeper and more lasting crisis is the cultural one. Changes in moral temper and culture—the fusion of imagination and life-styles—are not amenable to "social engineering" or political control. They derive from the value and moral traditions of the society, and these cannot be "designed" by precept. The ultimate sources are the religious conceptions which undergird a society; the proximate sources are the "reward systems" and "motivations" (and their legitimacy) which derive from the arena of work (the social structure).

American capitalism, as I have sought to show, has lost its traditional legitimacy which was based on a moral system of reward, rooted in a Protestant sanctification of work. It has substituted in its place a hedonism which promises a material ease and luxury, yet shies away from all the historic implications which a "voluptuary system"—and all its social permissiveness and libertinism—implies.

This is joined to a more pervasive problem derived from the nature of industrial society. The characteristic style of an industrial society is based on the principles of economics and economizing: on efficiency, least cost, maximization, optimization, and functional rationality. Yet it is at this point that it comes into sharpest conflict with the cultural trends of the day, for the culture emphasizes anticognitive and anti-intellectual currents which are rooted in a return to instinctual modes. The one emphasizes functional rationality, technocratic decision-making, and meritocratic rewards. The other, apocalyptic moods and antirational modes of behavior. It is this disjunction which is the historic crisis of Western society. This cultural contradiction, in the long run, is the deepest challenge to the society.

445

Notes

1. Compare these powerful statements by two contemporary writers. In Malraux' *Man's Fate (1933)* Old Gisors describes the Baron de Clappique and his desires:

> To be more than a man in a world of men. To escape man's fate. [To be] not powerful: all powerful. The visionary disease, which the will to power is only the intellectual justification, is the will to godhead: every man dreams of being god.

In Saul Bellow's *Mr. Sammler's Planet* (1970) old Sammler reflects:

> You wondered whether . . . the worst enemies of civilization might not prove to be its petted intellectuals who attacked it at its weakest moments—attacked it in the name of proletarian revolution, in the name of reason and in the name of irrationality, in the name of visceral depth, in the name of sex, in the name of perfect and instant freedom. For what it amounted to was limitless demand—insatiability, refusal of the doomed creature (death being sure and final) to go away from this world unsatisfied. A full bill of demand and complaint was therefore presented by each individual. Non-negotiable. Recognizing no scarcity of supply in any human department.

2. Frank Kermode, *The Sense of an Ending* (New York, 1967), p. 98.

3. Page Smith, *As a City Upon a Hill* (New York, 1968), pp. vii–viii.

4. Theodore Roszak, *The Making of a Counter-Culture,* (Doubleday, 1969) p. 13.

5. More technically, it was based on the welfare economics theorem of Pareto optimality, namely that one should seek a condition where some people would be better off without anyone being worse off. The direct redistribution of income is politically difficult if not impossible. However, from new or added national income, a higher proportion of the gains can be used to finance social welfare programs; and this was, as Otto Eckstein pointed out in "The Economics of the Sixties," *The Public Interest,* No. 19, Spring 1970, precisely what Congress was willing to do when economic growth was resumed in the Kennedy administration.

6. For a detailed discussion of some of the "structural revolutions" which underlie the more manifest crises, and for a discussion of political dilemmas of liberalism, see my essay "Unstable America" in the June 1970 issue of *Encounter* (London).

For Further Reading

Bell, Daniel. *The Coming of Post-Industrial Society* (New York: Basic Books, 1973).

———. *The Cultural Contradictions of Capitalism* (New York: Basic Books, 1976).

———. *The End of Ideology* (New York: Free Press, 1965).

———. *Toward the Year 2000: Work in Progress* (Boston: Beacon Press, 1969).

Brick, Howard. *Daniel Bell and the Decline of Intellectual Radicalism: Social Theory and Political Reconciliation in the 1940s* (Madison: Univ. of Wisconsin Press, 1986).

Kleinberg, Benjamin. *American Society in the Post-Industrial Age* (Columbus, Ohio: Charles E. Merrill, 1970).

Kristol, Irving. *Two Cheers for Capitalism* (New York: Mentor Books, 1978).

Lasch, Christopher. *The True and Only Heaven* (New York: Norton, 1991).

Lichtheim, George. *The Concept of Ideology and other Essays* (New York: Vintage, 1967).

Liebowitz, Nathan. *Daniel Bell and the Agony of Modern Liberalism* (Westport, Conn.: Greenwood Press, 1985).

Steinfels, Peter. *The Neoconservatives* (New York: Simon and Schuster, 1979).

Waters, Malcolm. *Daniel Bell* (New York: Routledge, 1995).

Waxman, Chaim I., ed. 1968. *The End of Ideology Debate* (New York: Funk and Wagnalls, 1968).

JEAN BAUDRILLARD (1929–   )

chapter 23

CONSUMPTION IS a feature of all human, indeed all organic, life, but a "consumer society" signifies a recent and distinctive phenomenon. In writings dating from around 1970, Jean Baudrillard endeavored to answer the question "What is a consumer society?" His approach is phenomenological—what is the experience of a consumer society?—and theoretical—what is the genealogy of consumer society? Where does it come from?

Abundance and conspicuous consumption are the features of a consumer society that first strike Baudrillard, but his observations quickly become more qualitative. Commodities often are not simply displayed but organized into networks, as when "Barbie" dolls come with clothing and accessories coordinated around themes such as "Surfer Barbie" or "Hospice Barbie." The makeover of merchandising involved in the shopping mall (or "drugstore") homogenizes and "culturizes" the consumer's experience. The relation of these modernist shopping environments to older business districts resembles that of Muzak to the music it simulates or *Reader's Digest* to the journals from which its articles derive. The leveling that Simmel so aptly described as the *subjective* effect of the commodity and money forms—money teaches us to see through all the differences of things to their common, quantitative core, their price—becomes an *objective* characteristic of consumer goods and the marketing ambience of a consumer society. Likewise, with the profusion of commodities a new brand of commodity fetishism takes hold. Marx described a situation where commodities interacting in the market take the place of conscious, social decisions about the production and distribution of wealth. Consumer society worsens this predicament because the intensification of "consumption" means our days often are spent in the pursuit, purchase, enjoyment, payment, replacement, storage, and disposal of commodities, leaving us increasingly absent to others and ourselves.

The mythology of consumer society suggests that shopping releases everyone into an arena of abundant choices and expressions of individuality. This popular notion is supported by the standard economic doctrine of "consumer sovereignty," according to which, individual consumer choices dictate what and how much will be produced. By contrast, Baudrillard insists that consumption is profoundly social and constrained. To identify what is most distinctive of a consumer society, Baudrillard appeals to the contrast between organic and psychosomatic illnesses. Ordinary desire for a specific useful object is like an illness which has a definite organic cause, but desire in a consumer society is like a hysterical illness, fluid and indeterminate. Consumers "go shopping" rather than "go to the store for," say, bread or one-inch nails. Consumer goods are cultural goods or *signs* (which Baudrillard contrasts with *symbols,* which are less malleable); they are coded to constitute a semiotic system through which we communicate and struggle for recognition. Our purchases "make a statement." Here Baudrillard draws both on structuralists like Roland Barthes and Claude Lévi-Strauss and on the fundamental critique of utility theory and *homo economicus* found in Durkheim, Mauss, Bataille, and Veblen. For Baudrillard, an adequate account of the commodity in a consumer society must attend not only to its use value and exchange value but also to its "sign value."

John Kenneth Galbraith described a "revised sequence" in which advertisers create artificial needs to enable producers to find buyers for their outpouring of goods. Baudrillard likes the debunking of the myth of consumer sovereignty here but is nonetheless sharply critical of Galbraith's approach. Baudrillard rejects the "humanist" and utopian assumptions supporting Galbraith's conception that needs can be sorted into true and false (artificial), and he thinks Galbraith naive to want to wish away the "logic of social differentiation" that makes consumption a ceaseless contest for rank. For a more compelling theory, Baudrillard turns to Marx and argues that consumer society represents a new stage of capital's domination. The sale of consumer goods is a necessary moment in the circulation of industrial capital; conversely, consumer goods in a capitalist society are offered for purchase only with a view to furthering the actual, if unspoken, goal of that society, namely, the boundless accumulation of capital. "Individual" consumption, then, belongs to a social activity that is constrained by that activity's goal.

Baudrillard cleverly compares the emergence of the consumer in this century with that of the industrial worker in the previous century. Battles were waged against traditional habits of work and consumption in order to produce the flexible "production force" and "consumption force" required for the expanded production of capital. Baudrillard's point could be put this way: whereas industrialization involved real subsumption of production under capital, "consumer society" amounts to real subsumption of consumption under capital. The hopes, fears, wants, and perceptions of the consumer are as relevant to commercial society as raw materials, parts, and labor. Baudrillard cites a telling remark of former U.S. President Eisenhower: "government best encourages economic growth when it encourages the efforts of individuals and private groups." To Baudrillard, this language of "effort" reveals how serious is the "work" of being a consumer. In contrast to Daniel Bell's view, the consumer's "fun morality" is really only Puritanism in drag.

FROM *SELECTED WRITINGS*

"CONSUMER SOCIETY"

Today, we are everywhere surrounded by the remarkable conspicuousness of consumption and affluence, established by the multiplication of objects, services, and material goods. This now constitutes a fundamental mutation in the ecology of the human species. Strictly speaking, men of wealth are no longer surrounded by other human beings, as they have been in the past, but by *objects*. Their daily exchange is no longer with their fellows, but rather, statistically as a function of some ascending curve, with the acquisition and manipulation of goods and messages: from the rather complex domestic organization with its dozens of technical slaves to the "urban estate" with all the material machinery of communication and professional activity, and the permanent festive celebration of objects in advertising with the hundreds of daily mass media messages; from the proliferation of somewhat obsessional objects to the symbolic psychodrama which fuels the nocturnal objects that come to haunt us even in our dreams. The concepts of "environment" and "ambiance" have undoubtedly become fashionable only since we have come to live in less proximity to other human beings, in their presence and discourse, and more under the silent gaze of deceptive and obedient objects which continuously repeat the same discourse, that of our stupefied (*medusée*) power, of our potential affluence and of our absence from one another.

As the wolf-child becomes wolf by living among them, so are we becoming functional. We are living the period of the objects: that is, we live by their rhythm, according to their incessant cycles. Today, it is we who are observing their birth, fulfillment, and death; whereas in all previous civilizations, it was the object, instrument, and perennial monument that survived the generations of men.

While objects are neither flora nor fauna, they give the impression of being a proliferating vegetation; a jungle where the new savage of modern times has trouble finding the reflexes of civilization. These fauna and flora, which people have produced, have come to encircle and invest them, like a bad science fiction novel. We must quickly describe them as we see and experience them, while not forgetting, even in periods of scarcity or profusion, that they are in actuality the *products of human activity,* and are controlled, not by natural ecological laws, but by the law of exchange value.

> The busiest streets of London are crowded with shops whose show cases display all the riches of the world: Indian shawls, American revolvers, Chinese porcelain, Parisian corsets, furs from Russia and spices from the tropics; but all of these worldly things bear odious white paper labels with Arabic numerals and the laconic symbols LSD. This is how commodities are presented in circulation.[1]

PROFUSION AND DISPLAYS

Accumulation, or *profusion,* is evidently the most striking descriptive feature. Large department stores, with their luxuriant abundance of canned goods, foods, and clothing, are like the primary landscape and the geometrical locus of affluence. Streets with overcrowded and glittering store windows (lighting being the least rare commodity, without which merchandise would merely be what it is), the displays of delicacies, and all the scenes of alimentary and vestimentary festivity, stimulate a magical salivation. Accumulation is more than the sum of its products: the conspicuousness of surplus, the final and magical negation of scarcity, and the maternal and luxurious presumptions of the land of milk and honey. Our markets, our shopping avenues and malls mimic a new-found nature of prodigious fecundity. Those are our Valleys of Canaan where flows, instead of milk and honey, streams of neon on ketchup and plastic—but no matter! There exists an anxious anticipation, not that there may not be enough, but that there is too much, and too much for everyone: by purchasing a portion one in effect appropriates a whole crumbling pyramid of oysters, meats, pears or canned asparagus. One purchases the part for the whole. And this repetitive and metonymic discourse of the consumable, and of commodities is represented, through collective metaphor and as a product of its own surplus, in the image of the *gift,* and of the inexhaustible and spectacular prodigality of the *feast.*

In addition to the stack, which is the most rudimentary yet effective form of accumulation, objects are organized in *displays,* or in *collections.* Almost

450

every clothing store or appliance store presents a gamut of differentiated objects, which call upon, respond to, and refute each other. The display window of the antique store is the aristocratic, luxurious version of this model. The display no longer exhibits an overabundance of wealth but a *range* of select and complementary objects which are offered for the choosing. But this arrangement also invokes a psychological chain reaction in the consumer who peruses it, inventories it, and grasps it as a total category. Few objects today are offered *alone,* without a context of objects to speak for them. And the relation of the consumer to the object has consequently changed: the object is no longer referred to in relation to a specific utility, but as a collection of objects in their total meaning. Washing machine, refrigerator, dishwasher, have different meanings when grouped together than each one has alone, as a piece of equipment (*ustensile*). The display window, the advertisement, the manufacturer, and the brand name here play an essential role in imposing a coherent and collective vision, like an almost inseparable totality. Like a chain that connects not ordinary objects but *signifieds,* each object can signify the other in a more complex super-object, and lead the consumer to a series of more complex choices. We can observe that objects are never offered for consumption in an absolute disarray. In certain cases they can *mimic* disorder to better seduce, but they are always arranged to trace out directive paths. The arrangement directs the purchasing impulse towards networks of objects in order to seduce it and elicit, in accordance with its own logic, a maximal investment, reaching the limits of economic potential. Clothing, appliances, and toiletries thus constitute object *paths,* which establish inertial constraints on the consumer who will proceed *logically* from one object to the next. The consumer will be caught up in a *calculus* of objects, which is quite different from the frenzy of purchasing and possession which arises from the simple profusion of commodities.

451

THE DRUGSTORE

The drugstore is the synthesis of profusion and calculation. The drugstore (or the new shopping malls) makes possible the synthesis of all consumer activities, not least of which are shopping, flirting with objects, idle wandering, and all the permutations of these. In this way, the drugstore is more appropriately representative of modern consumption than the large department store where quantitative centralization leaves little margin for idle exploration. The arrangement of departments and products here imposes a more utilitarian approach to consumption. It retains something of the period of the emergence of department stores, when large numbers of people were beginning to get access to *everyday* consumables. The drugstore has an altogether different function. It does not juxtapose categories of commodities, but practices an *amalgamation of signs* where all categories of goods are considered a partial field in a general consumerism of signs. The cultural center becomes, then, an integral part of the shopping mall. This is not to say that culture is here "prostituted"; that is too simple. It is *culturalized*. Consequently, the commodity (clothing, food, restaurant, etc.) is also culturalized, since it is transformed into a distinctive and idle substance, a luxury, and an item, among others, in the general display of consumables.

> A new art of living, a new way of living, claims advertising, (and fashionable magazines): a pleasant shopping experience, in a single air-conditioned location; one is able to purchase food, products for the apartment or summer home, clothing, flowers, the latest novel, or the latest gadget in a single trip, while husband and children watch a film, and then later you can all dine together on the spot.

Cafe, cinema, book store, auditorium, trinkets, clothing, and many other things can be found in these shopping centers. The drugstore recaptures it all in a kaleidoscopic mode. Whereas the large department store provides a marketplace pageantry for merchandise, the drugstore offers the subtle recital of consumption, where, in fact, the "art" consists in playing on the ambiguity of the object's sign, and sublimating their status and utility as commodity in a play of "ambiance."

The drugstore is neo-culture universalized, where there is no longer any difference between a fine gourmet shop and a gallery of paintings, between *Playboy* and a *Treatise on Paleontology*. The drugstore will be modernized to the point of offering a bit of "gray matter":

452

> Just selling products does not interest us, we would like to supply a little gray matter . . . Three stories, a bar, a dance floor, and shops; trinkets, records, paperbacks, intellectual books, a bit of everything. But we are not looking to flatter the customer. We are actually offering them "something": a language lab on the second floor; records and books where you find the great trends that move our society; music for research; works that explain an epoch. Products accompanied by "gray matter," this is the drugstore, but in a new style, with something more, perhaps a bit of intelligence and human warmth.[2]

A drugstore can become a whole city: such as Parly 2,[3] with its giant shopping center, where "art and leisure mingle with everyday life"; where each residential group encircles a pool club (the center of attraction), a circular church, tennis courts ("the least of things"), elegant boutiques, and a library. Even the smallest ski resort is organized on the "universalist" model of the drugstore, one where all activities are summarized, systematically combined and centered around the fundamental concept of "ambiance." Thus Idleness-on-the-Wasteful[4] simultaneously offers you a complete, polymorphic and combinatorial existence:

> Our Mt Blanc, our Norway spruce forest; our Olympic runs, our "park" for children; our architecture, carved, trimmed, and polished like a work of art; the purity of the air we breathe; the refined ambiance of our Forum, modeled after

Mediterranean cities where, upon return from the ski slopes, life flourishes. Cafes, restaurants, boutiques, skating rinks, night clubs, cinemas, and centers of culture and amusement are all located in the Forum to offer you a life off the slopes that is particularly rich and varied. There is our closed-circuit TV; and our future on a human scale (soon, we will be classified as a work of art by the department of cultural affairs).

We have reached the point where "consumption" has grasped the whole of life; where all activities are sequenced in the same combinatorial mode; where the schedule of gratification is outlined in advance, one hour at a time; and where the "environment" is complete, completely climatized, furnished, and culturalized. In the phenomenology of consumption, the general climatization of life, of goods, objects, services, behaviors, and social relations represents the perfected, "consummated,"[5] stage of evolution which, through articulated networks of objects, ascends from pure and simple abundance to a complete conditioning of action and time, and finally to the systematic organization of ambiance, which is characteristic of the drugstores, the shopping malls, or the modern airports in our futuristic cities.

PARLY 2

"The largest shopping center in Europe."

"Printemps, B.H.V., Dior, Prisunic, Lanvin, Frank et Fils, Hediard, two cinemas, a drugstore, a supermarket, Suma, a hundred other shops, all gathered in a single location!"[6]

In the choice of shops, from groceries to high fashion, there are two requirements: progressive marketing and a sense of aesthetics. The famous slogan "uglyness doesn't sell" is outmoded, and could be replaced by "the beauty of the surroundings is the precondition for a happy life": a two-story structure . . . organized around a central mall, with a main street and promenades on two levels; the reconciliation of the small and large shop and of the modern pace with the idleness of antiquity.

The mall offers the previously unexperienced luxury of strolling between stores which freely (*plain-pièd*) offer their temptations without so much interference as glare from a display window. The central mall, a combination of rue de la Paix and the Champs-Elysées, is adorned by fountains and artificial trees. Kiosks and benches are completely indifferent to seasonal changes and bad weather. An exceptional system of climate control, requiring eight miles of air conditioning ducts, creates a perpetual springtime.

Not only can anything be purchased, from shoestrings to an airline ticket, or located, such as insurance company, cinema, bank or medical service, bridge club and art exhibition, but one need not be the slave of time. The mall, like every city street, is accessible seven days a week, day or night.

Naturally, the shopping mall has instituted, for those who desire, the most modern form of payment: the "credit card." The card frees us from checks, cash, and even from financial difficulties at the end of the month. Henceforth, to pay you present your card and sign the bill. That's all there is to it. Each month you receive a bill which you can pay in full or in monthly installments.

In the marriage between comfort, beauty, and efficiency, Parlysians discover the material conditions of happiness which the anarchy of older cities refuses them.

Here we are at the heart of consumption as the total organization of everyday life, as a complete homogenization. Everything is appropriated and simplified into the translucence of abstract "happiness," simply defined by the resolution of tensions. Expanded to the dimensions of the shopping mall and the futuristic city, the drugstore is the *sublimation* of real life, of objective social life, where not only work and money are abolished, but the seasons disappear as well—the distant vestige of a cycle finally domesticated! Work, leisure, nature, and culture, all previously dispersed, separate, and more or less irreducible activities that produced anxiety and complexity in our real life, and in our "anarchic and archaic" cities, have finally become mixed, massaged, climate controlled, and domesticated into the simple activity of perpetual shopping. All these activities have finally become desexed into a single hermaphroditic ambiance of style! Everything is finally *digested* and reduced to the same homogeneous fecal matter (this occurs, of course, precisely under the sign of the disappearance of *"liquid" currency*, the still too visible symbol of the *real* excretion (*fécalité*) of real life, and of the economic and social contradictions that previously haunted it). All that is past (passed): a *controlled,* lubricated, and *consumed* excretion (*fécalité*) is henceforth transferred into things, everywhere diffused in the indistinguishability of things and of social relations. Just like the Roman Pantheon where the gods of all countries coexisted in a syncretism, in an immense "digest," the super shopping center,[7] our new pantheon, our pandemonium, brings together all the gods, or demons, of consumption. That is to say, every activity, labor, conflict and all the seasons are abolished in the same abstraction. The substance of life, unified in this universal digest, can no longer have any *meaning*: that which produced the dream work, the poetic work, the work of meaning, that is to say the grand schemas of displacement and condensation, the great figures of metaphor and contradiction, which are founded on the lived articulation of distinct elements, is no longer possible. The eternal substitution of homogeneous elements alone remains. There is no longer a symbolic function, but an eternal combinatory of "ambiance" in a perpetual Springtime.

TOWARDS A THEORY OF CONSUMPTION

The autopsy of homo economicus

There is a fable: "There once was a man who lived in Scarcity. After many adventures and a long voyage in the Science of Economics, he encountered the

Society of Affluence. They were married and had many needs." "The beauty of *homo economicus,*" said A. N. Whitehead, "was that we knew exactly what he was searching for." This human fossil of the Golden Age, born in the modern era out of the fortuitous conjunction of Human Nature and Human Rights, is gifted with a heightened principle of formal rationality which leads him to:

1. Pursue his own happiness without the slightest hesitation;
2. Prefer objects which provide him with the maximum satisfaction.

The whole discourse on consumption, whether learned or lay, is articulated on the mythological sequence of the fable: a man, "endowed" with needs which "direct" him towards objects that "give" him satisfaction. Since man is really never satisfied (for which by the way he is reproached), the same history is repeated indefinitely, since the time of the ancient fables.

Some appear to be perplexed: "Among all the unknowns of economic science, needs are the most persistently obscure" (Knight).[8] But this uncertainty does not prevent the advocates of the human sciences, from Marx to Galbraith, and from Robinson Crusoe to Chombart de Lauwe,[9] from faithfully reciting the litany of needs. For the economists, there is the notion of "utility." Utility is the desire to consume a specific commodity, that is to say, to nullify its utility. Need is therefore already embedded in commodities on the market. And preferences are manipulated by the arrangement of products already offered on the market: this is in fact an elastic demand.

For the psychologist there is the theory of "motivation" which is a bit more complex, less "object oriented"[10] and more "instinct oriented,"[11] derived from a sort of ill-defined, preexisting necessity. For the sociologist and psychosociologist, who arrived last on the scene, there is the "sociocultural." The anthropological postulate, of the *individual* endowed with needs and moved by nature to satisfy them, or of a consumer who is free, conscious and aware of his needs, is not put into question by sociologists (although sociologists are suspicious of "deep motivations"). But rather, on the basis of this idealistic postulate, sociologists allow for a "social-dynamics" of needs. They activate models of conformity and competition ("Keeping up with the Joneses")[12] derived from the pressure of peer group, or they elaborate grand "cultural models" which are related to society in general or to history.

Three general positions can be identified: for Marshall, needs are interdependent and rational; for Galbraith, choices are imposed by motivation (we will come back to this); for Gervasi (and others), needs are interdependent, and are the result of learning rather than of rational calculation.

Gervasi: "Choices are not made randomly. They are socially controlled, and reflect the cultural model from which they are produced. We neither produce nor consume just any product: the product must have some meaning in relation to a system of values."[13] This leads to a perspective on consumption in terms of integration: "The goal of the economy is not the maximization of production *for the purposes of the individual,* but the maximization of production in relation to society's value system" (Parsons).[14] Similarly, Duesenbury will claim that the only choice is, in fact, varying one's possessions according to one's position in the social hierarchy. In effect, the differences in choice from one society to another, and the similarity of choices within a society, compels us to view consumer behavior as a social phenomenon. The economist's notion of "rational" choice has been changed into the model of choice as conformity, which is significantly different. Needs are not so much directed at objects, but at values. And the satisfaction of needs primarily expresses an *adherence to these values.* The fundamental, unconscious, and automatic choice of the consumer is to accept the life-style of a particular society (no longer therefore a real choice: the theory of the autonomy and sovereignty of the consumer is thus refuted).

This kind of sociology culminates in the notion of the "standard package,"[15] defined by Riesman as the collection of products and services which constitutes the basic heritage of the middle-class American. Constantly on the rise and indexed on the national standard of living, the standard package is a minimum ideal of a statistical kind, and a middle-class model of conformity. Surpassed by some, only dreamed of by others, it is an *idea* which encapsulates the American way of life.[16] Here again, the "standard package" does not so much refer to the materiality of goods (TV, bathroom, car, etc.) as to *the ideal of conformity.*

All of this sociology gets us nowhere. Besides the fact that the notion of conformity is nothing more than an immense tautology (in this case the middle-class American defined by the "standard package," itself defined by the statistical mean of consumed goods—or sociologically: a particular individual belongs to a particular group which consumes a particular product, and the individual consumes such a product because he or she belongs to such a group), the postulate of formal rationality, which in economics determined the individual's relation to objects, is simply transferred to the relation of the individual to the group. Conformity and satisfaction are interrelated: the resulting similarity in the subject's relation to objects, to a group *posited as a distinct entity,* is established according to the logical principle of equivalence. The concepts of "need" and "norm" respectively are the expressions of this miraculous equivalence.

The difference between the economic notion of "utility" and the sociological notion of conformity is identical to the distinction Galbraith establishes between the pursuit of profit and economic motivation, which is characteristic of the "traditional" capitalist system, on the one hand, and the behavior of identification and adaptation, which is specific to the era of organization and of the technostructure, on the other. The *conditioning of needs* becomes the central issue for both the psycho-sociologists of conformity, and for Galbraith. This is never an issue for economists (and for good reasons), for whom consumers, with their ultimate rational calculation, remain ideally free.

Since Packard's *The Hidden Persuaders* and Dichter's *The Strategy of Desire* (and some others as well),[17] the conditioning of needs (particularly through advertising) has become the favorite theme in the discourse on consumer society. The celebration of affluence and the great lament over "artificial" or "alienated needs," together have fueled the same mass culture, and even the intellectual discourse on the issue. Generally this discourse is grounded in the antiquated moral and social philosophy of a humanist tradition. With Galbraith, however, it develops into a more rigorous economic and political theory. We will therefore remain with him, starting from his two books, *The Affluent Society* and *The New Industrial State*.

Briefly summarizing his position, we could say that the fundamental problem of contemporary capitalism is no longer the contradiction between the "maximization of profit" and the "rationalization of production" (from the point of view of the producer), but rather a contradiction between a virtually unlimited productivity (at the level of the technostructure) and the need to dispose of the product. It becomes vital for the system at this stage to control not only the mechanism of production, but also consumer demand; not only prices, but what will be asked for the price. Either prior to production (polls, market studies) or subsequent to it (advertising, marketing, conditioning), the general idea "is to shift the locus of decision in the purchase of goods from the consumer where it is beyond control to the firm where it is subject to control."[18] Even more generally:

457

> The accommodation of the market behavior of the individual, as well as of social attitudes in general, to the needs of producers and the goals of the technostructure is an inherent feature of the system [it would be more appropriate to say: a *logical* characteristic]. It becomes increasingly important with the growth of the industrial system.[19]

This is what Galbraith calls the "revised sequence," in opposition to the "accepted sequence" whereby the consumer is presumed to have the initiative which will reflect back, through the market, to the manufacturers. Here on the contrary, the manufacturers control behavior, as well as direct and model social attitudes and needs. In its tendencies at least, this is a total dictatorship by the sector of production.

The "revised sequence," at least, has the critical value of undermining the fundamental myth of the classical relation, which assumes that it is the individual who exercises power in the economic system. This emphasis on the power of the individual largely contributed to the legitimation of the organization; all dysfunctions, all nuisances, the inherent contradictions in the order of production are justified, since they enlarge the consumer's domain of sovereignty. On the contrary, it is clear that the whole economic and psychosociological apparatus of market and motivation research, which pretends to uncover the underlying needs of the consumer and the real demand prevailing in the market, exists only to generate a demand for further market opportunities. And it continuously masks this objective by staging its opposite. "Man has become the object of science for man only since automobiles have become harder to sell than to manufacture."[20]

Thus everywhere, Galbraith denounces the boosting of demand by "artificial accelerators," which the technostructure carries out in its imperialist expansion, rendering the stabilization of demand impossible.[21] Income, luxury goods, and surplus labor form a vicious and frantic circle. The infernal round of consumption is based on the celebration of needs that are purported to be "psychological." These are distinguished from "physiological" needs since they are supposedly established through "discretionary income" and the freedom of choice, and consequently manipulable at will. Advertising here of course plays a capital role (another idea which has become conventional) for it appears to be in harmony with commodities and with the needs of the individual. In fact, says Galbraith, advertising is adjusted to the industrial system: "It appears to place a significance on products only in so far as it is important for the system, and it upholds the importance and prestige of the technostructure from the social point of view." Through advertising, the system appropriates social goals for its own gain, and imposes its own objectives as social goals: "What's good for General Motors . . ."

Again we must agree with Galbraith (and others) in acknowledging that the liberty and sovereignty of the consumer are nothing more than a mystification. The well-preserved mystique of satisfaction and individual choice (primarily supported by economists), whereby a "free" civilization reaches its pinnacle, is the very ideology of the industrial system. It justifies its arbitrariness and all sorts of social problems: filth, pollution, and deculturation—in fact the consumer is sovereign in a jungle of ugliness, where *the freedom of choice is imposed on him*. The revised sequence (that is to say the *system* of consumption) thus ideologically supplements and connects with the *electoral system*. The drugstore and the polling booth, the geometric spaces of individual freedom, are also the system's two mammary glands.

We have discussed at length the analysis of the "technostructural" conditioning of needs and consumption because it is currently quite prominent. This kind of analysis, thematized in multiple ways in the pseudo-philosophy of "alienation," constitutes a representation of society which is itself part of consumerism. But it is open to fundamental objections that are all related to its idealist anthropological postulates. For Galbraith individual needs can be stabilized. There exists in human *nature* something like an *economic principle* that would lead man, were it not for "artificial accelerators," to impose limits on his own objectives, on his needs and at the same time on his efforts. In short, there is a tendency towards satisfaction, which is not viewed as optimizing, but rather as "harmonious" and balanced at the level of the individual, a tendency that would allow the individual to express himself in a society that is itself a harmony of collective needs, instead of becoming caught up in the vicious circle of infinite gratifications described above. All this sounds perfectly utopian.

1. Galbraith denounces the "specious" reasoning of economists on the issue of "authentic" or "artificial" gratification: "There is no proof that an expensive woman obtains the same satisfaction from yet another gown as does a hungry man from a hamburger. But there is no proof that she does not. Since it cannot be proven that she does not, her desire, it is held, must be accorded equal standing with that of a poor man for meat."[22] "Absurd," says Galbraith. Yet, not at all (and here classical economists are almost correct in their opposition to him: quite simply, they position themselves to establish the equivalency of satiable demands and thereby avoid all the problems). It is nevertheless the case that, from the perspective of the satisfaction of the consumer, there is no basis on which to define what is "artificial" and what is not. The pleasure obtained from a television or a second home is experienced as "real" freedom. No one experiences this as alienation. Only the intellectual can describe it in this way, on the basis of a moralizing idealism, one which at best reveals him as an alienated moralist.

2. On the "economic principle," Galbraith claims: "What is called economic development consists in no small part in devising strategies to overcome the tendency of men to place limits on their objectives as regards income and thus on their efforts."[23] And he cites the example of Filipino workers in California: "The pressure of debt, and the pressure on each to emulate the most extravagant, quickly converted these happy and easygoing people into a modern and reliable work force."[24] In addition in underdeveloped countries the introduction of Western gadgets is the best form of economic stimulation. This theory, which we could call economic "pressure," or disciplined consumption, and which is connected to forced economic growth, is seductive. It makes it appear that the forced acculturation to the processes of consumption is a *logical development* in the evolution of the industrial system. An evolution which progresses from the discipline of timetables and everyday behavior (to which workers have been subjected since the nineteenth century) to the processes of industrial production. Once having asserted this, we need to explain *why* consumers "take the bait," why they are vulnerable to this strategy. It is much too easy to appeal to "a happy and carefree" disposition, and mechanically to assign responsibility to the system. There is no "natural" inclination to a carefree disposition any more than there is to the work ethic. Galbraith does not take into consideration the logic of social differentiation. Hence, he is forced to represent the individual as a completely passive victim of the system. These processes of class and caste distinctions are basic to the social structure, and are fully operational in "democratic" society. In short, what is lacking is a socio-logic of difference, of status, etc., upon which needs

459

are reorganized in accordance to the *objective* social demand of signs and differences. Thus consumption becomes, not a function of "harmonious" individual satisfaction (hence limited according to the ideal rules of "nature"), but rather an infinite social *activity*. We will eventually come back to this issue.

3. "Needs are in reality the fruits of production," says Galbraith, pleased with himself for having put it so well. Expressed in a clear and demystified tone, this thesis, as he understood it, is nothing more than a subtle version of the natural "authenticity" of certain needs and of the bewitching character of the "artificial." What Galbraith means is that without the system of production a large proportion of needs would not exist. He contends that, in the production of specific goods and services, manufacturers simultaneously produce all the powers of suggestion necessary for the products to be accepted. In fact, they "produce" the need which corresponds to the product. There is here a serious psychological lacuna. Needs are strictly specified in advance in relation to *finite objects*. There is only need for *this* or *that* object. In effect, the psyche of the consumer is merely a display window or a catalog. Certainly once we have adopted this simplistic view of man we cannot avoid the psychological reduction: empirical needs are the specular reflections of empirical objects. At this level, however, the thesis of conditioning is false. We are well aware of how consumers resist such precise injunction, and of how they play with "needs" on a keyboard of objects. We know that advertising is not omnipotent and at times produces opposite reactions; and, we know that in reference to a single "need," objects can be substituted for one another. Hence, at the empirical level, a rather complicated strategy having a psychological and sociological nature intersects with the strategy of production.

The truth is not that "needs are the fruits of production," but that *the system of needs* is *the product of the system of production,* which is a quite different matter. By a system of needs we mean to imply that needs are not produced one at a time, in relation to their respective objects. Needs are produced as a *force of consumption,* and as a general potential reserve (*disponibilité globale*) within the larger framework of productive forces. It is in this sense that we can say that the technostructure is extending its empire. The system of production does not "shackle" the system of pleasure (*jouissance*) to its own ends (strictly speaking, this is meaningless). This hypothesis *denies* autonomy to the system of pleasure and substitutes itself in its place by reorganizing everything into a system of productive forces. We can trace this *genealogy of consumption* in the course of the history of the industrial system:

1. The order of production produces the productive machine/force, a technical system that is radically different from traditional tools.
2. It produces the rationalized productive capital/force, a rational system of investment and circulation that is radically different from previous forms of "wealth" and modes of exchange.

3. It produces the wage-labor force, an abstract and systematized productive force that is radically different from concrete labor and traditional "workmanship."

4. In this way it produces needs, the *system* of needs, the productive demand/force as a rationalized, controlled and integrated whole, complementary to the three others in a process of the total control of productive forces and production processes. As a system, needs are also radically different from pleasure and satisfaction. They are produced *as elements of a system* and not *as a relation between an individual and an object*. In the same sense that labor power is no longer connected to, and even denies, the relation of the worker to the product of his labor, so exchange value is no longer related to concrete and personal exchange, nor the commodity form to actual goods, etc.)

This is what Galbraith does not see and along with him all of the "alienists" of consumption, who persist in their attempts to demonstrate that *people's relation to objects, and their relation to themselves is falsified,* mystified, and manipulated, consuming this myth at the same time as the object. Once having stated the universal postulate of the free and conscious subject (in order to make it reemerge at the end of history as a happy end[ing]),[25] they are forced to attribute all the "dysfunctions" they have uncovered to a diabolic power— in this case to the technostructure, armed with advertising, public relations, and motivation research. This is magical thinking if there is such a thing. They do not see that, taken one at a time, needs are *nothing;* that there is only the system of needs; or rather, that needs are nothing but *the most advanced form of the rational systemization of productive forces at the individual level,* one in which "consumption" takes up the *logical* and necessary relay from production.

This can clear up a certain number of unexplained mysteries for our pious "alienists." They deplore, for example, the fact that puritan ethics are not abandoned in periods of affluence, and that an outdated moral and self-denying Malthusianism has not been replaced by a modern ethos of pleasure. Dichter's *Strategy of Desire* is determined to twist and subvert these old mental structures "from below." And it is true: there has not been a revolution in morals; puritan ideology is still in place. In the analysis of leisure, we will see how it permeates what appear to be hedonistic practices. We can affirm that puritan ethics, and what it implies about sublimation, transcendence, and repression (in a word, morality), *haunts* consumption and needs. It is what motivates it from within and that which gives needs and consumption its compulsive and boundless character. And puritan ideology is itself reactivated by the process of consumption; this is what makes consumption the powerful factor of integration and social control we know it to be. Whereas from the perspective of consumption/pleasure, this remains paradoxical and inexplicable. It can all be explained only if we acknowledge that needs and consumption are in

461

fact an *organized extension of productive forces.* This is not surprising since they both emerged from the productivist and puritan ethics which was the dominant morality of the industrial era. The generalized integration of the "private" individual ("needs," feelings, aspirations, drives) as a productive force can only be accompanied by a generalized extension, at this level, of the schemas of repression, of sublimation, of concentration, of systematization, of rationalization (and of "alienation" of course!), which, for centuries, but especially since the nineteenth century, have governed the structuration (*edification*) of the industrial system.

The Fluidity of Objects and Needs

Until now, the analysis of consumption has been founded on the naive anthropology of *homo economicus,* or at best *homo psychoeconomicus.* It is a theory of needs, of objects (in the fullest sense), and of satisfactions within the ideological extension of classical political economy. This is really not a theory. It is an immense tautology: "I buy this because I need it" is equivalent to the claim that fire burns because of its phlogistic essence. I have shown elsewhere[26] how this empiricist/teleologist position (the individual taken as an end in itself and his or her conscious representations as the logic of events) is identical to the magical speculation of primitive peoples (and of ethnologists) concerning the notion of mana. No theory of consumption is possible at this level: the immediately self-evident, such as an analysis in terms of needs, will never produce anything more than a consumed reflection on consumption.

The rationalist mythology of needs and satisfactions is as naive and "disabled" as is traditional medicine when confronted with psychosomatic or hysterical symptoms. Let us explain: within the field of their objective function objects are not interchangeable, but outside the field of its denotation, an object becomes substitutable in a more or less unlimited fashion. In this field of connotations the object takes on the value of a sign. In this way a washing machine *serves* as equipment and *plays* as an element of comfort, or of prestige, etc. It is the field of play that is specifically the field of consumption. Here all sorts of objects can be substituted for the washing machine as a signifying element. In the logic of signs, as in the logic of symbols, objects are no longer tied to a function or to a *defined* need. This is precisely because objects respond to something different, either to a social logic, or to a logic of desire, where they serve as a fluid and unconscious field of signification.

Relatively speaking, objects and needs are here interchangeable just like the symptoms of hysterical or psychosomatic conversion. They obey the same logic of shifts, transferals, and of apparently arbitrary and infinite convertibility. When an illness is *organic,* there is a necessary relation between the symptom and the organ (in the same way that in its role as equipment there is a necessary relation between the object and its function). In the hysterical or psychosomatic conversion the symptom, like the sign, is (relatively) arbitrary.

Migraine, colitis, lumbago, angina, or general fatigue form a chain of somatic signifiers along which the symptom "parades." This is just like the interconnection of object/signs, or of object/symbols, along which parades, not needs (which remain tied to the object's rational goal), but desire, and some other determination, derived from an unconscious social logic.

If we trace a need to a particular locus, that is, if we satisfy it by taking it literally, as it presents itself, as a need for a *specific* object, we would make the same error as if we performed traditional therapy on an organ where the symptom is localized. Once healed it would reappear elsewhere.

The world of objects and of needs would thus be a world of *general hysteria.* Just as the organs and the functions of the body in hysterical conversion become a gigantic paradigm which the symptom replaces and refers to, in consumption objects become a vast paradigm designating another language through which something else speaks. We could add that this evanescence and continual mobility reaches a point where it becomes impossible to determine the specific objectivity of needs, just as it is impossible in hysteria to define the specific objectivity of an illness, for the simple reason that it does not exist. The flight from one signifier to another is no more than the surface reality of a *desire,* which is insatiable because it is founded on a lack. And this desire, which can never be satisfied, signifies itself locally in a succession of objects and needs.

In view of the repeated and naive confusion one finds when faced with the continual forward flight and unlimited renewal of needs—which in fact is irreconcilable with a rationalist theory claiming that a satisfied need produces a state of equilibrium and a resolution of tensions—we can advance the following sociological hypothesis (although it would be interesting and essential to articulate both desire and the social): if we acknowledge that a need is not a need for a particular object as much as it is a "need" for difference (the *desire for social meaning*), only then will we understand that satisfaction can never be *fulfilled,* and consequently that there can never be a *definition* of needs.

The fluidity of desire is supplemented by the fluidity of differential meanings (is there a metaphoric relation between the two?). Between them specific and finite needs only become meaningful as the focus of successive conversions. In their substitutions they signify, yet simultaneously veil, the true domain of signification—that of lack and difference—which overwhelms them from all sides.

The Denial of Pleasure

The acquisition of objects is *without an object* ("objectless craving,"[27] for David Riesman). Consumer behavior, which appears to be focused and directed at the object and at pleasure, in fact, responds to quite different objectives: the metaphoric or displaced expression of desire, and the production of a code of social values through the use of differentiating signs. That which is determinant is not the function of individual interest within a corpus of objects, but rather the specifically social function of exchange, communication and distribution of values within a corpus of signs.

The truth about consumption is that it is *a function of production* and not a function of pleasure, and therefore, like material production, is not an individual function but one that is *directly and totally* collective. No theoretical analysis is possible without the reversal of the traditional givens: otherwise, no matter how we approach it, we revert to a phenomenology of pleasure.

Consumption is a system which assures the regulation of signs and the integration of the group: it is simultaneously a morality (a system of ideological values) and a system of communication, a structure of exchange. On this basis, and on the fact that this social function and this structural organization by far transcend individuals and are imposed on them according to an unconscious social constraint, we can formulate a theoretical hypothesis which is neither a recital of statistics nor a descriptive metaphysics.

According to this hypothesis, paradoxical though it may appear, consumption is defined as *exclusive of pleasure*. As a social logic, the system of consumption is established on the basis of the denial of pleasure. Pleasure no longer appears as an objective, as a rational end, but as the individual rationalization of a process whose objectives lie elsewhere. Pleasure would define consumption *for itself*, as autonomous and final. But consumption is never thus. Although we experience pleasure for ourselves, when we consume we never do it on our own (the isolated consumer is the carefully maintained illusion of the *ideological* discourse on consumption). Consumers are mutually implicated, despite themselves, in a general system of exchange and in the production of coded values.

In this sense, consumption is a system of meaning, like language, or like the kinship system in primitive societies.

A Structural Analysis?

In the language of Lévi-Strauss we can say that the social aspect of consumption is not derived from what appears to be of the realm of nature (satisfaction or pleasure), but rather from the essential processes by which it separates itself from nature (what defines it as a code, an institution, or a system of organization). Consumption can be compared with the kinship system which is not determined in the final analysis by consanguinity and filiation, by a natural given, but rather by the arbitrary regulation of classification. In the final analysis, the system of consumption is based on a code of signs (object/signs) and differences, and not on need and pleasure.

Rules of marriage represent the multiple ways of assuring the circulation of women within the social group. It is the replacement of a consanguineous system of relations of biological origin by a sociological system of alliance. Thus, rules of marriage and kinship systems can be seen as a kind of language, that is a set of operations intended to assure, between individuals and groups, a certain kind of communication. The same is true for consumption: a socio-logical system of signs (the level characteristic of consumption) is substituted for a bio-functional and bio-economic system of commodities and products (the biological level of needs and subsistence). And the essential function of the regulated circulation of objects and commodities is the same as that of women and words. It is designed to assure a certain type of communication.

We will come back to the differences between these various types of "lan-guages:" they are essentially related to the mode of production of the values exchanged and to the type of division of labor associated with it. Commodi-ties obviously are produced, whereas women are not, and they are produced differently to words. Nevertheless, at the level of distribution, commodities and objects, like words and once like women, constitute a global, arbitrary, and coherent system of signs, a *cultural* system which substitutes a social order of values and classifications for a contingent world of needs and pleasures, the natural and biological order.

This is not to claim that there are no needs, or natural utilities, etc. The point is to see that consumption, as a concept specific to contemporary soci-ety, is not organized along these lines. For this is true of all societies. What is sociologically significant for us, and what marks our era under the sign of consumption, is precisely the generalized reorganization of this primary level in a system of signs which appears to be a particular mode of transition from nature to culture, perhaps *the* specific mode of our era.

Marketing, purchasing, sales, the acquisition of differentiated commodities and object/signs—all of these presently constitute our language, a code with which our entire society *communicates* and speaks of and to itself. Such is the present day structure of communication: a language (*langue*) in opposition to which individual needs and pleasures are but the *effects of speech (parole).*

465

THE FUN-SYSTEM, OR THE CONSTRAINT OF PLEASURE[28]

The best evidence that pleasure is not the basis or the objective of consump-tion is that nowadays pleasure is constrained and institutionalized, not as a right or enjoyment, but as the citizen's *duty.*

The puritans considered themselves, considered their actual being, to be an enterprise to make profit for the greater glory of God. Their "personal" quali-ties, and their "character," which they spent their lives producing, were capital to be invested wisely, and managed without speculation or waste. Conversely, yet in the same way, man-as-consumer considers the *experience of pleasure an obligation,* like an *enterprise of pleasure and satisfaction;* one is obliged to be happy, to be in love, to be adulating/adulated, seducing/seduced, participating, eu-phoric, and dynamic. This is the principle of the maximization of existence by the multiplication of contacts and relations, by the intensive use of signs and objects, and by the systematic exploitation of all the possibilities of pleasure.

The consumer, the modern citizen, cannot evade the constraint of happiness and pleasure, which in the new ethics is equivalent to the traditional constraint of labor and production. Modern man spends less and less of life in production, and more and more in the continuous production and creation of personal needs and of personal well-being. He must constantly be ready to actualize all of his potential, all of his capacity for consumption. If he forgets, he will be gently and instantly reminded that he has no right not to be happy. He is therefore not passive: he is engaged, and must be engaged, in continuous activity. Otherwise he runs the risk of being satisfied with what he has and of becoming asocial.

A *universal curiosity* (a concept to be exploited) has as a consequence been reawakened in the areas of cuisine, culture, science, religion, sexuality, etc. "Try Jesus!" says an American slogan. *Everything* must be tried: since man as consumer is haunted by the fear of "missing" something, any kind of pleasure. One never knows if such and such a contact, or experience (Christmas in the Canaries, eel in whisky, the Prado, LSD, love Japanese style) will not elicit a "sensation." It is no longer desire, nor even "taste" nor a specific preference which are at issue, but a generalized curiosity driven by a diffuse obsession, a *fun morality*,[29] whose imperative is enjoyment and the complete exploitation of all the possibilities of being thrilled, experiencing pleasure, and being gratified.

Consumption as the Rise and Control of New Productive Forces

466

Consumption is a sector that only *appears* anomic, since, following the Durkheimian definition, it is not governed by formal rules. It appears to surrender to the individualistic immoderation and contingency of needs. Consumption is not, as one might generally imagine (which is why economic "science" is fundamentally averse to discussing it), an indeterminate marginal sector where an individual, elsewhere constrained by social rules, would finally recover, in the "private" sphere, a margin of freedom and personal play when left on his own. Consumption is a collective and active behavior, a constraint, a morality, and an institution. It is a complete system of values, with all that the term implies concerning group integration and social control.

Consumer society is also the society for the apprenticeship of consumption, for the social indoctrination of consumption. In other words, this is a new and specific mode of *socialization* related to the rise of new productive forces and the monopolistic restructuration of a high output economic system.

Credit here plays a determining role, even though it only has a marginal impact on the spending budget. The idea is exemplary. Presented under the guise of gratification, of a facilitated access to affluence, of a hedonistic mentality, and of "freedom from the old taboos of thrift, etc.," credit is in fact the systematic socioeconomic indoctrination of forced economizing and an economic calculus for generations of consumers who, in a life of subsistence, would have otherwise escaped the manipulation of demands and would have been unexploitable as a force of consumption. Credit is a disciplinary process which extorts savings and regulates demand—just as wage labor was a rational process in the extortion of labor power and in the increase of productivity. The case cited by Galbraith, of the Puerto Ricans who, having been passive and carefree, were transformed into a modern labor force by being motivated to consume, is striking evidence of the tactical value of a regulated, forced, instructed, and stimulated consumption within the modern socioeconomic order. As Marc Alexandre demonstrates, this is achieved through credit (and the discipline and budget constraints it imposes), by the mental indoctrination of the masses to a planned calculus and to "basic" capitalist investment and behavior.[30] The rational and disciplinary ethics, which according to Weber was at the origin of modern capitalist productivism, in a way, has come to inhabit a whole domain which previously escaped it.

We don't realize how much the current indoctrination into systematic and organized consumption is *the equivalent and the extension, in the twentieth century, of the great indoctrination of rural populations into industrial labor, which occurred throughout the nineteenth century.* The same process of rationalization of productive forces, which took place in the nineteenth century in the sector of *production* is accomplished, in the twentieth century, in the sector of *consumption.* Having socialized the masses into a labor force, the industrial system had to go further in order to fulfill itself and to socialize the masses (that is, to control them) into a force of consumption. The small investors or the sporadic consumers of the pre-war era, who were free to consume or not, no longer had a place in the system.

The ideology of consumption would have us believe that we have entered a new era, and that a decisive "human revolution" separates the grievous and heroic Age of Production from the euphoric Age of Consumption, where justice has finally been restored to Man and to his desires. But there is no truth in this. Production and Consumption are *one and the same grand logical process in the expanded reproduction of the productive forces and of their control.* This imperative, which belongs to the system, enters in an inverted form into the mentality, ethics, and everyday ideology, and that is its ultimate cunning: in the form of the liberation of needs, of individual fulfillment, or pleasure, and of affluence, etc. The themes of expenditure, pleasure, and non-calculation ("Buy now, pay later") have replaced the "puritan" themes of thrift, work, and patrimony. But this is only the appearance of a human revolution. In fact, this is the substitution of a new system of values for one that has become (relatively) ineffective: an internal substitution in a system essentially unchanged; a substitution within the guidelines of a more general process. What could have been a new finality, has become, stripped of any real content, an imposed mediation of the system's reproduction.

467

Consumer needs and satisfactions are productive forces which are now constrained and rationalized like all the others (labor power, etc.). From whichever perspective we chose (briefly) to examine it, consumption appeared quite opposite to the way we experience it as ideology, that is, as a dimension of constraint:

1. Governed by the *constraint of signification,* at the level of the structural analysis.
2. Governed by the *constraint of production* and the cycle of production in the analysis of strategies (socio-economico-political).

Thus, affluence and consumption are not the realization of Utopia, but a new objective state, governed by the same fundamental processes, yet overdetermined by a new morality. This corresponds to a *new* sphere of productive forces in the process of directed reintegration within the same expanded system. In this sense there is no objective "progress" (nor *a fortiori* "revolution"): it is simply the same thing and something else. What in fact results from the total *ambiguity* of affluence and consumption, which can be observed at the level of daily events, is that these are always lived as *myth* (the assumption of happiness, beyond history and morality), while they are simultaneously *endured as an objective process of adaptation* to a new type of collective behavior.

On the issue of consumption as a civic restraint, Eisenhower stated in 1958: "In a free society, government best encourages economic growth when it encourages the *efforts* of individuals and private groups. The government will never spend money as profitably as an individual tax-payer would have were he freed from the burden of taxation." He implies that consumption, not being directly imposed, could effectively replace taxation as a social levy. "With nine billion dollars of fiscal deductions," adds *Time* magazine, "the consumer went to two million retail stores in search of prosperity . . . They realized that they could increase economic growth by replacing their fans with air conditioners. They *ensured the boom* of 1954 by purchasing five million miniaturized television sets, a million and a half electric knives, etc." In short, they performed their civic duty. "Thrift is un-American" said William H. Whyte.[31]

Regarding needs as productive forces, the equivalent in the heroic epoch to "manual labor as natural resource," an advertisement for movie advertising claims:

> The cinema allows you, thanks to its large screen, to present your product on site: colors, forms, conditioning. Each week 3,500,000 spectators frequent the 2,500 cinemas in our advertising network; 67 per cent of them are between the ages of fifteen and thirty-five. These are consumers *in the fullness of their needs,* who want and are able to purchase . . .

Exactly, they are individuals in full (labor) force.

The Logistic Function of the Individual

> The individual serves the industrial system not by supplying it with savings and the resulting capital; he serves it by consuming its products. On no other matter, religious, political, or moral, is he so elaborately and skillfully and expensively instructed.[32]

The system needs people as workers (wage labor), and as economizers (taxes, loans, etc.), but increasingly they are needed *as consumers*. Labor productivity is increasingly replaced by the productivity obtained through technological and organizational improvements and increasingly investments are being redirected to the level of the corporation.[33] *But as consumer, the individual has become necessary and practically irreplaceable.* In the process of the extension of the techno-bureaucratic structures we can predict a bright future and the eventual realization of the individualist system of values, whose center of gravity will be displaced from the entrepreneur and the individual investor, figurehead of competitive capitalism, to the individual consumer, subsequently encompassing all individuals.

At the competitive stage, capitalism still sustained itself, for better or for worse, with an individualist system of values bastardized with altruism. The fiction of a social, altruistic morality (inherited from traditional spiritualism) "softened" the antagonisms of social relations. The "moral law" resulted from individual antagonisms, just as "the law of the market" resulted from competitive processes; they preserved the fiction of stability. For a long time we have believed in individual salvation for the community of all Christians, and in individual rights limited only by the rights of others. But this is impossible today. In the same way that "free enterprise" has virtually disappeared giving way to monopolistic, state and bureaucratic control, so the altruist ideology is no longer sufficient to reestablish a minimum of social integration. No other collective ideology has come to replace these values. Only the collective constraint of the state has thwarted the exacerbations of multiple individualisms. From this arises the profound contradiction of civil and political society as "consumer society": the system is forced to produce more and more consumer individualism, which at the same time it is forced to repress more and more severely. This can only be resolved by an increase in altruistic ideology (which is itself bureaucratized, a "social lubrication" through concern, social reform, the gift, the handout, welfare propaganda and humane relations). But this incorporation of altruism in the system of consumption will not be sufficient to stabilize it.

Consumption is therefore a powerful element in social control (by atomizing individual consumers); yet at the same time it requires the intensification of *bureaucratic control* over the processes of consumption, which is subsequently heralded, with increased intensity, as the *reign of freedom*. We will never escape it.

469

Traffic and the automobile provide the classic example of this contradiction, where there is the unlimited promotion of individual consumption; the desperate call to collective responsibility and social morality; and increasingly severe restraints. The paradox is the following: one can not simultaneously remind the individual that "the level of consumption is the just measure of social merit" and expect of him or her a different type of social responsibility, since in the act of personal consumption the individual already fully assumes a social responsibility. Once again, consumption is *social labor*. The consumer is conscripted and mobilized as a laborer at this level *as well* (today perhaps just as much as at the level of "production"). All the same, one should not ask the "laborer of consumption" to sacrifice his income (his individual satisfactions) for the collective good. Somewhere in their social subconsciousness, these millions of consumers have a sort of practical intuition of their new status as alienated laborer. The call for public solidarity is immediately perceived as a mystification. Their tenacious resistance here is simply a reflex of *political* defense. The consumer's "fixated egoism" is also the gross subconscious re-cognition of being the new exploited subject of modern times, despite all the non-sense about affluence and well-being. The fact that resistance and "egoism" drives the system to insoluble contradictions, to which it responds by reinforcing constraints, only confirms that consumption is a gigantic *political* field, whose analysis, as well as that of production, is still to be achieved.

The entire discourse on consumption aims to transform the consumer into the Universal Being, the general, ideal, and final incarnation of the human species. It attempts also to make of consumption the premise for "human liberation," to be attained in lieu of, and despite the failures of, social and political liberation. The consumer is in no way a universal being, but rather a social and political being, and a productive force. As such, the consumer revives fundamental *historical* problems: those concerning the ownership of the means of consumption (and no longer the means of production), those regarding economic responsibility (responsibility towards the *content* of production), etc. There is here the potential for a deep crisis and for new contradictions.

Ego Consumans

Nowhere, up to the present day, have these contradictions been consciously manifested, except perhaps in a few strikes among American housewives and in the sporadic destruction of commodities (May 1968, the *No Bra Day*[34] when American women publicly burned their bras). "What does the consumer represent in the modern world? Nothing. What could he be? Everything, or almost everything. Because he stands alone next to millions of solitary individuals, he is at the mercy of all other interests."[35] One must add that the individualist ideology is an important element here (even though, as we saw, its contradictions are latent): since it affects the collective domain of social labor, exploitation by *dispossession* (of labor power), it produces (at a

certain point) an effective solidarity. And this leads to a (relative) class consciousness. Whereas the directed *acquisition* of objects and commodities is in-
dividualizing, atomizing, and dehistoricizing. As a producer, and as a consequence of the division of labor, each laborer presupposes all others: exploitation is for everyone. As a consumer, humans become again solitary, cellular,
and at best *gregarious* (for example in a family viewing TV, the crowd at a sta-
dium or in a movie house, etc.) The structures of consumption are simultaneously fluid and enclosed. Can we imagine a coalition of drivers against car
registration? Or a collective opposition to television? Even if every one of
the million viewers is opposed to television advertising, advertisements will
nevertheless be shown. That is because consumption is primarily organized
as a discourse to oneself, and has a tendency to play itself out, with its gratifications and deceptions, in this minimal exchange. The object of consumption isolates. The private sphere lacks concrete negativity because it is collapsed on objects which themselves lack negativity. It is structured from outside by the system of production whose strategy is no longer ideological at
this level, but still political; whose strategy of desire invests the materiality of
our existence with its monotony and distractions. Or, as we saw, the object
of consumption creates distinctions as a stratification of statuses: if it no
longer isolates, it differentiates; it *collectively assigns* the consumers a place in
relation to a code, without so much as giving rise to any *collective solidarity*
(but quite the opposite).

In general then consumers, as such, are unconscious and unorganized, just
as workers may have been at the beginning of the nineteenth century. As such
consumers have been glorified, flattered, and eulogized as "public opinion,"
that mystical, providential, and *sovereign* reality. Just as The People is glorified
by democracy provided they remain as such (that is provided they do not interfere on the political or social scene), the sovereignty of consumers is also
recognized ("powerful consumers," according to Katona),[36] provided they do
not try to act in this way on the social scene. The People—these are the laborers, provided they are unorganized; the Public, or public opinion—these
are the consumers, provided they are content to consume.

471

Notes

1. Karl Marx, *Contribution to a Critique of Political Economy* (NY: International Publishers, 1970) p. 87. [Trans.]
2. Baudrillard appears to be quoting from an advertising brochure here, and elsewhere in the text. But at times they sound contrived, and can easily be read as fictional. [Trans.]
3. Parly 2: a planned community (etymologically and geographically) between
Paris and Orly (the airport in the southern suburb of Paris). Baudrillard offers his own
description in the next section. [Trans.]
4. "Idleness-on-the-Wasteful" would be one anglo-saxon version of "Flaine-la-
Prodigue," Baudrillard's parody of suburban communities around Paris. "Flaine": per-

haps the conjunction of "flemme" (laziness) and "flâneur" (idle/loafer); "Prodigue" (extravagant/wasteful). [Trans.]

5. See Chapter 2, note 24. [Trans.]

6. Printemps, B. H.V., Dior, Prisunic, Lanvin, Frank et Fils are department stores. [Trans.]

7. Originally in English. [Trans.]

8. Knight: unable to identify the source of this quotation. [Trans.]

9. A French sociologist, author of *Pour une sociologie des aspirations* (Paris: Denoël, 1969). [Trans.]

10. Originally in English. [Trans.]

11. Ibid.

12. Ibid.

13. The translator is unable to identify the source of this quotation.

14. The translator is unable to identify the source of this quotation from Talcott Parsons.

15. Originally in English. [Trans.]

16. A study in *Sélection du Reader's Digest* (A. Piatier: *Structure et perspectives de la consommation européenne*), found that consumption in Europe is the activity of a minority, in contrast to the large middle class in the USA, a consuming elite (the As) which serves as a model for a majority that does not yet have access to this display of luxury (sports car, stereo system, summer home), without which there are no Europeans worthy of the name.

17. For these references see chapter 2, nn. 9 and 11. [Trans.]

18. John Kenneth Galbraith, *The New Industrial State* (New York: Signet, 1967) p. 215. [Trans.]

19. Ibid., p. 222.

20. The translator and editor are unable to locate this wonderful reference from Galbraith.

21. This is the "anticoagulant" effect of advertising (Elgozy).

22. Galbraith, *The New Industrial State,* p. 281. [Trans.]

23. Ibid., p. 279. [Trans.]

24. Ibid., p. 280. [Trans.]

25. 'Happy end' was originally in English. [Trans.]

26. "The ideological genesis of needs," in *For a Critique of the Political Economy of the Sign,* trans. Charles Levin (St Louis: Telos Press, 1981).

27. Originally in English. [Trans.]

28. 'Fun-system' was originally in English. [Trans.]

29. Originally in English. [Trans.]

30. Marc Alexandre, "Sur la société de consommation," *La Nef,* 37.

31. Originally in English. The translator is unable to identify the source of this quotation.

32. *The New Industrial State,* p. 49. [Trans.]

33. Cf. Paul Fabra's article in *Le Monde,* June 26, 1969, "Les superbenefices et la monopolization de l'epargne par les grandes entreprises."

34. Originally in English. [Trans.]

35. *Le Cooperateur,* 1965.

36. Originally in English from George Katona, *The Mass Consumption Society* (New York: McGraw-Hill, 1964). The translator is unable to identify the page of this citation.

For Further Reading

Baudrillard, Jean. *America* (London: Verso, 1989).

———. *Fatal Strategies*. Translated by Philip Beitchman and W. G. J. Niesluchuowski (New York: Semiotext(e), 1990).

———. *For a Critique of the Political Economy of the Sign*. Translated by Charles Levin (St. Louis: Telos Press, 1981).

———. *Jean Baudrillard: Selected Writings*. Edited, with an introduction, by Mark Poster. (Stanford: Stanford Univ. Press, 1988).

———. *The Mirror of Production*. Translated by Mark Poster (St. Louis: Telos Press, 1975).

———. *Simulations* (New York: Simiotexte(e), 1983).

———. *Symbolic Exchange and Death*. Translated by Iain Hamilton Grant (London: SAGE Publications, 1993).

Barthes, Roland. *The Fashion System*. Translated by Richard Howard and Matthew Ward (London: Cape, 1985).

Berry, Philippa, ed. *Shadow of Spirit* (New York: Routledge, 1992).

Bourdieu, Pierre. *Distinction: A Social Critique of the Judgement of Taste*. Translated by Richard Nice (Cambridge: Harvard University Press, 1984).

Callinicos, A. *Against Postmodernism, a Marxist Critique* (Cambridge, England: Polity, 1989).

Certeau, M. *The Practice of Everyday Life* (Berkeley: Univ. of California Press, 1984).

Debord, Guy de. *The Society of the Spectacle*. Translated by Donald Nicholson-Smith (New York: Zone Books, 1994).

Deleuze, G., and F. Guattari. *Anti-Oedipus* (New York: Viking, 1977).

Descombes, V. *Modern French Philosophy* (Cambridge Univ. Press, 1980).

Ewen, Stuart. *Captains of Consciousness: Advertising and the Social Roots of the Consumer Culture* (New York: McGraw-Hill, 1976).

Fine, Ben, and Ellen Leopold. *The World of Consumption* (London: Routledge, 1985).

Galbraith, John Kenneth. *The Affluent Society* 4th Edition. (New York: American Library, 1985).

———. *The New Industrial State* 4th ed. (Boston: Houghton Mifflin, 1985).

Gane, Mike. *Baudrillard's Bestiary: Baudrillard and Culture* (New York: Routledge, 1991).

———, ed. *Baudrillard Live: Selected Interviews* (London: Routledge, 1993).

———. *Baudrillard: Critical and Fatal Theory* (London: Routledge, 1991).

Katona, George. *The Mass Consumption Society* (New York: McGraw-Hill, 1964).

Habermas, Jürgen. "Modernity versus post modernity" *New German Critique* 22 (1981): 3–14.

Kellner, Douglas. *Jean Baudrillard: From Marxism to Postmodernism* (Stanford: Stanford University Press, 1989).

Norris, Christopher. "Lost in the funhouse: Baudrillard and the politics of post-modernism" *Textual Practice* 3:3 (1989): 360–387.

Rojek, Chris, and Bryan S. Turner, eds. *Forget Baudrillard?* (New York: Routledge, 1993).

Simons, Herbert W., ed. *After Postmodernism* (London: SAGE Publications, 1994).

INDEX

action, 418
  contrasted with behavior, 417–418,
    422–424
  contrasted with work, 71, 417–419
Adorno, Theodor, 319, 419
alienation, *see also* gigantism, 18, 25 n.
    36, 224–234, 239, 255, 264–273,
    274–282, 333, 345–346, 349–350,
    387, 450, 470
Ambrose, St., 92–94, 97, 99
Aquinas, St. Thomas, 12, 17, 87–116
  on "retail trade," 100–102
  on capital, 89, 349
  on fair trade, 94–102
  on property, 91–94, 174–175
  on simony, 108–115
  on the commodity form, 89, 174–
    175
  on usury, 102–107
Arendt, Hannah, 417–428
Aristotle, 5, 7, 11, 22, 23–24, n. 18, 26 n.
    53 and 55, 28 n. 70, 41, 69–86, 118,
    155–156, 173–174, 205, 254, 318,
    335, 350, 367
  and Aquinas, 87–89, 89–116 *passim.*,
    174–175
  contra utility theory, 71
  on capital, 11, 70
  on *homo economicus,* 70–71
  on Plato's *Republic,* 78–84
  on the commodity form, 70–71,
    174–175
  on the value form, 7, 70, 272
Augustine, St., 87–88, 93–94, 96, 98,
    101, 109, 111
avarice, see greed

Bailey, George, 10
barter, *see also* gift exchange, 70, 73–74, 337–338
  contrasted with gift exchange, 365–367
  propensity to, 182–185
Barthes, Roland, 448
Bataille, Georges, 373–381, 448
Baudrillard, Jean, 11, 24 n. 28 and 34, 384, 430, 447–473
Bell, Daniel, 9, 25 n. 39, 429–446, 449
Bentham, Jeremy, 27 n. 62, 255, 291, 297–298
Berkeley, George, 216
Bible, the, 14, 19, 88, 92–116 *passim.*, 135, 137, 141, 353
Black, R.D. Collison, 27 n. 63 and 66
blasé attitude, 334, 339–341
Bloom, Alan, 14
Booth, William James, 28 n. 71
bourgeois world-view, 429–446 *passim.*
Brecht, Bertolt, 8
buyers and sellers, *see also* circulation of commodities, persons, contracts, wage labor, simony, 15, 21, 94–102 *passim.*, 110, 255, 272, 282–291, 334

Cadillac Man, 12
calling, 353, 358, 362–363, 409
Campbell, Martha, 23 n. 4
Camus, Albert, 384
capital accumulation, 4, 148, 185–189, 285–287, 318, 350, 398–399, 449
  duty to, see "the spirit of capitalism"
  its irrationality, 15–17, 349–350, 353, 398–399, 430,
capital, 1, 3, 13
  Aquinas on, 89, 349
  Aristotle on, 11, 292–293 n. 3
  as an automatic subject, 286–287
  as definite social form, 7, 15, 185–188, 350, 467
  contrasted with simple commodities, 282–287 *passim.*
  defined, 185–188, 285–287, 359
  fetish, 281, 286–287
  homogenizing effects of, 453–454
  industrial, 287
  interest-bearing, *see also* usury, 3, 70, 287, 383–384

Marx on, 256–293 *passim.*
  merchant, 3, 150, 191, 282, 287, 359
  Smith on, 185–188
Capital, 7, 254–255, 256–293
capitalism, 254, 256–293 *passim.*, 319, 334, 349–350, 354, 363, 373, 383–384, 390, 401–402, 444–445, 467, 469
  Adam Smith's advocacy of, 173–176, 297
  ancient vs. modern, 352–363 *passim.*
  as epoch making, 289, 293 n. 5
  contradictions of, 9, 430, 430–446 *passim.*, 457, 469– 470
  ideological breakdown of, 441–445, 469
  possible overcoming of, 7, 28 n. 71, 117–132 *passim.*, 277, 279–282, 291–292, 354, 391–392
Capra, Frank, 10
Castoriadis, Cornelius, 384
Chaplin, Charlie, 174
Christianity, 147–148, 155, 223, 227, 268, 280–281, 286–287, 292, 349–350, 362–363, 366, 429–430, 469
  Calvinism, 353, 409
  doctrines summarized, 87–88
Chrysostom, St. John, 88, 100–101
circulation of commodities, 16, 70, 275–276
  and capitalism, 23 n. 5, 255, 282–287
  contrasted with Christian love, 88
civil society, *see also* modern commerce, 223–225, 225–251 *passim.*
Clarke, Simon, 24 n. 19, 28 n. 68
class relations, 7, 24 n. 21, 40, 119, 121–122, 129–130, 156–157, 169, 176, 181, 188, 197–202, 205–206, 326–328, 245, 255, 298, 278–279, 385, 392, 426 n. 3, 440, 470–471
  and factions, 208–209
  estates, 234–239
classical political economy, *see also* Smith, Adam; Ricardo; Marx, 69
  and philosophy, 215–216, 335
  and "the social," 422–424, 426 n. 3 and 4, 426 n. 4
  Baudrillard's critique of, 454–462, 466
Club of Rome report, 25 n. 40
College of Sociology, 374

colonization, 8, 224–225, 247, 298
commerce, *see also* modern commerce,
    and the traditional, 3, 8–10, 14,
        39–41, 346, 355–363, 366, 430–446
        passim., 441–442
    bounds of, 11–13, 288
    emergence of, 39–41, 70
    in contrast to commercialism, 10–13,
        24 n. 29
    in relation to capitalism, 3–5, 281,
        282–291, 289, 334
    its side effects, 8–9
    marginalization of, 1, 4, 39, 280
commercial society, *see also* modern
    commerce, capitalism,
    defined, 3–4
    future of, 9–10
    not commercial to the bone, 1, 13
commercialism,
    as opposed to commerce, 10–13
commodity form, 1, 13, 173, 175, 273,
    275, 277, 448
    generalization of, 3–4, 13, 22–23, n. 3,
        191–197, 244, 255, 272, 277, 289,
        293 n. 5, 337–340, 387
    Marx on, 256–282
communism, *see also* Utopia, 77–84 *pas-
    sim.*, 118, 118–132 *passim.*, 384–5,
    388, 391, 400, 422, 426 n. 4
communitarianism, *see also* "tribal
    ethics," 5
conformism, *see also* individuality,
    420–422, 443, 456,
"conspicuous consumption," 9,
    317–318, 326–331, 447, 449–454,
consumer society, 118, 429–430,
    439–445, 447–449, 449–473 *pas-
    sim.*
    coding of commodities, 451,
        459–460, 462–465
    defined, 465
    "force of consumption," 460–461,
        466–468
    puritanism of, *see also* "fun morality,"
        449, 461–470
consumer sovereignty, 448, 456
    Galbraith's "revised sequence" cri-
        tique, 457–462
consumer, 2–3, 148, 233, 246–247, 254,
    304–305, 318, 330, 345–346,
    447–449, 451, 447–473 *passim.*

contract, *see also* person, wage labor, jus-
    tice, 5, 40, 134, 183–184
    international, 246
    restrictions on, 310,
    social, 135–145 *passim.*
corporations, 224, 229, 247–251
credit, 383–384, 387–390, 453–454
    as consumer indoctrination, 466–467
Critique of Political Economy, 292
Crusoe, Robinson, 278–279, 455
culture, *see also* modernism, postmod-
    ernism, 429–430, 431–446 *passim.*
    contrasted with social structure,
        431–446 *passim.*
custom, *see also* traditionalism, 8, 14,
    111–115, 148, 175, 240, 277, 330,
    334
customer, 2–3, 8, 337, 344, 360–361
Cynicism, 18, 233,

Darwin, Charles, 318
de Jouvenal, Bertrand, 415 n. 15
Debord, Guy, 11, 24 n. 34, 384
Diogenes, 18, 233
Discourse on the Origins of Inequality, 27 n.
    61
"disembedded economy," *see also* "em-
    bedded economy," 5–8, 13–16, 16,
    23 n. 9, 41, 253, 237, 319, 398, 418
divine command theory, 14–15,
    134–135, 135–146 *passim.*
division of labor, 142, 171, 205, 224,
    234, 261, 277, 335, 365, 425,
    426–427 n. 6
    and refinement of needs, 224, 234,
        344
    harmful effects of, 197–202, 215–216,
        216–222 *passim.*, 345–346,
        383–384, 426–427 n. 6
    in pin making, 176–177
    origin of, 182–185, 367, 426–427 n. 6
    productive power of, 171, 176–185
domination, *see also* patriarchy, rank,
    tyranny, 18, 291, 304, 384
    abstract form of, 25 n. 49, 255, 277,
        354, 363, 421, 448, 465–470
    contrast between personal and ab-
        stract, 278–279,
    domestic, *see also* patriarchy, 308
    personal, 134–135, 191–197, 237, 280
Douglas, Mary, 365

Durkheim, Émile, 365–367, 373–374, 429, 448

Eisenhower, Dwight, 449,
Ellul, Jacques, 384
"embedded economy," 5–8, 13–14
emulation, 319–331
"enclosure movement," 117
Epictetus, 18–19
Epicureanism, *see also* hedonism and utilitarianism, 18, 20–21, 27 n. 62 and 64, 418,
Essay concerning Human Understanding, 133
"evolutionary economics," 318–319
exchange value, *see also* value form, price, 182–185, 254–255, 256–258, 281–282, 318
    as goal of exchange, 73–76, 284–287, 292–293 n. 3
    as necessary form of appearance of value, 258, 264–273,
exploitation, 18, 206, 255

factions, 131, 167, 202, 206, 207–212 *passim.*
    defined, 207
family, 71–77 *passim.*, 78–81 *passim.*, 117–118, 120, 124, 139, 159, 164, 196, 223, 225–227, 231, 235–236, 242–244, 248–250, 279, 305–308, 320, 334, 341, 367–368, 400, 440, 443
    modern decline of, 420–421
Ferguson, Adam, 398
fetishism of commodities, *see also* value form, 16, 25 n. 50, 254–255, 274–282, 318, 444, 448
Finley, M.I., 69
foreign trade, 39, 118, 124–125, 150–153, 156, 161–163, 175, 190–197
Forrest Gump, 118
Foucault, Michel, 437
Franklin, Benjamin, 350–355, 359, 362, 430
free" labor, *see also* wage labor, 6
free-rider" problems, 298, 312, 402–403
friendship, 18, 70–71, 80, 82, 94–96, 106–107, 183
"fun morality," 430, 449, 466–470

Galbraith, John Kenneth, 444, 448, 455–462, 467
Galileo, 8
Gasset, Jose Ortega y, 399, 410,
gemeinschaft, 5, 223, 334
general and determinate abstractions, 5, 23 n. 12, 256, 261, 273
"general economy," 374, 375–381 *passim.*, 380–381 n. 1
generic humanity, *see also* natural function, "the economic," 26–27 n. 57, 319, 470
gesellschaft, 5, 223
gift exchange, *see also* potlach, 8, 71, 88, 105, 109–115, 191–197, 326–331, 365–366, 366–372 *passim.*, 374–381 *passim.*
gigantism, 345–346, 362, 383, 385–395, *passim.*, 422
God, see Christianity, divine command theory, 15, 87–89, 91–115 *passim.*, 135–141, 291–292, 324, 353, 366, 465
good, see the good
Gould, Carol, 25 n. 36, 26 n. 54
"Great Society," 399–414 *passim.*
"great transformation," *see also* Polanyi, 5, 418
greed, *see also* pleonexia, 101, 147–148, 150–153, 156, 161, 350
    "accursed love of gold," 15, 118, 125–128, 354–355
Gregory of Nyssa, St., 88, 91, 108
Gross Domestic Product, 2, 4, 444
Gross, David, 9, 24 n. 23
Grotius, Hugo, 175
Guinness, Alec, 17
Gyges, 40, 118

Hayek, Friedrich A., 148, 366, 397–416
hedonism, *see also* Epicureanism, utilitarianism, "fun morality," 27 n. 62, 28 n. 67, 41, 318–319, 430, 437, 440–441
Hegel, G.W.F., 5–6, 21, 25–26, n. 48, 174, 216–217, 223–252, 255, 293 n. 4, 385, 398, 435–436
Heilbroner, Robert, 25 n. 47
Hesiod, 427 n. 7
Hirsch, Fred, 25 n. 40
historical materialism, 193, 292 n. 2, 363

Bell's critique of, 430–446 *passim.*
Weber's critique of, 354–363
homo economicus, 22, 70, 71, 370, 398, 426
   n. 3, 448, 454–462
households, *see also* family, privacy, 71–85
   passim., 292–293 n. 3, 337–338,
   417–421, 423–425, 425–426 n. 1
   household management, 71–77
   "public household," 430
human needs, 2, 18–19, 26 n. 55, 224,
   256, 455–463
   and customs, 14, 334
   and social form, 71, 318, 334,
      418–419, 424–425, 448–449,
      455–461
   artificially conditioned, 455–461
   commensurability of, see utility theo-
      ry, 70, 459
   Hegel on, 224–237
   refinement of, 148–149, 189–197,
      224, 231, 234, 344
human rights, *see also* liberty, liberalism,
   9, 239–240, 243, 291, 455, 469
   "positive," 17–18, 239–240
human teleology, 21–22, 26 n. 55,
   155–156, 206, 216–221, 298,
   318–319
Hume, David, 1, 22, 148, 155–172, 191,
   206, 216, 318, 398
Hutcheson, Francis, 216
hype, *see also* public opinion, 11, 13
"hyperreality," 11, 384

Ignatieff, Michael, 25 n. 40 and 45, 26,
   n. 55
"improvement," 15, 19, 148–149, 150,
   157, 162, 168–169, 175, 207
   declining, 389
   Locke on, 133–135, 138, 140–145
   Smith on, 176–185 *passim.*, 188–191,
      195–197, 197–202 *passim.*
individuality, *see also* modern commerce,
   298, 335–336, 341–347, 413,
   420–422, 448, 469
   independence vs. personal peculiarity,
      346
industriousness, 15, 133–135, 138, 148,
   149–153, 156, 160–162, 167, 175,
   182, 197, 352
"infinite" self, *see also* "unencumbered
   self," 25–26, n. 48, 227, 229, 280,

429, 433, 435–436, 445 n. 1, 461
"instinct of workmanship," 9, 135, 319,
   325, 329
instrumentalism, 7–9, 11, 73, 75, 218,
   228
intellectualism, 336–347 *passim.*
"invidious comparison," 317–318, 322,
   325–326
"invisible hand," 174, 206, 224–226,
   232, 234, 248, 255, 291, 403, 409,
   415 n. 13, 423, 426 n. 3
It's a Wonderful Life, 10, 24 n. 29 and 30

James, William, 319
Jameson, Frederic, 9
Jesus of Nazareth, 88, 90, 100, 102, 130
Jews, 17, 103–104, 280, 286
joint-stock companies, 310
justice, 39–41, 41–68 *passim.*, 70,
   94–107, 206, 209, 239–242,
   404–406
   contrasted with love, 413
   emergence of, 401
   essence of, 407, 414 n. 7, 415 n. 10
   Hayek's critique of ("social justice"),
      397–398, 399–414 *passim.*
   in pricing, 94–96, 107, 241–242

Kant, Immanuel, 13, 14, 19, 25–26 n. 48,
   88, 174, 216, 221, 335, 398, 415 n.
   10
Kierkegaard, Søren, 25–26, n. 48, 383

"labor theory of property," 14–15,
   134–135, 135–145 *passim.*, 206,
   229–230, 255, 441
labor theory of value, 141–144,
   152–153, 160, 185–188, 233,
   254–255, 276–277, 280–282,
   291–292, 335
labor, *see also* division of labor, slavery,
   "unfree" labor,
laissez faire principles, 15, 299–315
   passim.
Lears, T.J. Jackson, 24 n. 24
Leibniz, Gottfried, 25 n. 46
Leiss, William, 22, n. 3
Lenin, Vladimir Iyich, 394
Levi-Strauss, Claude, 448
liberalism, 5, 7, 297–299, 399, 399–414
   passim., 443

liberalism *(continued)*
and utilitarianism, 21, 297–299, 426
n. 4
in disarray, 443
Marx's critique of, 255–256, 398–399
liberty, 7
and consumption, 447–449
and factions, 208, 301–302
and metropolitan life, 341–347, 409,
434, 441
and modern commerce, 15–16, 150,
155–156, 206, 223–224, 334
defined, 343–344
libertarian conception of, 16–17
Locke, John, *see also* "improvement," 14,
25 n. 45, 89, 133–146, 173, 206,
216, 255, 441
on measures, 134–145 *passim.*
Luke, Tim, 24 n. 30
luxury, 18–19, 118, 123, 134–135,
147–149, 182,
205, 224, 226–227, 233, 367, 369–370,
374–381 *passim.*, 445, 452
Hume on, 153, 156–157, 160–162,
163–171 *passim.*
"true" luxury, 380,

Machiavelli, Niccoló, 205
MacIntyre, Alasdair, 20, 23 n. 10, 25–26,
n. 48
Madison, James, 205–213
Maine, Henry Sumner, 5–6
Malinowski, Bronislaw, 367–368
Mandeville, Bernard, 19, 117, 147–154,
163–171 *passim.*, 164, 174, 370, 418
Mannheim, Karl, 334
Marcos, Imelda, 18
Marcuse, Herbert, 216
market, *see also* circulation of commodities, 4–5, 8, 15–17, 21, 23 n. 16, 28
n. 67, 148, 189, 223–225, 255,
297–299, 366, 397–399
contrasted with distribution (Mill),
298
its social form, 5–7, 16, 23–24 n. 18,
24 n. 19, 278–279, 289, 291–292,
298
contrasted with gift exchange,
106–107, 110, 365–366, 366–372
passim.
diminishing understanding of,

400–401
failure of it "correction," 406–407
Hegel on, 225–251 *passim.*
in eclipse, 383–384
limitations on, 242–242, 304–307
naturalistic or technical conception
of, 7, 23 n. 16, 25 n. 47
world, *see also* trade, foreign, 118, 206,
224–225, 246–247
Marx, Karl, 4–7, 16–17, 22, n. 2, 23 n. 5
and 6, 26 n. 51 and 53, 28 n. 71,
216–217, 253–295, 384, 390, 398,
423, 426 n. 3, 426 n. 5, 448, 455
on Aristotle, 7, 23–24 n. 18, 26 n. 53,
28 n. 70, 254, 272, 292–293 n. 3
on classical political economy, 24 n.
19, 253–255, 270, 276–278,
280–282, 291–291
on Epicurus, 27 n. 64, 280
on liberalism, 16, 255–256, 290–291,
398–399
on the value form, 7, 25 n. 50,
253–255, 291–292
on utility, 27 n. 66, 255–256, 298
on value, 25 n. 50, 254–255, 256–293
passim.
on wage labor, 287–291
"mass society," *see also* conformism, public opinion, 421, 424,
"matter-of-fact" mentality, 8, 337, 438
Mauss, Marcel, 365–372, 374–375, 448
"Mc-," 2
McCarthy, George, 24 n. 20
Midas, 16, 74
Mill, John Stuart, 19–20, 25–26, n. 48,
27 n. 62, 216, 297–316
miser, the, 16, 283, 375,
capitalist as "rational miser," 285
modern commerce, *see also* "disembedded economy,"
and "the social," 417–419, 419–427
passim.
and bureaucracy, 386, 390–391, 393,
421, 423, 469
and equality, *see also* wealth, buyers
and sellers, 232, 272, 274, 276, 280,
288, 291, 410, 420–421
and humanization, 155–156, 157–172
passim., 165–167, 197–202,
216–221, 280, 397–399, 399–414
passim.

and individuality, 232, 298, 334, 421
and liberty, 7, 15, 168–169, 195–197,
    226–227, 237–238, 291,302–303,
    334, 343–347, 397–399, 469
and military preparedness, 150, 156,
    157–162, 167, 197–202 passim.,
    205, 383–384, 390
and order, 119–120, 130, 150, 156,
    166, 174–175, 191, 196
and the growth of knowledge,
    133–134, 149–150, 156, 165–166,
    181, 197–202, 216–221, 303,
    398–399
and the state, 225–227, 250–251,
    297–299, 299–315 passim., 366,
    383–384, 390–394
demise of, 383–384, 388–390, 394,
    469
Hegel on, 225–251
interdependence in, 142, 183–185,
    217–221, 225–251 passim.,
    275–276, 338–339
its social form, 6–7, 9, 418–419,
    424–425
its spin-offs, 8–10
town and country, 189–197, 335–347
    passim., 391, 409, 440, 442
Modern Times, 174
modernism, 9, 335, 429–430, 433–436,
    443, 447–448
money, 1, 71, 289
and reputation, see also "pecuniary
    emulation," 249
as means of exchange, 70, 103, 237,
    285–286
as measure, 15, 18, 41, 96, 106
as root of evils, 118, 118–132 passim.
as signal of others' needs, 408
as social form, 16, 253–255, 265,
    333–334, 337–347
as store of value, 135, 139, 143–145
ceremonial, 367–372 passim.
coined, see also Gyges, 40
corrosive effects of, 39–41, 41–68 pas-
    sim., 139, 143–145, 226–227
fetish, 126–128, 254–255, 270–272,
    277, 281
genesis of, 70, 74, 95, 103, 135, 139,
    143–145, 292–293   n. 3
in the capital form, 282, 286–287
leveling effects of, 9, 286, 333–334,

337–340, 448
utopian eradication of, 130–131,
    459
moneymaking, see also capital accumula-
    tion, 7, 89
as an end in itself, 10–11, 13, 75, 101,
    284–285, 292–293 n. 3, 352–353,
    387
boundlessness of, 4, 7, 70, 73–76,
    89–90, 101, 135, 226–227, 233,
    255, 284–287, 292–293 n. 3, 318,
    352–353, 398
Plato on, 39–41, 41–68 passim.
More, St. Thomas, 18, 117–132
Murray, Patrick, 23 n. 12
Myrdal, Gunnar, 426 n. 4

natural function, see also state of nature
    theory, "instinct of workmanship,"
    18–21, 26–27 n. 57, 120–123,
    139–145, 227, 230–233, 329,
    418–419, 424–425, 454–463
"natural history," 155, 189–190, 318, 398
natural law theory, 91–115 passim.,
    135–145 passim., 297,
needs, see human needs
neoclassical economics, 27 n. 66, 28 n.
    68, 69–71, 255–256, 318, 335, 366
New Left, 216, 410, 430, 439–440, 443
New Palgrave, 27 n. 63 and 66, 28 n. 69
Nicomachean Ethics, 41, 89
Nietzsche, Friedrich, 336, 339, 346, 375,
    436
Nussbaum, Martha, 20

"Open Society," 398, 399–414 passim.
ordinary language, 2, 13, 25 n. 40
    passim., 227
altered by commercial forms, 2

passions, see also solidarity, industrious-
    ness, 81–82, 138, 148, 160–162,
    191, 206, 208–212, 304, 317–318,
    397–398,
patriarchy, 8, 121, 226, 236, 279, 298,
    308–309, 317, 320, 326–328,
    420–421, 426–427 n. 6
Paul, St., 88, 91–115 passim., 286
"pecuniary emulation," 150, 232,
    317–318, 459
Peirce, Charles Sanders, 319

persons, 231, 419
and property, 21, 134–145 passim.,
297
Christian doctrine of, 87–89
dignity of, 7, 13, 17–18, 128, 221,
394
Locke on, 134–135
phenomenology, 22, 447, 450
of human freedom, 17–18
Philosophy of Right, 223–224, 225–251,
293 n. 4
philosophy, 40–41, 41–68 passim., 77,
180–181, 185, 198, 418
and political economy, 215–216, 230,
335
Piccone, Paul, 24 n. 30
Plato, 2, 7, 25 n. 46, 39–68, 88, 118–119,
155–156, 226–227, 238, 350, 374,
397, 436
Aristotle on, 78–84 passim.
More on, 118–131 passim.
on Sophists, 39–41
pleonexia, see also greed, miser, 70
Polanyi, Karl, 5–8, 16, 398, 418
police, 166, 224, 229, 239–247, 250
Politics, 71–86, 101, 103–104, 205,
292–293 n. 3
Popper, Sir Karl, 414 n. 5
positivism, 319, 350
"postindustrial society," 430
Postman, Neil, 12
postmodernism, 9, 335, 429–430,
436–440
Postone, Moishe 24 n. 25, 25 n. 49
potlach (potluck), see also gift exchange,
10, 326, 368–369, 374–381 passim.
Poverty of Philosophy, 292
poverty, see also "rabble," 119, 148–154,
174, 197–202, 215, 224–225,
244–246, 249, 313–315, 329, 380,
401, 404, 414, n. 8, 425, 426–427
n. 6
voluntary, 90–91
Pretty Woman, 24 n. 29
price, see also money, 224, 273, 277
contrasted with dignity, 13
pride, 130–131, 147–148, 150–152,
196–197, 317
privacy, 300–301, 418, 425
contrasted with "the social," 419
contrasted with the intimate,

418–420, 424–425
contrasted with the public, 418–419,
424
production process, see also provisioning
process
"productive" and "unproductive" labor,
175–176, 185–188, 374
profit, see also surplus value, 4, 187
profitmaking, see also "retail trade," 2–3,
231, 285, 291
taste for, 75, 156, 162, 191, 285, 352
property, 7, 15, 21, 24 n. 21, 70–71,
88–89, 118, 118–132,
passim, 227
acquisition of, 71–77, 93
and freedom, 239, 288
Aquinas on, 91–94
common use of, 77–78, 81–84,
91–94, 135–145 passim., 161,
174–175, 185, 235–235
contrasted with wealth, 390, 418
limits on, 73, 134–135, 288, 298–299,
293 n. 4
Locke on, 133–145 passim., 255, 297,
441
love of what's mine, 79, 93, 120,
149–150, 304
modern use rights over, 173–175,
297, 291
origin of, 319–321
Utopian critique of, 118–120
women's exclusion from, 309
Protagoras, 41
Protestant work ethic, 9, 349–350,
350–363, 429–430, 438, 445
erosion of, 429–430, 439–445
irrationality of, 353, 362–363, 430
secularization of, 353–354, 362–363
provisioning process, see also production
process,
its determinate social form, 5–7, 9,
246, 252–255, 350, 418–419,
424–425
its proper social form, 14–22,
155–156, 225–251 passim.
public education, 199–202, 243,
305–307
public opinion, see also hype, 301–302,
340, 371, 383–384, 389, 392–393,
407, 471
public utilities, 241, 311

public-spiritedness, *see also* republicanism, 118, 147, 159, 168, 174,
205–206, 303
Pufendorf, Samuel, 175
Puritan Temper, 439–445, 449, 461

"rabble," 120, 122, 152, 202, 245, 249
rank, *see also* recognition, 369, 374–380,
421, 448–449
rationalism, *see also homo economicus,* "infinite" self, 18–20, 397–398, 438,
453–463
of utilitarianism, 20, 318
rationalization, 334, 349–350
reason, 138, 165, 182, 216
and metropolitan life, *see also* intellectualism, "matter-of-fact" mentality,
blasé attitude, 336–347, *passim.*
and rank 378–379
and self-love, 208
and will, 436
as God's image, 92
"constructivist rationalism," *see also*
unintended consequences, 398, 415
n. 13
formal rationality, *see also* instrumentalism, 217–221, 228–230, 235,
336–340, 350, 360, 370, 383–389,
445, 455
mutilated by the division of labor,
201–202, 216–221
nature of, 228–229
shaped by commerce and industry,
166, 225, 233–234, 235, 251,
322–323, 336–340, 360, 370,
383–389, 391, 393, 399–412
passim., 422–424, 438, 445, 455
substantive rationality, 216–217, 350
the test of, *see also* philosophy, 14, 15,
104, 135–145 *passim.*, 385, 388,
392–393, 398–399
recognition, *see also* rank, reputation,
224, 232, 238, 245, 249–250,
319–331 *passim.*, 344–347, 366
Republic, 39–68, 78–84, 88, 156,
226–227, 238
myth of the metals, 40, 84, 118,
126–128
republicanism, 157–163 *passim.*,
167–168, 200–202, 205–206,
207–212 *passim.*

"restricted economy," 374
"retail trade," *see also* capital, 70, 73–76,
89, 282–287
Ricardo, David, 230, 254, 291
rights, see human rights
Robinson, Joan, 25 n. 44
Rousseau, Jean-Jacques, 19, 411, 413,
415 n. 10, 415 n. 15, 419–421, 436
Running on Empty, 334
Ruskin, John, 339

Sabbath, 12, 15
sacred, the, 7, 11–13, 108–115 *passim.*,
373–375, 375–380 *passim.*
in a commercial society, *see also* wage
labor, 7, 13
Saint-Simon, Henri de, 432
Sandel, Michael, 23 n. 10, 25–26 n. 48
Saturday Night Live 12,
Schiller, Friedrich, 215–222, 375
Schmitt, Carl, 415 n. 11
Schuler, Jeanne, 24 n. 26
Scrooge, 16
Second Treatise of Government, 134–146
secularization, 8–9, 373–375, 429–430,
433
self-esteem, *see also* pride, recognition,
238, 245–246, 324, 334, 340,
344–347, 354
self-interest, *see also homo economicus,*
183–184, 197, 225–240, 291,
368–372 *passim.*, 409, 426 n. 3
and money, 194–197, 291, 337, 368,
408–409
origins of, 370, 408–409
selfishness, *see also* greed, 194, 235, 242,
248, 375–380 *passim.*
contrasted with self-love, 71, 82
Seneca, 425–426 n. 1
Senior, Nassau, 414 n. 8
Simmel, Georg, 9, 333–347, 448
simony, 11–13, 89, 108–115
"simulation," 11
slavery, 8, 71, 77, 82–83, 88, 117, 124,
127, 169, 247, 272, 303, 317,
319–320, 384, 388, 391, 419,
425–426 n. 1
Smith, Adam, 16, 135, 148, 173–203,
216–217, 230, 255, 291, 297, 366,
374, 414 n. 6, 426 n. 3
on commercial forms, 175–176

Smith, Tony, 24 n. 21
social form, 5–7, 9, 14, 253–256, 318,
    333–335
    commercial forms, *see also* capital,
        commodity, money, wage labor,
        buyers and sellers, 1, 7, 175–176
    equivocation regarding, 4–5
    power of, 175–176
socialism, 298, 336, 373, 373–375, 384
    Hayek's critique of, 397–398,
        399–414 *passim.*, 415 n. 13
solidarity, 18, 77–84 *passim.*, 365–366,
    373–375, 397–398, 407–408,
    429–430, 472
    renounced, 412–413
Sombart, Werner, 358–359
Sophists, *see also* Plato, 217
Sparta, 82–83, 118, 156, 158–159, 238
special interest groups, 403–406, 441
Spinoza, 25 n. 46, 374
"spirit of capitalism," 7, 350, 350–363
    passim.
state of nature theory, 18, 228–229, 232,
"status treadmill," 318, 324–325
Stoicism, 18, 88
strangers, 183–184, 194–197, 224,
    225–251 *passim.*, 335–347 *passim.*,
    407–410, 449
subsumption under commercial forms,
    2–3, 10, 13, 22, n. 2
    and commercialism, 13
    formal, 2–3, 10, 359–361,
    of earlier commercial forms, 4–5, 281,
        282–287, 289,   291
    real, 3, 10, 360–361, 384, 448–449,
        451–454, 467
summum bonum, see also the good, 16,
    89–90, 353
surplus value, 284–287

taxes, 158, 160, 163, 209, 226, 301, 306,
    311
Taylor, Harriet, 298
temporality, 434–435
    and commercial forms, 9–10
Thales, 77
The Cultural Contradictions of Capitalism,
    25 n. 39
The Division of Labor, 365
"the economy," *see also* "disembedded
    economy," 5–7, 16, 26 n. 51, 319

The Elementary Forms of Religious Life,
    374
The Fable of the Bees, 147–154, 370
"the fruit," 6–7
The Gift, 366–372, 375–381 *passim.*,
    380–381 n. 1
the good, 16, 21, 40–41, 41–68 *passim.*,
    88–91, 206, 353, 397–402,
    407–408, 410, 412–413, 440–445
    shared language of, 25 n. 40
    thick conceptions of, 15
The Man in the White Suit, 17
The Stranger, 2
The Theory of the Leisure Class, 26–27 n.
    57
the useful, *see also* luxury, "the instinct of
    workmanship," 19–20, 26–27 n. 57,
    27 n. 62 and 63 and 66, 98, 134–
    135, 143–144, 120–124, 319, 321,
    325, 330, 367, 369, 375, 378, 465
Thoreau, Henry David, 18
Tönnies, Ferdinand, 5–6
Toqueville, Alexis de, 420
totalitarianism, 391–392, 397, 399–401,
    411
tradition,
    and commerce, 8–10, 191–197,
        322–326, 355–363, 418, 449
    loss of, 9–10, 355–356, 434–435
traditionalism, *see also* custom, 8, 14,
    39–41, 350, 449
    Marx's critique of, 26 n. 53
    traditionalist capitalism, 359–361
    Weber on, 356–363
Treatise of Human Nature, 155–156
"tribal ethics," 397, 399–413 *passim.*, 415
    n. 15
Trotsky, Leon, 384
tyranny, see Gyges, 7, 40–41, 118, 124,
    169, 301–302, 303–304, 397,
    421–422

"unencumbered self," *see also* "infinite"
    self, 16, 25–26 n. 48, 255, 280, 419
"unfree" labor, 6, 8, 158, 169, 188,
    191–192, 221, 278–279, 319, 326,
    387–388
unintended consequences, *see also* "invis-
    ible hand," 174–175, 182, 189–197,
    226, 276, 398, 400, 409, 415 n. 13
USA Today, 2, 22 n. 1

use value, *see also* the useful, 27 n. 66,
254–256, 318
  as goal of exchange, 73–76, 284–285,
  292–293 n. 3
  contrasted with exchange value, 11,
  73, 254–256, 256–257, 260, 273,
  318
usefulness, see the useful
usury, 70, 76, 89, 102–107, 282, 292–293
  n. 3
USX, 11
Utilitarianism, 20, 25–26, n. 48
utilitarianism, *see also* Epicureanism, hedonism, 8, 19–22, 297–299,
  352–353, 366, 426 n. 4
  Durkheimian critique of, 365–372
  passim., 373–381 *passim.*
utility theory, *see also* utilitarianism,
  19–21, 27 n. 62 and 63 and 66, 28
  n. 68, 350, 418
utility, *see also* the useful, 19–21, 27 n. 62
  and 63 and 66, 255–256, 367, 375,
  378, 451, 455–456
  as opposed to the normative concept
  of the useful, 19–20, 27 n. 62
  as opposed to the useful, 19–20
Utopia, 117–131
Utopia, 9, 18, 117–131, 170, 468

value form, 25 n. 50, 253–255, 264–275
  "equivalent form," 255, 265–266,
  268–272
  its polarity, 265–273
  "relative form," 265–268
"value treadmill," 263–264, 318
value, *see also* Marx, labor theory of value,
  religious origins of, 367, 375, 450
Veblen, Thorstein, 9, 26–27, n. 57, 28 n.
  67, 135, 317–331, 366, 374–375,
  448
  critique of economic theory, 321, 325
voluntary associations, *see also* corporations, joint-stock companies,
  300–304, 311, 412–414

wage labor, 1, 3–4, 13, 15, 136, 149–154,
  156, 173, 185–188, 215–216, 255,
  287–291, 298, 356, 371. 426–427 n.
  6
  abstract, 234, 254–255, 258, 260–264,
267–268, 271
  and formal rationality, 350
  and the "unencumbered self," 255,
  288
  and women's liberation, 309
  concrete, 254–255, 260–264, 271, 278
  contrasted with labor power,
  287–291, 293 n. 5
  "corrupted," 11, 13, 55–61
  Hegel on, 233–234, 248, 293 n. 4
  in relation to freedom, 4, 16, 25 n. 36,
  134–135, 255, 288–291, 391–392
  inessential labor, 129
  social form of, 274–275, 298, 418,
  424–425
  "socially necessary," 254–255,
  258–260,   269, 277
waste, 15, 26–27 n. 57, 122–124,
  134–135, 195, 319, 329–331,
  373–375, 378, 390
Wealth of Nations, 16, 173–4, 176–202
wealth,
  accumulation of, 244, 256
  as an end in itself, *see also* wealthism,
  11, 17, 343
  as divinely entrusted, 88–89, 89–116
  passim., 134–135, 135–146 *passim.*
  excess of, *see also* "general economy,"
  luxury, 159–171 *passim.,* 191–197,
  319–331 *passim.,* 367–372 *passim.,*
  373–375, 375–381 *passim.,*
  450–451
  fetishism, *see also* wealthism, 323
  in the commodity form, 2–5,
  194–197, 254, 256–293, 272, 419
  in the commodity capital form, 4–5,
  175–176
  in the gift form, *see also* gift exchange,
  450
  proper end or measure of, *see also* utility theory, the good, human teleology, natural function, human rights,
  modern commerce, traditionalism,
  7, 10–11, 13–22, 40–41, 41–68 *passim.,* 69–71, 71–86 *passim.,* 88–89,
  89–116 *passim.,* 123, 168, 223–225,
  292–293 n. 3, 353, 358–359,
  362–363, 371–372, 401, 407–408,
  412–413, 430, 440–445
  and social form, 15–16, 191–197, 246,
  253–256, 277–278,   418–419

wealth *(continued)*
  "trickle down" theory of, 134–135,
    140–144, 156, 173–175, 181, 404,
    409, 414 n. 6
  unequal distribution of, 129–130,
    139–145, 162–163, 173–174, 206,
    208–210, 224, 235, 404
wealthism, 16–17, 21, 89–90, 418, 430,
  441
Weber, Max, 7, 14–16, 334, 349–364,
  430, 467
Weil, Simone, 383–395

critique of Marx, 384
Welch, C., 28 n. 69
welfare, 9, 17, 128–129, 224–225,
  238–240, 250, 298–299, 366, 401
  paradoxes of public assistance,
    243–246, 313–315
Welles, Orson, 2
Williams, Bernard, 25–26, n. 48, 28 n. 69
Winfield, Richard, 23 n. 16, 24 n. 21, 25
  n. 47

Xenophon, 426–427 n. 6